PROBLEMS IN MARKETING

Problems in Marketing

FIFTH EDITION

STEVEN H. STAR
Associate Professor

NANCY J. DAVIS
Research Associate

CHRISTOPHER H. LOVELOCK
Assistant Professor

BENSON P. SHAPIRO
Associate Professor

All of the
Graduate School of Business Administration
Harvard University

McGraw-Hill Book Company

NEW YORK   ST. LOUIS   SAN FRANCISCO   AUCKLAND   BOGOTÁ   DÜSSELDORF
JOHANNESBURG   LONDON   MADRID   MEXICO   MONTREAL
NEW DELHI   PANAMA   PARIS   SÃO PAULO
SINGAPORE   SYDNEY   TOKYO
TORONTO

Library of Congress Cataloging in Publication Data
Main entry under title:

Problems in marketing.

   (McGraw-Hill series in marketing)
   First-2d ed. by M. P. McNair and others.
     1. Marketing—Case studies. 2. Marketing management—Case studies.
I. Star, Steven H. II. McNair, Malcolm Perrine, date   Problems in marketing.
HF5415.P724   1977   658.8′007′22   77-488
ISBN 0-07-060835-0

PROBLEMS IN MARKETING

Case materials of the Harvard Graduate School of Business Administration are designed as the basis for class discussion rather than to illustrate either effective or ineffective handling of administrative situations.

The copyright on all cases and text materials in this book is held by the President and Fellows of Harvard College, and they are published here by express permission.

This book was set in Souvenir Light by Progressive Typographers.
The editors were William J. Kane and Laura D. Warner; the designer was Ben Kann;
the production supervisor was Dominick Petrellese.
The drawings were done by Fine Line Illustrations, Inc.
Fairfield Graphics was printer and binder.

CONTENTS

V
PRICING POLICY   *511*

VI
MARKETING RESEARCH   *599*

VII
MARKETING PROGRAMS   *699*

APPENDIXES   *819*

PREFACE

"The purpose of this book is to provide concrete problems in marketing for use in instruction." So wrote the late Melvin T. Copeland in his Preface to *Marketing Problems,* published in 1920, the first in a long line of marketing casebooks prepared by faculty members of the Harvard Business School.

Our purpose 57 years later—in the fifth postwar edition of *Problems in Marketing,* but actually the eleventh in the series—is essentially the same as Professor Copeland's. Like its predecessors, this book is designed primarily for classroom use. Its contents have all been pretested in the Harvard MBA program and include much of the material currently used in the required first-year marketing course at the school.

As this edition is the first to be published since "Doc" Copeland's death in 1975, at the age of 90, a brief historical overview seems timely.

Professor Copeland's book, later renamed *Problems in Marketing,* went through four editions before being taken over in 1936 by Edmund P. Learned. The somewhat specialized, wartime replacement volume, *Problems in Merchandise Distribution,* prepared by Professor Learned with Malcolm P. McNair and Stanley F. Teele, appeared in 1942. A successor to both books was published by McGraw-Hill in 1949 under the title *Problems in Marketing.* Second, third, and fourth editions appeared in 1957, 1961, and 1968. Among members of the present Harvard Business School faculty who co-authored these subsequent editions are our colleagues Harry L. Hansen, Milton P. Brown, John P. Matthews, Jr., and Walter J. Salmon.

In one respect, the present volume breaks with tradition. This is the first time that *Problems in Marketing* has not carried over cases from previous editions. All 33 cases are new, and 11 of the 13 accompanying introductory sections and appendixes have been specifically prepared for use in this volume.

The environment of marketing has changed in the nine years since the fourth edition was published. New technologies have resulted in new industries and products, or new ways of marketing established products. Marketing tools and concepts are now being applied in situations where they were previously neglected or only haphazardly employed, such as the operations of public and nonprofit organizations. Meantime, changes in societal expectations have resulted in increased powers for regulatory agencies such as the Federal Trade Commission. Readers will find a somewhat higher proportion of cases in the present edition devoted to service industries and the public sector than was true of its predecessor. However, the bulk of the 32 cases continue to deal with industrial and consumer goods in the private sector.

Our students, too, have changed. Among other things, they are capable of more thorough quantitative analysis of cases, reflecting both better prior training and the advent of the pocket calculator. Although none of the cases in this book is designed explicitly for use with sophisticated mathematical models or computer exercises, there are more opportunities than previously for thoughtful analysis of numerical data.

More than most authors, those who write and edit casebooks owe widespread acknowledgments. First, we should like to thank present and former colleagues on the Harvard faculty and research staff whose cases are included in this book—Robert D. Buzzell, F. Stewart DeBruicker, Darryl G. Clarke, Martin V. Marshall, Ralph Z. Sorenson II, Ulrich E. Wiechmann, L. Frank Demmler, Ronald Kurtz, and Harvey Singer—as well as Jean-Louis Lecocq, formerly of INSEAD in France.

We particularly appreciate the cooperation of the organizations (sometimes disguised) featured in the cases, since their willingness to share experience is the sine qua non of case development. No less significant is the provision of sufficient resources to finance the extensive costs of field research. We are very grateful to the Associates of the Harvard Business School, the 1907 Foundation, and the Harvard Business School Classes of 1947, who have contributed generously toward the cost of developing the cases featured in this book.

So many people have been involved in bringing the fifth edition to fruition that it is hardly possible to mention them all by name. However, we would like to acknowledge especially the help provided by our secretaries Bonnie Green, Emily Feudo, Mary Day, and Muriel Drysdale, and also the cooperation extended by the staff of the Intercollegiate Case Clearing House under its director, Charles N. Gebhard.

Clearly, case development is not a solitary task. Input comes from many sources, not least from students whose critical analysis in classroom discussions has served to sharpen and refine each of the cases included here. Neither case writing nor case teaching is an innate skill; both are developed and shaped over time under the guidance of more experienced teachers. Individually and collectively, we owe a special debt of gratitude to the authors of previous editions and to our colleague Theodore Levitt—formerly course head for first-year marketing—who has done much to teach all of us about marketing, teaching, and case writing.

Steven H. Star
Nancy J. Davis
Christopher H. Lovelock
Benson P. Shapiro

TO THE STUDENT

This book is intended as a basis for class discussion, with the student placed in the role of decision maker. Each case describes a real managerial situation, although names and data have sometimes been disguised. Dealing with these cases is not unlike working with the problems that men and women encounter in their jobs as managers.

THE CASE METHOD OF INSTRUCTION

The cases in this book provide students with a series of opportunities to act the role of real-world executives. You will be trying to resolve problems facing organizations, analyzing both qualitative information and quantitative data, evaluating alternative courses of action, and then making decisions about what strategy to pursue for the future.

From case study and discussions you will quickly discover the uncertainty of the real-world managerial environment. The information presented in a marketing case is rarely precise and unambiguous. The goal in using the case method is not to develop a set of "correct" approaches, but to learn to reason well with such data as are available. You will find, perhaps to your frustration, that there is no single correct solution to the problem presented in a given case. Instead, there may be a number of feasible strategies that management might adopt, each with somewhat different implications for the future of the organization.

Unlike lectures and textbooks, the case method of instruction does not present students with a body of tried and true knowledge about how to market goods and services successfully. Instead, it provides an opportunity to "learn by doing." As a teaching device, it can be successful only if you accept the role of involved participant rather than disinterested observer.

The 33 cases in this book cut across a wide range of organizations, industries, and marketing situations, and collectively provide much broader exposure than most managers experience in on-the-job activity over a period of many years. Typically, however, many or all of them will be presented to you for study within the space of just three to six months. As a result, it will become apparent that the problems with which managers deal are not unique to any particular organization or industry. This understanding forms the basis for developing a professional sense of management.

In spite of the realism that case writers try to build into their presentations, it is important to recognize that the cases do differ from real-world management situations in several important respects. First, the information is "prepackaged" in written form. By contrast, practicing managers accumulate information through such means as memoranda, discussions, research reports, observation, and external published materials.

Second, cases tend to be selective in their reporting of real-world phenomena. Most are designed with specific teaching objectives in mind. Each must fit a relatively short class period and focus attention on a defined category of marketing problems. To provide such a focus—and to keep the length and complexity of the case within manageable bounds—it may be necessary to omit information on problems, data, or personnel seen as peripheral to the central issue(s).

A case discussion in class is like a "snapshot" taken at a particular time. In the real world, however, management problems are most often dynamic in nature, calling for some immediate action and for further analysis and decisions at a later date. Managers are rarely able to wrap up their problems, put them away, and go on to the next "case." With this in mind, we have in a few instances included in this book two or more cases involving a single firm, thus giving you an opportunity to tackle continuing problems in the same organization.

A final difference between case discussions and the realities of management is that students have neither the responsibility for implementing their decisions nor the obligation to live with the consequences of these decisions. But this does not mean that you can be frivolous in making your recommendations in class. Your instructor and your classmates are likely to be critical of contributions to the class discussion that are not based upon careful analysis and interpretation of case facts.

PREPARING A CASE

Just as there is no one right solution to a case, so there is no single "correct" way of preparing a case. However, the following broad guidelines may help familiarize you with the task of case preparation. With practice, you should be able to establish a working style with which you feel comfortable.

First, it is important to gain a feel for the overall situation. What sort of organization is this? What problems does management appear to be facing? An initial skim reading of the case should provide you with some impression of what is going on and what information is being presented for analysis.

Now you are ready for a very careful second reading of the case. Seek to identify key facts, clarify the nature of the problem(s) facing management, and determine what decisions need to be made. Make some notes as you go along. Try to establish the significance of any quantitative data in the case (often presented in the exhibits). See if new insights might be gained by combining and manipulating data presented in different parts of the case. But do not accept the data blindly: in the case, as in real life, not all information is equally reliable or equally relevant.

After this careful study of the case, you should be in a position to identify alternative courses of action the organization might take. Consider the implications of each. Relate them to the objectives of the organization, as defined or implied in the case (or as redefined by you). Then develop a set of recommendations for future action, making sure that these are supported by your analysis of case data.

Up to this point, the best results are achieved through independent study. A useful next step, prior to class, is to discuss the case with a small group of classmates. Present your arguments and listen to theirs. The objective of this meeting is not to reach consensus but rather to broaden, clarify, and refine your own thinking.

CLASS DISCUSSIONS

In class sessions conducted according to the case method, you are likely to find that the instructor functions more as a moderator than a lecturer, calling on students, guiding the discussion, asking questions, and periodically synthesizing previous comments. And instead of being a passive notetaker, you will be expected to become an active participant in class discussions. Indeed, it is essential that you participate on a periodic basis. If nobody participated, there would be no discussion. And if you never participate, you will be denying other students the insights that you may have to offer. Moreover, there is significant learning in presenting your analysis and recommendations, and then debating these with classmates who may hold differing views or else seek to build on your presentation. But don't be so eager to participate that you ignore what others have to say. Learning to be a good listener is also an important element in the process of becoming a manager.

A few last words of general caution may be helpful. Avoid indiscriminate "rehash" of case facts in your presentations; the instructor and other students have already read the case, too. Avoid random comments, and instead work toward building a coherent class discussion. Before making a contribution, be sure that the points you plan to raise are relevant to what has gone before or will result in a timely redirection of the discussion.

Occasionally, it may happen that you are personally familiar with one of the organizations depicted in this casebook. Perhaps you are privy to information not included in the case, or else know what has happened since the time of the case decision. If so, keep this information to yourself unless the instructor specifically asks for it. There are no prizes for 20-20 hindsight, and injecting extra information which nobody else has is more likely to spoil the class discussion than to enhance it.

Learning comes through discussion and controversy. In the case method of instruction, students must assume responsibility not only for their own learning but also for that of others in the class. This is why it is so important that you be well prepared, willing to commit yourself to a well-reasoned set of analyses and recommendations, and capable of constructive participation in class discussions. If you and your classmates do not accept this challenge, you are likely to find the case method seemingly aimless and confusing. On the other hand, if you do accept it, then we are optimistic that you'll experience in the classroom that sense of excitement and stimulus that comes with being a manager in real-world situations.

Steven H. Star
Nancy J. Davis
Christopher H. Lovelock
Benson P. Shapiro

THE MARKETING PROCESS

Marketing has been defined in various ways by various writers, but for the purposes of this book we shall define marketing *as that process through which a business enterprise, institution, or organization (1) selects target customers or constituents, (2) assesses the needs or wants of such target customers, and (3) manages its resources to satisfy those customer needs or wants. Generally, although not always, the successful result of this process is the purchase by target customers of the firm's products or services in sufficient quantities and at sufficient prices to cover the enterprise's research and development, manufacturing, marketing, and administrative costs; and to provide a satisfactory profit.*

Viewed in this way, marketing is considerably broader in its purposes and activities than is generally recognized by the lay person or casual observer. While marketing is very much concerned with such specific functions as advertising, personal selling, distribution, and pricing, it is equally involved in determining what products or services the firm should offer, how they should be designed, and to whom they should be directed. Thus, at one level the marketing process is used by the firm to establish an overall product-market strategy: Which customers do we wish to serve with which products or services? At a second level, the marketing process is used to develop detailed marketing programs: What specific combination of product features, information (advertising and personal selling), convenience (physical distribution), attendant services (credit, delivery, repair service, customer training), and price will cause a specific customer or group of customers to purchase a particular product or service from us rather than from our competitors (or not at all)?

The materials in this casebook will be equally concerned with both levels of the marketing process. On the one hand, students should continually ask themselves, "What is this organization's (or corporate division's) overall product-market strategy? How sound is it in light of environmental trends, market characteristics, customer needs and wants, and competitive activities? Should it be modified? If so, how?" The object of asking these questions is, in effect, the establishment of a goal-oriented context within which to attach specific marketing problems. Widely disparate "solutions" to a marketing problem may be equally appropriate, depending on what it is that the organization is trying to accomplish.

On the other hand, virtually all the cases will require the development of a detailed plan of action to "solve" a specific marketing problem or to take advantage of a specific marketing opportunity. Generally, it will be necessary (1) to identify and define the problem or opportunity; (2) to develop alternative approaches and plans of action, (3) to analyze relevant market, customer, competitive, and economic data presented in the case, and (4) to use analysis to select and justify a specific plan of action. The emphasis throughout should be on analysis leading to managerial action, not on analysis for the sake of analysis.

THE MARKETING MIX

The marketing mix is a relatively simple conceptual scheme developed at the Harvard Business School in the 1940s and amplified considerably by later writers. Essentially, the marketing mix is based on the premise that a customer does not simply buy a physical product (or the functions that the product performs) but instead buys a bundle of satisfactions of which the physical product is only a part. A consumer who buys a stereo system, for example, willingly buys (and pays for) not just the stereo system itself, but also the information he or she has received through advertising, brochures, and retail salespeople; the physical convenience of being able to purchase the stereo from a local store rather than having to visit the manufacturer; and the reassurance of purchasing an established, reputable "brand name" with a strong warranty and an extensive after-sales service program. While consumers could, at least in theory, purchase a similar configuration of electronic components directly from another manufacturer at a much lower cost, many consumers clearly prefer to pay more for the complete bundle of product features, information, convenience, and attendant services. In this case, if we include retailer margins, the consumer is, in fact, paying considerably more to satisfy these other needs than for the physical performance of the product.

From the firm's point of view, each consumer need has a counterpart in the marketing mix. The consumer's need for performance or function is satisfied through decisions concerning which products to market and how they should be designed (product policy.) The consumer's need for information and reassurance is satisfied through decisions concerning brand names, advertising, personal selling, and public relations (communications policy.) Similarly, the consumer's needs for convenience in purchase, point-of-purchase information, and after-purchase service are satisfied through decisions concerning how the product or service should be distributed (channel policy.) Finally, the firm must determine how much a target group of consumers really needs or wants a particular bundle of satisfactions and how much they would be willing to pay for it (pricing policy.) As suggested above, a firm will generally only be able to satisfy a particular customer need or want if enough customers are willing to pay a price sufficient to cover the firm's R&D, manufacturing, marketing, and administrative costs, and also provide the firm with a profit.

This casebook is organized according to the elements of the marketing mix. Following a brief introductory module, it will focus sequentially on (1) product policy, (2) communications policy, (3) channel policy, and (4) pricing policy. Although each module will stress one element of the marketing mix, students will generally find that they cannot make decisions with regard to one element of the mix without careful attention to other elements of the mix. While the appropriate level of expenditure on advertising in support of a product will largely depend on the target consumer group's need for information, for example, it will also depend on the distinctive features (if any) of the product, on how widely the product is distributed, and on whether it can be priced high enough to provide an adequate margin to support advertising expenditures.

ANALYTICAL MODES IN MARKETING

The primary objective of the marketing process is to satisfy consumer needs and wants through the development and implementation of sound, profitable marketing programs. As already noted, effective marketing programs are made up of consistent sets of product, communications, channel, and pricing policies which satisfy the needs and wants of target groups of consumers.

The development of an effective marketing program is a difficult task which requires strong analytical abilities, a thorough understanding of environmental, institutional, and competitive factors, and a considerable amount of creativity and common sense. Fortunately, the accumulated experience of many years of marketing practice has led to the delineation of several analytical modes which are often quite useful to people engaged in the marketing process.

These analytical modes will be treated in considerable detail in subsequent notes. For now, it will suffice to list the most common analytical modes, with illustrative questions under each heading:

MARKET ANALYSIS

How large is the market for the product or service in question, and is it growing or shrinking? What are the determinants of market size? What are the demographic characteristics of the customers or potential customers in this market? Is the market segmented, and, if so, how? What are the market shares of the competitors serving this market? Are they changing, and, if so, why? Are there any major customer needs or wants which are not currently being satisfied?

CONSUMER ANALYSIS

Who are the current or potential customers in this market or market segment? Specifically, how do consumers use this product or service? Are the users of this product or service the same people who make the purchase decisions? What are the specific needs and wants of the purchasers(users) of this product or service? What (who) are the major influences on the purchase decision process? What sources of information are they exposed to? How do they process this information? Where and how do they purchase (or want to purchase) this product or service? What are the decision processes used in making purchase decisions? What are the major (potential) points of leverage on the customer's purchasing process?

TRADE ANALYSIS

What intermediaries (e.g., wholesalers, retailers), if any, are located between the manufacturer and consumer in the marketing process? What are the "demographics" of these intermediaries? What roles are they expected to perform (e.g., just physical distribution, or communications and attendant services as well)? How much influence do these intermediaries have over the customer's purchase decision? What are the needs and wants of these intermediaries? How do they decide which manufacturers to support, and with what intensity? What is the balance of power between manufacturers and the trade in this product or service category? What are the major (potential) points of leverage on the trade's merchandising behavior?

COMPETITIVE ANALYSIS

Who are the key competitors and potential competitors in this market or market segment? What are their major strengths and weaknesses (financial, technological, manufacturing, marketing)? What are their apparent product-marketing strategies? What specific marketing programs have they addressed to this market segment? How successful are they (market share, profitability)? How important is this market or market segment to them? If the firm under review takes a particular action, how would its competitors be likely to react and with what effect?

ECONOMIC ANALYSIS

What are the economics (fixed costs, variable costs, break-even point, profit impact target) of the proposed marketing program? What market share would this program require to achieve its profit impact target? What are the economics of alternative marketing programs? What market shares would they require? In the light of market conditions and the firm's objectives, which alternative (if any) has the highest probability of "success"?

SUMMARY

The marketing process is used by firms and other organizations to establish an overall product-market strategy and also to develop detailed marketing programs. Such programs involve, in varying degrees, decisions on each of the several elements of the marketing mix. Policies must be established on the nature of the product itself, how it is to be priced, the channels through which it is to be distributed, and what communications strategy shall be employed. Decisions on each should be oriented toward the needs and characteristics of target groups of consumers.

Several analytical modes are useful in developing marketing programs. These include market, consumer, trade, competitive, and economic analyses. However, when using these analytical modes, it is critical to remember that the objective is the development of sound plans of action, and not analysis for its own sake!

GILLETTE SAFETY RAZOR DIVISION
THE BLANK CASSETTE PROJECT

STEVEN H. STAR
Associate Professor
Harvard Graduate School of Business Administration

In late 1970, Mr. Ralph Bingham, vice president–new business development of the Gillette Safety Razor Division (SRD), was considering a proposal for SRD to market a line of blank recording cassettes. Like all Gillette divisions, SRD had received an earnings growth target as part of the corporate long-range planning process. SRD's forecast of demand for shaving systems implied that the division would not be able to achieve its earnings growth target several years out unless it added new product categories to its product lines. As vice president–new business development, it was Mr. Bingham's job to identify new business opportunities for the division, to assess their feasibility, and—working with functional managers in SRD—to develop plans for entering such new businesses.

THE COMPANY

The Gillette Company was founded in 1903 to manufacture and market the safety razor and blade invented by Mr. King Gillette. The company grew very rapidly and had achieved sales of $60 million and profits before tax of $20.4

Names of individuals and certain financial data have been disguised.

million by 1947. Until 1948, the company's product line was limited to safety razors, double-edge blades, and shaving cream.

In 1948, Gillette acquired the Toni Company, a leading manufacturer of women's hair preparations. This acquisition was Gillette's first effort outside the men's shaving business and was followed by acquisitions of the Paper Mate Corporation (1955), Harris Research Laboratories (1956), the Sterilon Corporation (1962), and the Braun Company (1967). Each of these acquisitions was intended as a diversification move, and the acquired companies were operated independently of the men's shaving business.

During this same period, Gillette had embarked on an extensive internal new product development program. At first, such development had been limited to the shaving business, with introductions of the first blade dispenser in 1946, Foamy Instant Lather Shaving Cream in 1953, the Gillette adjustable razor in 1957, and the Super Blue Blade in 1960.

In 1960, Gillette had entered the toiletries business with the introduction of Right Guard Deodorant for men. In time, Right Guard had come to be positioned as a deodorant for the entire family and had obtained 28 percent of the $250 million deodorant market by 1968. During the 1960s, Gillette had also introduced an aftershave lotion, a men's cologne, a talc, and several men's hair-grooming products. The Gillette name had been prominently featured in the advertising packaging of all these products, including Right Guard.

In 1967, it had been decided to split off the toiletries business from the razor and blade business, a move which was completed in 1968.[1] Organizationally, a separate Toiletries Division, with its own headquarters, manufacturing plant, and sales force, was now responsible for Right Guard, Foamy, and Gillette's other toiletry products. The Gillette Safety Razor Division (SRD) was now responsible for the development, manufacturing, and marketing of Gillette razors and blades in the United States, an activity which still accounted for a major share of corporate sales and profits.

In 1969, Gillette corporate sales were $609 million; profits before taxes were $119 million. Men's grooming products (razors, blades, and toiletries) represented 59 percent of sales, while women's grooming products represented 20 percent, Paper Mate 6 percent, and Braun 15 percent. According to the Gillette *Annual Report* for 1969, almost 50 percent of the corporation's assets were located outside the United States and Canada.

THE SAFETY RAZOR DIVISION

During the mid-1960s, as the toiletries business was in the process of being removed from its jurisdiction, the Safety Razor Division had concentrated on consolidating its position in the blade and razor business. In particular, it had

[1] The rapid growth of the toiletries business during the 1960s had led to the diversion of a considerable amount of SRD management time from the highly profitable razor and blade business. The establishment of separate profit centers for toiletries and razors and blades was intended to increase management focus on the major problems and opportunities of each business:

responded vigorously and successfully to competitive threats from Wilkinson, Schick, and Personna with the introduction of the stainless steel blade in 1963, the Super Stainless Steel blade in 1965, and the Techmatic shaving system in 1966. According to industry observers, these moves helped Gillette to maintain a high market share while significantly increasing the average selling price and unit profits of Gillette razors and blades.

The split-off of the Toiletries Division had, however, removed from SRD those product lines with the greatest potential for significant growth. By 1970, therefore, SRD was seeking new growth opportunities outside the blade and razor business.

In seeking new ventures for SRD, Bingham sought to identify "high growth markets where SRD's strengths would give it a competitive edge." Following discussions with other Gillette executives and trade sources, Bingham concluded that SRD was particularly strong in three areas: (1) shaving technology and development, (2) high-volume manufacturing of precision metal and plastic products, and (3) the marketing of mass-distributed packaged goods.

In the marketing area, distribution was generally considered to be SRD's most important strength. In 1968, Gillette razors and blades were sold by more than 500,000 retail outlets in the United States, including 54,000 chain and independent drugstores, 256,000 food stores, 21,000 discount and variety stores, and approximately 170,000 other outlets. Gillette razors and blades were stocked by 100 percent of the drugstores and discount stores in the United States, by 96 percent of chain and independent food stores, and by 83 percent of all variety stores. Wherever possible, SRD sought multiple displays of its products in a single outlet.

While SRD sold directly to large chain accounts, the majority of its retail accounts were served by 3,000 independent wholesalers. These wholesalers were of several types, including drug wholesalers, tobacco wholesalers, and toiletry merchandisers. The latter generally distributed to food and/or discount stores, often on a rack-jobbing[1] basis. According to SRD estimates, these wholesalers employed approximately 20,000 salesmen and were responsible for slightly less than 50 percent of SRD sales.

The SRD sales force consisted of 4 regional managers, a national accounts manager, 18 district managers, 109 territory representatives, and 27 sales merchandisers. Annual costs of operating this sales force (including compensation, expenses, and overhead) were estimated by industry observers to be between $5 and $6 million. The territory representatives focused their attention on whole-

---

[1] A rack jobber was essentially a wholesaler who undertook to set up displays and keep them stocked with merchandise. Rack-jobber personnel visited their retail accounts on a frequent basis; while in the store they replaced defective or worn merchandise, added new items, set up promotional displays, and did other work designed to maintain the strength of the business. While retailers using rack jobbers generally retained formal authority to determine which products and brands they would carry and how they would be priced, in practice these functions were often delegated to the rack jobber. It was considered unlikely, however, that a rack jobber would undertake to add a new product category (e.g., blank cassettes) without first obtaining formal approval from the retailer's merchandising personnel.

salers and the headquarters of direct retail accounts but also called on the top 10 to 20 percent of the retail outlets served by wholesalers. The sales merchandisers confined their efforts to the retail level, where they supplemented wholesaler salesmen's efforts to obtain special displays and promotions.

According to industry sources, the SRD sales force was extraordinarily effective in working with chain headquarters and wholesalers to achieve major impact at the retail level. As one observer put it:

> It's absolutely amazing, but when is the last time you went through a check out and didn't see a Gillette display? These things don't happen by themselves. Those guys [the SRD sales force] are great—well-trained, aggressive, and supported by effective sales programming.

In addition to distribution, SRD's marketing department was considered exceptionally strong in the fields of sales promotion and media advertising. In working with the trade, SRD often offered free merchandise or display racks in return for orders above a specified level. Consumer promotions were often price-oriented, such as a free razor with a cartridge of blades, or vice versa. SRD's media advertising had historically emphasized the sponsorship of sports events, a policy which continued in 1970. In recent years, however, SRD had begun also to sponsor prime-time movies and network series in an effort to reach female and nonsports-oriented male consumers. In 1970, SRD expected to spend approximately $10 million on media advertising, mainly on television.

THE BLANK CASSETTE PROJECT

Bingham had become interested in the blank cassette market in early 1970. At that time, a number of trade journals had carried articles on the rapid growth of recording tape sales, which were expected to exceed $500 million in 1970. While tape cassettes (as distinct from reel-to-reel tapes or 8-track cartridges) represented only a part of this market, it was Bingham's impression that the cassette share of the market was large and growing rapidly. Moreover, on recent visits to outlets of large discount stores and drug chains, Mr. Bingham had noted that many of these outlets were now carrying blank cassettes. In his judgment, the packaging and display of such cassettes was rather weak, and no single brand seemed to have obtained wide distribution. While admittedly not an avid viewer of television, Mr. Bingham could not recall having ever seen a television commercial for blank cassettes.

To learn more about the blank cassette market, Mr. Bingham hired a team of young consultants, all recent graduates of the Harvard Business School, to carry out a study of the industry. At the same time, he personally sought information from Gillette marketing and sales personnel and from his own contacts in investment banking and retailing. By October 1970, Mr. Bingham felt that he had obtained a reasonably good "feel" for the characteristics of the industry.

THE RECORDING TAPE MARKET

According to the consultants' report, the market for recording tapes of all types would be approximately $650 million (at retail list prices) in 1970; $500 million of these sales would be prerecorded tapes, while the remaining $150 million would be blank tapes. Of prerecorded tape sales, 77 percent would be 8-track cartridges (up 28 percent from 1969), 20 percent would be cassettes (up 53 percent from 1969), and 3 percent would be reel-to-reel tapes (up 5 percent from 1969.) In the blank tape market, roughly 85 percent of the market was represented by cassettes, 10 percent by reel-to-reel tapes, and 5 percent by 8-track cartridges.

Bingham believed that the potential future market for blank cassettes would depend largely on two factors: (1) the equipment configurations selected by consumers and (2) how consumers chose to use their equipment. At present, consumers had three basic choices: reel-to-reel tapes, 8-track cartridges, and cassettes.[1] Reel-to-reel tape recorders were the earliest form of tape recorders. They tended to be relatively large, heavy, and complicated to operate. In recent years most sales of such recorders had been at high price points (above $200). Bingham believed that reel-to-reel recorders were currently being used primarily for professional and business purposes and as components in elaborate home stereo systems. Reel-to-reel recording was thought to offer higher fidelity than either 8-track cartridges or cassettes and to have a very favorable image among serious audiophiles. In contrast to 8-track cartridges and cassettes, very large selections of prerecorded classical music were available on reel-to-reel tapes, although such "tape albums" tended to be relatively expensive.

Cartridge players, which had been introduced to the market in 1962, had rapidly gained a great deal of market acceptance. A cartridge was a continuous loop of tape enclosed in plastic. In contrast to reel-to-reel recorders, which required careful threading of the tape through recording heads and winding spools, cartridge systems were considered very easy to operate. The 8-track player had a slot (generally on the front panel) into which the cartridge was inserted. It was not necessary to align the cartridge or to perform complex manual operations. In a stereo configuration, an 8-track cartridge had a capacity of 90 minutes of recorded sound.[2]

In 1970, it was estimated that 6 million cartridge players were owned by consumers. Approximately 80 percent of these players were installed in automobiles, and 20 percent were used by consumers in their homes. According to the consultants' report, the heavy incidence of automobile use was attributable to two factors. First, the marketing strategy of the cartridge player industry had tra-

[1] See the Appendix for illustrations of the three types of equipment.

[2] Modern tape recording and playing equipment was capable of using multiple tracks on a single tape. Early cartridge systems utilized 4-track tape, but improved 8-track configurations had dominated this market since 1967. An 8-track cartridge provided approximately twice as much playing time as a 4-track cartridge. Four-track players could not play 8-track cartridges, but some 8-track players could also use 4-track cartridges.

ditionally been automotive-oriented. Second, until 1969 cartridge equipment had been capable of playing prerecorded cartridges but not of making recordings. This lack of recording capability was believed to have restricted the sales of cartridge players for in-home use. In 1969 and 1970, however, numerous manufacturers had introduced 8-track recorder-players to the market. This equipment retailed for $79.95 to approximately $200. Advertisements for 8-track cartridge recorder-players generally carried the theme: "Now you can record your favorite music at home, and listen to it both at home and in your car."

Cassette recording had been developed by North American Philips (Norelco) in 1963 and introduced to the United States market by Norelco and numerous licensees in 1965. A *cassette* was essentially a miniature reel-to-reel system encased in plastic. The cassette was approximately one-third the size of an 8-track cartridge ($2\frac{1}{2} \times 4 \times \frac{1}{2}$ inches versus $5\frac{1}{2} \times 4 \times \frac{3}{4}$ inches) and had a capacity of up to 120 minutes of recorded sound (60 minutes on each side of the tape). Material recorded on a cassette could easily be erased, thus permitting subsequent recording of new material on the cassette. If handled carefully, a high-quality cassette had an expected life of approximately 1,500 hours of recording or playing versus 500 hours for a high-quality 8-track cartridge.

From the outset, cassette systems had been marketed as recording and playing systems. At first, the bulk of sales had been of relatively inexpensive ($19.95–$50) portable monaural cassette recorders, often of relatively poor design, construction, and reliability. More recently, however, higher-quality stereo cassette decks[1] ($100 and up) for use with home stereo systems had been introduced, apparently with considerable success. These systems, used in conjunction with newly developed tapes, were generally believed to produce fidelity equal to the best 8-track cartridge systems. Several very expensive models (above $200), which incorporated Dolby noise reduction principles,[2] had been introduced in early 1970. According to audiophile magazines, these systems had sound reproduction capabilities comparable to all but the very best reel-to-reel recorders.

As of late 1969, it was estimated that 5.9 million cassette recorders had been sold in the United States. Virtually all these units were used as portables or as part of in-home stereo systems. The cassette system had not proved popular for automotive use, since the insertion of the cassette into the recorder required a considerable amount of attention by the user. Government agencies and consumer safety advocates had, according to trade sources, strongly discouraged

---

[1] In audio products terminology, a *deck* differed from a *player* in that it used the amplifier and loudspeakers of an independent high-fidelity system. A *player* contained its own amplifier and loudspeaker.

[2] A Dolby noise reduction system used advanced electronic techniques to reduce greatly the amount of mechanical and background sound which could be heard by the listener. Reel-to-reel and cassette recorders employing Dolby systems were generally used with specially coated tapes and cassettes. In early 1970, these tapes and cassettes were marketed exclusively by relatively small manufacturers of expensive tape recorders and cassette equipment. List prices for 60-minute blank cassettes containing specially coated tape ranged from $3.95 to $4.95.

the installation of cassette equipment in automobiles, apparently for safety reasons. Recent models of cassette equipment incorporated greatly simplified methods of cassette insertion and automatic reversal, however, and it was anticipated that cassettes would soon obtain a significant share of the automotive market.

In Bingham's opinion, portability, compactness, and ease of use were the primary reasons for the rapid market acceptance of cassette recorders. Typical portable cassette recorders had overall dimensions of $10 \times 5 \times 2\frac{1}{2}$ inches and weighed approximately 5 pounds; advances in electronic miniaturization had made possible even smaller units, which currently were intended primarily for the business dictation market.[1] According to the consultants' report, approximately 80 percent of the 1970 unit market would consist of portable units, ranging in price from $19.95 to $139.95. Some of the more expensive models included a built-in AM-FM radio, which facilitated off-the-air recording, and was believed to increase the cassette recorders' attractiveness to young people. In the consultants' judgment, portable cassette recorders selling for less than $50 frequently suffered from mechanical defects and offered only "minimum" sound quality, but the more expensive portable units generally provided fidelity equivalent to that of a good radio.

According to a study published by *Billboard* magazine, there was considerable variation in age and household income between cassette equipment owners and cartridge equipment owners (see Table 1).

[1] The "business-type" dictating equipment market was forecast to reach $60 million (at manufacturers' prices) in 1970 by *Electronics* magazine. Bingham estimated that this market consisted of about 500,000 units, perhaps half of which utilized cassettes. It was Bingham's opinion, however, that a considerable number of "standard" cassette recorders, which were not included in this forecast, were in fact being used for dictation and transcription.

TABLE 1
OWNERSHIP OF CASSETTE AND CARTRIDGE EQUIPMENT
BY AGE GROUP AND HOUSEHOLD INCOME

	U.S. population, %	Cassette owners, %	Cartridge owners, %
Age group:			
0–19	23.9	32	17
20–29	34.7	27	45
30–39	17.7	22	32
40+	23.7	19	6
	100	100	100
Household income:			
$5,000 and under	32	26	36
$5,001–9,000	25	27	24
$9,001–12,000	15	18	11
$12,001–15,000	17	14	13
$15,001+	11	15	16
	100	100	100

While little was known about how consumers used cassette recorders, it was believed that they were used by students for taking notes and recording lectures; by businessmen for dictating, recording conferences, and self-instruction; and by households for live recordings (e.g., "baby's" first words) and for the recording and playing of music. While virtually all new record albums were also available in cassettes, prerecorded cassettes represented only $100 million (at retail prices) of the $3 billion recorded-music market. (Prerecorded 8-track cartridges were expected to have 1970 sales of $385 million.) The relatively low share of the prerecorded-music market held by cassettes was attributed to two major factors. First, prerecorded cassettes were considerably more expensive than phonograph records; an album which had a list price of $4.98 in record form had a list of $6.98 in cassette or cartridge form.[1] Second, the recording at home of radio broadcasts (called off-the-air recording) was apparently quite prevalent among cassette recorder owners. FM stereo radio stations often played large portions of albums, or even complete albums without interruption, a practice which was believed to facilitate home recording. According to the consultants' report, the phonograph record industry was disturbed about the apparent trend to off-the-air recording (record industry growth had slowed to only 6 percent between 1969 and 1970) and was trying to find ways to limit the practice.

Trade sources estimated that 6 to 7 million cassette recorders would be sold by retailers in 1970, with perhaps 50 percent of these sales during November and December. Blank cassette sales were expected to reach $130 million (at retail prices), a 60 percent increase over 1969.

The consultants forecast that blank cassette sales would grow at an average rate of 30 percent per year through the 1970s. They based this estimate on an extrapolation of historical trends and on the following considerations:

1. Cassette players were expected to represent a major share of automotive applications by 1975. As the cassette share of this market grew, the practice of making "tapes" at home for use in the automobile would create a huge new market for cassettes.

2. As the teen-age group which was around when cassettes were introduced moved into college and business, a revolutionary increase in the use of recorders in study and business activities was predicted.

3. The rapid growth of the teen sector of the population indicated continued interest in the portable and fun features of the cassette.

4. Improvement in equipment and tape quality would allow cassettes to capture an increased share of the serious audiophile market.

5. Some industry observers expected cassettes to be commonly used for "letter" writing, home message centers, and a wide range of other consumer data storage and transmission purposes by the mid-1970s. In time, these observers believed, as many as 75 to 80 percent of the 65 million

---

[1] Records, cartridges, and cassettes were, however, all widely available at discounts of approximately 20 percent off list price.

households in the United States would own one or more cassette recorders.

PRODUCTS

Blank cassettes were produced in four basic capacity configurations: 30, 60, 90,
and 120 minutes. Since all four configurations used the same cassette case, they
could be used interchangeably with any standard cassette recorder. The most
popular 60-minute size seemed to be available in three quality-price configurations: (1) professional quality, with a typical list price of $2.98; (2) standard
quality, with list prices ranging from $1.75 to $2.00; and (3) budget quality, with
list prices of about $1.00.[1] Professional quality and standard quality cassettes
were generally sold under relatively well-known brand names (Sony, 3M, Mallory)[2] and were distributed through audio shops, the home entertainment departments of department stores, and some discount stores. According to the
consultants' report, even the leading brands had done "a minimum of advertising" and had "limited distribution, poor display and packaging, and generally
inferior merchandising." The consultants noted, however, that RCA and Capitol
Records had recently entered the business, and that Memorex, a leading supplier of tape to the computer industry, was about to do so. It was worth noting,
the consultants believed, that Memorex had hired two former Procter & Gamble
marketing executives to head its new blank cassette business.

Budget quality cassettes were believed to have captured 50 percent of the
dollar market in 1970. These cassettes were sold under a large number of relatively unknown brands and under the private labels of several large mass-
merchandising chains. Except for the private labels, it was rare for a particular
brand to be stocked by a retailer on a regular basis.

In 1969 and 1970, the rapid growth of the cassette market had attracted a
number of marginal firms into the industry. According to trade sources, 100 percent of the products of some of these firms were defective in some respect.
While a superior quality cassette had an expected life of 1,500 hours of normal

---

[1] Professional and standard quality cassettes utilized essentially similar cassette cases. The primary difference between the two types was in the materials used to coat the tape in the cassette.
Generally, standard quality cassettes had red, blue, orange, or yellow labels, while professional quality cassettes used some combination of black, white, and silver. Professional quality cassettes were
often packaged in a relatively rigid plastic box, while standard cassettes were packaged in either a
flexible plastic box or cardboard.

Budget quality cassettes were believed to use inferior cassette cases and tape. They often had
pastel or iridescent labels, and were typically packed in blister packs (for pegboard display) rather
than boxes. Budget quality cassettes were often promoted in newspaper advertisements and flyers
by discount stores, occasionally at prices as low as two for $0.98 for the 60-minute size.

[2] Sony was a well-known manufacturer of television sets, reel-to-reel tape recorders, cassette
recorders, and stereo systems. 3M manufactured a wide variety of consumer products (e.g., Scotch
tape) and was well established as the leading brand in the blank reel-to-reel tape market. Mallory
was well known as the manufacturer of long-life batteries, which were used primarily in electronic
and photographic equipment.

use, "the majority of cassettes produced in 1969 had on the average perhaps less than 50 hours of playing time. . . ." According to the consultants' report:

> Essentially, the problem boiled down to three parts: (1) oversize cassette cases which would not fit machines, (2) poor internal [cassette] construction in order to reduce costs, and (3) inferior quality tape resulting in poor recordings, limited high frequency response, and wear on machine recorder heads.

5. At the conclusion of their report, the consultants had attempted to ascertain the economics of the blank cassette industry. Using the 60-minute cassette as their example, they noted that such cassettes typically had retail list prices of $1.95 (standard quality) and $2.95 (professional quality). Retailer discounts, if they bought direct from a manufacturer, were typically 50 percent off retail list price. Wholesalers and rack jobbers, who currently handled about 70 percent of professional and standard quality cassette volume, also received a 50 percent discount from retail list price, plus periodic promotional allowances. A retailer who purchased cassettes from a rack jobber or wholesaler received a 35 percent discount. The extent to which wholesalers passed promotional allowances on to retailers was not known.

In the course of their study, the consultants had interviewed a number of suppliers to the cassette industry. Based on these discussions, they estimated that high-quality unloaded cassette cases could be purchased in large lots for $0.159 each. Standard quality recording tape could be purchased for $0.08 per 100 feet; professional quality tape would cost $0.12 to $0.14 per 100 feet.[1] (A 60-minute cassette contained 268 feet of tape.) The cost of loading, packaging, and inspecting was estimated to be $0.20 per cassette.

While supplier cost data were difficult to obtain, the consultants estimated that manufacturers of unloaded cassettes obtained gross margins of approximately 25 percent on large lot sales and that producers of tape realized gross margins as high as 50 percent. Despite the large increase forecast in cassette sales, the consultants believed that there was excess capacity in both unloaded cassette and tape manufacturing and that SRD would have no difficulty in contracting for whatever components and materials it might require.

The consultants had not investigated the feasibility of SRD's entering the blank cassette business from the standpoint of internal resources. Bingham had, however, held preliminary discussions on this subject with SRD sales and manufacturing executives. The SRD sales manager believed that his sales force could "squeeze cassettes in," giving cassettes as much as 10 percent of his sales force's time during the first year, provided that SRD did not introduce any other major new products during this period. The manufacturing manager assured Bingham that his operation could assemble cassettes, although he thought it might take as long as a year to achieve a rate of 1 million cassettes per month. "On a very rough basis," he estimated that fixed manufacturing costs and overheads at this level of operations might be approximately $500,000 annually.

---

[1] The new specially coated tapes for use in Dolby systems (see page 11) were not currently available from outside vendors.

DEVELOPING A PROGRAM

While Bingham considered the data he had obtained to be "still pretty rough and incomplete,"[1] he had discussed the cassette market with several high-level SRD executives, who had shown considerable interest. Based on these discussions, Bingham had agreed to prepare a "hypothetical business plan" which could be used as a basis for deciding whether SRD should proceed toward entry into the blank cassette business. In developing his plan, Bingham was especially concerned with the following considerations:

1   If SRD entered the blank cassette market, Bingham believed that it should initially limit its manufacturing activities to the assembly and packaging of purchased components. If the entry were successful, however, Bingham believed that SRD should manufacture its own tape within 1 year of the introduction and its own unloaded cassettes within 2 years.

2   SRD's advertising agency had suggested that the use of the Gillette name would be a decided advantage, since *Gillette* had a high connotation of quality and reliability, and consumers had recently been "burned" by low-quality cassettes. In discussions with SRD executives, Bingham had suggested the name *Gillette Cassette*, which had received an enthusiastic response. He wondered, however, whether it would be a good idea to associate the Gillette name so directly with blank cassettes. While he was sure that SRD manufacturing expertise could ensure that cassettes marketed under the Gillette name would be of consistently high quality, such cassettes, at least initially, would have no functional advantages over other "quality" brands.

3   According to the consultants' report, blank cassette unit sales were divided among categories of retailers as follows:

Discount and department stores	40
Electronics stores (one-third mail order)	18
High-fidelity stores	7
Drugstores	10
Variety stores	10
Stationery, TV, and appliance stores	5
Catalog stores (Sears, Wards)	7
Camera shops	3
	100%

Bingham knew that SRD's sales force and wholesalers called on discount stores, department stores, drugstores, variety stores, and catalog stores. He wondered whether it would be sufficient to distribute through these classes of outlets or whether electronics and high-fidelity stores should also be used. If he did seek to distribute through these outlets, he might wish to use audio products manufacturers' representatives, who received 10 percent commission on the billed price to the stores. Bingham also wondered whether some of SRD's other retail outlets (e.g., supermarket chains),

---

[1] In particular, he felt that the trade estimates of blank cassette sales might be inflated, perhaps by as much as $30 million (at retail prices).

which did not presently sell blank cassettes, should be included in his distribution plan.

4   Bingham assumed that media advertising, while uncommon thus far in the blank cassette industry, would play an important role in his marketing plan. In the past, SRD had spent more than $5 million to advertise the introduction of a new shaving system (e.g., Techmatic), but he doubted that such high expenditures would be required in a market where there was no significant competitive advertising. SRD's advertising agency, "on a very preliminary basis," had suggested a media budget of about $2 million for the first year and $1.2 million in ensuing years. While the agency's "thoughts on media" were "still pretty rough," the preliminary media advertising budget was based on the premise that virtual saturation of teen-oriented radio stations would be sought. Alternatively, the budget could be split (with reduced weight against each target) among teen-oriented radio, adult-oriented radio, and entertainment-oriented print media.

5   Most manufacturers of "quality" cassettes also marketed cassette accessories such as recording head cleaners and cassette storage cases. While Bingham doubted that such items would contribute significantly to profits, he wondered whether he should include them in his plan "in order to demonstrate to wholesalers, retailers, and consumers that Gillette is serious about getting into this business."

6   Bingham had not yet given much thought to pricing, but he felt that the Gillette image for quality might allow the *Gillette Cassette*, if that name were used, to command a premium price at retail. Competitive standard quality 60-minute cassettes (e.g., Sony, 3M, Mallory) had list prices of $1.95 but were typically discounted to $1.69–1.75. He wondered whether a standard quality Gillette Cassette might not carry a higher list price.

7   Wholesale and retail discounts from list prices were somewhat higher in the cassette industry than they were in the razor and blade business. While Bingham doubted that retailers would accept lower margins than were common in the cassette industry, he wondered whether SRD's wholesalers might not be satisfied with normal health and beauty aid wholesale margins (about 15 percent). In this regard, he noted that SRD's wholesalers sold competitors' shaving products but did not presently carry blank cassettes.

8   Several weeks previously, Bingham had asked selected members of the SRD sales organization "to check out this idea on a preliminary basis with trade sources." Excerpts from Bingham's notes on these investigations follow:

Competition is fierce, and completely price oriented. [Major off-brand suppliers] offer everyday margins up to 67%.

On the positive side, [many of our sources felt that] there is a real opportunity for an aggressive promoter to organize the market and assume a leadership position with the consumer.

Our investigation revealed that the absence of promotion against the consumer will not last long. Memorex, a West Coast firm, is building a 50-man sales force predominately staffed by ex-P&G men. They have also hired the Leo Burnett Agency to develop an ad campaign. Our information is that they plan to go in the direction of high quality audio shop distribution. It's difficult to imagine, however, that people with P&G backgrounds would refrain very long from attempting distribution in mass merchandising outlets.

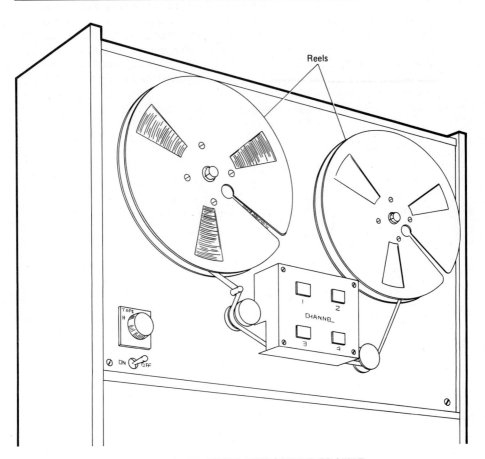

Reels

REEL-TO-REEL TAPE RECORDER-PLAYER

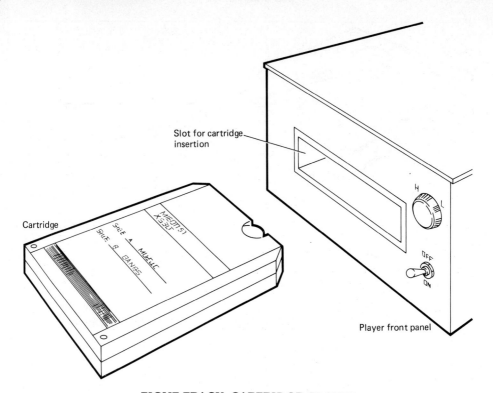

Slot for cartridge insertion

Cartridge

MEOTI-5)
X53µ
SωE A MµµµC
SωE B GAΠEP

Player front panel

EIGHT-TRACK CARTRIDGE PLAYER

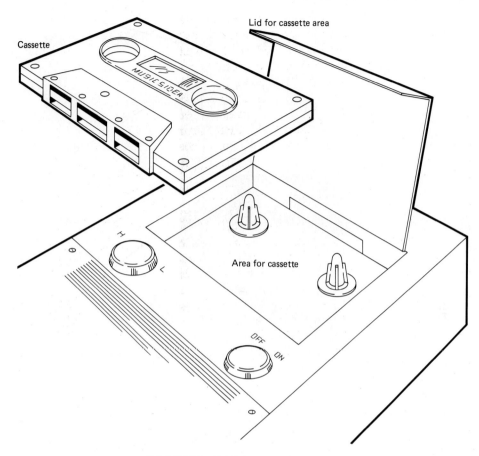

CASSETTE RECORDER-PLAYER

GOULD, INC.: GRAPHICS DIVISION

ULRICH E. WIECHMANN
Assistant Professor
Harvard Graduate School of Business Administration

RALPH Z. SORENSON II
President, Babson College

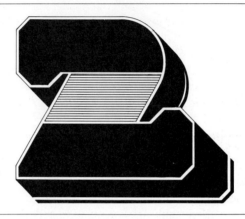

In August 1969, Mr. Willard C. Koepf, national sales manager of the Graphics Division of Gould, Inc., was asked by corporate headquarters to review the marketing possibilities for the electrostatic printer Gould 4800 and to formulate a marketing plan for the beginning fiscal year. The printer which was the division's only product, had been introduced with high expectations at the Spring Joint Computer Conference in Boston in May 1969. "Our feelings ranged from the belief that customers would break our door to take the device from our hands to the opinion of the engineers that the product was almost too good to be put on the market," Mr. Koepf commented.

So far, no orders for the printer had been received. During the computer show, however, potential end users had examined the product with interest and the printer had found an extensive coverage in the trade press. Leading original equipment manufacturers (OEMs), such as IBM, Honeywell, Burroughs, and Univac, had been equally interested in the product, but none of them had made a commitment to push it to end users and to provide the necessary interfacing and software support. As he was thinking about the most suitable marketing approach for the printer, Mr. Koepf wondered particularly whether he should concentrate his marketing efforts on the OEMs or whether the Graphics Division should try to sell the product directly to end users.

COMPANY BACKGROUND

The Graphics Division in Cleveland, Ohio, was one of 26 quasi-independently operating divisions of Gould, Inc., a diversified concern resulting from a merger, effective July 31, 1969, of Gould National Battery, Inc., and the Clevite Corporation.

Prior to the merger, the Graphics Division had been a department of Brush Instruments Division of the former Clevite Corporation. Clevite, an old, well-established company, was manufacturing and marketing such diverse products as copper foil for printed circuits; engine bearings and bushings; hearing aids; and torpedos; as well as a wide array of high-precision data display instruments for scientific, industrial, and aerospace applications, such as oscillographs, biomedical recorders, and plotters. Exhibits 1 and 2 show some of the instruments manufactured and marketed by Clevite's Brush Instruments Division.

In its chosen fields, and especially in the instruments sector, Clevite had enjoyed a solid reputation as a high-quality–high-price supplier. Selling the company's products required highly specialized technical sales teams as well as a close relation with customers. Its favorable acceptance in well-known markets had enabled the company to concentrate on the task of engineering and producing premium goods. Clevite did not undertake systematic market research, and its corporate marketing staff had been kept very small.

The merger of Clevite and Gould National Battery, Inc., had been initiated by Gould's president, Mr. William T. Ylvisaker. He had been appointed chief executive of Gould National Battery late in 1967. Gould National Battery, founded in 1905, had relied mainly on the manufacturing and marketing of automotive and industrial batteries, with a minor part of its revenues coming from the sale of engine parts and air-oil-fuel filters to machinery manufacturers and the automotive aftermarket. In 1967, the company was generally considered as an ailing member of a stagnant industry, facing a declining market share and a fall in earnings of 25 percent between 1962 and 1967.

To turn the company around, Mr. Ylvisaker looked for opportunities to broaden the base of Gould through a strategy of planned acquisitions of compatible businesses and emphasis on new product development. "We sat down and asked ourselves: 'What is this company?'" one company officer said.

The definition we came up with was not one of products or markets; we define our business in terms of technology. We thought that if we defined our business in terms of markets or products, we might finally find ourselves in a lot of unrelated technologies and be unable to stay in a leadership position. Since technology is usually the basis for new products, this could be most serious. I think it is harder to

*develop good technology than to revise a distribution system and a marketing
organization. If you define your business in terms of technologies, you have a
sounder basis for growth.*

*This is really why the Clevite Corporation was attractive for us. While there
was some similarity in terms of markets served and products produced between
Gould and Clevite, they were not serious direct competitors and were really different. But Gould National Battery has know-how in electrochemistry, electromechanics, and electronics from the battery business as well as in metallurgy from the
engine parts business. Similarly Clevite was dealing with electrochemistry in their
production of electroplated foil and bearings, with electromechanics and electronics
in their Brush Division and also with metallurgy. So the merger was consistent with
our concept of the business.*

*We want excellence in a few selected technologies. I don't mean neces-
sarily high technology—we are not breaking down new or fundamental barriers.
We don't do basic research, but good application research. We want to be on the
leading edge of existing technology, we want to be innovative in terms of products
and processes.*

*We are all committed to building a business on a good, sound, solid basis.
Our financial goals are to maintain a 15 per cent growth in earnings per share over
the next ten to fifteen years. To reach this goal requires two key things. (1) You
must be willing to invest at that rate in new products and engineering, fixed assets
and working capital. We are willing and able to do this. (2) You must be in markets
that are growing at a rate of 15 per cent a year. But we aren't yet and we must be.
Our major thrust, therefore, will most likely be in the electronics field in order to
get that growth. Statistically, we stand a better chance if we emphasize the electronics business. Certainly, one of the problems is to get into these growing
markets.*

The new electrostatic printer was seen by Gould's management as a way
to enter the rapidly growing computer peripheral market. Gould envisaged the
development of a complete line of computer peripheral devices and was prepared to invest up to $10 million in developing this line. Management was pre-
pared to forgo immediate profits on new investments but expected that such
investments should become profitable within at least 5 years.

The organization of Gould, Inc., after the merger of Gould National Battery and Clevite was based on the principal technologies used by the companies. Exhibit 3 shows an organization chart. Exhibit 4 gives a breakdown of sales
by product and major customer groups for fiscal year 1969.

THE ELECTROSTATIC PRINTER

The Gould 4800, a machine of about the size of a teletype console, was a nonimpact printer using the technology of electrostatic printing.[1] It was designed as an
output printing device for data from computers, magnetic tape, punched card
readers, cathode ray tube (CRT) memories, or telecommunication lines. It could

---

[1] For details on printing technologies, see the Appendix.

print both alphanumeric characters and graphs at a speed of 4,800/86-character lines per minute or the equivalent of one 8½ × 11 inch page per second. Exhibit 5 shows a picture of the Gould 4800 together with some product information from Gould's sales catalog.

The printer was a "by-product" of the Brush Division's activity in the field of data display instruments. In the course of the development of high-speed oscillographs, Brush engineers had gotten the idea that the oscillograph technology they were working on could be used in the creation of a high-speed printer for which, they thought, a wide market would exist in view of the fact that the existing computer printing devices were working at a much lower speed than the data-processing units to which they were connected. Indeed, one of the most widely discussed problems in the computer industry was the relative slowness of print-out equipment compared to the speed of computers themselves.

Development work on the electrostatic printer was started in 1963. Initially, two engineers were engaged in it full time; in 1966 the development group was enlarged to four engineers. No formal budget had been established for the development work. Management's attitude, as one executive described it, had been: "Just work on it and see what can be done." Total development costs, up to the market introduction in May 1969, amounted to roughly $500,000.

In 1968 a prototype of the printer had become ready, and shortly afterward the development group was separated from the Brush Division to form the Graphics Division, headed by a general manager, Mr. Koeblitz, who had been engineering manager of the Brush Division for approximately 12 years. A national sales manager, Mr. Koepf, was hired. He had worked in computer-related industries for approximately 4 years.

With its printing speed of 4,800 lines per minute, the Gould 4800 was at least four times faster than conventional line printers used for computer output. In contrast to these conventional line printers, the Gould 4800 could also print any kind of graphic output, such as charts, graphs, line drawings, curves and vectors. Exhibit 6 gives a sample of the range of possible output. Graphic output for engineering and scientific purposes was typically produced on high-precision–high-price XY plotters like the Brush 1000 (see Exhibit 2). The Gould 4800 printed graphic output 200 to 400 times faster than these plotters.

The major elements in the printing process of the Gould 4800 were an electromagnetic printing head and specially coated paper. Gould had applied for patents for both, but management of the Graphics Division thought that the process was not so unique that the patents could not be circumvented by competitors with similar technologies in less than 2 years.

The printing head contained a row of 600 styluses that could be selectively charged to 300 volts. As a web of the special paper passed beneath the styluses, the coating acquired an opposite electrical charge beneath each charged stylus. The charge then attracted a dark toner in a liquid suspension to form the characters as an array of black dots. The liquid evaporated and the printed output came out dry. Since there were few moving parts and no printing hammers as in a conventional line printer, the Gould 4800 operated noiselessly and presented relatively fewer maintenance problems.

Like all nonimpact printers, the Gould 4800 produced only single copies at a time. Since specially coated paper had to be used, the output could not be printed on preprinted forms. The copies from Gould's printer were brilliant white with a high-gloss surface, like the paper used in oscillographs and Brush analog recorders. They had the standard letter size of 8½ × 11 inches, which the design engineers believed to be the most acceptable format. The cost of the paper to users was set at 4.2 cents per 8½ × 11 inch page. This compared to the 0.14 cent per page of plain one-ply tab paper used in conventional impact printers.

The paper supply for the Gould 4800 was from a 300-foot roll. The paper-feeding mechanism moved the paper at a continuous speed of 10 inches per second on the average. The dominant form of paper supplied in conventional line printers came packaged "fanfolded," that is, in accordion fashion, with each sheet easily torn from every other sheet at the perforated creases that connected them.

The paper used in the Gould 4800 was unperforated, and so far, engineers had not developed a paper-output collecting, folding, or cutting device.

For use of the printer on-line with a computer, a translating or interface device was necessary to bring the data output of the computer into the format or arrangement desired by the user. The commercial utilization of the Gould 4800, therefore, required the creation of appropriate interfaces for computers of many manufacturers. It could also become necessary to create interfaces for different computer languages within each computer manufacturer's equipment. In addition, an extensive programming effort was required to develop software or application packages for various industry users. The prevailing experience in the computer industry had been that the end users of a particular piece of peripheral equipment like a printer or a card puncher were usually not willing to develop the necessary software or interfacing themselves. They expected this to be included in the "package." In addition, they were not favorably disposed to making modifications in existing programs to be able to run with a particular new peripheral device.

Production of the Gould 4800 was primarily an assembly operation and required the same technology as used in the Brush Instruments Division. Brush had free capacity available for up to 200 units per year which enabled the Graphics Division to utilize the manufacturing department of Brush Instruments for the initial production. Direct manufacturing costs amounted to roughly $4,500 per unit.

The paper used in the Gould 4800 was regarded equally as important to the printing process as the hardware. Management therefore regarded it as desirable to control the production of the paper to ensure reliability. A pilot paper coater had been built, but management had already started ordering items for a paper coater with a capacity of 50,000 rolls per shift. Completion of the facility requiring an investment of roughly $450,000, was planned for February 1970. The present paper costs to users of 4.2 cents per sheet reflected the Graphics Division's own manufacturing costs. With the larger paper coater, management expected to reduce manufacturing costs down to 3 cents per sheet.

THE MARKET FOR COMPUTER
PERIPHERAL EQUIPMENT

The computer peripheral market which the Graphics Division was about to enter had grown faster than the computer main-frame market in recent years, and although forecasts differed widely, the market was expected to continue its growth for some time to come.

The market was characterized by intense competition and rapid technological development. The major computer manufacturers, notably IBM, Honeywell, RCA, CDC, and NCR, were selling their own peripheral devices, competing against each other and against a number of smaller manufacturers such as Mohawk Data Sciences and Digitronics and against special-purpose terminal houses like Sanders Associates and Bunker-Ramo. Many new companies had recently been attracted to the peripheral equipment field.

Compatibility of the peripheral device with the communicating computer was a necessity and had been a major stumbling block to many of the smaller companies. To overcome this difficulty, a number of smaller companies with limited resources, e.g., Mohawk, had found it desirable to sell through one of the main-frame computer manufacturers. This approach relieved the peripheral company of the maintenance and marketing burden and enabled it to rely on the well-established customer relations of the computer manufacturer. It was realized, though, that total reliance on the marketing effort of the main-frame manufacturer might make it difficult for the peripheral company to establish an identity of its own in the market.

Peripheral-equipment purchase decisions among end users were normally in the province of the data-processing department manager or an executive with similar functions. The orientation of this group, according to a recent study, was strongly toward their traditional suppliers, the computer manufacturers, among which IBM held the dominant position. Reluctance to "experiment" was widespread, notably with regard to devices that might present compatibility problems. A survey among 1,600 computer users conducted by The Diebold Group[1] revealed a decided preference for a single vendor of both the computer and peripheral equipment for 31 percent of the respondents, but 19 percent mentioned multivendor preference and 50 percent remained uncommitted. As stated in the survey report, however, in cases where the main-frame manufacturer had all the desired peripheral equipment available, the user's expression of preference to use multiple vendors had to be taken with some precaution. Still, the rate of development of useful new peripheral products by new or non-main-frame manufacturers was so great that computer users generally felt it necessary to give serious consideration to these product sources.

---

[1] A major consulting company in the computer field.

THE MARKET FOR
ELECTROSTATIC PRINTERS

Little market research had been undertaken prior to or during the development work for the Gould 4800. "The engineers relied more on their own feelings," one executive observed. "Maybe they talked to some of the Burroughs[1] people who service our own computer; but on the whole contacts with the computer industry have been minimal."

Even after the prototype had become ready, very little market information was gathered before the printer was introduced in 1969. Mr. Koepf explained:

> We are a very small division. From the very beginning, we were running the division almost like our own little business. We don't have the time and the money to do much research. There is no planning group, no research group like in some of the larger divisions of Gould. All the planning and budgeting work splits essentially between Bill Koeblitz, our General Manager, and myself. In early 1968, The Diebold Group made a study for us on the printer market. They had data on conventional printers but when it came to electrostatic printers, they had to guess. Electrostatic printing is entirely new. Ours is not a "me-too" product. So, it's very difficult to say anything really firm about the market. But everybody knows that existing printers are much too slow.

The Diebold Group had undertaken to estimate the market potential for high-speed nonimpact printers for the period 1968 to 1972. Their estimate, which was based on extensive industry surveys, amounted to a total of 14,000 units for the 1968–1972 time period and included thermographic, electrostatic, and electrographic equipment.[2] Direct-ink printers were not included because of their low speed. This forecast posed the question of what portion of the potential market for high-speed nonimpact printers could be expected for electrostatic devices. As noted by the consultants, the factor that was most likely to affect this determination was the degree of support that major OEMs would give to the electrostatic printing technology. In the judgment of The Diebold Group, OEM support was necessary for electrostatic printers to capture a significant portion of the anticipated market for high-speed nonimpact printers. The consultants were confident that at least one major OEM would complement his product line with an electrostatic printer, and on the basis of this belief, they predicted that at least one-half the forecasted 14,000-unit market potential for high-speed nonimpact printers would be for electrostatic printers. The consultants assumed that 50 percent of the electrostatic market would subsequently go to this innovating OEM and thought it reasonable for Gould to obtain about 20 percent of the remaining market with an aggressive marketing policy.

So far, the Graphics Division had only one direct competitor, Varian Data

---

[1] A manufacturer of electronic data-processing equipment.

[2] See the Appendix.

Products, a smaller, but well-known, company manufacturing an electrostatic printer which was very similar in all its functional features to the Gould 4800. Varian had introduced its product in 1968 and tried to market it at prices between $15,000 to $18,000 direct to end users with discounts of 30 to 40 percent offered to OEMs. Mr. Koepf thought that manufacturing costs for the Varian printer were higher than those for the Gould 4800. Paper costs to users were identical, i.e., 4.2 cents per 8½ × 11 inch page. Mr. Koepf believed that Varian was not an important factor in the market and that their product had serious operational problems. No exact sales figures were available, but Mr. Koepf thought that Varian had sold only a few units.

The Graphics Division saw the Gould 4800 as a potential entrant into five basic functional areas of the information terminal market and into one broad area of miscellaneous new application not yet served by other devices: (1) computer line printer; (2) hard-copy printer of cathode ray tube (CRT) displays; (3) proof-copy or hard-copy printer for computer output to microfilm (COM) systems; (4) high-speed communications printer replacing teletype machines; (5) quick plotter from a computer-plotting program; and (6) in the miscellaneous area, servicing a multiplicity of scientific, medical, military, and commercial applications (like proofreading for computerized typesetters). Little information existed on the particular requirements for this last-mentioned market segment.

LINE PRINTER MARKET

The line printer market represented by far the largest market segment under consideration. The Graphics Division estimated that about 8,000 line printers had been installed during fiscal year 1969, equivalent to a shipment value of $160 million, and that the market was growing at a rate of 10 to 15 percent per year.

Virtually every traditional computer installation used a line printer as its main print-out device, and all the OEMs carried such printers as part of their product line. The purchase price of these machines ranged from $11,500 (Mohawk, 750 lines per minute) to $64,000 (Mohawk, 1,250 lines per minute). They could be rented for a monthly fee including full maintenance ranging from $315 to $1,020; IBM, for example, charged $875 per month for its 1403/3 model (1,100 lines per minute).

The existing printers were usually capable of printing up to six copies simultaneously on ordinary tab paper. They could also easily accommodate special-purpose preprinted forms of different sizes and thicknesses. The most common paper width used was 14⅞ inches. Most users of line printers required multiple copies of their output, and, for cost reasons, these had to be simultaneously produced, rather than serially or off-line on copying machines. Preprinted forms were used extensively, especially by organizations such as banks, insurance companies, credit card companies, or magazine publishers. Programming a printer to produce forms was generally not regarded as an alternative to the use of preprinted forms.

The speed of all existing line printers was many times slower than the rate at which the computer processor could generate data. Multiprogramming techniques had been developed, however, permitting the processor to activate more than one printer at a time and thus reducing the users' problem with jobs previously limited by printer speed.

CRT HARD-COPY MARKET

The market for the Gould 4800 as a device for printing permanent copies of data displayed on CRT screens was regarded as one of the fastest growing segments with an estimated annual growth of 30 to 40 percent. Shipments of CRT hard-copy printers in fiscal year 1969 were estimated at 700 units or $5 million. Among the users of CRT hard-copy printers were banks, stockbroker and insurance companies, as well as high-technology companies like aerospace firms who used CRTs for engineering purposes. In management's view, the almost perfectly silent operation of the Gould 4800, allowing its use in an office environment where the noise level had to be kept at a minimum, and the high printing speed, constrained only by the CRT or the telephone line, made the Gould 4800 well suited for application as a CRT hard-copy printer.

A number of CRT hard-copy printers were currently marketed by mainframe manufacturers and some of the larger computer peripheral manufacturers (IBM, 3M, Litton Industries, Beta Instruments Corporation). These machines used a thermographic or photographic process and were selling at user prices from $6,000 (3M) and $12,600 (Litton/Datalog) to $33,000 for a high-precision IBM machine. Printing costs of these devices were considerable since specially coated paper had to be used; they ranged from roughly 12 cents (3M) to about 18 cents (IBM, Litton/Datalog) per copy. The machines currently being marketed generally gave a higher resolution[1] than the Gould 4800, which was of particular interest in engineering applications.

CRT MICROFILM MARKET

The market for CRT microfilm printers was still a small segment of the computer peripheral market but growing at a rate of 30 to 40 percent annually. In fiscal year 1969, about 100 units had been shipped, representing a value of roughly $15 million. Manufacturers of these machines were Kodak, 3M, and Datagraphics. The Gould 4800 was not a substitute for these devices but rather a supplement for high-speed paper output. Some of the CRT microfilm machines were also equipped for paper output which they printed at the same or at an even higher speed than the Gould 4800.

---

[1] That is, dots per inch, determining clarity and accuracy of output.

COMMUNICATIONS PRINTER MARKET

The market for communications printers was dominated by the familiar tele-types, manufactured by a sizable number of specialized companies. More re-cently the traditional impact teletype had been supplemented by the Inktronic using direct-ink printing technology. In fiscal year 1969, an estimated 30,000 teletypes had been shipped, representing a value of about $35 million. Manage-ment expected this market to grow by 10 to 15 percent annually.

Impact teletypes reaching a speed of 10 characters per second were selling for roughly $1,000 to users. There was at least one faster unit available operating at 37 characters per second which was priced at $3,600. Direct-ink printers had a speed of 250 characters per second and ranged between $5,000 and $7,000 in price. Both impact teletypes and direct-ink printers printed on ordinary paper with an average cost per page to users of 0.5 cent for impact printers and 0.8 cent for the Inktronic. The impact teletype could also be equipped for multiple copies.

Theoretically, the Gould 4800 could print several thousand characters per second as a communications printer. Printing at such a speed required, how-ever, that a communications line was available which could transmit data at such a speed. So far, no equipment existed, either from a private company or from the Bell system for transmitting faster than 2,000 bits per second, i.e., 250 char-acters per second, on dial-up lines. The smallest telephone charge for a dial-up line was for 3 minutes; thus at printing speeds of 250 characters per second, the telephone charges for 1 and 10 pages (60 lines with 80 characters each) were the same since neither took more than 3 minutes (for example, 65 cents for transmission between New York and Philadelphia at a rate of 65 cents for the first 3 minutes and 15 cents for each additional minute). An increase in the speed of transmission for dial-up lines to 3,600 bits per second (450 characters) by the end of 1969 and to 4,800 bits per second (600 characters) in 1971 was expected.

Privately leased transmission lines were available for transmitting up to 9,600 bits per second (1,200 characters). The cost of a private line was propor-tional to the length of the line and was a fixed monthly fee independent of usage. For example, the cost for a private line from New York to Philadelphia was about $350 per month.

PLOTTER MARKET

The sales volume of plotters in fiscal year 1969 had been estimated by manage-ment at $10 million, equivalent to shipments of roughly 500 units. It was ex-pected that this segment would show an annual growth of 30 to 40 percent. In the judgment of Mr. Koepf, the Gould 4800 offered a number of advantages over the conventional digital XY plotters, such as higher speed, more versatility because of symbol-plotting and character-printing ability, and less service re-quirements since no ink and no moving pens as in XY plotters were used. The Gould 4800, however, did not offer the precision of conventional plotters: the smallest plotting increment possible with the Gould 4800 was 12.5 milli-inches compared to 0.01 milli-inches obtainable from conventional plotters. Many plotter users also required a wider paper web than 8½ inches and the flexibility to use different plotting surfaces, e.g., translucent paper.

Users of plotters fell into two broad categories: (1) scientific and engineering users and (2) nonscientific or commercial users.

1   Scientific and engineering users were the most important group requiring computer graphics and plotting techniques. Companies and institutions in this group included automobile companies, aircraft and aerospace manufacturers, universities, and scientific laboratories. Computer-aided plottings were required in the generation of high-accuracy engineering designs or in the solution of complex problems such as the plotting of missile trajectories. Most of these users had considerable computer experience and close contact with computer main-frame manufacturers. They required high accuracy and extensive software support for the plotter to meet these frequently changing, sophisticated plotting needs. The initial purchase price of the plotter was a less important consideration for them than accuracy, versatility, and an extensive software library provided. A number of large companies were currently serving this user group with digital XY plotters, among them IBM marketing plotters manufactured by California Computer Products, Inc., as part of IBM's full line of computers and peripheral devices.

2   The group of nonscientific, commercial users included companies and organizations requiring a plotter for fairly simple graphic representations of mathematical functions or time series (e.g., histograms, weekly or monthly sales and profit curves, line fitting). Minute accuracy was of less concern to this group of users. Their plotting needs appeared to be relatively stable over time and of limited sophistication. Consequently, it was expected that only a modest software library would be necessary. In the judgment of The Diebold Group, graphic output among commercial users of data-processing equipment was still in its very infancy, amounting to less than 1 percent of total printed output. Commercial users seemed to be largely unaware of the potential applications for a plotting device. The Diebold Group expected, however, an increasing popularity in graphic data output, primarily due to the emergence on the market of graphic CRT terminals.

INITIAL MARKETING PLANS

Management of the Graphics Division believed that most printing and plotting would ultimately be nonimpact to meet "instant information" requirements, to keep down sound pollution, and to provide absolute reliability. The Gould 4800, in management's view, met these needs completely, and it was expected that the design would receive rapid technical acceptance in its first year of exposure.

Management's sales forecast provided for a total volume of $800,000 in fiscal year 1970, $2.5 million in fiscal year 1971, and $5 million in fiscal year 1972. Exhibit 7 shows a breakdown of sales expectations in 1970 by market segments. It was expected that fiscal year 1970 would end with a loss, but management anticipated breaking even during fiscal year 1971.

The price to end users for the Gould 4800 had been set at $15,000 plus $4,000 for a character generator which was required to prevent excessive burdening of expensive computer memory space with output format instructions. Manufacturing costs of the character generator amounted to roughly $750. The price to OEMs was $9,900 for one to nine units of the Gould 4800 plus $3,200 for the character generator. Quantity discounts were available to OEMs as shown in Exhibit 8. Mr. Koepf explained:

> When we initially priced the product we didn't really know what to charge and what the market would bear. We thought that a larger spread between the users' price and the OEM price than was usually available for peripheral equipment would get us the interest of the OEMs for the product.

So far, no rental arrangements had been considered for the Gould 4800.

One of the major issues facing management was whether to concentrate sales effort for the Gould 4800 on end users or on the OEMs. The Diebold Group had prepared estimates for the required annual marketing expenditures for both approaches. A summary of their calculations is given in Exhibits 9 and 10. Based on the assumption that for direct selling to end users a total sales force of 20 salesmen would be needed and that the Graphics Division would do all its programming, interfacing, and equipment maintenance itself, the consultants arrived at a figure of $1.19 million as total annual marketing and support costs for selling direct to end users. For the approach of selling through OEMs and systems houses, they came up with a figure of $254,000 as average annual marketing and support costs. This estimate was based on the assumption that a sales force of five would be sufficient and that the OEMs would shoulder a large part of the programming, interfacing, and maintenance burden. The consultants concluded that it would be advisable for the Graphics Division to concentrate their marketing effort on the OEMs and systems houses.

Management's initial thinking essentially followed this recommendation. Mr. Koepf explained:

> We just wanted to sell the machine; if you go directly to end users you must have all the answers on programming, cost, and interfacing. We aren't quite ready for this. We thought that our product is so good that the OEMs would take it and run with it. We wanted them to do our homework for us, that is, provide users with interfacing, software, and maintenance.

Initial market response had been slower than expected. End users, in spite of a high expressed interest, had remained hesitant, and first discussions with OEMs had shown some signs of reluctance to push the product before end user pull had built up. Mr. Koepf commented: "The OEMs told us: 'Great, this is a wonderful machine; when you get some of our users interested to buy, come back and see us.' But people just don't like to be the first ones to try a new product."

20

BRUSH 816
8-Channel High Speed Multipoint Recorder

- Records up to 8 channels with One Precision Servo Penmotor
- Samples up to 16 points/second
- Permits Intensified Sampling of Important Channels
- Includes Single Channel Continuous Writing Capability
- 4.5 Inch Channel Span, 50 Divisions
- Convenient Z-fold Chart Paper
- ±2.5 Volt Sensitivity, Compatible with all Brush Signal Conditioners

Ideal for monitoring such variables as temperature, pressure, flow, etc. It utilizes felt-tip capillary writing. Sampling rates can be selected anywhere between 2 seconds per point to 16 points per second. Channels one or two can be intensified. Or it can write continuously as a single channel recorder. The Brush 816 can be used as a centrally located monitor of intensive care patients.

The Brush Multipoint is ideally suited for monitoring intensive care patients and in extended-term research. It provides a long term record of up to 8 parameters on a common time base (i.e. temperatures, pressures, flows, rates, volumes, etc.)
Brush 816 condenses data so that gradual variations that might be imperceptible, can easily be seen at a glance. In patient monitoring, Brush 816 greatly reduces demands on a nurse's time and simultaneously provides a continuous record for diagnosis and consultation.

35

34

Other quality Brush Recorders with specialized performance characteristics designed to meet your specific need.

BRUSH 1000 high performance XY plotter

Pressurized fluid writing permits skip-free, smooth writing at speeds to 100 inches/sec. Ultra fast response produced by high torque servo motors — 1750 in/sec² in X and 2750 in/sec² in Y directions. Non-contact servo loop feedback device insures pen positioning of 99¾% linearity. Maintenance free operation. No slide wires.

Accepts signals from Brush Bio-medical signal conditioners — records interaction of 2 independent variables or one variable against time or a dependent variable . . . i.e., producing pulminary flow — volume loops directly on-line (simulated on above trace). 10" x 15" writing area, 11" x 100' chart paper roll, sensitivity 5 mV/div.

Model 15-3327-00 (115V a-c ± 10%, 60Hz, 4:5 watts)
Model 15-3327-06 (230V a-c ± 10%, 50Hz, 475 watts)

BRUSH 280
2-channel high performance.
Double width 80mm channels assure highest resolution and quick and easy read-out. Built-in preamps provide a measurement range from 0.5 mV/div to 500V full scale. The finest 2-channel portable you can buy.

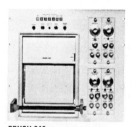

BRUSH 240
4-channel high performance.
It was designed for applications where versatility, maximum resolution and precision are required. Modular design permits use of interchangeable preamps. Rack, cabinet or cart mounted. It offers full scale frequency responses to 55Hz on 40mm and 35Hz on 80mm channels.

BRUSH 250
Single channel high performance.
Fastest, most versatile strip-chart recorder anywhere. To 10Hz f.s. 40 ms rise time. Detachable chart magazine. Accepts plug-in preamps. 4½" resolution. 12 chart speeds from 5 inches/sec. to 1/10 of an inch/min. (or 8 days of continuous recording).

BRUSH 2300
Lightbeam oscillograph.
This dual tungsten filament optical oscillograph provides fail-safe reliability, economy of operation, operator safety and application possibilities in high frequency ranges such as recording heart sounds and cartiac catheterization (superimposed traces) 1 to 16 channel, d-c to 1kHz with matched companion amplifiers and plug-in galvos.

CONTACT YOUR BRUSH INSTRUMENT SPECIALIST FOR ORDERING INFORMATION
AND TECHNICAL SPECIFICATIONS ON THE ABOVE INSTRUMENTS.

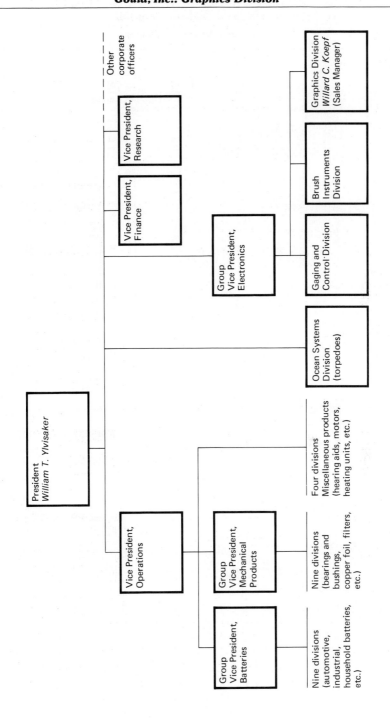

37

EXHIBIT 4
COMBINED SALES OF GOULD NATIONAL AND CLEVITE BY PRODUCT GROUPS AND MAJOR CUSTOMER GROUPS FOR FISCAL YEAR ENDED JUNE 30, 1969

Gould, Inc.: Graphics Division

Product groups	Percent of product group sales by major customer groups										
	Machinery mfrs.	Transportation	Heavy ind. eng. mfrs.	Auto mfrs.	Automotive after-market	Consumer	Government	Metal/plastics mfrs.	Medical/R&D labs	Community utilities	Electro. mfrs.
Batteries: Sales, $140.4 million % of total sales, 42.8	14.2	3.6		1.1	42.4	10.3	4.4	9.4	0.3	7.5	2.2
Mechanical products: Sales, $111.8 million % of total sales, 34.0	10.5	19.7	9.3	30.1	23.9		1.4	1.7		0.2	2.5
Electronic products: Sales, $76.2 million % of total sales, 23.2	2.4	2.1	0.5	1.4	0.1	6.3	38.3	1.9	1.9	1.8	43.2

* Includes miscellaneous products listed in Exhibit 3 and torpedoes.

Source: Company records.

EXHIBIT 5
Gould, Inc.: Graphics Division

GOULD® 4800

Gould 4800   electrostatic printer

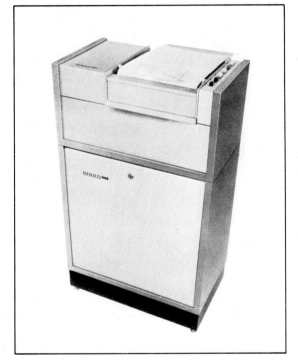

FEATURES

- 4800 lines/minute

- alphanumerics and graphics
- versatility of application
- built-in character generator-controller
- built-in control lines
- electrostatic printing—silent operation

- high-contrast smudge-proof hard copy
- programmed control of output forms
- minimum maintenance
- reliable low voltage operation

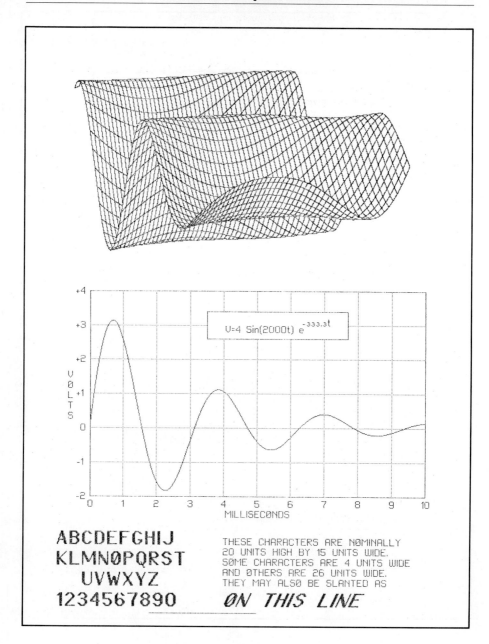

$$V = 4 \sin(2000t)\, e^{-333.3t}$$

ABCDEFGHIJ
KLMNØPQRST
UVWXYZ
1234567890

THESE CHARACTERS ARE NØMINALLY
20 UNITS HIGH BY 15 UNITS WIDE.
SØME CHARACTERS ARE 4 UNITS WIDE
AND ØTHERS ARE 26 UNITS WIDE.
THEY MAY ALSØ BE SLANTED AS

ØN THIS LINE

EXHIBIT 7
SALES FORECAST FOR FISCAL YEAR 1970 BY MARKET SEGMENTS
Gould, Inc.: Graphics Division

Segments or application	Graphics Division sales volume	
	Dollars	Units
Line printer	420,000*	34
CRT hard copy	45,000	5
CRT microfilm	0	0
Teletype	40,000	4
Plotter	180,000	20
Miscellaneous	115,000†	10
Total	800,000	73

* Includes 34-character generators.
† Includes paper and supplies.
Source: Company records.

EXHIBIT 8
OEM PRICE LIST
Gould, Inc.: Graphics Division

	Yearly unit quantity regularly scheduled	Unit price
Printer	1–9	$9,900
	10–19	9,158
	20–34	8,910
	35–49	8,663
	50–99	8,415
	100–499	8,168
	500–999	7,920
	1,000–up	7,670
Character generator		3,200

EXHIBIT 9
CONSULTANTS' ESTIMATE OF AVERAGE ANNUAL MARKETING AND SUPPORT COST SELLING DIRECT TO END USER MARKET
Gould, Inc.: Graphics Division

Sales considerations

Salesmen salaries (20 men)		
(excluding commissions)	$200,000	
Employee benefits	50,000	
Overhead	150,000	
Travel and business expenses	120,000	
Recruiting costs (including		
relocation)	18,000	
Training program	20,000	
Trade shows	80,000	
Advertising	50,000	
Total average annual sales		
considerations		$ 688,000

Support considerations

Programming:		
Programmers salaries	$145,000	
Employee benefits	36,000	
Overhead	109,000	
Recruiting costs (including		
relocation)	13,000	
Total average annual		
programming considerations*		$ 303,000
Maintenance:		
Maintenance engineers		
salaries	$108,000	
Employee benefits	27,000	
Overhead	81,000	
Recruiting costs		
(including relocation)	4,000	
Training program	6,000	
Travel and business expenses	43,000	
Revenue from maintenance		
contracts	(70,000)	
Total average annual		
maintenance considerations		$ 199,000
Total average annual marketing and		
support costs		$1,190,000

* Cost of computer time required to test and "debug" program not included.

Source: The Diebold Group.

EXHIBIT 10
CONSULTANTS' ESTIMATE OF AVERAGE ANNUAL MARKETING AND SUPPORT COSTS SELLING TO OEMs AND SYSTEM HOUSES

Gould, Inc.: Graphics Division

Sales considerations:

Salesmen* salaries (5 men), employee benefits, overhead, travel and business expenses, recruiting costs (including relocation), training program	$140,000

Programming considerations:†

Salaries, benefits, overhead, and recruiting costs	$ 60,000

Maintenance considerations:‡

Salaries, employee benefits, overhead, recruiting costs, training program, and travel	$ 54,000
Total average annual marketing and support costs	$254,000

    * Based on the assumption that five salesmen would incur about 20 percent of costs shown in Exhibit 9.

    † Based on 20 percent of programmers' expenses in Exhibit 9.

    ‡ Based on 20 percent of maintenance engineers' expenses (excluding revenue from maintenance contracts) in Exhibit 9.

    Source: The Diebold Group.

APPENDIX
DIAGRAM OF PRINTING TECHNOLOGIES

PRINTERS

IMPACT PRINTERS

Operation:
Each character printed separately as a hammer strikes against an inked surface and the paper

Advantages:
Multiple copies printed simultaneously
Specially coated paper generally not required
Preprinted forms may be used

Disadvantages:
Noise
Maintenance problems because of many moving parts

SERIAL PRINTERS

Operation:
Character types on hammer or drum transverse paper; columns printed sequentially

Speed:
10 to 37 characters per second

Principal application:
Telecommunication,
time-sharing,
low-cost computers

PARALLEL PRINTERS (line printers)

Operation:
Each column to be printed has its own set of character types, which allows simultaneous printing of columns

Speed:
330 to 1650 characters
per second

Principal application:
Most widely used printing device for high-speed computers

ELECTROGRAPHIC PRINTER

Operation:
Electric current is passed through chemically treated paper to burn in the image of each character

Speed:
N. A.

Note: The technique has fallen into disfavor because the burning of paper produces odor and hazardous gases

NONIMPACT PRINTERS

Operation:
Various nonmechanical printing techniques
(see below)

Advantages:
Generally faster than impact printers
Little or no noise
No or few moving parts; fewer
maintenance problems

Disadvantages:
Multiple copies not produced simultaneously
With one exception, special
(more expensive) paper needed

DIRECT INK PRINTER ("Inktronic")

Operation:
Each character is written on the
page by a burst of magnetically
deflected ink dots; special paper
not needed

Speed:
120 to 250 characters per
second; may still be increased

Principal application:
Telecommunication

ELECTROSTATIC PRINTER

Operation:
Characters are written by
bringing electrostatic charges
on dialectrically coated paper

Speed:
6900 characters per second
(Gould)

Principal application: ?

THERMOGRAPHIC PRINTER

Operation:
Characters are printed by
heating to between 120° and
200°F; specially treated paper

Speed:
300 characters per second; may
be increased to 3200 characters
per second without major
development work

Principal application:
CRT: hard copy output

MAN OF THE HOUSE, INC.

NANCY J. DAVIS
Research Associate
Harvard Graduate School of Business Administration

STEVEN H. STAR
Associate Professor
Harvard Graduate School of Business Administration

In January 1975, Mr. Lewis M. Weinstein, president of Man of the House, Inc., was faced with a threefold marketing problem. First, he had to formulate a plan to increase membership in his unique organization within his current market. Second, he needed to increase usage of his company's services among present members. Third, he had to decide how to position and merchandise his product as he expanded his operations and moved into a new market.

THE COMPANY

Man of the House, Inc. (MOH), was a Pennsauken, New Jersey, home service company which provided its members with over 60 services—major work such as roofing and remodeling, normal repair service on plumbing, heating, and electrical systems, decorative services such as painting and wallpapering, maintenance services such as major cleaning and lawn care, and small handyman jobs. The company began operations on January 1, 1973, after approximately 15 months of research and planning by Mr. Lewis M. Weinstein (34) and Mr. Richard L. Hutter (37).

A native of Camden, New Jersey, Weinstein received a B.S. in engineering from Princeton University in 1962 and an M.B.A. with highest honors from the Harvard Business School in 1965. After working for a time as a vice president of Management Data Corporation, Weinstein became director of finance and township manager of Cherry Hill, New Jersey. Hutter studied mechanical engineering at Drexel College and electrical and architectural engineering at the University of Pennsylvania. He had held a variety of jobs in which he was responsible for calculations and equipment selection of air-conditioning, heating, plumbing, and electrical systems for buildings ranging from single-family dwellings to an $80-million textile plant. Before joining MOH full time, he had been president of a mechanical contracting company which handled all types of refrigeration, air conditioning, heating, and electrical installation and service work.

Basically, the way that MOH worked was that customers paid a $12 annual membership fee and in return were eligible for MOH's maintenance, repair, and construction services. When members needed one of these services, they telephoned MOH, and a dispatcher contacted one of MOH's authorized service representatives, independent workers with whom MOH contracted. Emergency service was available 24 hours a day, 7 days a week, and response time on emergency jobs was often an hour or less. Normal service requests were usually handled the day they were received or the next day. Free estimates were available on any job other than a routine repair call. When the work was completed, customers made checks payable to MOH or charged the work on Master Charge or BankAmericard. An MOH dispatcher then telephoned the customer to make sure he or she was pleased with the service. Any problems were remedied immediately. Service representatives were paid by MOH only after member satisfaction had been verified.

Commenting on the origins of MOH, Weinstein stated that he, like many other people, had recognized the need for a professional home service delivery system for several years. He estimated that the total United States market for these services was as much as $20 billion per year just in homes. However, the industry was characterized by small, unorganized tradesmen whose business skills were secondary to their mechanical skills. According to Weinstein, thus far only a couple of other companies had managed to combine professional business approaches with top-notch mechanical talent, and these companies served very limited marketing areas. Since the summer of 1971, Weinstein and Hutter had discussed the possibility of starting such a company. Finally, in the fall and winter of 1972, they secured capital from seven investors, and Weinstein sold memberships while Hutter signed up contractors. "The fact that I had held public office and people recognized my name certainly increased the credibility of the company," Weinstein commented. "And Dick's contracts with various contractors whom he had worked with in the air-conditioning business enabled him to sign up excellent, reliable workers."

By January 1, 1973, MOH had 65 members and had contracted with 15 service representatives. It had also rented office space in Pennsauken, just across the town line from Cherry Hill, and had hired a man to serve as dispatcher and salesperson. "He didn't last very long," Weinstein commented later. "There was very little dispatching to do then—15 or 20 calls a week at the most. And he wasn't able to sell enough memberships to make enough money to live on." In the spring of 1973, Weinstein hired a woman to handle dispatching and general office work, two part-time salesmen to make door-to-door calls in an attempt to sell memberships directly, and other part-time people to sell memberships via the telephone. Talking about those early days, Weinstein said:

> We secured some new members that way, but it was to be impossible to control part-time people, especially since Dick and I ourselves were working here only part time. Our people promised customers the moon. Luckily we realized soon enough what was happening before our reputation was seriously damaged. We fired all the part-time people, I again became chief salesperson, and we spent a lot of time making sure our service lived up to the promises that had been made.

In the fall of 1973, the woman who had handled dispatching and general office work left, commenting that the place was "too dull and lonely to stay in." "She was really competent and we hated to lose her," Weinstein commented later, "but it proved to be a lucky break for us because it brought Flo Cohen into the organization, and she's done a lot to develop the personality for the whole company."

MOH's marketing efforts during the first part of 1973 were limited to a couple of ads written by Weinstein for the *Cherry Hill Shopper's Guide.* These early ads did not mention membership because Weinstein couldn't figure out how to use ads to sell memberships in a new company with a concept people had never heard of. "At that time, we'd do a job and then try to talk people into joining," Weinstein said. "We thought about not requiring membership at all, but a survey of members and nonmembers showed that jobs completed and dollars per job were much greater for members." (See Exhibit 1 for results of survey.) In September, Weinstein hired an advertising agency and began to put out brochures and do other things to gain recognition. For example, he set up a booth at the Cherry Hill Home Show, passed out about three helium-filled balloons per minute for 14 hours (the balloons carried the MOH logos), and discussed MOH's services with people who stopped at the booth. "This gained tremendous exposure for us," Weinstein said, "but it was hard to measure the direct response it generated."

MOH made money not by selling memberships but by billing customers 10 to 20 percent more than the amount it paid service representatives. MOH managed to keep its rates competitive with independent contractors, however, because its service representatives were willing to work for MOH at less than the

TABLE 1

	Sept. 30, 1973	Sept. 30, 1974
Number of members	325	1,398
Service income, YTD	$55,040	$161,246
Completed jobs, YTD	855	2,084

going market rate for several reasons. First, they were paid at the end of the week if their work had been completed satisfactorily. Thus, they did not have to carry receivables for 60 to 90 days as was customary in the business. Second, many were guaranteed a substantial amount of work from MOH. Third, if the service representatives went out to make an estimate, they had a higher than average chance of getting the job. Weinstein felt that other less obvious reasons contractors liked to work for MOH were that they received some helpful tips from Hutter about running their own businesses and that they simply liked to come into the MOH office, have a cup of coffee, and chat with the office staff.

By the end of 1973, the feasibility of providing services as planned had been proved. In December, Hutter joined MOH full time, and in January 1974, Weinstein did likewise. After securing additional capital, they began to expand marketing efforts. As a result of these efforts, membership, service income, and completed jobs increased considerably (see Table 1).

The jobs completed by MOH workers ranged from normal repair and maintenance to rather bizarre tasks, such as getting and keeping squirrels out of a hot-water heater, painting a mural on a bedroom wall, and pulling a 175-pound Great Pyrenees with a bulky cast on one of her legs out of a muddy creek.

CURRENT SITUATION, JANUARY 1975

In January 1975, MOH employed 12 people directly in addition to Weinstein and Hutter. The hub of the company was the central dispatch organization which operated on a 24-hour basis, 7 days a week, and never utilized an answering service or a telephone recording device. The chief dispatcher was Ms. Flo Cohen, MOH's office manager. Cohen had formerly managed a large apartment complex for which Hutter supplied heating and air-conditioning systems. She was described as "a crackerjack gal with sooty eyelashes and clanking gold bangles who comes across like a longtime good neighbor yakking over the back fence. When people call in a panic, Flo Cohen applies mustard plasters to the chest."[1] MOH's office staff was completed by Ms. Rebecca Wilkocz and Ms. Barbara Lewis. Wilkocz handled a good deal of MOH's dispatching, all its customer verification, and other general office work. Before joining MOH, she had

---

[1] Tilly Spetgang, "How Much Would You Charge to Pull Martha Out of the Mud?", *The Philadelphia Bulletin's Discover* magazine, April 14, 1974, pp. 16–18.

been the on-site office manager of a major construction firm. Lewis handled MOH's bookkeeping and did miscellaneous secretarial tasks. "Each of us has specific tasks we're responsible for," Lewis commented, "but we're flexible enough to pitch in and help each other when someone gets overloaded."

The office which Cohen "managed" was a rather chaotic operation with telephones ringing, service representatives wandering in and out chatting, drinking coffee, and picking up supplies or checks for work completed, incessant good-natured banter, and much concern about keeping customers happy. Cohen commented as follows:

> Most customers are very nice when they call for service, but we do get some people who are really obnoxious. Especially when the moon is full, all the crazies come out of the woodwork. A nasty guy called yesterday and ordered me to send someone out to fix his roof. I asked him if he was a member of MOH. "What do you mean by membership?" he asked, "What about my roof?" "Where does the water seem to be coming from?" I asked him. Then he shouted, "If I knew that, I wouldn't be calling you!" He slammed down the phone, and I hope we'll never hear from him again. But no matter what the callers say, we won't be provoked. We really spoil our members on purpose. We want them to know that we're always available to serve them, not to cause them more problems.

Wilkocz said that the only customers who really bothered her were the ones who lied. She elaborated as follows:

> Some people will complain that our service reps haven't called them and arranged to do their work. They'll swear they've been home every minute for the last week. But if our service reps have trouble reaching them, our night dispatcher will try until he gets them. The complaint that we neglect them just isn't true.
> When I call customers to see if they're satisfied with the work and they say "no," I first try to find out if they have a legitimate complaint. One guy complained that his brother-in-law could have fixed his television set faster than our repairman, only his brother-in-law lives in Milwaukee. Another argued that our prices were too high even though he had agreed to the price a week earlier. Now I don't consider these valid complaints. But if customers complain about inferior work or that our people left their houses in a mess, we do everything we can to rectify the situation. Sometimes Lew will talk with them or Dick will go do whatever is necessary to satisfy the customer, even though we'll lose money on the job. On the whole, however, we get relatively few complaints. My interest in my job stays high because I'm almost always being called for service, not complaints.

Commenting on the organization as a whole, Cohen said:

> This company is unique because Lew and Dick get along well together, are knowledgeable in the field, and put enough research and planning into the company to make it work. One big reason for the success we've had thus far is that Lew and Dick are easy to get along with, they're good to their employees, and they make everyone, including the service reps, feel comfortable. They don't pressure us because they know we're working hard to make a success of the company too. There's a rapport here that's lacking in many companies.

Cohen said that, as the company opened new branches, she would probably go from one office to another training people. "The company's Wandering Jew is what I'll be," she quipped.

MOH's night dispatcher was a victim of rheumatoid arthritis who worked out of his home. "He was doing nothing before we hired him," Weinstein commented. "He's on call seven nights a week from 4:30 P.M. until 8:30 A.M., and he loves it." The salaries of MOH's dispatchers and office personnel ranged from $150 to $175 per week.

MOH employed two telephone salespeople who called potential customers to set up appointments for a salesperson to visit their homes and explain MOH's services. No obligation was connected with this visit, and a small gift was given to the potential customer. Telephone salespeople were paid $2.50 per hour plus $2 per appointment plus a $10 bonus for every 12 appointments made in 1 week.

The task of turning leads into members was the responsibility of Ms. Phyllis Bonanno, Ms. Ginny Crawford, and Mr. John Corsonica. Bonanno had previously sold real estate and memberships in a health spa, and immediately before she joined MOH, she had been working as a secretary. "I hated typing and being stuck in an office all day," she said. "I was always talking back to the men. When Lew asked me to fill out an application for this job, I told him he could get all my data from my employment agency. I was really surprised when he offered me the job." Bonanno went on to say that she enjoyed the wide variety of experiences and the opportunities for growth which the job offered. "Lew has given me a good opportunity. He sees I have a lot of drive, and he listens to what I say. Of course I'm going to work hard, not just for the money but because I want to help make the company successful."

Bonanno was paid a $10 commission on regular membership sales and $6 on memberships sold to realtors to use as gifts for their customers. She was guaranteed $150 per week. Crawford and Corsonica both worked only part time for MOH. They were paid $6 per sale and received no guarantee. All received a 12-cents-per-mile travel allowance.

MOH's twelfth employee was a full-time mechanic whose salary and benefits amounted to about $250 a week.

In January 1975, MOH's membership totaled 1,849. MOH contracted with about 200 independent workers, and it represented anywhere from 10 to 60 percent of a contractor's total volume. During the week, MOH received up to 50 calls a day from members or prospective members, and on weekends it often received as many as 25 calls. Of MOH members who had called for service, 70 percent had called more than once. However, it now appeared that MOH would do only about $200 worth of business per member in 1974, as opposed to the projected $300 per member. Weinstein attributed this poor performance to generally bad economic conditions and to free memberships distributed by MOH or realtors which were not being used. (See Exhibit 2 for a statistical summary of MOH operations, and Exhibit 3 for operating expenses through November 1974.)

MOH had begun to get into the commercial market, i.e., small restaurants, office complexes, plants, shopping centers, apartment buildings, and so forth. Weinstein feared that these members could present problems because commercial bookkeeping procedures would probably require that MOH bill the company, and it would be at least 30 days before the bill was paid. Since MOH would still pay the service representatives as soon as they completed the work satisfactorily, its working capital requirements would be higher than at present. Weinstein thought that Corsonica would probably be MOH's chief commercial salesperson once a marketing program for these accounts was well underway. "It seems silly to sell a $12 membership to a $12 million corporation," Weinstein commented, "but the $12 will be easy to get, so why not?"

THE MARKET

In January 1975, MOH's marketing area consisted primarily of Cherry Hill and five surrounding communities—Moorestown, Mt. Laurel, Marlton, Cinnaminson, and Haddonfield. Within these communities, the prime candidates for MOH's services were thought to be residents who had lived less than 5 years in houses which were less than 10 years old and which according to the 1970 census had a median value of over $20,000. Weinstein estimated that, within a 5-year period, ownership of about 25 percent of these houses changed hands. He stated that MOH customers came from a wide variety of ethnic backgrounds, but that certain patterns seemed to be emerging. "We do better in newer Jewish neighborhoods because the tradition is to have people come in to do work," he commented. "It's very difficult to sell memberships to Italians, however. No matter how wealthy the family, the tradition of doing all one's own work around the house is still very strong."

Cherry Hill was by far MOH's dominant market. Located 6½ miles east of Philadelphia and adjacent to Camden, New Jersey, it covered 24.51 square miles. In 1940, this area had consisted primarily of fruit and vegetable farms and contained only 5,000 residents. After World War II, some industries moved in, but not until 1960 did major growth take place. By 1970 its population had reached 68,000, and it had been transformed into a cosmopolitan, suburban community. Residents came from a wide variety of ethnic and religious backgrounds. In 1972, Cherry Hill had over 18,000 single-family houses and over 3,000 apartment units. Each dwelling housed an average of 3¼ individuals and the median age was 30½ years. The township had 62 light industry manufacturing companies which together employed about 5,500 people. RCA Corporation alone had 1,700 employees, most of whom were electronic engineers and skilled workers. Other residents worked in outlying areas, and about 500 commuted 80 miles to jobs in New York City.

Moorestown covered a very large geographical area. The older part of the community consisted of very wealthy residents living in large colonial homes. New luxury homes were being built in the rural parts of Moorestown, and these were said to be "like the nicest parts of Cherry Hill."

TABLE 2

	Potential customers*	MOH members	Percent of penetration
Cherry Hill	15,000	1,200	8
Moorestown and Mt. Laurel	4,000	90	2
Marlton	3,000	60	2
Cinnaminson	4,000	32	1
Haddonfield	4,000	80	2
All others (Pennsauken and Merchantville primarily)	55,000	335	0.6

* Estimated by Weinstein.

Weinstein described Mt. Laurel as "essentially one development built around a golf course." He said the residents were upper middle class but not as wealthy as those in Moorestown. He estimated the top price of Mt. Laurel homes to be about $40,000.

Marlton was a brand new development. "There are no trees, and people who live there appear to be highly transient," Weinstein commented. "Homes worth $25,000 sell for $40,000." Marlton was expected to continue to be a major growth area.

Cinnaminson had a fairly heterogeneous population. The older sections were not as affluent as the newer sections, and the latter were not as wealthy as newer sections in MOH's other communities.

Haddonfield was said to be "older, more colonial, and even wealthier than Moorestown." It had very few new homes and no open land for any more construction. While MOH's success there had been minimal, Weinstein felt that any success at all indicated that MOH could market its services in older areas.

MOH's penetration of each community is shown in Table 2.

MOH'S MARKETING PROGRAMS

Weinstein had used a wide range of marketing programs to accomplish his first task, i.e., to secure members for MOH. He had found that direct selling was by far the best method of getting members who would use the services. He felt that, since the decision to join MOH was usually made by women, memberships were probably best sold by women. However, he felt that if the sales pitch were made to a couple a man could be equally successful. "John hasn't had the successes Phyllis has," he commented, "but neither has anyone else. Let's face it. Phyllis is a super salesperson for this business. It will be very hard to find anyone as competent when we open branches in other areas."

On the average, Bonanno sold about 21 memberships a week. Her sales calls averaged about 30 minutes, though they might last from 10 minutes to over an hour. She often made about eight calls per day, but she had done as many as twelve. Commenting on the selling task, she said:

The situations vary a lot. Last week I visited a sweet old lady who just wanted the free wine decanter and a little company. Other customers will be grumpy and fire questions at me, then end up buying. The ones that are most frustrating are women who have to ask their husbands if they can buy a membership. I'm irritated they can't make a $12 decision on their own, and it means I've got to follow up with another visit. If the husband is a real macho type, he probably won't admit that there's anything he can't do, and he's not a very likely prospect for our services.

When the cost of the gift which MOH gave the prospective member for agreeing to an appointment, the salesperson's commission, and the expenses involved in generating a lead were tallied, signing up a member cost considerably more than the $12 membership fee covered. Furthermore, MOH did not make money on membership renewals, and Weinstein was considering making the $12 membership fee a one-time requirement.

In the beginning, the telephone group tried to sell MOH memberships. This was unsuccessful, however, and its function was now limited to making appointments for salespeople to visit homes and explain MOH's program. In the past, MOH had four telephone salespeople, but two had produced very few leads and Weinstein had let them go. The telephone operation currently consisted of two women who together produced about 30 appointments per week, 50 to 60 percent of which resulted in memberships. "We need to increase the number of appointments considerably," Weinstein commented. "We'd like to get 100 new members a month from this source, so that means we need at least 150 appointments."

Weinstein described his telephone operation as "a rather informal outfit, pretty far removed from the traditional boiler room of most telephone sales operations." His telephone salespeople made calls on Monday through Thursday from 6:30 to 9:30 P.M. and on Saturday from 10:30 A.M. to 1:30 P.M. "We call in the evening because that's the best time to catch people at home," Weinstein commented. "Most of the women in the area don't stay home during the day."

The telephone salespeople had a set sales pitch which they could use or deviate from at will. (See Exhibit 4 for sales pitch.) Weinstein encouraged them to ask immediately if it was a good time to talk to a potential customer. "If people are busy, there's no point trying to get them to listen to us," he said. "That'll just alienate them, and we'll waste our time. It's better to get on to the next potential customer." He stated further that it usually took about 5 minutes for a telephone salesperson to complete the whole pitch and that if she got to the end she usually secured an appointment. The telephone salespeople had called all the residents of MOH's six major communities once, and they were now on the second round of calls to Cherry Hill residents.

Ms. Renee Bash, who had joined MOH as a telephone salesperson in September 1974, commented on her job:

*I never thought I could do telephone selling, but now I love it. Some nights I'm
really psyched up and can talk anybody into making an appointment, but if I'm depressed, I usually have trouble. If I can make two appointments before 7:00 P.M., I
know I'll have a good night. That's unusual, though, because people are tied up with
dinner the first half hour we're calling, and they're not very receptive to us.*

*I don't talk politics or try to raise anybody's consciousness. I just tell people
about MOH and see if they want to make an appointment. If they're not interested,
I want to get on to someone who is. Sometimes it's hard to get off the phone.
I must have an earth mother voice that inspires confidence because people tell me
about their suicide attempts, their divorces, their new babies, and anything
else that comes to mind.*

Bash went on to say that she believed in MOH, liked the people she
worked with and for, and appreciated the fact that Weinstein did not pressure
her to make more appointments. On her best night, she had made eight appointments, and she made anywhere from 20 to 65 calls in a 3-hour period.
Weinstein stated that Bash averaged one appointment for six calls made.

Ms. Pat McCabe, who had also joined MOH in September 1974, stated
that, when four people had been making calls, some competition had developed, but that, for the most part, everyone "cheer-leaded" each other. She said
it was especially easy to talk to someone who had seen an MOH advertisement.
She continued:

*Women are by far the easiest people to set up an appointment with. If teenagers
answer, they're hostile because you're tying up their phone. If men answer, you
have to do a whole number to make sure their egos aren't threatened. You've got
to let them know that signing up with MOH doesn't mean that they're not king of
their domicile.*

McCabe went on to say that she and Bash often approached customers in
markedly different ways.

*Renee gets right to the nitty-gritty of why she's calling, but I like to ease into the
presentation more slowly. Both of us bend over backwards to be courteous. If we
don't, it reflects badly on Lew and the company. A few people are already put off
by the name of the company. Lately we've gotten a lot of depressing stories—
people telling us they just got laid off from their jobs.*

Bash and McCabe said that, to fill the vacancies in their department, they
would recommend recruiting a mature person who had done some organizational work and who had rapport with people. They felt their current sales pitch
worked well but they had to be free to deviate from it, especially when people
started asking questions. They would not, however, try to sell memberships or
explain the whole service over the telephone.

In addition to telephone solicitation, direct-response advertising was used
to generate appointments. Most of the ads had been run in the *Cherry Hill*

Shopper's Guide and the weekly ~~Cherry Hill~~ *News,* both of which covered Cherry Hill, Moorestown, Mt. Laurel, and Marlton. A few ads had been run in the *Haddonfield Shopper's Guide* and in a small local paper in Cinnaminson. Some ads offered a free gift to people who called MOH and scheduled an appointment with a "membership representative," i.e., a salesperson. Weinstein stated that ads which included customer testimonials plus a free gift offer had generated high recognition for MOH and for the members who appeared in them. "Howard Felt claims that he has received more recognition by appearing in MOH ads then he ever received when he ran for Cherry Hill town council," Weinstein commented. Over 90 percent of all appointments generated by advertisements had been turned into sales. MOH had gotten 10 times better response from the *Cherry Hill Shopper's Guide* than from *The Cherry Hill News,* but Weinstein felt MOH should continue to advertise occasionally in *The Cherry Hill News* to strengthen the company's credibility. Weinstein had run one ad in the Camden daily newspaper (circulation 135,000). "It was a mistake to advertise in such a broad-based media," Weinstein commented. "Too many dollars got wasted in areas we can't cover. We spent $600 on that ad and got only fifteen responses within our marketing area." (See Exhibit 5 for examples of MOH's advertisements.)

MOH also advertised in the Cherry Hill *Blue Pages,* a publication similar to the telephone company's *Yellow Pages.* In November 1974, the book was circulated free to about 43,000 homes in Cherry Hill and two adjacent communities. MOH had been the first company to buy advertising in the *Blue Pages* and consequently had gotten excellent positions for its ads. It had a large ad on the first page and a three- or four-line listing under almost every category in the directory. Weinstein did not know how many members MOH had secured as a result of *Blue Pages'* advertisements, but he thought the book would keep MOH in people's minds and would increase the likelihood they would call MOH whenever they turned to the *Blue Pages* for services.

Also in November 1974, MOH made arrangements with Welcome Wagon[1] to be included in the approximately 200 presentations it made each month to new residents of the Cherry Hill area. There had not yet been sufficient experience to draw firm conclusions about this program, but Weinstein thought about 50 percent of the leads it generated would turn into membership sales. (See Exhibit 6 for the MOH letter included in the Welcome Wagon package.)

Another marketing device MOH used was to sell memberships at reduced rates to about 30 realtors who then gave the memberships to their customers as gifts. Realtors paid only $4 per membership. The number of new members derived from this source depended on the overall condition of the real estate market, and in recent months, the market had been very slow. Weinstein thought that, in normal times, MOH could expect about 75 to 100 memberships

---

[1] Welcome Wagon was an organization whose primary service was greeting new residents of a community and acquainting them with various institutions (hospitals, schools, etc.) and merchants within the community. The merchants they discussed were Welcome Wagon "sponsors," merchants who paid an annual fee for the service and who usually gave a small gift to the newcomers.

per month from realtors currently involved in the program. He was making concentrated efforts to expand the number of participating realtors. While he felt this was a good way to get members, experience had shown that these members did not use the services very much. He concluded that realtor salespeople either would not or could not do MOH's sales job, and he now had Bonanno take the free gifts and explain the program to the new home owners.

Weinstein had considered advertising on billboards, but he found that the few billboards in Cherry Hill cost about $700 per month, an amount which he considered "unquestionably prohibitive."

MOH had briefly run a program whereby members received a gift for getting their neighbors to make an appointment with an MOH salesperson. This program had not generated many leads, and Weinstein felt MOH members had actually been insulted by the free gift offer. "I'll recommend MOH if the service is good and the prices are right, but not just because you give me a wine decanter," one member had commented.

Weinstein thought one good way to generate new memberships would be for Bonnano to address women's groups. For this to be successful, however, the logistics of getting people to sign up immediately would have to be carefully worked out.

Weinstein's second marketing task was to increase the usage of MOH services by members. Thus far, MOH's limited resources had not permitted much in this area, but Weinstein felt it was essential to step up its efforts. His program consisted of three direct-mail items—a newsletter, a valuegram, and a tabloid. MOH had labels for the direct-mail pieces preprinted, and the office crew and telephone people put them on in their spare time. Sometimes they were assisted by Wilkocz's daughter and Weinstein's wife.

The newsletter had been sent monthly from December 1973 through September 1974. It was a folksy kind of communication designed to reinforce the pleasant continuing relationship between MOH and its members. It contained news about employees and new programs, helpful hints, and some special values. Weinstein had discontinued the newsletter because he felt that, though members enjoyed reading it, it actually did very little selling. For example, the September newsletter had drawn only five requests for special service. (See Exhibit 7 for sample newsletter.)

In December 1974, MOH introduced the Valuegram, an inexpensive direct-mail piece which offered one special value for MOH members. Weinstein planned to mail two Valuegrams each month. (See Exhibit 8 for sample Valuegram.)

In November, MOH began sending its members a four-page tabloid which offered reduced rates on services and various products. The products were usually installed items such as humidifiers, which, according to Weinstein, MOH could price competitively with discount houses. (He stated that it was difficult to price uninstalled items competitively.) He described the initial tabloid as "quite successful." Its preparation costs had been about the same as those of the newsletter, but it had produced 111 service requests and a 300 percent contribution to overhead and profit versus the costs of preparation and distribution. Weinstein planned to send out tabloids monthly. (*See* Exhibit 9 for sample tabloid, and Exhibit 10 for MOH's marketing expenses for 1974.)

PLANS FOR CORPORATE GROWTH

Weinstein and Hutter's goal was for MOH to become a nationwide corporation with branches in every metropolitan area. They considered the Cherry Hill branch a prototype that allowed experimentation and development of strategy, structure, and procedures which would be applicable elsewhere. "If we can eventually operate, say, fifty branches each of which has 7,000 members, and if each member generates $300 of service volume per year, not only will we have a large corporation, but we'll completely change the method of home services delivery in this country," Weinstein commented. He calculated MOH's potential annual service volume as follows:

- Per branch: 7,000 members
  $300 per year per member
  $2,000,000 service gross per year
- Total: $2,000,000 service gross per branch per year
  50 branches
  $100,000,000 total service gross per year

He calculated MOH's potential annual profitability as follows:

- Per branch: $2,000,000 service volume
  20 percent contribution
  $400,000 contribution
  $200,000 branch overhead
  $200,000 branch profit
- Total: $200,000 profit per branch
  50 branches
  $10,000,000 branch profit
  $1,000,000 corporate overhead
  $9,000,000 corporate profit

Weinstein thought MOH could achieve these profits with a total equity investment of less than $1 million plus cash flow generated by the earlier branches, and that MOH would very likely attract the needed equity. He noted furthermore that the projected $300 service volume per member included only the kinds of services already offered by MOH. With a nationwide market of 350,000 members from the top strata of the American consuming public, Weinstein felt it was "highly likely" that additional products and services could be sold in significant quantities and that product line expansion was a major long-

TABLE 3

	Total number of units	Units valued at $25,000 to $35,000		Units valued at $35,000 to $50,000		Units valued above $50,000	
Current market (i.e., Cherry Hill branch)	85,779	13,921	16%	5,319	6%	1,708	2%
Proposed market (i.e., northeast Philadelphia branch)	131,137	20,727	16%	8,705	7%	3,753	3%

term objective. He also felt that someday legislation would be passed requiring realtors to issue warranties on homes sold. He thought these warranties would probably last for 1 year and would cover anywhere from $150 to $300 in repairs after the home had been brought up to warranty level.

Weinstein enumerated four criteria which he felt MOH must meet before it opened new branches: (1) proof that the service delivery system could function effectively on a large scale; (2) proof that the marketing program could produce consistent growth in memberships and service usage; (3) development of a branch organization structure which could function without direct, day-to-day involvement of corporate officers; and (4) achievement of break-even service volume as proof that overhead projections were realistic. He felt MOH had made substantial progress in all four areas and that a second branch would be feasible in late 1975. He thought at least 1 year's experience with two branches would precede further expansion, but then expansion would follow at a more rapid rate.

The new branch which Weinstein and Hutter planned to open in 1975 would be located close to its current market and would encompass portions of northeast Philadelphia, lower Bucks County, and eastern Montgomery County. This area was very similar to MOH's current market (see Table 3). There was also a close correlation between ages of houses and length of time current residents had lived in the houses in the two markets. "If the factors we're looking at are the relevant ones for this business, we would expect our experience in the northeast Philadelphia branch to be similar to our experience in Cherry Hill," Weinstein said. "But we're still too new in the business to know if in fact we are using the appropriate criteria."

For the northeast Philadelphia branch, Weinstein would need a branch manager whose main functions would be to recruit and supervise service representatives and to oversee the operations of the branch office. Membership sales would be handled by branch salespeople, but they would be supervised by a corporate sales manager, probably Bonanno. Dispatching would be done by branch personnel.

Marketing activities would be controlled at the Pennsauken office. Weinstein thought that first-year operating and marketing expenses for the new branch would be about $100,000 and that the branch would not reach break-even until midway through its second year of operation. He felt, however, that MOH should raise about $400,000 to $500,000 before it opened the new branch. "Right now we're horribly undercapitalized," he commented. "I'm just plain tired of not having adequate working capital." He stated further that he wanted to stay away from franchising because it would not allow him to control adequately the quality of work performed.

As Weinstein contemplated moving into a new market, he wanted to position MOH properly. The first brochure used in the Cherry Hill market had stressed MOH's emergency service, and it had taken considerable effort to broaden the company's image to that of a total home service company. Weinstein was also concerned about what marketing programs he should use and what their order and magnitude should be. "Our marketing program is under tremendous pressure because we've got to start growing at a faster rate," he said. "We've done all right this year, but to reach our goals and open new branches as scheduled, we need to do two or three times as well as we did this year."

EXHIBIT 1
DATA REGARDING SERVICE FOR MEMBERS AND NONMEMBERS, AUGUST 1, 1973
Man of the House, Inc.

	Members*	Nonmembers
Number of service requests	634	342
Number of completed jobs	436	133
Close rate	69%	39%
Service dollars	31,800	6,300
Dollars per job	73	47
Percentage of job requests:		
For discretionary jobs	20	20
Close rate for discretionary jobs	26	6
Close rate for necessary jobs	79	47

* Included in the category are those who originally called as nonmembers requesting service and who subsequently became members.

EXHIBIT 2
STATISTICAL SUMMARY, 1973 AND 1974
Man of the House, Inc.

	Jan.	Feb.	Mar.	Apr.	May	June
Membership income:						
1973	876	216	312	528	1,020	240
1974	636	1,152	1,296	1,920	2,976	3,636
% '74 vs. '73	73	533	415	364	291	1,515
Service income:						
1973	980	2,352	1,291	4,902	8,445	14,339
1974	8,812	9,363	8,266	15,844	24,276	29,974
% '74 vs. '73	899	398	640	323	288	209
Requests for service:						
1973	74	61	84	265	262	307
1974	191	129	144	288	389	453
% '74 vs. '73	258	211	171	109	148	148
Completed jobs:						
1973	20	49	27	95	142	160
1974	91	129	128	204	328	306
% '74 vs. '73	455	263	474	215	232	191
Ratio completed jobs/requests:						
1973	27%	80%	32%	36%	54%	52%
1974	48%	100%	89%	71%	84%	68%
Dollars per job:						
1973	49	48	48	52	59	90
1974	96	73	65	78	74	98
% '74 vs. '73	195	152	135	150	125	109
Number of members:*						
1973	88	103	145	193	248	289
1974	378	451	545	663	863	1,119
% '74 vs. '73	429	437	375	344	348	387
Service dollars per member per month:						
1973	15	27	13	34	44	58
1974	24	25	18	29	37	35
% '74 vs. '73	160	93	138	85	84	60

* At end of each month.

62

EXHIBIT 2
Continued

July	Aug.	Sept.	Oct.	Nov.	Dec.	Total
108	60	72	72	312	360	4,176
1,716	1,452	996	1,284	1,644	1,464	20,172
1,589	2,420	1,383	1,783	527	407	483
7,249	8,037	7,445	7,224	5,036	7,499	74,799
19,978	21,483	23,250	20,751	18,570	23,815	224,382
276	267	312	287	369	318	300
234	224	133	147	163	93	2,047
377	426	316	311	487	391	3,902
161	190	238	212	299	420	191
147	115	100	118	83	78	1,134
309	320	269	284	277	359	3,004
210	278	269	241	334	460	265
63%	51%	75%	80%	51%	84%	55%
82%	75%	85%	91%	57%	92%	77%
49	70	74	61	61	96	66
65	67	86	73	67	66	75
133	96	116	120	110	69	114
305	319	325	332	358	374	3,079
1,224	1,329	1,398	1,497	1,633	1,735	12,835
401	417	430	451	456	464	417
25	26	23	22	15	21	323
18	18	18	15	13	15	265
72	69	78	68	87	71	82

EXHIBIT 3
APPROXIMATE OPERATING EXPENSES, 1974
Man of the House, Inc.

Corporate expenses:	
Salaries and wages	$ 68,000
General and administrative	34,000
Marketing	8,000
	$110,000
Cherry Hill branch:	
Salaries and wages	$ 28,000
General and administrative	14,000
Marketing	36,000
	$ 78,000
Total	$188,000

EXHIBIT 4
TELEPHONE SALES PITCH
Man of the House, Inc.

Mr./Mrs. _____? This is _____ from Man of the House. Did I catch you at a bad time? . . . I'm calling to tell you a little bit about Man of the House and also give you a chance to get a really super free gift.

Have you heard about Man of the House? . . . We have an outstanding home service program to do everything you need done in your home. When you find out about our program, I think you'll really be excited about it. We can save you a lot of money and a lot of aggravation.

Are you curious about what we do? . . . It takes about 10 minutes to cover all of the benefits we offer, and that's why we have Phyllis. Her job is to come to your home, explain the program, and answer all of your questions.

Now let me tell you about your free gift. Did you see it advertised this week in the Shopper or the News? It's a really super, unbreakable ice scraper. How many did you break last winter? . . . Well, you won't break this one! Everyone who's seen it wants one—and you can have one free—with no obligation—just for scheduling an appointment with Phyllis to learn about Man of the House.

Would you prefer an afternoon appointment, or would it be better for you in the evening?

EXHIBIT 5

Man of the House, Inc.

EXHIBIT 5
Continued

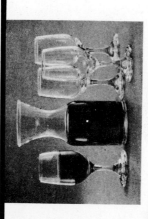

I thought Howard could fix everything. Then I found Man of the House.

by Carole A. Felt
Point of Woods,
Cherry Hill

My husband, the handyman. He can fix just about anything around the house. He wallpapered our bedrooms, built shelves for his study and installed a new brick patio out front. But there are some jobs Howard just can't handle. And when these jobs pop up, we call Man of the House.

We called MOH to do electrical work and install a new humidifier and were quite pleased. They've proven to us to be efficient and completely dependable and I highly recommend them to anyone I know.

After living in this area for four years, I have found that the only guaranteed work is from Man of the House. And, of course, from my husband, Howard.

In addition to Carole Felt, these local realtors also use and recommend MOH:

Borden ● Castle ● Erhardt ● Farrell & Hill ● Gitomer ● Kolton ● Lenny Manor ● Mancini & Tacknoff ● Paparone ● Parulak & Green ● Penthouse ● Pritchett Reinke ● Sayers & Runner ● Straub ● Todd ● Trengove

Need immediate help?
Call our 24 hour service line right now 663-2191.

MAN OF THE HOUSE INC.
7703 Maple Avenue
Pennsauken, N. J. 08109

☐ TELL ME MORE ABOUT MOH.
☐ HERE'S MY $12.00. I WANT TO
    JOIN MAN OF THE HOUSE.

Name _____
Address _____
City _____ State _____ Zip. _____
Phone Number _____

Free Cheers.*

A Free Wine Decanter Set Just For Talking With Us.

Here's an offer you can't pass up. Right now, when you call Man of the House and set up an appointment with one of our representatives, we'll present you with a handsome 5-piece wine decanter set. Free.

It's our way of saying "thanks" for allowing us to explain our unique program to you.

In as little as 15 minutes, our representative can show you how you can save a lot of time, money and aggravation.

* While supply lasts; comparable substitute thereafter.

And in today's economy, that's something every homeowner can appreciate.

Call Man of the House now at 663-2191. There's absolutely no obligation and, whether or not you join, the decanter set is yours to keep.

Now that's something you can drink to.

Man of the House inc.

663-2191

We'll fix your house. Without breaking your budget.

7703 Maple Avenue, Pennsauken, N.J. 08109

EXHIBIT 6
Man of the House, Inc.

7703 Maple Avenue ■ Pennsauken, N.J. 08109
609-663-2191

Welcome Wagon® INTRODUCES MAN OF THE HOUSE TO YOU!

You've just moved into a new home!
You want to make it distinctly yours.
Who can you call to help you?
Welcome Wagon has the solution for you;
Call Man of the House.

One great company, one telephone number,
over 60 services. Everything from changing
your locks to installing floodlights to
painting and paperhanging. Even cleaning
your windows or beautifying your lawn.
Plus 24 hour emergency repair service. Their
reputation is excellent and their prices are
reasonable.

Man of the House is for members only. It
costs just $12.00 to join, but you must be
a member to benefit from all the services
and special prices. We think it would be to
your advantage to call Man of the House and
arrange an appointment with their membership
representative. We're sure you'll be excited
about all the services Man of the House can
offer you, and you'll even get a useful gift.

You should call *Phyllis Bosanno*
at 663-2191. Call now.

Special P. S. Man of the House will even bring
Voter Registration forms for you
to complete without leaving your
home.

EXHIBIT 7
Man of the House, Inc.

A little news from
MAN OF THE HOUSE INC.

Volume 2 No. 7   August 1974   Telephone 663-2191

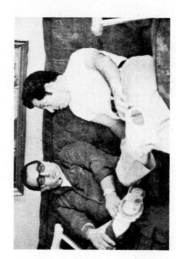

The Original Cast from Man of the House

Handyman Sam Loggia fell off a ladder, and air conditioning repairman Phil Weiss fell off a curb. What more can we say?

Man of the House Monthly Specials

It's Time to Treat your Trees.

The bugs are flying again. And, even if you treated your trees at the beginning of the season, it's time to spray them again. Man of the House can help protect your investment with our high pressure, non-toxic tree spray. And we can help you save money too.

High Pressure Tree Spray:

Area To Be Sprayed	Amt. of Trees	Regular Price	Special Price
½ acre	Heavy	$90.00	$80.00
"	Moderate	50.00	45.00
¼ acre	Heavy	60.00	40.00
"	Moderate	40.00	35.00
	Minimum	30.00	25.00

Tree Feeding:

No. of Trees	Regular Price Per Tree	Special	Special With Spray
Moderate 10 trees or less	$8.00	$7.00	$6.00
Heavy 11 trees or more	6.00	5.00	4.00

Gas Barbeque Special

Man of the House can help you save time and money with this deluxe barbeque grill. You can save time because the grill is a self-cleaning unit. It's also the only grill available with cast iron porcelain grates. You'll enjoy cooking on it all summer long because it features Turbo-air venting on the back to rotate the heat for more even cooking. The grates are 15'' x 22'' and there's also a cutting board and heat indicator.

And here's how Man of the House can save you money:

Regular Price of Barbeque	$156.54	
Installation	100.00	This Month's Special Price $199.00
	$256.54	Save $57.54

Color, Black; Weight, 60 lbs; not sold in stores.

MAN OF THE HOUSE INC.

7703 Maple Avenue
Pennsauken, N.J. 08109
663-2191

EXHIBIT 7

Continued

Dickie's Do's and Don'ts by Dick Hutter V.P.

Dear Member,

This column will appear periodically to provide you with some helpful tips on home maintenance we suggest you perform to keep your repair bills at a minimum. You may find this a bit unusual, especially coming from a company that specializes in repairing and renovating homes, but our policy has always been to save our members unnecessary and costly repair bills and to continue to help them in any way possible.

This month, I'd like to remind you about a very important and timely service you should be performing and that is changing the filter on your air conditioner. Most people are under the assumption that they only have to change the filter at the beginning of the season, Not so. The filter should be changed every THREE TO FOUR WEEKS. The cleaner the filter, the more efficiently your system will operate, and, therefore, lower electric bills. So, if you haven't changed the filter in the past month, do it now.

I'd also like to inform you that, due to the low voltage problem, sometimes your air conditioner will trip the circuit breaker. If your unit stops working, check the breaker panel before you call for service. If the breaker is tripped, shut it all the way off and then on. If the breaker continues to trip, there may be a problem. Call us and we'll check the unit.

DICK'S THOUGHT FOR THE MONTH
"If you want to forget all your other troubles, wear tight shoes".

663-2191. Call this number for . . . .

Air Conditioning	Fencing
Alarm Systems	Formica Counter Tops
Appliance Repairs	Heating
Asphalt Driveways	Kitchen and Bathrooms
Brick and Block Work	Lawn and Tree Care
Carpentry	Locksmith
Carpet Cleaning	Major Household
Carpet Installation	Cleaning
Concrete Driveways	Ornamental Wrought Iron
and Patios	Packing and Moving
Drapes & Curtains	Painting (inside or out)
Drapery Cleaning	Plant Arrangements
Electrical	Plumbing
Exterminator	Remodeling

Roof and Gutter
Room Additions
Sewer Cleaning
Siding
Storm Doors
and Windows
Tile (floor and ceramic)
TV Repair
Vanities
Wallpaper
Waterproofing
Window Glazing
and Cleaning
. . .plus the MOH Handyman

Remember . . . . .We Stand Behind Every Job.

These local Realtors Use and Recommend Our Services

Academy • Beckett • Bordon • Casel • Castle • Charleston • Chess • Erhardt
Farrell & Hill • Flinn • Gitomer • Kolton • Lenny • Manor • Mancini & Tacknoff
Paparone • Pawulak & Green • Penthouse • Pritchett • Reinke
Sayers & Runner • Stanton & Tobey • Straub • Todd • Trengrove • Vogdes

- [ ] Here's my $12. I want to JOIN Man of the House. Send me my membership certificate and service discount coupons.

Charge my
- [ ] BankAmericard # . . . .
- [ ] MasterCharge # . . . .

. . . .
Signature

Name . . . .

Address . . . .

City . . . . State . . . . Zip . . . . . . Phone . . . .

Today

THE PHILADELPHIA INQUIRER MAGAZINE

Serendipity

A WEEKLY GUIDE TO THE GOOD LIFE . . . .

SUNDAY, JUNE 23, 1974   EDITED BY ROBIN PALLEY

The Repairman Cometh

A Cherry Hill resident swears that when his hot water heater blew at 2 a.m. on Saturday, **Man of the House,** 7703 Maple Avenue in Pennsauken, had a new heater installed in time for Sunday morning bath. Man of the House offers a sort of "crisis insurance" for home owners. Members can take advantage of their men on call—plumbers, gardners, electricians, T.V. repairmen, painters, and locksmiths who offer home repair service—24 hours a day, seven days a week. Membership costs $12 and includes three $2 coupons to spend on work done in your home. After that, work is billed on a by-the-job basis. Every MOH visit is followed by a check-up call to make sure you're completely satisfied. In addition, an MOH newsletter offers special prices on certain jobs each month. Members receive free estimates on remodeling and major house cleaning, lawn and tree care. Call 1-609-663-2191 to join. Though the service is now limited to the Cherry Hill-Pennsauken area, cheer up Philadelphia: MOH plans to open in the Northeast sometime soon.

Our Services Are Growing.

We've Added Terrariums!

Now you can enhance the decor of any room in your home with a lovely terrarium from Man of the House. These terrariums are quite different from the ones you've seen because they're created with a natural look, not unlike that of a miniature forest or garden. They're made by none other than our chief dispatcher, Flo Cohen, and they're made to your order with no obligation to buy if you are not completely satisfied. The prices range from $10 (for a small one) to $45 (for the largest one imaginable.) So, if you'd like to beautify your home, or give someone an unusual gift, think of Man of the House and our terrariums.

Is Everybody Happy?

At Man of the House, we hope so. And we want to hear about it if you're not. You see, our policy is to stand behind all the work we perform. And that's why we follow the completion of every job with a check-up phone call to see if you're completely satisfied. We know we're good, but we also realize that we're not perfect. So, if there's ever any problem, please let us know about it. Immediately. You'll be surprised at how anxious we are to keep you happy.

The Next Time You Call Man of the House, Hang Up.

We're talking about our new drapery service, the latest idea from Man of the House to help you beautify your home. We can now offer you custom draperies and curtains for your house or office right in the convenience of your own home. Our representative will be happy to call on you and help you choose from a fashionable array of fabrics and styles. And all work is custom measured and cut and professionally hung. So take advantage of this unique new Man of the House service now. Call 663-2191 for an appointment.

EXHIBIT 8
Man of the House, Inc.

12-2-74
MAN OF THE HOUSE, INC.
7703 MAPLE AVE.
PENNSAUKEN, N.J.
08109

Man of the House inc.

Valuegram

BULK RATE
U.S. POSTAGE
PAID
Permit No. 389
Camden, N.J. 08101

Time Value

THIS VALUEGRAM WAS TRANSMITTED BY MAN OF THE HOUSE TO A POST OFFICE NEAR YOU FOR DELIVERY

➤ TO:

WE'LL CLEAN YOUR CARPETS........WITHOUT BREAKING YOUR BUDGET
DINING ROOM CARPET CLEANED FREE WHEN LIVING ROOM CLEANED AT NORMAL RATES....
12 x 15 LIVING ROOM $24.30....DINING ROOM FREE.......
15 x 20 LIVING ROOM $40.50....DINING ROOM FREE.......ETC......ETC.......
SHAMPOO METHOD......VACUUM, SHAMPOO, RE-VACUUM....DRY WITHIN 4 HOURS....
NOTE: SPECIAL TREATMENT FOR SPECIAL STAINS MAY BE EXTRA.....
TIME ALLOWS ONLY 50 SPECIALS BEFORE OFFER EXPIRES 12-31-74....SO CALL NOW!

...MAN OF THE HOUSE...

REPLY BY PHONE — CALL 663-2191 ······ 24 HOUR DISPATCH SERVICE ······ FOR MEMBERS ONLY

EXHIBIT 9
Man of the House, Inc.

71

EXHIBIT 9
Continued

We'll fix your house. With

Firewood Special

$50 per cord

delivered & stacked
reg. $70.00 **SAVE $20⁰⁰**

This winter Man of the House wants to light your fireplace! Imagine a warm, cozy fireplace to snuggle up to on cold winter nights. Shop around and compare prices. You'll find ours RED HOT. Members only.

Feel as comfortable at 68° as you would at 72° with this Thermal power humidifier. You can protect your family's health and save money at the same time. Humidifiers are recommended by area pediatricians. Members only. This model has the highest gallons per day rating of any unit in the same or higher price range: ARI — AIR CONDITIONING AND REFRIGERATION INSTITUTE CERTIFIED DIRECTORY RATING JULY 1 - DEC. 31, 1974.

Humidifier
$149⁹⁵

regularly $189.95

SAVE $40⁰⁰

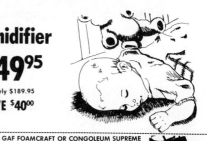

MANUFACTURER	MODEL	GAL. PER DAY
CARRIER	49BB001201	16.1
GENERAL ELECTRIC	BGHU500A	10.4
HERRMIDIFIER	447-1	10.3
SEARS	303.93251	16.0
SKUTTLE	98	17.2
WALTON	WA100	14.1
★ THERMAL	ST-200-6	20.0 ★

LEAF REMOVAL

Members only. Call 663-2191 now and schedule your lawn for a winter face-lift. Let our modern equipment give you the leisure time you deserve.

1/4 ACRE LOT **$24⁹⁵**

1/2 ACRE LOT **$39⁹⁵**

GAF FOAMCRAFT OR CONGOLEUM SUPREME
FLOORING SPECIAL

Beautify your kitchen with elegant and care free shinyl vinyl flooring that will be the envy of all your friends. Or give a bright new look to your drab, dreary den. Turn it into a real show place. Now's the time and the price is golden! Members only. Call today for samples and estimates in the convenience of your home. Comparable savings on all size rooms. What else would you expect from Man of the House?

12'x12' FLOOR reg. $220.00 . . . . . **$176**

12'x18' FLOOR reg. $330.00 . . . . . **$264**

Price includes metal thresholds & adhesives. (Preparation of floors when required is extra.)

CARPETS & DRAPES

Shop in the convenience of your home with our Interior Decorator to beautifully and professionally co-ordinate colorful Autumn values! Same top quality material and guarantee as all Man of the House service. Remember, when you increase the beauty of your home, you also increases its value. The estimates are free and the values are unbeatable. Call today. 663-2191. Members only.

G. E. GARBAGE DISPOSAL Model GFC 110
$69⁹⁵

INCLUDES INSTALLATION

SAVE $25.05   reg. $95.00

(Don't forget to check with us on the price of all other appliances you need.)

Get rid of unsightly garbage quickly and effortlessly. Disposal comes with a 1 year guarantee on parts AND labor. A great holiday gift. Order yours today. 663-2191. Members only.

EXTERMINATOR SPECIAL

If insects and field mice are driving you buggy, now's the time to get rid of them. Man of the House will spray the interior and exterior perimeter of your home and place extermination trays for field mice which causes them to leave the premises before they die.

$16 reg. $20.00 SAVE $4⁰⁰

A 1 year contract for a monthly exterminator service can save you more money! Members only. $6 per month, reg. $7 - save $12.00.

ASPHALT DRIVEWAY SPECIAL

NEW 2" THICK ASPHALT TOPPING OVER YOUR EXISTING DRIVEWAY. THIS IS NOT A TAR COATING BUT 2" OF ASPHALT!

$125   reg. $160.00   SAVE $35⁰⁰

(Average driveway 10'x36'. For larger areas $3.13 per sq. yd.)

A great example of how you get so much more for your membership in Man of the House! An extraordinary value that will add to the beauty of your home for years to come. This low price includes cutting away asphalt at garage apron and sidewalk to insure a level driveway at both ends. Plan to do it now before the weather changes and prices go up next spring. (Remember last year when no one could get asphalt due to the shortage?) Man of the House has it!

EXHIBIT 9
Continued

EXHIBIT 9
Continued

EXHIBIT 10
APPROXIMATE MARKETING EXPENSES, 1974
Man of the House, Inc.

January	$ 3,360
February	2,850
March	3,910
April	4,100
May	4,650
June	3,950
July	2,910
August	3,470
September	2,900
October	4,200
November	3,200
December	4,500
Total	$44,000

Note: Weinstein stated that it was difficult to determine the relationship between the company's marketing expenditures and its membership sales or usage of its services because marketing programs started one month often ran over into the next month or a program's cost might actually show up on the next month's marketing expenditures. "We just didn't monitor those early expenditures as carefully as we probably should have," he commented.

THE PEACE CORPS

STEVEN H. STAR
Associate Professor
Harvard Graduate School of Business Administration

Ralph Harmon,[1] who had been in charge of the professional services skills desk for 4 months, was pleased to receive the fall programs matrix. While it contained relatively few surprises (he had aided in its preparation), he finally had a relatively firm statement of his short-term responsibilities. As professional services coordinator, Ralph was responsible for the recruiting, selection, and placement of volunteers with skills ranging from master of business administration to engineers to nurses.

After reviewing the fall matrix, Ralph summarized the primary skills in the professional services area which would be required for the fall training program:

- B.S. nurses: 24
- R.N. nurses: 9
- Medical skills: 15
- Paramedical skills: 14

- B.B.A./B.S. economics: 192
- M.B.A./M.S. economics: 63
- Mechanical engineers: 3
- Civil engineers: 47

[1] Disguised name.

- Chemical engineers: 1
- Electrical engineers: 6
- Other engineers: 9
- Home economists: 43
- Geologists: 1

- Lawyers: 17
- City planners: 6
- Architects: 19
- Social workers: 1
- Miscellaneous: 15

These numbers, Ralph realized, were not as straightforward as they appeared. Within each category certain specialties were often required, as well as a particular marital status, family background (e.g., rural), or special ability (e.g., 2 years college French). Moreover, he knew that he would have to invite approximately 150 percent of the required number of trainees, since the acceptance rate of professional services volunteers had historically been somewhat lower than for most other skill categories.

As he studied the matrix, Ralph considered the changes which had taken place since he had joined the Peace Corps in 1965. He commented:

In those days, the basic concept underlying the Peace Corps was one of "hands across the sea." The Peace Corps consisted essentially of Bachelor of Arts generalists—young men and women with a great deal of enthusiasm and idealism, but little in the way of specific skills. Consequently, the Peace Corps would try to get as many young people as possible to apply, select those who seemed to be the best (whatever that was), and then teach them the basic rudiments of whatever it was they were supposed to do overseas. Since most of our programs were themselves quite general in those days, this approach worked pretty well. We were able to view our volunteers as virtually interchangeable parts until such time as they began training.

With time, however, the host countries became more sophisticated, and began to request increasing numbers of volunteers with specific skills. To some extent this was inherent to the process of development; as a country began to develop an administrative infrastructure it became more conscious of the specific areas where help would be useful. At the same time, it must be admitted, at least some countries were disenchanted with unskilled volunteers who insisted on giving advice to host country nationals who had more training (or better credentials) than they did.

When Joe Blatchford became Peace Corps Director in May, 1969, he recognized that host country requests had advanced far beyond our administrative ability to fill them. The countries were requesting farmers, skilled tradesmen, civil engineers, and MBAs, while we were still recruiting AB generalists. If we happened to get an engineer or an MBA, he generally got assigned to an appropriate program, but this was the exception rather than the rule. Increasingly, the host countries were complaining about the level of skill of our volunteers; when they requested an experienced teacher they wanted an experienced teacher, not a college graduate who had given some thought to teaching.

In September, 1969, Mr. Blatchford announced "New Directions," which was essentially a program to bring the Peace Corps more closely into line with the needs of the host countries. In essence, Mr. Blatchford directed that we give the countries what they want, even if it meant changing some of the traditional operating procedures of the Peace Corps. For example, we had always required that volunteers be single, unless married to a volunteer. And children were out of the question. But it is hard enough to find an experienced engineer or skilled worker who wants to go into the Peace Corps for two years—let alone one without a family.

The "New Directions" are certainly sound, and probably should have been instituted several years ago. But they complicate the recruiting and selection process. In the old days, the job was to recruit bodies, and assign them. Now, we have to recruit individuals with specific skills, specific backgrounds, and specific family situations. And they have to want to go to the country which has requested the specific cluster of attributes which they possess.

BACKGROUND

The Peace Corps was established in March 1961 in fulfillment of a campaign promise made by candidate John F. Kennedy in the fall of 1960. Through the use of volunteers, the Peace Corps was to "(1) help developing nations meet their needs for trained manpower; (2) help promote better understanding of the American people on the part of the peoples served; and (3) promote a better understanding of other people on the part of the American people." Between 1962 and 1969 the Peace Corps grew from 1,044 volunteers in the field during its first year to 9,752 volunteers in the field in 1969. During this same period, the annual appropriation for Peace Corps operations grew from $30 million to $114 million in 1966,[1] and to $102 million in 1969.

During this period, the Peace Corps was engaged in a wide range of programs overseas. Typical programs were in such fields as rural community development, primary education, English language instruction, and public health. All programs were initiated or approved by host country governments, which agreed to cooperate with the efforts of Peace Corps volunteers.

In 1969, the average Peace Corps volunteer was 24.2 years old (when entering training) and had a college degree (88 percent). Approximately 67 percent of the volunteers were male and 33 percent female. Volunteers were not allowed to be married, unless married to a volunteer who was assigned to the same country.

Service in the Peace Corps paid approximately $95 per month,[2] plus $75 per month which was paid to the volunteer as a readjustment allowance upon the completion of Peace Corps service. The major reason for the low living allowance (some of which was withheld) was to encourage the volunteer overseas to adopt a standard of living similar to that of host country nationals doing a similar type of work.

Peace Corps applicants were drawn from a variety of sources, but mainly from the college campuses. In the early years, heavy media advertising, placed

[1] In 1966, there were 12,000 volunteers in the field.

[2] This living allowance varied somewhat from country to country.

by the Advertising Council,[1] and a considerable amount of continuing publicity in all media produced a flood of applications[2] which were processed by Peace Corps Washington. During this period, each applicant was required to take an aptitude test, and the results of this test and recommendations submitted with the application were used by Peace Corps Headquarters to select applicants who would be invited for training.

Between June 1966 and June 1967, regional recruiting offices were established in four cities (San Francisco, Chicago, Atlanta, and Boston). During the next 2 years, these offices were supplemented by 30 area offices. These offices were typically staffed by returned Peace Corps volunteers, who planned and carried out a variety of recruiting programs, mainly on college campuses. In 1969, the Peace Corps employed approximately 120 persons in its field offices. Salaries of these personnel and other operating expenses were budgeted at approximately $1.5 million.

Prior to 1969, the emphasis at all times was on obtaining the greatest number of applicants possible. As one Peace Corps official explained:

> The idea was to keep the applications coming in. If we got enough applications, we could always pick enough good people to staff our programs. Our friends in Congress tended to look at number of applications as a key barometer of how we were doing. As long as our applications were up each year, and we had as few scandals in the field as possible, it was felt that we were doing a good job.

As the number of applications increased, processing became more and more of a problem. The Office of Volunteer Selection was responsible for screening all applications and selecting a pool of qualified applicants. The applications of these applicants were then sent to the Office of Placement, which determined which applicants were suitable for which assignments. The applications were then sent to the Regional Program Offices (e.g., Latin America), which decided which applicants to suggest for which country programs. Finally, the head of a particular program would decide which applicants to invite for training for his program.

At this point an invitation to training was sent to the applicant, who was generally expected to reply in 1 week. Training generally was to begin approximately 8 weeks after the invitations for a particular program were sent out. Peace Corps officials estimated that on the average 6 to 7 weeks elapsed between the time an application was submitted and the time an invitation was sent out.

[1] The Advertising Council was a branch of the American Association of Advertising Agencies. It arranged for the voluntary preparation of public service advertisements by member agencies and distributed such advertisements to appropriate media.

[2] Applications received:

1962	20,058	1966	42,656
1963	33,762	1967	36,548
1964	45,653	1968	31,111
1965	42,124	1969	24,336

TABLE 1

Resignations		Separations	
Not qualified for project	2.3%	Not qualified for project	0.5%
Motivation	22.6	Motivation	1.5
Personality	24.2	Personality	19.8
Skill	3.3	Skill	2.4
Language	0.4	Language	0.5
Married/engaged	2.7	Spouse	0.5
School	0.1	Full field investigation	0.9
Other	8.3	Peace Corps Washington	0.2
	63.9%	County Director	0.5
		Medical	6.1
		Legal	1.9
		Other	1.3
			36.1%

Peace Corps training was quite rigorous, typically lasting 12 to 14 weeks. During training, trainees were expected to gain reasonable fluency in the language of the country to which they were assigned, learn about the culture and history of the country, and become competent in whatever skills their particular program called for. In 1968, approximately 75 percent of trainees completed training successfully and were sent overseas. According to Peace Corps records, causes for noncompletion of training in 1968 are shown in Table 1.

Following training, the volunteer was sent to his assignment for 2 years. Between 1962 and 1969, 80 percent of Peace Corps volunteers completed 2 years of service. Those who did not finish left for a variety of reasons including "draft, death, sickness, family emergency, quitting, leaving two months or two weeks early to get a specific job or enter graduate school, etc." No quantitative data were available concerning specific reasons for attrition.

In May 1969, the new President, Richard Nixon, appointed Joseph Blatchford as director of the Peace Corps. Mr. Blatchford had founded ACCION, a private, nonprofit community development organization in Latin America in 1960. At the time of his appointment, he was working on plans to apply the experiences of ACCION to the Watts area of Los Angeles. At 35, Mr. Blatchford was the youngest agency head in the Nixon Administration.

At the time Mr. Blatchford became director, the Peace Corps had approximately 11,000 volunteers serving overseas, and expected to have approximately 10,000 volunteers during the next year. By this time, however, the Peace Corps was receiving much less public attention than it had during its early years, and was faced with a number of problems. Mr. Blatchford often told the story of his arrival in Washington to begin his new job. He had asked a cab driver at the airport to take him to Peace Corps Headquarters and had received the reply, "The Peace Corps? Is the Peace Corps still in operation?"

NEW DIRECTIONS

In September 1969, Mr. Blatchford announced "New Directions," a series of recommendations based on a careful analysis of Peace Corps operations and host country needs by Mr. Blatchford, the Peace Corps staff, and a number of task forces. The text of "New Directions" is reproduced in Appendix A.

RECRUITING AND SELECTION

When "New Directions" were announced, it was immediately apparent that they would have significant implications for the Peace Corps' recruiting and selection process. In particular, it would now be necessary to achieve much closer coordination between the overseas programming and recruiting functions. As one recruiter explained, "In the past we mainly recruited numbers. Now we will have to recruit specific types of people, with specific skills. If we are going to do this successfully, we will need detailed specifications with long lead times."

In addition to the question of specifications and lead times, there was the basic question of whether the Peace Corps would in fact be able to recruit adequate numbers of "New Directions" type personnel. While the Peace Corps had always met its targets for A.B. generalists, would it be possible to induce skilled farmers, engineers, blue-collar workers, and teachers to leave established jobs for 2 years of overseas volunteer service? If so, would the Peace Corps traditional recruiting approach be an effective means of recruiting such volunteers?[1]

FIRST STEPS

By mid-1970, the Peace Corps had instituted a number of changes intended to bring its recruiting and selection procedures into closer harmony with the "New Directions." As a first step, all recruiting and selection activities were combined in a single organizational unit, the Office of Volunteer Placement (OVP). This major objective of this organizational move was to "tighten up the recruiting and selection process, to achieve closer coordination between program specifications, recruiting, and the selection of volunteers to meet the specifications." (See Exhibit 1 for OVP organization chart, and Exhibit 2 for a typical OVP region.)

As part of the reorganization, five skill desks were established. These skill desks were respectively responsible for (1) mathematics, science, education; (2) professional services; (3) skilled trades; (4) agriculture; and (5) generalists. The skill desk coordinators were responsible for filling the programs which called for their assigned skills. On the one hand, they were to provide programming assistance to Peace Corps' recruiting efforts. Such programming assistance would consist of the translation and dissemination of volunteer specifications to the field

---

[1] See Appendix B for the results of an attitude study among teachers and skilled workers, and Appendix C for the results of a study among college seniors.

recruiting offices, headquarters advertising personnel, etc., and, where possible, the development of specific strategies to be used to recruit particular categories of volunteers. On the other hand, they were actually to fill the programs—to screen relevant application documents as they came in and recommend specific applicants for inclusion in specific programs. In cases where a shortfall was expected, they were to act as expediters, checking frequently on each step of the lengthy application process, and—where appropriate—maintaining close contact (usually by phone) with the applicant.

An almost immediate effect of the reorganization was a major shift in the orientation of Peace Corps' recruiting efforts, at least at headquarters. Where brochures and program descriptions had previously been almost always oriented to specific countries or geographic areas, they were increasingly structured on a skills basis. Regional brochures, e.g., Latin American Programs, were now supplemented by brochures describing programs in agriculture, education, health, home economics, the arts, architecture and city planning, physical education, engineering, business, skills and trades, and A.B. generalists.

Similarly, the Office of Volunteer Placement had instituted a program of weekly mailings to the field recruiting offices. These mailings were now organized by skill category, with one or two pages devoted to each skill desk. A typical entry in one of these mailings might be: "Do not recruit mechanical engineers unless they want to teach in Asia and have 18 credits in math, physics, *or* chemistry."

In addition, the skill desk personnel took the lead in designing special programs to be used in difficult recruiting situations. For example, a shortage of *experienced* teachers for fall 1970 programs was forecast by the Education Skill Desk in spring 1970. A special program was mounted in the Los Angeles area, consisting of a direct mailing to 128,000 teachers, personal calls on key education personnel, heavy newspaper publicity, and a formal conference. By June 1970, 102 applications had been received as a result of this program.[1]

Finally, there had been a shift in the Peace Corps' approach to media advertising. Since its establishment, Peace Corps advertising had been prepared by Young & Rubicam, a leading advertising agency. Young & Rubicam's advertisements for the Peace Corps were characterized by a subtle creative approach and had received a great deal of favorable comment from the advertising community. The best known of these advertisements was a 60-second television spot in which a young boy and girl lay on a towel on a beach for about 5 seconds, with the only sound being popular music being played on a portable radio. Finally, an announcer's voice was heard:

---

[1] According to Peace Corps records, miscellaneous and mailing costs for this program were $8,500, "No travel or labor costs were recorded, but much of this was time by recruiters in the immediate area, which was overtime not charged (i.e., recruiters worked over the weekend but did not collect overtime)."

In Somaliland last year, 90% of the children could not go to school because they had no teachers. Indians in Latin America lived on potatoes. That's all. Potatoes. In parts of Asia, people die of smallpox. Half the children in the Middle East die before their first birthday. It may be a wide wonderful world you live in, but the world you don't live in is filled with poverty, ignorance and disease. If you're not too busy, write the Peace Corps.

Until 1969, all Peace Corps media advertising was placed by the Advertising Council, of which Young & Rubicam (which received no profit on its Peace Corps account) was a member. The Advertising Council sent Peace Corps commercials to all major television stations. Stations which showed the commercials did so as a public service with no charge to the Peace Corps. According to Advertising Council estimates, Peace Corps advertising received approximately $10 million worth of free space in 1969, of which approximately $7 million was television and radio time.

In 1969, however, the Advertising Council removed the Peace Corps from its category of special accounts. The effect of this action was that Peace Corps commercials would now be sent to stations in a package with other public service commercials (rather than under special cover) and would, in general, receive less special attention. The reason for this change (according to the Advertising Council) was:

> . . . *because public service groups involved with environmental problems were increasing in number and required fuller advertising services, [and] because the Peace Corps planned to recruit fewer students, and concentrate more on attracting technicians and specialists, [which] would change the need for free advertising. . . .*[1]

When "New Directions" were announced, Young & Rubicam was given the assignment of preparing commercials oriented toward the new theme. At the same time, several other agencies were asked to work on the problem. After several months, Young & Rubicam resigned the account and the assignment was given to a small West Coast agency. This agency was not a member of the Advertising Council but would, presumably, be able to use the facilities of the Council for commercials distribution.

The new agency had proposed advertisements aimed at specific audiences. For examples of several of its early print advertisements, see Exhibit 5.

CURRENT PROBLEMS

By July 1970, in was generally agreed that OVP had made substantial progress in reorienting its operations toward the "New Directions" concept. Nevertheless, OVP headquarters personnel were increasingly concerned about a number of problems:

[1] Associated Press.

(1) Several members of OVP argued that program specifications still tended to be inaccurate, unreasonable, and too late. As an example of inaccuracy, they cited the following quotations from an internal memorandum:

> The "Country X" Agriculture Extension program calls for one MS AG economist and two BS agriculture degrees in horticulture. We already have the two BS AG degrees (accepts). On April 22nd, we received a call from the "Country X" desk relaying a message from the country—changing the program request to 1 MS AG economist, 1 BS AG degree in horticulture and 1 BS AG degree in animal husbandry, with names of people specially recruited by the PCV chief of the Ministry of Agriculture extension program (who never bothered to check in with this office). Not only were the two BS degrees specially recruited, but the "Country X" PTO had turned down earlier a BS AG degree in animal husbandry (with several years' experience) as acceptable in lieu of one of the horticulturalists. Written confirmation of the program change is expected from "Country X."

Specifications were unreasonable, they argued. They called for a short-supply skill (for example, M.B.A.s) when a surplus skill (for example, B.B.A.s) would have been adequate for the job. One staff member explained that there was a general tendency in less developed countries to place undue emphasis on educational attainment. Besides making programs more difficult to fill, this tendency often led to frustration and high attrition rates in the field when a volunteer felt that adequate use was not being made of his high skill levels. Similarly, many countries were still requesting unmarried, skilled blue-collar workers, even though this category of volunteer was virtually unavailable. In fact, it seemed likely that a large number of married skilled tradespeople would have to be rejected (with poor public relations effects), while a number of skilled trade programs would be understaffed, or even canceled, for lack of appropriate volunteers.

In the opinion of OVP staff members, the desire for single volunteers was understandable. Some assignments were in remote locations, where life would be very hard and boring for a nonworking wife, especially if she had children. Some countries simply did not want too visible a foreign presence, a problem which would be increased if wives and children were permitted. While sympathetic to these arguments, OVP personnel explained that they simply could not fill requests for unmarried personnel in certain skill categories. Overseas personnel would either have to negotiate the question with the host countries or it would be impossible to staff the programs.

With regard to the timing issue, there had been considerable improvement following a directive that all program specifications were to be received by Peace Corps Washington 5 to 11 months before training for the program was to begin. Nevertheless, changes and cancellations still took place "down to the wire," making it difficult to mount special recruiting programs, and, on occasion, making it necessary to cancel invitations to programs.

(2) A second area of concern was the recruiting and selection process itself. Despite elaborate PERT charts and systems diagrams, the process still re-

quired an average of 5 weeks from the time an application was received until the time a skill desk could act on it, and an average of 6 to 7 weeks until an invitation or a rejection notice was sent out. As a result, many applicants who were recruited only with considerable expenditure of resources were lost to the Peace Corps, as other attractive opportunities became available to them, or they simply got tired of waiting.

(3) Some staff members believed that the characteristics of the Peace Corps staff were themselves a major problem. As one staff member explained:

> Virtually our entire staff is made up of returned Peace Corps volunteers, which is a real advantage. They have a real feel for what's going on in the field, for what's between the lines of a program specification. And they have good credibility when talking with prospective applicants.
>
> The problem is that most of them were part of the "old directions." They find it difficult to talk to a farmer, or a skilled worker; or to figure out what kind of appeals we should use when recruiting this type of volunteer. Naturally, we're trying to recruit specialized recruiters with these kinds of backgrounds, but this will take time. And, more likely than not, they won't have been in the Peace Corps.
>
> Actually, the problem is more basic than that. Our spirit is still that of the AB Generalist. For example, we rely very heavily on personal recommendations in the selections process. But a farmer's friends, if they send in the forms at all, just don't write as well (or as convincingly) as an English professor at Dartmouth. As a result, a lot of good people are rejected.

(4) The Peace Corps had recently come under increasing congressional pressure to increase its effectiveness, reduce its costs, or both. A major consultant's study had recommended the application of "program budgeting" to the Peace Corps, with economic trade-offs being made between programs with identified, *measurable*, objectives. With regard to OVP, there was some feeling in Congress that costs were too high and that greater effectiveness could be achieved through a more rational allocation of resources. Recruiting and selection cost data for 1969 are presented in Exhibit 3.

RECRUITING M.B.A.s

One of the major problems facing OVP in the summer of 1970 was recruiting M.B.A.s. As "New Directions" began to be implemented in the field, requests for M.B.A.s increased significantly (see Exhibit 4 for descriptions of some typical M.B.A. programs). On the basis of early results, however, it seemed unlikely that enough M.B.A.s could be recruited to fill all programs. In early September 1970, for example, there were 36 M.B.A. slots for fall training (one project had been dropped and another had been reduced in scope since the publication of the fall matrix). Twenty invitations had been sent out, and another 10 applicants were in the process of being invited. On the basis of historical data, it was estimated that 65 percent would accept, leaving a shortfall of 16.

Several Peace Corps field recruiters had been asked to suggest means of improving the M.B.A. recruiting effort. One recruiter, for example, proposed the following program:

- **1** *Utilize one person as MBA recruiter for a region.*
- **2** *Utilize host country nationals or business/economics notables (e.g., Paul Samuelson) to gain entree to colleges and classrooms.*
- **3** *Mount intensive efforts exclusively for MBAs.*
- **4** *Utilize good films as entrees and to inform applicants.*
- **5** *Send form letters to MBAs, professors, teaching assistants, etc.*
- **6** *Utilize placement services effectively. (At some schools 95% of MBAs go through the placement service.)*
- **7** *Place articles and advertisements with* Business Week, Wall Street Journal, MBA *magazine. (Ads must feature adventure plus professional growth. Articles must be well written with same emphasis.)*
- **8** *Have detailed program information available for examination by MBAs. Establish a strong applicant-skill desk–country desk relationship to improve applicant follow-up and increase acceptance rate.*
- **9** *Initiate MBA intern programs with schools which have an international emphasis. (Under an intern program, applicants could receive some of their Peace Corps training [with credit] while still in school, and might receive graduate credit for some of their overseas work.)*

A second recruiter offered the following advice to recruiters seeking M.B.A.s:

Although Business Schools are physically located on college campuses, they might as well be on Wall Street in New York. The deans, professors, and even the students imagine themselves to be in the midst of the business community. They are in business school as a result of their focus on the business world. Ever since childhood their idols have worn business suits and have had a gift for gab. They are pragmatists.

None of the generalizations in the preceding eliminate the possibility of [recruiting M.B.A.s for] the Peace Corps. Leave the sensitizing to Peace Corps training. You'll never be able to sensitize these guys with a fifteen minute talk on social ideas anyway. They are much more apt to respond to an intelligent discussion of economic development schemes and the contribution the Peace Corps makes. Do not hesitate to point out that the Peace Corps experience will open up new job opportunities for them—possibly in international business. (No recruiter would be afraid to tell a teacher that they would have good job opportunities after P.C.—why do they shy away from this point in the case of business?) Be a good forceful speaker. Be short and organized.

Appearance is of vital importance. Forget about your own personality or image of what Peace Corps should do abroad. You are recruiting a specialized person to work in business development. This is what the country asked for. Most of the people in this category respond to neatly dressed (this means a tie and jacket, since a good percentage of the students do) businesslike people. Remember you wouldn't recruit a farmer wearing a suit.

TABLE 2

Region	No. of candidates	No. of institutions
Northeast	9,453	27
Midwest	9,177	36
West	8,267	27
South	7,084	38
	33,981	128

Business Schools are generally very well organized and run in a businesslike manner. Therefore, you should deal with the dean first. Once you have him sold, the rest will be easy.

According to Peace Corps records, approximately 15,000 M.B.A.s graduated in the United States each year. In 1970, there were 33,981 M.B.A.-degree candidates in 128 institutions, divided geographically as shown in Table 2.

EXHIBIT 1
OVP ORGANIZATION CHART
The Peace Corps

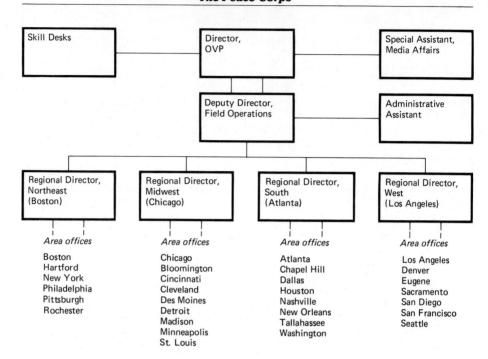

| Skill Desks | | Director, OVP | | Special Assistant, Media Affairs |

Deputy Director, Field Operations — Administrative Assistant

Regional Director, Northeast (Boston)

Regional Director, Midwest (Chicago)

Regional Director, South (Atlanta)

Regional Director, West (Los Angeles)

Area offices

Boston
Hartford
New York
Philadelphia
Pittsburgh
Rochester

Area offices

Chicago
Bloomington
Cincinnati
Cleveland
Des Moines
Detroit
Madison
Minneapolis
St. Louis

Area offices

Atlanta
Chapel Hill
Dallas
Houston
Nashville
New Orleans
Tallahassee
Washington

Area offices

Los Angeles
Denver
Eugene
Sacramento
San Diego
San Francisco
Seattle

EXHIBIT 2
A TYPICAL OVP REGION
The Peace Corps

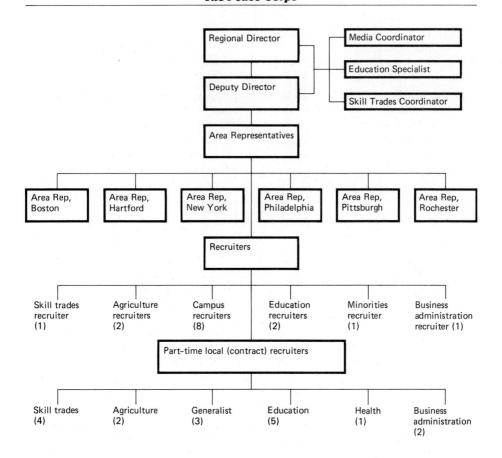

Regional Director

Deputy Director

Media Coordinator

Education Specialist

Skill Trades Coordinator

Area Representatives

| Area Rep, Boston | Area Rep, Hartford | Area Rep, New York | Area Rep, Philadelphia | Area Rep, Pittsburgh | Area Rep, Rochester |

Recruiters

| Skill trades recruiter (1) | Agriculture recruiters (2) | Campus recruiters (8) | Education recruiters (2) | Minorities recruiter (1) | Business administration recruiter (1) |

Part-time local (contract) recruiters

| Skill trades (4) | Agriculture (2) | Generalist (3) | Education (5) | Health (1) | Business administration (2) |

EXHIBIT 3
RECRUITING AND SELECTION BUDGET, PY 1969
The Peace Corps

Recruiting

Washington		Field offices	
Salaries	$ 433,600	Salaries	$ 859,200
Travel	45,800	Rents and utilities	136,100
Transportation	6,200	Secretaries	48,000
Printing	418,200	Travel	476,000
Advertising	141,900	Materials	4,500
Films	32,100	Distributions	20,300
Other	40,800		$1,544,100
	$1,118,600		

Recruiting total: $2,662,700
Applications received: 24,337

Trainee selection

Prescreening	$ 218,400
Evaluation	175,000
Program placement	343,600
Applicant liaison	307,700
Final folder review	84,600
Experimental programs	81,000
Invitation issuance	142,700
Selection total	$1,353,000

Invitations issued: 15,453

Source: Prepared by the casewriter (with the assistance of Mr. John Brock) from "Special Analytical Study of Recruitment and Selection in the United States Peace Corps," Washington, September 1969.

EXHIBIT 4
FALL 1970 MBA PROGRAMS
The Peace Corps

■ *Liberia education*

Needs M.B.A.s to teach accounting or business at the University of Liberia.

Volunteers may be male or female.

Single people preferred.

Training starts: 11/9/70

■ *Maharashtra (India) small industries*

Needs M.B.A.s to provide field extension service to small-scale units who request and need help. Work with industrialists to solve production problems.

Single males only.

Training: 11/16/70

■ *Andhra Pradesh (India) small industries*

Needs M.B.A.s to compile and analyze data to provide a solid basis for evaluating the feasibility of projects. These studies will be based on availability of equipment, skilled labor, raw materials, finances and market.

Single males only.

Training: 9/23/70

■ *Venezuela municipal management*

Needs M.B.A.s to work with the Venezuelan Association for Inter Municipal Cooperation of fiscal and administrative reforms.

Engineering of loans and creation of local planning offices.

Volunteers will be expected to train their counterparts in order to strengthen local governments.

Males only. Couples and some families acceptable.

Training: 10/11/70

■ *Colombia M.B.A./M.I.E.*

Needs M.B.A.s to work with government ministries on a "Directed Industrial Credit" program. Using cost accounting, finance, production and marketing skills to aid in the industrialization of the rural sector, incrementing production and income.

Male or female. Couples and families acceptable.

Training: 9/15/70

91

EXHIBIT 5
1970 PRINT ADVERTISEMENTS
The Peace Corps

Remember when the Peace Corps happened?

There was an electricity, a shared smile. Most of us said, "What a great idea!" And thousands of Americans said, "I want in."

Just like that. The Peace Corps was in business, exporting a product that the cynics had made jokes about for two hundred years: The American Innocence, the notion that people can change things.

The supply of volunteers was unlimited. Before the Sixties ended more than 40,000 Americans – most of them young and white and college educated – had joined the Peace Corps.

Whatever happened to the Peace Corps?

What happened was that America, the world's leading exporter of innocence, ran out of the product at home. Let's not go through the list again. Growing up anytime, anywhere is hard work. Growing up in America has become almost unbearable.

The Peace Corps had some growing up to do, too.

It had to stop telling young people that love alone conquers all, because it doesn't.

It had to stop saying that volunteers could be "agents of change" – political change – because it wasn't true.

It had to stop pretending it wasn't a United States government agency, because it is.

It had to learn that – believe it or not – people in faraway lands know more about what they need than we do. (And when they ask for help, they're very specific: an electrician, two city planners, five math teachers, an experienced farmer.)

Today the Peace Corps is in 60 countries. That's 59 more than it started in. It's changed a lot, but so has the world and so has America, and so – after all – have you.

The Peace Corps is still a remarkable idea for people who need to help, nose to nose. But it's not like it used to be.

It's better.

Peace Corps, Washington, D.C. 20525

92

EXHIBIT 5
Continued

If you speak cement blocks, talk to the Peace Corps.

Peace Corps
Washington D.C., 20525

NAME_____
ADDRESS_____
CITY_____ STATE_____ ZIP_____

(They've been looking all over for you.)

If you speak business, talk to the Peace Corps.

Peace Corps
Washington D.C., 20525

NAME_____
ADDRESS_____
CITY_____ STATE_____ ZIP_____

(They've been looking all over for you.)

If you speak agriculture, talk to the Peace Corps.

Peace Corps
Washington D.C., 20525

NAME_____
ADDRESS_____
CITY_____ STATE_____ ZIP_____

(They've been looking all over for you.)

If you speak nutrition, talk to the Peace Corps.

Peace Corps
Washington D.C., 20525

NAME_____
ADDRESS_____
CITY_____ STATE_____ ZIP_____

(They've been looking all over for you.)

93

APPENDIX A
The New Directions

The starting point for any Peace Corps program must be the needs of the country served. We begin by thinking about Bolivia, or Senegal or Korea, not the United States. First the country has to identify its greatest problems and set priorities. Then the Peace Corps and the country can begin a joint search for the best method to meet the problem together. I say "together" because there is simply no role for the Peace Corps apart from partnership with the country served. And I use the word "country" rather than government because this unique people-to-people organization will work closely with local governments but will also reach out to and work with all sectors of local society, private or governmental, that are committed to helping people. Following are ways that we plan to change our program to do a better job for them:

1 New ideas. *We must be sure the Peace Corps does not operate on out-of-date assumptions about what it can and cannot do. We should be prepared, for example, to suggest projects in such areas as educational television and radio, low-costing housing or curriculum reform; to work across national boundaries in regional development schemes; to operate mobile vocational education centers, leadership and middle-management training programs; to help equip vocational or television and radio facilities; to provide experts on a less-than-two-years basis or train host country people in the United States.*

2 Goal: a new resource. *Fron now on, no projects will be undertaken without establishment of specific long-range and interim goals, to the end that each project creates a new resource that will remain after the Peace Corps departs. To fail to take steps to create this resource would be to fail where we are needed most.*

3 Team approach. *In the future, Volunteers will be assigned in teams with varying levels of technical competence and experience. They will be concentrated in selected areas rather than scattered to many locations.*

4 More effective Volunteers. *The Peace Corps will aim at providing the skills in greatest demand overseas by providing better training to "Generalist" Volunteers (in most cases, the recent liberal arts graduate); improving the selection process to allow for placement of individual highly-skilled Volunteers, such as computer experts; designing programs for groups with special kinds of experience, such as teachers or former VISTA Volunteers; encouraging more Volunteers to extend a third year overseas; expanding post-service educational opportunities for returned Volunteers through programs with government, industry and universities; launching new recruiting programs by community or by occupational category and tailoring Peace Corps advertising to describe specific job opportunities; asking industry and labor to enable potential Volunteers to serve without sacrificing fringe benefits or seniority and asking industry to help Volunteers maintain mortgage or loan payments that would otherwise prohibit service; beginning a pilot program for married couples with dependent children, thus opening up a huge new pool of skilled and professional talent.*

5 Technical support. *We will provide the Volunteer with increased technical and logistic support by tapping other overseas agencies and local industries for assistance; by furnishing tools and other materials where needed; by tapping sources of assistance such as regional and international development banks, or foundations such as Ford and Rockefeller; by contracting with organizations such as VITA (Vol-*

unteers in Technical Assistance) *to supply the Volunteer with information on specific development problems; by increasing numbers of Peace Corps staff members in Washington and overseas who have professional training in such fields as agriculture, education, economic development; by recruiting experts as Volunteers on a short-term basis, to backstop generalist Volunteers and to provide in-service training for Volunteers.*

6 Binationalism. *When we speak of binationalism—or partnership—we speak of an outlook or an approach. But we also speak of a method, an imaginative action program that increases local capacity to solve problems. The idea of partnership does not exist for its own sake. Partnership has no other purpose than to mobilize and multiply local resources, to maximize impact on local problems. The work of the Peace Corps must be seen as an integral and indistinguishable part of each country's plan to meet its needs. In concrete terms this means insuring that the way Volunteers are recruited, selected, trained, placed, and directed is a joint responsibility. This will be done by: substantially increasing the number of non-Americans on Peace Corps staff, especially in higher-ranking positions, and establishing training programs for them if persons of sufficient training are not already available; involving our hosts directly in recruiting and selecting Volunteers; putting policy decisions in the hands of advisory committees composed in the main of host country people; establishing local advisory committees for each area of Peace Corps activity, such as health, agriculture, etc.; involving the local middle class, especially youth, in Peace Corps activities; conducting joint evaluations of Peace Corps activities; making support provided for Peace Corps Volunteers available for others in the same country.*

7 Building the resources of Volunteers. *People are the most valuable resource of any country. All our host countries recognize this truth, and encouraging the spread of volunteerism should be part of the Peace Corps' way of developing local resources. To this end, we will: encourage all our country directors to help create and assist local voluntary programs; offer to train in the U.S. or a third country participants for domestic voluntary programs; under an Exchange Peace Corps, bring to the U.S. those interested in voluntary action here and in their own countries and train them to replace Peace Corps Volunteers when they return home (discussed in more detail in Item 9); involve foreign students in voluntary service programs while they are in the U.S., preparing them for similar service at home; offer Peace Corps assistance to raise matching funds to create voluntary programs in other countries, through private sources or through appropriate use of U.S. funds.*

8 International programs. *Although I believe the Peace Corps should seek to maintain its own identity and programs, we look favorably on a proposal made by Iran this year for the United Nations to sponsor an international volunteer corps. This proposal has been placed on the agenda of the 1970 U.N. General Assembly. We are also exploring existing authority for assignment of up to 125 Peace Corps Volunteers to work with agencies of the United Nations, and we also believe the Peace Corps can participate in multi-national volunteer teams in specific countries.*

9 Exchange Peace Corps. *America has some serious problems, many of them more severe than those of comparable industrial countries. To acknowledge this fact is not news, but for a great country to acknowledge that other people, particularly those from less developed countries, could help solve these problems would have great value. It would add concrete substance to our ideas on partnership. It* *enables the United States to step back, if only in a small, symbolic way, from the client relationship with the aid recipient that inevitably strains the friendship of both countries. This is the spirit behind my proposal for an Exchange Peace Corps. Just as we send Americans abroad to help other nations begin self-help projects, and just as we value their contribution upon return, so we should bring to this country people who want to help the United States at the same time they are preparing to return and help their own countries. The main purpose of their year in the United States, in fact, would be to train them to form or work in new national service agencies once they return home. I hope to obtain the consent of Congress to operate a small pilot project for testing the Exchange Peace Corps idea this year.*

10 Returned Volunteers. *By the end of the year, there will be nearly 35,000 returned Peace Corps Volunteers in the United States. To date, the Peace Corps has not been of sufficient assistance to those who are looking for ways to serve their own country. A new unit in Peace Corps headquarters, the Office of Voluntary Action, will have specific responsibility for helping them. We will extend the period of time in which our Career Information Service furnishes returned Volunteers information leading to jobs and opportunities in education and social service; we will try on an experimental basis this year, a* Transitional Experience *for a limited number of newly-returned Volunteers, to provide them with an immediate and dramatic grasp of American problems and to stimulate them to explore ways to help solve those problems; we will try to establish in 1970 a* Peace Corps Development Fund *to make seed money available to returned Volunteers who are developing social action, education and other programs.*

11 The Peace Corps' home town. *Peace Corps staff for some time have been aware that their preoccupation with problems overseas tends to inhibit their understanding of problems in the District of Columbia and the nation as a whole. Through the new Office of Voluntary Action, we will try to counter this contradiction by developing opportunities for staff members and their families to volunteer for meaningful jobs in the District of Columbia. More than 100 such assignments have been identified so far by Mayor Walter Washington and his staff. We hope to demonstrate how a community's resources can be extended through voluntary involvement of professional and non-professional working people in their spare time, and to disprove the thesis that foreign and home-grown problems are mutually exclusive.*

12 Combined service. *Another way we intend to extend the resource of Peace Corps experience here at home is through a new program of combined service overseas and in the States. This does not mean the Peace Corps intends to launch its own domestic programs; our focus will continue to be overseas. But we can work out agreements with the Teacher Corps, local voluntary agencies or state, local or federal government programs that will allow a Peace Corps Volunteer to pursue career interests in several different service fields while putting his overseas experience to immediate use in a new context at home. I hope we can begin a pilot project for 100 Volunteers in combined services this year.*

The idea of combined service, the Volunteers to America, and our efforts to increase the effectiveness of returned Volunteers are all meant to break through the let-government-professionals-do-it attitude toward a fuller role for people in the affairs of this country. Compared to the magnitude of the world's problems, the palpable contribution of the Peace Corps is small. But by its example and inspiration the Peace Corps has multiplied its effect far beyond the sum of its manifest accomplishments, proving that in an age of realism, idealism is still a powerful instrument for change. Far from being exhausted, that idealism, renewed and rechanneled, has only begun its service to mankind. There is much to be done and much is expected of us. When he proposed to reform the welfare system in the United States recently, President Nixon talked about the need to reach beyond past expectations. He said,

> . . . abolishing poverty, putting an end to dependency—reaching the moon a generation ago, that may be impossible. But in the Spirit of Apollo, we can lift our sights and marshal our best efforts. We can resolve to make this the year, not that we reached the goal, but that we turned the corner. . . .

That message applies to the Peace Corps with its record of accomplishment as well as to the welfare system with its impotence against fundamental change. For those who care about bringing to each man the full life that should be his birthright, it is not how far we have come that counts but how far we have to go.

APPENDIX B
A RECRUITMENT STUDY AMONG TEACHERS AND SKILLED WORKERS
Roper Research Associates, Inc., June 1969

SUMMARY

In the early Spring of 1969, Peace Corps contracted with Roper Research Associates, Inc. to undertake a study of recruitment possibilities among experienced teachers and skilled workers, both married and single. Peace Corps needed to know the answers to the following questions:

1 What kind of image does Peace Corps have among experienced teachers and skilled workers?

2 How much do these groups know generally about Peace Corps' operation?

3 Do experienced teachers and skilled workers have any specific knowledge of Peace Corps?

4 Can Peace Corps attract more experienced teachers and skilled workers?

5 What changes in Peace Corps policy are needed in order to attract more of these groups?

Below are the findings most important for future Peace Corps policy:

1 The image of Peace Corps and of PCVs is strongly favorable among experienced teachers and skilled workers. While both groups are lukewarm in general toward government non-military aid, they strongly favor the Peace Corps because it helps others to learn to help themselves.

2 Most teachers, but less than half of the workers, demonstrated a broad general knowledge of what the Peace Corps is, what it does, and where it operates.

3 Specific knowledge of the Peace Corps is low. *For instance:*

a Half of potential teachers PCVs and over a third of potential worker Volunteers were aware that Peace Corps needed their skills.

b Less than one in three potential worker and teacher PCVs were aware that American doctors care for Volunteers abroad.

c Less than half of potential teacher PCVs and only a quarter of potential worker Volunteers were aware of the substantial separation allowance.

The absence of any prior and concerted effort by the Peace Corps to attract teachers and workers seems to be one of the major reasons why it has not attracted sufficient numbers in both groups to date. New efforts by PA and PI are needed here.

4 *It appears that Peace Corps can attract more teachers and, to a lesser extent, skilled workers, but certain changes in Peace Corps policy will have to be made (See 5. below). If these changes were made, 12% of married male teachers and 13% of single male teachers say they would definitely consider Peace Corps; among workers, only 2% of married and 4% of single males would definitely consider Peace Corps. Seven per cent of single female teachers questioned said they would definitely consider Peace Corps if changes were made.*

5 *The greatest single obstacle to Peace Corps service is the regulation barring persons with children under 18 from joining. The changes needed most by both groups are those which would:*

■*Permit them to take their families with them*

■*Pay more to meet these expenses*

■ *Guarantee that they would be able to meet long-term financial obligations*

Teachers also voiced the need for:

■ *Guarantees of getting their former job back*

■ *Guarantees of not losing tenure or seniority*

Potential worker PCVs stressed the need for:

■ *Clean housing and living conditions*

Neither the two-year service obligation, nor the need to be able to learn a foreign language were seen as real barriers by the great majority of potential teacher and worker PCVs.

RECOMMENDATIONS FOR PEACE CORPS PUBLIC RELATIONS EFFORTS AMONG EXPERIENCED TEACHERS AND SKILLED WORKERS

Roper Research Associates, Inc. were contracted in the Spring of 1969 to study the recruiting possibilities of Peace Corps among experienced teachers and skilled workers. One of the main findings of the research was that Peace Corps needed a more concerted public relations effort geared to teachers and workers. Below are the most important findings in this regard:

1 *About three-fourths of the teachers said that they remembered Peace Corps advertisements, while only 55% of the workers did. Of those who did remember Peace Corps advertising, very few said that they got the impression that the Peace Corps wanted people in their specific occupations. Most recalled that the Peace Corps needed idealistic and dedicated people. The report recommends that since Peace Corps' overall image is good among these groups, some changes in advertising copy or theme could be made with* more emphasis on the personal and career benefits which Peace Corps service can give to Volunteers *in teaching and skilled work.*

2 *Sixty-five percent of teachers and 24% of workers said they knew a PCV. Of those who knew a Volunteer and had discussed Peace Corps with him, most had a highly favorable impression. It appears that RPCVs communicate particularly well the ways in which Peace Corps service is of personal benefit. The report recommends that a* special recruiting program for teachers and skilled tradesmen using former Volunteers *could be highly effective.*

3 *Often the moderately interested married male is discouraged from applying for Peace Corps by his wife. The report recommends that* a strong selling effort will be needed among wives *of experienced teachers and skilled workers.*

CONSIDERATION GIVEN TO JOINING THE PEACE CORPS
(Base: 1,005 college seniors)

	Serious consideration, %			Some consideration, %			Hardly any consideration, %		
	'69	'67	'66	'69	'67	'66	'69	'67	'66
Total	13	13	16	39	33	32	48	54	52
East	14	14	16	39	35	32	47	51	52
Midwest	18	13	15	46	33	37	36	54	48
Plains	8	8	9	39	31	32	53	61	59
South	11	12	15	32	28	33	57	60	52
West	17	20	25	41	38	29	42	42	46
Private nondenominational	15	12	16	41	31	30	44	57	54
Private denominational	13	14	19	41	34	34	46	52	47
Public	13	14	14	37	33	33	50	53	53
Over 10,000	16	16	19	40	34	33	44	50	48
3,000–10,000	11	13	15	43	30	33	46	57	52
Under 3,000	13	11	13	35	35	32	52	54	55
Humanities and social sciences	15	22	X	44	37	X	41	41	X
Men	14	10	14	35	30	25	51	60	61
Women	11	20	20	46	39	46	43	41	34
Political activism scale:									
Most	23	24	33	42	41	X	35	35	X
Medium	17	17	19	43	38	X	40	45	X
Least	7	10	13	35	29	X	58	61	X
VISTA: Serious consideration	49	58	X	41	26	X	10	16	X
Black	4	X	X	21	X	X	75	X	X

X = not analyzed in previous surveys.

Columns headed "1966" or "1967" show comparable figures from the previous surveys.

Activism: An activism scale was developed to test the degree of activism among college seniors. Each senior was asked whether he or she had signed a petition, participated in a demonstration, joined a picket line, defied school authorities, risked a future security clearance, violated the law, gone to jail, or participated in civil disobedience. If the respondent replied affirmatively to at least four, he or she was classified as "most active"; if two or three, as "medium active"; if none or one, as "least active."

Source: From "College Seniors and the Peace Corps—1969" conducted for the Peace Corps by Louis Harris and Associates, Inc.

POLITICAL ACTIVISM SCALE

	Most active, %			Medium active, %			Least active, %		
	'69	'67	'66	'69	'67	'66	'69	'67	'66
Total	*18*	*11*	*7*	*33*	*29*	*28*	*49*	*60*	*65*
East	18	16	8	36	36	36	46	48	56
Midwest	18	8	6	46	29	30	36	63	64
Plains	13	3	4	28	21	20	59	76	76
South	13	7	7	25	25	26	62	68	67
West	28	22	13	31	31	23	41	47	64
Private nondenominational	19	17	7	36	32	31	45	51	62
Private denominational	10	5	7	38	31	29	52	64	64
Public	20	11	7	30	27	25	50	62	68
Over 10,000	23	16	10	34	26	27	43	58	63
3,000–10,000	21	13	9	32	30	26	47	57	65
Under 3,000	9	5	4	34	31	29	57	64	67
Humanities and social sciences	25	17	X	36	33	X	39	50	X
Men	21	13	9	33	27	28	46	60	63
Women	12	8	6	34	33	25	54	59	69
Peace Corps:									
Serious consideration	31	20	13	42	37	31	27	43	56
Some consideration	19	14	9	37	34	29	44	52	62
Hardly any consideration	13	7	3	29	24	25	58	69	72
VISTA: Serious consideration	40	21	X	31	30	X	29	49	X
Black	22	X	X	27	X	X	51	X	X

X = not analyzed in the earlier surveys.

Source: From "College Seniors and the Peace Corps—1969" conducted for the Peace Corps by Louis Harris and Associates, Inc.

PRODUCT POLICY

The determination of product policy is central to an organization's marketing effort. A firm's choice of products influences all the other elements in its marketing program and may have significant implications for such functional areas as finance, production, and personnel.

Product policy decisions center around what goods and services a firm should offer for sale and what characteristics these should have. They involve matching company resources and needs with market opportunities. Policy formulation, therefore, requires careful analysis of existing and potential products relative to the characteristics of both the market and the firm.

The word product connotes a physical good; however, in its generic sense as a marketing term it also includes intangible services offered in the marketplace. Although this note will emphasize product policy formulation from the standpoint of profit-making private firms, nonprofit organizations may also be faced with such decisions.

The following examples typify the varied product policy issues faced by managements of different organizations. A manufacturer of jellies and preserves wonders whether to introduce a tomato ketchup; a major automobile producer considers dropping its line of large luxury sedans and broadening its intermediate and small car lines instead; a well-known ski equipment firm debates purchase of a company which makes scuba and diving gear; a producer of electronic equipment for industrial users evaluates entry into the pocket calculator market; a supermarket chain wonders whether or not to discontinue sales of kitchen hardware; a liberal arts college reviews the feasibility of adding a professional degree program to its curriculum; a manufacturer of high-quality electric motors considers development of an inexpensive utility model with lower performance characteristics; a detergent company evaluates a proposal to introduce a new brand; and a candy manufacturer looks at the implications of discontinuing a certain size of chocolate bar.

For many companies, appraising the need for changes in the product line is a continuing process, reflecting the dynamic nature of the marketplace as well as changes in the nature and resources of the firm itself. One objective should be to eliminate or modify products which no longer satisfy consumer needs or fail to contribute significantly (either directly or indirectly) to the well-being of the firm. Another set of objectives relates to addition of new products or product features which will meet consumer needs better, enhance the company's existing product line, and improve utilization of present resources.

PRODUCT DECISIONS

Most companies are multiproduct organizations, often producing a variety of different product lines. This means that policy decisions may be made at three possible levels:

1   *Individual product items which have a separate designation in the seller's list.*

2 Product lines, *namely, a group of products which are related in the sense of satisfying a particular class of need, being used together, possessing common physical or technical characteristics, being sold to the same customer groups and/or through the same channels, or falling within given price ranges.*

3 The product mix, *which is the composite of products offered for sale by a firm. Although a particular product item—or even an entire product line—may not be profitable in itself, it may contribute to the well-being of the firm by enhancing the overall product mix. Some large corporations produce several thousand product items, grouped into a wide variety of different product lines, which together constitute the firm's product mix.*

Closely associated with these three levels of product decisions are the concepts of breadth, depth, and consistency of product mix.

Consistency of product mix refers to the degree of similarity between product lines in end use, technology and production techniques, distribution channels, and so forth. Breadth of product mix refers to the number of different product lines marketed by the company. Finally, the term depth of product mix refers to the average number of items (e.g., sizes, weights, colors) offered in each product line.

PRODUCT MIX DECISIONS

Product mix decisions tend to reflect not only the nature of the market and the resources of the firm but also the underlying philosophy of company management. Most firms are faced with several options over time. Some pursue a policy of diversity, while others prefer to concentrate their efforts on a narrow product mix offered in a limited number of sizes and varieties.

A firm's choice of product strategy should be determined by management's long-run objectives concerning profit levels, sales stability, and growth as modified by personal values and attitudes toward risk taking. Market opportunities for the firm's product mix serve to determine the upper limits for potential corporate profitability, while the quality of the marketing program tends to determine the extent to which this potential is achieved.

While the "ideal" product mix is likely to vary from firm to firm and may be hard to define, certain situations suggest a suboptimal mix:

- *Chronic or seasonally recurring excess capacity in the firm's production, storage, or transportation facilities*
- *A very high proportion of profits coming from a small percentage of product items*
- *Inefficient use of sales-force contacts and skills*
- *Steadily declining profits or sales*

Changes in product policy designed to correct any of the above situations or otherwise enhance the firm's ability to meet established objectives can take one of three basic forms:

1   Product abandonment *involves discontinuance of either individual items or an entire line.*

2   Product modification *involves changes in either tangible or intangible product attributes and may be achieved by reformulation, redesign, changing unit sizes, and adding or removing certain features.*

3   New product introduction *involves developing, test marketing, and commercialization of new product items or product lines.*

PRODUCT POSITIONING

The ability of an organization to compete effectively in any given market is determined in large measure by its ability to position its product(s) appropriately relative to the needs of specific market segments and the nature of competitive entries.

Development of an effective product-positioning strategy requires careful analysis of the ways in which the market is segmented and an evaluation of how well competing entries are meeting the needs of specific segments. Instead of competing head on against a strong competitor, a firm may choose to finesse the competition by appealing to a different segment.

Product positions often reflect not only intrinsic product characteristics but also the image created by promotional strategies, pricing decisions, and choice of distribution channels. Selective use of alternative brand names in multibrand companies may also contribute to achievement of the desired image. For instance, the name Oldsmobile carries different connotations for car buyers than does that of Chevrolet.

REPOSITIONING

As an alternative to physical modification of an existing product, firms sometimes elect to reposition the product simply by revising such marketing mix elements as advertising and promotion, distribution strategy, pricing, or packaging. However, a revision of the entire mix, including product features, may also accompany a repositioning strategy.

Sometimes repositioning may represent a deliberate attempt to attack another firm's product and eat into its market share; in other instances the objective is to avoid head-to-head competition by moving into alternative market segments with good potential whose needs are not presently well served by existing products.

Analysis of competitive offerings involves not merely a review of product features and other marketing mix strategies but also an evaluation of competitive advertising content. The image generated by advertisements and the nature of the slogans employed may constitute a major positioning tool, expecially for "commodity-type" products such as beer, cigarettes, or airline travel.

Repositioning along price- and quality-complexity dimensions is generally referred to as trading up *or* trading down. *However, repositioning may also involve sideways moves in which price and quality remain basically similar but tangible or image modifications are made to enhance the product's appeal to different types of consumers or for alternative end uses.*

Examples of repositioning existing products include adding improved performance features to a precision camera, advertising a deodorant formerly promoted only to men as "the deodorant for all the family," reducing the price of a felt-tip pen to take advantage of a perceived market need for a lower-price model, modifying the menu at a fast-food restaurant to improve its appeal to family groups, and giving an airline a more exciting image through changes in aircraft color schemes, introduction of new uniforms, and addition of on-board service frills, and then promoting these by a glamorous advertising campaign.

EVALUATING PRODUCT-COMPANY FIT

The fact that good opportunities exist in the marketplace for a new or repositioned product does not necessarily mean that the organization should proceed on such a product. Unless there is a good "fit" between the proposed product and the firm's needs and resources, the net result of a decision to proceed might be harmful, or at best, suboptimal.

Among the dimensions which need to be considered when evaluating product-company fit are:

1 *Technological skills of labor and management*
2 *Work-force size*
3 *Financial resources*
4 *Production resources and capacity*
5 *Logistics facilities*
6 *Feasibility of using existing sales force and distribution channels*
7 *Needs and behavior of existing consumers*
8 *Impact upon the market position of the firm's other products*
9 *Consistency with the organization's existing image*
10 *Seasonality of demand patterns for existing products (will the new product exaggerate existing fluctuations or counterbalance them?)*

The fact that a proposed product is not consistent with one or more of the above dimensions does not necessarily mean that the company should drop the idea. Indeed, the whole objective may be to diversify into new markets. However, the poorer the fit, the larger the financial resources that may be needed to develop the requisite new skills, production facilities, and market contacts.

SUMMARY

Product policy determination is an ongoing task, reflecting the changing nature of the marketplace. Because an organization's choice of products has such important implications for every facet of the business, it tends to be of great concern to top management.

Key considerations in the formulation of product policy are the skills, contacts, and other resources of the firm, its existing product mix, the corporate objectives established by management, the characteristics of existing and potential markets, and the nature of the competition. The process of evaluation, therefore, involves each of the analytical modes employed in marketing, namely, market, consumer, trade, competitive, and economic analysis.

LONDONTOWN CORPORATION

NANCY J. DAVIS
Research Associate
Harvard Graduate School of Business Administration

STEVEN H. STAR
Associate Professor
Harvard Graduate School of Business Administration

In June 1975, Mr. Jonathan Myers, president of Londontown Corporation, was considering the performance of his company's London Fog Division. After experiencing serious problems between 1968 and 1970, when sales dropped from 2 to 1.4 million units, the London Fog Division had managed to rebuild sales to 2 million units by 1973. However, in 1974 unit sales again stood at 2 million, and in mid-1975 company executives doubted that the division could break the 2 million barrier that year. Myers said:

> We could blame the depressed economy, but that's really dodging the issue. Maybe we need new selling techniques or different styling for different markets. It might be that our advertising or our high price structure isn't right for our customers. And perhaps we should reconsider our policy of selective distribution. Whether

our problem is in sales, advertising, pricing, styling, distribution, or whatever, we've got to identify and solve it if we're going to reach our goal of 2.5 million units by 1980.

COMPANY HISTORY

The Londontown Corporation traced its origins to a company which manufactured fine men's suits, overcoats, and formal wear during the early part of the twentieth century. In the early 1930s, the market for Londontown's products collapsed and the company was near bankruptcy. Israel Myers, an industrious young employee who had joined the company in 1923 at the age of 16, then purchased the company, got it back on its feet, and continued to produce a wide range of men's clothing. During World War II, Londontown supplied large orders of rubber raincoats to the Army, and when the war ended, Myers decided to concentrate on the raincoat business, which was then virtually devoid of competition. However, he wanted to manufacture garments whose fine fabrics, expert tailoring, and quality construction made them truly unique, attractive coats, not merely utilitarian products as he had made for the Army.

Myers' problem then was how to produce a coat that was both fashionable and water-repellent. Conventional fabrics could be made to repel water, but they were hot, heavy, and uncomfortable. The first step toward solving this problem came in the 1950s when the E. I. du Pont de Nemours & Co. developed a blend of Dacron and cotton which was both water-repellent and machine-washable. With this fabric, Londontown made lighter, more comfortable, more fashionable raincoats which provided warmth without weight, were made of wash and wear fabrics, and were appropriate for both casual and dress-up occasions. A second major technological breakthrough came when Du Pont developed Zepel, a special chemical blend which increased the water repellency of fabric.

In 1954, Londontown introduced a small line of men's raincoats under the London Fog label. The most revolutionary item in this line was Myers' new creation which he called the *Maincoat*. This was a year-round, all-weather garment with a zip-out lining for both the body and the sleeves, and it proved to be one of the most popular items ever to appear in the outer-garment industry. In 1955 Londontown introduced a London Fog raincoat line for ladies. Both the men's and women's raincoats had raglan sleeves, hidden buttons, and a loose fit, and this style constituted what came to be known as the "classic London Fog look." Throughout the fifties, London Fog's major consumers were college students and business executives. During this time, London Fog only gradually added new colors to its line. Mr. Stan Rubin, Londontown's vice president of styling and merchandising, later commented on this period as follows: "The fifties were the day of the uniform. *Esquire* and *Madamoiselle* magazines told students to buy three-piece suits, shirts with button-down collars, Villager dresses, Bass Weejuns, and London Fog raincoats, and they did." (See Exhibit 1 for examples of London Fog's line in the 1950s.)

In the sixties, major changes occurred in the raincoat market. "When the

Beatles came over from England in 1963, they brought the first fashion change," Rubin said. "However, this didn't get big until about 1965 or 1966 when the free speech movement was growing and students were switching from *Esquire* to *Rolling Stone.* Then they deserted department stores and college specialty shops and went en masse to Army-Navy stores." Also during the sixties, there was a major population movement to the West where more casual sports clothes were being worn.

In contrast to other companies which tried to respond to the rapid changes in the market, London Fog continued the styling and distribution strategies that had served it well in the past. Its products were still heavily demanded, but management did not recognize until the late sixties that the demand was coming from a different group of consumers. While college students were going to Army-Navy stores and executives were buying more fashionable clothing, London Fog's products were becoming prestige items for more affluent blue-collar workers and older people. Moreover, the westward population shift was not noticed because London Fog was still saturating other markets, especially in the Northeast, and was selling virtually all the raincoats it could make.

In 1968 and 1969, London Fog's remarkable success abruptly ended. Sales dropped from $42.8 million in 1968 to $35.5 million in 1969 and then to $30.0 million in 1970. Unit sales dropped from 2 million in 1968 to 1.4 million in 1970. Rubin commented on this situation as follows:

> Up until the late sixties, we operated on the principle that what was good for our factories was what people should wear. The combination of our missing new fashion trends and new markets and the recession of 1969 and 1970 caused our problem. All the symptoms were there by 1967, but our sales were still strong, so we didn't notice something was amiss until too late.

In 1969, London Fog executives addressed the problem of how to maintain the division's basic business while breaking into fashion in all three of its lines—men's raincoats, men's outerwear, and women's raincoats. At that time, the design staff consisted of three men who specialized in traditional lines. The salespeople did not know how to sell new fashion garments, and many had been doing much of their business by telephone. Moreover, there was a strong feeling that whatever changes were to be made should be done with the least possible confusion for the factory.

One of the first steps in the turnaround was to hire Mr. Mike Horen, formerly international services manager of Puritan Sportswear. Horen contracted with an advertising agency which was more marketing oriented than the previous one had been, and the company began doing market research to determine exactly who was buying its products. To increase the fashion orientation of the line, management contracted with a free-lance designer in New York who designed some models for London Fog on weekends. In the fall of 1969, the company came out with a line of men's fashion rainwear which was made of Dacron and cotton. A bigger step toward fashion was taken, however, in the fall of 1970 when the company introduced men's coats made of woven texturized polyester. This was a heavy, bulky fabric which maintained a fresh, crisp appearance and which was widely regarded as a wool replacement. These garments were oriented primarily to men 35 and older. Retailing at about $85, they were considered a replacement for wool coats which usually retailed for $120 and up. Also in 1970, the company hired Mr. Murray Kelberman, formerly vice president of sales at Hickok, to revitalize London Fog's sales organization. In 1971 London Fog opened a design room in New York, hired some new designers, and began to orient its women's line for the New York market. In 1973 the division began a major marketing effort with men's heavy outerwear, i.e., any outer garment other than raincoats or topcoats. It had carried a line of men's outerwear since 1967, but not until 1973 did this merchandise receive much attention.

As part of this reorganization in the early seventies, corporate management created Clipper Mist, Inc., to market moderate-priced men's rainwear. This subsidiary added women's rainwear in 1975. Also in 1970 the company acquired Star Sportswear Manufacturing Corporation, a 53-year-old company which produced popularly priced leather and suede coats, jackets, and leisure tops for men under the brand name Startown.

By 1974 Londontown's total corporate sales had reached $69,188,000 and net earnings were $2,750,000. Clipper Mist, Inc., had been the most successful of the new divisions, having become one of the top six men's rainwear brands in less than 4 years of existence. Myers felt that Clipper Mist offered the corporation extraordinary opportunites for the future. Clipper Mist's average retail price was $50, as compared to London Fog's $75.

Also by 1974, the London Fog Division had regained considerable strength, and despite Clipper Mist's success, London Fog still accounted for the majority of corporate sales and profits. London Fog's recovery had been aided by an act of nature—1972 had almost double the average rainfall of the last 50 years, and overall raincoat sales had skyrocketed. In 1973, however, rainfall was below average, economic conditions were uncertain, retail business was slowing throughout the economy, and the total raincoat market was shrinking. Nevertheless, London Fog managed to rebuild both market share and unit volume. In 1973 unit volume again reached 2 million. In 1974, however, though dollar sales climbed, unit sales were still at the 2 million mark.

THE MARKETS AND COMPETITION

The markets in which London Fog competed were highly fragmented. Moreover, because garment classifications were not clearly defined and manufacturers normally did not release sales figures by garment types, it was difficult to calculate market share data. This task was further complicated because some manufacturers' lines encompassed a wider price range than others. "You don't even know where the posts are in this race," commented Horen. In spite of these difficulties, London Fog management made estimates of total United States sales of each of its product lines and approximate London Fog shares in each category as shown in Table 1.

TABLE 1

	Total U.S. retail sales, 1974		Approx. London Fog shares	
	Dollars	**Units**	**% of dollars**	**% of units**
Men's rainwear	168,394,500	5,253,000	21.5	12.0
Men's outerwear	557,820,700	28,377,700	0.5	0.5
Men's jackets	344,845,400	26,629,100	2.5	1.6
Women's rainwear	401,902,000	12,666,000	11.8	6.4

These shares were not considered true indicators of London Fog's performance, however, because in the quality segments of the markets where London Fog actually competed, its shares were considerably larger.

At the very top of its men's rainwear line, London Fog competed with Aquascutum Ltd. and Burberry Ltd., English manufacturers whose coats retailed for $125 or more. Also in this category were a few French manufacturers. London Fog management thought that in the United States the combined sales of these manufacturers totaled less than $500,000.

The companies which competed most directly with London Fog were Harbor Master and Gleneagles. Their coats retailed for $50 to $120. Harbor Master, a division of Jonathan Logan Company, offered trench coats and a line of garmets with the "mature man's look." London Fog management estimated Harbor Master's sales of men's rainwear to be between $3 and $5 million. In the past, Gleneagles' rainwear line had been very similar to London Fog's but not nearly as successful. In recent years, Gleneagles had gradually moved out of rainwear into outerwear and had tried to develop a fashion image. Its sales in men's rainwear, outerwear, and leisure wear were thought to be between $4 and $6 million, about 80 percent of which was sold through the chain of retail stores operated by Gleneagles' parent company, Hart, Schaffner, and Marx.

Leaders in the medium-priced segment ($30 to $75), in which London Fog did not actually compete, were Rainfair and Clipper Mist who both offered the London Fog look but whose material, stitching, and lining were not comparable in quality to London Fog's. Rainfair's sales were estimated to be $11 million in 1974. Sears, Roebuck & Company and J. C. Penney were very strong in the lower-priced segment where coats retailed for $20 to $50. They had estimated 1974 sales of $30 and $18 million, respectively.

In men's jackets and outerwear, there were about 10 major companies in addition to London Fog. With 1974 sales of about $14 million, MacGregor was still the industry leader, though in recent years it had been declining, and about 25 percent of its sales were thought to be closeouts. Zero King had 1974 sales of about $9 million, primarily in heavy outerwear with some leisure suits. Mighty Mac (1974 sales, $8 million) and Strato Jack ($7 million) marketed lines similar to Zero King. Generally speaking, the average retail prices of these companies' garments were as follows: heavy outerwear, $85; spring jackets, $30; and leisure suits, $90. Other companies which were strong in men's outerwear were Puritan, Peters, Grais, Pacific Trail, and Catalina. The average retail price of their heavy outerwear was about $50. London Fog management stated that the outerwear market on the West Coast was very different from the market on the East Coast, and that active sportswear was heavily demanded everywhere while leisure sportswear was especially popular in the Southwest.

In ladies' rainwear, London Fog's chief competitor was Misty Harbor, a division of the Jonathan Logan Company. Misty Harbor had responded more quickly to the fashion trend of the late sixties and had gained considerable momentum when London Fog faltered. It had a sales force, but most of its sales were made out of its New York showroom. In 1974, its sales totaled $13 million. Its raincoats retailed for $55 to $100. The leading names in women's fashion raincoats, which retailed for $85 to $150, were Raincheeta, Burberry, and Aquascutum. London Fog management estimated that these lines together accounted for sales of about $15 million in 1974.

Other companies which marketed women's rainwear were Forecaster (1974 sales, $12 million), Cable ($3 million), Jerrold ($13 million), Main Street ($4 million), Drizzle ($7 million), Rain Shedder ($3 million), Totes ($3 million), and Weatherbee ($6 million). The lower-priced segment of the women's rainwear market was dominated by Sears, J. C. Penney, and mass merchandisers such as Zayres and K Mart.

CURRENT SITUATION, MAY 1975

In 1975 the London Fog Division marketed rainwear and outerwear for both men and women plus a small line of leisure suits for men. Leisure suits were matching slacks and jackets which Rubin described as "half dress-up suit, half-outerwear jacket, which can be worn for both dressy and casual occasions." London Fog's men's coats retailed for $55 to $135, and its women's coats retailed for $55 to $175. Retailer margins on these garments ranged from 45 to 53 percent. The seasonality of London Fog's lines is shown in Table 2.

London Fog's 1975 spring line consisted of 33 styles for men and 28 for women. The 1975 fall line consisted of 59 styles for men and 48 for women. (In 1964 London Fog's fall line had consisted of 14 styles.) On the average, each style was offered in three different colors. The division also offered a condensed, "holiday" line on a limited basis at Christmas. This line was used to test the market acceptance of new styles, fabrics, and ideas before large production commitments were made for the following season. For the Christmas holiday of 1975, this line was expected to consist of 12 items for men and 21 for women. Depending on the time of year, London Fog offered 50 to 60 different models in its regular retail lines. In addition, London Fog had "specialty" accounts, cus-

TABLE 2
PERCENT OF DOLLAR SALES BY CATEGORY AND SEASON, 1974

	Spring	Fall
Men's rainwear	31.5	68.5
Men's jackets	58.1	41.9
Men's heavy outerwear		100.0
Women's rainwear	47.9	52.1

tomers such as the military and other organizations. The division's final category of sales were closeouts, discontinued styles which were sold at somewhat less than full price at the end of a season. Closeouts accounted for about 6 percent of the division's total sales.

While London Fog's line had substantially more up-to-date fashion items than in the past, much of the line was still built around a few basic patterns. Special collars, linings, pockets, and trim were added to these patterns, with the result that the line appeared to have several distinctively different coats, but production processes in the company's four factories were not interrupted. As one executive commented:

> We try to maintain a facade of having a lot of fashion so that our line looks fresh and we get store windows, but we want to keep the number of really unique items small enough so they don't interfere with our basic business. For example, our four midi-coats get us lots of exposure, but they constitute only one percent of our volume.

The normal life cycle of London Fog's basic models was 3 to 5 years. Seventy percent of the men's lines and fifty percent of the women's lines consisted of basic garments. "We're really the corn flakes of raincoats," another executive said. "We're too big, and we like being an ongoing concern too much to get heavily into the fashion business."

For the fall of 1975, in men's rainwear, London Fog offered two distinct lines. The first consisted of 14 styles of the 41-inch-long classic coat with the "conservative gentleman's" look. The second line (18 styles) had a younger, more stylish look. The coats were 38 inches long, had higher armholes, and were trimmer. Coats in both lines were made from texturized polyester and Dacron and cotton. In men's outerwear, London Fog offered 22 styles, some styled for the mature man's market and others for the younger man's market. It also offered five styles of leather jackets. The 1975 fall line of women's coats included the company's first collection of women's outerwear, coats made of canvas, polyester and cotton, and 100 percent polyester and trimmed with real and fake furs. In women's rainwear, the company was introducing coats in a new textured polyester poplin weave and some lighter-toned colors for southern states. (See Exhibit 2 for examples of London Fog's lines in 1975.)

THE PLANNING PROCESS

About 8 months before the beginning of a particular selling season, Rubin presented a preliminary plan about the types of coats and fabrics to be included in the upcoming line to Myers, Kelberman, and Mr. Jerry Gilbert, vice president of manufacturing. This plan was put together by Rubin and the company's designers after lengthy study of trends in the European and American markets. Since Myers, Gilbert, and Kelberman were also very much interested in fashion and made a point of staying on top of fashion trends, they often made suggestions about Rubin's initial design plan.

About 5 months before the beginning of a selling season, Rubin took mock-ups, coats, and sketches to this committee, and the line was selected. The bulk of the fabric orders was then placed, though some fabrics would have to have been ordered as much as 3 months earlier. After the line was selected, models were sent to the New York showroom where they were previewed by some retail buyers. The buyers filled out questionnaires about each garment. "We've learned that if these buyers say they won't buy a particular coat, others won't either, so we eliminate the definite 'no's' from the line," Kelberman said.

About 3 months before the beginning of a selling season, this committee met to forecast sales by models. Of the previous year's lines, about 60 percent of men's rainwear, about 40 percent of men's outerwear, and about 30 percent of women's rainwear were retained. Sales forecasts for the retained lines were based on historical performance. Forecasts for the new lines were essentially the committee's best estimates, based on performance of new lines in previous years, market conditions, and an assessment of the population characteristics in the localities where the garments would most likely sell. "In a stable market for adult rainwear and outerwear, history is very important," Rubin commented. "The profit gains derived from smooth planning and steady production more than offset last minute changes in styles." Rubin went on to say that, once the sales force began to sell the line, 10 to 20 percent of the original models usually turned out to be such slow sellers that they were dropped from the line.

Although salespeople did not participate directly in the development of the line, they participated indirectly via written reports which detailed the performance of specific garments and any suggestions retailers or the salespeople themselves had about the garments. Moreover, Kelberman received weekly reports from regional managers about sales activity and trends in their region. (See Exhibit 3 for sample report from a London Fog salesperson.)

DISTRIBUTION

London Fog maintained a policy of selective distribution, choosing only those department stores and specialty shops whose image was consistent with its own quality image. In May 1975, the division had 8,100 accounts: 3,200 of these accounts carried both men's and women's lines, 2,700 carried men's only, and 2,200 carried women's only. "Requests for new accounts come into our office in Herculean numbers," commented Kelberman. "In major cities, there are only a handful of stores we'd like to sell and don't, and these are usually stores that insist on having only their names in the garments."

London Fog sold products at the same price to all its customers, and it did not accept returns. Because of the latter policy, many retailers preferred to order relatively small quantities initially and to reorder items which sold well. This buying pattern was directly opposed to London Fog's policy of relying on large opening orders and large manufacturing runs. The division's salespeople tried to convince customers that they needed London Fog products in their stores in depth because the products sold very quickly.

Because of regional differences in types of garments purchased, selling cycles for different lines began at different times of the year. Early in January, salespeople who sold men's outerwear met to learn about the new line. They then did the advance selling for the fall line of men's outerwear from mid-January through May. The balance of the fall line—men's rainwear and jackets and ladies' rainwear and outerwear—was introduced at a national sales meeting in early February, and advance selling of these garments ran from February 15 through June 30. In late July, regional meetings were held for salespeople in the South, Southeast, Southwest, and West. The purpose of these meetings was to introduce the Southland line, an early spring line of women's coats which the sales force began to sell on August 1 for delivery in mid-October. The complete spring line was introduced at a national sales meeting in early September, and it was sold between September 15 and January 31. Advance orders normally accounted for about 65 percent of London Fog's total orders.

During the rest of the year, the salespeople visited outlets, did inventory checks, took reorders, and talked to retailers about what was going on in the marketplace. The salespeople were encouraged to hold annual or seasonal breakfast meetings with major retail salespeople to teach them about London Fog's merchandise. Most salespeople preferred to use audio-visual training cassettes which headquarters had prepared because they felt that turnover among retail salespeople was too high for sales meetings to be effective. Kelberman stated that selling the men's line was a completely different process from selling the women's line. "Manufacturers come and go so rapidly in women's fashions that very few manufacturer-retailer loyalties develop," he said. "Selling women's apparel is really a no-holds-barred business."

London Fog's sales organization was headed by Kelberman. Six regional managers reported to him, and each of them was responsible for six to nine salespeople. Of the 36 salespeople, 11 handled primarily the men's line, though often in a small part of their territories they sold both the men's and women's lines. Seven salespeople handled primarily the women's line, though they too often sold some men's coats to a few of their retailers. Eighteen salespeople handled both the men's and women's lines. Salespeople were responsible for 50 to 150 accounts, and regional managers often handled a few accounts. London Fog's salespeople ranged in age from 30 to 72, with the average being about 38.

London Fog's sales territories were organized geographically, and almost all its salespeople handled both department store and specialty store accounts. In major markets, salespeople usually visited the buyer or merchandise manager of a single account as much as once a month, while in more remote areas of their territories, they might visit an account only two to four times a year. Salespeople reported that turnover among buyers was high because the position was frequently used as a training slot, and that buyers often relied heavily on them as authorities in the rainwear market.

As customary in the apparel industry, London Fog's salespeople were paid a straight commission—3 percent of sales—and they paid their own selling expenses. While this percentage was considered low for the apparel industry, the gross income of London Fog's salespeople was considered high. In 1974 it averaged over $40,000. Salespeople were charged 60 percent of the wholesale price for samples which they usually sold at the end of a selling season. Kelberman commented that:

> The biggest complaint we get from salespeople now is about the cost of travel. They like the styles we send them and are happy with the acceptance the London Fog name gives them in the marketplace. When I came here in 1970, morale was pretty low. Territories were not divided equitably; and some salespeople did most of their selling by phone. In 1970 we hired several professional salespeople and trained them to sell fashion goods. Since then, there's been almost no turnover in the sales force.

Kelberman thought that in the future the company might have separate forces for the men's and the women's lines if growth warranted such a split.

Kelberman maintained contact with top management of major accounts and directed the training of all sales personnel. He felt it essential to keep his salespeople informed about latest selling techniques so they could keep pace with the rapid changes occurring in retail outlets. He went on to say that for the division to offer a broad line of garments without wrecking its factories, it tried to direct the selling efforts from company headquarters:

> For the fall we're offering 48 ladies' coats, but we actually plan to make only 37. Therefore, our salespeople will really push what we plan to make and back off from the lines we don't want to make. Of course, if customers demand something we haven't planned to make, we can always change our mind and make it for them.

One way London Fog attempted to control sales was by preparing detailed merchandising plans for its major accounts. These plans included the retailer's historical dollar and unit sales of London Fog products, London Fog's objectives for the retailer, projected unit and dollar sales of London Fog products by model for the retailer's total operation, specific models, colors, number of units, and sizes for each of the account's retail outlets, and a recommended advertising program based on estimated purchases.

ADVERTISING PROGRAM

Through 1969 London Fog's advertising had consisted primarily of print ads in *The New Yorker*. It had offered a cooperative advertising allowance since 1955, but few retailers had used it. "London Fog ran clever, sophisticated, memorable ads for years, but we don't know if they sold any raincoats," commented Horen. "Merchandise was still on allocation then, so nobody worried much about the advertising's effectiveness." During this time, London Fog's annual advertising expenditures were about $1 million.

After joining London Fog in 1970, Horen began to look more closely at individual markets to determine where the company's business was coming from, where its greatest potential lay, and what its major problems were. With regard to advertising, he dropped the company's national program and developed fully paid "sell in" programs designed to get early orders from specific retailers in specific cities. During this time the company continued to offer its regular co-op program to all retailers in all segments of the country. In 1974 London Fog's measured media advertising expenditures had been $822,600, twice as much as all other manufacturers combined had spent. (See Exhibit 4 for comparative advertising expenditures.)

For 1975 London Fog's advertising program was specially designed for each of the company's major markets. London Fog paid the total advertising costs and handled all placements so that it could use the media which it considered most appropriate for its products. These media included television, newspapers, radio, and metro editions of *Time, Newsweek, U.S. News and World Report, Sports Illustrated, Redbook, McCall's,* and *Ladies' Home Journal.* Advertisements always included a retailer's name. For any given retailer, the amount of advertising he received depended on the share of London Fog's business he did in his particular market. This share was determined by the retailer's early bookings, which had jumped from 25 percent of sales in 1970 to 65 percent in 1975. Horen stated that, as a result of this program, London Fog was doing television advertising in more markets than ever before. About 25 percent of the television ads were run during weekday daytime shows, about 25 percent on prime time, and about 50 percent during news programs and late-night talk shows. He stated further that this program had the effect of increasing a retailer's actual markup on London Fog products by decreasing his advertising expenditures. Nevertheless, a few retailers would not use London Fog's ads because they didn't want their ads to look like everyone else's. The ads usually pictured London Fog's basic garments rather than its fashion items. (See Exhibits 5 and 6 for sample advertisements.)

The advertising budget for any given garment was determined by that garment's sales during the previous year. That is, built into the price of each garment was a certain dollar amount which was allocated for advertising expenditures for the following year. "This policy is based on the premise that, if advertising gets growth, we'll continue to grow," Horen said. "Unfortunately, however, we still don't have data that measures the impact of the ads," Horen said the company often used advertising to force specific items and to get some garments established.

Horen stated that he was just beginning to do some fairly sophisticated market research. Using various published data, he had determined the total United States market for each of London Fog's lines, and he had determined London Fog's share not only of the total United States market but of about 75 major target markets as well. He noted that London Fog's shares varied greatly from one market to another and from one product category to another. He summarized the ranges in the top 75 markets as shown in Table 3.

By looking at factors such as historical sales, weather, income, age,

TABLE 3

	Unit shares, %	Dollar shares, %
Men's rainwear	2.9–35.2	6.6–78.4
Men's outerwear	0.8–17.6	1.7–38.4
Men's jackets	0.5– 8.8	1.0–18.6
Women's rainwear	1.0–10.9	2.2–23.4

number of department stores and specialty stores, and the extent to which residents relied on public transportation, Horen projected the number of units London Fog would sell in any given city a year in advance. He also used a variety of factors to create an index to London Fog's sales by product line in each market. This index allowed management to determine the relative strength of each line by market and to step up marketing efforts wherever needed. Horen stated that if the company could bring all lines in these markets up to "average," which on his index was 100, the company's unit sales would sharply increase.

CUSTOMERS

In recent years, London Fog had also begun to do a fair amount of consumer research. The latest study, which was done in 1973, revealed that, though women represented a majority of the rainwear potential, London Fog was increasingly becoming a men's brand. While 45 percent of all raincoat owners were men, 62 percent of all London Fog raincoat owners were men. Moreover, while 57 percent of the men in the United States owned a raincoat, 22 percent of all male raincoat owners owned a London Fog.

The study indicated that, throughout the United States, raincoat ownership was declining. In 1973, 58 percent of the people surveyed owned a raincoat, while in 1972 the comparable number had been 69 percent. The decline was most pronounced among women, with a drop from 72 percent in 1972 to 58 percent in 1973, and among the 25–34 age group where ownership fell from 65 to 45 percent among males and from 68 to 41 percent among females. London Fog management felt these trends suggested that raincoats were discretionary items and that younger families, among whom the economic pinch tended to be tightest, might be deferring buying a raincoat for the wife in favor of getting one for the husband to wear to work.

London Fog owners tended to be distinctively upscale. Of the households surveyed, 61 percent of the homemakers who owned a London Fog had a high school education and 35 percent had been to college. Moreover, 42 percent of the London Fog owners had an annual income over $15,000. However, London Fog's share in the below-$15,000 group had also increased in recent years, largely, management thought, due to the total industry's declining in the past year while London Fog's unit sales had remained stable.

Regarding raincoat distribution, the survey indicated that 34 percent of all raincoats were owned by central city residents, 41 percent by suburban residents, and 25 percent by all other residents. London Fog's distribution closely paralleled these industry statistics. Ownership distribution by geographic region had not changed very much in recent years. Nearly half of all raincoats were owned by residents of New England, the Middle Atlantic states, and the South Atlantic states. London Fog's ownership distribution had changed somewhat since 1972, however. In New England it declined from 14 percent in 1972 to 11 percent in 1973, and it increased from 1 to 2 percent in the Mountain region and from 7 to 9 percent in the Pacific region. London Fog's share had climbed considerably in the North Central zone, an area which had received special attention in the past year and which represented 27 percent of the total United States potential.

Large metro areas (i.e., over 2 million population) accounted for 30 percent of all raincoats and 35 percent of London Fog raincoats. Medium-size metro areas (500,000–2 million) accounted for 27 percent of total industry sales and 27 percent of London Fog's sales. These figures had remained relatively stable in recent years.

The number of people owning more than one raincoat almost doubled between 1972 and 1973. In 1972 only 19 percent of all raincoat owners had more than one unit, but by 1973, 35 percent owned more than one. In 1973, 44 percent of London Fog owners had two or more units, as compared to 23 percent in 1972. Management thought this increase was due to styling advances which caused owners to want more fashionable garments.

Department stores accounted for 59 percent of all units sold and for 57 percent of all London Fog units. However, London Fog's unique strength was in men's and ladies' specialty shops which accounted for 35 percent of its sales, as compared to only 20 percent of total industry sales. The survey also indicated that the owners were keeping their raincoats longer than they had in the past. In 1972 the average raincoat had been 27 months old, while in 1973 it was 37 months old. London Fog units had a median age of 36 months. Management felt that the increased average age was caused by owners' keeping the "classic" units which they purchased before October 1969, while they had not held onto so many "fashionable" units purchased after that date.

PLANNING FOR THE FUTURE

Late in 1974, Horen put together a lengthy report on market and population changes which the company could expect through 1980. He was especially concerned that both men and women in the 45–54 age group, one of London Fog's prime markets, would decline in number. Moreover, he noted that the percentage of the population 65 and over was increasing, and that by 1980 this group, when combined with the 25–34 age group, would account for 45 percent of London Fog's total market. He felt that if the company did not design, price, and sell to the 25–34 age group and if inflation made London Fog raincoats too expensive for the 65-and-over group, then the company would lose a sizable share of the market by 1980.

Horen also predicted that many of London Fog's geographic markets would experience virtually no growth and perhaps even losses in population and in effective buying income. Growth in important cities, he said, would take place in the "Sun Belt" from southern California to Florida. He speculated further that the entire market for heavy outerwear might therefore be decreasing:

> A lot of people go from a climate-controlled home into the adjacent garage, get into a climate-controlled car and drive to a shopping center where they make a quick dash from the car to the climate-controlled stores. More and more, people can avoid bad weather if they want to.

Rubin also foresaw major problems ahead. He thought the unpredictability of the emerging youth market (20–30 years old) with regard to style would cause the company serious problems. He suspected that the more affluent members of this segment, which he estimated to be between 4 and 5 million people, would gravitate toward imported or high-style coats which retailed for $135 or more, but he said he didn't really know what the majority of the "former Army-Navy store crowd" would buy. He was certain that this group liked more individuality in dress and frequent change in fashion, however. These preferences would interfere with London Fog's long runs of garments in the factory and its planning from a good historical base. Secondly, Rubin was concerned about the decrease in the incidence of raincoat purchases. He thought the decrease had come about partly because rainwear was no longer as important a fashion item as it had been in the early sixties and partly because of the increased cost of living. "With inflation soaring, people are just buying fewer units of most items," he said. "We've got to be careful with our pricing structure. It's already high, and we just might eventually price ourselves out of the volume market."

Rubin said he was not sure how the population move to the South would affect London Fog's sales, but that the South had posed some problems in the past:

> In the South we sell only unlined raincoats, and these are sold at retail from October through January. In the North, unlined raincoats are sold from January through May, so we've always had some problems with our stock. Moreover, people in the South tend to buy less expensive goods. This has been partly due to overall lower income levels and partly to the fact that Southerners just can't be convinced of the need for an outer garment. No matter how much it rains or how cold it gets, most Southerners think the weather there is too nice for a coat.

Rubin stated that London Fog might also have some problems with their current retailers.

> Except for chain operations, a lot of the specialty stores we sell to are dying, and those that remain are becoming increasingly specialized. Moreover, big stores are getting increasingly difficult to do business with. They make all kinds of demands about returns, ad allowances, trade terms, and so forth.

A final problem Rubin pointed to concerned the mills which supplied their fabric. He said that the major suppliers had developed bigger, more sophisticated operations, and that they were more and more interested in doing larger runs for customers whose volume was substantially greater than that of rainwear manufacturers. This problem had been compounded by the proliferation of models causing raincoat manufacturers to want smaller and smaller runs of fabric.

In considering the future, Myers felt that the company had to determine exactly what geographic markets it should focus on and what product lines offered the greatest possibilities. The company's recent examination of its 75 major markets had revealed that the geographic distribution of its sales was very uneven. "In some markets we have unreal volume, and in others our volume is very low," he said. "We need to figure out how to get our low markets up to average while holding on to our share in the very high markets."

With regard to product mix, all agreed that the market was shifting even more toward leisurely life styles and that London Fog had to adapt its product mix accordingly. Rubin predicted that the men's heavy outerwear and jacket businesses would increase, but that men's rainwear would be under pressure because the 45–65 age group would increasingly be hurt by inflationary pressures and their raincoat purchases would decrease. He thought London Fog's business in women's rainwear and outerwear would increase because the demand for all-purpose coats was increasing. He predicted that the 2.5 million units which the company hoped to sell in 1980 would break down as follows:

Men's outerwear	650,000
Men's rainwear	700,000
Men's leisure suits	50,000
Women's outerwear	200,000
Women's rainwear	900,000
Total	2,500,000

EXHIBIT 1
SAMPLES OF LONDON FOG'S LINE IN THE 1950s
Londontown Corporation

TRUDI

EXHIBIT 2
Continued

MELANIE

EXHIBIT 2
Continued

BETTY

EXHIBIT 2
Continued

Deering

Rockfield

EXHIBIT 2
Continued

Baldwin

Pinehurst
(Leisure Outerwear)

EXHIBIT 3
SAMPLE REPORT FROM LONDON FOG SALESPERSON
Londontown Corporation

This is the retail reaction on the following coats:

Date 5/5/75
Salesperson M. Jones

Model	Excellent	Good	Fair	Poor	Comments
Valerie			X		
Shirley			X		
Jeannine				X	
Melissa			X		Selling not as good as last year.
Melinda	X				This shows us the need for more pattern coats. A good plaid would sell.
Kory		X			Sold well where placed.
Alison	X				Very good reaction at retail. I would like to have one more color in this coat. I think that we should expand our trench coat story.
Kathleen			X		Selling only fair. I do not know why this coat did not sell better but Tammy outsold this coat in every store.
Tammy	X				Best selling long coat. Could have done a much better job on this coat if we would put this coat in some new colors and also need this coat cut in size 20 in more colors. I could not develop the volume with this coat because we delivered it late.
Lainie			X		Fell because of Alison.
Glenda			X		Business on this coat fell for the first time in 3 years. I think that we should develop a new D.B. coat in Spring. This was my big volume coat now sales are just fair.
Beth				X	Delivered late but when delivered it did not sell.

130

EXHIBIT 3
Continued

Model	Excellent	Good	Fair	Poor	Comments
Lady Poole				X	Just another coat no real volume.
Celeste				X	This was the worst selling coat for Spring. It did not fit.
Lisa				X	Another poplin that just did not sell.
Wendy	X				Excellent selling coat. Should make to size 20.
Hope	X				Excellent selling coat. Should make to size 20.
Joy			X		Sold where placed. Could have sold better if it was not a raglan sleeve.

Competitive coats that are doing well in this area Poly coats doing very well. Also Misty Harbor short coats.
I need the following for Spring '76 for my territory POLY I feel that I could have done a much better job if we would expand our poly line. We need poly in short coats and we need more than one coat we should have 3 or 4 short coats. In long poly we could use a wrap coat. I also feel that we could use a plaid coat. In both a single breasted and a double breasted model. I have had very good reaction to the imagitex—poplin.

Long coats
1—I would like to see us expand our trench coat story.
2—We also need a coat to replace the Glenda coat.
3—A lot of my stores like the body style of the Colette coat, a double breasted Tammy model.
4—I also feel that we have too many raglan sleeve coats. I think we should expand our set-in sleeve picture.
5—Could use a new big woman coat—body similar to the Millie—shirt placket front in contrast color—Example: white with green—white with navy.

Short coats
1—We must cut short coats in size 18 and 20. I could do a big job on these sizes.
2—We need set in sleeve short coats.
3—Stores are looking at about 50% short coats for Spring '76.
4—Need poly in short coats.
5—We need at least 8 short coat models.

Colors
1—We should add some new colors for Spring '76. We could use some soft greens and some new light tones.

Super short coats
1—I am now getting calls for the super short coat 31 or 32 inches. I have had a very good reaction to the length of the Trixie coat.
2—This could be a new business.

EXHIBIT 4
COMPETITIVE ADVERTISING EXPENDITURES, JANUARY–DECEMBER 1974, IN THOUSANDS OF DOLLARS

Londontown Corporation

Brand	Total media	Magazines	Newspaper supplements	Spot TV
Aquascutum Ltd.:				
Aquascutum All Weather Coats, men	11.1	11.1		
Aquascutum All Weather Coats, women	14.0	14.0		
Braefair:				
All Weather Coats, women	2.2		2.2	2.2
Burberry Ltd.:				
Burberry All Weather Coats, men	17.2	17.2		
Burberry All Weather Coats, men & women	33.6	33.6		
Burberry All Weather Coats, women	9.0	9.0		
Cable Raincoat Co.:				
Snug All Weather Coats, women	76.4	27.6	48.8	
Drizzle:				
All Weather Coats, women	2.4		2.4	
Exylin Co.:				
Aqua-Sheen All Weather Coats, women	1.6	1.6		
B. W. Harris Mfg. Co.:				
Zero King All Weather Coats, men	35.2		35.2	
Jonathan Logan, Inc.:				
Harbor Master Ltd. All Weather Coats, men	18.5	18.5		
Misty Harbor Ltd. All Weather Coats, women	78.2	78.2		
Kopacorp Industries, Inc.:				
Rainfair Rain Topcoats, men	21.6	21.6		
Naman Rainwear:				
Raincheetahs All Weather Coats, women	11.9		11.9	
Rain Shedder:				
All Weather Coats, women	2.3		2.3	
Totes:				
Raincoats	89.6			89.6
Weatherbee Coats, Inc.:				
Weatherbee All Weather Coats, women	42.6	18.4	24.2	
Total	467.4	250.8	127.0	91.8
Londontown Corporation:				
London Fog Coats, men	123.4	33.9	89.5	
London Fog Coats, men & women	593.7			583.7
London Fog Coats, women	99.7	38.3	61.4	
London Fog Jackets, men & women	5.8			5.8
Total London Fog	822.6	72.2	150.9	589.5

Source: Leading National Advertisers, Inc., January–December 1974.

EXHIBIT 5
SAMPLE ADVERTISEMENTS, SPRING 1974:
STATEMENT ENCLOSURES
Londontown Corporation

LOVERS

Romantic things can happen in a London Fog.
So anywhere you wander, London Fog lets you laugh at the weather.

RENEE/HOPE

Romantic things can happen in a London Fog.
So anywhere you wander, London Fog lets you laugh at the weather.

MELISSA/CANDI

Romantic things can happen in a London Fog.
So anywhere you wander, London Fog lets you laugh at the weather.

GOLF

London Fog has gone to great lengths for a short coat . . . We call it The Golf.
Why? Why not? The Golf jackets from London Fog.

COOLIDGE BANK AND TRUST COMPANY

CHRISTOPHER H. LOVELOCK
Assistant Professor
Harvard Graduate School of Business Administration

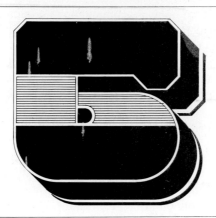

In June 1974, Mr. Milton Adess, president of the Coolidge Bank and Trust Company of Watertown, Massachusetts, was debating whether or not his bank should introduce NOW accounts.

Although modest in size, Coolidge had gained a national reputation for its innovative approach to banking. Among other things, in 1964 it had pioneered development of no-service-charge checking accounts. In 1972, however, a mutual savings bank in Worcester, Massachusetts, had begun offering negotiable order of withdrawal (NOW) accounts, which were effectively interest-bearing checking accounts. This concept was soon adopted by a number of other banks in Massachusetts. In the spring of 1974, Coolidge management recognized that some of their bank's large personal checking depositors were taking their business to NOW accounts at competing banks.

BANKING IN MASSACHUSETTS

Studies by the Federal Reserve Bank of Boston identified the existence of eight major banking markets in Massachusetts in the early 1970s. The largest of these, the Boston market, covered nearly all of eastern Massachusetts, extending from a few towns in southern New Hampshire, whose residents worked in the Boston area, down to the neck of Cape Cod (Exhibit 1). The wide geographic expanse of this market reflected Boston's position as the cultural and economic hub of New England as well as its role as the governmental center of the Commonwealth of Massachusetts.

Observers described the Boston retail banking market as "very competitive." This growing market had been the scene of active developments in recent years. The city of Boston was the home of a number of large and powerful banking organizations, headed by the First National Bank of Boston, the nation's tenth largest correspondent bank. As commuting into metropolitan Boston from the outlying areas had increased, banks located in this area had become alternative sources of banking to more people.

While the population of metropolitan Boston was approximately 2.8 million in 1974, that of the Boston banking market was estimated by the Federal Reserve Bank at 3.8 million. The total population of Massachusetts was 5.8 million.

State banking laws in Massachusetts restricted the operations of individual commercial banks to a single county. Banks were not allowed to open new branches or merge with other banks outside the county in which the home office was located. However, subject to regulatory approval, a bank holding company could acquire another bank anywhere in the state. This provided a means of circumventing the county-branching restrictions. Many large, Boston-based banks had recently formed holding companies which allowed them to take advantage of this situation, although subsidiary banks retained separate identities in each county. In the long run, observers anticipated that banking laws would be amended to permit statewide branch banking in Massachusetts.

The Boston banking market covered major portions of 5 of Massachusetts' 14 counties. Little Suffolk County comprised the cities of Boston, Revere, Winthrop, and Chelsea; Essex County comprised the so-called "North Shore" communities running up to the New Hampshire border; Middlesex, the most populous county in the state, included Cambridge, Watertown, and a large number of towns and cities west of Boston; gerrymandered Norfolk County included Brookline and many communities south and west of Boston; while Plymouth County extended south of Norfolk down toward Cape Cod (Exhibit 2).

Although not direct competitors in all commercial bank services, thrift institutions[1] in Massachusetts competed vigorously with commercial banks for savings deposits and were also important lenders of consumer credit. The introduction of NOW accounts by mutual savings banks in 1972 had enabled them to offer a substitute for commerical-bank demand deposits (checking accounts). In January 1974, the right to offer NOW accounts was extended to savings and loan associations, cooperative banks, and also commercial banks.

---

[1] The term *thrift institutions* comprised mutual savings banks, savings and loan associations, and cooperative banks. These were distinguished from commercial banks in that only the latter had authority to accept demand deposits (i.e., checking accounts) or make commercial loans. The three types of thrift institutions fulfilled essentially similar banking functions, and the primary differences between them lay in the source of their charters and whether they were regulated and insured by state or federal authorities.

In mid-1974, there were 167 mutual savings banks operating in Massachusetts plus 179 savings and loan associations and cooperative banks. These institutions controlled approximately $18.8 billion in total deposits, exceeding the total deposits of the state's 153 commercial banks.

COMPETITION IN RETAIL BANKING

Prior to the advent of "free" checking in the mid-1960s, retail banking institutions in Massachusetts and other states had avoided any significant price competition.

It was generally assumed that customers selected their banks primarily on the basis of convenience and, to a lesser extent, image. An article in the *New England Economic Review* noted:[1]

> Many banks have found that they can draw a larger volume of customers by increasing the accessibility of their facilities, for example by establishing branch offices in convenient locations, by adding parking space or opening drive-in windows, or by extending banking hours. Advertising is also an important mode of competition. Through creative use of the media, some banks have achieved an attractive image, stressing their friendly or personal services, or their status as a small bank underdog—trying harder, of course. Advertising campaigns are often combined with such gimmicks as baby photo contests, washing the windshields of customers' cars, or a wide variety of promotional giveaway offers to new customers, ranging from flatware to thermal blankets. Building attractive offices, adopting modern logos and offering "beautiful" checks are other items in the repertoire of appeals to retail customers.

Price competition, by contrast, was rare. In any given region, the prices of retail banking services (e.g., loan rates, checking account service charges, and other fees) had tended to settle at a competitive rate that was relatively uniform among all banks in the area, with only minor deviations in evidence. Price competition on a broad scale was restrained not only by a plethora of state and federal regulations designed to protect bank solvency, but also by customary industry practices and widespread distaste for "price-cutting" in banking circles. Coolidge Bank had shattered this situation in 1964 by introducing, and vigorously promoting, the concept of no-service-charge checking accounts.

THE GROWTH OF COOLIDGE BANK

The Coolidge Bank and Trust Company[2] received its charter from the Commonwealth of Massachusetts in July 1960. It was founded by a group of mer-

---

[1] Steven J. Weiss, "Commercial Bank Price Competition: The Case of 'Free' Checking Accounts," *New England Economic Review*, September–October, 1969.

[2] The bank was named after one of the seventeenth-century founders of Watertown.

chants and businessmen who, dissatisfied with the quality of service provided by the local bank in Watertown (a suburb of Boston), resolved to start their own.

The leader of this group, Mr. Milton Adess, became president of the new bank. Mr. Adess himself had no previous banking background. As a young man during the Depression, he had worked as a Fuller Brush salesman. From there, he went into retailing and subsequently built up a successful hardware business.

Coolidge Bank opened for service in a former store in December 1960 with a staff of 12 people. Initially, the operation was managed by the executive vice president, a former Rhode Island banker with 21 years' experience who had been recommended by one of the large Boston banks. However, after a year, this individual left Coolidge, and Mr. Adess, in his own words, "offered to come in and just watch the store."

Looking back, many years later, Mr. Adess discussed the background he brought to banking.

> I didn't know a thing about banking. I took a few AIB courses at night and learned a little bit about the language, but I certainly don't claim—even today—to have a strong banking background. I know a little about operations, but my forte is really marketing and loans. It's more of a straight businessman's view of what should be done.

Over the years, the president said, Coolidge had built up a strong professional management group with skills complementing his own. Regarding the bank's philosophy, he observed:

> We look at banking as another business and money as another commodity. We have one color to offer—green. And it's very much like selling any other commodity: we're selling money. And I've always been convinced that the individual or company who brings the best product to the public at the lowest possible price usually does very, very well.

The challenge during the bank's first years was to develop an asset base, since—as Mr. Adess noted—the bank's lending ability was limited by the size of its capital.

> I devoted half my time in the first formative year to just making cold calls. Strangely enough, a couple of my directors who are among our largest customers came as a result of those cold calls. We went out and knocked on doors, we got all our friends and cousins and everyone we could possibly grasp by the lapels and drag into the bank to open up an account of one sort or another, either savings or business.
>
> For the convenience of the public, we immediately started opening at 8 o'clock in the morning, rather than 9. And we extended the hours of banking. We were the first commercial bank to open Saturday mornings. We felt that Saturday mornings were times when the public, as a whole, had their leisure hours and were able to do their banking or sit down and talk to a bank loan officer.

Other early innovations for Coolidge included becoming the first bank in the Boston area to pay interest on Christmas Club accounts as well as the first to pay postage both ways for bank-by-mail accounts. Coolidge also reduced service charges for business checking accounts by one-third. Reproductions of billboards advertising these and later innovations are shown in Exhibit 13.

NO-SERVICE-CHARGE CHECKING

From total assets of $4 million at the end of its first year, "which was quite amazing to our friendly competitors and bankers in Boston," Coolidge Bank's asset base grew steadily, reaching some $12 million by the end of 1964. However, this still left Coolidge a very small bank by the standards of the major Boston banks, whose assets were in the hundreds of millions and higher.

During 1964, Coolidge began testing a radical departure in banking practice: no-service-charge (NSC) personal checking. Coolidge management had decided that the way to compete with the giants was, in Mr. Adess' words, "by trying to use our old hardware efforts—bring the best product to the people at the lowest possible cost." Commented the president,

> After doing an in-depth statistical study, we decided that service charges on personal checking accounts were really not necessary to operate a bank successfuly. I didn't think that the profit picture of a bank required service charges—and still don't!
>
> I thought it was a little unusual, really, that for all these years banks had been charging you for the privilege of leaving your money in their bank so that they could lend it out and make money on it. Now if you're going to be good enough to deposit your money with us, and we can make money on your money, why should we charge you for that privilege?
>
> Well, I thought of a plan in 1963 and it took me close to a year and a half to convince my Board, because it was really breaking all existing banking principles. And when our friendly competitors in Boston heard about our plan, their reaction was one of amazement. I received many telephone calls with gloomy forecasts that eliminating service charges on personal checking accounts would result in disaster. They said, "Do you realize what service charges amount to in banks?" And my response was, "Look, I don't know what your service charges amount to, but I know that mine don't mean too much because we haven't got very many customers."

After preliminary testing, Coolidge adopted NSC checking for all personal checking accounts in 1965, requiring a $100 minimum balance. After promoting this concept through billboards and newspapers, a limited advertising budget was assigned to WEEI, a talk-show radio station. The response to the radio advertising was described as "astounding." Coolidge Bank started getting accounts from "every city, town and hamlet in the state" and at one point, before the competition began following suit, was opening up to 200 accounts a day.

Many other banks soon followed Coolidge's lead, and within a few years NSC checking had become widespread in the Boston area. In 1969, Coolidge went one better, becoming the first to offer genuinely free checking by dropping its $100 minimum balance requirement.

A subsequent survey by the Federal Reserve Bank of Boston indicated that Coolidge's success in attracting new accounts as a result of its NSC plan had been replicated by many other banks in New England, mostly fairly new ones, which had been the first to offer NSC accounts in their local area. This survey found, fairly consistently, that "earlier entrants into the NSC competition in their areas generally have enjoyed a better response from new customers" (Exhibit 4).[1]

OTHER MARKETING ACTIVITIES AT COOLIDGE

Other innovations promoted by the bank included a program to market the American Express Gold Card—which carried a $2,000 credit line and was issued only through banks—to graduating M.B.A. students with verified job offers. Coolidge promoted this concept to business school students nationwide (and later to medical and dental students), and before long became the second largest retailer of such cards in the United States.

Beginning in late 1971, Coolidge introduced its *Cool Cash* concept by installing automated banking consoles, termed *Cool-O-Mats,* outside certain branches. These machines effectively provided 24-hour, 7-day banking transaction services for customers and were more sophisticated than existing cash-dispensing machines (which had been in use in Britain since 1967 and in the United States since 1969). Coolidge was the first bank in the Boston area to install automatic "total tellers," capable of performing the same range of banking transactions as a human teller (Exhibit 14). It promoted them aggressively, and by 1973 its Harvard Square machines were the most heavily used in the country.

Despite some early mechanical problems, later resolved, the Coolidge machines had generally performed well. Mr. Adess conceded that there had been occasional vandalism. "We've had some strange people in the Harvard Square area who poured bottles of Coke into the machines, but security has not been a problem." Viewed overall, he saw automatic tellers as a major opportunity to offer the public greater convenience.

Over the years, Coolidge had experimented with a number of communications approaches, including on-campus representatives, direct mail ("very expensive"), television ("outlandishly expensive"), newspapers, billboards, and radio. Commented Mr. Adess:

> I found that the greatest response came from radio. We checked this. Every new account was asked, "How did you happen to open an account at Coolidge?" And the greatest response came from talk programs. At one time, we were on three or four stations in the Boston area.
>
> We haven't had a direct mail piece now for years. We went out of the newspaper business. Our response from local newspapers has been minimal. Large Boston newspapers are very expensive and you're competing with some very big people in there.
>
> When you buy that minute on the radio, that's yours. And if that man—or woman—is driving in his car, or listening to that program at home, you've got his ear. And the results for us have been really great. Very, very good.

[1] Steven J. Weiss, op. cit.

Stimulated by a combination of innovative approaches to banking and aggressive advertising, Coolidge's deposits and assets grew rapidly (Exhibit 8). Although it had organized a holding company, First Coolidge Corporation, in 1970 to acquire the assets of Coolidge Bank and Trust Company, no attempt had been made to acquire subsidiaries outside Middlesex County. Nevertheless, Coolidge had succeeded in drawing some deposits not only from other parts of Massachusetts but from throughout the United States and even from depositors resident abroad.

Partly responsible for the growth in Coolidge assets and deposits were two mergers and the addition of several new offices. Branches were opened in Watertown in 1962 and in Cambridge in 1964, 1967, and 1970. In 1970 the bank also opened an attractive new four-story headquarters in Watertown Square, replacing its existing office there. 1971 was a particularly busy year for expansion. In April, Coolidge acquired the Industrial Bank & Trust Company of Everett, and in July it acquired the Arlington National Bank, with offices in Arlington, Lexington, and Bedford. In that same year, the bank moved its Harvard Square, Cambridge, office from a temporary location in a large trailer into a gaily painted, former garage. In Milton Adess' words, this was all part of Coolidge's attempt to "get away from that cold, granite-faced banker image that banking seems to have acquired over the years."

COOLIDGE BANK IN 1974[1]

By mid-1973, the First Coolidge Corporation ranked as the ninth largest commercial banking organization in the Boston banking market (Exhibit 3). Its operating income in 1973 exceeded $9 million and net income was some $668,000 (Exhibit 9), while year-end assets stood at $127 million (Exhibit 10).

In early 1974, the Coolidge Bank and Trust Company had a total staff of 201. There were 37 officers of the bank, headed by the president and executive vice president. Most of the senior officers had over 15 years' professional banking experience.

Five of the bank's nine offices were located in the densely populated cities of Cambridge and Watertown. Although five-sixths of its personal checking account holders in the Boston area resided in Middlesex County, Coolidge also drew a number of accounts from residents of neighboring counties, notably Suffolk. This was true of savings accounts too.

Coolidge had about 100,000 accounts of all categories. About 70 percent of these were personal checking accounts, while 23 percent were regular savings accounts held by individuals. There were no charges for transactions in either type of account. Savings account holders maintained a small passbook which was updated every time they made a deposit or withdrawal, and they received 5 percent interest on the outstanding balance. Management believed that a high proportion of their savings account holders also maintained checking accounts at

---

[1] Certain nonpublished data in the balance of the case are either disguised or approximations.

Coolidge. Other types of consumer deposits included 90-day notice savings accounts and longer-term savings certificates of deposit, all of which paid higher interest rates. Coolidge was more retail-oriented than most commercial banks, and accounts held by businesses represented only a small proportion of the total; however, the value of their deposits was quite substantial (Exhibit 11).

One significant difference between demand and time deposits was the reserve requirements. Under Massachusetts law, not more than 85 percent of demand deposits (i.e., checking accounts) could be reinvested by banks, whereas they were free to reinvest 100 percent of time and savings deposits.[1] NOW accounts were treated as time and savings deposits. Like most banks, Coolidge maintained cash balances and deposits with other banks exceeding this legal minimum. The treasurer indicated that, as of mid-1974, Coolidge was realizing an average yield on loans and securities of around 9½ percent.

THE COMPETITIVE SITUATION

Coolidge was one of 32 commercial banks and some 60 thrift banks in Middlesex County. Management saw the principal competition as banks with branches in the southeastern part of the county. A 1973 survey showed that Coolidge and two other commercial banks—Harvard Trust Company ($264 million assets, 13 branches) and Middlesex Bank N.A. ($302 million assets, 29 branches)—each had approximately 11 percent of the personal checking account market in Middlesex. Another significant competitor was Newton-Waltham Bank & Trust Company ($236 million assets, 21 branches) with an estimated 8 percent of this market. These three competing banks were all subsidiaries of the Baystate Corporation, a Boston-based bank holding company. A fourth competitor, County Bank N.A. (11 branches, $171 million assets), was a subsidiary of the Shawmut Association, Inc. Another Shawmut subsidiary, Community National Bank, was not viewed as a direct competitor since most of its branches were located in the western part of the county. Profiles of the personal checking customer base served by Coolidge and other selected Middlesex banks are shown in Exhibit 7.

Where savings accounts were concerned, competition was much stronger, coming from both thrift institutions as well as other commercial banks. Coolidge's market share of regular savings accounts was believed to be between 1 and 2 percent for the county as a whole. Thrift institutions had an advantage in that they could pay 5¼ percent on passbook savings versus the 5 percent legal maximum payable by commercial banks. Many of the thrift banks had multiple branches and a number were active in marketing their services.

Most of the locations served by a Coolidge branch were populated by several competing banks. The extreme example was at Harvard Square in Cambridge where, including Coolidge, four commercial banks and three thrift banks could be found within a 200-yard radius.

---

[1] Demand deposit reserve requirements were 20 percent in the city of Boston. Commercial banks which were members of the Federal Reserve System (Coolidge was not) had a 3 percent reserve requirement on time and savings deposits.

BANK CONSUMERS

A large-scale consumer survey in the Boston area found that nearly 82 percent of respondents maintained a checking account, while some 87 percent had savings accounts. However, there were significant variations in the pattern of checking and savings account ownership among households with different demographic characteristics (Exhibit 5).

In general, the survey found that respondents were more satisfied with their savings account bank than they were with their checking account bank. "Need better hours" and "poor personnel" were the principal complaints for both types of bank. About 10 percent of respondents had switched their accounts to different banks during the past year, but moving to a new house was given as a reason more frequently than dissatisfaction or ability to obtain a "better deal" at another bank. "Good service" was the most frequently cited reason for recommending a checking account bank, while "good rates" was cited most often for savings account banks (Exhibit 6).

In terms of location, branches close to home were preferred to those nearer to work. Of respondents with personal checking accounts, 50 percent said that the branch they used most often was closer to home than to work, 24 percent said the opposite, 16 percent said it was about equidistant, while 10 percent said they banked by mail. People in lower income and educational brackets were somewhat more likely to use a branch nearer home, while single people showed a greater tendency to patronize a bank near their work or to bank by mail than the sample as a whole.

THE ADVENT OF NOW ACCOUNTS[1]

Negotiable order of withdrawal (NOW) accounts originated as a device to expand the ability of mutual savings banks to attract deposits.

The first attempt to obtain regulatory approval of NOW accounts in the United States was made in July 1970 by the Consumers Savings Bank of Worcester, Massachusetts. The bank filed a plan with the State Banking Commissioner to allow its savings account customers to withdraw funds by means of a negotiable order, similar to a check, instead of presenting a passbook. Although the Bank Commissioner denied this application, a suit brought by Consumers Savings later resulted in a ruling in the bank's favor by the Massachusetts Supreme Judicial Court.

On June 12, 1972, Consumers Savings began offering NOW accounts, paying the maximum legal interest rate of 5¼ percent and charging 15 cents for each withdrawal order. Ten other mutual savings banks followed suit in August 1972. The following month, after it had been established that New Hampshire

---

[1] Information in this section was derived from Katherine Gibson, "The Early History and Initial Impact of NOW Accounts," *New England Economic Review,* January–February 1975, pp. 17–26.

law was similar to Massachusetts law, savings banks in New Hampshire began offering their own version of NOW accounts, paying a 4 percent interest rate but making no charge for withdrawals.

NOW accounts were soon adopted by the other mutual saving banks in the two states and attracted significant deposits. However, commercial banks saw these accounts as an unfair advantage in competing for household deposits, especially since they were prohibited by federal law from offering NOW accounts themselves. Although the commercial banks lobbied hard for abolition, state and federal regulatory agencies were unable to reach agreement on control of NOW accounts.

The issue was then brought to Congress where, after further debate, a compromise was reached. Public Law 93-100, signed in August 1973, extended authorization to issue NOW accounts to commercial banks, savings and loans, and cooperative banks but limited such accounts to Massachusetts and New Hampshire.

The various regulatory agencies then authorized commercial banks, savings and loans, and cooperative banks to begin offering NOW accounts from January 1, 1974, setting a maximum interest rate of 5 percent on these accounts for all institutions, including mutual savings banks. Advertising efforts were limited to media aimed primarily at residents of the two states. Although individuals and nonprofit organizations were allowed to hold NOW accounts, businesses were prohibited from doing so.

COOLIDGE BANK AND NOW ACCOUNTS

Coolidge management had followed the development of NOW accounts closely. Despite his bank's reputation for innovation, Mr. Adess' attitude toward them had, initially, been quite negative. As he explained, "To take away service charges, pay postage both ways, and give everything free—that's one thing. But to start paying 5 percent on top of that—now that's something else. That could become a real financial problem."

Coolidge held back in January 1974 when commercial banks first became entitled to issue NOW accounts. In that month, 11 of 153 commercial banks and 12 of the 179 savings and loans and cooperative banks in Massachusetts began offering the accounts. Some 75 mutual savings banks in the state already offered NOW accounts prior to 1974, and by the end of January the figure had jumped to 85, more than 50 percent of all such banks in the state. Data collected each month by the Federal Reserve Bank of Boston showed a steady increase in the number of banks offering NOW accounts, as well as in new accounts opened and the volume of deposits (Exhibits 15 and 16). However, not all commercial banks offering NOW accounts advertised the fact, although thrift institutions did so vigorously. The only commercial banks actively promoting these accounts in the Boston area were some small- and medium-sized banks in Essex County.

Many of the new accounts were opened by existing customers of the same bank, and quite a significant volume of funds deposited in these NOW accounts represented transfers from existing demand deposits or time and savings deposits at the same institution (Exhibit 17).

By June, Mr. Adess had noticed "quite a few decent-size, personal checking accounts" leave Coolidge for NOW accounts at nearby competing thrift institutions. He had also received "more than a few" calls from long-standing Coolidge customers, who had historically carried "decent balances" in their personal checking accounts, explaining the dilemma that they faced. Although they felt kindly disposed toward Coolidge for the innovative banking services that it had provided them over the years, they were nevertheless strongly tempted to move their checking business to other banks offering interest-bearing NOW accounts. The president felt that the time had come for the board to reassess the bank's position.

If Coolidge management decided to offer such accounts, then one issue would be what terms to offer. It was evident from the Federal Reserve Bank reports that significant variations existed between banks in the terms attached to NOW accounts, especially in the service charges levied per draft (Exhibit 18).

There were other inputs to this decision, too. Management knew the size distribution of existing demand and time deposits at Coolidge (Exhibit 12). The treasurer estimated that the direct cost to the bank of servicing a checking account transaction averaged around 10 cents, with overhead costs about the same. Costs for savings account transactions were substantially higher, due to the greater labor input required, not least by tellers. However, the number of savings account transactions each month was only a tiny fraction of those by checking accounts.

Also available was additional Federal Reserve Bank data on NOW account activity concerning the number of drafts issued by individual accounts each month (Exhibit 19).

"The priority," Mr. Adess told his fellow directors at the executive committee meeting called to discuss the NOW account issue, "is to hold the accounts that we have. We've taken a good hard look at every account that we've lost or are afraid of losing, and it's been the better ones—like those with an average monthly balance of over $1,000—not the 'garbage' accounts averaging $50."

EXHIBIT 1
BANKING MARKETS IN MASSACHUSETTS
Coolidge Bank and Trust Company

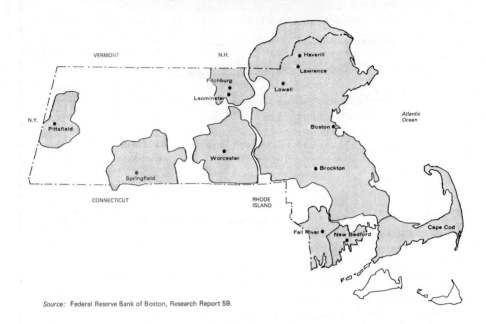

Source: Federal Reserve Bank of Boston, Research Report 59.

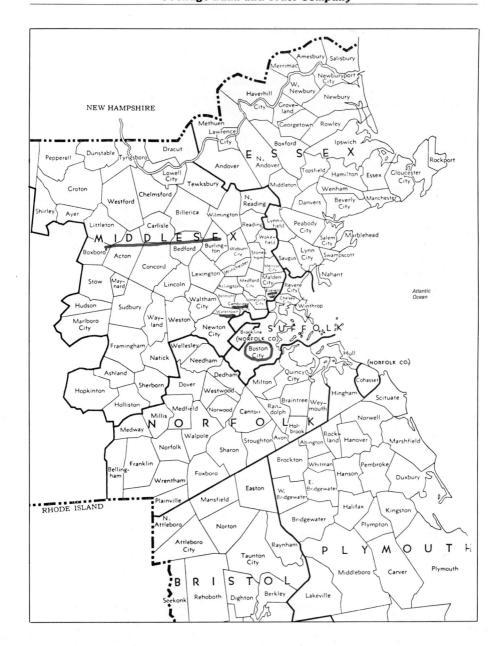

EXHIBIT 3
BOSTON BANKING MARKET, JUNE 30, 1973
Coolidge Bank and Trust Company

	Organization	No. of offices	Total deposits		Demand deposits <$20,000 (6/30/72)	
			$ million	%	$ million	%
1	First National Boston Corp.	42	3,137.8	30.7	202.3	15.3
2	Shawmut Association, Inc.	104	1,520.5	14.9	191.3	14.5
3	State Street Boston Financial Corp.	34	1,169.2	11.4	103.8	7.9
4	Baystate Corp.	125	1,138.4	11.1	239.9	18.2
5	New England Merchants Company, Inc.	17	921.2	9.0	72.7	5.5
6	Arltru Bancorporation	14	242.5	2.4	26.0	2.0
7	Multibank Financial Corp.	35	199.1	1.9	46.5	3.5
8	Essex Bancorp	14	118.2	1.2	26.4	2.0
9	First Coolidge Corp.	9	94.9	0.9	28.5	2.2
10	UST Corp.	9	93.3	0.9	21.6	1.6
11	Framingham Financial	15	87.2	0.9	19.4	1.5
12	Charterbank, Inc.	13	78.2	0.8	19.4	1.5
13	Atlantic Corp.	5	73.2	0.7	7.9	0.6
14	Hancock Group	14	68.3	0.7	21.5	1.6
15	Rockland Trust	15	68.2	0.7	22.7	1.7
16	Massachusetts Bay Bancorp	8	67.5	0.7	10.4	0.8
17	Security National Bank	9	66.1	0.6	14.4	1.1
18	Harbor National Bank	3	65.1	0.6	4.4	0.3
19	Commonwealth National Corp.	8	57.9	0.6	11.3	0.9
20	New England Bancorp.	15	53.4	0.5	12.9	1.0
21	North Atlantic Bancorp.	8	47.9	0.5	8.2	0.6
22	Capitol Bancorporation	3	47.7	0.5	4.9	0.4
23	Brookline Trust Co.	5	45.0	0.4	12.4	0.9
24	Cambridge Trust Co.	3	40.5	0.4	13.1	1.0
25	Malden Trust Co.	4	40.1	0.4	12.6	1.0
26	Yankee Bancorp.	5	37.5	0.4	7.9	0.6
27	The Haverhill National Bank	8	35.5	0.3	9.8	0.7
28	Naumkeag Trust Co.	3	34.7	0.3	8.2	0.6
29	Century Bancorp.	5	31.7	0.3	4.2	0.3
30	The First Natl. Bank of Malden	2	24.2	0.2	5.4	0.4
31	The Hudson National Bank	4	24.0	0.2	6.2	0.5
32	The Broadway Natl. Bank of Chelsea	1	19.7	0.2	4.4	0.3
33	Middleborough Trust Co.	4	19.5	0.2	4.7	0.4
34	Woburn National Bank	2	19.1	0.2	4.4	0.3
35	Natick Trust Co.	4	19.1	0.2	6.2	0.5
36	Saugus Bank and Trust Co.	3	19.0	0.2	3.8	0.3
37	The Home Natl. Bank of Milford	3	18.7	0.2	5.3	0.4
38	The Beverly National Bank	3	18.6	0.2	6.0	0.5
39	Charlesbank Trust Co.	3	18.0	0.2	4.9	0.4
40	Liberty Bank and Trust Co.	3	16.2	0.2	4.6	0.4
41	Massachusetts Bancshares	3	15.6	0.2	3.5	0.3
42	The First Natl. Bank of Ipswich	4	14.2	0.1	4.1	0.3
43	The Natl. Grand Bank of Marblehead	1	13.8	0.1	5.1	0.4
44	Lowell Bank and Trust Co.	1	13.5	0.1	3.3	0.2
45	Commercial Bank and Trust	3	13.2	0.1	3.4	0.3
46	First Bancorp.	6	13.2	0.1	3.9	0.3
47	Unity Bank and Trust Co.	1	12.9	0.1	2.4	0.2
48	The Peoples National Bank	3	12.9	0.1	3.4	0.3
49	Depositors Trust Co., Medford	3	12.9	0.1	3.7	0.3
50	Gloucester National Bank	1	12.3	0.1	2.4	0.2
	Next 30 banking organizations	48	188.6	1.8	48.4	3.7
	Total	658	10,220.7	100.0	1328.4	100.0

Source: Federal Reserve Bank of Boston, *Research Report* 59.

EXHIBIT 4
CUSTOMER RESPONSE TO BANKS OFFERING
NO-SERVICE-CHARGE BANKING
Coolidge Bank and Trust Company

Extent of new customer response to introduction of NSC plan	Timing of NSC introduction in local area, number of banks		
	First in area	Quick follower*	Later follower
Very successful—many new accounts	26	13	8
Moderately successful	16	14	17
Mediocre response	3	10	18
No significant volume of new accounts	5	15	24
Total usable responses	50	52	67

* Defined as within 3 months.

Source: Survey by Federal Reserve Bank of Boston, cited in Stephen J. Weiss, "Commercial Bank Price Competition: The Case of Free Checking Accounts," *New England Economic Review,* September–October 1969, pp. 3–22.

EXHIBIT 5
POSSESSION OF CHECKING AND SAVINGS ACCOUNTS IN THE BOSTON AREA BY DEMOGRAPHIC SEGMENTS
Coolidge Bank and Trust Company

Do you and your family currently have a checking account/savings account?

	Percent responding yes	
	Checking account	Savings account
All Boston area	81.8	86.9
Age:		
19–24	78.1	83.8
25–34	87.7	86.7
35–44	85.6	87.2
45–54	82.6	88.9
55–64	78.7	90.8
65+	69.0	83.9
Marital status:		
Married	84.9	89.1
Single	79.1	84.0
Other	69.5	80.2
Education:		
Not high school graduate	55.1	78.0
High school graduate	72.6	83.6
Some college	85.5	88.9
College graduate	92.6	91.6
Postgraduate work	96.7	90.7
Income:		
<$5,000	59.8	73.2
$5,000–10,000	73.2	81.6
$10,000–15,000	87.3	91.2
$15,000–25,000	95.1	94.7
$25,000+	98.8	94.7

Source: Survey conducted for Coolidge Bank, mid-1973.

150

EXHIBIT 6
COOLIDGE BANK: SELECTED RESPONSES TO BOSTON AREA CONSUMER BANKING SURVEY
Coolidge Bank and Trust Company

	Checking acct. bank	Savings acct. bank
What would you say is the most irritating characteristic of your checking account bank/savings account bank?		
Need better hours	4.2%	3.8%
Poor personnel	4.0	2.3
Want free checking	3.8	0.1
Long lines	2.2	2.0
Hidden charges	2.0	0.5
Bookkeeping errors	1.8	0.5
Slow bookkeeping	1.7	0.2
Low interest	0.1	1.0
Bad location/parking	0.8	0.5
Other complaints	5.2	2.7
No complaints cited	74.2	86.4
	100.0%	100.0%
Have you switched your account from another bank within the last year?		
Yes	10.3%	9.3%
No	89.7	90.7
	100.0%	100.0%
If yes, what was the major reason you switched your account?		
Moved	35.6%	35.1%
Dissatisfied with former bank	23.0	26.0
Better deal at new bank	9.2	15.6
Proximity to home or work	6.0	9.1
Other	25.3	14.3
	100.0%	100.0%
Why would you recommend this bank for checking accounts/savings accounts?		
Own experience*	10.7%	9.9%
Proximity*	8.6	10.6
Good service	35.1	24.0
Helpful, friendly personnel	10.5	10.6
Word of mouth	3.4	2.7
Good rates (Chkg. or Svgs.)	14.1	28.2
Full service	5.1	3.9
More branches	2.6	1.4
Liberal on loans	0.5	0.4
Large, stable	1.5	1.9
Good hours	1.5	1.4
Other	6.4	5.1
	100.0%	100.0%

* If respondent answered "own experience" or "proximity," interviewer was instructed to probe why the experience was good and circle another category if valid.

Source: Survey conducted for Coolidge Bank, mid-1973.

151

EXHIBIT 7
CONSUMER ACCOUNT HOLDER PROFILES OF BOSTON AREA BANKS, COOLIDGE BANK, AND SELECTED COMPETITORS

Coolidge Bank and Trust Company

	Income, $ thousand					Age					
	<5	5–10	10–15	15–25	>25	18–24	25–34	35–44	45–54	55–64	65+
All Boston area checking accounts	9.5%	25.4%	32.1%	24.4%	8.7%	12.6%	27.3%	20.2%	18.7%	11.5%	9.7%
Individual bank profiles:											
Coolidge Bank	13.6	21.4	31.4	25.7	7.9	19.1	47.1	15.3	10.2	5.7	2.5
Harvard Trust	12.0	28.0	22.7	28.7	8.7	17.9	31.5	19.1	14.2	8.6	8.6
Middlesex Bank	10.2	32.3	37.8	17.3	2.4	10.6	17.7	25.5	20.6	14.2	11.3
Newton-Waltham Bank	4.0	20.8	29.7	30.7	14.9	11.7	20.7	26.1	19.8	9.9	11.7
Community National Bank	1.5	22.7	34.8	33.3	7.6	12.7	35.2	26.8	14.1	8.5	2.8
All Boston area savings accounts	10.9	26.7	31.6	23.0	7.8	12.8	25.5	19.4	18.9	12.6	10.9

	Marital status			Education				
	Married	Single	Other	Some high school	High school graduate	Some college	College graduate	Postgrad work
All Boston area checking accounts	70.3%	18.4%	11.3%	6.8%	25.5%	25.3%	21.3%	21.0%
Individual bank profiles:								
Coolidge Bank	57.6	32.9	9.5	3.8	14.0	17.2	23.6	41.4
Harvard Trust	64.6	26.8	8.5	3.0	12.2	23.8	19.5	41.5
Middlesex Bank	77.3	10.6	12.1	10.0	40.0	23.5	13.6	12.9
Newton-Waltham Bank	73.2	13.4	13.4	7.2	17.1	23.4	27.9	24.3
Community National Bank	80.3	8.5	11.3	1.4	25.4	26.8	25.4	21.1
All Boston area savings accounts	69.5	18.3	12.1	9.1	27.6	24.9	19.9	18.6

Source: Survey conducted for Coolidge Bank and Trust Company, mid-1973.

EXHIBIT 8

COOLIDGE BANK AND TRUST COMPANY: YEAR-END DEPOSITS ($ MILLION), 1960–1973

Coolidge Bank and Trust Company

	Demand deposits*	Time deposits*	Total deposits†
1960	0.4	0.2	0.8
1961	1.9	1.0	3.5
1962	2.7	1.9	5.7
1963	3.8	3.0	8.0
1964	4.2	3.9	10.2
1965	6.7	5.4	13.9
1966	9.3	7.6	18.9
1967	16.2	10.7	29.8
1968	24.2	15.8	44.3
1969	25.4	11.1	44.3
1970	27.9	22.5	61.2
1971‡	43.1	29.9	84.8
1972	51.7	32.5	94.2
1973	54.5	46.1	113.6

* Deposits of individuals, partnerships, and corporations.

† Total deposits included deposits of the U.S. government ($1.7 million in 1973), of states and political subdivisions ($9.6 million in 1973), and of commercial banks, as well as certified and officers' checks.

‡ Coolidge acquired two other banks in 1971.

Source: Year-end reports by Coolidge Bank to FDIC.

72 - 73 change because of intro of NOW, Acc slowing increase.

EXHIBIT 9
FIRST COOLIDGE CORPORATION: CONSOLIDATED STATEMENT OF INCOME FOR THE YEARS ENDED DECEMBER 31, 1973 AND 1972
Coolidge Bank and Trust Company

	1973	1972
Operating income:		
Interest on loans	$7,952,215	$6,210,930
Interest and dividends on securities:		
U.S. government securities	304,233	277,300
Obligations of state and political subdivisions	199,672	332,103
Other securities	59,601	10,331
Other operating income	732,947	587,376
Total	9,248,668	7,418,040
Operating expenses:		
Salaries	1,895,640	1,705,963
Other employee benefits	159,723	203,117
Interest	2,471,277	1,790,298
Occupancy expense of bank premises	435,340	461,532
Loan loss provision (Note 4*)	626,228	451,860
Other operating expense	2,476,142	2,268,194
Total	8,064,350	6,880,964
Income before income taxes and securities gains	1,184,318	537,076
Less applicable income taxes (Note 6*):		
Current	178,299	(508,588)
Deferred	340,169	425,703
	518,398	(82,885)
Income before securities gains	665,920	619,961
Securities gains, less applicable income taxes of $2,158 and $41,785	1,843	35,737
Net income	$ 667,763	$ 655,698
Earning data per common share (based on 1,435,180 shares):		
Income before income taxes and securities gains	$ .83	$ .37
Applicable income taxes	(.37)	.06
Income before securities gains	.46	.43
Securities gains, less applicable income taxes	.01	.03
Net income	$ .47	$ .46

* Notes to financial statement not shown here.
Source: First Coolidge Corporation, *Annual Report,* 1973.

EXHIBIT 10
FIRST COOLIDGE CORPORATION,
CONSOLIDATED STATEMENT OF CONDITION
DECEMBER 31, 1973 AND 1972
Coolidge Bank and Trust Company

	1973	1972
Assets:		
Cash and due from banks	$ 14,175,427	$ 12,911,111
Investment securities (Note 2*):		
U.S. government obligations	5,009,926	5,049,377
Obligations of state and political subdivisions	8,949,981	3,516,426
Other securities	1,237,556	686,252
Total investment securities	15,197,463	9,252,055
Loans	89,803,957	78,335,088
Federal funds sold		800,000
Bank premises and equipment (Note 3*)	4,247,813	4,254,904
Customers' liability under letters of credit	2,528,392	3,404,040
Accrued interest receivable	657,558	375,564
Other assets and deferred charges	558,277	1,726,388
Total	$127,168,887	$111,059,150
Liabilities and capital:		
Demand deposits	$ 60,944,902	$ 57,722,105
Time deposits	52,576,676	36,186,015
Federal funds purchased		2,000,000
Unearned income	1,965,975	1,804,323
Letters of credit outstanding	2,528,392	3,404,040
Other liabilities	804,708	1,637,124
Total liablities	118,820,653	102,753,607
Reserve for loan losses (Note 4*)	882,989	882,989
Capital funds:		
Capital debentures (Note 5*)	190,000	241,000
Stockholders equity:		
Common stock, $0.60 par value, 2,000,000 shares authorized, 1,435,180 shares issued and outstanding	861,108	861,108
Surplus	5,645,020	5,645,020
Undivided profits	769,117	675,426
Total stockholders' equity	7,275,245	7,181,554
Total capital funds	7,465,245	7,422,554
Total	$127,168,887	$111,059,150

* Notes to financial statement not shown here.

Source: First Coolidge Corporation, *Annual Report,* 1973.

665,920
———————
127,168,887

EXHIBIT 11
COOLIDGE BANK AND TRUST COMPANY: DISTRIBUTION OF ACCOUNTS BY TYPE AND DEPOSIT VOLUME, MID-1974

Coolidge Band and Trust Company

Category	Percent of accounts	Percent of dollar deposits
Checking:		
Government	*	2
Business	4	22
Personal	70	26
Savings:		
Regular savings	23	24
Notice savings	*	3
Savings certificates of deposit	3	11
Commercial certificates of deposit	*	12
	100	100

* Less than 1 percent.

Source: Coolidge Bank records (disguised data).

EXHIBIT 12
COOLIDGE BANK AND TRUST COMPANY: DISTRIBUTION OF PERSONAL CHECKING AND SAVINGS ACCOUNTS BY SIZE OF AVERAGE MONTHLY BALANCE

Coolidge Bank and Trust Company

Average monthly balance	Personal checking accounts		Regular savings accounts	
	Percent of accounts	Percent of deposits	Percent of accounts	Percent of deposits
$50 and under	22.4	1.4	4.4	0.1
$51–100	29.9	5.6	2.1	0.2
$101–250	16.4	7.2	2.2	0.7
$251–500	11.3	10.6	13.2	7.3
$501–1,000	11.2	21.1	70.5	59.3
$1,001–2,500	7.6	30.3	4.0	7.0
$2,501–5,000	0.7	7.1	1.8	6.3
$5,001–10,000	0.4	7.0	1.3	9.7
$10,001–20,000	0.1	5.6	0.4	6.3
$20,001+	*	4.1	0.1	3.1
	100.0	100.0	100.0	100.0

* Denotes less than 0.1 percent.

Source: Coolidge Bank records (disguised data).

Source: Coolidge Bank, Annual Report 1970.

Cool Cash, introduced at year-end, represents a new concept in banking and yet another innovation for Coolidge Bank. Cool Cash permits the bank's customers, for the first time, to enjoy banking transaction services 24 hours a day, 7 days a week.

The base of Cool Cash is an automated banking console, the Cool-O-Mat outside the bank, which, when actuated by a specially coded card, can perform a wide variety of functions.

Small Loans — Up to $100 a day in cash can be obtained from the Cool-O-Mat, up to a credit limit of $500.

Checking Accounts — The Cool-O-Mat will accept unlimited checking account deposits. Checking account holders may withdraw up to $100 a day in cash.

Savings Accounts — The Cool-O-Mat will accept unlimited savings account deposits. Also, transfers between checking and savings accounts may be made.

Loan Payments — The Cool-O-Mat will receive, record, and give a complete receipt for loan payments of all kinds. It will also accept Master Charge, American Express Executive Credit, and Christmas Club payments.

The Cool Cash system is foolproof. The Cool-O-Mat will not operate unless it receives a special Cool Code number which the depositor supplies. Only the bank, the depositor, and the Cool-O-Mat know the special code number assigned to that particular Cool Cash card.

Coolidge Bank's first Cool-O-Mat is being installed at the Harvard Square Office. Other machines will be installed early in 1972 at the Fresh Pond Shopping Center Office, and at the Watertown Headquarters.

The Cool Cash system is an important new Coolidge Bank service, and should be a source of increased revenue for the bank.

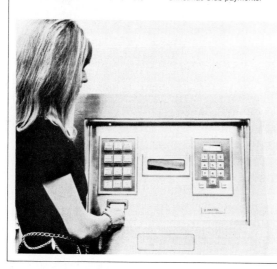

Source: Coolidge Bank, Annual Report 1971.

EXHIBIT 15
TYPE AND SIZE OF BANKS IN MASSACHUSETTS OFFERING NOW ACCOUNTS, 1974
Coolidge Bank and Trust Company

Type of bank and size of total asset base	No. of institutions offering NOW accounts, 1974					Total no. of banks in Mass., mid-1974
	Jan.	Feb.	Mar.	Apr.	May	
Commercial banks:						
Under $50 million	NA	5	7	8	9	101
$50–250 million	NA	5	7	8	8	41
Over $250 million	NA	2	2	3	3	11
Total	11	12	16	19	20	153
Mutual savings banks:						
Under $50 million	NA	22	26	29	29	69
$50–250 million	NA	54	58	61	65	84
Over $250 million	NA	13	14	14	14	14
Total	85	89	98	104	108	167
Savings & loans, cooperatives:						
Under $50 million	NA	11	21	27	34	156
$50–250 million	NA	10	11	11	12	22
Over $250 million	NA			1	1	1
Total	12	21	32	39	47	179

Source: Research Department, Federal Reserve Bank of Boston.

EXHIBIT 16
NOW ACCOUNT ACTIVITY IN MASSACHUSETTS
BY TYPE OF BANK, 1974
Coolidge Bank and Trust Company

	Jan.	Feb.	Mar.	Apr.	May
Commercial banks:					
No. of new accounts:					
Existing customers	917	409	478	799	461
New customers	347	557	642	613	774
No. of accounts closed	5	18	34	37	89
Total no. of accounts at month end	1,259	2,207	3,293	4,668	5,814
Deposits ($ million)	2.5	2.3	4.0	6.0	6.7
Withdrawals ($ million)	0.2	0.8	1.9	3.5	5.9
Balance at month end ($ million)	2.3	3.8	5.9	8.4	9.2
Mutual savings banks:					
No. of new accounts:					
Existing customers	4,660	4,061	4,960	4,784	5,033
New customers	3,360	3,715	4,157	4,021	4,860
No. of accounts closed	1,379	1,753	1,489	1,599	1,730
Total no. of accounts at month end	95,677	101,701	109,365	116,618	124,822
Deposits ($ million)	57.0	49.0	62.7	72.7	76.5
Withdrawals ($ million)	59.8	45.9	53.8	70.8	75.9
Balance at month end ($ million)	134.8	138.5	147.8	150.3	151.5
Savings & loans, cooperatives:					
No. of new accounts:					
Existing customers	784	809	1,242	1,499	1,355
New customers	464	763	1,043	739	1,077
No. of accounts closed	8	8	27	36	57
Total no. of accounts at month end	1,240	2,804	5,062	7,264	9,639
Deposits ($ million)	1.0	2.3	4.3	7.3	8.8
Withdrawals ($ million)	0.1	0.8	2.4	4.7	6.9
Balance at month end ($ million)	0.9	2.4	4.3	6.9	8.8

Source: Research Department, Federal Reserve Bank of Boston.

EXHIBIT 17
TRANSFERS TO NOW ACCOUNTS WITHIN AN INSTITUTION, 1974, IN THOUSANDS OF DOLLARS*

Coolidge Bank and Trust Company

	Jan.	Feb.	Mar.	Apr.	May
Commercial banks:					
Deposits from demand deposits	$215	183	223	430	276
Deposits from time and savings	$78	102	296	138	89
Mutual savings banks:					
Deposits from demand deposits†					
Deposits from time and savings	$1,604	1,196	1,505	2,533	1,673
Savings and loan associations:					
Deposits from demand deposits†					
Deposits from time and savings	$204	227	1,992	2,901	1,963

* Transfers to new NOW accounts, opened that month, from the institution's own demand deposits (i.e., checking accounts) or time and savings deposits.
† Thrift banks had no demand deposits.
Source: Research Department, Federal Reserve Bank of Boston.

EXHIBIT 18
NOW ACCOUNT TERMS IN MASSACHUSETTS, MAY 1974

Coolidge Bank and Trust Company

	Commercial banks	Mutual savings banks	Savings & loans, co-op banks
Interest rate paid:			
4.0%	1		
5.0%	19	108	47
Basis for calculation of interest rates:			
Average daily balance	4	2	1
Minimum balance	1	2	
Day of deposit to withdrawal	15	103	44
Other		1	1
Frequency of compounding:			
Continuous	3	72	30
Daily	5	22	6
Monthly	7	11	4
Quarterly	5	3	7
Charge per draft:			
Free	3	36	16
10 cents	1	19	12
15 cents	13	48	15
Other*	3	5	4

* "Other" includes institutions using a combination of free drafts plus a charge for each draft over a specified number.
Source: Research Department, Federal Reserve Bank of Boston.

EXHIBIT 19
VOLUME OF DRAFTS ISSUED BY NOW ACCOUNTS IN MASSACHUSETTS, 1974
Coolidge Bank and Trust Company

	Jan.	Feb.	Mar.	Apr.	May
Commercial banks:					
Total volume of NOW drafts, thousands	3.2	4.7	11.1	19.2	25.1
% distribution of NOW accounts by no. of drafts per account:					
0 drafts	51.8	55.0	47.8	43.9	44.5
1–9 drafts	46.1	34.7	39.1	41.4	39.6
10–20 drafts	2.0	9.0	10.7	11.7	12.2
> 20 drafts	0.2	1.3	2.5	3.0	3.7
Average no. of drafts per active account	5.4	4.7	6.4	7.3	7.7
Mutual savings banks:					
Total volume of NOW drafts, thousands	493.7	498.2	598.5	708.8	757.5
% distribution of NOW accounts by no. of drafts per account:					
0 drafts	25.1	27.2	26.9	27.2	26.6
1–9 drafts	56.5	55.7	56.3	53.2	52.9
10–20 drafts	14.6	13.2	13.5	15.3	15.5
> 20 drafts	3.8	3.9	3.3	4.3	4.9
Average no. of drafts per active account	6.8	6.7	7.4	8.3	8.2
Savings & loans, cooperatives:					
Total volume of NOW drafts, thousands	2.1	9.9	25.5	46.8	66.4
% distribution of NOW accounts by no. of drafts per account:					
0 drafts	59.5	30.0	36.0	25.7	20.0
1–9 drafts	37.6	57.5	44.0	47.2	49.1
10–20 drafts	2.9	11.2	15.9	20.7	23.1
> 20 drafts		1.3	4.1	6.4	7.8
Average no. of drafts per active account	4.2	5.0	7.7	8.5	8.4

Source: Research Department, Federal Reserve Bank of Boston.

THE STAR-ADVOCATE COMPANY

NANCY J. DAVIS
Research Associate
Harvard Graduate School of Business Administration

STEVEN H. STAR
Associate Professor
Harvard Graduate School of Business Administration

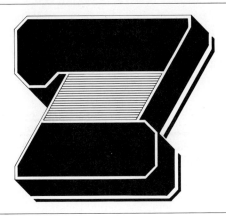

The Star-Advocate Company in Murfreesboro, Yosemite, a western state bordered by Columbia, Jackson, and Texarkana, published the *Morning Star* (circulation 73,350) and the *Evening Advocate* (circulation 146,700) 6 days a week. With 70 percent penetration of all Yosemite households and 90 percent of Murfreesboro households, it was by far the leading daily newspaper in the state.

In September 1974, company management recommended to the board of directors that the company also start publishing a Sunday newspaper. The chief competitors, management thought, would be *The Carson Gazette* and *The Texarkana Post.* While these papers together sold only 19,000 of the 260,800 daily newspapers sold in Yosemite, they sold about 126,000 of the 202,000 newspapers sold on Sunday. *Star-Advocate* executives stated that the Texarkana papers were strong products but that they contained only token news for

All names and figures have been disguised.

Yosemite residents. They thought that if the *Star-Advocate* could put out a similarly strong Sunday paper with more complete Yosemite news, the paper could achieve a net paid circulation of 140,000 to 145,000 within 2 months of publication.

COMPANY HISTORY

The *Morning Star* and *Evening Advocate* traced their origins to the mid-1800s when Murfreesboro was widely known as a booming mining town. Over the years, ownership of the papers changed hands several times, and for a brief period, it was held by *The Carson Gazette* in nearby Texarkana. The editorial stance generally shifted to reflect the views of whoever owned the papers at the time. At various times it had editorialized both for and against capital punishment, for and against price supports for farmers, and for and against strip mining.

It was not until the mid-1960s when a group of local businessmen purchased the papers and began to hire first-rate managerial and editorial personnel that the papers achieved a degree of stability. Their circulation, advertising linage, and profitability grew steadily. Moreover, their editorial stance showed a surprising degree of independence as the owners maintained a laissez faire attitude toward them. For example, though the Murphy family, who owned the mines and part of the newspapers, adamantly defended strip mining as being essential to the economic stability of the town, the papers took the position of the area's conservationists who argued that strip mining would not only destroy the aesthetic qualities of the land but would also harm the large segment of the population which was dependent on tourists who were drawn to the area's rivers, lakes, and mountains.

In 1969 the *Star-Advocate* owners began to acquire several small evening newspapers throughout Yosemite and to merge them into the *Star-Advocate's* operations. One result of this was that the *Evening Advocate's* circulation increased substantially so that by 1974 it was double that of the *Morning Star*. Another result was that the *Star-Advocate* for all practical purposes became a monopoly newspaper within Yosemite. Its only remaining in-state competitor was *The Yosemite News*, a small paper published in the state capital and oriented primarily toward state political news. When the *Star-Advocate* owners had tried to purchase *The Yosemite News*, Yosemite owners replied that they had "no intention of selling out to the Eastern leftists who are now running the *Star-Advocate*."

Also in 1969, Mr. Stanton B. Lionel, a 40-year-old Texan with reportorial and editorial experience at four previous newspapers, took over as executive editor. He made innovations in the papers' typography, continued switching their emphasis from "school lunch and Masonic Club" stories to harder news from news bureaus, and hired young writers from other papers and from universities. By 1974 the combined circulation of the two papers had reached

220,000. On 1973 revenues of $24,813,370 the company's after-tax earnings were $2,647,249.

THE MARKET

Almost 90 percent of the *Morning Star* and *Evening Advocate*'s circulation was concentrated in Yosemite, and over 75 percent was in its home market, Brunswick County. Most of the remainder was in Evans County, Columbia, Clark County, Jackson, and two counties in Texarkana, though there was also some circulation in four other Columbia counties. Population throughout the market had been relatively constant over the last 5 years, and no major growth was predicted in the near future. (See Exhibit 1 for map of the market.)

The state of Yosemite had a total population of 930,000, about 80 percent of which lived to the east of the Brunswick River. This river divided the state into two distinct areas. East of the river was an urban, business-oriented center surrounded by generally affluent suburbs. In addition to the Murphy mines, White Trucking Company, and Cummins Engine Company assembly lines, a large Revlon distribution center, divisions of Shell Oil and United Chemical Company, and several other industries were located there. Within the eastern half of the county, the fastest growing area was around Abilene, where Yosemite University was located. *Star-Advocate* management had begun to view this area along with parts of Evans County, Columbia, and a county in Texarkana as a distinct market because residents tended to shop in the same places. The *Star-Advocate* had recently begun to publish a weekly supplement, *Phoenix,* aimed at this audience.

EAST

Though Murfreesboro had undertaken major urban renewal programs, it was still losing population to suburban areas. There were few night spots in the city, and the streets were virtually deserted after 8:00 P.M. Most entertaining was done in private homes. Previous political patterns appeared to be breaking down, but in the past, Murfreesboro had tended to vote for Democratic party candidates, while Brunswick County as a whole had voted for Republican party candidates.

Brunswick County to the west of the Brunswick River and San Jose and San Simeon Counties were primarily rural areas. Farming, especially cattle raising, was the primary source of income. In 1972 the average net income per farm was $14,700. In San Jose County where Monroe, the state capital, was located, major employers included the state government and a large Air Force base. In San Simeon County, the major industries were another Murphy coal mine, two-medium-sized slaughterhouses, a fishery, and several tourist resorts. Much of the counties' social life centered around churches and granges, and residents of Monroe were said to be "obsessed with state politics." Traditionally, San Jose residents had voted for Democratic party candidates, and San Simeon residents had voted for Republican party candidates.

Clark County, Jackson, was considered similar to San Jose and San Simeon Counties in that it had some light manufacturing and a good deal of farming. Evans County, Columbia, had some light manufacturing, but its main industries were boating and recreation. In the western part of the county, and in the other Columbia counties where *Star-Advocate* products were circulated, were several farms and ranches. Evans residents were said to be "totally disinterested" in Yosemite politics. Only the very western portions of the two Texarkana counties were considered part of the *Star-Advocate's* marketing area. They were very sparsely settled, rural areas.

In the past, Yosemite residents had done much of their shopping in Carson. This had changed in recent years, however, as more and more shopping centers were built in Yosemite. In 1974 there were 17 major shopping centers in Brunswick County, 3 in San Jose County, and 5 in San Simeon County. (All but two of the Brunswick County shopping centers were located to the east of the Brunswick River.) Major retailers included Sears, Bullocks, Grants, Penneys, Woolworth, I. Magnin, Rich's, Sakowitz, and White Frost. Leading food chains were A&P, Safeway, Ralph's, Pantry Pride, Kroger, and Shop Rite. The advertising budgets for some large retailers such as Sears, Bullocks, and the large chain food stores were usually controlled by regional offices in Carson or Las Rivas.

COMPETITION

While there were numerous papers circulated throughout Yosemite, the *Morning Star* and *Evening Advocate* managers considered *The Carson Gazette, The Texarkana Post,* and *The Yosemite News* to be their prime competitors. (See Exhibit 2 for comparative circulation data, and Exhibit 3 for regular features of the various papers.)

Lionel described *The Gazette* (total circulation 977,200) as "the good grey *Gazette,* a little stuffy but generally well-written and well-edited." He said it was especially strong in sports and that its editorial page was good though it was usually "a little to the right of the *Star-Advocate.*" It was a privately owned newspaper and was thought to be in trouble financially but capable of holding on for some time.

Lionel considered *The Post* (total circulation 707,200) a "first class editorial product." He said it often did "magazine-type trend stories" as opposed to the straight reporting in *The Gazette.* "Since the Welles Company purchased *The Post* in 1972, its news hole has been increased dramatically, and it has hired a lot of smart young editors," Lionel commented. He considered *The Post's* editorial stance slightly more liberal than the *Star-Advocate's.* He thought *The Post* was also having financial difficulties and that the Welles Company was probably pressing it to improve its profit picture. "Both *The Gazette* and *The Post* have improved a lot editorially in the last few years," Lionel said. "They're waging a real war with each other, and they just about have the Carson area saturated. The only place they have to go is into peripheral areas."

Both *The Gazette* and *The Post* had opened bureaus and contacted several stringers in Yosemite within the last year. Both now published a Yosemite edition of their Sunday papers, and Lionel had heard that *The Gazette* was looking for someone to sell advertising in Yosemite.

The *Star-Advocate*'s other major competitor, *The Yosemite News* (total daily circulation 37,300) was published in Monroe. It published an evening paper Monday through Friday and a Sunday paper but not a Saturday paper. Its Sunday paper had been started in the fall of 1968. Lionel considered this paper "a generally poor product which is markedly more conservative than the *Star-Advocate.*" He said it had no editorial policy as such, but that editors often argued among themselves on various issues. He said its emphasis was "political to the point of obsessiveness," but that many people considered reading it essential to keep up with Yosemite state politics.

Also vying for the advertising dollars in the Yosemite market were nine weekly papers in Yosemite and a daily and Sunday paper in Doral, Columbia, just over Yosemite's western border. The latter paper had made some inroads into southwestern San Simeon County primarily, management thought, because of its ads. It did not cover Yosemite news.

CURRENT POSITION, SEPTEMBER 1974

In addition to the main office in downtown Murfreesboro, the *Star-Advocate* had bureaus in Abilene, Monroe, and Alexandria, the largest city in San Simeon County. The Abilene bureau consisted of six reporters, three part-time students, and three clerks, one of whom handled some advertising. The Alexandria bureau had four reporters and one clerk, and the Monroe bureau had six reporters, two clerks, one librarian, and one advertising salesperson. The *Star-Advocate* also kept one reporter in Washington, and three stringers more or less regularly contributed to the papers. In all, the company employed almost 1,000 people. (See Exhibit 4 for organization chart, and Exhibit 5 for breakdown of expenses by department.)

In September 1974, the Star-Advocate Company published two editions[1] of the *Morning Star* (circulation 73,350) and three editions of the *Evening Advocate* (circulation 146,700). Both papers were published 6 days a week.

The press time and circulation of the various editions are shown in Table 1. The single-issue newsstand price for either paper was 15 cents, and the price for 6-day home delivery was 75 cents. About 73 percent of the papers were home-delivered.

The editorial stance of both papers was described as "primarily local." The papers endorsed candidates of both political parties as well as independents, but they did not necessarily take a stand on every political race. They differed in

---

[1] In this instance, an edition was a separate printing of essentially the same newspaper. Editions differed primarily in that some pages were replated so that news could be targeted to specific geographic areas and later editions could contain later-breaking news.

TABLE 1

	Press time	Circulation	Circulation area
Morning Star:			
State edition	12:30 A.M.	19,560	San Jose and San Simeon Counties and Columbia counties excluding Evans
Final edition	2:00 A.M.	53,790	Brunswick, Evans, and Clark Counties plus two Texarkana counties
Evening Advocate:			
State edition	11:45 A.M.	19,560	San Jose and San Simeon Counties and Columbia counties excluding Evans
Abilene edition	12:45 P.M.	45,640	Abilene area, Evans County, and two Texarkana counties
City edition	2:00 P.M.	81,500 220,050	Murfreesboro area, Clark County

that the *Morning Star* was primarily a "hard news" product while the *Evening Advocate* generally included more features. The average news hole of both papers was 33 percent.

The *Morning Star* consisted of four sections. The first was devoted to "hard" international, national, and state news, and it contained the editorial and op-ed pages. Regular columnists included Art Buchwald, David Broder, Harriet Van Horne, Jules Feiffer, James Kilpatrick, Laurie Ranin, and some local editorial writers. The front page of the second section of each edition contained news aimed at residents of that edition's market, and this section often contained some advertising from that particular market. It also contained arts and entertainment news, but this was not necessarily "zoned" for specific areas. The third section was the sports and financial section. The final section regularly contained "Living" or society features, comics, obituaries, and classified advertising. On the average, about eight pages were made over from the first to the second edition. The average size of the *Morning Star* was 36 pages.

The *Evening Advocate* consisted of two sections. The first contained state, national, and international news, a page of local news for residents of each edition's market, a couple of pages of business news, often some travel features, three to five pages of sports news, and the editorial and op-ed pages. Names regularly appearing on the latter pages were Tom Wicker, Arthur Hoppe, and Russell Baker. Another regular feature was "Speaking Out," a column which allowed knowledgeable people to show their expertise and concern about various issues. Section two contained several "People" pages which included various features, wedding announcements, and other social activities. It also contained theater and arts pages, comics, television listings, obituaries, an astrological forecast, a crossword puzzle, and classified advertising. On the average, about four pages were made over from the first to the second editions, and about five from the second to the third. The average size of the *Evening Advocate* was 32 pages.

Since 1972, the *Star-Advocate*'s circulation and advertising linage had been stagnant in Brunswick County and actually declining in San Jose and San Simeon Counties and in Columbia counties other than Evans. Employees in the Monroe and Alexandria bureaus believed it was only a matter of time before *The Yosemite News* started a major program to squeeze the *Star-Advocate* out of San Simeon County as it had begun to do in San Jose County. They said San Jose residents were dissatisfied with *The Yosemite News* but felt it was their main source of local advertising and news. They pointed out that most of the San Jose and San Simeon population was not aware that the *Star-Advocate* had bureaus in Monroe and Alexandria.

In August 1974, in an attempt to counter competitive pressures from a strong weekly newspaper in Abilene, the *Star-Advocate* began publishing *Phoenix,* a preprinted tab[1] which was inserted into some copies of the Abilene edition of the Thursday *Evening Advocate* and into some copies of the final edition of the Friday *Morning Star. Phoenix* contained news and advertising from Abilene, Evans County, Columbia, and one Texarkana county. It was circulated to about 52,000 households. Its editor worked out of the Murfreesboro office, but relied heavily on the Abilene bureau writers and on 13 stringers. The front-end costs of *Phoenix* had not been very high, and it was expected to break even at 16 tab pages of advertising and 8 tab pages of news. *Star-Advocate* management thought that, if *Phoenix* proved to be successful, it would publish it more often than once a week. However, *Phoenix* had failed to attract the advertising hoped for, and in September its size was down to about 20 pages per issue.

In September 1974, *Star-Advocate* management recommended to the board of directors that the company publish a Sunday paper, while concurrently cutting back Saturday publication from two papers to one (i.e., two editions of the *Morning Star*). In support of its proposal, management cited a survey of executives of 19 companies which had recently started Sunday papers. According to the executives, adding a Sunday newspaper would (1) improve profits through increasing circulation and advertising revenue, and through more efficient use of existing facilities, equipment, and personnel; (2) protect one's own market by stunting threats from outside competition; (3) offer better service by being a 7-day factor in the lives of readers and advertisers; (4) smooth out the week's work without loss of momentum due to a "dark" day; and (5) shed the small-town image associated with papers which did not publish on Sunday. Fourteen of these nineteen new Sunday papers made money or broke even during the first year, three were marginal, and two were too new to evaluate.

The proposal also cited factors peculiar to the *Star-Advocate* which argued for starting a Sunday paper. In the first place, the management team pointed out that, in an independent consumer study, 78 percent of the people interviewed said they would purchase a Sunday *Star-Advocate* if one was published. Second, the management team felt that the Sunday reading habit was ap-

---

[1] A tab, the colloquial term for tabloid, was a newspaper, usually half the ordinary size, with many pictures and short news stories.

parently well established among Yosemite residents. Though the Carson papers' Yosemite circulation had been declining in recent years, together they still sold 126,000 Sunday papers in Yosemite. In addition, *The Yosemite News* had a Sunday circulation of about 44,000, and other newspapers were thought to sell about 30,000 papers in Yosemite. (See Exhibit 6 for historical trends in Yosemite Sunday circulation.)

A third reason in favor of starting a Sunday paper was that once the recently purchased automated typesetting equipment was installed and working well, the company would have excess production capacity. This meant that many sections of a Sunday paper could be printed during the week and that additional production costs would be very low. The proposal further stated that starting a Sunday newspaper would be a good way to improve the stagnant circulation within Brunswick County and to arrest the decline in San Jose and San Simeon. Finally, it asserted that a Sunday paper should enable the company to significantly improve its rate of return and that it might be the only way to attain its 1975 financial goals.

Several *Star-Advocate* managers were in favor of a "forced" circulation policy—that is, a policy whereby current subscribers to either the *Morning Star* or the *Evening Advocate* would be required to subscribe to the Sunday paper if they were to continue their daily subscriptions. However, most top executives and board members felt strongly that readers should be able to choose or reject the Sunday paper without tying the decision to the daily papers. Even though executives of recently started Sunday papers provided ample evidence that forcing circulation was far more attractive economically than not forcing circulation, the numerical calculations in the proposal which management submitted assumed that Sunday circulation would not be forced. (See Exhibit 7 for the financial analysis presented in support of the proposal.)

STRUCTURE OF THE ORGANIZATION, SEPTEMBER 1974

Mr. Stanton B. Lionel, president and editor-in-chief, occasionally sat in on daily editorial board conferences at which the executive editor, the chief editorial writer, six other editorial writers, and the cartoonists determined the papers' editorial stance on current issues. Other than this, however, Lionel had little to do with the editorial side of the paper. In managing the newspaper, he relied heavily on an Executive Committee which consisted of Mr. Donald Samuelson, chairman of the board; Mr. Ned Adams, assistant to the president; Mr. Nick Thompson, marketing director; Mr. Fred Caine, executive editor; Mr. John Mueller, vice president and general manager; Ms. Cynthia Mill, administrative assistant; Mr. Bert Jones, advertising director; Mr. Van Green, classified advertising director; Mr. Hank Hawley, circulation director; Mr. Don Pennel, production director; Mr. Jack Schroeder, controller; and Mr. Greg Thurner, personnel director. This committee met every Monday afternoon to discuss a wide range of issues such as rate increases, introduction of new technology, company finances, new ventures, market studies, product and circulation policies, salary increases, and personnel requirements.

The *Star-Advocate* had three other standing committees: Revenue and New Ventures, Technology, and Cost Reduction. These were chaired by a member of the Executive Committee and Adams sat on each of them, but otherwise they were composed of operating personnel. "Our intent is to involve as many people as possible in the decision making processes of the papers," Lionel said. "They're much more willing to carry out policies which they've helped make."

As assistant to the president, Adams had been involved primarily in research studies which dealt with circulation in the western market, the possibility of starting a Sunday newspaper, and an evaluation of the papers' newsprint situation. He was currently working with Thompson to determine how the advertising and circulation departments could be better managed, and he had begun revising the company's budget-planning process.

EDITORIAL DEPARTMENT

Executive editor Fred Caine supervised a 218-person news and editorial staff. Reporting directly to him were two managing editors, one for the *Morning Star* and one for the *Evening Advocate.* Also, the editor of the editorial page, three investigative reporters, and the metro, lifestyles, sports, public affairs, and photography editors reported to him. Nineteen editors reported to the *Morning Star* managing editor and twenty-one to the *Evening Advocate* managing editor. They were responsible for putting together all but the sports and editorial pages of their respective papers. Both papers drew on the same pools of reporters, though reporters were assigned to specific departments. The metro editor supervised 8 assistant editors and 44 reporters. The lifestyles and sports editors each supervised 22 reporters, and the photography editor supervised 13 photographers. Caine also supervised the Monroe, Abilene, and Alexandria bureau chiefs, who together were responsible for 17 news and editorial people. Also included in the editorial department were 11 librarians and 27 copy boys, wire room attendants, clerks, and photo lab technicians.

Caine stated that, with about eight additional people, the editorial department could adjust easily to publishing a Sunday paper. He continued as follows:

> My people would welcome a Sunday paper because they don't like to see their stories in other newspapers. If we go to a single paper on Saturday, the editorial staff would still have to put out twelve editorial and op-ed pages each week. The lifestyle department would probably just shift some items like travel news and weddings to the Sunday issue and would use more of the wire material that we already get. We'd need additional photographers and graphic arts people, and there would be some pressure on the metro staff to come up with more features. The greatest impact would be on the sports department. Late-breaking news is very important there, and we might need to hire some people for that department. We would also have to hire a Sunday editor who would function as a third managing editor.

MARKETING DEPARTMENT: ADVERTISING, PROMOTION, CIRCULATION

Mr. Nick Thompson, marketing director, supervised the company's advertising, promotion, and circulation activities. After 16 years in the editorial department, he had been assigned to this position to develop a unified marketing strategy. He and his subordinates were attempting to develop a long-term plan which would raise the papers' profile. He thought that starting a Sunday paper would be one of the most important steps in this regard. He thought further that a Sunday paper, even without extensive promotion in Yosemite's western counties, would arrest the decline in circulation in those counties, but he was not convinced it would do much to increase circulation there. "People in the western counties consider our products to be city-oriented, liberal publications," he said. "We need to do a lot more zoned news before they'll start thinking of our products as 'local' newspapers."

ADVERTISING AND PROMOTION

Mr. Bert Jones, director of advertising and promotion, headed a 132-person department. Reporting directly to him were Mr. Rob Seaton, display advertising manager, Mr. Van Green, classified advertising manager, and Mr. Jim Richards, promotion manager.

Seaton supervised 15 retail salespeople, 13 of whom operated out of the Murfreesboro office and sold ads primarily in Brunswick, Clark, and Evans Counties, and one of whom operated out of the Monroe bureau and sold primarily in San Jose and San Simeon Counties. One handled *Phoenix* advertising almost exclusively. Each had about 150 accounts, only 60 of which were considered "active" (i.e., they had run ads within the last 3 to 6 months). Active accounts were visited at least once a week. Retail salespeople received annual base salaries ranging from $11,400 to $14,800 plus commissions which sometimes went as high as $400 a month. Seaton stated that the *Star-Advocate* had lost considerable ROP[1] linage in recent months due to bad economic conditions throughout the country. "If it weren't for a tremendous influx of preprints,[2] we'd be in real trouble," Seaton said. "But we're still ahead of last year in actual revenue because preprints are much more profitable than ROP." Retail advertising accounted for about 68 percent of the *Star-Advocate*'s advertising revenue.

Seaton also supervised the *Star-Advocate*'s national advertising manager, Mr. Stuart Newston, who with his assistant made some visits to national advertisers and also worked closely with the company's national advertising represen-

---

[1] "Run of the paper" advertising.

[2] Preprints were advertisements printed separately from the main part of the papers and inserted into them. Sometimes they were printed by companies other than the newspaper company which distributed them.

tative agency[1] in Las Rivas. National advertising accounted for about 8 percent of the papers' advertising revenue.

Mr. Van Green, classified advertising manager, supervised seven full-time and two part-time outside classified salespeople. Each was responsible for about 100 accounts, about 65 of which were "active" (i.e., they ran ads daily). Salespeople visited active accounts daily to monthly. They earned a base salary of from $12,500 to $14,000 plus a commission. Green also supervised seven telephone advertising counselors who accepted copy from and made recommendations to real estate and employment agencies who ran daily advertisements. These counselors were paid about $10,000 to $11,000 annually. Green was also responsible for 29 "transient advisors" who accepted incoming calls from people who placed ads only occasionally. Each day, the transient advisors telephoned all customers whose classified ads were expiring to see if they wanted them renewed. The advisors were paid $7,500 to $8,500 annually. Transient ads represented about 33 percent of the *Star-Advocate*'s total classified revenue, and all classified ads represented 24 percent of the papers' total advertising revenue. Green stated that over the last few months, in spite of the general downturn in the economy, employment advertising had held steady though real estate and automotive advertising had fallen. He thought auto advertising had gone as low as it would go but that real estate would probably fall about 8 percent and employment advertising about 5 percent during 1975.

Jones was confident that his department could generate considerable additional revenue with a Sunday paper. The continued development of Sunday shopping in Yosemite was a valuable asset, he felt, and representatives of Sears, Bullocks, and other retailers had indicated interest in advertising in a local Sunday paper. He thought that automotive and especially real estate advertising would increase considerably because the real estate dealers who advertised regularly all week would probably run display ads on Sunday.

Jones's major concern was that big customers would merely transfer ads from weekly to Sunday editions. To prevent this, he thought the paper might initially allow customers to run their weekday ads with no copy change on Sunday at half price. Even with this incentive, however, he expected about 10 pages of advertising to be transferred from daily to Sunday papers. After the introductory period, the rates would be adjusted according to the Sunday paper's circulation. For example, if Sunday circulation were 140,000 as compared to weekday circulation of 220,000, Sunday advertising rates would be about 64 percent of weekday rates. Jones estimated that during the first year a Sunday paper would increase classified advertising volume by 10 to 12 pages per week, retail volume by 8 pages per week, and national volume by ½ page per week, after taking into account the transfer of about 10 pages per week from daily to Sunday. Ad-

---

[1] An advertising representative agency was an independent company which sold advertising for several newspapers to the advertising agencies or advertising departments of major national companies. Their salespeople, known as *reps*, usually received about 10 percent and the agencies about 15 percent of the rates charged to advertisers.

vertising managers of recently started Sunday newspapers stated that their Sunday publications experienced an immediate and substantial increase in classified advertising. In retail advertising, however, some showed no gains and others showed only moderate increases in the first year. Eventually, however, Sunday retail advertising revenue became a major source of additional revenue. Most reported that national advertising showed virtually no increase at the outset. (See Exhibit 8 for comparative milline advertising rates.)

Jones thought starting a Sunday paper would require five additional full-time and five additional part-time people to sell ads. He thought further that, regardless of whether the *Star-Advocate* started a Sunday paper, he needed an additional salesperson in San Jose and San Simeon Counties to counter the downward trend in advertising volume and share there. He thought that doing more zoned advertising and gaining identification by means of a Sunday paper would probably increase circulation in the western counties.

The *Star-Advocate*'s promotion manager, Mr. Jim Richards, also reported to Jones. Richards did a good deal of market research, produced sales aids and promotional pieces for the advertising and circulation departments, and wrote in-paper promotional pieces and billboard and radio copy. Jones and Richards felt they would need about 6 months of intensive promotional efforts to prepare the public to accept a Sunday publication. For the first 3 months, they planned to do an "image campaign" consisting of billboard and radio advertising and direct mailing. This campaign would not be related directly to the Sunday publication but would remind people that the paper performed a valuable service in their lives. The last 3 months would be devoted to extensive general promotion efforts which would emphasize the start of the Sunday paper. It was thought that this campaign would cost about $150,000.

CIRCULATION

Mr. Hank Hawley, circulation director, supervised a 117-person circulation department. The mailroom foreman and the district managers were the company's primary link with 36 independent contract haulers whose sole task was to drop off papers at assigned locations. Hawley's assistant was primarily responsible for 5 circulation supervisors who in turn directed 59 district managers. The district managers worked with carriers on sales campaigns, collection, record keeping, and customer service, and they picked up extra papers and collected newspaper revenues from newsstands in their districts. Hawley said that the highest paid district manager made about $15,000 annually. The *Star-Advocate*'s 3,211 carriers were independent contractors, each of whom had about 50 customers. A carrier made 21 cents per week per subscriber. Circulation accounted for 33 percent of the *Star-Advocate*'s revenue.

Hawley stated that starting a Sunday paper would require three new circulation clerks, three new mailers, several miscellaneous circulation people, and a lot of negotiating on his part. "The truckers already work six days a week, and those who want to work seven will bid on the Sunday runs we come up with," he said. "We'll also have to determine whether the *Morning Star* or *Evening Advocate* carriers will deliver the Sunday paper." All other negotiations would be with unionized employees who currently worked a 5-day week. "We will be asking mailroom people to work early Sunday morning instead of Saturday afternoon, and they're not going to be ecstatic about doing that," he said.

Hawley stated further that the initial circulation costs of a Sunday paper would be high because the paper would be delivered free to all current daily subscribers for 2 weeks. Truckers and carriers would have to be reimbursed for delivering these papers, though they would not yet be generating any revenue. Hawley thought the district managers and carriers would try to convert the readers to paying subscribers during the third week. "Our job would be much easier if we could use a forced circulation policy," he commented. "But our top management is adamantly against it, so we'll have to put on a major circulation drive."

In spite of the difficulties, Hawley was in favor of starting a Sunday paper. He said:

> We'd be able to provide a total package for the week, and this should be useful in attracting new subscribers, especially if the Sunday edition is a complete, well rounded product. However, a Sunday paper alone will not be adequate to reverse the downward spiral in the western counties. We need better local news and advertising in the daily package to do that.

Hawley stated that one strong point in favor of starting a Sunday paper was that the *Star-Advocate* already had a good distribution system in place, and that neither of the Carson papers had been able to accomplish this. Both papers had local subcontractors who distributed their papers in Yosemite both during the week and on Sunday, but the turnover among them was said to be very high. Hawley estimated that about 70,000 of the Carson papers' Sunday sales were home-delivered and about 56,000 were sold at newsstands. In many areas of Yosemite, Carson papers were sold only at newsstands.

PRODUCTION, ACCOUNTING, AND EMPLOYEE AND COMMUNITY RELATIONS

Mr. John Mueller, executive vice president, general manager, and treasurer, was responsible for all noneditorial and nonmarketing functions, i.e., production, accounting, and employee and community relations.

The *Star-Advocate*'s production department was converting from hot metal to cold type,[1] and Mueller expected the process to be completed by December

---

[1] The hot metal production system was based on the Linotype machine, a large typesetting contraption on which matrices of letters were assembled and into which molten lead was injected to form a line of type. Once copy was set in lead type, it went through several elaborate, cumbersome, time-consuming steps before the page mold was ready for the printing press. Cold type production was based on photocomposition machines, computers, and other electronic equipment which greatly increased the accuracy and speed of the production process.

1, 1974. This would completely eliminate the stereotype department and would reduce the 407-person production department to 380 employees. (The composing room and pressroom staffs would remain unchanged.)

Some executives had feared that employee cutbacks would create serious problems among the company's heavily unionized labor force. The problems had been averted, however, because the company agreed to extremely liberal settlements including immediate pensions for many employees and liberal severance pay for others. Furthermore, the vast majority of the *Star-Advocate*'s production employees had job guarantees built into their contracts, and they would not be laid off regardless of the lessened work requirements resulting from the new processes. The time required to retrain people meant that all employees were currently kept busy. However, once the cold type conversion was completed and the employees retrained, the company would have excess production capacity. This was not expected to occur before 1976, however, and if a Sunday paper were started before then, additional personnel would be needed.

Mueller stated that the major production problems in going to a single Saturday paper and starting a Sunday paper would be spreading the work force over 7 days. He commented:

> No one wants to work Saturday night, so we'll have to do some fancy negotiating with the people who now produce the Saturday Evening Advocate to get them to work Saturday night instead of Saturday afternoon. That may cause some serious "people problems." Our production employees are already upset because of the conversion to cold type and the retraining it requires. Asking them to work on Saturday night just might be the final straw.

Mueller felt that a Sunday paper would not cause major problems for his other departments though it would mean additional paperwork for the accounting department, which would need eight new people. He thought, however, that there were strong arguments against starting a Sunday paper besides those he had advanced regarding production employees. He commented as follows:

> The biggest reason I can see for having a Sunday paper is prestige, and from where I sit as treasurer, prestige isn't enough. I'm not at all convinced we'll get enough additional advertising and circulation to pay for a Sunday paper. Our advertisers say they're interested, but they won't give concrete assurances that they'll increase their total expenditures with us. Furthermore, San Jose and San Simeon counties are pretty well covered by the Yosemite News. Even in good times, Sunday papers can't be assured of a profit within the first couple of years, and the generally bad economic conditions right now suggest we'd have an uncommon amount of trouble. We need to get better at what we're doing now. Our profit level has been on the downroad for several years. 1973 was a turnaround year, but our profitability still isn't strong enough to launch into new ventures.

PRODUCT POLICY CONSIDERATIONS FOR A SUNDAY STAR-ADVOCATE

To launch a successful product, *Star-Advocate* managers thought they had to steer a middle course between the Carson papers and *The Yosemite News*. The Sunday edition of *The Texarkana Post* (Yosemite Sunday circulation 59,000) was by far the heftiest of the three papers. The main part of the paper consisted of about 12 sections which together accounted for over 200 pages. In addition, the paper contained eight pages of color comics, a general-interest magazine produced by the *Post's* staff, a TV magazine, and numerous advertising inserts. The Sunday *Post* which was circulated in Yosemite was labeled "Yosemite Edition," and the pages which dealt with Yosemite news were listed on the front. It also carried a skyline about the results of Yosemite University's sports activities. *The Sunday Gazette* (Yosemite circulation 67,000) consisted of about 130 pages divided into seven sections, eight pages of color comics, a TV magazine, *Parade* magazine, and some advertising inserts. Its papers circulated in Yosemite were labeled "Latest Yosemite News." The Sunday edition of *The Yosemite News* was printed in four sections and contained about 36 pages. It also contained 12 tab pages of color comics, a television section, and *Family Weekly* magazine. (See Exhibit 9 for specific contents of samples of each paper.)

The Sunday *Star-Advocate* which managers currently envisioned would contain about 52 pages of regular news and advertising, 8 pages of color comics, a "TV Guide"-type magazine listing all area television programs including cable television, and a nationally syndicated Sunday magazine, probably *Family Weekly*. They thought that the main part of the paper would probably consist of four sections, but the specific content of those four sections had not yet been determined.

Discussions with publishers who had recently started Sunday papers led the managers to believe that acceptance of a Sunday *Star-Advocate* would depend on a penetrating and knowledgeable coverage of the local scene. Thus, they felt the publication should stress local news, complete late local sports, and significant stories and features that probed an aspect of contemporary life in Yosemite. They felt furthermore that the Sunday paper should report the latest available national and international news and national sports news. Lionel stated that both Carson papers and *The Yosemite News* were "very weak" on national and international news. He went on to say that a real plus for the *Star-Advocate* was that its Sunday product would go to press about midnight and therefore could provide later news than its competitors. The Yosemite editions of the Carson papers went to press around 9:00 P.M. and *The Yosemite News* around 7:00 P.M.

One issue which *Star-Advocate* managers would have to decide if the board approved the proposal was how to price the Sunday paper. Many felt that they should charge 25 cents for home delivery and thus make the total price for 7-day home delivery an even $1. The circulation manager felt, however, that this would eliminate tips and cause dissatisfaction among the carriers.

One way to get around this would be to increase daily home delivery rates to 90 cents for 6 days and then charge $1.15 for 7 days. This was considered a viable alternative since the paper had not had a home-delivery rate increase since September 1968, and the increase to 90 cents would merely equalize home-delivery and single-copy rates. The latter had been increased from 10 to 15 cents in August 1972. Most executives thought the newsstand price for a Sunday Star-Advocate should be 35 cents as compared to 50 cents for the Carson papers and 25 cents for The Yosemite News.

Another issue which Star-Advocate management still had to resolve was the matter of timing. Some executives thought the new Sunday paper should be started in March 1975 to prevent competitors from becoming more firmly entrenched in the Yosemite market. Others argued, however, that the starting date should be postponed until September 1975 to give adequate lead time to all departments to assure a top-notch product. Still others thought the Star-Advocate should phase the new paper in gradually. For example, it might start producing only a morning Saturday paper, put an improved television-guide book in that paper, and thereby try to get people to change their reading habits from evening to morning. Once this was successful, they reasoned, the company could start producing a Sunday paper. Opponents of this proposal argued that it would introduce readers to the wrong package and that they would be reluctant to switch to the Sunday paper later on.

Both Star-Advocate management and the board of directors knew that the Carson papers were aware that the Star-Advocate was thinking about starting a Sunday paper. Both had recently stepped up their coverage of Yosemite news. Recently, The Gazette had approached the Star-Advocate with a proposal that the Star-Advocate distribute the Sunday Gazette and obtain publication rights to certain daily Gazette features. While this proposal had met with a cold response from Star-Advocate management, Lionel felt that negotiations could be reopened if it were decided not to publish a Sunday newspaper.

EXHIBIT 1
MAP OF THE *STAR-ADVOCATE*'S TRADING AREA
The Star-Advocate Company

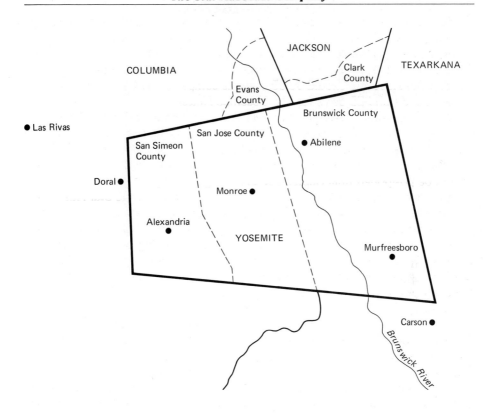

EXHIBIT 2
COMPARATIVE CIRCULATION OF NEWSPAPERS IN THE *STAR-ADVOCATE*'S MARKETING AREA
The Star-Advocate Company

	No. of households	Average household E.B.I.	Circulation of Morning Star	Circulation of Evening Advocate	Circulation of Texarkana Post		Circulation of Carson Gazette		Circulation of Yosemite News	
					Morning	Sunday	Evening	Sunday	Evening	Sunday
Brunswick County, Yosemite	197,000	$13,724	51,252	122,871	12,301	51,886	4,097	55,701		
San Jose County, Yosemite	39,100	9,641	4,956	3,116	635	2,934	1,532	6,627	37,273*	42,763*
San Simeon County, Yosemite	40,500	9,768	9,731	8,299	NA	4,844	NA	5,524		
Total Yosemite	276,600		65,939	134,286	12,936	59,664	5,629	67,852	37,273	42,763
Clark County, Jackson	30,400	12,020	1,406	797	5,931		7,261			
Evans County, Columbia	22,700	11,103	1,714	5,607						
All other Columbia counties	57,200	NA	1,380	2,469						
Texarkana counties	425,600	14,013	2,244	3,569	107,174		176,491			
All other			511	462						
Total			73,194	147,190						

* Includes circulation within all three Yosemite counties. *Star-Advocate* management stated that San Jose was by far *The Yosemite News'* major market.
Source: ABC Audit Report for 12 months ending December 31, 1973.

EXHIBIT 3

REGULAR NATIONAL FEATURES OF COMPETITIVE NEWSPAPERS IN THE *STAR-ADVOCATE*'S MARKETING AREA

The Star-Advocate Company

	Wire services	Syndicated columnists	Comics		
The Morning Star	Washington Post New York Times Chicago Tribune Newhouse, AP, UPI Reuters, Newsday Los Angeles Times	Art Buchwald David Broder Harriet Van Horne James Kilpatrick Laurie Ranin Jules Feiffer	Woody's World Marmaduke Eb and Flo Smidgens The Dropouts Moon Mullins	Grin and Bear It Mr. Tweedy Buz Sawyer Snuffy Smith Miss Peach Nancy	Conchy Li'l Abner Henry Hogar the Horrible
The Evening Advocate	Washington Post New York Times Chicago Tribune Newhouse, AP, UPI Reuters, Newsday Los Angeles Times	Anthony Lewis John Heritage Russell Baker Sydney J. Harris	Heathcliff Alley Oop Tumbleweeds Phantom Frank and Ernest Eek and Meek	Benjy Captain Easy Judge Parker The Born Loser The Smith Family Norbert	Luther
The Carson Gazette	New York Times AP, UPI	Carl Rowen Marquis Childs Vic Gold Clayton Fritchey Keven P. Phillips Sandy Grady Art Buchwald Erma Bombeck Dear Abby	Peanuts Andy Capp Li'l Abner Miss Peach Blondie The Better Half Good Earth Almanac Hints from Heloise Mary Worth	Beetle Bailey Kerry Drake Rex Morgan, M.D. Brenda Starr Ziggy Doonsbury The Family Circus The Phantom Snuffy Smith	Prince Valiant The Wizard of Id Mutt and Jeff The Small Society Tumbleweeds Funky Tales B.C.

EXHIBIT 3
Continued

	Wire services	Syndicated columnists	Comics		
The Texarkana Post	Agency France-Presse AP, UPI Washington Post Chicago Tribune Los Angeles Times Knight News Service London Observer Service	Ann Landers Charles W. Bowser Nicholas Von Hoffman William Rusher Andrew M. Greeley	Hager the Horrible Dick Tracy Funky Winkerbean Fred Basset Animal Crackers Juliet Jones Winnie Winkle Gahan Wilson Sunday Comics The Lockhorns	Steve Canyon Big George Tank McNamara Rivets Momma Nancy Broom Hilda Freddy Henry Donald Duck	Catfish Ferd'nand The Flintstones Johnny Wonder Junior Jumble Archie Mark Trail Conchy Marmaduke
The Yosemite News	AP	Jack Anderson William Hoffman William F. Buckley, Jr. Dear Abby	Dick Tracy Uncle Nugent's Funland Do You Know??? Peanuts Marmaduke Broom Hilda	Smith Family Blondie Juliet Jones Moose Miller Archie Berry's World They'll Do it Every Time	Popeye The Small Society Trudy Steve Canyon Yogi Bear

EXHIBIT 4
ORGANIZATION CHART, SEPTEMBER 1974
The Star-Advocate Company

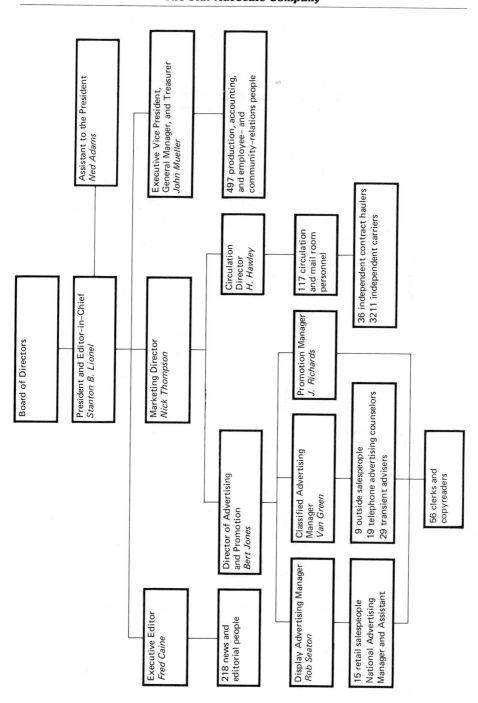

Board of Directors

President and Editor-in-Chief
Stanton B. Lionel

Assistant to the President
Ned Adams

Executive Vice President, General Manager, and Treasurer
John Mueller

497 production, accounting, and employee- and community-relations people

Marketing Director
Nick Thompson

Circulation Director
H. Hawley

117 circulation and mail room personnel

36 independent contract haulers
3211 independent carriers

Director of Advertising and Promotion
Bert Jones

Promotion Manager
J. Richards

Classified Advertising Manager
Van Green

9 outside salespeople
19 telephone advertising counselors
29 transient advisers

Display Advertising Manager
Rob Seaton

15 retail salespeople
National Advertising Manager and Assistant

56 clerks and copyreaders

Executive Editor
Fred Caine

218 news and editorial people

EXHIBIT 5
EMPLOYEES AND PERCENT EXPENSES BY DEPARTMENT
The Star-Advocate Company

Department	No. of employees	% of expenses
Production, accounting, and community and employee relations	497	32
Newsprint		17
Editorial	218	15
Advertising and promotion	132	7
Circulation	117	13
General and administrative	9	16*
	973	100

* Included funds for pensions.

EXHIBIT 6
YOSEMITE SUNDAY CIRCULATION
The Star-Advocate Company

	1969	1970	1971	1972	1973
Texarkana Post	71,831	69,068	65,779	62,647	59,664
Carson Gazette	74,351	75,583	74,101	67,983	67,852
Yosemite News	NA	NA	40,914	39,341	42,763
Other	38,768	36,016	34,742	32,466	32,000 (est.)
Total	184,950	180,667	215,536	202,437	202,279

184

EXHIBIT 7
SUNDAY *STAR-ADVOCATE*
The Star-Advocate Company

Projected weekly revenue and expense analysis for 1975*

Revenue:

Advertising	$ 41,300	
Circulation	28,960	
Total	$ 70,260	

Cost of production:

Salaries (75% fixed; 25% variable)	$ 7,200
Newsprint (100% variable)	12,200
Other (25% fixed; 75% variable)	2,100
Total	$ 21,500

Other operating expenses:

Editorial (100% fixed)	$ 14,900
Advertising (100% fixed)	2,100
Circulation (25% fixed; 75% variable)	9,100
Business (75% fixed; 25% variable)	2,700
Total	$ 28,800

Weekly operating profit	$ 19,960
Annual operating profit	$1,037,920
Rate of return on revenue	28%

— Start-up costs

New employee training	$ 20,200
Sunday newspaper design	16,300
Computer programming	32,600
Invoices	8,100
Promotion	163,000
Total	$ 240,200

Revenue and cost breakdown

Revenues:
Advertising:
Linage:

Retail	13 pages/Sunday *Star-Advocate*
Classified	14 pages/Sunday *Star-Advocate*
National	1.3 pages/Sunday *Star-Advocate*
TV Magazine	9,988 lines/Sunday *Star-Advocate*
Inserts	16 inserts/year

Rate:

Retail	75% of combination rate
Classified	75% of combination rate
National	75% of combination rate
TV Magazine	$0.55/line
Inserts	$3,000/insert
Daily advertising	May decline as much as 10 pages per week, at least initially

Circulation:

Sunday circulation†	143,000: 94,400 home delivery
	46,200 newsstands
	2,400 mail

* This revenue and expense analysis does *not* take into account (1) economic impact of possible transfer of advertising from daily to Sunday or (2) projected loss of Saturday circulation due to cannibalization.

† Management forecasted that this circulation would break down as follows: (Brunswick) 111,300 + (San Jose) 10,600 + (San Simeon) 14,500 + (out of state) 6,600 = 143,000.

EXHIBIT 7
Continued

Revenue and cost breakdown (*continued*)

Price	$0.25 home delivery (less $0.05 carrier margin) 0.35 newsstands and mail (less $0.05 newsstand margin on newsstand sales)
All day Saturday	— Saturday's circulation should decrease approximately 20,000 due to duplication. Net revenue loss will be approximately $0.09/copy, after carrier and newsstand margins.

Expenses:

Production:
Salaries:
Composing room	+8 situations @ $8/hour
Pressroom	+10 situations @ $10/hour
Electrician	+2 @ $250/week
Custodian	+1 @ $140/week
Stereo	0

— Newsprint:
Cost	$255/ton
Consumption	48 tons/week (@ 78 pages/pound)
Average size	52 pages

Other: Includes ink, supplies, electricity, repairs

Editorial:
Salaries, +8 employees	$ 3,300/week
Comics	3,600/week
Family Weekly	1,200/week
TV Magazine	5,800/week
Supplies	400/week
Syndicates	600/week
	$14,900/week

Advertising:
Salaries:
+5 employees	
+5 part-time employees	$ 1,450/week
Mats	300/week
Promotion	350/week
	$ 2,100/week

Circulation:
Salaries:
+3 clerks	$ 588/week
+3 mailers	862/week
Other (motor routes, supervision, drivers, inserting)	7,000/week
Supplies	300/week
Promotion	350/week
	$ 9,100/week

Accounting:
Salaries:
+5 clerks	$ 625/week
+3 switchboard operators	375/week
Computer operations	100/week
Taxes and benefits associated with new employees	1,600/week
	$ 2,700/week

EXHIBIT 8
MILLINE ADVERTISING RATE COMPARISONS*
The Star-Advocate Company

Weekday:

Star-Advocate (morning and evening)	$ 5.57
Carson Gazette (evening)	4.57
Texarkana Post (morning)	5.78
Yosemite News (evening)	9.62

Cost / 1000 lines

Sunday:

Star-Advocate (proposed)	$ 6.31
Carson Gazette	4.07
Texarkana Post	3.78
Yosemite News	10.61

* The milline advertising rate was the cost per thousand lines per thousand circulation. A standard-size newspaper page contained 2,400 lines. These rates were "basic" rates, before quantity discounts, commissions, etc. On the average, the *Star-Advocate* obtained net advertising revenue equal to approximately 60 percent of its basic rates.

5.57
$\times 2.4$

CIRCULATION

DAILY

Rate per page

$(5.57 \times .220 \times 2.4 \times .6) = 1,225.4$

$= \$1,764$ Rate SAT.

subtract news print savings

At 33¢ per copy how many more sell.

EXHIBIT 9
CONTENTS OF SAMPLE ISSUES
OF SUNDAY PAPERS[1]
The Star-Advocate Company

YOSEMITE NEWS

■ *Section 1*

8 pages of national and local news, with heavy emphasis on local news

2 "Opinion" pages (editorial and op-ed)

■ *Section 2*

3 pages of local, national, and international news

2 "Entertainment" pages

3 complete pages of J. C. Penney advertisements

■ *Section 3*

5½ pages of sports news

1½ pages of J. C. Penney advertisements

1 page of business news

1 complete page of Sears advertisements

1 page of obituaries and miscellaneous news

■ *Section 4*

4 pages of local news

4 pages of classified advertising

■ 12 tab pages of color comics

■ 16 tab page magazine with various features and complete television listings

■ 4 tab page section entitled "The Mini Page" for children

■ *Family Weekly* magazine

THE SUNDAY GAZETTE

■ *Section 1*

56 pages: national, international, and state news

This section was printed in three parts. The front page and 2 other pages of the third part were devoted to Yosemite news.

■ *Section 2*

8 pages "News and Views": editorials, Washington Report, News Spotlight, book reviews

188

[1] ROP advertisements were, of course, scattered throughout the papers.

EXHIBIT 9
Continued

■ *Section 3*

16 pages: sports and classified automotive advertising

■ *Section 4*

16 pages of "Focus": This section contained various features about a range of "modern living" issues. It also contained wedding and engagement announcements.

■ *Section 5*

8 pages of "Entertainment and The Arts": movies, theater, music, art

■ *Section 6*

16 pages of real estate articles and advertisements, miscellaneous classified advertisements, obituaries

■ *Section 7*

10 pages of "Travel and Resorts"

■ *TV Time:* television listings and articles

■ *Parade* magazine

■ *Looking:* a 24-page magazine produced by the *Gazette* staff

■ 8 tab pages of Sears advertising

■ 7 pages of color comics

■ 1 page of "The Mini Page" for children (This page was attached to the comics section.)

THE TEXARKANA POST

■ *Section A*

26 pages of primarily national and international news with some local news

■ *Section B*

16 pages of "Yosemite and Metro": about 8 pages of this section were actually devoted to national and international news. In all, about 2 pages were devoted to Yosemite news.

■ *Section C*

14 pages of "General News": miscellaneous national and international news

■ *Section D*

26 pages of "Sports": 20 pages of sports news and 6 pages of business and financial news, including stock quotations.

EXHIBIT 9
Continued

- *Section E*

30 pages of automotive articles and all classified advertising

- *Section F*

18 pages of "Living": miscellaneous features, consumer news, fashion, stamps and coins, garden news, weddings

- *Section G*

8 pages of "Today's World": miscellaneous news analyses, editiorial and op-ed pages, education and science pages

- *Section H*

12 pages of "Food": some articles but primarily advertisements

- *Section I*

10 pages of "Travel"

- *Section J*

Missing from sample copy, presumed to be classified advertising

- *Section K*

26 pages of "Home and Real Estate": articles and classified advertising

- *Section L*

12 pages of "The Arts": movies, theater, concerts, art museums, book reviews

- *TV Week:* magazine produced by the *Post* staff
- 4 page tab insert of Sears advertising
- *World:* 40 page magazine produced by the *Post* staff
- 20 tab page insert of special condominium advertising
- 6 tab pages of miscellaneous advertising
- 8 pages of color comics

POLAROID FRANCE (S.A.)

ROBERT D. BUZZELL
Professor
Harvard Graduate School of Business Administration

JEAN-LOUIS LECOCQ
Directeur des Études
École Supérieur de Commerce et d'Administration
des Entreprises de Rouen

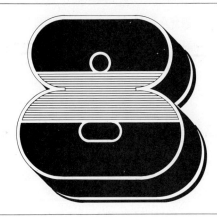

In July 1967, M. Jacques Dumon, general manager of Polaroid France (S.A.), was preparing a preliminary marketing plan for 1968. M. Dumon was scheduled to present his proposals to the marketing executives at the headquarters office of the American parent firm, Polaroid Corporation, in September. Following this review, a final version of the plan would be adopted as a basis for Polaroid's operations in France during the forthcoming year.

In preparing his recommendations for 1968, M. Dumon was especially concerned with problems of pricing and promotion for the Model 20 Swinger camera. The Swinger had been introduced in France during the fall of 1966 and was the first Polaroid Land Camera available to French consumers at a retail price under Fr. 300.[1] Sales of the Swinger during 1966 and early 1967 had not reached expected levels, and M. Dumon was aware that the basic attitude of headquarters management toward overseas operations in 1968 was cautious, because Polaroid's unconsolidated foreign subsidiaries had incurred a combined loss of $907,000 in 1966. He recognized, therefore, that all proposals for 1968 would be subject to extremely careful scrutiny.

COMPANY BACKGROUND

Polaroid Corporation, with headquarters in Cambridge, Massachusetts, produced a wide line of photographic and related products for household and business uses, including cameras, film, photographic equipment, polarizing products, and x-ray products. Total 1966 sales in the United States amounted to $316.5 million, more than three times the amount of business done in 1962. Worldwide sales in 1966, including Polaroid's 13 subsidiaries, totaled $363 million. A summary of sales and profits for the period 1950–1966 is given in Exhibit 1.

The company was founded in 1937 by Dr. Edwin H. Land to produce polarizing products, including sunglasses, photographic filters, and glare-free lamps. By 1941, sales had reached $1 million. Following World War II, Dr. Land developed a new method for developing and printing photographs. The Polaroid Land Camera was announced in 1947, and the first models were sold in November 1948. The Polaroid Land Camera utilized a "one-step" process, in contrast with the "three-step" process required for conventional photography. In conventional still photography, the sequence involved in producing a black-and-white picture is as follows:

1   A photosensitive material (film) is exposed to light. The light converts grains of silver bromide into specks of silver, the amount of silver deposited in a given area depending on the amount of light reaching that area.

2   The film is developed by immersing it in a chemical solution which converts the exposed grains into black silver. The unexposed grains are then dissolved with a second solution and washed away. This yields a finished negative in which all the natural tones are reversed; i.e., black appears as white, and vice versa.

3   The negative is placed in contact with a sheet of light-sensitive paper and exposed to light. The developing process is then repeated to produce a finished positive print.

The second and third steps of conventional photography require that ex-

[1] Franc = 20 cents (approx.) in 1967.

posed film be processed in a commercial laboratory or in a home darkroom. For most amateur photographers, this means a delay of several days between taking a picture and receiving a finished print of it.

The technique developed by Dr. Land yielded finished prints from the *camera itself*, with no delay for processing. Basic discoveries in photographic chemistry, and new materials based on these discoveries, permitted the entire process to be completed in 60 seconds (later, in 10 seconds) with no equipment other than the camera and film.

The Polaroid Land Camera was commercially successful almost from the beginning. In 1949, sales of cameras and film amounted to over $5 million.

PRODUCT LINE

Between 1949 and 1964, research and development activities at Polaroid provided the basis for a continuous improvement and diversification of Polaroid's camera product line.

The earliest versions of the Polaroid Land Camera produced sepia-colored prints of a quality inferior to that of conventional films. Subsequent improvements in the film permitted clear black-and-white photographs and, beginning in 1963, color pictures as well. Another major innovation in 1963 was the introduction of the Automatic 100 Land Camera. The Model 100 utilized a film pack rather than the film roll which had been used in all earlier Polaroid cameras. With a film pack, the camera could be loaded more easily and quickly since it was not necessary to wind the film around a series of rollers. Instead, the user simply opened the camera, inserted the pack, and closed the camera. In addition to the pack-loading feature, the Model 100 incorporated several other improvements over the earlier models. It weighed less than earlier models and had a better exposure control.

Following the introduction of the Model 100, Polaroid introduced three lower-priced pack cameras: the Model 101 in 1964 and Models 103 and 104 in 1965. In early 1967, a redesigned line of five pack cameras was introduced. Thus, in mid-1967, the models offered and their suggested retail prices in the United States were as follows:

- Model 250 $159.95
- Model 240   124.95
- Model 230   94.95
- Model 220   69.95
- Model 210   49.95

All these cameras produced both black-and-white and color photographs in a 3¼ × 4¼ inch format, and all had electric-eye mechanisms for automatic exposure control. The main differences among the various models were in lens qualities and in materials. For example, the Model 250 featured a Zeiss rangefinder-viewfinder, a three-piece precision lens, an all-metal body, and a leather carrying strap. The Model 210 had a plastic body, a nylon strap, a less expensive focusing system, a two-piece lens, and was not designed to accommodate the accessories (such as a portrait lens) which could be employed with the higher-priced models.

In late 1965, Polaroid introduced the Model 20 Swinger Land Camera in the United States.[1] The Swinger was a roll-film camera, capable of taking black-and-white photos only, in a 2¼ × 3¼ inch format and with a 15-second development time. It was made of white plastic; the suggested retail price, emphasized in national advertising, was $19.95. The introduction of the Swinger enabled Polaroid to compete for the first time in the large-volume market for inexpensive cameras; around three-fourths of all still cameras purchased each year sold for less than $50 at retail. Thus, the launching of the Swinger was a major contributing factor in the dramatic growth of the company's sales during 1965 and 1966 (see Exhibit 1). According to company reports, by "sometime in 1967" over 5 million Swinger cameras had been sold by Polaroid.

All Polaroid cameras were produced for the company by outside contractors. The company itself manufactured black-and-white and color film rolls (for pre-1963 cameras), film packs for pack cameras, and film rolls for the Swinger.

In addition to amateur cameras and film, Polaroid produced one camera (the Model 180) for professional photographers and highly skilled amateurs, as well as several different types of industrial photographic equipment and supplies. Special-purpose industrial products included a system for producing identification cards and badges; x-ray equipment and film; and the MP-3 Industrial View Land Camera, designed for such applications as photomicrography.

Polaroid Corporation did not publish sales figures for individual products. According to the company's annual reports, photographic products accounted for between 93 and 97 percent of sales during the 1950s and 1960s. The remaining 3 to 7 percent of total volume was derived from sunglasses, polarizers, and other nonphotographic products. Trade sources estimated that cameras represented about 55 to 60 percent of Polaroid's sales volume in the mid-1950s and around 40 percent in the mid-1960s.

THE UNITED STATES CAMERA MARKET

The market for still cameras in the United States expanded dramatically during the early 1960s. According to trade estimates, some 14 million still cameras

[1] The name *Swinger* was chosen to emphasize the appeal of the new camera to teen-agers and young adults. The word *swinger,* in American slang, designated a youthful and exciting person. Presumably this usage was related to the much older word *swing,* a popular type of jazz music in the 1930s and 1940s. Because of the worldwide popularity of this kind of music, the word *swing* had essentially the same meaning (and pronunciation) throughout Western Europe as in the United States. The term *swinger* was, however, strictly American.

TABLE 1

Year	Industry sales,* million units	Polaroid market share,* percent
1954	4.5	4–5
1958	4.9	
1960	4.6	8
1962	5.3	
1964	8.4	11
1965	11.0	
1966	14.0	30–35

* Industry sales estimates published in annual statistical reports, prepared by Augustus Wolfman of *Modern Photography* and *Photo Dealer* magazines; Polaroid market share estimates from various trade sources; for 1964, from Duncan M. Payne, *The European Operations of the Eastman Kodak Company,* Institut d'Etudes Européenes de Geneve, 1967, p. 28.

were sold in 1966, three times as many as in 1960. Estimates of total industry sales and of Polaroid's market share (in units) are shown in Table 1. According to trade estimates, Polaroid camera sales in 1966 represented approximately 50 percent of the total *dollar value* of United States retail camera sales.

The rapid growth of the camera market was due, in the opinion of industry observers, to rising levels of consumer income and to the introduction of new products by Polaroid and by the Eastman Kodak Company. As described in the preceding section, Polaroid had introduced a series of new models in 1963, 1964, and 1965 at progressively lower prices and with various improvements in operating features.

In 1963, Kodak had introduced its new line of Instamatic cameras. Instamatic cameras used pack-in film rolls, like Polaroid's earlier models. Instamatic cameras were designed to use 35-mm film enclosed in a special cartridge produced only by Kodak. Thus, although Kodak licensed other companies to manufacture cameras using Instamatic film, it was the only source of film for all such cameras.

Kodak's own line of Instamatic cameras included simple, fixed-focus models selling at retail for around $12 and more sophisticated models priced as high as $100. Thus, Instamatics competed in virtually all price segments of the camera market except the under-$10 category. According to trade estimates, Instamatics accounted for around a third of all still cameras sold in the United States in 1964 and 1965.

Still cameras were purchased primarily by "amateur" users for personal recreational use. In 1966, 70 to 75 percent of all United States households owned one or more still cameras. Some cameras, and a significant proportion of all film, were bought by business, institutional, and governmental users for use in research, sales promotion, record keeping, etc. The principal objective of Polaroid's marketing programs was, however, the sale of Polaroid Land Cameras to household consumers.

TABLE 2

	Purchasers of:			
Income group	All still cameras	Polaroid pack cameras	Polaroid Swingers	All U.S. households
Under $3,000	4%	1%	3%	17%
3,000–4,999	11	9 ⎤	20	18
5,000–6,999	21	16 ⎦	20	20
7,000–9,999	31	31	38	26
10,000 or more	34	43	39	19
Age of principal user				**All U.S. individuals**
19 or younger	30%	23%	26%	22%
20–49 years	53	63	65	50
50 years or more	16	14	9	28

Household consumers used several different types of cameras, ranging from very simple, inexpensive "box" cameras up to very complex 35-mm instruments. According to Polaroid estimates, 35-mm cameras (exclusive of Instamatics) represented only about 5 to 7 percent of total camera purchases in 1965. In terms of retail price categories, around 15 percent of all cameras were sold at retail prices under $10, between 60 and 65 percent were priced between $10 and $49, and 20 to 25 percent cost $50 or more. Nearly half of all cameras were for the purchasers' own use, over 40 percent were purchased as gifts, and almost 10 percent were obtained as prizes, premiums, or in return for trading stamps.

Because of the importance of gift giving, camera sales were highly seasonal. November and December accounted for over 50 percent of total annual retail sales. The second most important selling season, May to July, accounted for nearly one-fourth of annual sales.

Up to 1963, the dominant type of customer for still cameras costing over $10 was the relatively affluent family with small children. The introduction of the Instamatics, the Swinger, and the relatively inexpensive Models 104 and 210 pack cameras resulted in a substantial broadening of the household market. The estimated distribution of purchasers by income groups and age groups in 1965–1966 are shown in Table 2.

POLAROID MARKETING IN THE UNITED STATES

Polaroid had no direct competition in the instant-photography field. Although the patents on the original version of the Polaroid Land Camera had expired in 1965, Polaroid still held some 750 unexpired patents on various improvements in film chemistry and camera design that had been developed during the 1950s and 1960s. The company's products were, however, in active competition with many conventional types of cameras and films.

POLAROID ADVERTISING

At the time of its introduction in 1948, the first Polaroid Land Camera was a radical product innovation in photography. According to *Fortune* magazine,[1] "Land's revolution was at first derided by all the experts . . . (including) virtually every camera dealer in the country, every 'advanced' amateur photographer, and nearly everyone on Wall Street." To overcome the skepticism of consumers and dealers, Polaroid placed considerable emphasis on national advertising. According to trade estimates, the company's advertising expenditures increased during the 1950s and 1960s as shown in Table 3.

Especially during the introductory phases of Polaroid marketing, the Land Camera lent itself ideally to the medium of television, where the method of operation and its results could be demonstrated. The company was among the first major sponsors of "big-time" network television programs in the 1950s, such as the Garry Moore and Perry Como music-variety shows. Advertising trade publications estimated that around 45 percent of Polaroid's total advertising budget was devoted to network television in the mid-1960s, about 30 percent to magazines, and less than 5 percent to newspapers.

Early Polaroid advertising in the United States was designed to acquaint consumers with the basic idea of instant photography. An illustrative advertisement from the mid-1950s is shown in Exhibit 2. Later, after the majority of prospective buyers were familiar with the concept of "a picture in a minute," the company's advertising efforts were devoted to announcements of successive changes in product features, such as color film and pack-loading cameras, and to publicizing the availability of lower-priced cameras. An example of a 1966 Swinger advertisement is given in Exhibit 3.

[1] Francis Bello, "The Magic that Made Polaroid," *Fortune*, April 1959.

TABLE 3

Year	Estimated advertising expenditures*
1954	$ 1,700,000
1957	3,000,000
1958	4,000,000
1960	7,500,000
1963	8,000,000 }(Color film and pack
1964	8,500,000 ∫ cameras introduced)
1965	12,000,000 (Swinger introduced)
1966	18,000,000

* Estimates by *Advertising Age* and other trade sources.

DISTRIBUTION AND PRICING

In the United States, Polaroid sold its cameras and film directly to around 15,000 retailers. Pack cameras were sold primarily by specialty photographic stores, department stores, and general-merchandise discount stores. Swinger cameras and Polaroid films were carried by a greater number and variety of outlets, including many drugstores. Sales were made to many of the smaller outlets via wholesalers, but the bulk of Polaroid sales was made directly to stores and to buying offices of chain and mail-order firms.

Polaroid Corporation established "suggested" retail prices for cameras and film, but there were no legal or other restrictions on the freedom of dealers to set their own resale prices. The suggested retail prices provided gross margins for the retailers of around 33⅓ percent on the Model 250, 28 percent on the Model 210, 33⅓ percent on the Swinger, and 33⅓ percent on pack films. Because Polaroid Land Cameras were regarded by the larger retailers as attractive products to feature in discount promotions, the prevailing retail prices were often well below suggested levels. In mid-1967, consumers in large metropolitan areas could buy the Model 250 at a discount price of around $129.95, the Model 210 for around $39.95, and the Swinger for as little as $14. The smaller conventional photographic stores sold Polaroid cameras and films at lesser discounts and, often, at full list price. Polaroid films were also often sold at prices significantly below the suggested or list figures (see Table 4).

Discounting by retailers was also common in the sale of competing cameras. Some of the larger and more aggressive discount stores sold cameras at prices very slightly above cost, and the smaller conventional stores found it very difficult to compete with such outlets. Partly for this reason, a substantial proportion of total retail camera sales were made by a relatively small number of dealers. For example, 40 percent of Polaroid's total sales were accounted for by 10 percent of its total number of sales accounts, and 60 percent of total sales by 20 percent of the accounts.

Sales were made to dealers by Polaroid's field sales force of some 55 salespeople who were responsible for calling on dealers periodically, setting up displays in the stores, training retail salespeople, assisting dealers in planning retail advertising of Polaroid products, and introducing new products. From time to time, the salespeople conducted special promotional campaigns, such as used-camera trade-in campaigns. For these programs, Polaroid would provide display and advertising materials to the dealers and the salespeople would assist them in

TABLE 4

Film type	Suggested retail price	Discount price
107: Black-and-white pack	$2.85	$1.99–2.49
108: Color pack	5.39	3.99–4.99
20: Black-and-white Swinger	2.10	1.49–1.79

promoting the sale of new Polaroid cameras via special trade-in allowances on used Polaroid cameras.

The frequency of salespeople's calls depended on a dealer's size and location. Small dealers located in remote areas were visited only once every 4 to 6 months. Large dealers located in major metropolitan areas were visited weekly. Dealers' orders were almost always placed by telephone or mail to one of Polaroid's six regional warehouses.

Polaroid salespeople were compensated on a salary basis. A typical salesperson's territory included about 300 regular dealers, along with wholesalers and other types of accounts.

POLAROID OVERSEAS OPERATIONS

Up to 1964, Polaroid's sales outside the United States and Canada were relatively small. Cameras and film were exported from the United States and were subject to the high tariffs which most countries imposed on photographic producers. As a result, prices of Polaroid products were so high as to make them virtually luxury items.

Beginning in 1965, Polaroid undertook a more aggressive program of developing international markets. Mr. Stanford Calderwood, marketing vice president of Polaroid, commented on this development at an international distributors' meeting in September 1966:[1]

> In 1965, things began to change somewhat and the international curve began perking up as we introduced the Models 103 and 104. . . . In 1966, international sales began to climb very sharply because of the introduction of the Swinger. It is our goal—and we think it is an achievable goal—that in the next decade we can make the international business grow so it will be equal in size to the U.S.A. total.

According to the company's *Annual Reports,* sales to dealers by Polaroid's overseas subsidiaries in 1966 amounted to $36 million, compared with $18.2 million in 1965. Beginning in 1965, the company had adopted a policy of pricing cameras and film "as if they were being made behind the Common Market and Commonwealth tariff barriers." Also in 1965, Polaroid established manufacturing facilities for Swinger film at Enschede, The Netherlands, and at the Vale of Leven, Scotland. Swinger camera production in the United Kingdom commenced in late 1965 at a plant set up by one of Polaroid's Amercian camera suppliers.

Along with the establishment of manufacturing facilities, Polaroid:[2]

---

[1] *Intercom,* Polaroid International Communique, October 1966.

[2] Polaroid *Annual Report* for 1966, p. 13.

> . . . embarked on a program designed to stimulate increased demand for its products overseas. Margins were adjusted downward to bring prices to the foreign consumer more in line with those to U.S. consumers. . . . Greatly expanded magazine and newspaper advertising, as well as commercial television where available, carried the Polaroid instant-picture message in many languages.

The costs of the expanded marketing program, coupled with delays in providing Swinger cameras from the new overseas factory, contributed to an operating loss of $907,000 by Polaroid's unconsolidated subsidiaries (excluding Canada) in 1966.

A portion of Polaroid's organization for international marketing, showing the activities affecting operations in Europe, is depicted in Exhibit 4. As shown there, the general managers of the European subsidiary companies reported to a European coordinator, located at the Polaroid International headquarters in Amsterdam, who in turn reported to Polaroid's vice president–sales, Mr. Thomas Wyman. Mr. Wyman and his assistant manager for international sales also had frequent contact with the subsidiary managers by mail and through periodic visits.

Advertising policies were established by the company's vice president–advertising, Mr. Peter Wensberg, in consultation with representatives of Doyle Dane Bernbach, the company's advertising agency. The agency was also charged with directing the work of its subsidiary and affiliate agencies in other countries. Thus, advertising campaigns for European markets were developed by the overseas agencies within broad guidelines established by Mr. Wyman and by DDB–New York. Mr. Wensberg stated that ". . . we are great believers in the power of advertising," and that "much of the success of our advertising efforts over the years has been due to the fact that we have what we feel is the world's best advertising agency—Doyle Dane Bernbach, in New York."

INTERNATIONAL PLANNING AND CONTROL

During 1965, Polaroid's marketing executives had developed a new planning and control system for overseas marketing operations. This system included a standardized format for financial accounting, standardized monthly performance reports, and annual operating plans for each subsidiary company. The system required that an annual operating plan be developed and submitted to Cambridge each fall, covering proposed operations during the next calendar year. The format of the plan called for:

1   A review of market conditions, including trends in total industry sales, competitive developments, distribution, and changes in consumer buying habits.

2   A statement of objectives for the year, expressed in concrete terms (e.g., "increase distribution by adding at least 20 more department stores and 100 more photographic stores").

3 A summary of planned marketing activities, including sales force, advertising budget and media, publicity, market research, and customer service.

4 Estimated operating results for the year, including monthly sales forecasts for each major product, operating expenses, estimated profits, and cash flow.

Monthly reports to Cambridge indicated actual results in comparison with the plan, and significant discrepancies were explained via accompanying correspondence.

POLAROID FRANCE (S.A.)

Polaroid France (S.A.) was established in November 1961 as a wholly owned subsidiary of Polaroid Corporation. Up to 1964, sales in France were relatively small. With the introduction of the Models 103 and 104 cameras in 1964 and 1965, followed by the Swinger in late 1966, sales of Polaroid France increased rapidly.

M. Dumon became general manager of Polaroid France early in 1966. During 1966, he was responsible for making preparations for the introduction of the Swinger, which took place in September. The addition of the Swinger involved a significant expansion of sales volume, advertising and promotional efforts, and retail distribution for Polaroid France. Consequently, M. Dumon had devoted most of his efforts during 1966 to discussions with the major advertising media, hiring additional personnel, and working with retailers to obtain distribution and promotional support for the new camera.

In mid-1967, Polaroid France employed 86 persons. The company's headquarters office and warehouse were located at Colombes, a suburb of Paris. Reporting to M. Dumon were the sales manager, the advertising manager, and the administration manager. An organization chart is given in Exhibit 5.

THE FRENCH CAMERA MARKET

The market for still cameras in France was about one-tenth as large as that in the United States. According to estimates by Polaroid's marketing research department, total camera sales to household and business users in France had increased slowly since 1963 (see Table 5).

TABLE 5
STILL CAMERA SALES (THOUSAND UNITS)

Year	Total	Over $50	Under $10
1963	1,200	210	390
1964	1,350	220	390
1965	1,300	220	400
1966	1,350	230	420

In comparison with the United States market, cameras selling for less than Fr. 50 ($10) comprised a larger proportion of total camera sales—around one-third. These inexpensive cameras were primarily simple, fixed-focus "box" cameras, many of which were imported. In France and elsewhere in Europe, Kodak offered less expensive models in the Instamatic line than those available in the United States. According to one source, Kodak sales represented about half the French camera market in 1965–1966.

Altogether, there were some 11,000 retail outlets for cameras in France.[1] Specialty photographic stores sold around three-fourths of all still cameras bought by French household consumers. Other important types of outlets included department stores (5 to 10 percent of total sales), supermarkets (5 percent), and opticians (2 percent). There were fewer general-merchandise discount retailers in France than in the United States, and this type of outlet sold only 1 to 2 percent of all still cameras.[2] Some of the larger photo retailers were aggressive discounters, however, especially in the Paris metropolitan area. The large department stores, such as Galeries Lafayette and Au Printemps, also sold cameras at substantial discounts from suggested retail prices. Outside Paris, smaller conventional photo stores dominated the retailing scene. These smaller stores typically had markups on photographic products of 25 to 30 percent, while the larger stores operated on margins of around 20 percent. As in the United States, the dealers earned their highest margins on film processing (35 to 40 percent).

Market studies by Polaroid indicated that about one-third of total camera sales were made in Paris, although only 17 percent of the population lived in the region. An additional 15 percent of camera sales were accounted for by other major cities (population over 100,000).

In France, about a third of all still cameras were purchased to be given as gifts. This compared with a gift proportion of nearly half in the United States. Because gift giving played a lesser role in the market, Christmas season sales naturally represented a smaller percentage of annual industry volume than in the United States. The peak selling season in France was during the spring and summer: May, June, and July accounted for more than half of annual camera sales, and November–December represented less than 15 percent.

According to Polaroid estimates, sales of Kodak Instamatic cameras amounted to over a fourth of the French market; 35-mm cameras, including the Agfa Rapid line manufactured in Germany and designed to compete with Instamatics, had market share of over 20 percent.

Camera purchases were relatively concentrated in the higher income groups (Table 6). About two-thirds of all French camera users were men. Among both men and women, persons under 24 years of age accounted for 34 percent of all camera users.

[1] Payne, op. cit., p. 98.

[2] Some French "supermarkets" carried diversified lines of general merchandise in addition to food, however, and were essentially combinations of United States food supermarket and discount-department store types of outlets.

TABLE 6

Annual income, francs	All still camera buyers, %	All French individuals over 15 years, %	Polaroid buyers, %	
			Pack	Swinger
≤6,000	3	17	1	1
6,001–8,400	14	17		
8,401–12,000	29	26	1	1
12,001–24,000	36	30	4	9
>24,000	18	11	94	89

Among Polaroid Swinger buyers, nearly 20 percent were under 21 years of age, and another 20 percent between 21 and 30. The corresponding figures for all cameras selling for less than Fr. 100 were 30 and 35 percent.

POLAROID MARKETING IN FRANCE

Prior to the introduction of the Models 103 and 104 pack cameras, Polaroid products were distributed in France on a limited scale. In 1963, only around 400 outlets carried Polaroid cameras. During 1965 and 1966, the marketing program had undergone a complete transformation. A broadened product line, lower prices, increased distribution, and more aggressive promotion all contributed to the company's growth.

DISTRIBUTION AND SALES FORCE

The number of outlets handling Polaroid products increased steadily from 1,300 in 1964 to 1,600 in 1965 and 3,400 in 1967. By mid-1967, M. Dumon estimated that Polaroid accounts represented around two-thirds of total retail camera sales among all photographic specialty stores, and 60 percent in the department store category. The largest 15 percent of Polaroid's accounts represented about 80 percent of the company's total sales.

Polaroid's sales force, which consisted of 10 men in mid-1966, had grown to 22 by July 1967. On average, each salesman made eight calls per day. The salesmen were compensated on a straight salary basis. They called on the dealers, took orders, arranged for in-store promotions of Polaroid cameras, and handled dealer problems relating to camera repairs, deliveries, etc.

PRICING

While Polaroid Corporation did not release cost figures for individual products, Polaroid France's gross margin on total sales (cameras and film) was approximately 30 percent (see Exhibit 8).

According to industry sources, Polaroid France's gross margin on the Swinger was probably slightly less than earned on other cameras. These sources also indicated that gross margins on cameras were typically about twice what they were on film. If Polaroid was typical of the French camera industry, these sources added, it probably sold about eight rolls of film for each camera during the first year in the user's hands.

Experience with other cameras suggested that the Swinger would probably have a useful life of 5 to 6 years.

Because cameras were easily shipped from one country to another, Polaroid felt that it was essential to coordinate prices on an international level. Consequently, all selling prices for Polaroid France were prescribed within narrow limits by management in Cambridge. Following the changes in Polaroid's marketing policies in 1965, prices to dealers were reduced substantially. The price paid by a dealer depended on quantities ordered. On the average, dealer costs for Polaroid pack cameras and film provided gross profits for the retailer of about 33 percent if he resold at full list price. Typical retail selling prices for Polaroid cameras and film and for major competing products in the United States and France are shown in Exhibit 6. These prices were from 15 to 20 percent below suggested retail prices.

When the Swinger was introduced, it was believed that small dealers would be reluctant to handle it unless there were some kind of guarantee of obtaining adequate margins. Resale price maintenance was permitted in France only when specifically authorized. Polaroid applied for, and received, permission to establish a retail price of Fr. 99 ($19.90) for the Swinger; under French law, dealers were permitted to deviate from this price by up to 5 percent, and the prevailing price in larger retail outlets was quickly established at Fr. 94. The price paid by the dealer to Polaroid was Fr. 84.

Retail prices of Polaroid cameras and films are shown in Exhibit 6.

ADVERTISING AND PROMOTION

During 1966, Polaroid France spent some $600,000 on advertising, of which slightly over half was devoted to the introduction of the Swinger. The budget for 1967 was somewhat lower at around $550,000. About 40 percent of the total was devoted to magazines, 50 percent to newspapers, and 10 percent to cinema advertising.[1]

Because Polaroid cameras were much less well known in France than in the United States, a major objective of Polaroid advertising was to increase consumers' awareness and understanding of the "instant picture" idea. According to studies by the company's marketing research department, in early 1966 fewer than 5 percent of French consumers demonstrated "proved awareness" of Polaroid Land Cameras, and the level of awareness had increased only slightly by early 1967. A consumer was classified as having "proved awareness" if he or she (1) indicated knowledge of the Polaroid brand name *and* (2) knew of the instant-picture feature. The French level of awareness compared with an esti-

[1] Total advertising expenditures by all photographic manufacturers in France were estimated at $1.8 million in 1965.

mated 85 percent in the United States, 70 percent in Canada, 15 percent in Germany, and 26 percent in the United Kingdom. An illustrative Swinger advertisement from the 1966 introductory campaign is shown in Exhibit 7.

A major obstacle to increasing awareness of Polaroid was the fact that commercial television was not available in France. Polaroid marketing executives believed that television had been a major factor in the growth of Polaroid sales in the United States, and in other countries where commercial television was available—such as Germany and the United Kingdom—it was used extensively.

To demonstrate the concept of instant photography to French consumers, Polaroid placed considerable reliance on in-store sales demonstrations. The company encouraged dealers to perform demonstrations by offering a free roll or pack of film (eight exposures) for each 14 demonstration photos taken by the dealer. To qualify for this partial reimbursement, the retailer had to send the negative portions of 14 film exposures to the company.

In-store sales demonstrations were also conducted by Polaroid demonstrators. These demonstrators, who were paid Fr. 35 per day, visited retail stores on prearranged schedules to conduct demonstrations of Polaroid cameras before groups of potential customers. Polaroid France provided the films for the demonstrations, provided that the dealer ordered cameras in advance. For example, if the dealer ordered 15 pack cameras, the company provided six packs of black-and-white film and three packs of color film for use in the demonstrations.

Total expenditures for promotion in 1966 amounted to $200,000 and approximately the same amount was budgeted for 1967. Polaroid marketing executives were not satisfied with the dealers' participation in the promotion program. Mr. Wyman, vice president–sales of Polaroid Corporation, wrote to M. Dumon in May 1967, stating that "it appears that the dealer is not demonstrating cameras as frequently and as skillfully as we should like."

1966–1967 RESULTS AND 1968 PROSPECTS

Sales and profits of Polaroid France during 1966 and the first half of 1967 had not lived up to expectations. As shown in Exhibit 8, a net loss was incurred in 1966. Moreover, by July it was apparent to M. Dumon and to the Polaroid headquarters marketing staff that the goals set for 1967 would not be attained. Hence, a revised plan was prepared calling for lower sales volume and lower levels of expenditure.

Polaroid's other European subsidiaries were also below the levels planned for 1967, but not to the same degree as in France. In several countries, including Italy, Switzerland, and Belgium, Polaroid's estimated share of the camera market was significantly higher than in France. Polaroid's market penetration was about the same in France, Germany, and the United Kingdom, however, despite much higher levels of consumer awareness in the latter countries. In some other countries, the company's advertising expenditures were proportionately higher than in France; with the French 1966 expenditure per camera sold set as 100, indexes of cost per unit for Germany, the United Kingdom, and Italy were 112, 133, and 120, respectively.

For 1968, it was anticipated that the French camera market would grow very slightly, if at all. No major competitive new product introductions were anticipated. Polaroid was contemplating the introduction of a new camera model in the United States around mid-year, but production would probably not be adequate to meet worldwide demand until the end of the year. Consequently, M. Dumon's plans for 1968 were to be based on the same basic product line as in 1967.

In considering his marketing program for 1968, M. Dumon was especially concerned with the problems of pricing and promoting the Swinger. With regard to pricing, he wondered whether he should recommend that the company apply for a 1-year continuance of government approval for resale price maintenance. The current approval was due to expire on August 1, 1967, and M. Dumon felt that there might be some advantages in allowing completely free pricing after that date. On the other hand, he did not want to lose any of the distribution which had been so carefully built up during the preceding year, on account of "cutthroat" price competition by the discount stores.

The problem of promotion was a chronic one for Polaroid. Awareness of the Polaroid name and instant-picture feature had increased only slightly between early 1966 and early 1967, and even Polaroid camera owners displayed a lack of full understanding of some important features. For example, among a group of 100 Swinger owners interviewed in June 1967, nearly half did not realize that it was possible to obtain duplicates of Polaroid pictures from the company's print copy service.

Although the need for further consumer education about Polaroid photography seemed great, it was also clear that advertising had played a very important role in building demand during 1966 and 1967. Among a sample of Swinger owners interviewed in November 1966, 53 percent mentioned advertising as their original source of information about the camera; 5 percent mentioned conversations with photo dealers, and 5 percent in-store demonstrations.

M. Dumon wanted to recommend a program which would contribute to the company's longer-term marketing goals in France. At the same time, he was aware of the need to improve current operating results. He had recently received a letter from Mr. Wyman, indicating that "we must be in a position, with a prepared advance plan, to reduce expenditures and limit our activities to insure that we are producing a profit for the year."

EXHIBIT 1
SALES AND NET EARNINGS OF POLAROID CORPORATION IN THE UNITED STATES AND CANADA, 1950–1966
Polaroid France (S.A.)

Year	Sales (\$ thousand) U.S. only	Sales (\$ thousand) U.S. & Canada	Net earnings (\$ thousand) U.S. only	Net earnings (\$ thousand) U.S. & Canada
1950	NA	\$ 6,390	NA	\$ 726
1951	NA	9,259	NA	512
1952	NA	13,393	NA	597
1953	NA	26,034	NA	1,415
1954	NA	23,500	NA	1,153
1955	NA	26,421	NA	2,402
1956	NA	34,464	NA	3,667
1957	NA	48,043	NA	5,355
1958	NA	65,271	NA	7,211
1959	\$ 89,487	89,919	\$10,750	10,743
1960	98,734	99,446	8,838	8,813
1961	100,562	101,478	8,008	8,111
1962	102,589	103,738	9,872	9,965
1963	122,333	123,459	11,078	11,218
1964	138,077	139,351	18,105	18,323
1965	202,228	204,003	28,872	29,114
1966	316,551	322,399	47,594	47,963

Source: Company annual reports.

207

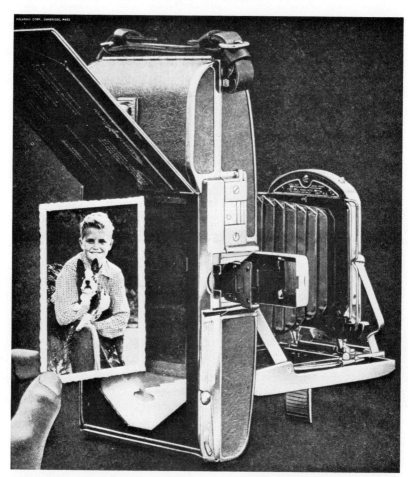

How to take a picture 1 minute and see it the next! Today's Polaroid Land Camera is a magnificent photographic instrument that not only takes beautiful pictures—but develops and prints them as well. With this camera in your hands, you are a magician, who can produce a finished print in 60 seconds. You are a professional photographer, fully equipped to produce expert pictures—clear, sharp, lasting black and white prints—on the spot. Whether you own several cameras or have never even owned one, you will have to own a Polaroid Land Camera. Ask your dealer to show you this remarkable instrument. There are three to choose from, including a new smaller, lower-priced model. *the amazing* **POLAROID** *Land* **CAMERA**

American Girl July 1966 Pg. B/W Bld
This Advertisement prepared by DOYLE DANE BERNBACH, INC
For Polaroid Corp. Job no. PO 611

EXHIBIT 4

PARTIAL ORGANIZATION CHART: EUROPEAN MARKETING ACTIVITIES, 1967
Polaroid France (S.A.)

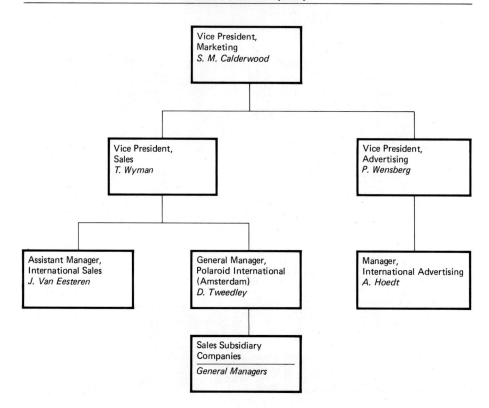

EXHIBIT 5
ORGANIZATION CHART, 1967
Polaroid France (S.A.)

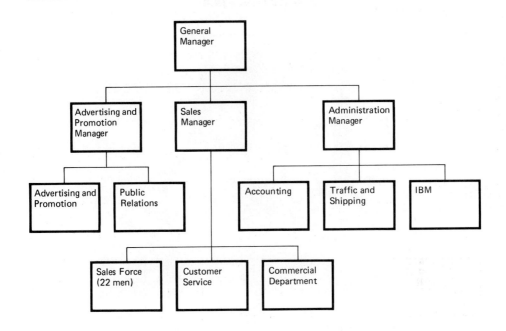

EXHIBIT 6
RETAIL PRICES OF POLAROID CAMERAS AND FILM AND OF MAJOR COMPETING PRODUCTS: UNITED STATES AND FRANCE, 1967
Polaroid France (S.A.)

Camera model or film type	U.S. typical prices	France* Typical prices	France* Lowest discount prices
Cameras:			
Polaroid Swinger	$17.00		$19.08
Polaroid Model 104	40.00	$70.04	67.40
Kodak Instamatic 104	13.50	15.00	
Films:			
Polaroid Type 20	1.77	2.01	
Pack Film, color	4.49	5.03	
Pack Film, black and white	2.09	2.48	
Kodak Instamatic color film:			
Per pack (12 prints)	1.24	0.97	
Per finished print	0.44	0.45	

* French prices include taxes on "value added" of approximately 20 percent of retail price.

"POLAROID" est la marque déposée de Polaroid Corp. Cambridge, Mass. U.S.A.
"SWINGER" est la marque déposée de Polaroid Corp. Cambridge, Mass. U.S.A.
"POLAROID" (France) S.A. 115 Rue des Champarons 92 - Colombes

Maintenant
vous pouvez avoir une photo en 15 secondes
avec un appareil Polaroid qui ne coûte que

99 F

Le nouveau "Swinger" Polaroid, c'est vraiment autre chose.

Pour 99 F seulement, voilà un appareil qui vous donne des photos noir et blanc parfaites, bien contrastées, des gros plans et des scènes rapides sensationnels.

Et vous avez en main l'épreuve terminée en 15 secondes.

C'est à peine croyable. Si vous n'avez pas vécu ces 15 secondes, ces 15 "interminables" secondes, vous ignorez encore tout du vrai plaisir de la photo !

Et c'est si facile. Visez, tournez le bouton de temps de pose : quand le mot YES apparaît dans le viseur, déclenchez.

Tirez le film hors de l'appareil et comptez jusqu'à 15 . Détachez l'épreuve du négatif. Et voici, terminée, votre épreuve sur papier.

Le "Swinger", c'est un appareil comme vous n'avez jamais rêvé d'en posséder pour seulement 99 F.

Ne vous privez pas de ce plaisir. Offrez-vous le nouveau "Swinger" Polaroid. Il est sensationnel.

SWINGER POLAROID

15 secondes après, la voici.

212

EXHIBIT 8

CONDENSED OPERATING STATEMENT AND UNIT SALES OF CAMERAS, 1966–1967, IN THOUSANDS OF DOLLARS

Polaroid France (S.A.)

	1966 actual	1967 original plan	1967 revised estimate
Net sales	$ 5,640	$ 8,800	$ 7,300
Cost of goods sold	3,950	6,170	5,150
Gross margin	$ 1,690	$ 2,630	$ 2,150
Advertising and promotion costs	800	750	630
Selling costs	150	370	370
General and administrative costs	1,000	850	750
Operating profit	($ 260)	$ 660	$ 400
Unit sales:			
Pack cameras	25,000	30,000	25,000
Swinger cameras	85,000	115,000	95,000

COMMUNICATIONS POLICY

A. ADVERTISING AND PROMOTION

B. PERSONAL SELLING

Communications policy is a critical ingredient in virtually all marketing programs. Even a well-designed product or service, intended to satisfy a pressing consumer need, will have scant opportunity to do so unless target consumers (1) are aware that it exists, (2) understand what it is supposed to do for them, and (3) have at least some idea of where or how to obtain it. While communications policies frequently have objectives which are considerably more elaborate and complex than those suggested above, it is difficult to imagine any marketing program that does not have to accomplish at least these minimum objectives.

In developing a communications program, the marketer must determine (1) who are to be the targets of its communications program, (2) what is to be communicated, (3) how much communication will be necessary, (4) which means of communication are to be used, and (5) whether the expected results of the proposed communications program will produce a positive profit impact after taking communications costs into account.

TARGETS

The appropriate audiences for a communications program generally depend on (1) the target market segment(s) of the overall marketing program and (2) the nature of the purchase decision process in these market segments. Based on an understanding of his or her firm's marketing strategy, the marketing manager must determine which households or organizations are to be communicated with, and which individuals in those households or organizations will either make the purchase decisions or influence it to a significant degree.

Consider, for example, a specialized manufacturer of ceramic crucibles used to pour molten steel produced by blast furnaces. In selecting the appropriate audiences for its communications program, such a manufacturer might usefully develop a complete listing of all blast furnaces in the United States, categorized by geographic location, capacity, size and nature of the firm, and (possibly) current purchasing behavior. Using these data, the crucible manufacturer might then determine which segment or segments of this market should be the target(s) of its overall marketing strategy, and what priorities to assign to each market segment or even to each potential customer.

Having thus decided which organizations are to be the targets of its market-ing program, the crucible manufacturer would then determine which individuals (or positions) in the target firms play significant roles (as purchasers or in-fluencers) in the purchase decision process for crucibles. In this case, it might be determined that purchasing agents play the decisive role in the purchase of rou-tine items consumed in the manufacturing process (such as crucibles), but that production foremen have strong views regarding the ostensible advantages of competitive brands of crucibles, and that top executives of steel mills regularly review supply arrangements for items such as crucibles to be assured of guaran-teed availability during periods of strikes or shortages. Under these circum-

stances, the crucible manufacturer might decide that all these members of the purchase decision-making unit (DMU) should be recipients of its communications, although to different degrees.

Defining target audiences for consumer goods is generally an equally complex process. The manufacturer of a new children's breakfast cereal, for example, might define its target market segment as households with children, or as households with two or more children below the age of 12 who currently are or are not heavy users of children's breakfast cereals, or even as households which, for one reason or another, are currently heavy users of a particular competitive brand.

Once the cereal manufacturer has decided which households are to be the targets of its marketing program, it must then determine which members of these target households are instrumental in the breakfast cereal purchase decision process. While the purchase may be made by an adult member of the household, the children themselves may provide major inputs to the decision process. As in the case of the ceramic-crucible manufacturer described above, the appropriate audience for this manufacturer's communications program might usefully include several members of the DMU.

MESSAGES

The marketer's next task is to determine what message or messages to communicate to each of the audience segments. At a conceptual level, such messages may be viewed as satisfying each audience segment's need or desire for information relevant to the purchasing process.

An audience segment's need for information may generally be ascertained by answering such questions as: (1) what stage is our product or service in the product life cycle; (2) at what stage is the audience segment along the awareness → trial → repurchase continuum; (3) what, specifically, is our product or service intended to do for members of the audience segment; (4) how does our product or service compare with available alternatives; (5) what role does this audience segment play in the household or organizational purchase decision process?

The position of the product in the product life cycle will often determine what information it is desirable to communicate. For a totally new product category (e.g., an optical scanner to be used in automated typesetting), the initial communications task may simply be to create awareness that it is now possible to do something which was not previously feasible. However, for a new entry in an existing product category, such as a new type of potato chip, it may be necessary not only to announce that the new product is now available but also to describe its benefits relative to alternatives.

Once the target audience is aware that the new product or service exists, and—in general terms—of what it is supposed to do, a common communications objective is to obtain trial or direct exposure. In the case of frequently purchased consumable goods (e.g., ceramic crucibles, potato chips), it is generally necessary to communicate convincing reasons why the target should deviate from a relatively well-established, routinized purchasing pattern. In the case of infrequently purchased durable or capital goods (e.g., furniture, typesetting systems), the most appropriate communications objectives may be (1) to convince members of the target audience to consider the product or service when they next enter the market and (2) to explain how they should go about doing so.

After the target audience has been directly exposed to the new product or service, whether through actual trial or (say) a demonstration, the marketer's communications objectives may shift to ensuring that the target audience is fully aware of the various uses and advantages of what is being marketed. While also relevant earlier in the communications cycle, it is at this stage that the differing information needs of individual members of the DMU may be most significant. In the case of the optical scanner cited above, for example, it may initially be critical to inform all members of the target DMU that the new product exists, that it is made by the XYZ Company, and that it is now possible to get further information, observe the equipment in operation, etc. Once these communications objectives have been accomplished, however, it may be appropriate to convey different messages to the potential customers' top managements, technical staffs, production people, and (perhaps) stockholders and bankers.

In designing messages for specific audience segments, it is generally useful to determine what the product or service being marketed is intended to do for the recipient of the message. While it may be noteworthy that the ceramic crucible described above is baked at an exceptionally high temperature and allowed to cool slowly, these aspects of the crucible manufacturer's production process are unlikely to be of obvious relevance to that firm's target audiences. The manufacturing process may, however, be highly relevant to the purchasing agent if it is related to fewer rejects at the time of delivery; to the shop foreman if it is related to greater consistency and thus fewer problems at the critical moment when molten steel is being poured; and to steel mill top management if it is related to a large buffer stock which can be deployed at times of peak demand or product shortages.

In a similar vein, the consumer products manufacturer will generally find it useful to focus on what its product is intended to do for individual members of its target audience, rather than on the product itself. A good-tasting, nutritious children's cereal may, for example, provide a parent with a convenient way of preparing a quick, wholesome breakfast during the morning rush of getting the kids off to school, or simply with something a 3-year-old will eat rather than throw on the floor. For the child, however, the most salient message may be that the cereal tastes good, or that it is fun to eat, or that the box contains a "Buck Rogers Super Laser Space Ring," in that eating this cereal makes one feel like a big game hunter, secure against childhood fantasies of rampaging lions and tigers.

INTENSITY

Having selected the target audiences for a communications program and delineated the messages to be communicated to these audiences, it is then necessary for the marketing manager to determine what level of communications effort is necessary to achieve the desired effects. To a considerable extent, the appropriate intensity of a communications program will be a function of (1) the nature of the message to be communicated, (2) the number of targets to be reached, (3) the receptivity of the audience to the message, (4) the intensity of competitive communications activities, and (5) the amount of funds available for the communications effort.

Some messages simply require more time and effort to communicate than others. At one extreme, a new entry in an existing product category (e.g., a new flavor in an established line of soft drinks), which requires no major behavioral change of the target consumer, generally calls for only a low level of communications intensity. In effect, all that is necessary is to inform the target consumer that the new flavor is now available and is worthy of trial. At the other extreme, a complex new product such as the optical scanner cited above, which performs a new function in a new way and necessitates major changes in the production process where it is to be used, is likely to require an extremely intensive communications effort.

In general, a greater intensity of communications effort is required when a new product is introduced than later in the product life cycle. At the time of product introduction, it is often necessary to inform the communications targets (1) that the new product exists, (2) what it is supposed to do, (3) what its major features and benefits are, (4) what it costs, and (5) where or how to buy it. As an increasing percentage of the target audience becomes aware of the product's existence and major attributes, it may only be necessary to remind potential customers of these facts or to stress particular product benefits.

The number, heterogeneity, and receptivity of members of the target audience have a significant influence on the necessary level of communications effort. In general, a greater level of communications effort is needed to reach a lot of people than to reach a few people, or to reach separate audiences with different messages than to reach a single audience with a single message. Similarly, it often requires less effort to communicate a message when the audience is actively seeking information of the kind being communicated (e.g., gasoline mileage data in 1975) than to communicate the same message to a relatively passive audience (e.g., gasoline mileage data in 1965).

In situations where the purpose of a communications program is to convince potential customers to purchase one brand rather than another which purports to provide a similar benefit, the intensity of competitive communications efforts will often establish a minimum threshold which must be surpassed if the communications program is to achieve its desired effects. If, for example, one brand of analgesic communicates the importance of "getting rapidly into the bloodstream" to the target consumers (say) 10 times per week, it is unlikely that a competitive analgesic, which emphasizes "gentleness to your stomach" will have much impact if it reaches the target only once per week. Similarly, even an exceptional salesperson will find the going tough if a buyer he or she visits only twice a year has lunch weekly with the sales representative of a major competitor.

Ultimately, however, the intensity of a communications program will depend largely on the extent of the target audience's need for information and the willingness of the purchaser to pay for such information. In the case of private label grocery products competing with advertised brands, for example, the higher price necessitated by the communications programs of the advertised brands will only be paid if the target consumer finds the information thus communicated to be worth the difference in price. Not surprisingly, private labels tend to do least well in product categories which present the consumer with considerable perceived risk, or in which it is difficult for the consumer to determine the respective merits of competitive brands. Similarly, consumers who have the least confidence in their purchasing ability are most likely to purchase the more expensive, advertised brands, even though their income levels may be such that they would most benefit from the savings available on the private labels.

MEANS

In seeking to convey messages to its target audiences, a marketer generally has a wide range of possible means of communication: It might, for example, use mass advertising media (e.g., outdoor billboards, television, mass circulation magazines, newspapers), selective advertising media (e.g., FM radio, specialized magazines, the Wall Street Journal*), point-of purchase advertising (e.g., displays, in-store "boutiques," counter cards), direct mail, or personal selling. In choosing among such communications means, a number of considerations are especially significant. First, it is necessary to find a communications means which will actually reach the target audience. Second, it is essential that the communications means is appropriate for the message to be conveyed. Finally, the relative costs of alternative communications means vary widely and must be taken into account in establishing an efficient communications mix.*

In virtually all cases, personal selling is considerably more expensive than the various types of media and nonmedia advertising. According to Sales Management magazine, the typical industrial sales call in early 1975 cost almost $70. By way of contrast, it can be estimated that 20 minutes spent by a retail salesperson explaining the features of a major appliance to a consumer costs perhaps $3; that a high-quality direct-mail piece costs between 25 cents and $1 (including the cost of the mailing list); that selective media cost between 5 and 10 cents per impression (cost per thousand readers or viewers); and that mass media cost as little as 1 cent or less per impression.

Generally, the marketer of a complex technical product (e.g., the optical scanner described above) has no choice but to rely on personal selling, despite its costs, for the bulk of its communications effort. For a product such as this, personal selling effort directed to the various members of the DMU is virtually essential to get the message across. The use of personal selling under these circumstances makes certain that the relevant decision makers and influencers are exposed to the message, makes it possible to custom tailor the message to the information needs of each individual, allows the communicator to respond to questions and objections, and provides an opportunity for feedback. Nevertheless, the salesperson's task, even under these circumstances, can often be simplified or even made possible by an effective media advertising campaign intended to establish credibility and stimulate a need for the information which the salesperson is to provide.

In the case of infrequently purchased, high-ticket shopping goods such as major appliances and furniture, the bulk of the target audience's information needs will generally be satisfied in the retail store through visual inspection, descriptive tickets and price tags attached to the merchandise, and personal selling. Under these circumstances, the marketer's communications effort will generally emphasize retailer "push" rather than direct consumer "pull." Even under these circumstances, however, it may be possible to use media advertising to stimulate primary demand, to presell desirable product features, or to draw consumers to those outlets which carry a particular manufacturer's brand.

At the opposite extreme, marketers of frequently purchased low-ticket convenience goods generally rely on impersonal communications through print or electronic media for the bulk of its communications effort. While package copy or in-store display in a self-service store may communicate part of the message, such means are generally used to reinforce or supplement previous communications through the media.

Depending on the targets of the communications program, the marketer may find it more economical to use either mass media (intended to reach everybody) or selective media (intended to reach targets with specified characteristics). A marketer of disposable diapers, for example, might pay less per impression for a mass medium that reaches both mothers with infants and a lot of other people than for a selective medium which has a higher concentration of mothers with infants in its audience. In making the decision as to which medium to use, the marketer should consider the probability of a particular message getting through to its targets, and the economics of reaching the segments it actually wishes to reach.

The nature of the medium is also relevant to the media selection decision. Certain products (e.g., food preparation gadgets) seem to require visual demonstration as part of their communication programs; television is generally regarded as an excellent medium for this purpose. Other products (e.g., stereo components) seem to need a good deal of detailed descriptive copy, for which magazines seem to be highly appropriate. Supermarkets which seek to communicate reduced prices on specific items for limited periods find newspapers to be an excellent medium because of their low cost, mass audiences, large-page formats, and precisely timed immediate impact on the reader.

ECONOMICS

With few exceptions, the types of communications efforts described in this note require the expenditure of funds by the marketer. Such expenditures can vary from a few hundred dollars for a small retailer, which simply wishes to announce its existence, to many millions of dollars for firms with large sales forces or extensive advertising programs. Whatever the size of a firm's communications budget, however, its costs must ultimately be paid by the purchaser of the firm's products or services.

Alternative communications means differ significantly in the timing with which expenditures take place. A new product introduced with a "pull" advertising campaign, for example, requires an investment in communications "up front," which (hopefully) will be recovered through subsequent purchases. A marketer employing a "push" strategy, conversely, is often able to compensate distribution channels for their communications efforts through extra discounts, in effect a "pay as you go" method of covering communications costs.

Whatever the timing of communications costs, they can only be justified economically if they lead to either a higher price (and unit contribution) or a greater volume than would occur if the communications effort had not taken place. In either event, the product of incremental contribution (if any) multiplied by incremental volume (if any) must exceed the expenditure on communications. The appropriate time frame in which communications costs are to be recovered will, of course, depend largely on the objectives of the communications effort.

SUMMARY

An effective communication policy requires (1) identification of the targets of the communication, (2) development of messages which fulfill the marketer's communications objectives and satisfy the information needs of the targets, (3) determination of the level of communications intensity necessary to achieve the marketer's objectives, (4) selection of the communications means which will reach the marketer's target audiences with the desired messages most effectively and efficiently, and (5) an indication that the economic benefits of a proposed communications program will exceed its cost.

In this note, these steps in the development of a communications policy have been presented in a fixed sequence, as if it were always appropriate for the marketer to begin with step 1 and proceed serially until step 5 is reached. In actual practice, it is generally more fruitful to consider all five steps more or less simultaneously, adjusting the various elements in the communications policy as the program is developed. In this way, consistency among target, message, intensity, means, and economics can be achieved. Such consistency is the primary requisite of an effective communications program.

A. ADVERTISING AND PROMOTION

ACTIVE DETERGENT

STEVEN H. STAR
Associate Professor
Harvard Graduate School of Business Administration

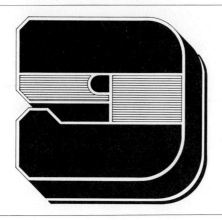

In the late fall of 1974 the Witco Chemical Company of Paterson, New Jersey, announced that it was introducing *Active,* a new, "non-advertised national brand" of laundry detergent in the New England and Washington–Baltimore markets. According to Dr. Marvin Mausner, vice president of Witco's Ultra Division, laundry detergents were one of the most heavily advertised product categories in the United States, with 1974 industry media advertising expected to reach $80 million, 8 percent of industry sales (at manufacturers' prices). Since detergents were a mature product category, such high advertising expenditures were unwarranted in Dr. Mausner's view, especially in an era when consumerism and intense concern over inflationary price increases were so pronounced. In light of this analysis, Witco planned to position Active as a de-

This case has been written from published sources, an address by Dr. Mausner to the Marketing Club of the Harvard Business School, and a number of industry sources who prefer to remain anonymous.

tergent which was "as good as" the nationally advertised brands, but which would sell at a lower price because no money would be spent on consumer advertising. To acquaint consumers with its new product, Witco planned to rely on a public relations program, package copy, and visible shelf locations in supermarkets.

COMPANY BACKGROUND

The Witco Chemical Corporation was one of the world's larger manufacturers of specialty chemical products, with 1974 sales of slightly more than $550 million. Witco's product line covered a wide range of industrial and consumer applications, from private label laundry detergents to diatomaceous earth and urethane chemicals and systems (see Exhibit 1). In 1973, "consumer" markets represented between 18 and 19 percent of Witco's sales. Witco's major consumer products included the Amalie and Kendall brands of motor oil, private label detergents, and lubricants.

Witco had been a major manufacturer of detergents and ingredients used in the manufacture of detergents for many years. In 1973, Witco had detergent sales of approximately $28 million, most of which represented sales of private label detergents to such major retailers as Stop & Shop, Jewel, and Shop Rite. The remainder was sold to other detergent manufacturers. According to industry sources, Witco was, by far, the largest manufacturer of private label detergents in the United States.

Witco's decision to enter the branded detergent business had the twin objectives of increasing Witco's detergent volume and of increasing Witco's profit margin. While a manufacturer of private label detergents (such as Witco) received only about $0.27 per pound (including transportation) for packaged detergents, a national brand manufacturer (such as Procter & Gamble, Lever Brothers, or Colgate) received between $0.33 and $0.37 per pound. No matter how they were marketed, detergents cost from $0.19 to $0.21 per pound to manufacture in late 1974 (including transportation and packaging).

Dr. Marvin Mausner, vice president and technical director of Witco's Ultra Division, was in charge of the technical aspects of the Active project. A Ph.D. in chemistry, Dr. Mausner had specialized in detergents research and development for many years, and had—in his own words—"seen and cleaned more piles of dirty laundry than any woman in the room." By late 1974, Witco had hired several persons with extensive packaged goods marketing experience to develop the Active marketing program.

THE UNITED STATES DETERGENT MARKET

The United States laundry detergent market was estimated at $1.105 billion (at retail prices) in 1974, up 1.4 percent over 1973. While product category unit sales had grown by as much as 5 percent per year in the late 1960s, this rate of growth had slowed considerably in the early 1970s. According to industry observers, this reduction in the industry's growth rate could be attributed to a tendency by consumers (1) to use less detergent in each wash load, (2) to wash more clothes in each load, and (3) to form households later and have fewer children than they had during the 1960s.

The detergent industry was dominated by three large multinational companies: Procter & Gamble, Lever Brothers (a subsidiary of Unilever), and Colgate-Palmolive. These three companies accounted for 91.9 percent of the United States market in 1974, up 1.5 percent from 1973. Private label laundry detergents were estimated to account for less than 5 percent of the United States market in 1974, a notably lower percentage than in most other household-products product categories.

The three industry leaders pursued marketing strategies based on multiple products aimed at individual market segments and on heavy advertising and promotion expenditures. In 1974, Procter & Gamble, with 54 percent of the total market, marketed nine brands of laundry detergent; Lever Brothers (22 percent share) marketed seven brands; and Colgate (15.9 percent share) marketed six brands. During that year, only seven brands had more than 4 percent market share: Tide (P&G), 27.3 percent; Cheer (P&G), 9.3 percent; All (Lever), 9.3 percent; Wisk (Lever), 8 percent; Fab (Colgate), 5 percent; Cold Power (Colgate), 4.7 percent; and Bold (P&G), 4.5 percent. Comparative data on the leading detergent brands are shown in Exhibit 2.

In 1974, P&G, Colgate, and Lever were the first, sixth, and seventh largest advertisers in the United States, allocating the vast bulk of their advertising expenditures to television. According to industry estimates, P&G spent $42.7 million on laundry detergent advertising in 1974, Lever spent $18 million, and Colgate spent $17.2 million. While all three firms used nighttime television to advertise some of their products, the majority of their detergent advertising was on daytime television, especially the so-called "soap operas." (See Exhibit 3 for examples of detergent advertising.) It was estimated that the leading manufacturers in the detergent category spent approximately as much on consumer promotion (e.g., cents-off coupons) and trade promotions (e.g., allowances for special displays) as they did for media advertising.

The vast bulk of laundry detergent sales were through food stores. Detergents were an important product category to food retailers, which frequently sold them at relatively low margins to reinforce their low-price images with consumers. One large supermarket chain in New England devoted 24 linear feet (48 square feet of floor space) to laundry detergents in a "typical" store. During the fourth week of October 1974, this "typical" store sold 384 units of powdered laundry detergents and obtained $522.89 in sales and $61.93 in gross margins from the powdered laundry detergent product category. (See Exhibit 4 for a detailed analysis of an average weeks's laundry detergent sales in this store, and Exhibit 5 for a "Plan-O-Gram" showing shelf locations of individual brands and sizes in this store.) According to the groceries merchandising manager for this chain, detergents were a stable product category which required little management attention.

During recent years, there had been trends in the industry toward low- or nonphosphate detergents, toward larger package sizes, and (most recently) toward phosphate-free liquid detergents. Looking ahead toward 1975, industry observers believed that the laundry detergent product category would grow very little, if at all, in unit volume, although dollar sales might increase as a result of inflation-induced price increases. The new category of liquid laundry detergents was expected to increase in market share, but low- and nonphosphate powdered detergents, such as Arm & Hammer, were not expected to make further inroads. While P&G and Colgate had each increased their market shares by about 1.5 percent in 1974 (Lever and "others" had each lost about 1.5 percent in 1974), no major changes in manufacturers' market shares were anticipated for 1975. It was expected, however, that increased pressure on retail inventories and shelf space might cause major supermarkets to reduce their numbers of stockkeeping units (a single size of a specific brand) in 1975.

The major new branded detergent on the market in 1974 was P&G's Era, a nonphosphate heavy-duty liquid positioned to compete with Lever's Wisk. P&G introduced Era in Oklahoma City and in Portland, Oregon, in November 1972 and gradually expanded east into Kansas City, Wichita, St. Louis, Milwaukee, Chicago, Cincinnati, Cleveland, and Pittsburgh. In each of these markets, it did massive sampling and couponing programs, gave dollar allowances to the trade, and ran saturation TV advertising. Lever countered with a "buy one, get one free" promotion on Wisk, but according to P&G's sales literature, Era still beat it handily. In some markets, Era became the best-selling liquid detergent 2 months after its introduction, and the best-selling of all competitive powders and liquids within 3 months. P&G sources said Era had leveled off to a 6 percent share in its test markets. In October 1974, P&G had begun to introduce Era into New York and New England markets.

Industry sources would not speculate on P&G's total introductory expenditures for Era, but it was known that P&G had spent as much as $25 million to launch Bold detergent in 1965. During the first half of 1973, according to measured media figures, P&G spent $236,400 on Era in Oklahoma City and Portland ($204,400 in spot TV and $32,000 in Sunday newspaper supplements). Measured media sources put spot TV expenditures on Era through the first 6 months of 1974 at about $800,000, but that did not include subsequent outlays for Chicago, Cincinnati, Cleveland, and Pittsburgh. In Milwaukee, during a 1-week period, TV advertising expenditures came to $7,000. According to P&G sources, the TV spots reached "nine out of ten women every four weeks with an average of six Era spots." All spots were 60 seconds. Their theme was "The new detergent that could make your present one obsolete. New Era. Outpowers the powders." P&G did not emphasize the fact that Era did not contain phosphates, largely, it was thought, because P&G still asserted that a small amount of phosphorus was necessary to make an effective powdered detergent.

For the introduction of Gain, P&G had distributed about 40 million samples door to door across the country. The total Era sampling was not expected to be as large, however, because only major metropolitan areas got free samples. Smaller towns got free coupons via mail. In Chicago the sampling consisted of about 1.2 million samples of 16-ounce-size Era (55 cents retail) in sealed bags containing a sales brochure, a 25-cents-off coupon for Downy fabric softener, and a 10-cents-off coupon for two bars of Zest. The Milwaukee distribution was estimated at over 1 million.

ACTIVE

Witco's marketing strategy for Active was based on the premise that a significant segment of consumers would be attracted to a new detergent positioned as equivalent to the nationally advertised brands in ingredients and performance, but considerably less expensive to purchase. According to Dr. Mausner, a homemaker who used Active would receive performance at least as good as that of such national brands as Tide, Cheer, or All. As a mature product category, Dr. Mausner continued, detergents were all essentially the same in performance, although they could differ significantly in color, fragrance, and density. With regard to density and performance, Active was formulated to be "virtually identical" to the best-selling brands.

The package for Active was brightly colored (red, yellow, and blue) to attract consumer attention and contained more body copy than was typical on detergent packages. The Active message, "As good as the advertised brands; less expensive because it is not advertised," was featured in the body copy, as was a "double your money back guarantee if not completely satisfied." According to Dr. Mausner, the Active package was intended to induce consumer trials and to reinforce the Active message once it was in the consumer's home.

Active was to be distributed as intensively as possible through supermarkets and independent grocers. The manufacturer's selling price was to be $9.45 per case of ten 49-ounce packages. Most supermarkets were expected to sell Active for $1.10 to $1.15 per unit. Supermarkets typically obtained 5 to 12 percent gross margins on advertised brands of detergents, which they sold at retail from $1.25 to $1.35 for the 49-ounce size. While supermarkets could obtain gross margins of more than 20 percent on their private label laundry detergents, such private labels, as noted above, accounted for only a small share of industry volume.

Witco planned to use food brokers to sell to retailers, beginning in the New England and Washington–Baltimore markets. These two areas were believed to account for approximately 8 to 10 percent of the laundry detergent market. Food brokers, who did not take title to the merchandise they sold, typically acted as agents for a number of noncompeting manufacturers. They received compensation in the form of a commission on their sales, usually 5 percent of the manufacturer's selling price. In recent years, food brokers had increased in importance in many product categories. While most of the lines they carried were specialty products manufactured by companies which could not afford their own sales forces, there had been a recent tendency for large packaged-food manufacturers to use food brokers for some of their products and their own direct sales forces for others. In following this course, such manufacturers seemed to value highly the long-standing relationships between leading food brokers and major supermarket accounts, and to believe that food brokers could give more focused attention to certain brands than their own multiproduct sales forces.

In the laundry detergent product category, none of the leading manufacturers utilized food brokers. P&G was believed to have the strongest sales force in the packaged-goods industry, while Colgate's and Lever's sales forces were considered very effective. Witco had been able to sign up the leading food brokers in the New England and Washington markets, both of which were highly enthusiastic about having an entry in the detergent product category. Based on early indications from the food brokers, it was anticipated that Active would achieve 80 percent distribution in the New England and Washington–Baltimore markets by mid-1975.

While Active would not be advertised to the consumer, Witco planned some trade advertising in late 1974 and early 1975. These advertisements, which would be placed in such trade publications as *The Griffin Report* of New England and *Food World,* would stress the benefits of the product to the retailer. Among the major benefits to be cited were higher gross margins, a better value to the consumer during a period of rapid inflation, and an image of being responsive to the consumerism movement.

Public relations was to be the primary instrument for acquainting consumers with the fact that Active was on the market. Dr. Mausner and other Witco personnel were to speak to women's groups, educational institutions, trade associations, and consumerist groups throughout the Washington, D.C., and New England markets, to be interviewed by newspaper and magazine "consumer affairs" reporters, and to appear on radio and television talk shows. Based on previous experience, the public relations firm employed for this purpose estimated that as many as 1 million persons would be exposed to Active through the news media by the end of the first quarter of 1975. In support of this projection, they explained that high prices and consumerism issues in general were very topical in early 1975 and that newspapers were always looking for interesting material for their weekly food sections.

EXHIBIT 1
MARKETS SERVED BY WITCO CHEMICAL
Active Detergent

Markets served*	Estimated % of 1973 sales	Typical products furnished
Consumer	18–19	Amalie Motor Oil, detergents, gasoline, Kendall Motor Oil, private label lubes
Plastics	15–16	Cross-linking agents, fillers, mold-release agents, organic peroxides, petrolatums, plasticizers, poly-butylene, process oils, stabilizers, stearates, sulfur-derived chemicals, surfactants, urethane chemicals, waxes, white oils
Rubber	10–11	Antioxidants, carbon blacks, emulsi-fiers, extender oils, mold-release agents, process oils, stabilizers, urethane chemicals
Industrial lubricants	9–10	Blending stocks, bulk lubricants, natural and synthetic petroleum sulfonates, stearates
Construction	6–7	Asphalts, dust control agents, road oils, urethane systems, wood-treating oils
Detergents	5–6	Anticaking agents, detergent alkylates, hydrotropes, surfactants
Drugs, cosmetics, pharmaceuticals & toiletries	5–6	Diatomaceous earth, petrolatums, stearates, sulfur-derived chemicals, surfactants, white oils
Textile	4–5	Antistatic agents, dye assists, sur-factants, urethane chemicals, white oils
Paper and packaging	3–4	Defoamers, polybutylene, stearates, urethane systems, waxes
Agricultural chemicals and animals feedstuffs	2–3	Emulsifiers, larvicides, spray oils, white oils
Primary and fabricated metal products	2–3	Cleaners, coolants, corrosion inhib-itors, defoamers, degreasers, electrode binder pitch, emulsifiers, forming compounds, rust preventives
Energy	1–2	Diesel fuel, fuel oil, kerosene
Food and food processing	1–2	Defoamers, diatomaceous earth, emulsifiers, petrolatums, stearates, white oils
Automotive, chemicals and chemical processing, coatings and inks, furniture and bedding, insulation, oil well drilling	12–13	Activated carbon, asphalts, carbon blacks, chemical intermediates, defoamers, diatomaceous earth, driers, emulsifiers, ink oils, lacquer bases, lubricants, mildewcides, petrolatums, petroleum sulfonates, plasticizers, rust preventives, stearates, undercoatings, urethane chemicals and systems
Total	100	

* Markets served represent areas where the "typical products furnished" by Witco, as listed, are used either by the consumer directly or by industry in further manufacture.

Source: Witco Chemical Annual Report, 1973.

EXHIBIT 2
LEADING LAUNDRY DETERGENTS: MARKET SHARES AND MEDIA ADVERTISING, 1974
Active Detergent

Manufacturer	Brand	U.S. market share, %	New England market share, %	Measured media advertising, $ million
Procter & Gamble	Tide	27.3	18.3	11.5
Lever	All (powder & liquid)	9.3	13.3	7.8
Procter & Gamble	Cheer	9.3	4.8	10.0
Lever	Wisk (liquid)	8.0	13	8.4
Colgate	Fab	5.0	6.2	3.8
Colgate	Cold Power	4.7	6.6	4.0
Procter & Gamble	Bold	4.5	4	4.0
Procter & Gamble	Gain	3.6	1.7	3.3
Procter & Gamble	Dash	3.0	3.8	4.7
Colgate	Ajax	3.0	4	3.2
Procter & Gamble	Oxydol	2.7	3.1	3.2
Colgate	Dynamo (liquid)	2.0	2.6	5.6
Procter & Gamble	Duz	2.0	NA	1.2
Lever	Breeze	1.5	NA	0.7
Lever	Drive	1.3	NA	1.0
Colgate	Punch	1.0	NA	nil
Procter & Gamble	Bonus	1.0	NA	0.1
Church & Dwight	Arm & Hammer	NA	4.9	NA
All others		NA	NA	7.5
		100	100	80

Source: Advertising Age, April 7, 1975; Leading National Advertisers, January–December, 1974; SAMI (courtesy of a supermarket chain which prefers to remain anonymous).

EXHIBIT 3

TELEVISION ADVERTISING (ALL MAJOR BRANDS)

Active Detergent

PRODUCT: TIDE DETERGENT
PROGRAM: EDGE OF NIGHT
WCBS-TV
9/16/74 (NEW YORK)
60 SEC.
2:55 PM

1

WOM: Did you ever watch your little boy when he's helping his father?

2

MAN SINGS: Gary is daddy's little helper.

3

You can tell by his knees how hard he's tried.

4

You get a lot of dirt with children. You get a lot of clean with Tide.

5

Helping dad, a kid gets hungry,

6

and his shirt gets covered with cherry pie.

7

You get a lot of dirt with children. You get a lot of clean with Tide.

8

WOM: Somehow Gary gets twice as dirty as his father.

9

And the dirt's not only on his clothes, it's in them. Ground right through to the inside.

10

Kids' dirt's the worst kind of dirt, but it's the kind of dirt I depend on Tide to get out.

11

See. The shirt's nice and clean.

12

And look how clean Tide got the pants — outside and inside.

13

All ready for Gary to help his father again.

14

MAN SINGS: Tide was designed with mothers in mind. It gets out the dirt kids get into. You get a lot of dirt with children. You get a lot of clean with Tide.

15

ANNCR: Get Tide. 'Cause Tide gets out the dirt kids get into.

231

EXHIBIT 3
Continued

```
PRODUCT:    ALL
PROGRAM:    GIRL IN MY LIFE
            WABC-TV
5/17/74     (NEW YORK)
30 SEC.
2:38 PM
```

1	**2**	**3**	**4**
MAN: Where you going? WOM: To that laundry test.	MAN: But that's my favorite shirt. WOM: Well, it's my favorite laundry problem, greasy oil.	MAN: Move over. If my shirt goes, I go.	Look at these problems.
5	**6**	**7**	**8**
WOM: But our greasy oil is the toughest.	ANNCR: Let's see.	We're dropping greasy oil	into three leading detergent solutions.
9	**10**	**11**	**12**
MAN: Hey, a demonstration. WOM: Don't get excited. Nothing's - -	MAN: Hey, this one's breaking up. WOM: And the others aren't.	ANNCR: What did it? "all" with Bleach, Borax and Brighteners.	WOM: Look. MAN: The greasy oil's gone.
13	**14**		
"all's" what you need to clean the tough stains.	WOM: It's what I need to clean everything.		

EXHIBIT 3
Continued

PRODUCT: LIQUID ALL
PROGRAM: NEWS
WABC-TV
10/8/74 (NEW YORK)
30 SEC.
6:33 PM

1	2	3	4
MAN: She's all set. Here's your warranty,	and here's a surprise. I call it the out-cleaner.	WOMAN: Thanks, but I use this.	MAN: The leading all-temperature powder?

5	6	7	8
Liquid All out-cleans that, in hot, warm and cold water.	WOMAN: Even this greasy shirt?	MAN: Watch. Liquid All is penetrating.	It's lifting out the dirt now.

9	10	11
See? Liquid All out-cleans your powder.	WOMAN: Mine. Yours. I'll take the out-cleaner.	ANNCR: Liquid All — the out-cleaner. In hot, warm and cold water.

233

EXHIBIT 3
Continued

PRODUCT: CHEER DETERGENT
PROGRAM: ANOTHER WORLD
WNBC-TV
7/5/74 (NEW YORK)
60 SEC.
3:15 PM

1

BOY: Hey Mom! Look at Dad's old sweater. 1960, what an antique!

2

WOMAN: Hey Jeff. I was class of '60 myself.
BOY: Unbelievable.

3

You wear stuff like this too?

4

WOMAN: Back then your dad and I looked keen!
BOY: Keen?

5

WOMAN: Groovy
BOY: Huh?
WOMAN: Uh, out of sight.

6

BOY: Right. Can I wear it?
WOMAN: Not till we wash it.
BOY: Okay.

7

WOMAN: Jeffrey, that's hot water. That's a cold thing.
BOY: Cold thing?
WOMAN: Look at the Cheer.

8

See? Different clothes need different temperatures.

9

BOY: Right. Hot or cold?
WOMAN: Uh huh. Cheer's made for all temperatures. Hot for whites, warm for permanent press.

10

BOY: And cold for old stuff.
WOMAN: Cold's for the bright stuff; to protect it from fading.

11

Three temperatures.
One detergent.
BOY: Far out!
WOMAN: Permanent press, whites.

12

BOY: And these colors. Wow!
WOMAN: Jeff, those aren't just colors. That's old pomegranate and puce.
BOY: Pomegranate and puce? Far out!

13

ANNCR: All-temperature Cheer. For the way you wash now.

14

All-Tempa Cheer.

EXHIBIT 3
Continued

```
CLIENT:    LEVER BROTHERS
PRODUCT:  WISK
TITLE:     "CALYPSO"
TIME:      30 SEC.
```

1	2	3	4

MAN: (SINGS) You are doing fine. Now watch your shoulder. Oh, you've got a ring.

Ring around the collar!

Ring around the collar! ANNCR: Those dirty rings.

You try scrubbing,

5	6	7	8

soaking,

and you still have . . . MAN: (VO) Ring around the collar!

ANNCR: Now try Wisk.

Liquid Wisk sinks in

9	10	11	12

and starts to clean

before you start to wash.

MAN: (SINGS) Here's a man with everything. Pretty wife and no more ring. MAN: No more ring.

ANNCR: Wisk around the collar beats ring around the collar every time.

EXHIBIT 3
Continued

PRODUCT: FAB
PROGRAM: MOVIE
            WNBC-TV
2/19/74   (NEW YORK)
30 SEC.
5:29 PM

1	2	3	4

ANNCR: Who can resist them.

Clothes so fresh you know they're deep-down clean.

The kind you get from Fab with Lemon-Freshened Borax.

Lots of things get clothes clean.

5	6	7	8

But only Fab gets all your wash that lemony fresh clean.

Come home to Fab

with Lemon-Freshened Borax.

CHORUS: Oh Fab, we're glad, there's Lemon-Freshened Borax in you.

236

EXHIBIT 3

Continued

PRODUCT: COLD POWER DETERGENT
PROGRAM: PEYTON PLACE
WNBC-TV
1/2/74 (NEW YORK)
30 SEC.
3:39 PM

1	2	3	4

MEADE: This is Julia Meade in Milwaukee, Wisconsin

with the William Paluzzi family. They're concerned about the energy crisis, too.

MAN: We're turning our thermostat down. Not using as much electricity.

WOMAN: And I'm washing in Cold water with Cold Power.

5	6	7	8

I've done so much washing with Cold Power

I'm really convinced clothes come out clean and bright without fading.

MAN: Not using hot water cuts fuel costs, too.

MEADE: Wash with Cold Power.

9

The detergent specially formulated to get your clothes really clean in cold water.

EXHIBIT 3
Continued

PRODUCT: BOLD
PROGRAM: SOMERSET
WNBC-TV
1/8/74 (NEW YORK)
60 SEC.
4:27 PM

1

MAN: Engine trouble, eh Joey?

2

BOY: No. Adjusting the carburetor.
MAN: Dual carburetors?

3

BOY: Of course, Grandpa. All racing cars have dual carbs.

4

(MUSIC) CHORUS SINGS: He's the bold one.
MAN: Your mom's gonna love me when she sees all this dirt.

5

BOY: Race you to the house, Grandpa.

6

CHORUS SINGS: He's the bold one. He's the one for Bold.

7

MAN: Joey sure got dirty.
WOMAN: He always gets dirtier than anyone in the family. But fortunately there's—

8

MAN: Bold huh?
WOMAN: Bold's got so much cleaning energy, I think they made it special for your grandson.

9

MAN: Enough for this, I hope.
WOMAN: The next time Joey wears that shirt he'll look as nice as anyone in the family.

10

You watch. Thank you. Well? MAN: It's dandy.

11

BOY: Want to go to the moon? MAN: The moon?

12

BOY: In my rocket.

13

CHORUS SINGS: He's the bold one. He's the one for Bold.

14

ANNCR: Try Bold.

15

CHORUS: Bold can make the bold one bright.

238

EXHIBIT 3
Continued

PRODUCT: GAIN DETERGENT
PROGRAM: GUIDING LIGHT
WCBS-TV
8/22/74 (NEW YORK)
60 SEC.
2:03 PM

1	2	3	4

GIRL: I hate Norman Brown.
WOM: What happened?
GIRL: He tripped me.

WOM: He sure did.
GIRL: I wanted to wear this to the movies,

and now it's had it. I never want to see him again.

WOM: Norman Brown's form of courtship.
WOM: Gain? I thought we both used —

5	6	7	8

WOM: I switched.
WOM: Switched?

WOM: It smells nice but it's not why I switched.

This dirt, gravy stains, ground-in dirt and grass stains?

Come on, no detergent will get all this out.
WOM: No detergent gets out everything.

9	10	11	12

But Gain's dynamite on dirt and on tough stains like these. You'll see.

WOM: The dirt came out! And the gravy and the grass stains.

WOM: But that's not why I switched to Gain.

GIRL: You got it clean!

13	14	15

WOM: Oh, Molly, she noticed the wash.

WOM: That's why I switched.

ANNCR: Gain gets clothes so clean, people actually notice the difference.

239

EXHBIT 3
Continued

PRODUCT: DASH DETERGENT
PROGRAM: SEARCH FOR TOMORROW
             WCBS-TV
3/21/74   (NEW YORK)
60 SEC.
12:32 PM

1	2	3	4
WOMAN: Richard, I thought the wife did the laundry?	MAN: Momma. While Joan's in school we share the house-work.	WOMAN: Well, you sure didn't learn that from your father. Well, I'll wash later.	MAN: Oh, no. You're our guest. You just have a few things.

5	6	7	8
I'll throw them in with my regular load. This is a big machine.	WOMAN: Are you sure the whole load will get clean? MAN: Uh, huh.	WOMAN: Your apron is mighty dirty. MAN: Momma. That's Joan's.	Don't worry. Joan got Dash.

9	10	11	12
With Dash you can wash a big load and still get it clean. It's concentrated.	Here. Feel. WOMAN: Wow! MAN: Yeah!	WOMAN: You were right about Dash. My extra stuff got really clean.	And look how clean your apron is now. MAN: Momma. I told you. That's not my apron.

13	14
This is my apron.	ANNCR: Try it yourself. Get more clothes really clean. With big machine Dash.

240

EXHIBIT 3
Continued

PRODUCT: AJAX
PROGRAM: ROOKIES
WABC-TV
2/18/74 (NEW YORK)
30 SEC.
8:19 PM

1	2	3	4
WOMAN: Give me strength.	ANNCR: You've got it when you put your wash	in Ajax. (MUSIC)	WOMAN: Oh, give me strength.

5	6	7	8
ANNCR: You've got it when you put your wash in Ajax.	Ajax Laundry detergents. Whiteners, brighteners, sure.	But above all Ajax cleaning strength to really dig dirt. Next time you think . . .	WOMAN: Give me strength.

9	10	11
ANNCR: Think	Ajax.	Ajax gives you strength.

EXHIBIT 3
Continued

PRODUCT: OXYDOL
PROGRAM: SEARCH FOR TOMORROW
WCBS-TV
6/17/74 (NEW YORK)
60 SEC.
12:32 PM

1

JENNY: Ah. There.
You can carry this easily.
WOMAN: Sure Jenny. When
it's empty.

2

MAN: Well, you can practice
by carrying these home.
WOMAN: Oh, no. We're not
buying white jeans.

3

MAN: Why not? WOMAN:
Do you know how dirty
they'll get?

4

JENNY: Oh, what's a
little dirt. Where's your
pioneer spirit?

5

WOMAN: What pioneer
spirit? I can't get white
clean. JENNY: Well chances
are you're not getting colors
clean either.

6

Every try Oxydol?

7

MAN: You mean you sell
detergent too? JENNY: No.
But I do sell clothes. And that's
why I tell folks

8

about Oxydol with bleach.
Bleach whitens. And that's
not all.

9

Oxydol bleach actually
helps break up dirt.

10

Sort of like this. While the
detergent washes it away.

11

WOMAN: Bet even Oxydol
couldn't get this clean.

12

JENNY: You lose. This
smock was as dirty as that.

13

WOMAN: Okay. Pack up the
white.

14

JENNY: I'll even pack up
the Oxydol.

15

Oxydol. For the white
that says the wash is clean.

242

EXHIBIT 3
Continued

PRODUCT: DYNAMO
PROGRAM: MIKE DOUGLAS
              WCBS-TV
5/31/74   (NEW YORK)
30 SEC.
5:48 PM

1	2	3	4
(SILENT)	WOMAN: Oh. Motor oil on your shirt.	WOMAN: You''ll never get that clean.	WOMAN: (LAUGHS) Dynamo will mother.

5	6	7	8
WOMAN: A liquid? WOMAN: Uh uh. A quarter cup cleans the whole wash.	And gets out these oily stains on Clarence's shirt.	No powder can do all that. WOMAN: Sounds expensive.	WOMAN: Uh, uh. Wash for wash costs the same as powders. See. A quarter cup cleaned the whole wash.

9	10	11
WOMAN: Dynamo does more than powders do. ANNCR: For the whole wash.	WOMAN: Right, mother.	ANNCR: With greasy stains Dynamo works better than powders.

EXHIBIT 3
Continued

PRODUCT: DUZ
PROGRAM: LET'S MAKE A DEAL
WABC-TV
8/27/74 (NEW YORK)
30 SEC.
1:48 PM

1	2	3	4

WOMAN: Know what a wool sweater costs now?

Frank could work almost six hours just to pay for a sweater for a ten year old.

So I learned to knit.

When you don't have money, it pays to know little tricks

5	6	7	8

like knitting. Like Duz.

Duz is famous for getting things clean. It costs a little more,

but there's a pretty blue glass in every box. So I don't have to buy glasses.

I'm smart to buy Duz. Even Frank thinks so.

244

EXHIBIT 3
Continued

```
CLIENT:    LEVER BROTHERS
PRODUCT:  BREEZE
TITLE:     "SURPRISE-DOLLY"
TIME:      30 SECONDS
```

1	2	3	4
DOLLY: Folks, I've got something for you.	A surprise package.	That's right. A surprise package.	Because this season, Breeze Detergent is full of new surprises.

5	6	7	8
New rose towels, new solid color towels, and even new candy stripe towels.	Nine colorful towel surprises.	And you can mix 'em or match 'em,	but you can't buy 'em.

9	10	11
You can only get them in boxes of Breeze.	And that's no surprise.	You always collect beautiful towels in Breeze.

EXHIBIT 3
Continued

CLIENT: LEVER BROS.
PRODUCT: DRIVE
TITLE: "LIPSTICK SUN STAIN"
DATE: 11/5/74
LENGTH: 30 SECONDS

1	2	3	4
(GIRLS GIGGLING)	MOTHER: Oh no! Lipstick!	How'll my detergent wash that out? LADY: Relax.	We'll use Drive with Stain Eraser . . .(PULLS OUT STICK)

5	6	7	8
Ta da!!	MOTHER: Drive's Stain Eraser?	LADY: Puts extra cleaning power where you need it . . . right on the stain.	MOTHER: You rub it on? LADY: Yeah . . . It's got concentrated stain fighters.

9	10	11	12
Then Drive's powder does the rest.	They team up to fight tough stains.	LADY: Ta Da!!! MOTHER: Lipstick's gone! It's clean!	ANNCR: Only Drive has Stain Eraser. Puts extra cleaning power where you need it.

EXHIBIT 3
Continued

PRODUCT: BONUS DETERGENT
PROGRAM: HOGAN'S HEROES
           WKPC-TV
7/27/73   (CINN.)
60 SEC.
6:32 PM

1

WOMAN: Okay, open your eyes.

2

GIRL: Oh mom, the bathroom looks so pretty.

3

MAN: It's all red, white, and blue.

4

WOMAN: I just did a few things here and there.

5

GIRL: Look, we got new towels. Oh, red, white, and blue ones.

6

MAN: Sara, they really cheer up the old bathroom. But they look so expensive. They're textured.

7

WOMAN: Honey, they're the new red, white, and blue towels you get from Bonus Detergent.

8

GIRL: It's so soft.

9

BOY: Smells good too. WOMAN: You get a fluffy red, white, and blue one in every box of Bonus.

10

MAN: In the Bonus we use?

11

WOMAN: That's right. The same Bonus that gets Jimmy's baseball shirt really white.

12

BOY: Yeah, it was really dirty. MAN: That's terrific. And the red, white, and blue towels are great too.

13

GIRL: They really are pretty, Mom.

14

BOY: Yeah. Now at least it'll be fun to take a bath.

15

ANNCR: From Bonus. New red, white and blue towels.

247

EXHIBIT 4
SALES OF POWDERED LAUNDRY DETERGENTS IN ONE "TYPICAL" SUPERMARKET: OCTOBER 21–26, 1974
Active Detergent

Item	Cost/ unit	Retail/ unit	Weekly sales units	Weekly sales dollars	Weekly gross profit	Approx. linear feet
Tide:						
20 oz.	$0.47	$0.53	56	$ 29.68	$ 3.36	3.4
49 oz.	1.12	1.27	39	49.53	5.85	7.2
84 oz.	1.87	2.13	18	38.34	4.68	2.4
All:						
49 oz.	$0.99	$1.15	32	$ 36.80	$ 5.12	7.2
157 oz.	2.97	3.29	11	36.19	3.52	2.4
320 oz.	5.95	6.29	6	37.74	2.04	3.0
Cheer:						
49 oz.	$1.12	$1.27	18	$ 22.86	$ 2.70	2.4
84 oz.	1.87	2.13	6	12.78	1.56	1.8
Fab:						
20 oz.	$0.47	$0.53	26	$ 13.78	$ 1.56	1.8
49 oz.	1.12	1.27	15	19.05	2.25	3.0
84 oz.	1.87	2.13	6	12.78	1.56	1.8
Cold Power:						
49 oz.	$1.12	$1.27	18	$ 22.86	$ 2.70	2.4
84 oz.	1.87	2.13	8	17.04	2.08	1.8
Bold:						
84 oz.	$1.87	$2.13	7	$ 14.91	$ 1.82	1.8
Gain:						
49 oz.	$1.12	$1.27	9	$ 11.43	$ 1.35	1.8
Dash:						
49 oz.	$0.99	$1.15	8	$ 9.20	$ 1.28	2.4
157 oz.	2.97	3.29	5	16.45	1.60	1.8
Ajax:						
49 oz.	$1.12	$1.27	9	$ 11.43	$ 1.35	2.4
84 oz.	1.87	2.13	1	2.13	0.26	1.8
Oxydol:						
49 oz.	$1.12	$1.27	9	$ 11.43	$ 1.35	2.4
Duz:						
50 oz.	$1.35	$1.47	4	$ 5.88	$ 0.48	2.4
Miracle White:						
49 oz.	$1.08	$1.27	3	$ 3.81	$ 0.57	1.8
Instant Fels:						
49 oz.	$1.13	$1.27	5	$ 6.35	$ 0.70	1.8
Arm & Hammer:						
30 oz.	$0.47	$0.54	15	$ 8.10	$ 1.05	1.8
70 oz.	1.08	1.25	16	20.00	2.72	1.8
115 oz.	1.68	1.99	6	11.94	1.86	3.0
Private label:						
49 oz.	$0.82	$1.05	12	$ 12.60	$ 2.76	5.4
84 oz.	1.38	1.62	12	19.44	2.88	8.4
160 oz.	1.86	2.09	4	8.36	0.92	1.8
Total			384	$522.89	$61.93	83.2

EXHIBIT 5
PLAN-O-GRAM OF LAUNDRY DETERGENTS SECTION:
ONE "TYPICAL" SUPERMARKET, OCTOBER 1974
Active Detergent

Dimensions across top: 24½ inches | 13 inches | 15½ inches | 19 inches

Related product category

Other	Dash 49 oz	Duz 50 oz	Instant Fels 49 oz	Arm & Hammer 30 oz	Tide 20 oz	Miracle White 49 oz	Fab 20 oz.
All 157 oz	Private label 84 oz	All 49 oz	Private label 49 oz	Private label 160 oz	Arm & Hammer 70 oz	Ajax 49 oz	Oxydol 49 oz
All 320 oz	Dash 157 oz	Fab 84 oz	Private label 49 oz	Cheer 49 oz		Tide 49 oz	
	Arm & Hammer 115 oz			Private label 84 oz			Tide 84 oz

Gain 49 oz | All 49 oz | Cold Power 49 oz | Fab 49 oz | Ajax 84 oz

Other | Bold 84 oz | Cheer 84 oz | Cold Power 84 oz | Bold 84 oz

24 linear feet

6 feet

249

SOUTHWEST AIRLINES: I

CHRISTOPHER H. LOVELOCK
Assistant Professor
Harvard Graduate School of Business Administration

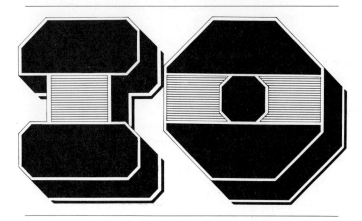

"Y'all buckle that seat belt," said the hostess over the public address system, "because we're fixin' to take off right now. Soon as we get up in the air, we want you to kick off your shoes, loosen your tie, an' let Southwest put a little love in your life on our way from Big D to Houston." The passengers settled back comfortably in their seats as the brightly colored Boeing 737 taxied down toward the takeoff point at Dallas's Love Field airport. Moments later, it was accelerating down the runway and then climbing away steeply into the Texas sky on the 240-mile flight to Houston.

On the other side of Love Field from the airport terminal, executives of Southwest Airlines ignored the noise of the departing aircraft, which was clearly audible in the company's modest but comfortable second-floor offices next to the North American–Rockwell hangar. They were about to begin an important meeting with representatives from their advertising agency. In just 2 weeks' time, on July 9, 1972, the airline would be raising its basic fare from $20 to $26. One problem was how to break the news of this increase to the public. This issue had to be resolved within the context of developing future advertising and promotional strategy for the airline as it moved into its second year of revenue operations.

COMPANY BACKGROUND

Southwest Airlines Co., a Texas corporation, was organized in March 1967. The founder, Rollin W. King, had graduated from the Harvard Business School in 1962 and was previously an investment counselor with a San Antonio firm. From 1964, Mr. King (who held an airline transport pilot's license) had also been president of an air taxi service operating from San Antonio to various smaller south Texas communities.

From the middle 1960s onward, Rollin King and his associates became increasingly convinced that there was an unmet need for improved air service within Texas between the major metropolitan areas of Houston, Dallas–Fort Worth, and San Antonio. These four cities were among the fastest growing in the nation. By 1968 the Houston standard metropolitan statistical area had a population of 1,867,000. Dallas's population was 1,459,000, San Antonio's 850,000, and Forth Worth's 680,000. The cities of Dallas and Fort Worth were located 30 miles apart in northeastern Texas but were frequently thought of as a single market area. Although each had its own airport—with Dallas's Love Field the busier of the two and the only one served by the airlines—construction had recently begun on the huge new Dallas–Forth Worth Regional Airport, located midway between the two cities and intended to serve both.

Air service between these market areas was provided primarily by Braniff International Airways and Texas International Airlines. In 1967, Braniff operated a fleet of 69 jet and turboprop aircraft on an extensive route network, with a predominantly north-south emphasis, serving major United States cities, Mexico, and South America. Total Braniff revenues in that year were $256 million, and it carried 5.6 million passengers. Texas International Airlines (then known as Trans-Texas Airways) was a regional carrier serving Southern and Southwestern states and Mexico. In 1967, it operated a fleet of 45 jet, turboprop, and piston-engined aircraft on mostly short-haul routes, carrying 1.5 million passengers and generating total revenues of $32 million. Both Braniff and TI were headquartered in Texas.

Service by these two carriers within Texas represented legs of much longer, interstate flights, so that travelers flying from Dallas to San Antonio, for example, might find themselves boarding a Braniff flight which had just arrived from New York and was calling at Dallas on its way to San Antonio. Local travel between Dallas and Houston (the most important route) averaged 483 passengers daily in each direction in 1967, with Braniff holding an 86 percent share of this traffic (Exhibit 1).[1] Looking back at the factors which had first stimulated his interest in developing a new airline to service these markets, Mr. King recalled:

The more we talked to people, the more we looked at figures of how big the market was and the more we realized the degree of consumer dissatisfaction with the services of existing carriers, the more apparent the opportunities became to us.

[1] Local travel figures excluded passengers who were traveling between these cities as part of a longer journey.

We thought that these were substantial markets, and while they weren't nearly as large as the Los Angeles–San Francisco market, they had a lot in common with it. We knew the history of what PSA had been able to do in California with the same kind of service we were contemplating.[1]

But the main reason Southwest ever got into the business was the lousy job that Braniff and TI were doing. When you went into somebody's office, from whom you were trying to raise money, you weren't faced with telling them why there ought to be another airline serving these markets. Because they all hated Braniff—and to a less extent, TI. So you didn't have the problem of convincing people that there was a need for good air service. The only problem we had was convincing them that we were going to do the thing first class, so that there was a chance of having some success financially.

On February 20, 1968, the company was granted a Certificate of Public Convenience and Necessity by the Texas Aeronautics Commission, permitting it to provide intrastate air service between Dallas–Fort Worth, Houston, and San Antonio, a triangular route structure with each leg ranging in length from roughly 190 to 250 miles (Exhibit 2). Since the new airline proposed to confine its operations to the state of Texas, its executives maintained that it did not need certification from the federal Civil Aeronautics Board.

The following day, Braniff and Texas International initiated a lawsuit in the Texas courts, seeking to enjoin issuance of the Texas certificate. These two airlines already offered service on the proposed routes and considered the market insufficiently large to support entry of another airline. More than 3 years of legal maneuvering followed, including a refusal by the U.S. Supreme Court to review the case (thus upholding the issuance of the Texas Certificate to Southwest). Failing in their efforts, Braniff and TI then went before the Civil Aeronautics Board, arguing that Southwest should be regulated by that Board. Without CAB regulation, Southwest would have a great deal more freedom of operation than its competitors, and could set fares without CAB approval.[2] The CAB turned the complainants down, stating that it had no jurisdiction over an intrastate carrier. These legal battles cost the new airlines $530,000 before its first flight ever left the ground and reportedly cost Braniff more than twice as much.

Although this extensive litigation delayed the start of Southwest operations by several years, management felt that the net effect had been beneficial in terms of both the equipment finally purchased and the makeup of the management team.

During the summer of 1970, Rollin King was approached by M. Lamar Muse, an independent financial consultant, who had resigned the previous fall as president of Universal Airlines—a Detroit-based supplemental carrier—over a

---

[1] Pacific Southwest Airlines had built up a substantial market share on the lucrative Los Angeles–San Francisco route, as well as on other intrastate operations within California.

[2] The Civil Aeronautics Board regulated the activities of all interstate airlines in matters such as fares and routes, but had no authority over airlines operating exclusively within a single state. [The CAB should not be confused with the Federal Aviation Administration (FAA), which regulated safety procedures and flight operations for all passenger airlines, including intrastate carriers.]

disagreement with the major stockholders on their planned purchase of Boeing 747 jumbo jets. Mr. Muse had read of Southwest's legal battles and told Mr. King and his fellow directors that he would be interested in helping them transform the company from "a piece of paper" into an operating airline.

The wealth of experience which Lamar Muse could bring to the new airline was quickly recognized. Before assuming the presidency of Universal in September 1967, he had served for 3 years as president of Central Airlines, a Dallas-based regional air carrier. Prior to 1965, Mr. Muse had served as secretary-treasurer of Trans-Texas Airways, as assistant vice president–corporate planning of American Airlines, and as vice president–finance of Southern Airways. After working informally with Southwest for a couple of months, Mr. Muse became an employee of the company in October 1970 and was elected president, treasurer, and a director on January 26, 1971. Mr. King was named executive vice president–operations at the same time.

One of the reasons he was attracted to Southwest, Lamar Muse explained, was that:

> I felt the interstate carriers just weren't doing the job in this market. Every one of their flights was completely full—it was very difficult to get reservations. There were a lot of cancelled flights; Dallas being Braniff's base and Houston TI's base, every time they had a mechanical problem it seemed like they always took it out on the Dallas–Houston service. From Dallas south to San Antonio and Houston is the tag end of Braniff's system, everything was turning around and going back north to Chicago or New York or wherever. There was so much interline traffic that most of the seats were occupied by those people. While Braniff had hourly service, there really weren't many seats available for local passengers. People just avoided flying in this market—they only went when they had to.

In discussing the characteristics of Braniff and Texas International, Mr. Muse stated that the former's reputation for punctuality was so poor that it was popularly referred to by many travelers as the "world's largest unscheduled airline."

Optimistic about the outcome of Southwest's legal battles and content to leave such matters to the company's lawyers, Messrs. Muse and King spent many weeks on the West Coast in late 1970 and early 1971 prospecting for new aircraft. There was a recession in the airline industry at the time, and prospective aircraft purchasers were being courted assiduously. High-pressure negotiations were therefore initiated by Southwest with representatives of McDonnell-Douglas, Boeing, and several airlines for the purchase of new or used jet aircraft.

These negotiations included detailed discussions with Pacific Southwest Airlines (PSA), which was interested in selling Southwest not only aircraft but also crew training, manuals, technical advice, and consulting services. PSA had revolutionized commuter air service in California in the early 1960s, quickly obtaining a significant market share in the face of entrenched competition from United and Western with the aid of reduced fares and aggressive promotion (Exhibits 5 and 6 show examples of PSA advertising in 1969–1970). Although nothing eventually came of the PSA negotiations, Mr. Muse and Mr. King felt that the understanding they had gained of that carrier's activities would prove extremely useful in designing Southwest's own smaller, but not dissimilar operations. Finally, the Boeing Company, which had overproduced its Boeing 737 twin jet (in a speculative assessment of future orders which had failed to materialize), offered both a substantial price reduction and also very favorable financing terms. In March 1971 the Southwest executives signed a contract for three Boeing 737-200 aircraft, some months later increasing their order to four. The total purchase price for the four 737s was $16.2 million and compared with a previous asking price for this aircraft of approximately $4.6 million each.

Mr. Muse and Mr. King were delighted to have obtained such good terms on the 737s, which they regarded as a better aircraft for their purposes than the McDonnell-Douglas DC-9 or other alternatives. The Boeing 737 was a more modern aircraft than the DC-9, having first been introduced into airline service in 1968. It was specially designed for short-distance routes and had been developed by Boeing from their successful long-range, four-engine 707 and intermediate-range, tri-jet 727 airliners. The new model 737-200 had a seating capacity of 112 and incorporated a number of refinements and improvements to the basic design. Nicknamed "Fat Albert" by pilots because of its short, stocky fuselage, the 737 offered the same spacious cabin interior as the larger Boeing 727 (six-abreast seating versus five-abreast in the DC-9) but required a smaller crew.

PREPARING FOR TAKEOFF

Returning to Texas from their successful negotiations in Seattle, Messrs. Muse and King faced some urgent problems and an extremely tight deadline. The start of scheduled operations had been tentatively set for June 18, a little over 4 months away. During this period, Southwest had to raise additional capital to finance both start-up expenses and what might prove to be a prolonged period of deficit operations. The existing skeleton management team had to be expanded by recruiting several new specialist executives, while personnel had to be hired and trained for both flight and ground operations. Meantime, numerous marketing problems had to be resolved and an introductory advertising campaign developed to launch the new airline. Finally, Braniff and Texas International were continuing their legal battles with a view to stifling Southwest.

Southwest's initial proposal had called for the use of fully depreciated, turboprop Lockheed Electra aircraft, and the schedules proposed in the original application before the Texas Aeronautics Commission reflected this fact. The airline's purchase of the Boeing 737 gave Braniff and TI (which operated 727s and DC-9s, respectively, on most of their Texas schedules) an excuse for a last-ditch effort to ground Southwest. Arguing that the purchase of jets was never contemplated in the original application, they jointly obtained a court order enjoining the TAC from allowing Southwest to provide any service other than that originally proposed in 1967—with old equipment and relatively slow schedules. However, on appeal, the injunction was stayed by the Texas Supreme Court and Southwest permitted to initiate operations with the new fleet and schedules.

Once again, legal matters were left to the company's lawyers while the Southwest executives moved quickly to attend to financial, personnel, and marketing problems. An urgent need was to improve the airline's financial position, since at year's end 1970 the company had a mere $183 in its bank account (Exhibit 3). Between March and June 1971, Southwest raised almost $8 million through the sale of convertible promissory notes and common stock. The cover of the stock prospectus, issued on June 8, carried the warning, in heavy black type: "These securities involve a high degree of risk."

Vacancies on the existing management team were soon filled. The man selected as vice president–maintenance, John A. Vidal, had previously been manager of line maintenance for Braniff International and had experience in airline maintenance with four different airlines, dating back to 1946. Recruited as vice president–ground operations was William W. Franklin, a veteran of 23 years' service with Texas International, whose most recent assignment had been 7 years as TI's vice president–customer service. The position of vice president–flight operations was filled by Captain Donald G. Ogden, a 34-year veteran of American Airlines, whose management experience included positions as chief pilot and manager of flying at American's bases in Dallas–Fort Worth, Memphis, Tulsa and Nashville, in addition to his latest position as director of flight standards. To fill the position of vice president–marketing, Southwest succeeded in hiring Richard Elliott, a hard-driving marketing manager formerly with Braniff, who had also held marketing positions with Mohawk Airlines and Central Airlines. Messrs. Vidal, Elliott, and Franklin had all been recently fired by their former employers, Braniff and TI—a fact which Mr. Muse considered one of their strongest recommendations for employment with Southwest.

Considerable marketing planning had taken place while the new staff members were being recruited and initiated into their new jobs. Some decisions, such as route structure and schedules, had already been made earlier. Initially, two of the three Boeing 737s would be placed in service on the busy Dallas–Houston run and the third would fly between Dallas and San Antonio. For the time being, Southwest did not plan to exercise its rights to operate service on the third leg of the triangle between Houston and San Antonio.

Schedule frequency was constrained by aircraft availability. Allowing time for turning around the aircraft at each end, it was concluded that flights could be offered in each direction between Dallas and Houston at 75-minute intervals and between Dallas and San Antonio at intervals of every 2½ hours. Both services were scheduled for 50 minutes. The Monday–Friday schedule called for 12 round trips daily between Dallas and Houston and 6 round trips daily between Dallas and San Antonio. Saturday and Sunday schedules were more limited, reflecting both the lower travel demand at weekends and the need for downtime to service the aircraft.

The pricing decision, meantime, had been arrived at during the Southwest executives' visit to PSA. Rollin King recalled:

What Andy Andrews [President of PSA] said to Lamar and me one day was the key to out initial pricing decision. Andy told us that the way you ought to figure your price is not on how much you can get, or what the other carriers were charging or anything, but that you had to sort of go back and forth. He said, "Pick a price at which you can break even with a reasonable load factor, and a load factor that you have a reasonable expectation of being able to get within a given period of time, and that ought to be your price. It ought to be as low as you can get it without leading yourself down the primrose path and running out of money."

After estimating the amount of money required for preoperating expenditures and then carefully assessing both operating costs and market potential, Muse and King settled on a $20 fare for both routes, with a break-even point of 39 passengers per flight. This compared with existing Braniff and TI coach fares of $27 on the Dallas–Houston run and $28 on the Dallas–San Antonio service.[1] The two executives felt that an average of 39 passengers per flight was a reasonable expectation in light of the market's potential for growth and the frequency of flights Southwest planned to offer, although they projected a period of deficit operations before this break-even point was reached. They anticipated that while Braniff and TI would probably reduce their own fares eventually, Southwest could expect an initial price advantage.

Immediately after returning from Seattle, Lamar Muse got together with vice president–marketing Dick Elliott to select an advertising agency (the company already employed a public relations agency to handle publicity). Several advertising agencies were invited to make presentations for the airline's account, among them The Bloom Agency, which had come to the Southwest executives' attention as a result of a beer advertising campaign which they liked. Messrs. Muse and Elliott were highly impressed by The Bloom Agency's presentation and 2 days later gave them the account. The assignment: Come up with a complete communications program—other than publicity—within 4 months. "We've got no hostesses and no uniforms and no airplanes and no design and no money," Mr. Muse told the agency people, "But we're going to have an airline flying in 120 days!"

Bloom, a large regional advertising agency conveniently headquartered in Dallas, immediately set to work assigning personnel to the account. As account group supervisor, they selected Raymond J. Trapp, an M.B.A. graduate of Northwestern University, who had previously worked for the Ogilvy & Mather agency in New York on Lever Brothers and General Foods accounts.

The account group approached Southwest Airlines, in Ray Trapp's words, "as though it were a packaged goods account." Their first task was to evaluate the characteristics of all American carriers competing in the Texas markets. To facilitate comparisons, Mr. Trapp prepared a two-dimensional positioning diagram, rating each airline's image on "conservative-fun" and "obvious-subtle" dimensions (Exhibit 7). This was based primarily on a content analysis of recent

---

[1] Braniff also offered first class service at a higher fare.

airline advertising, with a view to determining the image conveyed by each carrier.

Texas International was immediately dismissed as dull and conservative with a bland image (Exhibit 11 shows typical TI advertisements of that period). Braniff's advertising, however, presented an interesting contrast in styles. From 1965 to 1968, Braniff had employed the New York agency of Wells, Rich, Greene, which had developed an innovative marketing and advertising strategy for their client, with a budget that exceeded $10 million in 1967. Instead of the traditional, rather conservative airline color schemes then current (typically white and silver with thin, colored stripes along the fuselage), the agency president, Mary Wells, had Braniff's entire fleet of nearly six dozen aircraft painted in a variety of brilliant colors covering the entire fuselage and tail fin. Braniff hostesses were outfitted in "couture costumes" created by the Italian fashion designer Emilio Pucci, while the advertising sought to make flying by Braniff seem a glamorous and exciting experience.

This strategy was believed by many observers to have been an important factor in Braniff's rapid growth during the second half of the 1960s. The airline enjoyed a fruitful relationship with Wells, Rich, Greene until 1968 when the agency resigned the account following Ms. Wells' marriage to Harding Lawrence, president of Braniff International.[1] By 1970, under Clinton E. Frank Inc., the advertising was down to approximately $4 million. The Frank agency still retained Ms. Wells' brightly colored aircraft and Pucci uniforms, but had adopted a subtler, more conservative advertising style (Exhibit 8). Bloom executives concluded that Braniff's image was changing; they had abandoned their initial fun image in favor of chic, leaving a vacuum for Southwest Airlines to occupy. The agency decided to position Southwest even further out on the "fun"-"obvious" side of the old Braniff image.

With this in mind, the account group developed what they termed "an entire personality description model" for the new airline. The objective was to provide the agency's creative specialists with a clear understanding of the image that Southwest should project, so that this might be reflected consistently in every facet of the communications campaign they had to design. This personality statement, which was also used as a guideline in staff recruiting, saw Southwest as "young and vital . . . exciting . . . friendly . . . efficient . . . dynamic."

While copywriters were busy developing advertising themes, other specialists at The Bloom Agency were working feverishly on projects which included research, overall marketing plans, and media evaluation. Personnel from Ernest G. Mantz & Associates, industrial designers, flew out to Seattle to work with Boeing on designing the aircraft interior. Mr. Mantz who had been retained to develop the exterior color scheme and all related corporate image collateral material, worked closely with the agency people. The result was a striking-looking aircraft, painted in red, orange, and earth tones with bold white lettering; the same colors gave a bright, cheerful appearance to the cabin. Meantime,

---

[1] Shortly after, Mary Wells Lawrence won the even larger TWA account.

fashion specialists at Bloom were designing uniforms for the airline personnel. Straightforward navy blue suits and uniform caps were selected for the flight crew, but eye-catching colors and patterns were chosen for the hostesses and counter staff; the hostesses' uniform consisted of orange knit tops, red hotpants, and high, bone-colored boots.

At one point, as many as 30 different people at Bloom were working on the Southwest account, which had a first-year budget of $700,000. An office was found at the agency for Dick Elliott, the airline's marketing vice president, and he, Lamar Muse, and other Southwest personnel were constantly in and out of the agency during this preoperating period. Looking back, one member of the Bloom account group observed, "It was almost as if we were an arm of the airline."

One constraint which restricted marketing activities in the months and weeks prior to passenger operations was the planned issue of over $6 million worth of Southwest stock on June 8. The company's lawyers had advised that a media campaign promoting the airline prior to the stock issue might violate Securities and Exchange Commission regulations against promotion of stock. Virtually the only advertising conducted prior to this date, therefore, was for personnel.

Recruitment advertising in one area proved outstandingly effective, with over 1,200 young women responding to advertisements placed in national media for positions as air hostesses with Southwest. Forty applicants were selected for training, and while airline officials made no secret of the attractive looks of the successful candidates, it was also pointed out that their average scores on the required FAA proficiency test placed the Southwest hostesses among the highest ranked in the nation.

The prohibition on advertising did not entirely keep Southwest out of the news. The airline's continuing legal battles with Braniff and TI received wide press coverage in the mass media, while Southwest's public relations agency put out a number of press releases which subsequently appeared as news or feature stories.

INAUGURATION OF SERVICE:
THE FIRST SIX MONTHS

On June 10, 1971, The Bloom Agency's advertising campaign for Southwest finally broke. It began modestly with small "teaser" advertisements in the newspapers, containing provocative headlines such as "The 48-Minute Love Affair," "At last a $20 ticket you won't mind getting," "Love can change your ways," and "A fare to remember." The ads were unsigned, but contained a telephone number for the reader to call. On phoning, a caller in Dallas would hear the following message:

> Hi. It's us. Southwest Airlines. Us with our brand new, candy-colored, rainbow powered Boeing 737 jets. The most reliable plane flying today. And we start flying June 18, to Houston or San Antonio. You choose—only 45 minutes non-stop. In

that time, we'll be sharing a lot of big little things with you that mean a lot. Like love potions, a lot of attention and a new low fare. Just $20. Join us June 18. Southwest Airlines. The somebody else up there who loves you.

There were approximately 25,000 telephone calls as a result of these teaser ads.

On Sunday, June 13, all newspapers in the three market areas ran a four-color double-truck[1] advertisement for Southwest (see Exhibit 13). On each succeeding day for the next 2 weeks, full-page newspaper ads were run in all markets, each one focusing on the various advantages Southwest Airlines offered the traveler, including new aircraft, attractive hostesses, low fares, fast ticketing, and inexpensive, exotically named drinks. Television advertising was also heavy and included 30-second spots featuring the Boeing 737, the hostesses, and what was referred to as the "Love Machine" (Exhibit 14). Whereas the competition used traditional, handwritten airline tickets, Southwest counter staff accelerated the ticketing process by using a machine to print out tickets and a pedal-operated tape recorder to record the passengers' names for the aircraft manifest as they checked in—both these ideas having been copied from PSA. Rounding out the advertising campaign were strategically located billboards containing painted displays at entrances to all three airports served by Southwest. Nearly half the year's promotional budget was spent in the first month of operations (Exhibit 15 shows a media breakdown of expenditures in 1971 and 1972).

Scheduled revenue operations were inaugurated in a blaze of publicity on Friday, June 18, but it soon became evident that the competition was not about to take matters lying down. In half-truck and full-page newspaper ads, Braniff and TI announced $20 fares on both routes. The CAB had disclaimed authority over intrastate fares, and Texas law barred jurisdiction by TAC over carriers holding Federal Certificates of Public Convenience and Necessity; thus, the CAB carriers were free to charge any fare they wanted. Braniff's advertising stressed frequent, convenient service—"every hour on the hour," hot and cold towels "to freshen up with," beverage discount coupons, and "peace of mind" phone calls at the boarding gate; it also announced an increase in frequency of service between Dallas and San Antonio, effective July 1 (Exhibits 9 and 10). TI, meantime, announced that on July 1 it would inaugurate hourly service on the Dallas–Houston route, leaving Dallas at 30 minutes past each hour. TI also introduced "extras" such as free beer, free newspapers, and $1 drinks on those routes competing with Southwest (Exhibit 12). Southwest then countered with advertising headlined "The Other Airlines May Have Met Our Price But You Can't Buy Love."

Initial results for Southwest, however, were hardly spectacular; between June 18 and 30, there were an average of 13.1 passengers per flight on the Dallas–Houston service and 12.9 passengers on the Dallas–San Antonio route (Exhibit 16). Passenger loads during the month of July showed only a marginal improvement. Southwest management concluded that it was essential to improve schedule frequencies to compete more effectively with those of Braniff

---

[1] *Double truck* is a printer's term used to describe material printed across two full pages. A *half-truck* ad is one printed across two half pages.

and TI. This became possible with the delivery of the company's fourth Boeing 737 in late September 1971. Effective October 1, therefore, hourly service was introduced between Dallas and Houston and flights every 2 hours between Dallas and San Antonio.

Advertising and promotional activity continued with regular television advertising and frequent publicity events, usually featuring Southwest hostesses. A direct-mail campaign was targeted at 36,000 influential business executives living in Southwest's service areas. Each of these individuals received a personalized letter from Lamar Muse describing Southwest service and enclosing a voucher good for half the cost of a round-trip ticket; about 1,700 of these vouchers were subsequently redeemed.

Surveys of Southwest passengers departing from Houston showed that a substantial percentage would have preferred service from the William P. Hobby Airport, 12 miles southeast of downtown Houston, rather than from the new Houston Intercontinental Airport, 26 miles north of the city. Accordingly, arrangements were completed in mid-November for 7 of Southwest's 14 round-trip flights between Dallas and Houston to be transferred to Hobby Airport (thus reopening this old airport to scheduled commercial passenger traffic). Additional schedule revisions made at the same time included a reduction in the number of Dallas–San Antonio flights to four round-trips each weekday, inauguration of three round trips daily on the third leg of the route triangle between Houston (Hobby) and San Antonio, and elimination of the extremely unprofitable Saturday operation on all routes. These actions contributed to an increase in transportation revenues in the final quarter of 1971 over those achieved in the third quarter, but Southwest's operating losses in the fourth quarter fell only slightly, from $1,006,000 to $921,000 (Exhibit 4). At year's end 1971, Southwest's accumulated deficit stood at $3.75 million (Exhibit 3).

THE SECOND SIX MONTHS

In February 1972, Southwest initiated a second phase of the advertising campaign, hired a new vice president–marketing, and terminated its public relations agency (hiring away the agency's publicity director to fill a newly created position as public relations director at Southwest).

The objective of this new phase was to sustain Southwest's presence in the marketplace after 8 months of service. Heavy frequency advertising, employing a wide variety of messages, was directed at the airline's primary target, the regular business commuter. Surveys had shown that 89 percent of Southwest's traffic at that time was accounted for by such travelers. Extensive use was made of television in this campaign, which featured many of Southwest's own hostesses.

Mr. Elliott, whom the president described as having performed a "Herculean task" in getting Southwest off the ground, had resigned to take a position with a national advertising agency. The new vice president–marketing, Jess R.

Coker, had spent 10 years in the outdoor advertising business after graduating from the University of Texas. His most recent assignment, before joining the airline, had been as vice president of Southern Outdoor Markets, a company representing 85 percent of all outdoor advertising facilities in the 14 southern and southeastern states. As marketing vice president at Southwest, Mr. Coker became responsible for all marketing functions of the airline, including advertising, sales, and public relations. Jess Coker typically met with the account executive from The Bloom Agency to discuss not only media advertising but also the numerous other small activities handled by the agency. These included preparation and execution of pocket timetables, point-of-sale materials for travel agents, and promotional brochures.

Although the majority of ticket sales were made over the counter at the airport terminals, sales were also made to travel agents and corporate accounts. Travel agents, who received a 7 percent commission on credit card sales and 10 percent on cash sales, would often arrange package deals for travelers, such as a weekend in San Antonio, including airfare, hotel, and meals. Corporate accounts—companies whose personnel made regular use of Southwest Airlines—received no discount but benefited from the convenience of having their own supply of ticket stock (which they issued themselves) and of receiving a single monthly billing. Jess Coker was responsible for a force of six sales representatives, whose job was to develop and service both travel agents and corporate accounts, encouraging maximum use of Southwest through distribution of point-of-sale materials, development of package arrangements, distribution of pocket timetables, etc. Sales representatives also promoted the availability of Southwest's air freight business, which featured a special rush delivery service for packages. Each representative, as well as most company officers, drove an AMC Gremlin car, strikingly painted in the same color scheme as Southwest's aircraft.

Also reporting to Mr. Coker was Southwest's new public relations director, Camille Keith, formerly publicity director of Read-Poland, Inc., the public relations agency which had up till then handled the airline's account. Ms. Keith, a graduate of Texas Christian University, had joined WFAA Television in spring 1967 while still in college. After 4 years with this Dallas-based ABC station as promotion assistant and then publicity director, she had joined Read-Poland and there spent much of her time working on the Southwest account. Ms. Keith's responsibilities focused on obtaining media coverage for the airline, and also included publication of Southwest's in-flight magazine and development of certain promotions jointly with the advertising agency.

Exhibit 17, a partial organization chart, summarizes the organization of the marketing staff at Southwest and its relationship to other areas of management.

Between October 1971 and April 1972, average passenger loads systemwide increased from 18.4 passengers per flight to 26.7 passengers. However, this was still substantially below the number necessary to cover total costs per trip flown, which had been tending to rise. It had become evident that the volume of traffic during the late morning and early afternoon could not realistically support flights at hourly intervals. It was also clear that most Houston passengers preferred Hobby Airport to Houston Intercontinental. Over time, the number of Southwest flights to Hobby had been steadily increased, and the decision was now taken to abandon Houston Intercontinental altogether.

On May 14, a new schedule was introduced, which reduced the total number of daily flights between Dallas and Houston from 29 to 22, primarily by reducing service in the 9:30 A.M. to 3:30 P.M. period from hourly to every 2 hours. Eleven flights daily continued to be offered on the Dallas–San Antonio route and six between San Antonio and Houston, with some minor schedule modifications. Hobby Airport was to be used exclusively for all flights to and from Houston. Braniff quickly retaliated by introducing its own service from Dallas to Hobby and undertaking an extensive publicity program promoting this airport.

From a financial viewpoint, the most significant aspect of Southwest's actions was that the new schedule made it possible for the company to dispose of its fourth Boeing 737. Experience had shown that the 737s could be turned around (i.e., loaded and unloaded) at the gate in as little as 10 minutes. This meant that an hourly schedule on the Dallas–Houston run could be maintained with only two aircraft instead of three. With the slack provided by the reduced midday frequencies and a schedule which involved periodically flying an aircraft around all three legs of the route triangle, management concluded that a total of three aircraft would suffice and that the fourth could be sold. By mid-1972, the airline industry had recovered from its 1970–1971 slump and aircraft manufacturers had waiting lists for their more popular models. Southwest had no trouble finding a ready buyer for its now surplus 737 and made a profit of $533,000 on reselling it. The combination of this capital gain, lower operating costs, and a continued increase in revenues resulted in a reduction of the quarterly net loss from $804,000 to $131,000 between the first and second quarters of 1972 (Exhibit 4).

For some months, Southwest had been experimenting with a $10 fare on Friday evening flights after 9:00 P.M. In May, this reduced fare was extended to post-9:00 P.M. flights on a daily basis. The result was sharply higher load factors on these discount flights relative to the average achieved on standard-price flights.

June 1972 saw Southwest Airlines celebrating its first birthday. This provided Camille Keith with an opportunity for more of the publicity stunts for which the airline was already becoming renowned. Posters were hung inside the aircraft and in the waiting lounges, the aircraft cabins were decorated, and there was an on-board party every day for a week, with birthday cake for the passengers and even balloons one day for the children. This activity, promoted by newspaper advertising, generated considerable publicity for the airline and, in management's view, reinforced Southwest's image as the plucky, friendly little underdog which had now survived an entire year against powerful, entrenched competition. Discussing her job, Ms. Keith observed:

> One good point was that Mr. Coker and I didn't have airline backgrounds. Our backgrounds were in the areas that we're serving—public relations and marketing

and sales. Nobody had ever told me "You can't have a flying birthday party" and I didn't know you're not supposed to have Easter bunnies on airplanes. So we did things that other people who'd been brought up in the [airline] business never did. We went out and tried things and if they didn't work, then we tried something else. And we had more flexibility in that area to do it. We were new, we knew all our employees and everybody knew that if the company went under we were all out of a job. Mr. Muse has been great and let me do a lot of crazy things. And our really great bunch of hostesses has made it easy. How many airline stewardesses would dress up in Halloween costumes on a flight and pass out trick-or-treat candy? Or wear bunny costumes at Easter or reindeer horns at Christmas?

Not all public relations activity was just hoopla, Ms. Keith stressed, mentioning that she worked quite closely with the advertising agency to coordinate the airline's mass communication strategy.

I keep them informed and I sit in on their meetings and they sit in on some of our brainstorming sessions, because it has to go together. I can't do one kind of PR campaign if they're doing an opposite advertising campaign. Neither can we have advertising running that I'm unaware of, in case the media should ask me about it.

One example of a specialized promotional campaign involving inputs from both Camille Keith and The Bloom Agency was the Southwest Sweetheart's Club. Using a specialized mailing list, a direct-mail piece was sent to executive secretaries in Southwest's market area, offering them membership in this club. For each reservation on Southwest she made for her boss, the secretary received a "sweetheart stamp," and for each 15 stamps, she obtained a free ride on Southwest. Additional bonuses for members included a twice-yearly drawing for a big Mexico City vacation.

While recognizing that interesting, well-written press releases could generate some publicity, Ms. Keith believed that for Southwest to get far more than its fair share of media coverage, the airline had to be constantly alert to opportunities for newsworthy stories or incidental coverage.

The unusual is what's going to get covered. The standard thing that we flew everyday on time (which is what we're supposed to do), and that we didn't lose any bags (which is an obligation under our certificate), and that the passengers were happy (which is our responsibility to them), is not news. It's supposed to happen. The news is that Senator Bentsen flew on Thursday afternoon and the girls knew him and spoke to him, and that I was in Houston when he landed and had a nice talk with him. . . . Lots of times, PR is getting the TV people to pan your airplane when someone like this gets off, instead of just taking his picture inside the terminal building.

On several occasions, Southwest had been featured in articles appearing in such national media as *Business Week*. Ms. Keith stressed that, typically, these articles did not just "happen," but were often the result of a long-term selling effort on her part to interest the editors of a particular publication.

PLANNING AHEAD

After a year of operation, Southwest management decided it was time to take a hard look at the fare structure and its relationship to costs and revenues. They soon concluded that the airline could no longer afford a $20 fare on daytime flights. New tariffs were therefore filed with the Texas Aeronautics Commission, effective July 9, 1972, which raised Southwest's basic one-way fare from $20 to $26, provided for a round-trip fare of $50, and offered a $225 Commuter Club Card providing unlimited transportation for the purchaser on all routes for a 30-day period.

One problem was how to break news of the increased fares to the public. A meeting was therefore called to discuss appropriate strategy. An important consideration was how the competition would react. Braniff and TI offered $20 fares on routes served by Southwest, but it was not certain that they would necessarily follow suit with increases to $26; however, Southwest management knew that both airlines were losing money on these routes.

At this meeting, Southwest executives also planned to discuss future marketing communications strategy. Mr. Muse felt that it was an appropriate time to take stock of the airline's position in the market and formulate a strategy for its second year of operations.

EXHIBIT 1
SOUTHWEST AIRLINES AND COMPETITORS: AVERAGE DAILY LOCAL PASSENGERS CARRIED IN EACH DIRECTION, DALLAS–HOUSTON MARKET*

Southwest Airlines: I

	Braniff† Psgrs.	Braniff† % of mkt.	Texas Int† Psgrs.	Texas Int† % of mkt.	Southwest Psgrs.	Southwest % of mkt.	Total market passengers
1967	416	86.1	67	13.9			483
1968	381	70.2	162	29.8			543
1969	427	75.4	139	24.6			566
1970:							
First half	449	79.0	119	21.0			568
Second half	380	76.0	120	24.0			500
Year	414	77.5	120	22.5			534
1971:							
First half	402	74.7	126	23.4	10	1.9	538
Second half	338	50.7	120	18.0	209	31.3	667
Year	370	61.4	123	20.4	110	18.2	603
1972:							
Jan.	341	48.3	105	14.9	260	36.8	706
Feb.	343	47.6	100	13.9	277	38.5	720
Mar.	357	47.5	100	13.3	295	39.2	752
Apr.	367	48.3	97	12.8	296	38.9	760
May	362	48.5	84	11.3	300	40.2	746
June‡	362	46.8	81	10.5	330	42.7	773
First half	356	48.0	93	12.5	293	39.5	742

* The numbers should be doubled to yield the total number of passenger trips between the two cities.

† These figures were calculated by Mr. Muse from passenger data which Braniff and TI were required to supply to the Civil Aeronautics Board. He multiplied the original figures by a correction factor to eliminate interline traffic and arrive at net totals for local traffic.

‡ Projected figures from terminal counts by Southwest personnel.

Source: Company records.

EXHIBIT 2
SOUTHWEST AIRLINES ROUTE MAP
Southwest Airlines: I

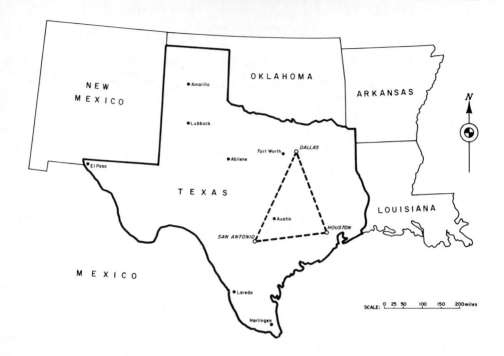

EXHIBIT 3
SOUTHWEST AIRLINES: BALANCE SHEET AT DECEMBER 31, 1971 AND 1970

Southwest Airlines: I

Assets

	1971	1970
Current assets:		
Cash	$ 231,530	$ 183
Certificates of deposit	2,850,000	
Accounts receivable:		
Trade	300,545	
Interest	35,013	
Other	32,569	100
	368,127	100
Less allowance for doubtful accounts	30,283	
	337,844	100
Inventories of parts and supplies, at cost	171,665	
Prepaid insurance and other	156,494	31
Total current assets	3,747,533	314
Property and equipment, at cost:		
Boeing 737-200 jet aircraft	16,263,250	
Support flight equipment	2,378,581	
Ground equipment	313,072	9,249
	18,954,903	9,249
Less accumulated depreciation and overhaul allowance	1,096,177	
	17,858,726	9,249
Deferred certification costs less amortization	477,122	530,136
	$22,083,381	$539,699

Liabilities and stockholders' equity

	1971	1970
Current liabilities:		
Notes payable to banks (secured)	$ 355,539	$ 30,819
Accounts payable	54,713	79,000
Accrued salaries and wages	301,244	
Other accrued liabilities		
Long-term debt due within 1 year	1,500,000	
Total current liabilities	2,211,496	109,819
Long-term debt due after 1 year:		
7% convertible promissory notes	1,250,000	
Conditional purchase agreements— Boeing Financial Corporation (1½% over prime rate)	16,803,645	
	18,053,645	
Less amounts due within 1 year	1,500,000	
	16,553,645	
Contingencies:		
Stockholders' equity:		
Common stock, $1.00 par value, 2,000,000 shares authorized, 1,108,758 issued (1,058,758 at Dec. 31, 1971)	1,058,758	372,404
Capital in excess of par value	6,012,105	57,476
Deficit	(3,752,623)	
	3,318,240	429,880
	$22,083,381	$539,699

Notes to financial statement not shown here.
Source: Southwest Airlines Company *Annual Report*, 1971.

267

EXHIBIT 4
SOUTHWEST AIRLINES: QUARTERLY INCOME STATEMENTS
Southwest Airlines: I

Income statements, $ thousand	1971		1972	
	Q3	Q4	Q1	Q2 (projected)
Transportation revenues*	887	1,138	1,273	1,401
Operating expenses:				
Operations & maintenance	1,211	1,280	1,192	1,145
Marketing & gen. admin.	371	368	334	366
Depreciation & amortiz.	311	411	333	334
Total	1,893	2,059	1,859	1,845
Operating profit (loss)	(1,006)	(921)	(586)	(444)
Net interest revenues (costs)	(254)	(253)	(218)	(220)
Net income (loss) before extraordinary items	(1,260)	(1,174)	(804)	(664)
Extraordinary items	(571)†	(469)†		533‡
Net income (loss)	(1,831)	(1,643)	(804)	(131)

  * Includes both passenger and freight business.
  † Write-off of preoperating costs.
  ‡ Capital gain on sale of one aircraft.
  Source: Company records.

EXHIBIT 5
PACIFIC SOUTHWEST AIRLINES MAGAZINE ADVERTISING, MAY 1969
Southwest Airlines: I

It's a rare passenger who can't give the blues the brush flying PSA. Big exhibitions like our snappy new all-jet fleet, and 900 flights a week serving San Francisco, Oakland, San Jose, Ontario, Los Angeles, Hollywood-Burbank, San Diego and Sacramento. Nice little shows like impromptu parties, kids' gifts, crossword puzzles. Call your travel agent or PSA and put on a happy face.

When the big hand is on 12 and the little hand is on

7 am
8 am
9 am
10 am
11 am
12 noon
1 pm
2 pm
3 pm
4 pm
5 pm
6 pm
7 pm
8 pm
9 pm **PSA flies between Los Angeles and San Francisco**

Plus the Midnight Flyer Monday through Friday. **PSA gives you a lift**

EXHIBIT 7
ADVERTISING AGENCY'S POSITIONING DIAGRAM
OF U.S. AIRLINES ADVERTISING/COMPETING
IN TEXAS MARKETS
Southwest Airlines: I

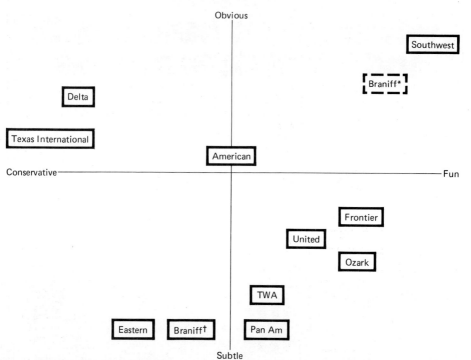

*Former advertising by Wells, Rich, Green ("The End of the Plain Plane," "The Air Strip")
†Clinton Frank advertising
Source: Bloom Agency (2/11/71)

Welcome to "747 Braniff Place." The most exclusive address in the sky.

Braniff's new 747 is more than flight. It is a place to live well in flight. We put in contoured chairs, not straight-backed seats. Three of six lounges are in Coach. The menu was created by Braniff's International Board of Chefs. In all, we've made this the most exclusive address in the sky. Join our first 747 Braniff Place non-stop flights between Dallas/Fort Worth and Hawaii starting January 15. For reservations and connections to Dallas/Fort Worth, call Braniff or your travel agent.

Come up to the International Lounge.

Our upstairs Lounge is like an intimate club overlooking the world. You'll find superb beverages. And an hors d'oeuvre buffet that's going to be a legend.

Relax in one of our six Lounges.

No more gathering in the aisles. We have lounges for everyone—three in coach alone. More lounges than any other 747. And they are furnished handsomely, with comfortable chairs and couches.

You reserve a chair, not a seat.

No ordinary straight-back airplane seat. You're wrapped in a contoured chair that curves forward for privacy. And from Pucci, another flight of fancy. New hostess ensembles. Inside each, a young lady to pamper you outrageously.

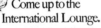

We set a beautiful table.

You'll appreciate the gleaming linens, fine china and crystal. Select your six-course meal from an international menu. Coach cuisine? The best you've ever savored. With a choice of entrees, too.

747 Braniff Place
The most exclusive address in the sky.
BRANIFF INTERNATIONAL

[1] Prepared by Clinton E. Frank, Inc.

EXHIBIT 9
Continued

Houston
(every hour on the hour)

(a) with the experience of Braniff's million-mile Captains.
(b) with Braniff's big 3 & 4 engine jets.
(c) in Braniff's reclining seats.
(d) and because you have a choice of either 1st class or coach service.
● **Special Service Representatives At The Boarding Area** . . . to help speed and ease things up.
● **Peace-Of-Mind Phone Calls** . . . made for you at the last minute.
● **Hot or Cold Towels** . . . to freshen-up with in the morning and afternoon.
● **Local Newspapers and The Oil Daily or Other Special Interest Journals Available** . . . because you requested them.

● **"747 Braniff Place" Hors D'Oeuvre Sampling** . . . on selected flights.
● **Commuter Refreshment Discount Book Available** . . . to save you money on any Braniff flight.

*Braniff Style Commuter Service: On the hour flights to Houston from 7 am to 9 pm and on the hour flights to San Antonio from 7 am to 7 pm (San Antonio on the hour flights start July 1, 1971). Coach fare —tax included. $20 fare effective June 18.

You'll like flying
Braniff Style.

. . . Braniff Style.

HOUSTON
(every hour on the hour)

SAN ANTONIO
(every hour on the hour*)

$20
Coach — Tax Included

BRANIFF
Call Braniff at 357-9511 or Your Travel Agent

*Starting July 1

[1] Prepared by Clinton E. Frank, Inc.

if we listed all the 66 cities in the 9 states and mexico that we jet to it would take up this entire costly page. we'd rather spend the money getting you there on time.

Texas International
We run an intelligent airline.

[1] The original of each advertisement occupied only a small corner of the newspaper page.

EXHIBIT 11
Continued

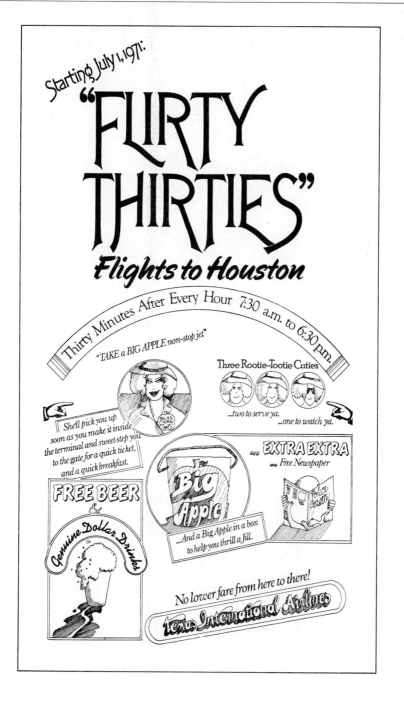

EXHIBIT 13
SOUTHWEST INTRODUCTORY ADVERTISING
Southwest Airlines: I

At last, there's somebody

The planes are new. The pilots are not. We've talked to, tested, and evaluated very good, reputable, reliable pilots that any major airline would hire. Out of them all we've selected a group — maybe an elite — of the very best in the business, with an average of 15,200 hours in the air.

Our ground crew is no small potatoes, either. They're well-trained in dozens of skills that insure your comfort aboard Southwest Airlines.

It's us, Southwest Airlines.

Us, with our brand new Boeing 737's.

We fly to Dallas/Ft. Worth, Houston and San Antonio. Your choice, all flights non-stop.

In that time you're going to feel there really is somebody else up there who loves you.

By sharing a lot of little things with you. Big, little things that mean a lot to travelers.

Three years ago the Boeing 737 was introduced to the public all over the world. Today — as of this morning — the Boeing 737's have accumulated 1,000,000 flight hours, carrying nearly 70 million passengers approximately 430 million miles. The Boeing 737 is the super reliable jet specially designed for short haul traffic. Obviously, it is more than just a beautiful body. No other airlines will be flying 737's on these routes. And Southwest Airlines won't be flying anything else.

And we give trading stamps. Not the ordinary kind. Ours are Love Stamps. You get one from our hostess if for any reason she finds you unhappy in any way with our service. The basic idea is that we want you to trade in your bad feelings for good ones. The Love Stamp hopefully will make amends—with a free drink or something, and then you'll feel better about us right away. And want to ride our airplanes again, and again.

JUNE 18

LOVE STAMP
GOOD FOR ONE FREE LOVE POTION ON YOUR NEXT FLIGHT

Dallas/Ft. Worth to Houston (and back)
Dallas/Ft. Worth to San Antonio (and back)
All flights non-stop.

Dallas/Ft. Worth to Houston		Houston to Dallas/Ft. Worth	
Depart	Arrive	Depart	Arrive
7:30 a*	8:18 a	7:30 a*	8:18 a
8:45 a*	9:33 a	8:45 a	9:33 a
10:00 a	10:48 a	10:00 a*	10:48 a
11:15 a*	12:03 p	11:15 a	12:03 p
12:30 p	1:18 p	12:30 p*	1:18 p
1:45 p**	2:33 p	1:45 p	2:33 p
3:00 p	3:48 p	3:00 p**	3:48 p
4:15 p**	5:03 p	4:15 p	5:03 p
5:30 p	6:18 p	5:30 p*	6:18 p
6:45 p**	7:33 p	6:45 p	7:33 p
8:00 p	8:48 p	8:00 p**	8:48 p
9:15 p**	10:03 p	9:15 p**	10:03 p

Dallas/Ft. Worth to San Antonio		San Antonio to Dallas/Ft. Worth	
Depart	Arrive	Depart	Arrive
7:00 a*	7:50 a	8:15 a*	9:05 a
9:30 a	10:20 a	10:45 a	11:35 a
12:00 n	12:50 p	1:15 p	2:05 p
2:30 p	3:20 p	3:45 p	4:35 p
5:00 p	5:50 p	6:15 p	7:05 p
7:30 p**	8:20 p	8:45 p**	9:35 p

* Except Sunday
** Except Saturday

EXHIBIT 13
Continued

EXHIBIT 14
SOUTHWEST AIRLINES INTRODUCTORY
TV ADVERTISING, JUNE 1971
Southwest Airlines: I

SOUTHWEST AIRLINES

CODE NO: SWA-3-30-71
TITLE: "TV Love Machine"

TELEVISION STORYBOARD
THE BLOOM AGENCY

1. (Natural sfx, people talking up and under)...

2. ...

3. ...

4. ...

5. (Wm Anncr VO) If you're standing in line...

6. ...you're not flying...

7. ...Southwest Airlines.

8. Because our Love Machine gives you a ticket...

9. ...in under ten seconds.

10. HOSTESS: Have a nice flight.

11. (Sfx: music and jet engine) 12 flights each day to Houston...

12. ...6 to San Antonio, for a loveable $20...

13. ...on Southwest Airlines.

14. "The somebody else up there...

15. ...who loves you."

B R Y C H I C A G O

280

EXHIBIT 15
SOUTHWEST AIRLINES: ADVERTISING AND PROMOTIONAL EXPENDITURES, 1971 AND 1972
Southwest Airlines: I

| | 1971 | | | 1972 |
	Preoperating	Operating	Total	(budgeted)
Advertising:				
Newspaper	$139,831	$131,675	$271,506	$ 60,518
Television	36,340	761	37,101	127,005
Radio	5,021	60,080	65,101	95,758
Billboards	26,537	11,670	38,207	90,376
Other publications	710	20,446	21,156	28,139
Production costs	52,484	43,483	95,967	83,272
Other promotion and publicity:	29,694	27,200	56,894	48,366
	$290,617	$295,315	$585,932	$533,434

Source: Company records.

EXHIBIT 16
SOUTHWEST AIRLINES
MONTHLY FLIGHTS AND PASSENGER COUNTS ON EACH ROUTE
Southwest Airlines: I

Month	Dallas–Houston		Dallas–San Antonio		San Antonio–Houston	
	# psgrs.	#flights	# psgrs.	# flights	# psgrs.	# flights
June 1971*	3,620	276	1,910	148		
July	10,301	642	5,158	346		
Aug.	11,316	672	4,805	354		
Sept.	11,674	612	4,766	327		
Oct.	14,522	764	6,492	382		
Nov.	14,060	654	4,167	240	888	72
Dec.	14,665	687	4,004	165	1,707	134
1971 total	76,568	4,307	31,302	1,962	2,595	206
Jan. 1972	16,122	634	2,788	141	1,954	128
Feb.	16,069	640	2,755	142	2,088	134
Mar.	18,285	669	4,270	209	2,803	146
Apr.	17,732	605	4,617	189	2,301	130
May	18,586	584	4,254	198	2,461	138
June†	19,782	521	5,198	201	2,628	140
First half total	106,576	3,653	23,882	1,080	14,235	816

* Part-month only
† Projected figures
Source: Company records.

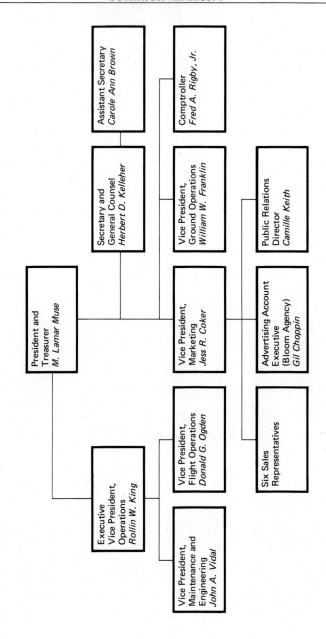

282

HONEYWELL INFORMATION SYSTEMS
1974 ADVERTISING PROGRAM

NANCY J. DAVIS
Research Associate
Harvard Graduate School of Business Administration

STEVEN H. STAR
Associate Professor
Harvard Graduate School of Business Administration

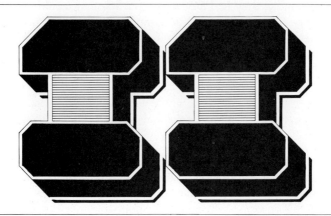

There is no way that we can continue to increase awareness of Honeywell as a computer manufacturer without maintaining a high level of advertising exposure. We have managed to stake out the number two awareness position over the years, but we can't afford to let up or we'll find the rest of the pack breathing down our necks—Director of Advertising.

Inflation has driven our marketing costs out of line. We've got to cut costs across the board, and that includes advertising. Besides, our market is primarily our present customers. We don't need to blanket the country with advertising to tell our customers about our new line—Director of Finance.

This new product announcement is our most important event since we took over General Electric's computer operation. It will do more for our image than anything else we can advertise. We need to get this story across not only to prospects, but to the financial community—Corporate Vice President.

This new product announcement is important, but we have to make our '74 goals with our current product line. Our total ability to satisfy our customers' needs is the story we must get across. This capability is enhanced by the new line, but it's only part of the story—Branch Manager.

These were the arguments facing Christopher J. Lynch, vice president of marketing, and Daniel E. Callanan, director of communications, for the data-processing operations of Honeywell Information Systems in September 1973 as they pondered the advertising budget and creative format for 1974.

They recognized the need for continuing to stress Honeywell's overall capabilities and ability to achieve results in a marketplace dominated by one competitor. Secondly, they had a new product line that would require a major promotional investment. They felt it was important in this promotion to position the new line as an enhancement to the existing product line which would have to continue to generate revenue and profits for some time. Third, inflation was beginning to squeeze profits, and there were increasing pressures to slash costs wherever possible.

COMPANY HISTORY

In 1973, Honeywell Information Systems was a division of Honeywell, Inc., an international industrial corporation whose worldwide sales totaled $2.39 billion. The Information Systems Division accounted for $1.177 billion or 49 percent of sales and $93 million or 41 percent of corporate earnings before interest and taxes. It controlled about 8 percent of the United States computer market as measured in dollars. While Honeywell's corporate headquarters was located in Minneapolis, main offices for North American Operations of Honeywell Information Systems were on Boston's Route 128 in Waltham, Massachusetts.

Honeywell Information Systems traced its origins to Datamatic, a joint venture with Raytheon established in 1955 when Honeywell, Inc., recognized that evolving computer (or digital) technology would have a profound effect on the controls business—the primary thrust of the company.[1] In 1957 Honeywell bought Raytheon's 40 percent, and Datamatic became a division of Honeywell. In 1963 Honeywell introduced a medium-sized computer, the Model 200, which it called the *Liberator* because it was designed to be compatible with IBM's 1401 system and therefore was able to free the customer from having to stay with IBM. The Model 200 was expanded into a full series of computers and proved to be the backbone of Honeywell's computer line throughout the sixties. Despite its success, however, company management decided that Honeywell could not stay in the computer business without a larger market share and a

---

[1] Various control systems, especially heating, air conditioning, and process control systems, had been the basis for Honeywell's formation and early growth. By 1973, the Control Systems Division, the counterpart of the Information Systems Division, manufactured sophisticated monitoring and control systems for the environment, guidance systems for the United States space program, industrial process control systems, and cameras.

broader customer base. Therefore, in 1970 Honeywell, Inc., acquired General Electric's computer operations, merged it with its own, and formally created Honeywell Information Systems. (Hereafter *Honeywell* refers to Honeywell Information Systems, not to the total corporation.)

General Electric's line of large and small computers, when combined with the Series 200, made Honeywell a full-service computer company with as wide a range of computers and services as any competitor and a customer base equal to a 10 percent share of the worldwide market. Since General Electric's computer operations extended throughout the world, Honeywell's computer business immediately became a worldwide concern. In all, it reached into 58 countries which comprised 97 percent of the worldwide data-processing market. It had production and engineering facilities in the United States and five other countries. It was divided into four operating units, each responsible for marketing and financial control in their respective geographic territories, and with certain manufacturing, design, and development activities. This case is concerned only with the North American Operations which was responsible for all business in the United States and Canada.

Between 1970 and 1973, a great deal of time, effort, and money was spent merging the two lines and building a functioning operation out of the two organizations. Especially, present General Electric and Honeywell customers had to be reassured that they would not need to switch nor reprogram their entire systems, and that any improvements developed by Honeywell would be compatible with their systems. Honeywell management stated that the customers' concerns were justified since immediately after the merger Honeywell had 10 different product lines, 12 major operating-systems software packages, and 157 different kinds of peripheral equipment.

By 1973 the product lines had been consolidated so that Honeywell marketed essentially five lines of general-purpose computers. These ranged from the Series 50 family of small computers, which were aimed primarily at small businesses, up to the Series 6000, which were giant computers used by such diverse organizations as Ford Motor Company, Pillsbury, and the Department of Defense's Worldwide Military Command and Control System. Small systems rented for about $2,000 a month, medium-sized systems for about $20,000, and large systems for about $100,000 per month. Sale prices ranged from $50,000 to $7 million. Honeywell was planning to introduce a new line, known as the Series 60, during 1974—ideally in April. This line would include the full range from mini- to supercomputers, would be compatible with all other Honeywell models, and would be Honeywell's major product for the future. Its development had cost more than $300 million.

THE COMPUTER INDUSTRY

The computer industry got started during World War II when the U.S. government initiated several research projects oriented toward rapid data processing. The first commercial installation was in 1954 when Univac delivered a computer to General Electric. By 1956 the competitive structure of the industry was emerging. Though about 15 companies were manufacturing computers, IBM had captured about 80 percent of the market. (See Exhibit 1 for worldwide market share data, 1953–1973.)

Over the next several years, the industry was characterized by rapid growth in demand, intense competitive activity, and rapidly changing technology. Several solid companies such as RCA, Bendix, Raytheon, Philco-Ford, and General Electric had gotten into the computer business but were either unwilling or unable to invest the necessary funds in research, development, and marketing and eventually dropped out of the industry. Technological changes had indeed been enormous. During the fifties relatively slow, limited-memory-capacity computers were used primarily for massive, often repetitive calculations in scientific application. Beginning in the early sixties, significant strides were made in increasing computers' speed and memory capacity, and manufacturers began to distinguish more between computers for businesses and those for scientific applications. Later in the sixties, solid-state technology, remote terminals, improved programming, and other innovations were introduced, making much of the earlier equipment obsolete.

In 1964, IBM introduced the Series 360, whose development costs were estimated to be $5 billion. This was followed 6 years later by the Series 370 which, though recognized as a technological leader, was not nearly so revolutionary. Customers proved to be less ready to switch from their present computers than they had been in the past. In 1973, Honeywell was making plans to introduce its new Series 60 during 1974. Other than this, most new products being introduced by the industry were peripheral accessories rather than main computer-processing units.

By 1973 almost all organizations were considered potential computer customers. Customers could either purchase or rent the equipment. Sales of large computers which cost over $1.5 million generally required 6 to 12 months of selling and negotiating, and top management was almost always involved. Medium-sized units, i.e., those which sold for $200,000 to $1.5 million, were also usually purchased by experienced and sophisticated managers in companies which were expanding their operations. When small units (purchase value $40,000 to $200,000) were sold to large organizations for specific purposes which their larger computers did not perform, a data-processing executive who was a sophisticated buyer usually made the purchase decision.

In smaller organizations that were buying small computers, however, the purchase decision almost always involved top management which usually was not at all sophisticated in computers. Often, it was the company's initial computer purchase, and it represented a substantial financial commitment. In such situations, the salesperson had to understand the customer's business well enough to explain clearly how the computer would be installed and used. However, the limited revenue from a small computer sale did not justify so large a selling effort as did the revenue from larger units, and the sale of a small computer was expected to be consummated within 2 months.

Once a customer purchased a particular computer, he usually stayed with that brand because there was little compatibility among different manufacturers' hardware and software. In fact, from 1971 through 1973 roughly 80 percent of Honeywell's shipments were delivered to firms that already had some type of Honeywell equipment installed.

COMPETITION

In 1973 IBM, Honeywell, Sperry-Rand/Univac, and Burroughs were the leading full-line computer companies. IBM was by far the market leader with about 70 percent of the market. While IBM was strong in every area, it was considered especially strong in medium-sized computers. Its 6,000-person sales force and $2.2 million space advertising[1] budget (plus an estimated $5 million in TV and radio) were also the largest in the industry. Honeywell management expected IBM's advertising expenditures to increase in the near future, particularly to promote their small computers. The increase was expected to be evident in the pages of general news and general business publications, the media IBM already utilized most. IBM had not previously advertised in key market publications such as those edited for manufacturing, distribution, financial, and education audiences (as Honeywell had been doing), nor had IBM advertised to any extent in computer publications. As had been the case with many other computer companies, IBM had changed its advertising theme fairly often and had used a wide variety of formats.

Sperry-Rand/Univac controlled about 8 percent of the market, primarily with large computers. However, its medium-sized computers appeared to be increasing in popularity. Its advertising expenditures were second only to IBM's. Its advertisements in general publications such as *Business Week* and *Fortune* usually consisted of human interest stories in which a computer played a significant role. In key market and computer publications, human interest stories were sometimes used, but more often the ads consisted of pictures and descriptions of computers.

Burroughs, perhaps best known for its strong line of office machines for routine bookkeeping chores, was strong in both large and small computers. Its smaller computers were sold by its office machine sales force and its other computers by a special sales force. It usually concentrated on selected markets such as banking and retailing where it had strength. It controlled about 6 percent of the United States market. It traditionally had confined its advertising largely to product announcements consisting of pictures of equipment with nontechnical functional descriptions.

Honeywell considered three other companies—Control Data, National Cash Register, and Digital Equipment Corporation—as competitors, even though they did not market full lines of computers. Control Data specialized in very large special-purpose computers for scientific and government applications,

[1] Space advertising referred primarily to magazine and newspaper advertising.

areas in which it had early demonstrated competence. National Cash Register (NCR) marketed a broad line of computers and was especially strong among retailers. Digital Equipment Corporation (DEC) had been extremely successful in producing minicomputers, many of which were sold to other manufacturers to be incorporated into their products. DEC had recently begun to sell small computer systems for educational, scientific, and general-purpose uses.

According to data which Honeywell had compiled from magazine and newspapers in which it regularly advertised, from 1970 through 1973 computer manufacturers' space advertising expenditures had been fairly erratic. Generally speaking, the introduction of a new line or special emphasis on an old line was accompanied by very large expenditures which might well drop off sharply the next year. NCR, for example, had spent over $1 million in both 1971 and 1972, but in 1973 it had spent only $385,000. Sperry-Rand/Univac, which had dropped from over $1 million in 1970 to $85,000 in 1971, had jumped to $972,000 in 1973. Except for 1971, IBM's expenditures had consistently been over $2.2 million, though its 1973 level was below its 1970 level. In recent years, Honeywell had been spending approximately $1 million per year. (See Exhibit 2 for sample advertisements of Honeywell's competitors.)

STRUCTURE OF THE HONEYWELL ORGANIZATION

In September 1973, Honeywell's North American Operations (NAO) was headed by Mr. Robert P. Henderson, vice president and general manager. Reporting to Mr. Henderson were the vice presidents of finance, administration, field engineering, and manufacturing, and four marketing executives—two concentrating on federal government and Canadian accounts, plus Mr. Christopher J. Lynch, vice president of marketing for the data-processing operations, and Mr. Richard R. Douglas, vice president of marketing operations and planning. (See Exhibit 3 for an abbreviated organization chart of data-processing operations.)

THE FIELD MARKETING ORGANIZATION

The line sales organization for United States commercial accounts was headed by four vice presidents of field marketing who were responsible for different geographic sections of the country and who reported directly to Mr. Lynch. They managed 12 regional marketing directors who in turn supervised over 2,000 people in 50 branch offices. This organization accounted for more than 75 percent of NAO's computer revenues. (The remaining 25 percent was derived from various Canadian and U.S. government accounts which were handled by other NAO sales organizations.)

Some branch offices, especially those in large metropolitan areas, were organized by customer industry, while others were organized geographically. Some salespeople specialized by customer type, while others covered a wide variety of industries. Salespeople were committed to serving customers' needs and were paid on commission using a formula which considered both rental and sales revenue.

In 1973, Mr. Lynch instituted a formal program of account management, a system that called for each salesperson to investigate and record each customer's future needs for information systems. This system included the current system, the next system, when it should be ordered, when it should be installed, and so forth. This was an important step in assuring customer continuity when making the transition from present systems to the new Series 60. It also aided the marketing organization in planning priorities and recommending factory schedules and helped define the promotional and educational requirements that would be needed at announcement time. It was a key tool in defining the total capability that Honeywell planned to stress in launching the new product line.

THE HOME OFFICE MARKETING ORGANIZATION

Honeywell's home office marketing functions included marketing operations and planning, NAO communications, and finance and administration. Marketing operations and planning, under the direction of Mr. Douglas, helped develop broad strategies for the company with regard to product lines, pricing, industry specialization, market research, competitive evaluation, and so forth. Specialists within this department worked closely with internal departments, outside sources, and progressive customers to develop information systems for specific industries. They also manned exhibits at trade shows and actually assisted in much of the company's high-level selling.

NAO communications, directed by Mr. Daniel E. Callanan, consisted of four well-defined functions: merchandising, public relations, communications services, and advertising.

The merchandising function was concerned with assisting the marketing activity by developing promotional programs and materials such as brochures, product briefs, visual aids, and other items used by the sales force in sales calls and presentations. A key activity was producing case histories of customer success stories. They also provided the editing, illustrating, composing, and much of the writing for the technical literature required by customers for the operation, installation, and maintenance of Honeywell information systems. Others activities included planning and conducting national sales conferences and seasonal motivational meetings, administering special incentive sales contests, publishing a weekly newsletter, and videotaping a 15-minute news program which was distributed every other week to branch offices.

The public relations function was conducted by four resident employees and the full resources of Carl Byoir & Associates, an independent firm which handled public relations for all of Honeywell, Inc. This group was responsible for counseling management on public postures, establishing press relations, conducting press conferences, generating articles, and writing press releases and executive speeches. It also helped produce films and various programs and promotional pieces designed to communicate a positive Honeywell image to the general public.

Communications services was created initially to be the production facility for NAO communications. It included the print shop and offices which purchased outside printing, and warehoused, distributed, and invoiced all literature used by field marketing and its customers. Manuals were sold to customers. With its extensive distribution, list maintenance, and billing facility, it gradually took over the marketing of basic supplies such as magnetic tape reels, disk packs, and printer ribbons.

Communications services also included the marketing of items such as animal posters, pewter replicas, coffee mugs, place mats, decals, and book matches—all featuring the same animals used in Honeywell advertising and illustrated in an animal "gift catalog" sent to all marketing personnel. Honeywell marketing people liked to present token gifts to their customers as contracts were signed, equipment installed, or leases renewed. Customers who wanted additional items and employees who wanted items for personal use were encouraged to order directly by sending personal checks. In 1973, sales of animal items totaled $98,000, of which nearly half were ordered by individuals. Communications services was a self-financing operation—all its costs were recovered either from customers or from Honeywell departments and individuals.

The advertising function came under the direction of Mr. Morris D. Dettman, a 25-year Honeywell employee, who had established his reputation as an ad executive in Minneapolis before his 1956 transfer to the computer group in Boston. Dettman's organization handled Honeywell's exhibits, direct-mail, and media advertising. Exhibits were the responsibility of an exhibits manager who set up displays and equipment at various trade shows. Frequently these exhibits featured a selection of the original computer component sculptures. Honeywell normally avoided general computer conventions which catered to a wide range of computer-specialist audiences and required massive budgets. It preferred to concentrate more directly on the specific needs of an audience. Direct mail was used to communicate with customers when new products were announced, to elicit responses from prospects for specific products, and to respond to inquiries generated by media advertisements and editorial items.

HONEYWELL'S ADVERTISING PHILOSOPHY

Honeywell's current media advertising program dated back to 1962 when the industry was, in the words of one executive, "like Snow White and the Seven Dwarfs—IBM led with an 80 percent share and the rest of us little guys tagged along behind." A survey of several financial executives that year had revealed that only 31 percent were aware that Honeywell sold computers, only 11 percent could recall any Honeywell advertising, and only 14 percent said they would consider investigating Honeywell as a supplier if they needed equipment. Until this time, Honeywell's advertising, like that of most computer companies, had consisted of straightforward pictures of computers with copy describing their capabilities.

Company executives and Honeywell's advertising agency, Batten, Barton, Durstine, and Osborn (BBDO), then decided that the company's advertising aimed at managerial and financial personnel should be switched from solely promoting computer hardware to putting more direct emphasis on creating awareness of Honeywell as a computer manufacturer. The idea was that an increase in share of mind had to precede growth in share of market. The BBDO creative staff then went to work on a new campaign format. They came back with the idea of using four-color illustrations of animals sculpted out of computer parts. This idea had several advantages. The electronic sculptures related to the product. They could be used with a wide variety of subjects, hardware, software, applications, even philosophy. They provided a continuity to all advertising so the program would build as more and more ads were produced. Most important, they resulted in advertising uniquely different from anything else in the industry. Parts for the animals were selected from assembly lines and scrap bins and were bona fide computer components. Once a sufficient stable of animals had been created, fewer and fewer new animals were necessary since they could be used in different ads for different publications and modified slightly with props or accessories and reused. Some animals had been used in as many as eight different advertisements. (See Exhibit 4 for typical computer component ad, and Exhibit 5 for examples of one sculpture used in several different ads.)

In 1968 Mr. Dettman began looking for a theme line for the company. In a conversation with a customer in Chicago, the customer commented, "You know, you really are the only logical alternative to IBM." Mr. Dettman seized the line as the basis for a theme or positioning statement. The agency's creative team took it and came back with the line "The Other Computer Company: Honeywell" which, after testing, was installed as Honeywell's advertising signature. (See Exhibit 6 for sample advertisements.)

The function of the animals in Honeywell advertising was twofold. First, they had proven to be uniquely effective attention getters, which Honeywell advertising executives considered the first objective of any advertisement. Second, they had provided continuity and identity for Honeywell advertising and helped to set the tone or personality of Honeywell.

The campaign proved to be quite successful. Studies of financial officers revealed that many more of them began to recognize Honeywell as a computer company, and if they needed equipment, more were likely to consult Honeywell than had been the case in 1962. (See Exhibit 7 for historical trends.) Similarly, the ads ranked high in advertising recall studies done by *Business Week,* and the magazine reported that the campaign had consistently scored better than any other ad campaign ever run in the weekly. (See Exhibit 8 for sample *Business Week* reports.) Moreover, in 1970, color reproductions of four sculptures were offered for $1 in ads in *Computerworld* and *Datamation.* During the first week of the offer, Honeywell received 2,000 orders. One industry observer commented, "When people start paying for your advertising illustrations, your ads must be pretty damn good."

Mr. Callanan commented as follows:

> One strength of our print campaign is its consistency. The longevity of the theme has built a strong, widely recognized reputation for us. Our customers and our prime prospects immediately think of Honeywell when you say "The Other Computer Company" or when they see animals sculpted from computer parts. If we switch our format or theme now, we'll be wasting all the money Honeywell has spent to develop its present image. At today's prices, launching a new advertising campaign in 1974 would cost at least twice as much as we're spending in 1973 to maintain our present program.

Honeywell segmented its potential audiences into three categories and designed media advertisements to appeal to each. The first category consisted of general managers and financial officers earning more than $15,000 per year and working in companies which employed more than 100 people. Advertisements for this group were run in general business publications such as *Forbes, Fortune, Business Week,* and *The Wall Street Journal* and in news weeklies such as *Time, Newsweek,* and *U.S. News and World Report.* They were designed to make executives aware of Honeywell as a major computer manufacturer. Mr. Eustis Walcott, Honeywell's account supervisor at BBDO's Boston office, commented on advertising to this market as follows:

> Ads for general managers and financial officers are not designed to promote hardware directly. Rather, they are designed to sell Honeywell's concept of data processing, and this encompasses hardware, software, and knowhow. We want the ads to stop the reader and establish in his mind that Honeywell is different from any other computer company and is a logical alternative to IBM. Even if he doesn't read the whole ad, he is made aware that Honeywell is a computer company. He will remember Honeywell the next time he is asked to approve a computer recommendation or needs to install or change a system.

The second audience category was referred to as key-market prospects, and it included senior and operating management in fields such as finance, manufacturing, government, hospitals, distribution, and education. This was essentially the program which supported the industry marketing specialists. Ads aimed at this category focused on specific applications of Honeywell's equipment and were designed to make managers aware of Honeywell's interest and capabilities in specific industries. Unlike ads for general managers and financial officers, these contained somewhat more technical information, particularly with respect to software designed for specific industries. Typical publications used included *Iron Age, Banking, Modern Hospital, Nation's Schools, The American City,* and *Electrical Wholesaling.*

The third category consisted of data-processing professionals. Ads for this category emphasized technical facts about the different systems. They were run in magazines such as *Computerworld, Datamation,* and *Computer Decisions* and often involved multiple-page units due to the amount and level of detail incorporated.

Mr. Dettman commented as follows on this philosophy:

We realize that eyeball-to-eyeball contact provided by a salesperson is what sells computers, not advertising. Nevertheless, our program for general managers and financial executives serves two important purposes. First, it makes prospects aware that Honeywell is a computer company so that when a salesperson visits the prospect, he or she is not walking into totally uncharted territory. Second, after the sale is made, our advertising program helps keep customers aware of what is going on with Honeywell. It projects the image of a growing, dynamic company which the customer can be proud to associate with. Hopefully, this will make him less susceptible to rival products.

In addition, our advertising to data processing professionals does go into more technical detail for those who are looking for, and can appreciate, detailed product information.

Of our three major programs, the management campaign essentially sells Honeywell as a computer company worthy of consideration. Our key market program sells our capability and dedication to meeting needs of specific industries. Our data processing manager program sells our technological capability to computer professionals.

Traditionally we spend about half our budget to reach our management target, one-third on key markets, and one-sixth to reach the data processing professional. This particular emphasis is due more to the size of the audience (which determines costs) than it is to the relative importance of the categories.

PROPOSED CAMPAIGNS FOR 1974

Honeywell's advertising department and BBDO assumed a maximum budget of $1 million and prepared the following two alternative recommendations:

1 To achieve maximum impact for the new product announcement, no advertising will run in 1974 prior to the late April announcement date. Starting with the press conference, two-page "announcement advertising" will run in management publications (Business Week, The Wall Street Journal, Newsweek, Fortune, and Forbes), and "announcement advertising" will continue with one-page units for the balance of the year. This advertising will emphasize features, functions, and benefits of the new product line as distinguished from the more general capabilities (responsiveness, cost effectiveness, time sharing) which were subjects of prior management advertisements. This effort will use approximately $250,000 of the $1 million annual budget.

Space advertising will be supplemented with a 13-week spot television campaign on network golf and news programs to provide additional impact and coverage of middle and top management executives on behalf of the new line. This will cost $500,000 or half the annual budget.

The final $250,000 will be invested in a major exhibit at the National Computer Conference which happens to coincide closely with the announcement date. The conference tends to attract data processing professionals and will take the place of space advertising normally addressed to this audience.

Under this proposal, there will be no funds available for key market advertising during 1974, and the full budget will be spent to maximize the market impact of the new product line—75 percent aimed toward the management audience and 25 percent toward data processing professionals.

2 *We will continue to advertise to traditional management and key market audiences from January to April, emphasizing customer success stories and deemphasizing hardware and software specifics.*

At announcement time, we will produce major "announcement advertising" (2-page units) for management publications and continue to emphasize the new product line with follow-up one-page units for the balance of year. This will require $500,000 or half the annual budget. We will use the same product announcement advertisements in key market publications.

Under this plan, we will hold back on advertising addressed to the data processing professional until announcement time and then produce an 8-page supplement on the new line for two computer publications, Computerworld *and* Datamation. *Then we will follow with 2-page semitechnical units for the balance of the year.*

This proposal will result in an expenditure of $500,000 or one-half the total budget to reach the management audience, and the remaining half to reach key markets and data processing professionals, with key markets getting the larger share. From an emphasis standpoint, this proposal devotes roughly one-third of the total budget to results-oriented capability advertising and two-thirds to the new product announcement.

OBJECTIVES OF THE 1974
ADVERTISING PROGRAM

In September 1973, Mr. Lynch outlined the broad objectives for the 1974 advertising program as he saw them:

A computer-buying decision is generally looked on as a significant long-term relationship. For this reason, the stature and commitment of the supplier can be as important as the performance of the system. Moreover, as the marketplace becomes more sophisticated, our users become increasingly concerned with a system's ability to achieve an overall result and less interested in the specifications and performance of bits and pieces of the system. As a result of these conditions in the market-place, we want to be known as a company fully committed to satisfying the information system needs of its customers, and we will continue to position our company as a fully-capable contender and logical alternative to IBM. Moreover, rather than emphasizing specific hardware and software features, we want to stress the overall results which our systems can achieve. In doing this, we can capitalize on the acceptance we have achieved at major, well known companies.

Many users have had traumatic experiences in converting from one computer system to a newer generation or even a newer model. Our new line has been designed to make the transition as painless as possible. In announcing it, we must stress that it enhances the continuity of our users' past and present investments in information systems.

Our objectives must be accomplished within a budget that recognizes the tremendous pressures for profitability in a lackluster, if not deteriorating, national economy. We'll have to do the job with no more, and perhaps less, money than we had last year. Fortunately, we've got a lot going for us. Our signature, "The

Other Computer Company: Honeywell," is well-recognized and right on target as a corporate positioning statement. And we've got a device in the computer component animals that is a proven attention-getter and identifier.

It was with these objectives in mind that Mr. Lynch and Mr. Callanan would review the proposals which the advertising department had presented and decide how to build a successful advertising campaign for 1974.

EXHIBIT 1
COMPUTER INDUSTRY SHARE OF MARKET WORLDWIDE
Honeywell Information Systems

	1953 $150 million	1958 $650 million	1963 $4.1 billion	1968 $7 billion	1970 $7.1 billion	1971 $7.2 billion	1972 $8 billion	1973 $9 billion
IBM	36%	73.7%	78.7%	69.7%	71.1%	67.9%	64.2%	63.9%
Honeywell		0.6	1.7	4.3	7.3	9.6	10.6	10.5
GE			1.2	4.0				
Univac	49	13.7	6.5	5.9	5.9	7.8	8.0	7.5
Burroughs		3.1	2.0	3.2	3.2	4.3	4.6	4.7
Control Data			2.7	4.3	4.2	4.0	4.4	4.2
RCA		1.5	2.5	3.4	2.3			
NCR			1.6	2.2	2.1	2.1	2.5	2.5
Others	15	7.4	3.1	3.0	3.9	4.3	5.7	6.7
	100%	100%	100%	100%	100%	100%	100%	100%

Source: International Data Corporation.

EXHIBIT 2
Continued

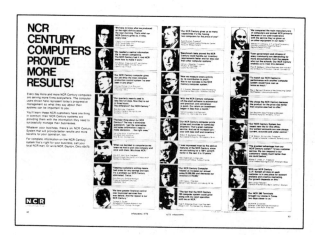

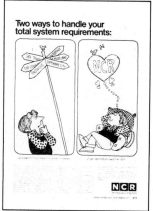

EXHIBIT 2
Continued

EXHIBIT 2
Continued

EXHIBIT 3
ABBREVIATED CHART OF DATA-PROCESSING OPERATIONS, 1973
Honeywell Information Systems

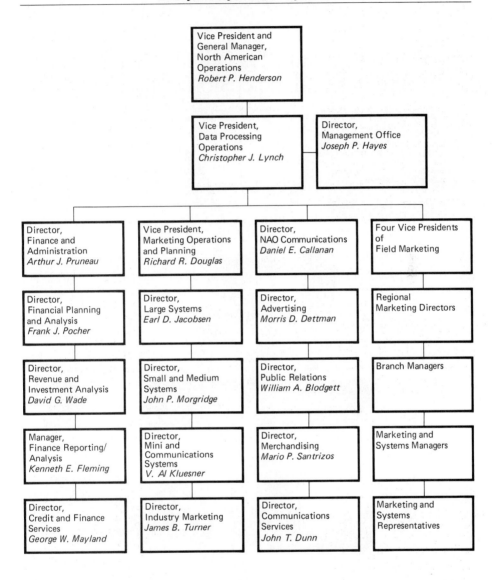

When you haven't got all the customers, you fight for all the customers you've got.

The way we see it, the only way to get ahead in this business is to do right by the business you've got.

So we make sure our customers are happy customers. We make sure our computer systems are doing what our customers expect them to do: solving the right problems—faster, better, more economically.

We've got a world-wide force of support specialists who make sure your investment in a Honeywell computer system pays off for you. Now. And in the future.

And best of all, Honeywell offers basic software, systems support, application packages, and education at no extra cost.

Sure, we'll fight for new customers. More aggressively than any other company in the business.

But after we get the business, we knock ourselves out.

EXHIBIT 5
EXAMPLES OF ONE SCULPTURE USED IN SEVERAL DIFFERENT ADVERTISEMENTS ADDRESSED TO DIFFERENT AUDIENCES
Honeywell Information Systems

EXHIBIT 5
Continued

EXHIBIT 6
EXAMPLES OF PRINT ADVERTISING CAMPAIGNS
Honeywell Information Systems

MANAGEMENT CAMPAIGN

Objective: To build awareness of Honeywell as a computer manufacturer that:

- Is the logical alternative to IBM
- Is committed to delivering results
- Has a total capability that combines people, products, and services
- Is dedicated to the long-range continuity of its customer's investments in information systems

Target audience: Middle and top managements of present and potential computer user organizations.

KEY MARKET CAMPAIGN

Objective: To emphasize Honeywell's commitment and communicate its industry-specific capabilities to selected key markets.

Target audience: Operating and top management personnel in selected industries.

DATA-PROCESSING PROFESSIONAL CAMPAIGN

Objective: To build awareness of Honeywell's technological expertise among data-processing professionals.

Target audience: Managers of data-processing installations, key systems personnel, and consultants (specifiers of computer equipment).

EXHIBIT 6
Continued

Management

Management

Management

Management

Key Market — Banking

Key Market — Manufacturing

Key Market — Hospitals

Key Market — Education

Key Market — Distribution

EXHIBIT 6
Continued

Key Market — Local Government

Merger Announcement

Data Processing Professionals

Data Processing Professionals

EXHIBIT 7
RESEARCH TRENDS
Honeywell Informations Systems

	1962	1964	1966	1968	1970	1972
Number surveyed......	400	410	300	302	300	378
	100%	100%	100%	100%	100%	100%

When asked to name the leading computer manufacturers, a sample of executives gave the following responses:

	1962	1964	1966	1968	1970	1972
IBM	93%	97%	98%	97%	98%	96%
Honeywell	31	55	66	67	75	68
Univac	56	58	51	49	49	44
NCR	42	41	42	42	41	35
Burroughs	39	39	39	32	41	33
RCA	29	37	39	32	41	
GE	14	21	33	27	40	
Control Data	7	23	30	30	38	28

When asked what manufacturers they would consult if they were seeking new computer equipment, the executives responded as follows:

	1962	1964	1966	1968	1970	1972
IBM	83%	89%	92%	91%	90%	87%
Honeywell	14	32	46	43	48	44
Univac	33	36	30	20	19	17
NCR	24	23	24	29	31	22
Burroughs	19	19	17	20	20	20
RCA	16	14	20	14	21	
GE	5	9	16	12	16	
Control Data	2	5	7	10	12	9

Source: Financial Executive Benchmark Studies conducted annually by BBDO.

EXHIBIT 8
BUSINESS WEEK ADVERTISING READERSHIP RESEARCH SCORES, 1971—1973
Honeywell Informations Systems

Issue	Ad subject	% recalling	Issue norm	Rank	Cost efficiency index	Rank
1/20/70	Small computer (frogs)	20	14	3	176	3
2/17/70	Cost effectiveness (bull)	32	9	1	440	1
3/17/70	Maintenance (owl)	38	14	1	266	3
4/14/70	Maintenance (owl)	25	7	1	408	1
5/12/70	Small computers (frogs)	34	8	1	687	1
6/09/70	Maintenance (owl)	27	7	2	676	1
7/07/70	Small computers (frogs)	34	9	1	387	1
8/04/70	Small computers (frogs)	33	13	1	246	1
9/01/70	Maintenance (owl)	27	10	1	289	1
9/29/70	Cost effectiveness (bull)	25	9	1	357	1
10/27/70	Maintenance (owl)	24	8	2	310	2
3/20/71	Time-sharing (tub)	32	7	3	226	2
4/17/71	Time-sharing (tub)	31	8	2	247	2
5/15/71	Responsiveness (St. Bernard)	25	11	3	209	4
6/05/71	Responsiveness (St. Bernard)	31	9	1	179	5
7/10/71	Complete line (steer)	43	11	1	425	1
8/07/71	Complete line (steer)	36	10	1	430	2
10/02/71	Complete line (steer)	38	9	1	628	1
10/30/71	Time-sharing (tub)	23	8	3	249	2
1/22/72	Response 2000 (eagle)	36	11	1	321	2
4/15/72	Customer support (kangaroo)	23	9	3	400	2
5/13/72	System 700 (bees)	26	7	2	474	2
6/24/72	System 700 (bees)	31	9	1	452	2
7/08/72	Responsiveness (poodle)	40	12	1	165	5
8/05/72	Cost effectiveness (grizzly)	21	11	4	182	3
10/28/72	Responsiveness (poodle)	28	7	1	468	1

Source: "Multimeasure Proved Advertising Recall Studies," conducted for *Business Week* by Opinion Research Corporation, Princeton, N.J. Studies show ability of readers of publication to recall (unaided) advertisements appearing in each issue. Note that the Honeywell ad ranked first in 16 of the 26 insertions listed, based on recall percentage, and first 11 times based on cost efficiency.

L'eggs PRODUCTS, INC.

HARVEY SINGER
Research Associate
Harvard Graduate School of Business Administration

F. STEWART DEBRUICKER
Assistant Professor
The Wharton School, University of Pennsylvania

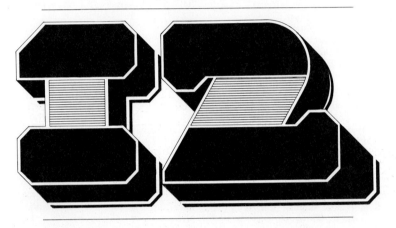

Jack Ward sat down at his desk one day in the summer of 1973 to resolve a problem which required a decision that week. As group product manager of L'eggs Products, Inc., he had to decide what supplemental advertising and promotional activities, if any, to employ for L'eggs Pantyhose during the coming fall season.

L'eggs Products, Inc., was a subsidiary of the Hanes Corporation, producers of hosiery, knitwear, and foundation garments. L'eggs Pantyhose was the first major nationally branded and advertised hosiery product distributed through food and drug outlets. It had been remarkably successful since its first test market introduction in 1970, through market-by-market roll-out, and now was distributed through grocery stores and drugstores in 90 percent of the country. By mid-1973 it accounted for over 25 percent of the hosiery volume done by food and drug outlets. These outlets represented between 20 and 25 percent of total United States hosiery sales. The resulting 5 to 6 percent overall market share made L'eggs Pantyhose the largest selling single brand in the hosiery industry.

With success, however, had come increased competitive efforts from other major manufacturers and from private label brands. In response, and in keeping with the L'eggs philosophy of aggressive marketing utilizing packaged goods techniques to reinforce consumer purchase behavior, L'eggs was considering various types of advertising and promotional activities for the fall season of 1973. These would coincide with the back-to-school season and the advent of cooler weather, both traditional stimuli to hosiery sales.

DEVELOPING THE L'eggs STRATEGY, 1969–1972[1]

L'eggs was the first brand in the hosiery industry to utilize a "packaged goods" marketing program to advertise, promote, display, and sell hosiery to the consumer through food and drug outlets. This represented a departure from the traditional methods used to merchandise hosiery.

Before the introduction of L'eggs, branded hosiery sales by major industry producers (including Hanes) were made exclusively through department and specialty stores. Starting in 1965, however, sales of private label hosiery through supermarkets and drugstores had grown dramatically and by 1969 represented a significant share—6 percent for drugstores and 12 percent for supermarkets—of the $1.5 billion retail hosiery market.

Noting these trends, Hanes investigated possible entry into these mass-merchandising outlets on a branded basis. Extensive market, consumer, and product research studies were made to determine (1) the actual size, composition, and nature of the market; (2) consumer attitudes and behavior toward hosiery in general and supermarket hosiery in particular; (3) whether new products developed by Hanes would fulfill planned advertising promises and the consumer expectations these generated.

Market information received from the A. C. Nielsen Company store audits in 1969 verified the existence of a substantial market, but indicated problems to be overcome if food and drug hosiery sales were to reach full potential (as compared with health and beauty aid products, for example, where mass outlets accounted for 50 percent of industry volume). Further channel research isolated these problems:

1   A very fragmented market. Over 600 different hosiery brands were sold in mass outlets, and no brand had more than a 4 percent share.

---

[1] Material in this section is taken from a speech made to the American Marketing Association in November 1972 by David E. Harrold, the original marketing director of L'eggs Products, Inc., and now president of Hanes Knitwear Division.

2   Advertising and promotion to stimulate sales were based on price only—rather than informing the consumer about product qualities or why she should consider buying in a particular outlet.

3   Stock-outs ran as high as 25 percent—manufacturers did not anticipate needs, keep stocks in balance, nor provide necessary service.

4   Retail turnover lagged behind the average of all food and drug products—the retailer's return on investment was unattractive.

Consumer research provided insights into what had to be done to establish a permanent branded franchise:

1   The consumer felt that supermarket and drugstore hosiery had a low-quality image.

2   There was no brand loyalty.

3   Products lacked consistency from package to package.

4   Frequent stock-outs diluted the consumer's confidence in product availability and drove her back to traditional hosiery outlets where such problems did not exist.

Despite these problems, the research indicated a strong desire by consumers to purchase hosiery regularly in convenience outlets if they could develop a lasting confidence in the product.

Hanes concluded that the trade and consumer needed a completely new hosiery product and a marketing program which would build consumer loyalty by virtue of unique product benefits: a distinctive name, package, and display; heavy advertising to build awareness of the brand name, the product's benefits and consistency, and where the product was to be available; and promotional techniques to stimulate both trial and repeat purchases.

The company had developed a new and superior product (preferred over any product tested against it, including the consumer's own brand). It was a one-size, superstretch pantyhose which had no shape until placed on the woman's leg, and which then shaped itself to conform to her leg structure, thereby providing an excellent fit for 70 percent of all wearers. This product was more expensive to manufacture than conventional pantyhose. However, with only one size required, Hanes could drastically reduce the inventory and display space required at retail and could consider major innovations in packaging and display.

Hanes sought to develop an integrated hosiery program for food stores and drugstores in which all elements including name, package design, display configuration, advertising, and promotion would complement each other. The name, package, and display would have to be dramatic and different if they were to attract the consumer's attention in the store. Other objectives were (1) a package which would differentiate the Hanes product from competitive offerings, minimize pilferage, simplify consumer choice, and facilitate stocking; and (2) a display which would hold an adequate amount of inventory to minimize stock-outs, while utilizing the smallest practical amount of costly square footage and the greatest practical amount of "free" vertical space. In addition, it was hoped that the display could be designed in such a way that it would be of use to Hanes but not to competitive brands, and that the display would be able to provide service and education to the consumer via information panels, literature racks, etc. In essence, Hanes management hoped to use display and packaging techniques to duplicate, in self-service channels, the personalized service available in department and specialty stores.

Working with a package design consultant, the Hanes new product group developed the brand name *L'eggs*. The name, in turn, suggested the package, an actual plastic egg held in color-coded cylinders (for various colors and styles) that was modular and distinctive from competition. They developed a plastic display (called the *L'eggs Boutique*) that carried through the egg concept. It had only a 2-foot diameter, carried 24 dozen pairs, lent itself to placement in high-traffic locations of the store, and proved to be a highly effective point-of-purchase device. Exhibit 1 illustrates the L'eggs Boutique.

The L'eggs program was supported by advertising and promotion spending equal to that of a new cigarette or detergent introduction. Introductory advertising was at the rate of $10 million nationally, a level twice as high as total advertising expenditures for the entire industry in support of name brands. Media included daytime and prime-time (7:00 P.M. to 11: P.M.) television, magazines, Sunday supplements, and local newspapers. In L'eggs' test market cities, two out of three hosiery advertisements seen by consumers were for L'eggs—a brand available only in supermarkets and drugstores. As Mr. David Harrold, the original marketing director of L'eggs Products, explained:

> Given the unstructured market, the nonexistent brand awareness of food and drug hosiery, and the need to reinforce brand permanency to the consumer and the trade, we wished to: (a) build strong brand awareness and recognition of our logo and package; (b) let the consumer know where L'eggs was available, that it was new and different, and that it would become a permanent grocery and drugstore fixture; (c) stress our major product attribute, that L'eggs fit better than any other hosiery product—our theme was "Our L'eggs fit your legs"; (d) show the display and package in all advertising to make them synonymous with the L'eggs program.

In addition to media advertising, a $5 million market-by-market consumer promotion plan was tested, using introductory direct-mail coupons worth 25 or 35 cents off the purchase of one pair, as the products were introduced in each test market. This was the hosiery industry's first use of heavy couponing as a strategic trial-generating device to increase consumer awareness and product experience.

The L'eggs marketing strategy also included a major innovation in the distribution system offered to the trade. L'eggs hosiery was delivered through the front door of the store directly to the retail display by L'eggs sales personnel in distinctive L'eggs trucks. These salespersons saw that a full range of styles and colors was always in stock. They ensured attractiveness and cleanliness of the display. They rotated and balanced inventory for each store's display rack to maximize sales velocity at each location. Accordingly, the displays had excellent turnover. The company estimated that L'eggs dollar sales per square foot were more than seven times the retailer's average for all goods, and—since the products were consigned[1]—the retailer had no investment. The sales-route force also acted as a detail force to implement promotions and other merchandising events at store level.

Another innovation was a computerized, on-line marketing and sales information network to support the distribution system. It tracked product movement for each display, and through its reports L'eggs could assure balanced product availability on every route van, in every warehouse, and along the pipeline from factory to each market. An outside management consulting firm was hired to design and implement this information and control system. In use, it coordinated manufacturing, warehouse distribution, retail inventory balancing, sales and market analysis, and billing and accounts receivable. Each sales call to a display unit provided a body of inventory and sales information to the system. This information was then assembled by display, by account, by route, by market, and by branch warehouse on a weekly basis and provided an excellent and timely data source for analysis of sales performance. In addition, extensive marketing information was routinely gathered in all markets via store audits and diary panels purchased from syndicated information sources. Special field survey research in specific markets conducted by outside research contractors, plus concept tests and focus group interviews conducted by the company's own market research personnel, supplemented the routine syndicated information.

SALES RESULTS THROUGH 1972

Test marketing was conducted from March to October of 1970. After the first 6 months of test market, 40 percent of all potential women users had tried L'eggs at least once. Over two-thirds of those triers repeated with one or more subsequent purchases. Brand awareness and advertising awareness exceeded 80 percent after only 7 weeks of advertising in the test markets. L'eggs became the leading brand of pantyhose, regardless of outlet, in the test markets. At the end of 6 months, almost 25 percent of all women listed L'eggs as their regular brand.

Market-by-market roll-out commenced in the fall of 1970. At its introduction into each geographic market, L'eggs was accompanied by high levels of advertising, demonstration, introductory coupons, and cents-off deals to induce initial trial. This introductory program was often continued for 13 weeks or more, until the product group felt that the introductory objectives had been met. Additional coupon promotions in specific markets were generally repeated several

---

[1] That is, the retailer was not billed for the product until after it had been purchased by a consumer.

times per year. The L'eggs brand quickly became the dominant factor influencing the entire industry's approach to consumer marketing of hosiery products.

In 1970, L'eggs retail sales were $9 million, representing only 9 months' sales experience in test markets accounting for 3½ percent of the United States and 2 months' sales in the first roll-out market. In 1971, retail sales were over $54 million. L'eggs became firmly established as the best-selling hosiery brand in the country, regardless of outlet, with over a 3 percent share of the total $1.6 billion market. This level was reached with distribution which in 1971 covered only 33 percent of the United States, on the average.

The L'eggs program dramatically expanded hosiery sales through food and drug outlets. Prior to the introduction of L'eggs, only one out of four women had purchased hosiery in these outlets. After 6 months in test markets, over 40 percent of all women had tried L'eggs, which were available only through food and drug outlets. Nielsen data confirmed that total hosiery sales through convenience outlets had expanded substantially; L'eggs sales were thus primarily "add-on" sales. Trade acceptance and distribution levels in all market areas equalled the penetration that an established marketing company such as Procter & Gamble or General Foods would expect to achieve on a major new product introduction—even though this was Hanes' first exposure to mass-merchandising channels.

By the end of 1972, the program had expanded into 75 percent of all retail markets. Fifty major markets had been opened in the span of 18 months. About 45,000 stores were under contract to display the L'eggs Boutique in prominent, high-traffic locations.

1973: MARKETING ORGANIZATION AND STRATEGY

As of mid-1973, the success of the L'eggs program had continued. As market by market roll-out proceeded, and L'eggs attained deeper penetration of each successive market, retail sales climbed to over $110 million in 1972 and were projected to top $150 million for the fiscal year ending December 31, 1973. By mid-1973, L'eggs had achieved distribution in over 90 percent of the United States and was represented in every major market except New York City. The company's goal was to become fully national by late 1973.

The marketing organization had expanded from an in-house group that in 1969 consisted only of a marketing director, one product manager, an assistant, and one merchandising manager. The present structure included product managers for each of L'eggs major product extensions; assistants and merchandising managers for each; managers for new products and market development; and a marketing research group. This was in addition to some 700 sales and administrative personnel. An organization chart is shown in Exhibit 2.

Since introducing the original L'eggs Pantyhose and stockings, the company had introduced several successful product extensions under the L'eggs brand: Sheer From Tummy to Toes pantyhose, Queensize pantyhose, Sheer

TABLE 1
L'eggs SHARE OF TOTAL HOSIERY SOLD
THROUGH FOOD AND DRUG OUTLETS (Unit basis, pairs)

	Jan.– Feb.	Mar.– Apr.	May– June	July– Aug.	Sept.– Oct.	Nov.– Dec.
1972	20%	22%	25%	27%	27%	27%
1973	29%	30%	31%	29%		

Source: Nationally syndicated retail audit service.

Energy (a support-hosiery product positioned toward nonsupport-hose wearers), and L'eggs Knee Highs. All these product extensions cannibalized the original L'eggs brand to some extent, but the majority of sales were pure incremental sales—coming at the expense of competitors in the market place and expanding the total unit and dollar sales of L'eggs Products, Inc.

The use of packaged goods marketing techniques continued to receive the same emphasis in 1973 as it had during the original test market period. Now that L'eggs was approaching 100 percent national distribution, the initial test market advertising and promotion spending of $15 million on an equivalent national basis had evolved to an annual spending level of nearly $20 million for advertising, promotion, market research, and new product development.

The sales effectiveness of this strategy was readily apparent, as detailed in Table 1.

THE INDUSTRY

L'eggs was introduced into a mature, stable industry. After some expansion in the 1960s with the widespread introduction of pantyhose, the industry had stabilized at a dollar volume of about $1.5 billion and was not expected to increase. Unit sales had increased moderately over the previous several years, but this increased demand had not expanded dollar volume, since the increased sales had only come in the wake of decreased prices. Many purchasers had merely shifted from name brand department store hosiery at an average price of around $3 to discount hosiery sold in food and drug outlets at prices typically ranging from $0.99 to $1.39. Trade publications had estimated that up to 50 percent of food and drug private label hosiery sold at prices as low as $0.39 per pair.

Grocery and drugstore outlets represented the fastest growing hosiery channel. Estimates in the trade were that these outlets had accounted for only 5 percent of the units (pairs) sold in 1968. They accounted for 22.1 percent of unit sales in 1972 and were expected to account for as much as 50 percent of unit sales by 1976. L'eggs Products, Inc., had prepared its own estimates of distribution channel changes which are shown in Exhibit 3.

The major companies in the industry appeared to be hastening this trend with huge amounts of marketing spending to advertise and promote food and drug hosiery. Estimates of industry spending ran as high as $33 million in each of 1972 and 1973 by three companies alone, although this figure was probably based on announced intentions and not actual spending.

COMPETITION

Although there were almost 600 different brands of hosiery competing in food and drug outlets, many were private label and house brands, and the large majority of these were distributed only locally or in a grocery chain's own outlets. L'eggs' only identifiable branded competition in 1972 and 1973 were those products marketed by the Hanes Corporation's major competitors in the hosiery industry: Kayser-Roth Corporation and Burlington Industries. These companies, like Hanes, witnessed the stagnation of hosiery in department store outlets, and soon after L'eggs appeared brought out their own heavily advertised and promoted brands for food and drug outlet distribution. Kayser-Roth's entry was called *No Nonsense Pantyhose,* and Burlington called its product *Activ Pantyhose.*

These competitors were companies with considerable financial resources in comparison to the Hanes Corporation. Hanes' 1972 sales were $245 million, of which women's hosiery accounted for about $140 million. Hanes' other divisions manufactured and marketed men's and women's knit outerwear and underwear, foundation garments, and swimwear. Kayser-Roth had sales of $519 million in 1972, of which women's hosiery was estimated to account for less than 20 percent. Kayser-Roth also manufactured men's sportswear and clothing, women's sportswear and swim suits, textiles, and Supphose, the industry's leading support-hosiery brand. Burlington Industries was even larger, with 1972 sales of $1.8 billion, of which women's hosiery sales were $101 million. Burlington also manufactured many other products, such as fabrics, yarns, hosiery for private label marketers, carpets, furniture, sheets and pillowcases, and industrial textiles. Additional financial information for the three companies is given in Exhibit 4.

These competitors each utilized a somewhat different marketing strategy for hosiery products sold through food and drug channels. Kayser-Roth marketed its No Nonsense brand through supermarket warehouse distributors, who delivered to the back door inventory area of the store—a system typical of packaged goods products. To compensate the store or chain for stocking and cleaning retail displays, No Nonsense offered a retail margin of 42 percent versus L'eggs' 35 percent. The No Nonsense retail prices started at $0.99 versus $1.39 and up for L'eggs.

Burlington distributed its Activ brand in a manner similar to that used by L'eggs. Activ salespersons and vans delivered via the "front door" to the Activ display fixture in food and drug outlets. In addition, Burlington distributed Activ through the General Cigar Corporation, which placed the product in cigar stores and newsstands to achieve a retail base beyond food and drug outlets. Like No Nonsense, Activ's suggested retail price of $1 was substantially below that of L'eggs.

L'eggs responded to this price competition neither by direct price-cutting policies of its own nor by permitting the retailers to reduce normal L'eggs prices at the store level. L'eggs was a fair-trade item, and indeed the maintenance of the fair-trade policy was strictly enforced by the company. Management had not hesitated to drop individual stores or even chains from the retail network when they became aware of discounting and abuse of suggested prices for L'eggs products (via information gathered by the route salespersons during store visits). Retail price maintenance was an important part of L'eggs' overall marketing strategy.

The L'eggs response to competitive price differences was to continue the original strategy of competing in food and drug channels on bases other than price, particularly superior fit. L'eggs management believed that higher prices were necessary and justified because their product was more expensive to produce, due to specially developed high-quality yarn and 100 percent inspection. L'eggs management preferred over the long run to pursue a strategy of maintaining prices and using the resulting margins to support product improvements and advertising to the consumer. In 1973, L'eggs contribution was about $5 per dozen pairs.

An additional reaction to branded price competition came in 1971 when L'eggs Products, Inc., test-marketed its own $0.99 brand, First To Last. The First To Last marketing strategy did not utilize price as the primary sales quality differentiating the product—because there were numerous house brands and private label pantyhose in all retail outlets that sold at prices considerably below $0.99. Rather, the durability and long-lasting qualities of the product were stressed. Advertising and promotion for First To Last made a conscious effort to minimize any linkage in the consumer's mind between First To Last and L'eggs brands, thereby reducing the degree of cannibalization. The First To Last roll-out proceeded cautiously, with the objective of profitable penetration before further expansion, and in mid-1973 First To Last was distributed in less than 10 percent of the United States.

Although Activ and No Nonsense each announced at their respective introductions planned advertising and promotion spending levels of $10 million nationally, the actual figures were much less. Industry estimates were that No Nonsense would spend no more than $3 million and Activ no more than $1.5 million in 1973. This was partially due to a slower distribution growth than originally planned. While Kayser-Roth had announced that No Nonsense would be distributed in 60 percent of the United States by the end of 1973 and 100 percent by 1974, Mr. Ward estimated that actual distribution had reached less than 15 percent of the country by mid-1973 and would be no more than 40 percent by the end of the year. Similarly, while Burlington had planned for Activ to be distributed in 35 percent of the United States by the end of 1973 and 50 percent by 1974 or 1975, Mr. Ward estimated that actual distribution had reached less than 10 percent of the country by summer of 1973 and would be no more than 30 percent by late fall.

Market shares for No Nonsense and Activ reflected this lack of national distribution and penetration in comparison to L'eggs: In late summer 1973, national market shares in food and drug outlets were 1 percent for both No Nonsense and Activ, compared to 29 percent for L'eggs Pantyhose. Mr. Ward noted, however, that actual spending levels indicated that these competitors could be major factors in geographic markets where they had achieved distribution.

DEVELOPING A SUPPLEMENTAL
PROGRAM FOR FALL, 1973

In considering various supplemental advertising and promotion programs for the fall season, Mr. Ward was acutely aware of the fact that L'eggs seemed to have at least two distinct types of markets characterized by different levels of consumer response to its products. Like many mass marketers, L'eggs used as a measure of this responsiveness a quantity called the BDI (brand development index). For L'eggs, BDI was defined for each geographic market as the number of L'eggs pairs sold per thousand target women per week divided by the national average number of L'eggs pairs sold per thousand target women per week, then multiplied by 100. An area with BDI below 100 was an area where L'eggs lagged in penetration versus its national average. Exhibit 5 presents a listing of markets, their BDIs, and share of L'eggs sales accounted for by each.

In certain regions of the country, the BDIs were consistently less than 80. Mr. Ward's rationale was that these areas had longer warm seasons that might explain lower pantyhose sales. Consumer surveys and panels conducted frequently by L'eggs' market research group, by the advertising agency, and by hired outside research organizations had shown that these low-BDI markets almost uniformly had low—and unsatisfactory—L'eggs trial rates. Typical comparisons between markets are shown in Exhibits 5 and 6. Thus, a major objective in low-BDI areas was to increase trial rates.

In other areas of the country trial rates had peaked at around 50 percent in 6 to 12 months after markets were opened. The brand group did not feel that trial rates in these areas could be increased profitably, or at least would not sustain increases long enough to generate profitable long-run sales. The major problem in high-BDI areas, therefore, was to increase the repurchase rate among L'eggs purchasers.

From different sources of research data, Mr. Ward inferred that much brand switching was taking place: In consumer market surveys, typically 20 to 30 percent of consumers would say that L'eggs was their usual brand. However, actual sales figures taken from the company's sales-tracking system and from syndicated store audits indicated that L'eggs had achieved only about a 10 percent share of the total market in high-BDI areas. Therefore, the most important objectives in these areas were to change users (even repeaters) from casual users to loyal users, to increase their repurchase rate, and to load users with the product to decrease the probability they would switch to competitive brands. Both Activ and No Nonsense were running introductory promotions as part of their roll-outs in many market areas during the fall season.

THE ALTERNATIVES

Mr. Ward was considering two basic approaches to accomplishing L'eggs' marketing objectives. On the one hand, he could boost L'eggs' planned media advertising expenditures for August through October from the currently planned level of approximately $2.5 million to, perhaps, $3.5 million. Such an increase in media advertising would ensure media dominance in all markets and would be expected to have a significant positive effect on both trial and repurchase. Advertising copy would stress L'eggs quality advantages (especially fit and durability), and subtly carry the message: "You get what you pay for." If spot TV rather than national television were purchased (at a cost penalty of about 20 percent), separate campaigns could be run in high-BDI and low-BDI areas, or expenditures could be concentrated in selected markets.

On the other hand, Mr. Ward was attracted by the idea (developed by the product group) of maintaining media advertising expenditures at the planned level but using in-store price promotions as a direct means of inducing consumer trial and/or repurchase. The product group had developed two such promotions: (1) a 40-cents-off twin-pack offer (see Exhibit 7) and (2) a 20-cents-off single-pack offer (see Exhibit 8).

In focusing on these alternatives, the product group had reasoned as follows about their likely effects: the 40-cent twin pack probably would achieve the objective of loading the consumer in high-BDI areas (for her next pair, the consumer would have the second pair of L'eggs in the twin pack already and would have no need to go out and purchase, perhaps, a competitive brand). Hopefully, more product use and experience with two pairs rather than one would predispose the consumer to repurchase L'eggs the next time she needed hosiery. However, Mr. Ward thought the twin pack might not be effective in low-BDI areas because, with low-trial and low-market share in these areas, sufficient numbers of consumers might not purchase the twin pack often enough to make the promotion effective. Besides, the consumer, not a L'eggs user anyway, might balk at having to purchase two pairs in order to try L'eggs.

The 20-cent single pack seemed to have a good potential in both types of markets. In low-BDI areas, consumer take-away for the promotion (the number of consumers purchasing) would presumably be higher because the new trier would not be forced to purchase two pairs. In high-BDI areas, the consumer might buy two or more single packs, satisfying the objective of consumer loading and raising repeat rates. There was nothing, however, to encourage the consumer (or force the consumer, as did the twin pack) to purchase more than one pair.

Under either alternative, L'eggs would bear 65 percent of the cost of the price reduction and the retailer would bear 35 percent (the same ratio as the retailer's gross margin). For example, for the 20-cents-off single pack, the retailer would absorb 7 cents (35 percent of 20 cents) and L'eggs would absorb 13 cents (65 percent of 20 cents).

Since L'eggs was a fair-traded item, Mr. Ward knew that it could not appear in any store under a cents-off deal except for a limited time only and could not appear in any store under two different prices for the same quantity (such as a regular-priced boutique pack and a 20-cents-off promotional single pack) simultaneously. This meant that to implement the single-pack offer, L'eggs would have to move all existing inventory out of stores at the beginning of the promotion, replace them with special 20-cents-off single packs, remove all special packs at the promotion's end, and move all regular inventory back in.

have to increase sales people

A possible solution was for L'eggs to make the special single pack a simple variation of the regular pack. At the promotion's start all existing store packs could have a flag inserted, then removed at the promotion's end. (Exhibit 8 shows a discount flag inserted into a regular L'eggs pack.) Because the L'eggs route persons were fully occupied by their normal stocking, accounting, and boutique cleaning operations in over 70,000 outlets, a temporary work force would have to be hired to travel with the route persons to insert flags. Mr. Ward estimated each of the 600 L'eggs route persons would need a temporary assistant for one 3-week cycle. These temporaries could be hired from well-known agencies at the rate of $30 per day per person. After the promotion was begun, the temporary labor would be replaced by factory labor because flags would be inserted in boutique-destined replacement packs at the factory. The product group recommended that the route persons be used for unflagging boutique packs at the promotion's end, even though their route schedules could be delayed considerably by the extra work.

To supplement the boutique in the stores during the promotion, the factory would also make up special "shippers"—self-contained cardboard floor displays packed at the factory to minimize setup time at the retail store, but which (if accepted by the retailer) would require allocating additional floor space to L'eggs (see Exhibit 9). Mr. Ward estimated the cost of the single-pack shippers, freight, point-of-sale material, etc., would average out to $0.35 per dozen pairs. These shippers could simply be removed at the promotion's conclusion.

The twin pack required no such expensive field labor to implement. Because the quantity in the promotional twin packs would differ from regular boutique packs (one pair each), the twin-pack shipper display could be utilized to implement the promotion (see Exhibit 10 for a mock-up of the twin-pack shipper) without boutique flagging. The shipper and promotional packs for it could be completely factory-made and placed in the store to coexist with regular-priced boutique packs, then simply removed at the promotion's conclusion. Fair-trade laws would not be violated, since the cents-off promotional twin packs would hold different quantities than the regular-priced boutique packs. Mr. Ward estimated the cost of making up these shippers, freight, point-of-sale material, and twin packs at $0.38 per dozen hosiery pairs.

He anticipated a bit of increased trade resistance to the twin-pack alternative since the shippers were absolutely necessary in the case of the twin packs, and thus the retailer would have to devote roughly 6 more square feet of selling space to L'eggs during the promotion. In contrast, the 20-cents-off single-pack alternative could be accomplished solely via flagged boutique packs if the retailer refused the additional single-pack shippers. However, Mr. Ward expected this resistance to be minimal because of L'eggs' outstanding sales velocity. In addition, retailer acceptance for the twin-pack alternative might be greater: The retailer could be shown that because the boutique packs at regular prices (and margins) were still in the store, consumers could elect to purchase a single pack at normal prices and margins instead of the twin pack with its commensurately lower margins per pair.

Mr. Ward recognized, of course, that it would theoretically be possible to use both the 40-cents-off twin-pack promotion in high-BDI markets and the 20-cents-off single-pack promotion in low-BDI markets. While conceptually attractive, such an option would be undesirable, in his view, because of increased costs and difficulty of implementation. Under either in-store price promotion alternative, for example, L'eggs planned to devote a substantial portion of its *normal* media advertising budget to advertising the promotion on television and in local newspapers. If the 20-cents-off single pack were used in some markets and the 40-cents-off twin pack in others, it would be necessary to switch from national network advertising to local spots at considerable additional cost.

Moreover, the mechanics of implementing two promotions simultaneously would cause headaches for L'eggs production and warehouse personnel, who would have to produce and ship several different types of point-of-sale materials, special packages, and shipper displays of merchandise. Finally, selling a "mixed" promotion to national and regional accounts, with stores in both high-BDI and low-BDI markets, would be exceedingly difficult. As Mr. Ward explained, "How do you convince Safeway's national buyer to take the promotion when you also have to tell him why his Little Rock stores have to take single-packs and his Los Angeles stores have to take twin-packs?"

ESTIMATING SALES RESPONSE TO PROMOTION

Relying on his personal judgment, and his experience gained during the national roll-outs, Mr. Ward estimated some of the sales response effects of the 20-cent single-pack and the 40-cent twin-pack promotions. For the 20-cent single pack, he reasoned that during the 4 weeks the promotional packs were actually in the stores, about 80 percent of what would have been L'eggs purchases at normal prices would be made instead at the reduced price. The other 20 percent would represent stores that did not accept the promotion, lost flags, and similar factors. Since normal L'eggs volume was running at 150,000 dozens per week, or 600,000 dozens per 4 weeks, Mr. Ward estimated that normal purchases at reduced prices would thus total 80 percent of 600,000, or 480,000 dozen.

It was more difficult, of course, to estimate the effect of a promotion on incremental business. Mr. Ward made the working assumption that the single-pack promotion would generate a 10 to 11 percent net cumulative sales increase[1] over an immediate period of 20 weeks during and following the promotion, plus a 10 percent long-term (sustained) sales increase.

For the 40-cent twin-pack alternative, Mr. Ward judged that during the 4

---

[1] That is, sales during the 20 weeks would be 10 to 11 percent greater (in aggregate) than they would have been without the promotion.

weeks the packs were actually in the stores, about 60 percent of what would have been L'eggs purchases at normal prices would be made instead at the reduced price. This estimate was lower than the 20-cent single-pack figures because:

1   Single pairs at regular prices would be coexisting in the stores with promotional packs, and women—even L'eggs users—who did not want two pairs would still have the opportunity to purchase one pair at regular prices.

2   Mr. Ward expected the twin-pack alternative to have less effect with non-loyal L'eggs users who might resist buying two pairs at a time, but might pick up one pair, even at regular price.

3   Some stores might not accept the promotion.

Taking these factors into account, Mr. Ward estimated that the twin-pack alternative would generate a 10 percent net cumulative sales increase over the immediate 20-week period during and following the promotion but would produce no long-term increase in sales.

Consumer response to an increased media advertising budget was exceptionally difficult to estimate, Mr. Ward believed, but would almost certainly not be as great (in the short run) as to either of the cents-off promotional alternatives. Nevertheless, he was strongly attracted to the ease of implementation of this alternative and to the possible strategic advantages of not focusing the consumer's attention on price at this point in the development of competition in the market. At his request, the L'eggs advertising agency had prepared rough copy boards for a series of 30-second vignettes, which stressed L'eggs superior quality, especially with regard to fit. (See Exhibit 11 for an example of the proposed copy.)

CONCLUSION

As he reviewed the alternatives, Mr. Ward remained convinced that some form of supplemental advertising or promotion should be employed during the fall of 1973. While L'eggs had had considerable market success during the 3 years since it had first begun test marketing, he considered it imperative that actions be taken to sustain that success, especially in the face of increasing competition. Moreover, he remained concerned about those low-BDI markets where L'eggs' apparent penetration was well below its national average.

Since the fall season was rapidly approaching, Mr. Ward knew that he would have to make a firm decision as to what course to follow before the end of the week.

Stress Quality RATHER than price

Advertise: Physical Attribute attractive legs - Psychological

EXHIBIT 1
L'eggs Products, Inc.

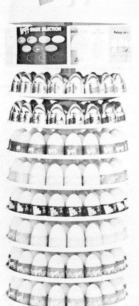

The classic
L'EGGS Boutique.

—A traffic-stopping showpiece.

—Easy to shop.

—Displays 288 of the most attractive packages ever seen in the hosiery industry.

—Stands on a 2-foot circle of floor space.

EXHIBIT 2
ORGANIZATION CHART
L'eggs Products, Inc.

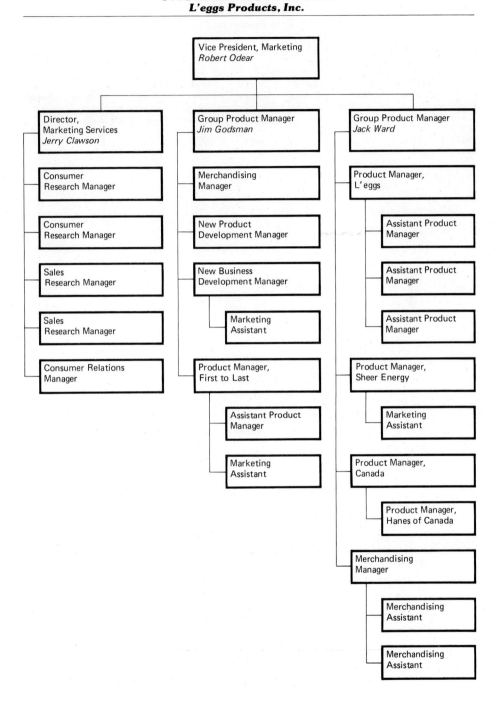

Vice President, Marketing
Robert Odear

Director, Marketing Services
Jerry Clawson
- Consumer Research Manager
- Consumer Research Manager
- Sales Research Manager
- Sales Research Manager
- Consumer Relations Manager

Group Product Manager
Jim Godsman
- Merchandising Manager
- New Product Development Manager
- New Business Development Manager
  - Marketing Assistant
- Product Manager, First to Last
  - Assistant Product Manager
  - Marketing Assistant

Group Product Manager
Jack Ward
- Product Manager, L'eggs
  - Assistant Product Manager
  - Assistant Product Manager
  - Assistant Product Manager
- Product Manager, Sheer Energy
  - Marketing Assistant
- Product Manager, Canada
  - Product Manager, Hanes of Canada
- Merchandising Manager
  - Merchandising Assistant
  - Merchandising Assistant

EXHIBIT 3
WOMEN'S HOSIERY UNIT SALES
1971–1973 ESTIMATED, 1974 FORECAST*
L'eggs Products, Inc.

	All hosiery				Pantyhose			
	Total volume	% of change	In food and drug	% of change	Total volume	% of change	In food and drug	% of change
1971	123		28		82		20.8	
1972	121	−2	29.5	+5	92	+12	24.4	+17
1973	114	−6	29.9	+2	85	−8	25.6	+5
1974	110	−4	30.5	+2	79	−7	25.0	−2

* Units: millions of dozens of pairs.
Source: Company estimates.

EXHIBIT 4
COMPANY FINANCIAL DATA*
L'eggs Products, Inc.

	Hanes	Kayser-Roth	Burlington
1972 total sales	245	579	1,816
1972 women's hosiery sales (est.)	142	80–100	101
1972 total net income	8.2	11.9	49.6
1971 total sales	176	467	1,727
1971 women's hosiery sales (est.)	88	70–95	115
1971 total net income	3.5	12.3	40

* All figures in millions of dollars.
Source: Annual Reports; Corporate 10-K forms filed with the Securities and Exchange Commission.

EXHIBIT 5
1972 PERFORMANCE IN MARKETS OPENED
DURING 1971 AND EARLIER
L'eggs Products, Inc.

Markets	BDI	Share of sales, %	Markets	BDI	Share of sales, %
Portland	80	1	Binghamton	110	1
Sacramento	60	1	Springfield	140	1
Milwaukee	90	2	Hartford/New Haven	90	2
Kansas City	70	1	Erie	160	*
Chicago	110	6	Buffalo	100	2
Los Angeles	120	7	Rochester	110	1
Eugene	80	*	Syracuse	150	2
Medford	60	*	Utica	50	*
Klamath Falls	80	*	Columbia/Jefferson City	90	*
St. Joseph	80	*	Macon	60	*
Topeka	60	*	Chattanooga	70	1
Madison	40	*	Grand Junction	170	*
Rockford	70	*	South Bend/Elkhart	100	1
Santa Barbara	70	*	Cincinnati	120	2
Philadelphia	130	9	Dayton	100	2
Reno	80	*	Indianapolis	110	2
Chico/Redding	90	*	Harrisburg/York	120	2
San Francisco	90	6	Green Bay	60	1
Salinas/Monterey	120	1	Terre Haute	60	*
San Diego	90	1	Eureka	130	*
Detroit	140	6	Las Vegas	130	*
Flint/Saginaw	150	2	Grand Rapids/Kalamazoo	150	2
Lansing	180	1	Fort Wayne	100	1
Boston	130	8	Boise	100	*
Providence	100	2	Twin Falls	110	*
Cleveland	110	5	Idaho Falls/Pocatello	130	*
Youngstown	90	1	Fresno	80	1
Atlanta	90	2	Phoenix	100	1
Denver	150	2	Tucson	60	*
Colorado Springs	100	1	Salt Lake City	80	1
Cheyenne	200	*	Miami	50	1
Toledo	90	1	Tampa	80	1
Columbus	150	2	West Palm Beach	60	*
Lima	110	*	Fort Myers	60	*
Zanesville	120	*	Pittsburgh	100	1
					100%

* Less than 0.5 percent.

EXHIBIT 6

PENETRATION MEASURES IN HIGH- AND LOW-BDI AREAS

L'eggs Products, Inc.

Market	Kansas City (low-BDI)			Philadelphia (high-BDI)		
Time after introduction	13 weeks, %	6 months, %	12 months, %	13 weeks, %	6 months, %	12 months, %
Brand awareness	90	90	90	100	100	100
Advertising awareness	60	60	60	80	70	70
Trial	20	20	30	30	40	50
Repurchase rate*	60	70	70	60	70	80
Product satisfaction	70	70	70	90	90	90
L'eggs is usual pantyhose brand	10	10	10	10	20	20

* Defined as percentage of triers who bought more than once in last 3 months.
Source: Company data.

EXHIBIT 7
40-CENTS-OFF TWIN-PACK
L'eggs Products, Inc.

EXHIBIT 8
20-CENTS-OFF SINGLE PACK
L'eggs Products, Inc.

EXHIBIT 9
SINGLE-PACK FLOOR DISPLAY
L'eggs Products, Inc.

EXHIBIT 10
TWIN-PACK FLOOR DISPLAY
L'eggs Products, Inc.

EXHIBIT 11
POSSIBLE ADVERTISING COPY FOR
FALL 1973 SUPPLEMENTAL CAMPAIGN
L'eggs Products, Inc.

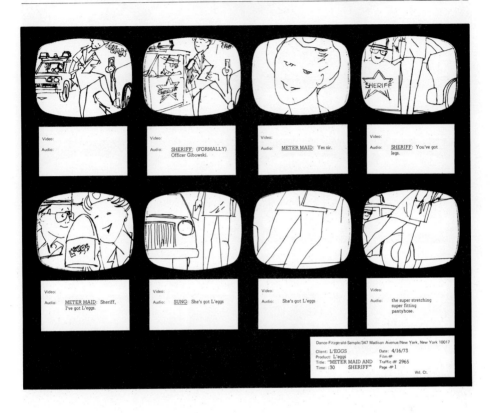

EXHIBIT 11
Continued

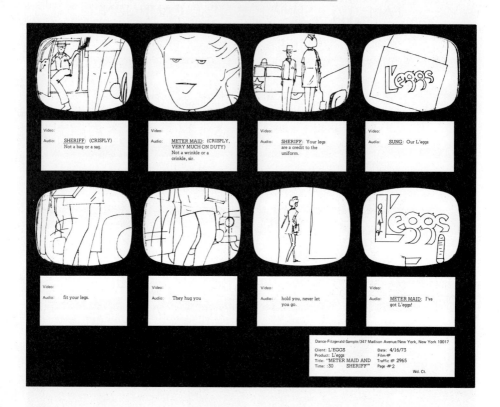

Video:

Audio: SHERIFF: (CRISPLY)
Not a bag or a sag.

Video:

Audio: METER MAID: (CRISPLY,
VERY MUCH ON DUTY)
Not a wrinkle or a
crinkle, sir.

Video:

Audio: SHERIFF: Your legs
are a credit to the
uniform.

Video:

Audio: SUNG: Our L'eggs

Video:

Audio: fit your legs.

Video:

Audio: They hug you

Video:

Audio: hold you, never let
you go.

Video:

Audio: METER MAID: I've
got L'eggs!

Dance-Fitzgerald-Sample/347 Madison Avenue/New York, New York 10017

Client: L'EGGS   Date: 4/16/73
Product: L'eggs   Film #
Title: "METER MAID AND   Traffic # 2965
Time: :30   SHERIFF"   Page #2
                                  Wd. Ct.

THE FEDERAL TRADE COMMISSION (1971)
IN RE: FIRESTONE

STEVEN H. STAR
Associate Professor
Harvard Graduate School of Business Administration

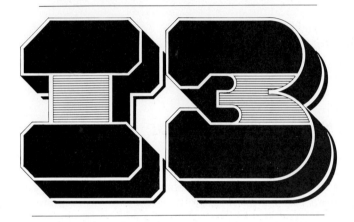

In July 1971, Mr. Robert Hughes, hearing examiner for the Federal Trade Commission, was considering the recent FTC complaint against the Firestone Tire & Rubber Company. In this complaint, the FTC had alleged that Firestone had engaged in deceptive advertising practices during 1966, 1967, and 1968. Hearings had been held in March, April, and May of 1971, and final arguments had been filed in June. It was now Mr. Hughes' responsibility to decide whether

This case was prepared from published sources and legal documents filed in the actions described in the case. It is intended for discussion by graduate students of business administration, and simplifies many of the legal issues under consideration. In addition, considerable evidence and certain arguments have been omitted for the sake of brevity. Consequently, this case should not be viewed as a complete summary of the actions it describes.

In several instances, the sequence of events has been modified; paraphrases and summaries of testimony are often presented as direct quotations. The hearing examiner described in the case is purely fictitious, as are the thought processes and opinions attributed to him.

Firestone had engaged in deceptive advertising, and, if he found that it had, to determine what remedies should be ordered.

Mr. Hughes' task was complicated by the intervention in the case of Students Opposed to Unfair Practices (SOUP) and the Association of National Advertisers (ANA). SOUP had argued that the FTC's traditional remedy, a "cease-and-desist" order, was inadequate in this case, since the effects of Firestone's allegedly deceptive advertising would continue to be felt even after the cessation of such advertising. To mitigate these long-term effects, SOUP had contended, Firestone should be required to "affirmatively disclose" its previous alleged deceptions in future advertisements. ANA, conversely, had argued (1) that the FTC lacked the authority to require "affirmative disclosure," (2) that the long-term effects of advertising were minimal, and (3) that affirmative disclosure, if adopted as a remedy by the FTC, would be injurious to the process of competition.

THE FEDERAL TRADE COMMISSION[1]

The FTC was established in 1914 as an independent regulatory agency. The FTC's primary responsibility was to enforce certain provisions of the antitrust laws, especially with regard to "unfair methods of competition in commerce." Since the meaning of the provisions in question was somewhat unclear, the FTC was intended to serve as a "forum" for the interpretation of the law as well as an enforcement agency. According to most legal scholars, the FTC's authority was thus limited to the issuance of cease-and-desist orders, which required that a party charged with specific "unfair practices" not engage in those unfair practices in the future. The FTC did *not* have the authority to impose penalties or sanctions unless one of its cease-and-desist orders was disobeyed.

Throughout its history, there had been considerable controversy concerning the scope of the FTC's authority and jurisdiction. During the 1920s, for example, the FTC became increasingly involved in consumer protection on the grounds that deceptive trade practices were a form of unfair competition. In 1931, the U.S. Supreme Court ruled that deceptive trade practices did not necessarily fall under the FTC's jurisdiction, since deceptive practices were not injurious to competition in an industry where most major competitors engaged in such practices. In 1936, however, Congress amended the Fair Trade Commission Act to give the FTC explicit jurisdiction over "unfair or deceptive acts or practices in commerce."

The FTC consisted of a Chairman and four Commissioners appointed for staggered 7-year terms. In 1970, the Commission staff included approximately

---

[1] This section of the case is based on the *Report of the ABA Commission to Study the Federal Trade Commission,* September 1969; E. Cox et al., *The Consumer and the Federal Trade Commission* (the "Nader Report"), 1969; G. J. Alexander, *Honesty and Competition,* Syracuse University Press, Syracuse, N.Y., 1967; and John Osborne, "Reform at the FTC," *New Republic,* October 2, 1971.

400 lawyers and 200 economists and other professionals. In general, the staff was expected to identify and investigate "unfair or deceptive practices in commerce" and bring them to the attention of the five Commissioners. If the Commissioners agreed that the practices in question were in fact either unfair or deceptive, the FTC staff could seek their curtailment through either formal or informal means. If the formal procedure were followed, the FTC staff would issue a formal complaint and proposed "order" or "remedy." The party against whom the complaint had been issued could then either agree to cease-and-desist from the practices in question or demand a formal hearing before a hearing examiner. At such hearings, the FTC staff and the respondent each presented briefs and oral arguments to the hearing examiner who then reached a decision and issued an order. Either party could then appeal the hearing examiner's decision to the five Commissioners. If the respondent were dissatisfied with the Commissioners' decision, he could appeal to the federal courts.

During the 1960s, the FTC placed increased emphasis on informal procedures, none of which had the force of law. Among the more important of these procedures, as summarized by the American Bar Association, were:

> **1** Industry Guides. *These constitute advice to the business community of the FTC's views of the legality of specific conduct in selected areas. . . .*
>
> **2** Advisory Opinions. *These opinions are rendered in response to individual inquiries concerning the legality of a proposed course of action. Opinions can be requested, for example, with respect to proposed advertising claims. . . . While the FTC may reconsider its advice, particularly in light of changed circumstances, the advice affords a businessman a dependable assurance that the agency will not move against the business conduct in question.*
>
> **3** Trade Regulation Rules. *These rules are published after hearings, at which all businessmen who are likely to be affected have an opportunity to present their views. . . .*
>
> **4** Assurances of Voluntary Compliance and Informal Corrective Actions. *"Assurances" are written agreements to discontinue objectionable practices, which now include a provision for the submission of a subsequent compliance report by the business unit.*

In the late 1960s, the FTC began to receive very strong criticism from a number of sources. In early 1969, for example, a group of law students working with consumer advocate Ralph Nader issued a report entitled *The Consumer and the Federal Trade Commission.* This report concluded that:

> *Among other failings, the agency's methods of detecting statutory violations were inadequate, its consumer protection program (particularly in the area of false advertising) was largely ineffective in coping with modern forms of deceptive advertising, its heavy reliance on voluntary enforcement techniques was failing to secure real compliance with the law, [and] that the overall performance of the FTC was "shockingly poor."*

Later in 1969, a special commission of the American Bar Association issued a report on the FTC.[1] While somewhat more temperate than the Nader group's report, the ABA commission was also highly critical of the FTC, especially in the area of consumer protection.

For example, the ABA commission was not favorably impressed with the methods used by the FTC to detect deceptive advertising:

> *The FTC's monitoring program is limited almost exclusively to examination of commercial advertising on national television. . . . Although vast amounts of material are accumulated dealing with national and local magazine advertising, national and regional radio scripts, regional television, and local newspaper advertising, no personnel have been assigned to screen this material. . . .*

The commission was extremely critical of the FTC's enforcement procedures:

> *The failure to put some bite into enforcement is illustrated by the long history of the FTC's dealings with the J. B. Williams Company over advertising campaigns for Geritol. After more than three years of investigation, the FTC, in December, 1962, directed the issuance of a complaint in which it alleged, among other things, that respondents had misrepresented the efficacy of Geritol in the treatment of tiredness, nervousness, loss of strength and irritability. No preliminary injunction was sought. About three years later a cease and desist order was entered which was eventually affirmed with slight modification by the Court of Appeals. . . . In March, 1969, almost 10 years to the day after the beginning of the investigation, the FTC found that certain of Geritol's commercials still violated the cease and desist order. . . . No further action has been taken.*

The ABA commission charged that the FTC had done a poor job of allocating its admittedly limited resources. A great deal of effort seemed to be going into relatively trivial matters (e.g., that "Navy shoes" were not made by the Navy; that "Indian" trinkets were not manufactured by Amercian Indians) rather than into the detection and prevention of deceptive practices which had a major impact on consumers. For example, in 1969, according to the ABA commission, only 12 attorneys were assigned to work on:

> *. . . misbranding of softwood lumber, cigarette advertising and labeling, fair packaging and labeling, encyclopedia and magazine subscription frauds, failure to publish or deceptive publication of gasoline octane ratings, advertising campaigns dealing with gasoline additives, promulgation of product safety standards, automobile warranty claims, and several other matters which are still confidential. . . . The predictable result is that investigations, once initiated, disappear from public view and surface, if at all, many years later.*

In 1970, President Nixon appointed Mr. Miles Kirkpatrick, who had been chairman of the ABA special commission, to be Chairman of the FTC. This ap-

---

[1] This study had been undertaken at President Nixon's request shortly after the publication of the Nader report.

pointment was widely interpreted in the press as a mandate for the FTC to increase its effectiveness. In his first few months, Mr. Kirkpatrick induced a number of promising young lawyers to join the FTC staff, including Robert Pitofsky, a New York University law professor who had been counsel to the ABA commission. Mr. Pitofsky became head of the FTC's Consumer Protection Bureau.

By July 1971, FTC activities in the field of consumer protection had increased noticeably. In recent months, for example, the FTC had obtained an injunction to prevent the insertion of razor blade samples in Sunday newspapers, asserted its authority to require affirmative disclosure, given increased attention to advertising directed at children, entered into a consent decree requiring affirmative disclosure,[1] and undertaken a major study of the processes through which television advertising affected consumer behavior.

THE FIRESTONE COMPLAINT

The FTC had issued its initial complaint against Firestone in June 1970. This complaint was directed at Firestone advertisements which had appeared in 1966, 1967, and 1968. According to the complaint, certain advertisements used by Firestone during this period had been deceptive with regard to pricing, product quality, and/or product safety.

PRICING

In the tire industry it was common to advertise price reductions on specified tires for limited periods of time. During the summer of 1966, for example, Firestone had run the following advertisements in a number of newspapers:

Gigantic July 4th Offer.
10 Day Offer Now Thru Sat. July 2

TIRE JAMBOREE

Low, low prices on our popular high quality nylon cord tire . . . the Firestone Safety Champion.
Jamboree Prices Start at $16 Plus $1.61 per tire Fed. Excise tax, sales tax and trade-in tire with recappable cord body 6.00-13 tubeless blackwall.

---

[1] On July 2, 1971, the FTC and ITT Continental Baking Company announced provisional acceptance of a voluntary consent order under which Continental would devote 25 percent of advertising expenditures for "Profile" bread for 1 year to affirmative disclosure of the fact that "Profile" was not effective for weight reduction, contrary to possible interpretations of prior advertising. Interestingly, the FTC staff had decided not to seek affirmative disclosure in a similar case against Swift Baby Food, since Swift was "an extremely weak company in this particular market (no. 4 in the four-member baby food field) and it was not thought desirable to impose an advertising requirement which might make it more difficult for Swift to become a more effective competitor in that product category. More significantly, this very weak position in the market indicated that . . . there must have been little residual effect on the consumer from the false advertising, one of the reasons for requiring corrective advertising in the first place. . . ." (Address by Gerald J. Thain, July 7, 1971.)

[Advertisement includes listing of other sizes of Safety Champion tires with price listed for each.]

* * * *

Now thru Sept. 3 SAVE BIG! BUY NOW AT DISCOUNT PRICES

FIRESTONE
Pre-Labor Day
TIRE SALE

Prices slashed on
FIRESTONE
Safety Champions

Sale Prices Start at $16 Plus $1.61 Fed. excise tax and trade-in tire off your car.

[Advertisement includes listing of other sizes of Safety Champion tires with price listed for each.]

According to the complaint, these advertisements clearly implied that:

> The tires advertised were being offered at prices which were significantly reduced from the actual bona fide prices at which those tires had been sold to the public at retail by respondent in the recent regular course of its business prior to the publication of the advertisement and purchasers would thereby realize bona fide savings in the amount of such reduction.

The complaint went on to allege that the tires in question were rarely sold at prices higher than those stated in the advertisements, and that the advertisements were thus deceptive.

PRODUCT QUALITY

During 1967, Firestone had used the following advertisement:

THE SAFE TIRE—FIRESTONE

When you buy a Firestone Tire—no matter how much or how little you pay—you get a safe tire: Firestone tires are custom-built one by one. By skilled craftsmen. And they're personally inspected for an extra margin of safety. If these tires don't pass all of the exacting Firestone inspections, they don't get out.

The complaint contended that this advertisement conveyed the impression that:

> A purchaser of a tire bearing the brand name "Firestone" is assured of receiving a tire which will be free from any defects in materials or workmanship or any other manufacturing defects. . . . Although [Firestone] may exercise due care in the course of manufacturing its tires, [Firestone] cannot assure that tires containing defects in materials or workmanship or other manufacturing defects will not reach the hands of the purchasing public.

PRODUCT SAFETY

The following statements had appeared in Firestone advertisements during 1967 and 1968:

> *Firestone—The Safe Tire. At 60,000 Firestone Safe Tire Centers. At no more cost than ordinary tires.*
>
> * * * *
>
> *Like the original Super Sports Wide Oval Tire. It came straight out of Firestone racing research.*
>
> *It's built lower, wider. Nearly two inches wider than regular tires. To corner better, run cooler, stop 25% quicker.*

According to the complaint, these statements implied that Firestone tires would be "safe under all conditions of use," and that Firestone:

> *. . . had established through adequate scientific tests that any car equipped with Firestone Super Sports Wide Oval tires could be stopped 25 percent quicker under typical road and weather conditions . . . when compared with the performance of the same vehicle under the same conditions when equipped with any [other] manufacturer's tires. . . .*

These implications were deceptive, the FTC alleged, because (1) the safety of any tire was dependent on the conditions (e.g., inflation pressure, vehicle weight) under which it was used and (2) Firestone had not established the performance claims for Super Sports Wide Oval tires through "adequate scientific tests."

REMEDY

The complaint concluded by requesting that Firestone be ordered to cease and desist from the allegedly deceptive practices described above.

THE HEARING

At the hearing, arguments were presented concerning the pricing issue, the product quality issue, the product safety issue, and the remedy itself.

THE PRICING ISSUE

On this issue, Firestone agreed with the complaint's allegation that the advertisements in question offered significant price reductions to consumers for specified periods of time. Arguments at the hearing thus focused on whether consumers had, in fact, been able to obtain significant price reductions during the "sale" periods.

In support of its complaint, the FTC presented a tabulation of data from a sample of 357 "sales slips" examined at Firestone stores in Washington, D.C., Philadelphia, and Baltimore. These sales slips covered sales of advertised tires during the summer of 1966. Of the 357 sales slips, 104 reflected purchases at or below advertised prices during periods when price reductions had been advertised. An additional 208 sales slips reflected purchases at prices at least 10 percent higher than advertised prices during periods when price reductions were not being advertised. According to the FTC, the remaining 45 sales slips reflected purchases either at or below advertised prices during "nonsale" periods, or purchases above advertised prices during "sale" periods.

The FTC contended that these pricing irregularities were highly significant, since price reductions played a major role in the sale of tires. Several years previously, for example, Firestone's Counsel had written to the FTC:

> Our Advertising Department feels, and this is supported by surveys they have made from time to time, that the only advertising which effectively produces greater than normal sales [is that] which pertain[s] to promotions which specifically refer to price reductions.

In response, Firestone contended that 28 of the sales slips at issue were explained by special situations, and that the remaining 17 sales slips represented an insignificant proportion of the total sample. According to Firestone, the 28 sales slips which reflected special situations were accounted for by employee discounts, discounts to employees' friends and relatives, tires sold after "sale" periods which had been ordered during "sale" periods, and, in one case, "a special price as a reward for [a customer's] honesty in returning the [higher-priced] tires put on his car by mistake." Firestone's allegations in these 28 cases were supported by affidavits of employees of the stores where the sales had taken place.

THE PRODUCT QUALITY ISSUE

On this issue, Firestone argued that the complaint's interpretation of how consumers would perceive these advertisements was erroneous. Firestone had hired an expert consultant to conduct a survey of how prospective tire buyers perceived the advertising claims in question. According to this survey, 52.7 percent of those interviewed "thought the advertisement said that [Firestone] did all it could to use the best procedures to make its tires safe and as free as possible of defects"; 30.2 percent "understood the advertisement to say that 'almost all' of [Firestone's] tires were safe under normal conditions" or "that 'each model' of [Firestone's] tires at least met minimum Government safety standards"; and 15.3 percent "thought the advertisement said that [Firestone's] tires were absolutely safe or absolutely free from defects." On the basis of this survey, Firestone argued that "no significant segment of the tire-buying public would actually purchase its tires by construing 'The safe tire' text as alleged in the complaint."

In response, while agreeing that the survey had been conducted in "a professional and competent manner," the FTC questioned whether a structured survey of this kind could measure a consumer's true perception of an advertisement under nonsurvey conditions. Moreover, the FTC argued, 15 percent was not an "insignificant segment," especially when safety was at stake.

THE PRODUCT SAFETY ISSUE

This issue was complex, and included references to advertisements which are not described in this case. Fairly typical, however, was the argument concerning the "stop 25% quicker" claim. The FTC contended that Firestone had not conducted scientific tests to establish this claim. Firestone alleged that its wide oval tire would, in fact, stop a vehicle 25% quicker than would ordinary tires on glare ice, and that it had test data to support this claim. Firestone did not, however, claim to have test data which demonstrated that the wide oval would stop 25% quicker on ordinary surfaces. The FTC did not dispute the wide oval tire's alleged perfomance on glare ice and did not present evidence suggesting that the wide oval tire would not stop 25% quicker on ordinary surfaces. In essence, the FTC was not disputing the performance claim, per se, but the fact that it was being made without the support of "adequate scientific tests."

A second dimension of this issue was concerned with the brand name used by Firestone for its "second level" line of tires prior to 1969. During the 1960s, Firestone had marketed this line of tires under the brand name *Safety Champion*. According to the FTC, this brand name implied that the tires:

> . . . had unique construction or performance features which rendered them safer than other tires; [but] that the tires so designated did not have any unique construction or performance features that rendered them safer than other tires; and that there were other tires available that were as safe as those designated Safety Champion.

At the hearing, the FTC counsel argued that "the literal meaning of the term 'safety champion' is that it is supreme over all competitors, unexcelled, and first rate." In support of this contention, he cited a dictionary definition of the word *champion* and argued that "it is reasonable to infer that this term represents that the tires were supreme over all competitors as to safety."

Firestone responded by citing a study it had conducted which indicated that the brand name Safety Champion did not connote a safer tire than competitive brand names such as Safety All-Weather, Safety-Traction Tread, Grip Safe, Super Safety 800, and Safety Master. Moreover, Firestone argued, it had submitted the brand name Safety Champion to the FTC for approval in September 1958 and had received an FTC staff opinion that ". . . we would interpose no objection, provided, of course, that the tire so designated is safe under the conditions outlined in your letter." In its letter requesting approval, Firestone had stated that "under normal driving conditions, including driving at maximum legal limits on super highways, this tire has exclusive Firestone construction features and will give excellent performance from a safety standpoint."

THE REMEDY

As noted above, the FTC complaint had requested that an order be issued requiring Firestone to cease and desist from the allegedly deceptive practices described in the complaint. In July 1970, Students Opposed to Unfair Practices (SOUP) had requested permission to intervene in the case on behalf of the public. In essence, SOUP had contended that a cease-and-desist order would not be an effective remedy in the case since the effects of the allegedly deceptive advertisements would continue to be felt long after the cessation of such advertisements. An appropriate remedy, SOUP had argued, would be for Firestone to admit its previous alleged deception in future advertisements so as to mitigate the residual effects of that deception.

After considerable debate, the five Commissioners overruled the hearing examiner, and SOUP was allowed to intervene in the proceedings. SOUP's intervention was limited to the question of remedy. Shortly thereafter, the Association of National Advertisers (ANA) was also granted permission to intervene.

SOUP

SOUP was an organization of law students at George Washington University. The stated purpose of SOUP was:

> . . . the protection of consumer interests, and advocacy of their interests before the federal administration agencies. . . . Incorporated as a non-profit organization, SOUP [was] totally independent[;] all decisions concerning policy, strategy, and goals [were] the sole product of a majority vote of its members.

THE CAMPBELL SOUP CASE. SOUP had first come to public attention in 1969 when it had attempted to intervene in FTC proceedings against Campbell Soup Company. The FTC and Campbell had agreed to a consent order under which Campbell would cease and desist from certain allegedly deceptive practices. In particular, the FTC had alleged that Campbell had exaggerated the quantity of solid ingredients in Campbell Soups in certain advertisements by placing marbles at the bottom of the bowl of soup being photographed. In the proposed consent order, Campbell had agreed not to use such advertising techniques in the future.

In a lengthy brief, SOUP had argued that the proposed consent order was not adequate in this case because it did not take account of the way in which modern advertising actually worked. Citing dozens of marketing textbooks, studies of advertising effectiveness, and popular books (e.g., Packard's The

Hidden Persuaders, McLuhan's *Understanding Media,* and Galbraith's *The New Industrial State),* SOUP argued that advertising was often most effective on a subconscious (subliminal) level and that its effects on consumer behavior often persisted long after the advertisement had been viewed. In a typical passage, SOUP contended:

> *Campbell's Soup ads ensure that the message (the product) is impressed in the memory.*
>
> *Women, according to Fransesco Nicosia (a behavioral scientist), are especially prone to learning from pictures rather than from copy.*[1] *Campbell exploits this proclivity by using distracting pictures, and by symbolizing the message within the picture rather than writing it. Thus, resistance to the message is broken, and the information enters the woman's memory. As described* supra *by Krugman, eventually the information enters the subconscious, where it becomes a motivating force in crisis (purchase) situations.*
>
> *Besides the fact that Campbell scenes are highly filled with identification, they are also fairly unstructured. That is, very rarely is the bowl of soup so emphasized as to overpower the rest of the scene. Often, the family—e.g., the children or the husband—are as important to the ad as the bowl of soup. The family scene is pleasant, and permits the woman to contemplate the better side of family life. While she is meditating, Campbell's central message—the superiority of its product—is learned without resistance and without consciousness. The woman learns that Campbell's Soups are superior to other soups because of the numerous vegetables (or beans or dumplings) which it contains. By serving soup with such rich garnish, the woman is truly performing well: not only is she feeding her family, she is feeding them soup (with all of its rich connotations); not only is she feeding them soup, she is feeding them the richest and most nutritious brand.*
>
> *Thus, women are consciously persuaded to choose Campbell's Soups to attain the image of the appreciated efficient important provider; and they are subconsciously persuaded that Campbell's is a superior brand, though this knowledge may not be realized until after the purchase is made. Campbell's Soup ads have accomplished a prodigious feat in mass persuasion, as verified by increasing sales and earnings.*

[1] *Francesco Nicosia,* Consumer Decision Processes in the Behavioral Sciences, *1966, at 165.*

Because of the nature of Campbell's advertising, SOUP had argued, a cease-and-desist order would not adequately protect the public interest. Cease-and-desist orders were not widely publicized, and the public thus had no practical means of learning that it had been deceived. As a result, it would continue to believe that Campbell soups contained more solid ingredients than they in fact did and would continue to buy Campbell soups on the basis of false information.

The only appropriate remedy, according to SOUP, was to inform the consumers who had been deceived. Since the FTC had limited resources, SOUP recommended that Campbell be required in a specified percentage of its advertisements for a specified time period to "affirmatively disclose" that:

Campbell Soup Company has been charged with deceptive advertising in violation of the Federal Trade Commission Act. Pictured bowls of soup appeared to contain more solid ingredients than a bowl actually contains if prepared according to the dilution directions on the can.

Such affirmative disclosure, SOUP argued, would counteract the effects of the allegedly deceptive advertising and deter such deceptive advertising in the future.

In a split decision, a majority of the FTC Commissioners denied SOUP's intervention in this case. According to the majority opinion, the alleged deception, while "tawdry," was not one which warranted the affirmative disclosure proposed by SOUP. Nevertheless, the opinion continued:

We have no doubt as to the Commission's power to require such affirmative disclosures when such disclosures are reasonably related to the deception found and are required in order to dissipate the effects of that deception. . . . All that is required is that there be a "reasonable relation to the unlawful practice found to exist."

According to a number of observers, the Commissioners had, in effect, reasserted their authority to take action which would "remedy" the effects of unfair or deceptive business practices. They had not claimed the right to "punish" a company which had engaged in unfair or deceptive practices, or to use the threat of such punishment to deter future unfair or deceptive practices. While it was expected that the FTC's authority to require affirmative disclosures would eventually be determined by the U.S. Supreme Court, it was generally believed that hearing examiners would now assume that the FTC had such authority until such time as the courts decided otherwise.

THE FIRESTONE CASE. As noted above, SOUP had received permission to intervene in the Firestone case. In its brief, SOUP argued that the Commission had the authority to require affirmative disclosure and that affirmative disclosure was both appropriate and necessary in this case. Essentially, SOUP's position was:

The good will created by the advertising alleged in the complaint to be false is still contributing to Firestone's tire sales.

1 Memory, both conscious and unconscious, of [Firestone's] 1967–1968 advertising campaign is still favorably affecting [Firestone's] tire sales.

2 Firestone's 1968 advertising will significantly continue to contribute to its sales through 1972 as a result of the lagged effect of its advertising.

In support of this position, SOUP relied heavily on the testimony of three expert witnesses, all of whom testified without compensation. The first to testify was Dr. Darrell B. Lucas, professor of marketing at New York University, author of numerous "standard" marketing texts and monographs, and consultant to many organizations (including ANA). Twenty years previously, Dr. Lucas had studied the ability of consumers to remember advertising claims which had appeared in a single issue of *Life* magazine. In that study, Dr. Lucas had found that at least 20 percent of those who had seen a single advertisement could remember having seen that advertisement when it was shown to them a year later. According to Professor Lucas:

> *Individual advertisements differ greatly in memorability and no claim is made for the precision of this memory measurement, but the evidence tended to confirm my judgment that vivid individual advertisements, and especially whole advertising campaigns, can and do leave a lasting impression that is significant. . . .*
>
> *I think it is important to point out when we talk about the memory of an advertisement or campaign in the conscious sense, that advertising creative people are told to write advertisements which cause people to buy the product, not to remember the specific advertisement. . . .*

Dr. Lucas also noted that both economists and advertisers increasingly viewed advertising expenditures as capital investments which were expected "to pay out" well into the future. In addition, he testified that:

> *There is a growing body of evidence supporting the psychological theory that advertising has a "sleeper effect."*
>
> *The meaning of that ["sleeper effect"] is that the impressions which one receives from a source which he doesn't credit as being particularly reliable or important, and often advertising is in that category in the mind of the person exposed, these impressions may carry on and not be accepted fully at the time they are made. But at some later date when one has forgotten the source of the impression, he may assume that it was told to him by a more important source, like a friend or someone who is capable of giving him authentic advice. So he may then accept and act upon impressions or ideas that he would not have accepted or acted upon at the time they were made.*

SOUP's second expert witness was Assistant Professor Douglas F. Greer of the University of Maryland. At SOUP's request, Dr. Greer had developed an econometric model which estimated the lagged effects of Firestone's 1968 tire and tube advertising.[1] Using this model, Dr. Greer estimated that "the lagged effect of *all* Firestone's tire and tube advertising in 1968 was approximately 35% in 1969; 12% in 1970; 4% in 1971; and 1.5% in 1972. If 1967 advertising is included, this last figure is increased to 2%." He then testified that:

> *These estimates provide rough approximations of the goodwill created by Firestone's advertising in 1967 and 1968 that continued to generate sales. . . . It is*

[1] Under cross-examination, Dr. Greer had stated (1) that he had only a very short period of time to do the work on which his testimony was based; (2) that the model he had used was a relatively unsophisticated model which had been developed many years before for a study of the cigarette industry; (3) that the quality of his work in this case (because of limitations of time and available data) was not such that he would have submitted it to a professional journal; and (4) that Dr. Kuehn (an ANA witness—see later) was one of the world's leading experts in advanced model-building techniques.

not possible, with the information and techniques available, . . . to estimate quantitatively the lagged effect of a specific advertising campaign for a specific line of tires.

SOUP's third expert witness was Dr. Harvey Resnik, chief of the Center for Suicide Prevention of the National Institute of Mental Health. Dr. Resnik testified that on the basis of his clinical experience as a psychiatrist, specializing in suicidology and high-risk-taking patients, an undetermined but relatively small proportion of the car-driving population could be classified as high-risk takers, and that this class of drivers tended to use equipment up to and beyond the limits of what it believed to be its safety. In his opinion, those high-risk takers who believed that the tires were safe and stopped 25 percent quicker could be expected to drive less carefully. In addition, Dr. Resnik testified that an undetermined number of persons who might be classified as average-risk takers who read and believed that Firestone wide oval tires were safe and would stop 25 percent quicker could also be expected to drive less carefully.

In addition, SOUP argued that Firestone had known that its advertisements were deceptive at the time it had used them. After considerable debate, SOUP had been able to obtain access to a survey of consumer reactions to an *earlier* Firestone advertisement containing language virtually identical to that in the advertisements under consideration. According to this survey:

- *20% of the persons surveyed stated that they thought the idea of a "safe tire" "is the main idea they are trying to get across in this ad."*
- *When asked "what did you learn from this ad that you didn't know before," 15% stated "quicker stops."*
- *93% did not find anything in the advertisement "unbelievable."*
- *86% of the persons interviewed said that from this advertisement alone they derived the impression that the tire advertised was "safer than most tires."*

SOUP contended that these data demonstrated that Firestone had *knowingly* engaged in deceptive advertising, and that the public should thus have the benefit of any doubt concerning an appropriate remedy.

In conclusion, SOUP asked for an order which would require that Firestone, for a period of 1 year:

. . . cease and desist [from making] any claims, directly or indirectly, in connection with the advertisement of Firestone tires as to . . . the safety or stopping ability of Firestone tires . . . unless it is clearly and conspicuously disclosed in any such advertisements . . . that the Federal Trade Commission has found that certain of [Firestone's] previous advertisements of Firestone tires were false, misleading or deceptive . . . ; [and] the respects in which . . . [such] advertisements were false, deceptive, or misleading.[1]

---

[1] This is one of four alternative wordings suggested by SOUP.

ANA's INTERVENTION

The Association of National Advertisers, Inc. (ANA), was a trade association consisting of approximately 500 manufacturers and others who advertised on a national or regional basis. As a leading professional advertising organization, it felt that it should intervene in opposition to SOUP's position, since SOUP's proposal, if adopted, would have important implications for other advertisers. In its brief, ANA essentially argued (1) that the FTC did not have the authority to require affirmative disclosure; (2) that advertising's delayed impact was considerably less than SOUP contended; and (3) that SOUP's proposed remedy, if adopted, would be detrimental to the competitive process.

On the second point, ANA relied heavily on expert witnesses.[1] Its first witness was Dr. Alfred Kuehn, a highly respected econometrician. Dr. Kuehn testified that he had:

> . . . studied, analyzed, and estimated lagged effects of advertising outlays, and his total research experience establish[ed] that the direct delayed advertising effect is very small compared to the repeat purchase or habit effect . . . [having] an annual delayed effect ranging from zero to approximately 3%, but generally under 1%.

In fact, Dr. Kuehn stated, the lagged effects of advertising were "so small compared to those of other variables that [he] frequently no longer even include[d] lagged advertising as a variable factor in his market analysis and predictive models and studies." Dr. Kuehn also criticized Dr. Greer's econometric model, contending that it was greatly oversimplified and thus attributed effects to advertising which in fact were highly dependent on other variables. In this regard, Dr. Kuehn noted that Dr. Greer's model had originally been developed in a study of the cigarette industry, and that advertising had a much greater effect on cigarette sales than it did on tire sales.

ANA then presented evidence through three other witnesses that the great bulk of advertising claims is quickly forgotten. Mr. Ernest A. Rockey of Gallup & Robinson (G&R), a leading marketing research firm, reported the results of a study G&R had conducted at ANA's request. G&R had access to considerable data from previous studies concerning consumers' ability to remember specific advertisements. While these data varied considerably from product category to product category and from specific advertisement to specific advertisement, Mr. Rockey claimed that they demonstrated that the vast majority of consumers could not remember the main features of advertisements they had seen on television or read in magazines the previous day. For example, only 6 to 8 percent of consumers could typically remember the "featured idea" of a television commercial for tires they had seen the night before.

Mr. Charles D. Jacobson of Daniel Starch & Staff, Inc., also a leading marketing research firm, then testified concerning a Starch study conducted in At-

---

[1] According to SOUP, ANA's witnesses were compensated at rates up to $600 per day for time spent in conducting studies, preparing to testify, and testifying.

lanta, Georgia, in the spring of 1969. In that study, persons who had viewed a particular television channel during a specified 30-minute period had been questioned within 2½ hours concerning a commercial which had been aired during that period. Only 32 percent reported having seen the commercial, and only half of that group (16 percent) were able to identify the brand which had been featured in the commerical.

ANA's next witness was Mr. Edward G. Gerbic who had 30 years' experience in marketing and advertising for various firms, and most recently had been vice president and director of marketing for Johnson & Johnson. Mr. Gerbic agreed with Dr. Lucas that:

> *In order for advertising to be profitable it must leave some impression on the respondent's memory until he has an occasion to buy . . . but . . . in actual practice, advertisers consider it pretty hazardous to buy consumer advertising at the wrong time and at the wrong place and in the wrong way . . . [While] I think in the very nature of things it is possible for one to remember something that made a deep impression on him years ago and for no good reason . . . , such instances . . . do not represent any substantial ratio of the total advertising claims that were made during the same period as they ran. . . .*
>
> *[Moreover] advertising for infrequently purchased products [such as tires] commands an even lower degree of attention than other kinds of advertising. . . . If one is not in the market for an automobile, or carpeting, or a battery, or a refrigerator, he has a lot more things to do than [to] read advertising for these products. So, instead of five million people, . . . one might actually reach fifty thousand. . . . Of these, how many will remember a month later, or two months later, or three . . . ?*

ANA's final witness was Mr. Walter Bregman, chief operating officer of Norman, Craig and Kummel, a major advertising agency. Mr. Bregman argued that the adoption of the SOUP proposal would greatly inhibit effective advertising, and thus lessen competition:

> *We would lean over so far backwards, in my opinion, that much of our advertising would be what we call in the trade compliments-of-a-friend advertising. In other words, we would probably not provide the information—that, as I understand it, is one of the directions, one of the hoped-for benefits—we would not provide the information, as we probably could, because we would be afraid, we would be concerned about it, and I guess we would pull back a little too far.*
>
> *. . . I can see myself sitting on a creative review committee and saying to someone, I don't think we had better recommend that demonstration because it could be a problem, and I don't want to have to run this advertising for my client in the future or have him run it for himself, even though, in our judgment, that is a perfectly valid claim and we may have support for it—I mean, for example, a genuine product claim.*
>
> *Under the old guidelines—and I believe most of us, all of us, genuinely believe that what we were saying about a product was honest, ethical, and true—if, for some reason, the guidelines changed, or the rules changed, someone would come to you and say you can't do this anymore, a cease and desist order would be*

passed or given to us, and we would stop. And that would be that. In this case, if we do this thing, which we in truth believe to be absolutely correct and proper at the time, and subsequent to that time something changes, it is no longer a question of you can't say that anymore—it is now a question of not only you can't say it anymore, but you have to tell people that what you have been saying, presumably, has been found by someone to be deceitful or fraudulent, or whatever. I don't want to be put in that position. It is a great concern to me as an advertising man not to put my client in that position. That is why I would refrain probably, and perhaps incorrectly, but I would probably refrain from getting involved in that closeness to the problem.

I suspect we would end up in areas of very sort of general image, this is a nice product, why don't you buy it, kind of thing. This is what I mean by compliments-of-a-friend advertising.

THE DECISION

Before he could write his decision, Mr. Hughes, the hearing examiner in the Firestone case, would have to reach a conclusion on four major issues:

1   Were Firestone's July 4th and Labor Day "sale" advertisements deceptive?
2   Was Firestone's "The Safe Tire" advertisement deceptive?
3   Was Firestone's "Stop 25% quicker" advertisement deceptive?
4   If he found that any or all of these advertisements had been deceptive, should SOUP's proposed remedy be adopted?

With regard to the fourth question, Mr. Hughes had already decided to assume that the FTC had the authority to order "affirmative disclosure" if the facts of the case warranted it. While the Supreme Court might later "knock the props out from under his assumption," he believed that such questions were best left to a court higher than his.

B. PERSONAL SELLING

GILBERT PRINTING COMPANY

WARREN D. NELSON
MBA, Class of 1973
Harvard Graduate School of Business Administration

BENSON P. SHAPIRO
Associate Professor
Harvard Graduate School of Business Administration

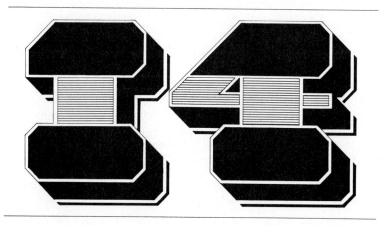

In August 1972, Mr. Bob Peterson, executive vice president of the Gilbert Printing Company, was seeking an approach to increasing sales $500,000 in the next 2 years. In the past few years he had participated actively in two programs—the move of Gilbert Printing Company into a new plant in a suburb of Baltimore and major acquisitions of new printing equipment. The move and expansion had been quite successful, but Mr. Peterson was concerned about the performance in his primary area of responsibility, sales. For the past 5 years, sales volume had remained essentially stable, slightly above an annual level of $3.5 million (see Exhibits 1 and 2). Mr. Peterson wondered if he could increase the sales output of his present four-man sales force and how he should go about recruiting new salesmen.

INDUSTRY BACKGROUND

PRINTING PROCESSES

In 1972 the major printing processes in commercial application were letterpress, offset lithograph, gravure, flexography, and screen. Gilbert Printing Company had concentrated on quality letterpress work until the mid-1960s, when it began a shift to offset lithography (see Exhibit 1).

Offset presses were of two types, sheet-fed and web-fed. Sheet-fed presses received paper one sheet at a time, while web-fed presses printed from continuous rolls. Most web-fed presses, printed on both sides of the paper at the same time. Sheet-fed offset printing applications included general commerical printing, such as annual reports and brochures, direct-mail advertising, catalogs, calendars, labels, letterheads, business forms, greeting cards, posters, packaging, folding boxes, coupons, trading stamps, and art reproduction. Web offset was used in printing business forms, newspapers, preprinted newspaper inserts, catalogs, books, encyclopedias, and magazines. It was fairly widely believed that web offset, with its faster feeds and greater output volume, could not quite match the quality of printing obtained from sheet-fed offset, but this question was subject to some dispute. A large 4-color sheet-fed offset press might cost approximately $2,000,000

INDUSTRY CHARACTERISTICS

Printing and publishing was the seventh largest industry in the Baltimore metropolitan area according to "value added," and the largest according to number of plants employing more than 10 persons, roughly 800 compared to a total of 5,000 plants listed in the directory. Approximately 70 percent of all commercial printing firms in Maryland employed nine or fewer persons. Only 15 commercial printing plants in Maryland employed 100 or more persons, and only three of these employed 250 or more. The printing industry had the largest number of individual firms in the United States.

A 1966 study of the printing industry, commissioned by the printers' trade association, Printing Industries of America, Inc., found that the printing industry was healthy and growing. Growth of printing and publishing had roughly paralleled the growth of all manufacturing. The study also found that the printing industry was more profitable than three-quarters of American industries, with an average return on investment of 10 percent. However, the study found a highly uneven distribution of profits among printing firms—out of every five printing firms one lost money, three averaged about 6 percent return on assets, and one earned three times more (return on assets) than all the rest.

COMPANY BACKGROUND

PRODUCTION

In 1968 Gilbert moved from an old three-story plant to a new single-level facility in a suburb convenient to downtown Baltimore. Gilbert personnel designed the plant and oversaw every detail of the construction and moving efforts. They continued to operate the old plant while moving equipment—some old and some new—into the new plant. According to trade sources the move went smoothly and customer service continued satisfactorily throughout the move.

In 1972 total company employment was approximately 150. Production equipment was geared to the product mix in 1972—85 percent offset and 15 percent letterpress. Two modern 4-color sheet-fed offset presses, two 2-color offset presses and two single-color offset presses were operated on two shifts during most of the year. Older letterpress equipment, including 17 presses of various sizes, handled the declining portion of letterpress jobs.

The first step in preparing a printing job to be run on an offset press was work-up of a "board," or layout of the artwork in full color. A full-time artist was retained on Gilbert's staff to prepare layouts or consult with customers and salesmen on art problems.

After a job was printed, it was usually further processed. Stitching machines were available to bind sheets into pamphlets or books. Cutting, folding, and packaging were also standard operations often performed after printing. Gilbert maintained its own delivery fleet. To ensure that jobs could be processed promptly, an extensive inventory of paper was maintained in a warehouse adjacent to the pressrooms. A typical job could be shipped within 2 weeks after a final specification was received, and faster if desired. Roughly 2,500 jobs per year were processed during the 1970–1971 period.

The specifications for each order were transmitted by the individual salesman to the production supervisor. An estimator assisted during the initial work-up of specifications and estimation of price and delivery time for the salesman to submit to the customer, especially on those jobs requiring competitive bidding. Gilbert's estimator was able to handle the estimating function by devoting only half his time to it. Thus he was also able to handle a large portion of the company's purchasing activity. Four "customer men" worked in the production department in liaison capacities between the salesmen and customers, and the production department. These men received customer phone calls and handled the customer's request or problem when that customer's salesman was not in the office. The duties of these men also included expediting orders, making sure that the jobs were processed exactly according to specifications, and in general following through to satisfy the customer after the salesman had obtained the original order. According to Mr. Peterson, this backup capability was a unique strength of the Gilbert Printing Company, since many competitive printing companies required the salesmen themselves to perform the duties handled by these customer men. The customer men ranged in age from 40 to 50 and

TABLE 1

Step	Time required, minutes
1 Salesman records initial customer specifications	15–30
2 Salesman completes specification form	5
3 Salesman transmits form to estimator	5
4 Estimator prepares bid from standard rates	30–45
5 Salesman reviews bid	5
6 Salesman decides on his price quotation	15
7 Salesman submits and explains bid to potential customer	10
8 Salesman prepares written confirmation of bid	5
9 Written confirmation typed and mailed by secretary	5

earned between $12,000 and $16,000 per year. All had substantial printing production experience. Each tended to work with a particular salesman and a particular group of customers.

The process for preparing bids, on those jobs requiring competitive bidding, consisted of the steps shown in Table 1, with average times estimated for each step.

ORGANIZATION AND MANAGEMENT

Steve Gilbert, president, was a grandson of the founder, Abraham D. Gilbert, who started out as his own salesman and pressman in 1890 in Baltimore. Steve had been president since 1965 when his father, David Gilbert, retired from the presidency at the age of 80. Bob Peterson, executive vice president, had started out as a printing salesman with no background in the industry after a stint in the service in World War II. He had been so successful as a salesman that in 1958 he was offered status as a principal stockholder, which he accepted. In 1972 Messrs. Gilbert and Peterson controlled all the stock.

Mr. Gilbert and Mr. Peterson were joint decision makers on all management questions. Mr. Gilbert concentrated on the operations end of the business, while Mr. Peterson concentrated on sales, but both principals conferred frequently and preferred to reach concurrence before making management decisions. Alex Petroski, sales manager, assisted in managing the sales effort.

Steve Gilbert gave his views on the present status and on the future of the Gilbert Printing Company (as paraphrased by the casewriter):

> We are a very tightly run company. I personally review internal operating and financial data every day. Our production crew is young and well trained. Our craftsmen and supervisors are very company-minded, and they really care about doing good work. There is no union.[1] We pay very good wages and we have lib-

---

[1] Casewriter's note: Few competitors were unionized either.

eral fringe benefits—group hospital and medical plans, dental insurance, a profit-sharing retirement plan, free flu shots, free eye exams, and even a tax expert who comes in to help employees with their income tax returns. We are a quality-minded company, and the main element in quality is our top production crew—they give us a real competitive advantage. Our approach has paid off in the past—we have been in the top 20% of printing companies as far as profitability is concerned, except for one or two of the past five years. Right now, unfortunately, sales volume is static.

As for the future, I am enough of a realist to admit that we cannot succeed by remaining static. If we could be assured of maintaining a static, profitable level it would be ideal. But we cannot—we have to grow just to stay even. Right now we are not as profitable as we should be. Our existing plant could produce an added $2–3 million of work, and we have allowed room for expansion to handle more. Expanding our production capacity is absolutely no problem.

We do not use so-called "sophisticated" management techniques. We do not set our sights on future targets and push to make them. As to how we grow, it is somewhat "in the clouds"—we follow the market and respond to it rather than trying to anticipate where the market is headed and get there first. I would not say we have the inventive kind of management that could develop new techniques —we stay with the stable, established technology. This is because we have a sound company and good strategy right now—naturally we avoid risks we do not have to take. We have a lot to lose if we make mistakes.

Our main problem for the future is to increase sales. But we do not want to increase sales volume unless it can be done profitably. The trouble with a lot of the high volume work is that it is low margin. We are profit oriented, not sales volume oriented. What we need is to hire some proven, experienced salesmen who have some accounts to bring along, and who would appreciate our company for the excellent production support we can give them. If we could hire an entire four-man trained sales force from outside, and have them bring their business along, it would be Utopia.

MARKETING PRINT IN THE BALTIMORE AREA

The major characteristics of print marketing—huge primary demand, intense competition, wide diversity of demand, and long established customer-vendor relationships—were both the keys to success and the barriers to expansion of Gilbert's marketing efforts, in Mr. Peterson's opinion.

To a considerable extent the print market in Baltimore followed the trends and practices in the major customer groups served—retailers, manufacturers, advertising agencies, publishers, financial companies, educational institutions, etc. For example, in the late 1960s the trend was away from "showpiece" annual reports, coveted business for reasons of both prestige and profit, because companies had become more frugal in response to the recession and the sagging stock market. Another recent trend among many print buyers was toward requests for competitive bidding for printing jobs. In the past many buyers had done business primarily on the basis of past service and quality rendered by the printer or on the basis of the printer's reputation. One Gilbert salesman estimated that 60 percent of his jobs were sold on a bid basis 4 years ago, but that 90 percent of his jobs were sold on a bid basis in 1972.

The casewriter accompanied a Gilbert salesman during a call on a typical customer, a publisher. During the call the buyer commented to the casewriter that he had an average of six print salesmen calling on him every day. Following the call the Gilbert salesman commented that he would estimate that 10 print salesmen per day called on major buyers of print, such as the publisher. The salesman commented that, while the group of companies competing for business from such a buyer was too long to list, he believed that his serious competition came from seven of the larger and more highly regarded printing firms in the area (see Exhibit 3).

MARKETING STRATEGY

Mr. Bob Peterson's description of Gilbert's marketing strategy was paraphrased by the casewriter as follows:

> Our product is the best there is in the area, for the kind of work our customers want. We provide the highest quality work, absolutely on-time delivery, strict adherence to customers' special instructions or changes, and expert professional consulting and personal service from our salesmen. We do have a reputation for being higher priced than most of our competitors. Our prices are up to 10% higher than the low bid on many jobs. As a result, we have to hire the best salesmen we can get, because it is entirely up to them to carry out our strategy and make sure that our customers are satisfied that they get the service they are paying for.
>
> Our profits for the past five years have been somewhat erratic, and we have been unable to increase our sales volume, but we are confident that our strategy is sound. Our problem has been implementation.

SALES FORCE

All customer accounts were classified either as *house* accounts or as *salesmen's* accounts. House accounts were handled directly by Mr. Gilbert or Mr. Peterson and often involved long-standing "understandings" or relationships that required minimal effort to maintain. Many of these understandings had existed for as long as 25 years. Almost all printers, according to Mr. Peterson, had a few such accounts. It was standard practice in the industry for owners of the companies to handle their own house accounts. Salesmen's accounts were handled by a four-man sales force including Alex Petroski, who was the sales manager. A breakdown for major accounts for the past 5 years, by salesman, is given in Exhibit 4. Further information on the salesmen is given in Exhibit 5.

Mr Peterson described the Gilbert philosophy of managing salesmen as "laissez-faire." He commented that the salesmen had to be "creative," and adapt themselves to each unique situation. This required, according to Mr. Peterson, that each salesman be allowed to work independently, develop his own style, and learn for himself the kinds of customers he could succeed with.

Salesmen were paid a commission of 7½ percent of sales.[1] In the event that a salesman cut price to obtain a sale, however, his commission was reduced for that sale. The amount of reduction was negotiated with Bob Peterson and varied according to company need for business and other factors. In no case, however, was the commission reduced below 5 percent. During sales slumps a salesman's draw could be continued even if it were not covered by commission, but he was then expected to make it up during following months so that his annual salary worked out to 7½ percent of his sales. In addition to commission, each salesman was furnished a company car and expense account.

Exhibit 5 includes two salesmen who were no longer employed with Gilbert. Frank Barr was considered a high-potential salesman when he was hired, and he had been highly successful selling locks in quantity to motels, hotels, and office buildings. The locks were purchased in large quantities by a few buyers. However, he was unable to sell print, and he was fired. Bob Peterson commented on Frank's failure:

> He was the stereotype of a good salesman—if he walked in here tomorrow, unknown, I would hire him immediately. He was well-groomed, well-spoken, smooth and likeable. But selling print is unlike selling anything else, and it is almost impossible to tell beforehand who will be able to sell print. Frank's problem may have been a failure to learn the technical aspects of printing, or possibly that he was simply calling on the wrong customers. We do not really know why he failed. There was no attempt to diagnose the reasons he could not close sales.

Robert Darman, on the other hand, had been highly successful. He had some art talent and could sell well to ad agencies. He was selling $400,000 of print per year when ad agency business was booming, then, when their business turned down, his sales fell off, and he got behind in his ability to "make up" the salary he was drawing. Also, he encountered some problems in his personal life. He quit actually "owing" back salary. As of August 1972, he was working as a printing salesman for another company.

SELLING APPROACHES

The casewriter interviewed Bob Peterson and each of the Gilbert salesmen. All the following comments are paraphrased.

BOB PETERSON (who continued to sell in addition to his management responsibilities):

> A big problem in selling print is that it is like selling "blue sky." There is nothing tangible to sell—the product is just press time, along with some attendant services. Of course, we offer premium service and strict attention to quality, but these are

[1] New salesmen were paid salaries of between $10,000 and $15,000 (plus automobile) until they had developed enough sales so that their commissions were equal to their salaries.

intangibles and it is often difficult to find a customer who appreciates these factors, let alone convince him that we are better than the competition. Of course, after getting an initial order we have to live up to our claims in order to get repeat business.

Selling blue sky requires salesmanship at its creative best. A good print sales-man has to have all the usual qualities—good appearance, charm, and empathy with the buyer. Also, a print salesman has to use all the other influences expected of him—tickets to athletic events or the theater, holiday presents, and wining and dining. But a top salesman has to do these things plus something else—the extra variable that clinches the sale.

When I first began selling after the service, I had no printing background at all. Nor did I have much knowledge of practices or terminology in the industries I was selling to. But I was extremely successful because I relied on my intuition and tried to do something extra besides the things all the competitors were doing. Prob-ably the most effective thing I did was to make sure that I invited the buyer's wife and my wife to the occasion or event where he was my guest. I made him feel comfortable and welcome as a friend, not just a business prospect. Getting the buyer's wife to like my wife and me was a major breakthrough. Many of the peo-ple my wife and I have met through this process have remained good friends, above business considerations. Because I had a good deal of charm and taste in this type of "social selling," many buyers were willing to overlook some of my shortcomings in the technical areas. One factor about selling print in the Gilbert Company that allows this "social selling" to succeed is that a salesman needs only 10 good accounts to be earning a good income for himself and the company. He has ample time to concentrate on each one of his top customers.

In cultivating customer relationships, of course, it is vital to know who really influences the purchase decision. Most buyers in purchasing departments base deci-sions on price and delivery—only a few really care about quality and special ser-vice. It is usually the creative people—the ones in the advertising depart-ment—who are willing to pay a higher price to get exactly the quality they want. So we concentrate on the people in the advertising departments of companies. In some companies, though, the purchasing department will not take suggestions from the advertising people, or there is a purchasing director with set ideas, a lot of power, and little sympathy with the "creative types" who care more about quality than price. We have a great deal of trouble with such companies. Fortunately, most companies do have creative people in influential positions, and many of these persons like their work and stay in their positions for a long time. This has been the case with some of my best customers I have served for up to 25 years.

One tendency many young salesmen have is to withhold information about their customers from their company. Our salesmen do not do this—they cannot and still be successful. The opposite is true. They can help themselves by bringing their customers in to see our plant and meet our men in production and customer service. Then if a customer calls when a salesman is not in the office, one of our production men or "customer men" can handle this call. If the call had to be turned away, the first thing the customer would do would be to call another printer who could help him right away. Another reason our salesmen must be open with our inside customer men is that they can help them immensely by handling many of the details of customer orders. To earn a really good salary of, say, $50,000, a salesman would have to do $670,000 of business a year. Servicing even one-half that much business would be next to impossible without relying on our inside men *to handle a good deal of customer work. This adds another dimension to the talents required of our salesmen—they have to be able to coordinate their work with our inside men, keep them informed, and maintain excellent working relations with them.*

The four inside customer men we have are very important in providing the high quality service we promise our customers. Few of our competitors use such inside men to beef up their service capability.

In a small company like ours, we don't have time to do market analysis. We just get out and call on as many customers as possible. I don't really even have time to be talking to you—I have six phone calls I should be making right now.

We do not have the time or money to "train" salesmen. They have to be top people who can make it on their own. Most salesmen prefer it that way, in fact.

ALEX PETROSKI The casewriter traveled with Alex Petroski, the salesman–sales manager, for 1 day:

9:00 A.M. The first-hour of the day was spent in the office on paperwork. Along with other work, Alex dictated a letter inviting a high-potential company buyer and his wife to spend a weekend in September at the Petroski's summer home in a nearby resort area. Alex indicated that the buyer had expressed interest in the resort area during his last sales call. Alex spent a few minutes with the estimator.

Alex then explained his first sales call. He had obtained an order for 10,000 copies of a four-color direct-mail flyer. He indicated that he had shaved the price to $1,200 from $1,260 to get the order, but that the standard price for a volume of 15,000 copies was only $1,600 due to economy of scale. He said he would convince the buyer to take 15,000 copies, and this would allow Alex to earn his full commission.

9:30 A.M. Left the office for first call, a publishing company. While driving to the call in a suburban location, Alex commented that he would make $120 for the morning's work.

10:00 A.M. Arrived in the customer's lobby. The receptionist admitted Alex to see the buyer.

10:10 A.M. Alex introduced the casewriter to the buyer, then began small talk. When the talk turned to details of the printing job, Alex said to the casewriter that he would now see a "professional" buyer dealing with a professional salesman—and he requested the buyer to act out his usual professionalism as well as he could. After several details were taken care of, Alex suggested that what he would do if he were the buyer would be to order 15,000 copies instead of 10,000 because of the great price break, which Alex then explained. The buyer became noticeably tense and commented that he would like to order the higher volume but that he was already in trouble with his budget. Alex did not comment further and left the conversational initiative with the buyer for the next major portion of the visit. The conversation turned to small talk and the buyer asked if Alex had heard of another printing firm that was about to go out of business. Alex expressed interest and ignorance on the matter. Later in the discussion Alex agreed to take the "boards" to the buyer's artist in downtown Baltimore later in the day. Toward the end of the call the buyer appeared more relaxed and said he would purchase 15,000 units instead of 10,000.

10:40 A.M. First call was completed, and Alex headed back to the office to set up two sales calls in downtown Baltimore. During the return trip, Alex answered questions about Gilbert's sales program and selling print in general.

> *No, our salesmen have no way of knowing the actual profit to the company of various kinds of orders. This is somewhat of a problem to management, but we have not had time to solve it.*
>
> *I am recognized as one of the three or four best non-owner print salesmen in the Baltimore area, and I have been in the business 14 years. The only generalization I can make about how to sell print is that each sale is different.*
>
> *I have toyed with a possible sales idea—a new marketing outlet for the Gilbert Company. Students on many university campuses would be our sales representatives to their schools. They ought to be in a better position to find out who buys the print, and on what basis, than our regular salesmen. And the 7½% commission should look quite attractive to them.*
>
> *A print salesman could probably make at most five meaningful sales calls in a single day.*
>
> *I did at one time request our salesmen to fill out call records so we could begin to establish some data on numbers of calls, where the calls were, etc. But the salesmen lost interest after the first few weeks, and started "fudging" the data. So we dropped the program.*

11:10 A.M. Back at the office, Alex promptly set up two calls in Baltimore.

11:25 A.M. Left office for second call.

11:35 A.M. Arrived at customer's store, an old-line specialty retail outlet catering to the carriage trade. The objective was a repeat order for a color catalog. Throughout the call, Alex acted as if it were a foregone conclusion that Gilbert would get the repeat order. He said that in situations like this the objective was to make it as easy as possible for the potential customer to give him the order. During the call Alex obtained a "dummy" of the catalog from the advertising manager. After the call Alex mentioned that last year was the first time he had obtained the order for the catalog. He then commented that he had called on the advertising manager for 3 years before getting the order, and that his problem had been in thinking that the advertising manager himself had responsibility for the catalog. Alex finally learned that it was actually the president of the company who made the decision about the design and printing of the catalog. With this knowledge, Alex said it was easy to get the order because he talked directly to the president, who had been somewhat displeased with the service rendered by printers who had done the last catalog.

12:00 P.M. The next stop was to drop off the material at the studio of the artist who did the work for the publisher called on earlier in the day. The studio was two doors away from the previous call. Alex made small talk and expressed a great deal of interest in an old nickelodeon that the artist, a young fully bearded man dressed in an open pullover shirt, old jeans, and sandals, was playing full blast. Alex told a story of how he barely missed purchasing an old nickelodeon from a boardwalk arcade that had gone out of business a few years ago.

12:20 P.M. After the call, Alex asked the casewriter if he had noticed the layout that the artist had been doing. Alex said it was obviously a big printing job and that he would keep in touch with the publisher to find out when selection of a printer was to begin. He said that keeping in touch with a customer's artist was a good way to learn of potential printing jobs.

12:40 P.M. Arrived at the office of the next call, a recently founded, four-man investment banking firm. Gilbert would be printing an advertising brochure, and a principal of the firm was making the selection of paper from samples Alex had brought. The customer was quite hesitant about choice of paper, and Alex expressed confidence in his choice. Alex then turned the discussion to some oceanfront real estate the firm was developing, and Alex got the principal to talk about the project. Alex then mentioned that he had a chance to buy a sizable piece of land in a particular resort area, and the customer said no one had ever lost money buying land in that area. Alex said his problem was coming up with the cash, and the principal said that was what banks were for. Following the call Alex stopped in at his bank, located a few doors away, and confirmed that financing was indeed available for this type of investment. The bank visit took approximately 5 minutes.

1:15 P.M. During lunch Alex asked if the casewriter thought that a job selling print would have an appeal for an M.B.A. graduate from a top-rated business school. Alex asked about aspirations of M.B.A. graduates and how they might view working for a family-owned and managed company. He commented that if he had held an M.B.A. degree when he first started working, he would have expected his business efforts to earn some equity, since that was the only way to really make money. The discussion then turned to the problems and opportunities of owning one's own business.

2:00 P.M. On the return trip to his office, Alex talked further about his role as sales manager:

> It is frequently difficult to get a salesman to give up an account he has cultivated without success. For example, one of our salesmen had called on an account for years without success, but refused to give it to another salesman because the buyer had become such a good personal friend and golfing partner.

DAVE SHEA. Dave had the strongest technical background of the Gilbert salesmen. He had worked for Gilbert in production and estimating for 10 years, and subsequently moved to the sales position which he had held for the past 5 years. Dave talked about himself, his work, and other aspects of printing sales:

> In my job in estimating and production I became interested in sales because I could see the potential earnings that were available. Before that I had never wanted to be

a salesman, and at times I still question my interest in a sales career. I was convinced by others that I could succeed in sales, so I tried it with the knowledge that I could always fall back on my production knowledge if I could not succeed in selling.

I am not a strong "stand-up" salesman like Alex Petroski, and I have no design talent or artistic taste. That is a serious flaw for a print salesmen. But I have been successful because of my strong technical background. I sell best to two types of buyers—the ones who are true professionals and demand a true technical salesman, and the ones who know little or nothing about print and need the education I can give them. My part-time job as a professor, teaching graphic arts cost estimating, helps my image as a competent technical man and educator.

A salesman could probably make six "hello" calls in a day, but four calls per day to active accounts is the maximum. After the two calls in the morning, it is invariably necessary to return to the office to do some paperwork in support of the sales calls.

During a sales call I spend a good deal of time working with the technical aspects of the job itself. Frequently I am in two- or three-on-one situations, trying to solve problems, looking at details of preliminary proofs. Frequently I will have to refer back to the preliminary proof book or the original outline to solve the problem. Also, during a sales call to an active account, there is a check list of technical information that has to be obtained and this takes time.

The customers I prefer the most are the ones with a good deal of technical expertise. For example, paper companies or consumer manufacturers who are large enough to have a competent professional purchasing department. I have thought about ranking print buyers on the basis of expertise, and I would give the following rankings on a 1 to 10 basis: paper companies, 10; publishers, 9; mutual funds, 7–8; miscellaneous medium to large industrials, 3 to 7; and advertising agencies, 1. All small buyers I would rank 1. The reason funds are sophisticated is that they buy so much print and can afford to have good buyers. But I cannot sell to funds because I do not "talk the language" of investments, stock market, etc. I should probably make more of a study of the mutual fund industry and learn their terminology.

One of my best customers is a large consumer-goods manufacturer. They have one purchasing department that does all of the purchasing for other departments in the company. It took me three years to get a sizable order from them. The way they operate is to investigate vendors and classify them on their ability to handle certain types of work. Then when a job comes along, they will ask the qualifying print vendors to bid—usually I am competing against five or six other vendors—and they generally give the business to the low bidder. However, they make sure to cultivate their vendors by spreading the work around—if they didn't, a printer would probably stop bidding. For this reason the potential of this business is limited on the upside, but there is also some minimum amount of business a vendor can count on as long as he continues to deliver good service and quality at reasonable prices.

When I started selling I quoted strictly list price, even with padding in some cases. But lately I have been negotiating more closely, and I will cut my commission if I feel it is desirable to do so on a particular job. Another technique I have been using more lately is quoting alternates to the specifications that a purchaser has submitted for bids. By altering the paper, the largest single cost component of most printing jobs, I can sometimes meet the intent of the specifications at a lower

cost. Of course, a danger in this technique is that the buyer may adopt my standard the next time he requests bids and my advantage disappears.

One of the things I dislike about selling is making cold calls. I do have somewhat of a lack of confidence, and the thing you have to do on a first call is sell
yourself. It takes a strong "stand-up" salesman to do that. I am more of a service
man than a stand-up salesman like some of our other men are.

When I deliver a speech, people frequently say they think I must be a strong
stand-up man. I once trained four weeks to sell pharmaceuticals. Their method was
to memorize a canned sales pitch to deliver to the pharmacist on the first call, but I
found that I was extremely averse to the approach. The first Monday morning after
the training program, I sat in the car with the district manager outside my first drug
store and argued about the canned approach. I resigned on the spot.

DICK PETERSON. Bob Peterson's son Dick had joined the firm in 1971 after receiving an M.B.A. from Columbia:

The key to selling print is having a personality that will win the buyer over. It helps
to have something in common with the buyer—age, for example. I can usually sell
better to younger buyers than older ones.

Eight calls in one day are probably the most a salesman could make. I
average four or five every day. We try to spend as much time as possible making
calls. I may spend more time in the office—one and a half hours per day—than
the other salesmen because I spend a lot of time on the phone.

It is not possible to predict how a customer will react ahead of time. The
only way to find prospects is to keep your eyes open. I use the classified section of
the newspaper to get leads since companies hiring personnel frequently will also
have more activity in other areas of their business—and make a lot of calls.

It might take three months of making calls before a buyer will even trust you
enough to ask you to quote on a job. Then he will be suspicious if your first bid is
low, but he may still give you a chance if he has any desire at all to do business
with you. This is largely a function of how well his other printers are serving him.

I bid on six different jobs at an insurance company, which I initially considered a good prospect. I finally concluded that they always took the lowest bid, and
that quality of work did not enter into the purchase decision. As soon as I discovered that fact, I dropped them as a prospect.

Our company's image is that we have no late deliveries, and consistently
high quality. We have to live up to it because we also have a reputation for being
more expensive than our competitors.

The recent trend toward competitive bidding may be hurting our sales prospects. We did a study a couple of years ago showing that we obtained roughly one
job for every three bids submitted. Now the ratio is probably worse—I would guess
one sale is closed for every four jobs we bid on. The problem is that many buyers
have the idea that they should be able to get the high quality service we offer for
the lower prices they paid during the recent recession, or for the lower prices our
competitors quote. I would guess that prices for printing sales in this area have
risen 10% in the last 15 months.

Many purchase decisions by print buyers are based on politics or social connections. For example, a buyer may throw business to a printer if he represents a
company with a service that the printer uses—accounting, legal, etc. A salesman

always has to be careful not to waste his time on buyers with established ties that cannot be broken on the basis of a better printing service.

Most of our salesmen have not intentionally tried to match their customers to their special talents. But through the process of making many sales calls, that fit is usually established naturally.

HARRY COHEN. Harry had the most design talent of the salesmen. He held undergraduate and graduate degrees in graphic arts designing. Harry was hired as art director at the Gilbert Printing Company, a position he held for 2 years before he became a salesman:

When I first started selling, I had no background in sales at all. I would have liked more training and guidance than I received, but it is company policy that a salesman learns mostly on his own.

Of course with my background I go after the accounts that can use my talent. What I do is to give away a design service to obtain the printing order. The trouble with this approach is that it limits the volume of business I can handle, since it takes time to produce good designs.

When I began selling I got leads on prospective customers any way I could—I even wrote down names from trucks I passed on the road. One of my best customers today I read about in the Sunday paper when the company first moved to Baltimore. I got in touch with the advertising manager and gave him a lot of good advice about art services in Baltimore. I set him up with an agency and helped on initial designs. I was able to make sure that the design specifications fit our printing capability best, so I naturally got the printing business.

I accumulated more than 600 entries in a notebook on potential customers. I don't use it any more, however. I really spend less time prospecting for new customers than I should. It is much easier to concentrate on my present customers.

I become deeply involved in all phases of processing an order for my customers. I follow it all the way through the production sequence—this ensures that the job is done in exactly the way I know the customer wants it.

In a sales situation, I sell myself—all aspects. For example, I have a farm and I bring it into conversations. At Christmas I do not give my customers the usual gift certificate or liquor that most salesmen do—my wife cans jams and pickles and I give these. They mean a lot more—they're something personal.

I stay away form purchasing agents because all they know is the unit cost at the bottom of the line. They do not see the total package. Also, I cannot relate to most purchasing agent types. I also stay away from most ad agency production managers for the same reason. The last thing ad agencies need is my design talent. Some of my best customers are mutual funds who can really use my design talent. If I design a piece it saves them a fee—I am really selling on the basis of economics when I give away free design work.

Every printer tells his potential buyers that he has a high quality. That is all right for getting the first order, but you do have to provide acceptable quality to get repeat business. A print jobber[1] once won a competitive bid from me, and the

---

[1] A print jobber was an independent salesman who obtained orders from his customers, then selected a printer to do the work. The jobber earned his profit from the difference between the price he charged his customer and the price he paid the printer to do the work.

job he delivered looked like an out-of-tune color television picture. I had no trouble with competition from the jobber after that.

THE SITUATION IN AUGUST 1972

Bob Peterson had several courses of action in mind for increasing Gilbert's sales. He was actively trying to recruit salesmen from other printers, but it was always difficult to lure away a good salesman. Another possibility was to promote an employee with good technical knowledge of printing production, but no sales background, to a sales position. Such a salesman could certainly service existing accounts, freeing up more experienced salesmen to call on potential new accounts.

The success of his son, Dick, had led Mr. Peterson to consider recruiting a salesman from an M.B.A. program. He was confident such a person would have the talent, general knowledge of business, and personal drive required of the high-caliber salesman he was seeking. However, he was still unsure of how to select a person who had the particular qualities that would make a good print salesman. Mr. Peterson knew there was a considerable element of chance involved in hiring an unproven salesman. Also, he wondered what it would take to attract and motivate a high-caliber M.B.A. to a career in printing sales. He thought that the monetary incentive was a strong lure to potential printing salesmen and that the broad range of customers should interest and challenge an M.B.A. graduate.

Mr. Peterson had compiled some data on potential customers (see Exhibit 6). He wanted to have a new salesman to call on these customers. He knew that some printing companies had succeeded by hiring persons with knowledge of certain customer groups and then training these persons to sell to those customers. But any training effort would have to take time away from present sales efforts and could cause a net loss to the company, especially in the short run.

Mr. Peterson believed that the sales plateau of the Gilbert Printing Company would result in decreases in profit as costs in general rose faster than revenues. He wanted a plan to increase the sales in the short run and to build a foundation for longer-term growth at a good profit level.

EXHIBIT 1
ANNUAL SALES
Gilbert Printing Company

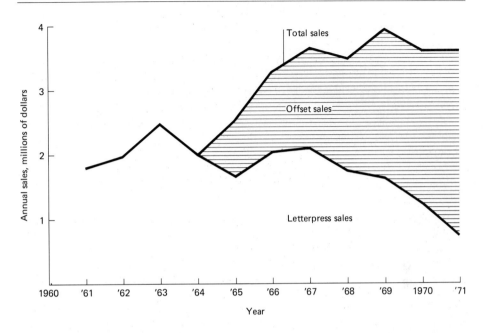

Total sales

Offset sales

Letterpress sales

Annual sales, millions of dollars

4

3

2

1

1960　'61　'62　'63　'64　'65　'66　'67　'68　'69　1970　'71

Year

EXHIBIT 2
INCOME STATEMENT, 1971
Gilbert Printing Company

Net sales		$3,640,000
Cost of sales:		
Materials	$1,353,000	
Direct labor	1,142,000	
Variable factory expense	160,000	
Fixed factory expense	220,000	
Total		2,875,000
Gross profit		$ 765,000
Selling and administrative expenses		625,000
Net profit (before taxes)		$ 140,000

EXHIBIT 3
PRIMARY COMPETITORS
Gilbert Printing Company

Name of competitor	Estimated sales 1971, $ millions	Comments*
Foremost Printing Co.	3.5	Quality closest to Gilbert in 4-color work
Wood Printing Co.	4.0	Recently purchased large web-offset press
Quality Press	2.0	
A. T. Berg Co.	3.5	Lower prices, lower quality
Morris Printing Co.	1.5	Lower prices. No 4-color capability
AAA Lithographers	2.0	
Robinson Printing Co.	1.0	Has one top-notch salesman

* Comments based on opinions expressed by Gilbert salesmen.

EXHIBIT 4
SALES DATA, THOUSANDS OF DOLLARS
Gilbert Printing Company

	1967	1968	1969	1970	1971
Accounts over $100					
House accounts:					
Old Ironside Distiller & Bottler	162	201	219	188	142
XYZ Paper Co.	204	169	153	199	99
Industrial Valve Co.	75	54	79	85	126
Consumer Package Goods Co.	1,790	1,582	1,528	1,083	1,607
Sterling Silver Co.	233	195	206	228	125
Subtotal	2,464	2,201	2,185	1,783	2,099
Alex Petroski:					
ABC Mutual Fund	88	78	123	107	100
Dave Shea:					
TVW Paper Co.	7	44	44	116	73
Educational Associates	167	30	9	30	37
Over $100 total	2,726	2,353	2,361	2,036	2,309
% of total company sales	74	68	60	56	64
Accounts $30 to $100					
House accounts:					
Clothing Mfg., Inc.	37	21	27	26	18
White Paper Co.	43	55	6	10	0
Black Paper Co.	26	29	35	34	14
Subtotal	106	105	68	70	32
Alex Petroski:					
Misc. Indust., Inc.	0	0	4	62	1
AA Publishing Co.	96	7	73	34	12
BB Publishing Co.	55	65	50	49	87
AA Mutual Fund	78	62	67	36	20
CC Publishing Co.	34	17	3	2	6
Top Food Co.	0	46	35	29	34
Church Press	17	38	5	16	*
Indust. Goods, Inc.	0	2	52	52	5
BB Mutual Fund	21	42	49	91	51
Subtotal	301	279	338	371	216
Dave Shea:					
Ace Consumer Mfg.	0	5	12	79	6
Ideal Ad Agency	39	42	49	37	50
Industrial Mfg. Co.	0	4	98	10	1
Plastics Mfg. Co.	0	0	0	37	0
Home Products, Inc.	0	3	8	19	90
DD Publishing Company	0	0	0	2	31
Creative Ad Agency	36	54	60	61	8
Subtotal	75	108	227	245	186
Harry Cohen:					
Admirable Ad Agency	11	31	20	0	20
CC Mutual Fund	0	4	25	57	53
Industrial Electronics Co.	0	1	41	28	26
DD Mutual Fund	0	20	54	37	0
Subtotal	11	56	140	122	99

* Gone out of business.

EXHIBIT 4
Continued

	1967	1968	1969	1970	1971
Accounts $30 to $100 (*continued*)					
Dick Peterson:					
Eastern University	54	80	60	38	63
Andrew Ad Agency	0	11	32	41	40
Consumer Electronics Mfg.	38	36	81	18	5
EE Mutual Fund	0	0	0	0	35
Subtotal	92	127	173	97	143
Frank Barr:†					
Arnold Ad Agency	0	0	0	44	1*
Albert Ad Agency	31	20	26	15	5*
Subtotal	31	20	26	59	6
Robert Darman:†					
$30 to $100 total	616	695	972	964	682
% of total company sales	17	20	25	26	19
Accounts under $30‡					
% of total company sales	9	12	15	18	16
Total Company Sales	3,689	3,458	3,910	3,664	3,597
"House" Sales $	2,570	2,306	2,253	1,853	2,131
"House" Sales %§	70%	67%	58%	51%	59%

* Gone out of business.

† Some of Frank Barr's and Robert Darman's sales are included in sales of persons to whom their accounts were reassigned.

‡ 150 accounts in this category in 1971.

§ For first 6 months of 1972 "house" sales were 57 percent of total.

EXHIBIT 5
SELLING PERSONNEL
Gilbert Printing Company

Name	Age	Years of service	Background	Sales volume, thousands of dollars			
				1972 1st 6 mos.	1971 1st 6 mos.	1971 Total	1970 Total
Steve Gilbert, President	42	20	Administrative			2,324 (house sales)	2,054 (house sales)
Bob Peterson, exec. VP	53	25	Sales				
Alex Petroski, sales manager–salesman	39	13	Sales; qualified as stockbroker	320	192	507	498
Dave Shea, salesman	34	15	Sales, 5 years; estimating and production, 10 years	234	212	450	324
Harry Cohen, salesman	32	7	Sales, 5 years; art director, 2 years; extensive art education	195	115	200	363
Dick Peterson, salesmen	25	4	M.B.A. '71, Columbia; extensive part-time printing experience prior to 1971	98			
Frank Barr*	28	2	Sales, industrial	24		11	
Robert Darman†	30	4	Sales; art education		48	105 (through Sept.)	425

* Dismissed June 1972.
† Quit September 1971.

EXHIBIT 6

MARKET INFORMATION: PRINT BUYERS WITH POTENTIAL
OF $25,000 AND UP PER YEAR

Gilbert Printing Company

Customer group	No. of potential accounts	No. of accounts sold	Purchase decision maker
Mutual funds	20	10	Advertising manager*, Purchasing agent
Advertising agencies	15	6	Production manager
Paper companies	12	6	Advertising manager
Universities, colleges	75	6	Special print buyers, P.R. directors, others
Consumer and industrial manufacturers	100+	20	Product managers, advertising managers, purchasing agents, art directors
Insurance companies	4	0	Purchasing agents
Banks	6	1	Advertising manager, purchasing agent
Publishers	3	3	Advertising manager, others
Financial report buyers†			Vice presidents of finance,
Annual reports	200	20	advertising managers,
Proxies, prospectuses	100–200‡	5	treasurers, or attorney who works on documents

    * The title advertising manager was used as a proxy for any marketing executive with influence over printer selection.

    † While many other customer groups included financial report buyers, this segment was important enough to form a special group.

    ‡ If the firm were to enter this market in a major way it would need $75,000–$100,000 worth of new equipment, most of it for typesetting. The company presently had no typesetting equipment and relied on outside contractors for that function. This market segment demanded fast delivery. Prospectuses would often be delivered early in the evening with delivery required at the start of the following working day.

UNION CARBIDE CORPORATION: LINDE DIVISION

BENSON P. SHAPIRO
Associate Professor
Harvard Graduate School of Business Administration

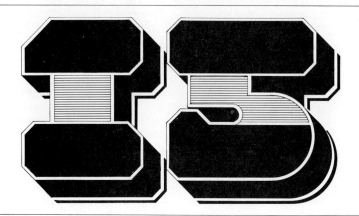

In May 1970 the Linde Division of Union Carbide Corporation officially entered the wastewater treatment business with its patented UNOX[1] System. By the fall of 1971, several systems had been sold[2] in both the municipal and industrial markets. The division's management, however, was concerned about the loss of a sale to the city of Bakerton in a midwestern state and the extremely time-consuming nature of the selling process in general.

---

[1] UNOX is a registered trademark of Union Carbide Corporation.

[2] The word *sold* had an unusual meaning in this context. Six systems were under contract and being installed. Another 20 treatment plants were being designed to use the UNOX System but contracts had not been issued on them yet. However, once a wastewater treatment plant was designed to utilize the UNOX System, competitive systems could not be incorporated into the plant without a total redesign.

THE LINDE DIVISION

The Linde Division was one of 16 domestic operating divisions of the Union Carbide Corporation. The corporation was one of the largest chemical companies in the world with 1970 sales of over $3 billion and net income of $157 million. Total assets as of December 31, 1970, were over $3.5 billion including almost $2 billion in depreciated fixed assets. The corporation spent over $78 million for research and development in 1970.

The Linde Division was a part of the Gases, Metals and Carbons Group which had 1970 sales of $1.156 billion and income contribution of $153 million. Gases and related products accounted for sales of $379 million. The division was described as follows in the 1970 *Annual Report*:

> *A major activity of this Division is the production of purified gases—primarily oxygen, nitrogen, argon, hydrogen, helium, and acetylene. They are used in the production and fabrication of steel and other metals, in the aerospace program, in chemical and petroleum processing operations, and in wastewater treatment. The Division manufactures equipment used in various industrial processes, such as welding, flame-cutting, and POLARSTREAM liquid nitrogen refrigeration for in-transit preservation of food.*

THE UNOX PROCESS

By 1971, the Linde Division had invested several million dollars and several years in the development of the UNOX System. The UNOX System was designed to significantly improve the secondary treatment of wastewater, both municipal and industrial. Primary treatment typically consisted of large settling tanks in which some biological breakdown of organic waste took place and where solid materials settled out of wastewater. In many areas of the nation, the typical sewage system consisted of a set of collecting pipes and a primary system only. In those systems the partially treated sewage was discharged into a nearby waterway.

Other areas also had secondary treatment plants in which the organic wastes were further broken down by biological action. There were two available methods for secondary treatment: activated-sludge and trickling-filter. In the activated-sludge process the sewage was treated in a large tank in which a biomass containing bacteria and air and the sewage were mixed together. The bacteria needed the oxygen in the air to decompose the sewage. The trickling-filter operation used different equipment to accomplish the same process. The sewage was sprayed over a bed of small stones or plastic pieces on which the bacteria grew. As the sewage seeped through the bed the bacteria broke down the organic material. The outgoing stream from the trickling-filter process was considered in the industry to be of lower quality than that from the activated-sludge process. That is, less of the organic material was broken down. In both processes the treated sewage was discharged into a nearby waterway.

The UNOX System was essentially an improvement over the standard air-activated sludge process which had been developed in the early 1900s. In the UNOX System the air was replaced by relatively pure oxygen which considerably speeded the process because the oxygen in the air dissolved poorly and slowly in the sewage. The UNOX System provided:

1   A process of, and apparatus for, highly efficient oxygen mixing, dissolution, and utilization

2   The delicate controls and advanced know-how necessary to maintain the operation at peak efficiency

The UNOX System reduced the typical wastewater retention time of 3 to 6 hours to 1 to 2 hours. While a conventional air aeration system could remove only 30 to 60 pounds of BOD[1] per 1,000 cubic feet of tank capacity per day, the UNOX System could remove 150 to 200 pounds per 1,000 cubic feet per day. The electrical mixing power, which was a large operating cost of an activated-sludge plant, was much more efficiently used in the UNOX System. According to the Linde Division, the UNOX System provided:

1   Better treatment quality

2   Reduced capital cost

3   Reduced operating cost

4   Reduced sludge-disposal cost (because the system generated less sludge)

5   Reliable process control

6   Effective odor control (the UNOX System processing tanks were covered whereas conventional tanks were open)

7   Reduced land area necessary for tankage and equipment

Exhibits 1 and 2 show cost comparisons.

Linde management believed that in selling the UNOX System it was selling an advanced technological process embodied in a particular combination of equipment elements. It provided the design and hardware for an oxygen dissolution system and an instrument and control system. If requested by the customer, Linde also made available an oxygen-producing facility. Although customers could order the oxygen-producing facility from a competitor, all UNOX Systems which had been sold or were in the design stage incorporated a Linde oxygen-generating facility. Linde assembled and fabricated the equipment and sometimes installed it. Installation was typically provided only on the larger, more complex units where outside contractors might be less familiar with appropriate installation procedures. Linde coordinated specifications with consulting engi-

---

[1] BOD was biological oxygen demand, a measure of the amount of organic material present in sewage.

neers for other parts of the wastewater system and supplied drawings and plans which enabled the UNOX System to be connected to these.

The system was priced on the basis of the number of pounds of organic material which had to be removed from the wastewater per day.

The profit margin for the UNOX System compared favorably with those of other products in the division and corporation and reflected the high market risk and substantial amounts of valuable technical manpower which had been devoted to the project. Furthermore, because the UNOX business was not capital intensive its return on assets was very good. Return on assets was the criterion that the corporation used in measuring the performance of a business.

The Linde Division had several competitors who were also anxious to improve wastewater treatment. One competitor, another very large chemical firm, sold advanced wastewater treatment plants utilizing the best available standard technology. The firm sold complete plants (turn-key installations) totally designed, engineered, and constructed by the firm. While a few plants had been sold to industrial users, none had been sold in the municipal market. One reason was that federal government funding regulations specified that an independent engineering organization such as a consultant had to be used on municipal wastewater treatment plants receiving federal funds. Since the firm did the engineering work itself, no independent consulting engineer would be used in the turn-key installation.

Another competitor, a large supplier of industrial gases (1970 sales of $437 million) was attempting to gain federal government support to develop another form of the oxygen-using system. As of 1971 it had not received any government research funds. Union Carbide had earlier received just over $500,000 of government funding to demonstrate the UNOX System in a small municipal wastewater treatment plant.

A smaller supplier of industrial gases (1970 sales of $261 million), regarded in the chemical industry as a very alert aggressive competitor, was also known to be developing a system. It was also negotiating with the Linde Division to license the patents covering the UNOX System. Under the proposed arrangement, Linde would receive a fee for each installation the competitor sold, with the fee being based on the size of the installation. Linde personnel expected a licensing agreement to be consummated in the spring of 1972. Linde desired to license its pertinent patents because of its projections of the large size of the market and because management considered it better to have a competitor when selling to public sector markets.

Several other firms were working to improve the efficiency of the trickling-filter technology by improving the shape of the plastic pieces used in the beds. Linde management was relatively unconcerned about this form of competition.

The chief competition was from standard air-activated sludge systems which had worked reliably for many years and which were familiar to municipalities, consultants, and state and federal agencies.

Because of the size of the potential market for the UNOX System, the Linde Division had set up a separate organization to pursue the wastewater treatment market. Exhibit 3 shows the organization chart. Six salesmen and a sales manager were employed in the selling effort. There were also two product managers in the marketing organization, one for the industrial market and one for the municipal market.

THE INDUSTRIAL MARKET

Linde management divided the industrial from the municipal market on the basis of the nature of the funding of the project. Most industrial waste was in fact treated in municipally owned plants. Even when a municipality financed a wastewater treatment plant solely to process industrial wastes (e.g., for several factories located near each other), Linde personnel considered it a municipal installation because of the financing and purchasing methods. Thus, to Linde the industrial market consisted of wastewater treatment plants purchased and financed by industrial firms.

Only large plants could justify their own wastewater treatment facilities. Such an installation would cost between $1 and $20 million with a $20 million plant equivalent in size to that needed for sanitary waste (regular household waste) by a city of 300,000 people. The UNOX System proportion of the installation would account for between 10 and 50 percent of the cost, with a higher percentage for smaller plants. The UNOX System proportion of industrial treatment facilities thus might sell for between $500,000 and $2 million, with some occasionally selling for as little as $100,000 or as much as $5 million.[1]

The removal of organic materials from wastewater was most important to plants in three industry categories: pulp and paper, food products (including canning, distilling, brewing, and meat packing), and chemical and petrochemicals (see Exhibits 4 and 5 for details). According to Linde executives these categories accounted for 90 percent of the industrial market and differed substantially from each other but had some important common characteristics. According to the industrial systems product manager, wastewater treatment systems were purchased in the same manner as any other large, technically complex systems:

> The technical organization is in reality the buyer. The purchasing agent or operations personnel take part in the discussions but they seldom have even the power to veto a proposal. Top management, of course, has that power. Typically we deal primarily with the manager of engineering although the purchasing agent may arrange and attend the early meetings.

Linde management believed that most industry wastewater treatment facilities had been installed because of legal requirements or public pressure. Each individual industrial system was different in terms of its requirements. In general, industrial waste was more concentrated (higher amount of BOD per gallon of wastewater) than sanitary waste.

---

[1] These same dollar and percentage figures would generally apply in the municipal market, but the relative cost of the UNOX System in the larger plants might go somewhat below 10 percent. Municipal plants would also tend to be larger.

The pulp and paper industry consisted primarily of a few large firms and had a strong industry trade association which performed wastewater treatment research and provided technical support to member firms. Installations were typically large by industrial standards but were usually in sparsely populated areas where land was cheap and pollution control problems less urgent.

The food industry, on the other hand, was highly fragmented and consisted primarily of smaller firms and plants. Each particular segment of the industry (e.g., brewers, meat packers) had unique problems. Industry trade associations were typically not actively involved in research. Most of the firms did not have large engineering groups and had to rely on consulting engineers (described below). Most of the plants were in urban areas where pollution control standards were tight and land very expensive. Odor problems could be particularly important in such areas. Other segments of the industry, such as canneries, were in rural or semirural areas.

The chemical industry was even more concentrated than the pulp and paper industry. Many firms, especially large ones, had wastewater treatment engineering capabilities.

Linde management believed that there was less economic incentive for industrial plants to use the UNOX System than for municipalities to use it. Because industry was more parsimonious in its building and purchase policies,[1] generally built structures with shorter life spans, tended to use used equipment, and often built wastewater treatment facilities with its own labor and equipment, industrial wastewater treatment facilities were less costly for industry to build than for municipalities and thus the capital savings from the use of the UNOX System were often relatively smaller. On the other hand, capital investment dollars were more dear to private firms than municipalities because municipalities often received state or federal financial aid to build wastewater treatment facilities.

The UNOX System also offered intangible benefits which were of more importance to industry than municipalities. Odor control was a major intangible benefit. Because the tanks used in the UNOX System were closed they did not allow odor to escape the plant. This was important because industrial wastewater treatment facilities were often built in populated areas and often processed waste with very offensive odors. Land savings resulting from fewer tanks were important because factories had often grown to the limits of their available space and private industry could not obtain land through eminent domain as municipalities could. Finally the UNOX System had excellent ability to absorb shock loads which were more frequent and serious in industrial plants than in municipal ones. Such unpredictable peak loads were caused by unplanned production variations, safety considerations, and operator error. Peak loads in municipal plants were highly predictable and could be handled by traditional plants, although the UNOX System offered some added efficiency in handling even predicted peak loads.

---

[1] Wastewater experts, for example, often commented that industry typically built earthen dikes for its settling ponds while municipalities usually built concrete dikes.

Industry differed from municipalities in that industry was often able to affect the amount and nature of the wastewater it generated by changing its production processes. One way was to recycle its wastewater. A large brewer, for example, was reported to be working on a system to recycle spent fermentation fluid, which was the primary organic component of brewery wastewater.

On some occasions other chemical firms had resented using a technology developed outside their own laboratories. One Linde executive described this as the "Not Invented Here" syndrome. He went on to say that, on the other hand, companies which competed with other divisions of Union Carbide had no unusual hesitancy in purchasing UNOX Systems. "The chemical industries are a complex relationship of suppliers, customers, and competitors all woven together. They are used to buying and selling to each other even though they compete with each other."

THE MUNICIPAL MARKET

Linde executives felt that it was a complex job to sell a UNOX System to a municipality. Four parties were involved in the purchase: (1) the municipality, (2) the consulting engineer, (3) the state, and (4) the federal government.

In most cities or sewage districts the purchase of a secondary wastewater treatment facility was a major undertaking. The city engineer (or equivalent) would typically be directly involved in the process. He was a professionally trained civil or sanitary engineer and usually not a political appointee. In some cities, the engineers had very large staffs while in others they had almost none. The Chicago Metropolitan Sanitary District employed about 350 engineers. The city of Miami also had a staff large enough to design its own secondary treatment plant. The city of Buffalo, on the other hand, had only a small engineering staff. The smaller cities and towns typically had no professional staff. The water and sewage officials depended heavily on consulting engineers.

Consulting engineers were involved in some way in almost every municipal waste treatment plant, and in most cases they were heavily involved. According to Linde executives there were "a vast number" of consultants ranging from small operations (several engineers and draftsmen) up to large firms with several hundred employees. The smaller firms tended to operate regionally while the large ones tended to have several offices across the nation. Sometimes a national and regional firm would combine efforts to obtain a particular job. It was estimated in the industry that the 10 largest consulting firms did about three-fourths of the "big" jobs.

The consultants were prevented by what was called "professional ethics" from cutting fees. In fact the trade association of consulting engineers published a schedule of fees for various sizes and types of installations. The consultants were paid a percentage of the cost of the installation, with the percentage varying from 5 to 8 percent. Occasionally there had been rumors of some slight fee cutting by some consultants, but in 1971 fees were firm because business was good due to the large number of wastewater treatment plants being installed. Consultants tended to rely on their professional reputations and personal relationships in selling their services. They typically spent a great deal of time explaining their competence to prospective customers. It was exceedingly unusual for a municipality or sewer district to use the same consultants for more than one plant at the same time. That is, if a municipality were building several plants simultaneously, each would be analyzed or designed by a different consulting engineer.

Many experts thought that municipal installations differed substantially from each other and each required its own engineering and design work. However, some of the same equipment components were often used in different designs.

Many consulting engineers had been somewhat hesitant to incorporate the UNOX System into their designs. They were concerned about the newness of the system. New products or procedures often took many years to gain strong acceptance from consulting engineers. Linde executives believed that they were fortunate because the technology of oxygen-generating plants was well established and because their process was a refinement of the well-regarded activated-sludge process.

It was the standard procedure on the part of even the largest consulting firms to recommend the use of a large new development like the UNOX System on only one or two of their projects at one time. Because of the long design and engineering cycle, this presented a major problem to Linde. The consultants told Linde that they were willing to accept only a limited amount of risk.

The consulting organizations themselves differed in the manner in which they worked. Almost all were partnerships. In some firms the partners worked relatively autonomously, while in others they shared projects. In smaller and medium-sized firms, a partner was in charge of each job. In larger ones, a project engineer would supervise the groups of engineers who worked on each wastewater treatment facility. Sometimes, if an installation were small, a project engineer would supervise it even in the smaller firms. A partner was almost always involved on each UNOX System installation because the system was new.

The consultant's involvement with a project began with a definition of the problem. This was usually a general survey of the municipality's needs and was typically a low-price contract. Linde management was not interested in projects at this stage.

The next step was a preliminary study of alternative solutions to the problem which had previously been defined. This stage, called a *facilities analysis,* was sometimes combined with the problem definition. The facilities analysis report began with the analysis of such considerations as size of the treatment plant or plants to be built, number of plants to be built, quality of outgoing wastewater, and an estimate of the cost. While generally interested in these matters, Linde's major involvement was in the second part of the analysis which focused on the choice of the process to be used. Here physical (e.g., land availability) and financial constraints were carefully considered. This led to a preliminary design for the plant and a relatively complete estimate of costs. To Linde management this was the critical stage at which they had to demonstrate the cost effectiveness of the UNOX System to the municipality and its consultants. Success at this stage led to a "commitment."

The problem definition and facilities analysis stages of the process typically cost the municipality between several hundred thousand and several million dollars on a fixed fee basis and took 1 to 2 years to complete.

Upon receipt of the facilities analysis report, a municipality might immediately authorize the preparation of a detailed design for the plant. But, at other times there might be a long delay before detailed design was authorized. It was not unusual for a municipality to hire a different consultant to design the plant than the one which prepared the facilities analysis report.

The chosen consultant would then design the treatment plant by setting up the detailed specifications for each piece of equipment and would develop engineering drawings for the tanks and other large custom pieces of equipment. Sometimes the project consultant would subcontract parts of the design work to other consultants. The consultant was usually paid a percentage of cost of the total installation for this detailed design.

Before the final designs were completed they generally had to be approved by state authorities, and if the plant were to be built even partially with federal funds they also had to be approved by the Environmental Protection Agency, a federal agency. Typically, the state agency responsible for authorization was either a public health agency or an environmental protection agency. Each state tended to have its own design guidelines. One group of 10 Northeast states had developed a set of joint guidelines of design criteria. Some of the guidelines, however, were not designed to accommodate new processes such as the UNOX System.

The state agencies typically were conservative in their approach to certifying new types of equipment and processes. In general, their emphasis was on protecting the people of the state from financial or health risks. Large cities often could influence the decisions of state authorities. At other times, however, the state was totally independent of municipal wishes.

The federal Environmental Protection Agency, on the other hand, was anxious to encourage the development of new equipment and methods. It had, for example, provided funds for the demonstration of the UNOX System. The Agency was also willing to fund the installation of new equipment and processes. Sometimes federal and state authorities disagreed about the usefulness of new processes. In such cases the federal personnel exerted no overt influence on the state personnel because, according to industry sources, the Environmental Protection Agency was anxious to avoid encroaching upon state prerogatives.

The funding of municipal projects varied, although most were constructed with one-third federal funds. In almost all cases state and federal agencies provided more than 50 percent of the funds, and in some they provided as much as 90 percent.

If the design included the UNOX System, Linde management considered it "sold." At this stage, however, Linde still had no order or contract. It could, in fact, be up to 2 years before Linde received the contract. It was also still possible that Linde would not eventually get the order. For example, the plant might not be built because a bond issue to finance the project would not be passed by the voters. Sometimes it took so long for the bond issue to be voted that the design apparently became obsolete and would have to be redone. In other cases wastewater treatment plant designs were modified, for example, so that two plants were combined. At still other times the consultant might be replaced and a new consultant would redesign the plant.

Once a proposed project was fully designed and then approved by municipal, state, and federal authorities it was put up for bid. The specifications in the bids were written in varying degrees of detail, but typically the specifications neither encouraged nor discouraged the use of the UNOX System directly. Instead they would include specifications which many, few, or sometimes only a single manufacturer could meet. Because of the unique nature of the UNOX System, the specifications would typically either enable only Linde to get the job or would totally prevent it from getting the job. Since their reputation for objectivity and reliability was crucial to consulting engineers, they were generally reluctant to write specifications so narrowly that only a single manufacturer could qualify.

General contractors bid for the contract, which included everything (equipment, piping, installation, electrical work, etc.). Much of the actual contract work would, however, be performed by subcontracting specialists like electrical contractors, foundation contractors, etc. If the UNOX System were relevant to a particular project, the general contractor would have to obtain a subbid from Linde in the same way as he normally obtained subbids from, say, electrical contractors. Linde provided the same price and subbid to all the general contractors bidding on a job.

Linde executives expected that in the future a general contractor would be able to get other subbids from licensees of the Union Carbide patents, or even from competitors.

The sale of a UNOX System typically was the culmination of a great deal of effort on the part of Linde sales executives. The salesmen or sales executives usually had a great deal of advanced information concerning a prospective major wastewater treatment facility. They typically learned of these in the early stages of the thinking which preceded the formal facilities analysis. The Linde executives might learn of proposed projects from municipal, state, or federal officials, consulting engineers, or the trade press.

As the facilities analysis progressed, Linde salesmen attempted to have details which defined the UNOX System written into the specifications for the project. They called constantly on the municipal, state, and federal officials involved and upon the consulting engineer. The sales manager and product managers were typically involved in the selling process. Larger potential sales received the attention of the manager of the UNOX System marketing organization and the head of Linde's new venture operation. The selling effort continued for many months. Typically the sales approach stressed the lower operating and investment cost of the UNOX System and the other benefits described earlier. Frequently the Linde sales team made presentations to groups of officials and consultants concerned with a particular project.

Linde management was concerned that "municipal prospects would not believe our claims of performance for the Linde process." One sales development device which had worked quite well in this regard was trailer-mounted miniature UNOX Systems used for local demonstration purposes. The division had eight of them. The units would be delivered to a site and hooked up to the incoming wastewater pipes for between several months and 1 year. The units acted as both tests and demonstrations. They generated information for the final design of a full-size unit and data for use in operating the full-sized plant.

Linde charged each prospective customer as much as $25,000, plus up to $300 per day for a demonstration unit. This, according to Linde executives covered Linde's direct cost (not including amortization and overhead). The units were described as a "great selling tool." Ninety percent of the places where a demonstration unit had been installed ended up deciding to design their plant on the basis of the UNOX System. But the demonstration units cost almost $100,000 each to build. Linde executives wondered whether they could be more effectively used and indeed whether they justified their expense.

According to one Linde executive, the demonstration units were used in three different types of situations. First, they were sometimes used where the municipal wastewater executives and consultants wanted UNOX but needed justification. Second, they were used where more data were needed by the decision makers. The data needed would either relate to treatability or to economics. In the first situation the unit was used to ascertain whether or not the UNOX System was appropriate for the wastewater. This was important because sometimes the UNOX System would effectively treat waste which could be only marginally treated with a standard air-activated sludge process. In the second case the data were used to design the actual plant which would range from 100 to 10,000 times larger than the demonstration unit and to develop data on operating costs. The third type of use was in cases where "they don't want the UNOX System but they go through the motions."

The same executive described the demonstration units as a marketing tool. "It gives the engineers and politicians credibility." He indicated that the data on treatability and economics were generally available from Linde's laboratory-size unit. When the laboratory testing was done, several barrels of the wastewater to be treated would be delivered to the division's laboratory.

Of specific concern was the situation in the Midwestern city of Bakerton. Bakerton had a population of about 100,000. It badly needed an improved wastewater treatment plant. State authorities felt that the situation was so bad that they would not allow the city to issue any more building permits until the wastewater treatment facility was improved. Although such action was unusual the state officials had the power to take that action because they feared the effect the untreated wastewater would have on underground water supplies. They considered the situation a potential health hazard. The consulting engineer who was working on the project was totally behind the UNOX System concept. The city engineer and the city council approved the consultant's plans quickly and easily. Linde executives were sure that the system would be written tightly into the specifications.

The state, however, balked. State authorities would not approve design specifications in which the amount of BOD to be processed was more than 70 pounds per day per 1,000 cubic feet of aeration capacity. The UNOX System operated most efficiently when processing 200 pounds of BOD per day per 1,000 cubic feet of aeration space. State authorities chose the 70 pounds of BOD because the UNOX System being installed in the city of Aldrich (population 120,000) in the state was to operate at the 70-pound figure. According to Linde executives the economics of the Aldrich installation were such that the UNOX System was more economical than competing systems even if it had to be restricted to the 70-pound figure. They expected that as the Aldrich operating personnel gained experience and confidence in the system its capacity could be raised by raising the BOD loading above 70 pounds. In the Bakerton case, however, the economics were such that at the 70-pound loading, the UNOX System was not economical. This was explained to the state authorities who wanted to ponder the matter.

The Bakerton city council was not willing to wait. It instructed the city engineer to tell the consultant to develop plans for a system of standard design even though it might be more expensive to construct and operate. To Linde executives, the city council seemed hesitant, even afraid, to consider the UNOX System after the state limited its approval.

In reviewing the situation one Linde executive stated:

> We were, of course, terribly disappointed. We thought that the sale was a foregone conclusion. In fact, it looked like one of the surest sales we had ever been involved with. I just don't know how we can make the benefits of the system more clear. We have a great product here which obviously meets a crying consumer need—a need which everyone recognizes—yet it's so difficult to sell.

On the other hand Linde had been successful in selling other installations. Exhibit 6 gives some examples.

The division did not utilize journal advertising. It depended upon press publicity and technical papers because division management believed it did not need journal advertising.

The actual selling was performed by the main sales force with the assistance of the product managers and sales manager. The salesmen had been trained in selling UNOX Systems and were provided with leads and industrial directories for their territories. Leads for industrial installations typically came from three sources: (1) consulting engineers, (2) other Union Carbide Corporation salesmen who learned of a prospective installation in the course of their sales activities, and (3) firms who contacted Linde by mail. The salesmen were paid by salary. The division of their selling time between industrial and municipal systems was determined by negotiations between the product managers and the sales managers. In 1971 the sales budget was 20 percent industrial, 80 percent municipal, and in 1972 this would be changed to 35 and 65 percent.

These figures were weighted averages because the percentage varied by region. Thus, the Houston salesman, whose territory included many large chemical plants, spent a larger percentage of his time on industrial prospects than did other salesmen whose territories had less industrial potential.

It was believed that the elapsed time between an initial sales call and sale of the system varied between 1 and 2 years for industrial systems and between 3 and 5 years for municipal systems. This difference, according to Linde executives, was because industry had more freedom in purchasing procedure (it didn't have to have public bids or state or federal approval), and often was under greater time pressure to have the system installed. The cost of selling a system to industry was typically the equivalent of 4 to 6 man-months, or $20,000 to $30,000. Municipal projects could take up to 50 man-months, or $250,000.

The nature of the sales effort was also different. Industrial firms sometimes did not make as much use of consulting engineers as municipalities and usually did more of their own engineering. This was especially true of large paper, petroleum, and chemical firms which had large staffs of engineers. The industrial installations thus required a higher portion of selling time and a smaller proportion of presales engineering time. The presales engineering typically consisted of feasibility studies involving the nature, size, and costs of equipment and operating procedures. According to Linde management industrial customers typically issued single contracts for both the design and construction of a treatment plant. Municipalities, on the other hand, had the design work done first and then received bids for construction of the plant. The industrial market product manager believed that the gross margin per dollar expended in sales effort (including both actual personal selling and presales engineering) was equal as between industrial and municipal sales.

EXHIBIT 1
TOTAL TREATMENT COST "UNOX" SYSTEM AND
AIR AERATION TYPICAL RANGE
Union Carbide Corporation: Linde Division

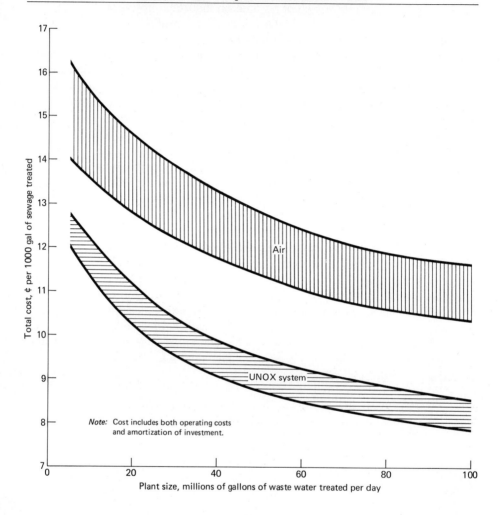

Note: Cost includes both operating costs and amortization of investment.

Air

UNOX system

Total cost, ¢ per 1000 gal of sewage treated

Plant size, millions of gallons of waste water treated per day

EXHIBIT 2
AIR VERSUS OXYGEN PLANT COSTS
FOR EXISTING PLANTS
Union Carbide Corporation: Linde Division

| | Design flow,* million gal/day | | | | | |
| | 6 | | 30 | | 100 | |
	Air	Oxygen	Air	Oxygen	Air	Oxygen
Capital cost, $1,000	$640	$540	$2,200	$1,700	$6,100	$4,950
Horsepower	290	105	1,470	515	4,880	1,580
Operating and maintenance, $/yr.	$61,300	$32,100	$226,000	$106,000	$632,000	$283,000
Total cost in cents/1,000 gal	9.1¢	6.3¢	9.5¢	6.6¢	7.9¢	5.5¢
Percentage cost savings of oxygen system, %	31		31		30	

	Design flow,* million gal/day	Cost, millions
Cost of original Batavia plant† (1965)	2.2	$1.35
Cost of new plant using air (1970)	10	$4.50
Cost of conversion to oxygen system (1970)	10	$1.25

* Design flow is the size of the plant in millions of gallons of treated wastewater per day.
† Batavia was the original UNOX demonstration grant.
Source: The Oil and Gas Journal, June 29, 1970.

EXHIBIT 3
ORGANIZATION CHART
Union Carbide Corporation: Linde Division

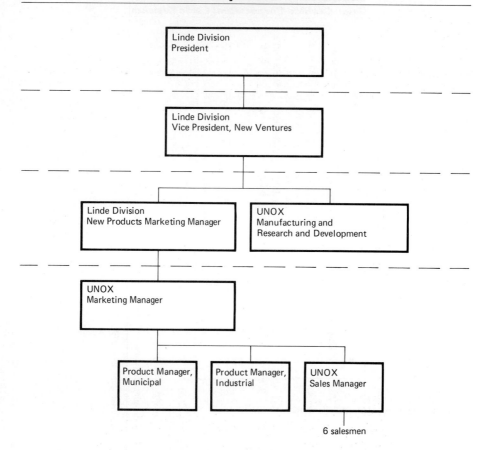

EXHIBIT 4
THE ESTIMATED MUNICIPAL WASTEWATER TREATMENT MARKET, TOTAL FOR 1972–1976, BY SIZE RANGES
Union Carbide Corporation: Linde Division

Size range, MGD*	No. of municipalities	% of total units	Total estimated treatment capacity in this size range, MGD	% of total treatment capacity in this size range
10–35	265	68	5,300	27
36–75	63	16	3,100	16
76–150	35	9	4,000	21
151+	26	7	7,100	36
	389	100	19,500	100

Projected timing (using index numbers)

1972	1973	1974	1975	1976	Total
21%†	28%	21%	17%	14%	100%

Note: In some cases numbers have been disguised.

* MGD means millions of gallons of wastewater to be treated per day.

† To be read "21% of the treatment capacity to be added between 1972 and 1976 is projected to be added in 1972."

Source: Company reports and estimates.

EXHIBIT 5
ESTIMATED INDUSTRIAL WASTEWATER TREATMENT CAPITAL EXPENDITURES 1971–1980, BY SECTORS AND DOLLARS*
Union Carbide Corporation: Linde Division

Segment	Selected major industry sectors, Total 1971–1980		
	Gross capital expenditures	Amount to be spent by municipalities	Amount to be spent by industry
Food products	$1,694	$1,051	$ 643
Textile	423	316	107
Pulp and paper	1,497	290	1,207
Chemical (incl. petroleum)	1,689	145	1,544
	$5,303	$1,802	$3,501

Total of these selected sectors, each year

1971	1972	1973	1974	1975	1976	1977	1978	1979	1980	Total
$307	$334	$364	$394	$427	$275	$300	$325	$365	$410	$3,501

* Dollar amounts are in millions based on 1971 costs and no inflation.

Source: Company reports and estimates.

EXHIBIT 6
EXAMPLES OF UNOX SYSTEMS WHICH HAD BEEN
SOLD (MUNICIPAL MARKET)
Union Carbide Corporation: Linde Division

Size, MGD	Total cost	UNOX proportion of the total cost
180	$50 million	$3.5 million
100	$50 million	$4.5 million
100	$27 million	$3.9 million
20	$ 9 million	$900,000

THE SMITHVILLE COMPANY[1]

DIRCK SCHOU
MBA, Class of 1973
Harvard Graduate School of Business Administration

BENSON P. SHAPIRO
Associate Professor
Harvard Graduate School of Business Administration

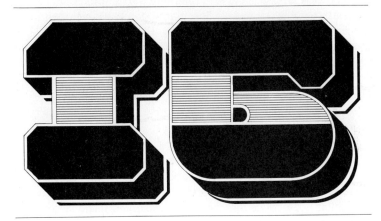

In March 1973 Ms. Katherine O'Brien, vice president—marketing, was attempting to decide whether or not the Smithville Company should discontinue the use of manufacturers' representatives[2] in favor of a company-owned sales force. The president of the firm, Mr. James Petrosky, had expressed great interest in the idea. It was clear, however, that the primary input into the decision would be Ms. O'Brien's.

The Smithville Company had been founded just before World War I and had remained a modest, family-run operation, producing crocks, pots, and miscellaneous garden and kitchen ceramic articles until the late 1950s. At that time, Mr. Petrosky assumed the responsibilities of chief executive officer and put the

[1] Confidential company data have been disguised.

[2] Manufacturers' representatives or reps were independent selling organizations which sold lines of complementary but noncompetitive items of different manufacturers. The representatives usually were compensated with a commission on merchandise shipped and paid their own expenses. They did not take possession of the merchandise. Commission rates and standard policies differed by industry.

company on a course of developing and selling complete lines of stoneware[1] dinnerware and related kitchen and table accessory items. The projected sales of $6.7 million for 1973 represented a doubling in volume since 1970. Mr. Petrosky desired to maintain a growth rate of at least 20 percent per year in both sales and profits for the foreseeable future. Exhibit 1 provides recent income statement information.

In 1973 the company was producing and selling three lines of dinnerware and an assortment of mugs, and was devoting approximately 18 percent of its production to contract work for other manufacturers. Its oldest line of dinnerware, the Greenwich line, was begun in the late 1950s and contained approximately 70 separate items. Its newest line, Saratoga, was developed in the late 1960s and comprised approximately 40 items. Exhibit 2 gives a list of the items in the Greenwich line, and Exhibit 3 contains pictures of several of the items. Exhibit 4 provides item sales. Smithville distributed its branded lines through an estimated 12,000 active accounts. Although department stores, chain stores, and mail-order catalog outlets were becoming increasingly important, it was estimated that as of the end of 1972, over 60 percent of sales revenue (exclusive of contract work) came from small gift shops.

Ms. O'Brien believed that Smithville products were purchased as gifts as often as they were purchased for personal use, and that most of the purchases resulted from in-store displays. Some unsophisticated market research conducted by the company through the use of warranty cards seemed to verify this assumption. (Exhibit 5 describes the results of this survey.) The larger dollar volume in all lines came from the related items rather than the dinnerware sets. She attributed this to three factors. First, once a consumer had either purchased or received as a gift a 45-piece set (eight 5-piece place settings and five serving dishes), she would add, or receive as a gift, pieces related to her original set on a continuing basis. Second, the related items were sufficiently attractive and functional in their own right to serve as welcomed additions to any home, whether the core dinnerware set was possessed or not. Finally, most of the articles were moderately priced and widely distributed. This thinking led Ms. O'Brien to conclude that the relevant definition of the Smithville market was the entire gift and decorative accessory market as well as the dinnerware market.

Ms. O'Brien was optimistic about the future for stoneware articles in the United States. For one thing, the clearly recognized trend toward casual and convenient living remained strong. And, it was reasoned, as Americans spent more leisure time in their homes, they would seek both artistic and functional ware to fill their environment. Stoneware was more craft-oriented than traditional fine china, and its low price and rugged nature (it could be placed in the oven directly from the refrigerator) made it particularly well suited to take advantage of these trends. Americans were also building more second homes which would mean an increase in the need for inexpensive furnishings. In addition to these considerations, the more general economic developments such as the de-

[1] Stoneware was a form of pottery which was considerably cheaper than china. It was also considered to be less fragile.

valuation of the dollar, the increasing amounts of import taxes being placed on foreign goods, and the rapidly increasing wages in both Europe and Japan all contributed to the increasing competitiveness of American-made stoneware, which had suffered considerably at the hands of foreign imports in the late fifties and early sixties.

The Smithville lines were sold primarily by a nationwide system of manufacturers' representatives. The manufacturers' representatives varied widely in their method of operation. Some were one-person operations. Others were members of small organizations composed either of unrelated representatives or family members. These organizations generally comprised one or more principals and several subrepresentatives and/or detail men. The subreps and detail men differed from the reps in that they normally received half the manufacturer's commission on all the merchandise they sold, with the other half going to the rep organization that employed them. Detail men were sometimes compensated by salary. Subreps were usually given a territory within which they would sell and service accounts. Detail men would often only service[1] large, established accounts. A list of the reps, the territories they covered, and brief sketches of their principal characteristics are given in Exhibit 6. Smithville's reps accounted for approximately 87 percent of the branded-line sales. Exhibit 7 gives a breakdown of the sales and commissions of the reps. The remaining 13 percent of captive-line sales were accounted for by the following sources: Mr. James Fletcher, the company sales manager who also covered all the territory within a 50-mile radius of company headquarters, 2 percent; jobbers, 6 percent; and house accounts, 5 percent. The Appendix contains a review of the casewriter's travel with two salesmen.

Should it be decided to start a direct force, not all the reps would probably be replaced. The decision on whether to replace a man or organization depended upon such things as the size of his territory versus the present and potential sales from that territory, the nature of the outlets he was serving, and the geographic location of his territory. Ms. O'Brien had tentatively selected those reps whom she would replace and those whom she would keep based upon her personal knowledge of their volume, territories, and outlets. That list is reproduced in Table 1.

To calculate the monetary effects of the potential change in the sales force, the data in Table 2 were collected.

Ms. O'Brien's tentative plan called for hiring 20 field salesmen. Of these 20, she estimated that approximately 3 would come from the existing reps or their subreps, leaving 17 people to be recruited and trained. To allow for possible dropouts and for some rejection discretion, she assumed that she would initially hire and train four more people than would be ultimately needed. All the people hired would have to have at least 1 year of successful housewares-selling experience because Ms. O'Brien believed that to achieve the transition with a minimum disruption in sales volume, all territories must be switched simulta-

---

[1] In this context servicing means the maintenance of displays, taking of inventories, and other such tasks. It did not include the actual selling.

TABLE 1

Name	To be replaced		Replacements	
	No. of reps	No. of showroom personnel	Direct men	Showroom personnel
Austin	7	3	6	2
Blumberg	2	2	3	1.5
Pote	1	0	2	0
Shutzer	2	2	0	0
Kammer	1	0	1	1.5
Blinn	1	0	1	0
Whitwer	1	0	1	0
Norton	1	0	1	0
Martin	4	0	2	0
Riggs	7	2	3	2
	27	9	20	7

Reps to continue with company

Flinton: Alaska and Pacific Northwest
Miller: Rocky Mountain States
Fries: Hawaii

Orlinoff: Military exchanges
Gerard: Caribbean countries

neously. If the switch were to take place one territory at a time, over a period of 6 months to a year, or longer, she knew that the reps in those territories which had not yet been converted would be devoting their time to increasing the volume of their other lines, and looking for new lines, at the expense of Smithville. Therefore, the people who replaced the reps would have to be qualified to service existing accounts without much assistance from the home office initially.

Whereas it would be more expensive to hire experienced people, it was assumed that it would be less expensive to train them and the initial turnover rate would be much lower. It was estimated that 1 month of training would be sufficient to acquaint the people with the product line, familiarize them with the marketing program and the sales administrative system, and give them refresher training in selling technique. The three men who were to come from the existing rep force would not go through this program, since it was planned that they be recruited during the weeks immediately preceding the switch. They would

TABLE 2

Average cost to locate and train salesmen	$6,073
Average annual compensation of highest paid housewares salesmen	$20,550
Average annual expenses as percent of gross pay	42.7 percent
Average annual turnover	10 percent
Average training time	7 months
Average annual volume per salesman, hardware, tools, and housewares	$501,000

Source: Compensation of Salesmen, A Dartnell Management Guide.
The Dartnell Corporation, Chicago.

receive individual attention from the sales manager after they had joined Smithville.

Ms. O'Brien estimated the costs of recruiting and training the field salesmen as follows:

Recruiting and training	$1/7 \times \$6,000 \times 21 =$	$\$18,000$
Salary while training	$1/12 \times 15,000 \times 21 =$	$\underline{26,250}$
		$\$44,250$

In addition to recruiting and training the field salesmen, four of the showroom personnel would be recruited and trained at the same time. These four would then train the additional showroom personnel once they had begun working. These people would also have to have at least 1 years' selling experience in housewares. Their responsibilities would include supervising the operation of the showroom, servicing the key accounts in their area, and some actual field selling.

The costs of recruiting and training these people was estimated to be:

Recruiting and training	$1/7 \times \$6,000 \times 4 =$	$\$3,429$
Salary while training	$1/12 \times 15,000 \times 4 =$	$\underline{5,000}$
		$\$8,429$

This was developed as follows: The Dartnell data mentioned previously suggested that $6,000 was the cost of a 7-month recruiting and training period. Ms. O'Brien estimated that it would take her only 1 month to recruit and train a new salesman. There would be 21 people recruited and trained. The $15,000 salary during training was estimated.

On a continuing basis, the following additional overhead and per person costs were anticipated if a direct force were started:

Overhead (per annum)

1 field sales manager at 133% of estimated salesman compensation[1]	=	$\$ 27,000$
Recruiting and training 3 people per year to allow for turnover $(\$7,000 \times 3) =$		$21,000$
Salaries of recruits while training $(7/12 \times \$9,000 \times 3)$	=	$15,750$
Showroom expense:		
Rent and maintenance[2] $(4 \times \$7,000)^+$	=	$28,000$
Salaries for personnel (4 at $20,000; 3 at $7,500)	=	$\underline{102,500}$
		$\$194,250$

Salesmen (per person–per year)

Pay (base and incentive)	=	$\$20,000$
Expenses (42.7% of pay based on current experience)	=	$8,540$
Benefits	=	$\underline{2,000}$
		$\$30,540$

The analysis in Table 3 compared the costs of a rep force to the estimated costs of a company-owned sales force over the next 5 years.

---

[1] The assumption that the field sales manager's salary would be 133 percent of salesman compensation was an industry rule of thumb.

[2] The $7,000 estimate of showroom rent and maintenance came from company experience. It was presently maintaining a showroom in New York.

TABLE 3

	Projected, in thousands				
	1974	**1975**	**1976**	**1977**	**1978**
Branded-line sales (20% per annum growth)	$6,766	$8,215	$9,858	$11,830	$14,196
Reps:					
Sales by reps (87% of total)	5,886	7,147	8,576	10,292	12,351
Rep's commissions (assume 12%)*	706	858	1,029	1,235	1,482
Company-owned sales force:					
Retained reps (5% of sales at 12%)	35	43	51	62	74
Direct people:					
Number of people	20	20	22	22	24
Overhead	194	194	194	194	194
Salesmen pay	612	612	672	672	763
Total direct force costs	$ 841	$ 849	$ 917	$ 928	$ 1,031
Savings (cost) of direct versus reps	(135)	9	112	307	451
Start-up costs (recruiting and training) = $52,679					

* Twelve percent was the standard industry commission rate.

In addition to and perhaps more important than the economic side of the analysis, according to Ms. O'Brien, were many qualitative factors that had to be considered before making a switch. For example, she believed that by and large a company-owned sales force would make it easier for the retailers to buy Smithville products. The company salesmen would be spending less time with each account, and the time saved would allow them to get at least one and possibly more calls in per year per account. Retailers would appreciate this, since they would then be able to order (and inventory) smaller amounts of merchandise and yet not have to worry about missing sales because they were out of stock. During the time that he did spend with each account, the salesman would spend time maintaining the displays, educating the retail clerks, backing up national ads with better in-store merchandising, and educating the buyers. Negative attitudes caused by problems in delivery, back orders, cancellations, and quality could, she thought, be more credibly countered on the spot by a company person.

A company sales force, she expected, could be directed and managed so that Smithville could receive broader placement in department stores. Very few reps in her experience were good at or liked servicing the larger department stores. One of the reasons for this was that it took a long time for an order placed by the department store buyer to receive funding. A rep, she reasoned, couldn't be bothered to follow up with the store as necessary to ensure that funding was obtained. She also thought that a rep wanted orders that were sent to the factory immediately so that he could get his commission quickly. Furthermore, it was more expensive to visit the downtown areas where the department store buyers were usually located; a rep's expenses came right out of his pocket. Finally, the buyers in department stores expected a salesman to take stock, arrange displays, and educate retail clerks at the main store and all the branches. She believed that reps avoided these duties whenever possible.

Placement with department stores was important to Ms. O'Brien for several reasons in addition to the increased sales revenue to be obtained from a new account. The department stores typically ordered in larger quantities and were thus able to receive and use cooperative advertising allowances from Smithville. Ms. O'Brien thought that local advertising not only helped sell more at the department store but had a spillover effect on the outlying gift shops. Also, a consumer who might purchase a 45-piece set at a department store would be likely to purchase accessory pieces when visiting a local gift shop.

Ms. O'Brien hoped that in addition to broadening placement with department stores the company sales force would be able to gain additional placement in the smaller outlets as a result of additional cold calls made at the suggestion of the home office. She had found it extremely difficult to make some reps perform missionary selling work. Many reps appeared to believe that once a rep had established himself in an area, he could either write more business than he could handle or he could add another line more easily than he could open new accounts.

She hoped that company sales people would be able to obtain broader product coverage with the existing accounts. Since they would be selling fewer products than the reps, they could concentrate their selling efforts. This was particularly important to Smithville since much of the projected growth was to come from new lines and new products within existing lines.

One of the most important reasons for having a company sales force in Ms. O'Brien's mind was the fact that a direct force could provide the company with much more information about the marketplace than could the reps. Actions of competitors, new product ideas, and new styling and color trends would all flow back to the marketing office much more frequently, given a good communications system.

Ms. O'Brien believed that the advantages of a company sales force revolved around the greater control which was possible with a company sales force. With the reps, the company did have the option of replacing a rep if he was not performing adequately. However, this was a complicated process. For one thing, most of the individual reps with whom the company dealt were members of an organization of more than one rep. Therefore, if the company was displeased with the conduct of one of the reps, it had to take into consideration the relationship that person might have with the rest of his organization before recommending his removal. Even in the cases where Smithville was an organization's major source of income, this was a problem. And when a rep was removed, it was not an easy task to find a replacement who had the right product mix to enable him to continue serving his existing accounts as well as Smithville.

Perhaps the most concern in Ms. O'Brien's mind relative to the switch was the question of initiative in the company sales force. Would direct men in fact have the requisite initiative and resourcefulness to sell new accounts, educate the retail clerks and buyers, develop creative in-store displays, and work with the department stores? Furthermore, what would prevent the more creative sales people from becoming manufacturers' representatives themselves? This concern tended to force Ms. O'Brien to focus the issue on a question of size. Perhaps, she reasoned, a company sales force was appropriate only when a company was large enough to have either a strong consumer or retail franchise so that it could afford to turn its selling function over to its own sales people, who would then be required to do little more than detail work. She wasn't sure that the company salesmen could "sell" as well as the better reps.

She also wondered about the nature of the administrative system needed to properly utilize and control a direct sales force. For example, how fast could the recently hired marketing administrative manager develop the needed tools to process and present the added information the sales force could generate. He appeared to have a good working knowledge of electronic data processing, and Ms. O'Brien was confident that together with the electronic data processing department manager he could eventually develop the appropriate tools. However, both executives had a great many everyday responsibilities that would limit their ability to devote maximum effort to the development of a more complete sales information system.

Ms. O'Brien also wondered how many accounts would discontinue carrying Smithville because of their loyalty to the reps. While she did not feel that this would be a major factor, when coupled with the fact that a company sales person would mean one more salesman for the buyer to see, she estimated that a few marginal accounts would be lost.

Finally, Ms. O'Brien knew that she must factor expansion plans into her thinking. In addition to the 20 percent growth planned, the company was presently investigating the possibility of acquiring a small pewter operation for the production of a full line of pewter serving and decorative accessories. Furthermore, a small German pottery which Smithville owned had just recently begun exporting a limited line of earthenware, and while its volume was very small at present (estimated to be $300,000 in 1973), it would hopefully grow and perhaps more lines would be imported in the future. Finally, a new pottery was to be built in the near future which would greatly increase capacity. Ms. O'Brien wondered if it might not be wise to let the existing rep organization develop the sales to support this plant, and then make the switch.

EXHIBIT 1
STATEMENTS OF INCOME,
THOUSANDS OF DOLLARS
The Smithville Company

	1970	1971	1972	1973 (proj.)
Net sales	3,500	4,142	5,611	6,712
Cost of sales	2,484	2,868	3,866	4,365
Gross profit	1,016	1,274	1,745	2,347
Selling expenses	500	621	703	936
G&A expenses	195	213	232	262
Total expenses	695	834	935	1,198
Net profit (loss) before other income and expense	321	440	810	1,150
Other income (expense) net	(73)	(27)	(14)	(50)
Net profit before tax	248	413	796	1,100

Breadkown of selling expenses

Salaries		95	79	132
Commissions		353	403	490
Advertising and promotion		84	118	166
Travel and entertainment		6	4	12
Office expense		33	42	53
Shows (primarily china and glass show in Atlantic City)		12	14	22
Royalties (paid for the design of one of the lines)		38	43	54
Training and meetings				7
		621	703	936

Breakdown of net sales figure for 1972

Sales by representative	4,025
Sales by sales manager	99
Sales to jobbers	300
Other house accounts	222
Total captive line sales	4,646
Contract sales	965
Net sales	5,611

EXHIBIT 2
ORDER FORM: GREENWICH LINE
Smithville Company

WHOLESALE PRICE LIST

TERMS: 1% 15 DAYS, NET 30

F.O.B. FACTORY

Sold to: _____ Ship to: _____

_____ _____

Zip Code _____ Zip Code _____

Order No. _____ 14-23	Direct/Indirect _____ 36	Common Code _____
Order Date _____ 24-29	Ship Date _____ 37-42	53 54
Dept. _____ 30-34	Cancel Date 49-50 51-52 43-48	Ship Via _____ 55-68
Pricing Code _____ 35	Salesman #1 #2	New Cust. Code _____ 69

CREDIT INFORMATION: ☐ OLD ACCOUNT ☐ D&B RATING ☐ CREDIT REFERENCES ON REVERSE SIDE   H.F.C. ☐ YES ☐ NO   BUYER

GREENWICH STONEWARE

QTY.	ITEM NO.	DESCRIPTION	STD. PACK	PRICE	EXT. AMT.	CODE	QTY.	ITEM NO.	DESCRIPTION	STD. PACK	PRICE	EXT. AMT.	CODE
	1G	CUP, 9 OZ.	24	.60 EA.		001-01311		249G	OVAL ROASTER, 16"	3	3.50 EA.		249-01316
	2G	SAUCER	24	.50 EA.		002-01319		250G	OVAL ROASTER, 16" ON WARMER	1	5.50 EA.		250-01314
	3G	SALAD PLATE, 7"	24	.50 EA.		003-01317		265G	OVAL RAREBIT, 9½"	6	1.00 EA.		265-01312
	4G	DINNER PLATE, 10"	24	.85 EA.		004-01315		270G	OVAL RAREBIT, 11"	6	1.50 EA.		270-01317
	5G	LUNCHEON PLATE, 8½"	24	.60 EA.		005-01312		282G	MUG, 12 OZ.	24	.55 EA.		282-01317
	6G	BARBEQUE PLATE, 11"	6	1.25 EA.		006-01310		286G	MUG, 16 OZ.	12	.75 EA.		286-01318
	7G	STEAK PLATE	12	1.25 EA.		007-01318		288G	4 PC. MUG SET, 8 OZ.	6 SETS	2.00 SET		288-01314
	8G	FRUIT, 4½"	24	.40 EA.		008-01316		300G	4 PC. IND. CASSEROLE SET	6 SETS	3.00 SET		300-01317
	9G	4 PC. BOWL SET, 5½"	6 SETS	2.00 SET		009-01314		305G	CASSEROLE, 12 OZ.	12	1.00 EA.		305-01316
	10G	BOWL, 7"	12	.65 EA.		010-01312		310G	CASSEROLE, 1 QT.	6	2.00 EA.		310-01316
	11G	ROUND VEGETABLE, 9"	6	1.25 EA.		011-01310		315G	CASSEROLE, 2 QT.	1	2.50 EA.		315-01315
	12G	FLANGED SOUP BOWL	12	1.00 EA.		012-01318		316G	CASSEROLE, 2 QT. ON WARMER	1	3.50 EA.		316-01313
	14G	DIVIDED VEGETABLE	4	2.25 EA.		014-01314		325G	CASSEROLE, 3 QT.	1	3.50 EA.		325-01314
	16G	PLATTER, 14"	6	2.25 EA.		016-01319		326G	CASSEROLE, 3 QT. ON WARMER	1	4.50 EA.		326-01312
	17G	PLATTER, 16"	4	3.00 EA.		017-01314		330G	CASSEROLE, 4 QT.	1	5.00 EA.		330-01314
	20G	SUGAR & CREAMER SET	6 SETS	2.25 SET		020-01311		335G	CASSEROLE, 2QT. ROUND ON WARMER	1	3.00 EA.		335-01313
	25G	SALT & PEPPER SET	6 SETS	1.75 SET		025-01310		340G	TWN CASSEROLE SET, 2 QT. ON WARMER	1 SET	7.00 SET		340-01313
	28G	COVERED BUTTER DISH	6	1.75 EA.		028-01314		405G	INDIVIDUAL SOUFFLE/RAMEKIN	12	.50 EA.		405-01314
	34G	16 PC. SET-SERVICE FOR 4	1 SET	6.00 SET		034-01312		406G	SOUFFLE, 1 QT.	6	1.25 EA.		406-01312
	36G	45 PC. SET-SERVICE FOR 8	1 SET	17.50 SET		036-01317		408G	SOUFFLE, 2 QT.	6	1.75 EA.		408-01318
	39G	SERVER, 3 COMPARTMENT, 11"	1	2.50 EA.		039-01311		415G	PITCHER, 1½ QT.	6	1.50 EA.		415-01313
	40G	CHEESE & RELISH DISH, 15"	4	2.50 EA.		040-01319		416G	PITCHER, 2 QT.	4	2.00 EA.		416-01311
	43G	JAM & RELISH SERVER	1	2.50 EA.		043-01313		433G	GRAVY BOAT ON SAUCER	4	1.75 EA.		433-01316
	44G	DEVILED EGG DISH	1	2.50 EA.		044-01311		434G	GRAVY BOAT/BUTTER MELTER ON WARMER	6	1.75 EA.		434-01314
	46G	4 PC. CORN DISH SET	6 SETS	2.50 SET		046-01316		453G	3 PC. MIXING BOWL SET, 6", 8"; 10"	1 SET	2.50 SET		453-01314
	70G	BEAN POT, 2½ QT.	6	2.50 EA.		070-01316		495G	COFFEE CARAFE ON WARMER	1	3.50 EA.		495-01315
	80G	BEAN POT, 3½ QT.	6	3.00 EA.		080-01315		500G	4 PC. SUGAR & CREAMER SET	1 SET	3.00 SET		500-01312
	81G	BEAN POT, 3½ QT. ON WARMER	1	4.00 EA.		081-01313		511G	SPOON REST	6	1.00 EA.		511-01319
	120G	TIER TRAY	4	2.50 EA.		120-01319		520G	4 PC. CANISTER SET	1 SET	7.00 SET		520-01310
	130G	LAZY SUSAN, 14"	1	4.00 EA.		130-01318		540G	COOKIE JAR	1	2.50 EA.		540-01318
	140G	LAZY SUSAN WITH CASSEROLE, 16"	1	6.50 EA.		140-01317		550G	TEA POT, 6 CUP	4	2.50 EA.		550-01317
	150G	SOUP TUREEN, 2½ QT.	1	4.00 EA.		150-01310		551G	TEA POT, 6 CUP ON WARMER	1	3.50 EA.		551-01315
	170G	SOUP TUREEN, 5 QT.	1	5.00 EA.		170-01314		574G	CHAMBERSTICK	6	1.00 EA.		574-01317
	180G	CHIP AND DIP ON STAND	1	3.00 EA.		180-01313		578G	6 PC. CUSTARD CUP SET	6 SETS	1.50 SET		578-01318
	200G	SAMOVAR, 20 CUP	1	7.50 EA.		200-01319							
	220G	3 PC. SALAD SET	1 SET	3.00 SET		220-01317							
	221G	4 PC. SALAD SET ON STAND	1 SET	3.00 SET		221-01315							
	225G	7 PC. SALAD SET	1 SET	4.50 SET		225-01316							
	230G	SPAGHETTI DISH, 14"	4	2.50 EA.		230-01316							
	231G	SHIRRED EGG DISH, 6"	12	.75 EA.		231-01314							
	240G	OVAL BAKER, 7"	6	.75 EA.		240-01315							
	241G	OVAL BAKER, 9½"	6	1.00 EA.		241-01313							
	247G	OVAL ROASTER, 14"	3	2.75 EA.		247-01310							

YOU MUST ORDER IN STD. PACK QUANTITIES

FORM 1-1-72

TOTAL _____

400

EXHIBIT 3
GREENWICH LINE
Smithville Company

EXHIBIT 4
SALES OF THE GREENWICH LINE
The Smithville Company

Item number	Description	Unit sales	Dollar sales
	Primary items (dinnerware)		
1G	Cup, 9 oz	21,288	$11,883
2G	Saucer	13,145	6,025
3G	Salad plate, 7''	29,328	13,107
4G	Dinner plate, 10''	33,226	26,006
5G	Luncheon plate, 8½''	17,415	10,209
6G	Barbeque plate, 11''	3,552	4,296
7G	Steak plate	7,307	8,681
8G	Fruit, 4½''	30,557	11,937
9G	4 pc. bowl set, 5½''	13,359	24,974
10G	Bowl, 7''	17,796	11,377
11G	Round vegetable, 9''	11,042	13,154
12G	Flanged soup bowl	10,246	9,900
14G	Divided vegetable	7,324	16,182
16G	Platter, 14''	8,720	19,203
17G	Platter, 16''	4,366	12,506
20G	Sugar & creamer set	11,336	25,299
25G	Salt & pepper set	12,533	21,813
28G	Covered butter dish	9,741	16,938
34G	16 pc. set—service For 4	9,662	55,481
36G	45 pc. set—service For 8	6,661	114,669
39G	Server, 3 compartment, 11''	2,260	5,509
	Secondary items (related accessory)		
40G	Cheese & relish dish, 15''	2,316	5,610
43G	Jam & relish server	6,739	15,084
44G	Deviled egg dish	2,364	5,749
46G	4 pc. corn dish set	2,889	7,013
70G	Bean pot, 2½ qt	5,118	12,069
80G	Bean pot, 3½ qt	2,889	8,100
81G	Bean pot, 3½ qt on Warmer	1,453	5,620
120G	Tier tray	2,360	5,881
130G	Lazy susan, 14''	3,645	14,041
140G	Lazy susan With casserole, 16''	9,799	58,107
150G	Soup tureen, 2½ qt	4,210	16,348
170G	Soup tureen, 5 qt	4,941	24,143
180G	Chip and Dip on Stand	3,019	8,699
220G	3 pc. salad set	3,085	8,903
225G	7 pc. salad set	978	4,295
230G	Spaghetti dish, 14''	4,877	11,660
231G	Shirred egg dish, 6''	4,464	3,039
240G	Oval baker, 7''	7,470	5,680
241G	Oval baker, 9½''	10,040	10,054
247G	Oval roaster, 14''	3,949	10,298
249G	Oval roaster, 16''	3,782	11,982
250G	Oval roaster, 16'' on warmer	2,009	$10,702
265G	Oval rarebit, 9½''	8,778	8,970
270G	Oval rarebit, 11''	5,988	8,717
282G	Mug, 12 oz	33,702	18,235
286G	Mug, 16 oz	10,742	8,179

EXHIBIT 4
Continued

Item number	Description	Unit sales	Dollar sales
Secondary items (related accessory)			
288G	4 pc. mug set, 8 oz	18,409	35,439
300G	4 pc. ind. casserole set	5,136	15,004
305G	Casserole, 12 oz	14,477	14,716
310G	Casserole, 1 qt	5,408	10,441
315G	Casserole, 2 qt	7,665	18,431
316G	Casserole, 2 qt on warmer	4,703	16,113
325G	Casserole, 3 qt	3,822	12,592
326G	Casserole, 3 qt on warmer	2,198	9,789
330G	Casserole, 4 qt	2,081	9,883
335G	Casserole, 2 qt round on warmer	7,824	22,454
340G	Twin casserole set, 2 qt on warmer	5,805	37,094
405G	Individual souffle/ramekin	4,617	2,264
406G	Souffle, 1 qt	4,717	5,769
408G	Souffle, 2 qt	7,135	12,296
415G	Pitcher, 1½ qt	3,101	4,601
416G	Pitcher, 2 qt	3,974	7,907
433G	Gravy boat on saucer	7,441	12,564
434G	Gravy boat/butter melter on warmer	4,497	7,586
453G	3 pc. mixing bowl set, 6″, 8″, 10″	6,268	15,045
495G	Coffee carafe on warmer	4,323	14,505
500G	4 pc. sugar & creamer set	1,356	3,978
511G	Spoon rest	11,449	11,102
520G	4 pc. canister set	3,158	21,205
540G	Cookie jar	4,299	10,517
550G	Tea pot, 6 cup	5,344	12,778
551G	Tea pot, 6 cup on warmer	2,875	9,812
574G	Chamberstick	4,176	6,035
578G	6 pc. custard cup set	15,391	20,346

4 nbo 46,000

12,000

$387. Avg. Sales.

EXHIBIT 5
STONEWARE MARKETING SURVEY
The Smithville Company

	Saratoga		Greenwich		Columbia		Total	
	Amt.	%	Amt.	%	Amt.	%	Amt.	%
Received as a gift	601	56	340	65	244	56	1185	58
Purchased for own use	471	44	182	35	190	44	843	42
Where purchased:								
Dept. store	377	39	239	54	162	43	778	43
Gift shop	370	38	82	18	119	31	571	32
Stamp plan	4	1	8	2	0	0	12	1
Other	217	22	116	26	98	26	431	24
Newly wed:								
Yes	237	21	76	17	51	12	364	18
No	868	79	360	83	382	88	1610	82
First Smithville:								
Yes	741	76	352	69	339	83	1432	76
No	235	24	160	31	67	17	462	24
Cause to purchase:								
Magazine ad	71	8	23	8	29	11	123	9
Newspaper ad	11	1	4	1	3	1	18	1
TV	0	0	0	0	1	0	1	0
Sales clerk	21	2	2	1	17	6	40	3
Store display	749	88	260	90	214	81	1223	87
Live in:								
City	397	37	174	34	155	38	726	36
Suburbia	672	63	338	66	257	62	1267	64
Income:								
Under $8,000	281	27	111	22	78	15	470	23
$8,000–$12,000	336	33	200	39	143	28	679	33
Over $12,000	411	40	199	39	287	56	897	44
Age:								
18–25	397	36	128	26	99	23	624	31
26–35	298	27	166	34	115	26	579	29
36 and over	403	37	191	39	220	51	814	40

EXHIBIT 6
SMITHVILLE'S MANUFACTURERS' REPRESENTATIVES[1]
The Smithville Company

AUSTIN COMPANY TERRITORY: Conn., N.J., Del., N.Y., D.C., R.I., N.H., Vt., Mass., Maine, Md., Pa.

Jim Henderson. Manager of Austin Company.

Jim is a shrewd manipulator. He comes across as a crass blowhard, but there is a lot behind the huff 'n puff exterior. Henderson now has the power as well as the know-how to get the Austin reps up out of the trenches.

Louise Boyer. Rep for Austin. Territory: D.C., Md., Del., Pa.

Louise does a good job with the major department stores and larger independents. Doesn't want to be bothered with small accounts. Louise is one of the people who feels that she and the other Austin reps shouldn't go out opening up a flock of new accounts because her various manufacturers can't produce enough to keep their existing accounts well stocked.

Bob Spoerri. Rep for Austin. Territory: Conn., N.J., N.Y.

Bob is a more quiet type. He is well-liked and respected by his customers. He is thorough and works to a plan. Bob projects a very professional image.

Doug Burns. Rep for Austin. Territory: N.H., Vt., R.I., Maine.

One of the newer Austin reps, he's been with them for 2 or 3 years. Prior to that he had worked for NCR. Doug is a young and aggressive rep and does a fine job opening up new accounts. He is too customer oriented. [See the Appendix for a description of 2 days with Doug Burns.]

Joe Schotz. Rep for Austin. Territory: N.Y., Pa.

Another newcomer to the Austin ranks, Joe is an ex-machinery salesman and a personal friend of Jim Henderson. Joe is a professional BS artist and a detail nut. He is very thorough and believes in working to a plan. Unfortunately, sometimes his plans aren't too well laid.

Sandy Boothby. Rep for Austin. Territory: Mass.

This will probably be his last year as a rep. He'll be handling only the state of Massachusetts for '73. Sandy is an old timer who is not willing to put up with the frustrations involved in dealing with major department stores. He is not willing to get involved in detail work. [See the Appendix for a description of a day with Sandy Boothby.]

Bernard Metnik. Rep for Austin. Territory: N.Y.

Buddy does a reasonably good job with the Mom & Pop type stores, but has done a deplorable job with Manhattan department stores. Buddy simply isn't of high enough caliber to sell to major accounts. He's the kind of salesman buyers love; a pushover.

[1] Opinions from James Fletcher, sales manager.

405

EXHIBIT 6
Continued

GARY BLINN. Independent. Territory: N.C., S.C., Va.

Gary is an old timer. His arrival is a big event for his customers. He is very well-liked, understands the importance of cooperative advertising, and has pretty good control of his territory. Blinn has substantial outside income and doesn't have to work. The thought that he may actually be working on a semi-retired basis has crossed my mind. I feel we could get more out of him.

BLUMBERG & ASSOCIATES, INC. Territory: Ala., Fla., Ga., Tenn.

Mitch Blumberg. Manager of Blumberg & Associates, Inc.

Mitch is the son of an old timer in the gift field. He's a reasonably good rep, but a poor manager. He has little if any control over his sub-reps. He carries too many lines. He carries lots of lines to guard against losing Normandy which is his biggest source of income. He is the only rep that Normandy now uses.

HAROLD POTE. Independent. Territory: Ind., Ky., Ohio, W. Va.

A genuine smile and shoe shine type. Hal SELLS, but is terrible on detail work. Despite his allergy to paper work he is a sales manager's joy. Aim him at a target and most of the time he'll hit it.

WILLIAM SHUTZER ASSOCIATES, INC. Territory: Mich.

William Shutzer. Manager of William Shutzer Associates, Inc.

Another smile and shoe shine type. Bill has good lines, owns a portion of the major exhibit building in Detroit, and knows everybody in the industry. He also runs a small but very profitable import operation. Bill is a stickler for detail.

GERRY KAMMER. Independent. Territory: Ill., Wis., Ind.

Gerry believes in loving his customers to death. Any one of his customers' problems must be taken care of at once or he'll have a nervous breakdown. He is thorough to a fault and does a fine job selling to all classes of customers. Kammer worries too much. I'm sure he goes to bed every night worrying he's going to lose one of his lines.

LONNIE MARTIN AND ASSOCIATES. Territory: Iowa, Minn., S. Dak., N. Dak., Neb., Wis.

Lonnie Martin. Manager of Lonnie Martin and Associates. Territory: Minn.

Lonnie is a pain. He expects lots of cooperation from the home office but isn't willing to reciprocate. It's a constant prod, prod, nudge, nudge, with him. He is a nitpicker and loses sight of major objectives. He requires constant super-vision. Though he's done a reasonably good job in his territory, I feel that there is much room for improvement.

406

RIGGS & FIELDS. Territory: Miss., Kans., Okla., Ark., Mo., La., Tex.

EXHIBIT 6
Continued

Mike Riggs. Manager of Riggs & Fields.

I'm very impressed with Riggs. I feel that he is probably one of the most professional reps we have. His major difficulty has been attracting and holding on to good sub-reps. Mike is hungry, aggressive, and doesn't let too many things stand in his way.

THE MILLERS. Territory: Ariz., Colo., N. Dak., S. Dak., Mont., Utah, N. Mex., Wyo.

Ed Miller. Manager. Territory: Mont., Neb., Wyo., N. Dak., S. Dak.

Miller and his sub-rep, Don Tiner, are coming through with substantial increases in their sparsely populated territory. Miller has a tendency to be just a little bit on the nitpicky side. He is the son of an old time gift and glassware rep. He comes across as being a bit introverted.

V. A. DEMERY. Independent. Territory: Ariz., N. Mex., Utah, Mont., Colo., Idaho, Wyo.

JACK FRIES. Independent. Territory: Hawaii.

JENNIFER FLINTON. Independent. Territory: Alaska, Ore., Idaho, Wash.

Jennifer is full of ideas, which she presents in a very logical and convincing manner. The problem is that the ideas when implemented turn into nightmares because she didn't know what she was talking about. She is a very strong willed, good basic salesperson. Jennifer would do a better job if she simply worked harder and concentrated on selling rather than getting into areas that aren't her bag.

GLENN WHITWER. Independent. Territory: S. Calif., Nev.

Glenn is now producing several times his predecessor's volume. He requires a lot of reassurance and coddling. However, the extra effort that he requires is worthwhile since he usually achieves his objectives. Glenn is a nervous, sensitive guy who isn't allergic to pounding the pavement.

HUGHES NORTON. Independent. Territory: N. Calif.

Norton does a reasonably good job with major department stores in Northern California; he does a poor job with independent gift shops. He has fallen into a rut and wants to keep calling on the same familiar faces. He is probably our poorest rep when it comes to pioneering. He is lazy and lethargic.

CARL, INC. Territory: Military exchanges.

Dave Orlinoff. Rep for Carl, Inc.

Orlinoff heads up Carl, Inc. They handle our military representation. Orlinoff has some good high volume electronics lines and handles our line as a side line. Constant pressure is required to keep him on the ball. He is thorough and perceptive. If we can provide the motivation we can get a lot better results.

407

EXHIBIT 7
SALES AND COMMISSION DATA FOR MANUFACTURERS' REPRESENTATIVES
The Smithville Company

Name	No. of sales-people	Sales, $ thousands			Commissions, $ thousands			Smith-ville CPM,† $ thousands	Total CPM, $ thousands	% of comm. by Smith-ville‡
		Smith ville	Other*	Total	Smith ville	Other	Total			
Austin Co.	10	$1,746	$1,229	$2,975	$174	$195	$369	$17.4	$36.9	47
Gary Blinn	1	170	152	322	16	15	31	16.0	31.0	52
Blumberg Assoc.	4	225	NA	NA	17	NA	NA	4.2	NA	NA
Pote	1	360	218	578	37	29	66	37.0	66.0	56
Shutzer	3	204	1,300	1,504	19	196	215	6.3	72.0	9
Gerry Kammer	1	315	153	468	25	16	41	25.0	41.0	61
Martin Assoc.	4	278	430	708	27	63	100	6.7	25.0	27
Riggs & Fields	9	240	NA	NA	23	NA	NA	2.6	NA	NA
The Millers	4	122	250	372	16	33	49	4.0	12.2	33
Jack Fries	1	2	NA	NA	0.4	NA	NA	0.4	NA	NA
Jennifer Flinton	2	60	709	769	8	63	71	4.0	35.5	11
Glen Whitwer	1	86	212	298	11	26	37	11.0	37.0	30
Hughes Norton	1	114	318	432	12	40	52	12.0	52.0	23
Dave Ortinoff	8	93	3,000	3,093	11	287	398	1.4	50.0	3
Gerard and Son	NA	10	NA	NA	2	NA	NA	NA	NA	NA

* Estimates of a reps sales and commissions in other lines was made from information furnished by the reps, and hence is highly suspicious.
† CPM is commission per man and is arrived at by dividing the commissions by the number of men listed in the second column.
‡ This figure is the percentage of a rep's total income that comes from Smithville.

The casewriter accompanied two salesmen, Sandy Boothby and Doug Burns. The following is a brief diary of their activities. The trips were made in April 1973.

A DAY WITH SANDY BOOTHBY

GENERAL

Sandy Boothby was one of the original members of the Austin Company, Smithville's largest and most important representative organization. He was 64 years old, had 2 years of college, had been an insurance and pickle salesman before becoming a giftware manufacturer's representative, chain-smoked, drove a Cadillac, and had 11 grandchildren. Sandy's son was also a giftware rep.

Half the commission paid by the manufacturers of the lines he sold for the Austin Company was paid directly to him, the other half was paid to the Austin Company.

First call: Arbor Gift Shop (10:15 A.M.–12:30 P.M.) The store was a family-owned and operated gift store located in a mall south of Providence, Rhode Island. It was an account which Sandy opened 6 years ago when he was still covering Rhode Island and which he had kept even though he now only covered Massachusetts.

The store carried a large variety of gifts ranging from plastic flowers to lead crystal. The most important lines in the store were lamps (115 styles ranging in price from $30 to $115), casual wood furniture, wooden accessories, pottery (stoneware dinnerware), glassware, metalware (wrought iron, brass, copper, pewter and aluminum), clocks, and framed pictures. The store owner estimated his inventory at $50,000 and, together with a second store he had some 30 miles away, he got approximately nine turns per year. The store this meeting took place in had 1,900 square feet. The second store had 1,100 square feet. As the buying-selling session began, the owner pulled up a stool for Sandy, remarking that he was the only salesman that gets to sit down while working in this shop.

After first asking what Sandy had on special (promotion), the owner and Sandy began to systematically thumb through the catalogs of the lines Sandy carried, selecting the items to be ordered. In determining what to order, the store owner referred to the very limited stock he had in the room and to an order form on which he kept a record of the inventory he had in a nearby warehouse, scurrying back and forth from the shop floor. At the end of this 2-hour session, Sandy casually mentioned the new product line Smithville had introduced. Sandy did no merchandising of the store displays. The total order taken was $3,100.

Second call: Peach Tree (2:00–2:15). No sale. Owner did not want to reorder before paying his outstanding bills with Sandy's companies. Sandy left a promotion flyer with the owner.

Third call: Revolutionary Shop (3:00–3:45). This store was owned by a man and his wife and was a separate standing operation (in back of their house) in the middle of nowhere. The woman ran the gift shop while her husband operated the small lamp-assembly shop upstairs. The lines carried were essentially the same as those in the first store. Again, the owner offered Sandy a small stool and took physical inventory as he ordered.

When asked if she had a fixed dollar amount she would order from a given salesman, she replied no, that she ordered whatever she needed. However, even though she had recently sold out of one of Sandy's lines, she did not reorder it. Her order amounted to $475.

Fourth and final call: The Carriage (4:00–4:15). This shop was not more than 3 miles from the previous shop. It was by far the most professionally merchandized store. The store had approximately 4,000 square feet and carried essentially the same lines as the preceding store, with a very large selection of casual furniture and earthenware.

As Sandy walked in, the manager, who was very busy, told Sandy to write up a well-rounded $250 order of Sandy's metalware line.

As we departed, the owner remarked about how well his club plans[1] had been doing, accounting for as much as 50 percent of his sales in recent days. Sandy remarked that approximately 25 percent of his customers had club plans.

MISCELLANEOUS NOTES

Sandy serviced about 300 accounts, calling on each account once every 40 days or so.

He stated that it took him from 6 months to a year to gain the confidence of a new account.

He planned his day so that he was virtually assured of placing at least one major order for his two largest lines.

He would always order his best lines first, leaving little time for pushing new products. By the time he would get to the new products, the buyer was tired of talking, taking inventory, and spending money.

The buyers estimated that they saw an average of two salesmen a day, every day.

---

[1] Club plans are arrangements whereby a group of women make periodic visits to the gift shop and purchase gifts over time by depositing the money with the gift shop until the selected item is payed for. The organizer of the plan periodically receives free gifts as do the club members upon making X amount of purchases.

TWO DAYS WITH DOUG BURNS

GENERAL

Doug was a man in his early thirties with 3 years of gift-selling experience, all with the Austin Company. He had worked for a small computer software company before joining Austin. Doug lived in Concord, New Hampshire, centrally located to service Maine, New Hampshire, Vermont, and Rhode Island, his assigned territory. Since joining the Austin Company, he had more than doubled the volume they did in his territory.

FIRST DAY. The territory covered on this trip was Rhode Island, primarily around the city of Providence. This territory was given to Doug on January 1, 1973. Prior to January, the territory was nominally assigned to Sandy Boothby. However, Boothby had done very little selling in Rhode Island for the past 5 years, and many of the accounts called on had not seen a salesman in at least 5 years.

Woodlawn Drug and Gift (10:00–10:20). This combination drugstore and gift shop was owned by a pharmacist and his wife. The wife did the giftware buying and merchandising. She had recently ordered one of Doug's lines for the first time at a trade show, and Doug was interested primarily in seeing that it was properly displayed.

The wife was not in and the line was not displayed. Doug spent some time talking with the husband. However, he would not let Doug arrange a display of the line since his wife was not there.

Arlington Country Store (10:45–11:45). This was a retail outlet associated with a manufacturer of decorated linens. It carried a full line of gifts and casual furniture, and it served as a seconds outlets for the linen company. The store was a free-standing operation in the middle of the country with no other commercial buildings within at least 1 mile. It had approximately 6,000 square feet of usable floor space and was very professionally merchandised.

The buyer for this store had never seen a Smithville salesman or anyone connected with the company and yet carried every product made by the company. She stated that Smithville products were one of her five largest volume lines.

Doug spent most of his time listening to her complaints about breakage and suggested methods for her to expedite claim settlements with the trucking companies.

Cassis's Hardware (12:15–12:45). As the name implied, this store was primarily a hardware store. When Doug arrived, the owner-buyer was making out a Smithville order and writing a letter to the company concerning an inaccurate dunning notice he had received. Doug promised to settle the dunning mix-up. He also attempted to get the buyer to let him write up the order that the buyer had been working on when we arrived but was not successful. (Doug received credit for all sales in his territory, whether or not he wrote the order.)

Belmont Jewelry and Gifts (1:00–1:30). This store carried a very small assortment of cheap jewelry and gifts. They did very well with Doug's metalware line. They had not seen a salesman for this line in approximately 9 years. They ordered approximately $500 of the metalware line.

When asked (after departing the store) how he ensured that an account was credit worthy, Doug stated that since they were being shipped the line, they were OK.

Oak Lane Gift Shop (2:30–2:35). The buyer was out, and the clerk who was minding the store knew very little.

Kewish's Gifts, Furniture, and Housewares (2:50–3:00). The buyer was out, and the store attendant was unwilling to discuss Doug's lines with him.

Jacque's Gifts and Interiors (3:15–3:45). The owner was in, but not in a buying mood. He spent considerable time complaining about the damage done to the Smithville products in transit and talking about how slow things were.

Morse's Jewelry Store (4:00–4:10). This jewelry store, located in a new shopping center, did not carry any of Doug's lines. It carried several china patterns and several ironstone patterns of dinnerware in addition to moderately priced jewelry. Doug spoke to the store manager, suggesting that the Smithville line of casual dinnerware would serve to round out the store's selection of dinnerware. While the store manager did not buy, stating that this was a recently opened store and hence was proving to be a cash drain on the original store (located downtown in a nearby village), he did take a catalog, customer brochures, and several promotion fliers from Doug. The store manager was concerned about where the nearest outlet offering Smithville was located. Doug told him, adding that as he drove by that particular outlet today he saw a "for sale" sign posted on it. (It was this "for sale" sign and the knowledge that the account had traditionally been a small-volume account that led Doug to make this cold call in the first place.)

SECOND DAY. The territory covered on this trip was southern New Hampshire. This territory had been Doug's territory since he joined the Austin Company. The nature of these calls was completely different from those made in Rhode Island a month earlier. All the buyers knew Doug very well.

Free Spirits (10:40–11:00). Free Spirits was a free-standing furniture and gift store with furniture becoming more and more the primary business. The owner's brother was a furniture sales representative. The owner and his wife both did the buying.

The owner's wife stated that she had just sent in an order for some of Doug's products and was not interested in buying any more at this time.

Archer's Department Store (11:15–12:15). This store was one of many stores making up Baltimore, Inc., a chain of department stores in the Northeast. Each store did its own buying. All orders were approved at headquarters located in Boston. Doug had been working for sometime on getting the headquarters to allow him to write orders for each store as Doug deemed necessary within an assigned budget. To get them to approve this method of buying, Doug kept his own inventory report on his items carried by the store. He then attempted to show the individual store buyers and the approving authrorities that his items turned over rapidly. He reasoned that their buyers could not keep as close a watch on his products as he could and would often order less than the optimal product mix and insufficient quantities of the faster-selling items. He also noted that during the particularly busy season before Christmas, when the buyers and other seasoned store personnel were busy with part-time, inexperienced help and with in-store selling, he could order on his own without taking up their time. Doug reminded them that he would do all their inventorying, would maintain their in-store displays, and would educate the retail clerks when he came in.

On this particular stop, recent store actions played directly into his hands. A newly assigned buyer had not ordered sufficient quantities of two of Doug's lines in February because of a tight budget and poor planning, and hence was completely out of stock of many of the items. This buyer had recently made out an order on his own to fill in the gaps he was now suffering, but because the items needed were so many, the buyer again had bought short for fear of spending too much money. After taking inventory (at which time Doug discovered that several of the items the buyer had thought he was out of were in the storeroom), Doug was able to convince the buyer to let him make out a more complete order.

Following lunch, Doug returned to the store to talk to the assistant manager about this situation. The recounting of the above-described chain of events to the assistant manager fell on fertile soil, and he urged Doug to get approval from the central office as quickly as possible and assured Doug that he would also contact headquarters on Doug's behalf.

Olde Tavern Gift Shop (1:30–1:40). This shop was a free-standing building in a small village that housed three shops: a toy shop, a gift and candle shop, and a dress shop.

Doug was very well known by all personnel at this establishment, but since the buyer (who had just returned from Europe the night before) was out, no business was done.

Monroe Trading Post (2:00–2:20). This store did not carry any of Doug's lines. However, its owner was the sister of a representative who was a good friend of Doug's and who had suggested to Doug that he try to get his lines into the store. Doug had become increasingly concerned over the deterioration he had been witnessing in the management of a store nearby that presently carried his lines. Doug, therefore, hoped to get this store to carry his lines.

The store owner, Mrs. Monroe, liked the Smithville products very much, and considerable time was spent talking about how well they had served several of her relatives. However, she felt that her store was presently too crowded to be able to allow her to carry Smithville and do it justice. She said she was planning to build an addition and would like to carry Smithville when the addition was finished.

Bonnie's (2:30–2:50). This was another free-standing, man and wife gift shop at which Doug stopped mostly because he happened to be in the area. The owner happened to be collecting items for a Rotary auction and so Doug reluctantly donated a sample he had in the car. No order was taken, but arrangements for a buying session for the middle of June were consummated.

Harris' Department Store (3:00–3:10). The owners of this store had declared bankruptcy on May 1 and were not interested in talking with Doug.

Concord Gift and Candle (4:00–4:30). This store was adjoining an animal hospital where the owner's husband practiced. The owner had approximately two to three times as much inventory as she needed in all items. Doug had recently sold her a starter assortment of one of his lines she had not previously carried and was interested in finding out how well the line was moving. The order had just arrived that day and stood crated on the receiving dock. After helping the owner find space to store some other recently received merchandise, Doug attempted to assist the owner in selecting an appropriate display location for the new line. This attempt was only moderately successful as the conversation kept drifting to a discussion of the store's cash and tax problems.

MISCELLANEOUS NOTES

One of the more subtle problems Doug found he had in dealing with his customers was ensuring that they kept an adequate supply of merchandise on hand at all times. Without statistical tabulations to keep precise track of a line's performance, the buyer would often not buy the amount needed to support the display necessary to properly merchandise the line. The buyer was more likely to buy based on his or her subjective experiences at the time he or she decided to buy, experiences which were often not related to the line's performance. Occasionally, when this behavior caused the whole line to go unordered for an order cycle, the buyer would find himself completely out of a line and yet unwilling to make the larger-than-normal expenditure to "buy back into the line."

Hence, once Doug had achieved placement of a line, he saw his primary responsibility as being to ensure that the line never became so depleted that it became necessary to get the buyer to "buy back into the line."

CHANNEL POLICY

A channel of distribution is the means through which a product or service is transmitted from the location where it is produced to the point where it is purchased for ultimate use or consumption. In some cases, manufacturers will find it advantageous to perform the distribution function themselves (direct distribution), *while in other cases they will prefer to delegate the distribution function to one or more levels of independent intermediaries* (indirect distribution). *In either case, the distribution channels used by the manufacturer will generally be expected to perform functions beyond that of physical distribution. A retailer or industrial distributor, for example, in addition to distributing a manufacturer's products to its customers, may also be expected to provide information* (through display, local advertising, or personal selling), *credit, repair service, etc.*

In formulating a channel policy, a manufacturer must determine what pattern of ultimate distribution is appropriate for its products and target customers, what functions this ultimate level of distribution should perform, how to motivate this ultimate level of distribution to perform these functions, and what system of intermediate distribution most effectively and efficiently meets the needs of the final level of distribution.

ULTIMATE DISTRIBUTION POINTS

As a general rule, manufacturers prefer to distribute through as few ultimate distribution points as feasible, given the needs and shopping behavior of their target customers. This preference is based on the premise that a small number of retailers or industrial distributors is (1) *relatively inexpensive to service,* (2) *likely to be loyal to the manufacturer,* (3) *able to afford sizable inventory and advertising levels, and* (4) *unlikely to engage in competitive practices which could damage the image or profitability of the manufacturer's products.*

In actual practice, customer needs and shopping behavior tend to force manufacturers to use more ultimate distribution points than they would like. A large category of products, known as convenience goods, *are characterized by low price, frequent purchase, near-commodity status, and a relatively low level of importance to most consumers. In purchasing such products, few consumers are willing to go very far out of their way to obtain a preferred brand if it is not available at a convenient retail outlet or at their "regular" industrial distributor. In such cases, manufacturers generally find it advantageous to market their products through as many ultimate distribution points as possible* (intensive distribution). *Generally, the "convenience outlets"* (e.g., supermarkets, drugstores, industrial mill supply houses) *which carry such products sell a number of competing brands in a particular product category and are unlikely to provide a single brand with strong, consistent preferential support.*

A second category of products, known as shopping goods, *are typically high-priced, infrequently purchased, and of considerable importance to the consumer. In seeking to buy such products, most consumers tend to "shop around," looking for just the right style or specifications, considerable product or application information, and/or the lowest price. Unlike convenience goods, which are typically sold largely on the basis of retail displays or industrial supply houses' catalogs, the sale of shopping goods often depends on intensive personal selling, very large retail or distributor inventories, and a considerable amount of preferential support by the ultimate distribution point. In marketing such products, manufacturers generally prefer to focus on a carefully selected set of outlets in a given market area* (selective distribution). *Given customer shopping behavior for such products, a selective distribution pattern is based on the premise that the manufacturer's target customers, in shopping around, will eventually visit—or receive a sales call from—the selected outlets through which the manufacturer distributes its products. In effect, such manufacturers seek to obtain a large share of the business of a few, effective outlets rather than a small share of the business of many outlets.*

A final category of products, known as specialty goods, *is characterized by infrequent purchase, considerable importance to the consumer, and an exceptionally high level of brand preference. Customers for such products generally know what they want prior to purchase and are willing to go to considerable trouble to obtain it. Manufacturers of specialty goods are thus often able to market through only a single, relatively inconvenient outlet in a given market area* (exclusive distribution).

As might be expected, many products do not fall neatly into one or another of these categories. An exotic sports car, for example, may be a specialty good for some consumers (who will go to the factory in Europe if necessary to buy it) and a shopping good for other consumers. Depending on the consumer, and that consumer's intended applications for the product, home furnishings or wearing apparel can have the characteristics of specialty goods, shopping goods, or convenience goods. Even the razor blade, a convenience good by all criteria, took on the aspects of a specialty good for some consumers when Wilkinson Sword introduced stainless steel blades through a very small number of retail hardware stores.

DIRECT VERSUS INDIRECT DISTRIBUTION

In an ideal world (from their point of view), most manufacturers would prefer to market directly to their customers, through company-owned ultimate distribution points, rather than through independent intermediaries. In theory, at least, the direct-marketing manufacturer would have more control over the entire marketing process than would a manufacturer which marketed through independent intermediaries. In addition, the direct-marketing manufacturer would, at least in theory, be able to obtain the profit margin otherwise earned by independent retailers and distributors.

As might be expected, company-owned ultimate distribution points are rarely feasible for convenience goods, since products of this type generally require very extensive distribution. To provide the convenience required by customers, such distribution points generally have to carry an assortment of merchandise which is wide enough to obtain adequate sales volume from a relatively small customer base. Few convenience goods have enough per capita consumption to justify "convenient" specialized distribution, and few manufacturers find it worthwhile to invest in distribution systems in which their own products play only a small part.

Manufacturers of shopping goods, conversely, might find it advantageous to integrate forward since preferential support at the ultimate distribution point is often critical to success in such product categories. In practice, however, very few manufacturers of shopping goods own and operate their own ultimate distribution points. The major reasons why they have not integrated forward to this level are (1) consumers are believed to desire greater variety at the point of sale than the manufacturer could provide; (2) the investment required for even a selective distribution system would be very high; (3) manufacturers often feel that they lack the skills necessary to manage the ultimate distribution function; (4) independent merchants and distributors are often able to engage in marketing practices at the local level (e.g., price cutting) which would be dysfunctional if carried out by the manufacturer; (5) some consumers may prefer to buy from locally owned independent businesses which they consider more "responsive"; and (6) the United States courts have not looked favorably upon the acquisition of independent distribution outlets by manufacturers if the objective or effect is to increase preferential support for the acquiring manufacturer's products at the expense of competitive brands.

Forward integration by manufacturers of specialty goods is, however, quite common. Since such products are marketed through relatively few outlets, generally on an exclusive basis, the amount of investment required is relatively low. In such cases, the exclusive distributor of a manufacturer's products is likely to be considered a branch of the manufacturer whether or not it is company-owned. As a general rule, manufacturers of such products do integrate foward, unless limited financial or managerial resources make it impractical for them to do so.

WHOLESALE DISTRIBUTION

In almost all cases, the ultimate level of distribution takes place at a great many more geographic locations than does the manufacturing process for a particular product. As a result, having decided upon the pattern of ultimate distribution, the manufacturer must then decide how to distribute the merchandise to its ultimate distribution points.

The needs of these ultimate distribution points determine what functions must be performed by the manufacturer's first level of distribution. If retailers require rapid delivery, for example, the manufacturer's distribution system will either have to make use of remote warehouses or of relatively high-cost transportation methods (e.g., air freight). If a manufacturer's ultimate distribution points wish to be supplied by a single source supplier, the manufacturer will either have to distribute through full-line independent wholesalers, or, in effect, undertake to operate such a wholesaler itself. If personal selling to the ultimate distribution points is a major influence on their behavior, the manufacturer may have to perform some or all of the selling function (missionary selling), even though relying on independent wholesalers for physical distribution.

There are two major types of independent wholesalers: exclusive and non-exclusive. An exclusive wholesaler carries only one manufacturer's product in a given product category, while a nonexclusive wholesaler carries competing brands. Generally, a nonexclusive wholesaler is only appropriate for products for which intensive distribution is sought, since such a wholesaler could not be expected to maintain a pattern of selective or exclusive ultimate distribution for one brand in a category, and alternative patterns of ultimate distribution for other brands in that category. Manufacturers with selective or exclusive ultimate distribution patterns thus generally use either exclusive independent wholesalers or their own direct distribution systems.

As is true for ultimate distribution levels, most manufacturers would prefer company-owned and operated intermediate levels of distribution to the use of independent wholesalers. In making the decision between direct and indirect intermediate distribution, the manufacturer must determine (1) whether direct or indirect distribution would best satisfy the needs of the ultimate distribution points and (2) whether the increased unit contribution and (possibly) increased volume obtainable through direct distribution would outweigh the costs of setting up and operating an independent distribution network. In making this calculation, it is, of course, necessary to take into account the rather considerable investment in working capital (inventories, accounts receivable) that is characteristic of most intermediate levels of distribution.

SUMMARY

In formulating a channel policy, manufacturers are sometimes faced with a choice between direct and indirect distribution strategies. While the latter strategy inevitably involves loss of control by the manufacturer over the final point of sale, economic considerations are often compelling. The nature of the product, as well as customer needs and shopping behavior, are important inputs to this decision. Few manufacturers can afford to provide both the extensive distribution and wide assortment of merchandise typically demanded by buyers of convenience goods. Ability to provide specialized services to the customer may be another determinant.

In many instances a similar decision has to be made concerning choice of wholesale distribution points between the manufacturing location and the ultimate distribution point. Again, the needs of the ultimate distributor and the economic trade-offs involved are major inputs to the decision.

ROCKWELL INTERNATIONAL: MICROELECTRONIC PRODUCT DIVISION

NANCY J. DAVIS
Research Associate
Harvard Graduate School of Business Administration

STEVEN H. STAR
Associate Professor
Harvard Graduate School of Business Administration

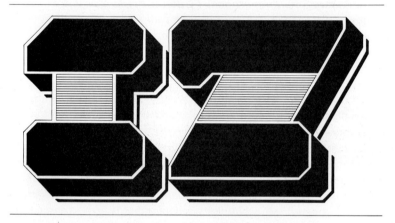

In February 1975, top executives of the Microelectronic Product Division of Rockwell International were reviewing Rockwell's recent entry into the consumer calculator market. While pleased with Rockwell's early results, they were not certain that a continuation of Rockwell's introductory marketing strategy would be the best course to follow. In particular, Rockwell's introductory program had been designed to obtain maximum support from leading department stores and calculator specialty stores. Rockwell executives felt this strategy had been quite effective, but there were signs that the market might now be shifting from department stores and specialty stores to mass-merchandising channels of distribution as industry price levels continued to drop. According to trade rumors, the industry leader, Texas Instruments (TI), was planning to broaden its distribution to include mass merchandisers in mid-1975. Rockwell executives had to decide whether to continue their planned roll-out through emphasis on department stores and calculator shops or to anticipate TI's move into mass distribution.

COMPANY BACKGROUND

Rockwell International was a large, diversified firm with fiscal 1974[1] sales of $4.4 billion and profits after taxes of $130.3 million. It was divided into five major operations: automotive, aerospace, electronics, utility and industrial, and consumer. In recent years, the company had been decreasing the portion of its business represented by government defense and aerospace contracts. While government contracts had represented 74 percent of its business in 1967, this figure had dropped to 36 percent by 1974.

Rockwell's Microelectronic Product Division was one of three parts of the electronics operations whose fiscal 1974 sales had approximated $900 million. Microelectronic was a manufacturer of sophisticated semiconductor devices, business machines, and consumer calculators. It was one of the world's largest manufacturers of large-scale integrated (LSI) circuits, displays, and keyboards, the major components in electronic calculators. In an industry in which rapidly declining component costs and learning-curve pricing had established the competitive climate, and nonintegrated or small-volume manufacturers appeared to be at a serious competitive disadvantage, industry sources estimated that Rockwell's manufacturing costs were as low as those of any other firm in the industry.

• Prior to the fall of 1974, Rockwell had not marketed a calculator under its own name. It had, however, been a principal supplier of components for 36 brands of calculators and had produced over a million of the private label calculators sold by such firms as Sears, Roebuck & Company, Unicom, and Lloyds Electronics. Up to mid-1974, the Microelectronic group produced more than 65 models of private label calculators. According to industry estimates, Rockwell had been the third largest manufacturer of calculators (after TI and Bowmar Instruments Corporation) in both 1973 and 1974.

In early 1974, Rockwell management decided to enter the branded calculator business with a line of Rockwell calculators, while maintaining its large private label and components businesses. At that time, it was becoming increasingly clear that the cost advantages and aggressive pricing of such integrated firms as TI and National Semiconductor were about to cause an industry shakeout which would most seriously affect those firms that relied on components purchased from larger electronics companies such as Rockwell.

[1] October 1, 1973–September 30, 1974.

THE UNITED STATES CALCULATOR INDUSTRY

The development of integrated circuits (ICs) in the early sixties made possible the creation of the first electronic calculators. Sumlock Comptometer Co., Ltd., an English firm acquired by Rockwell in 1973, developed the first electronic calculator in 1961 as a replacement for electromechanical machines. Its high cost prevented widespread use, however. In the mid- to late-1960s, a number of American business equipment manufacturers, using more advanced ICs, brought machines in the $1,000 + range on the market. In 1969–1970, using American ICs manufactured by TI and Rockwell, the Japanese surprised United States business machine manufacturers with a wide range of calculators costing as low as $395 for a four-function (+, −, ÷, ×) unit. By 1971 Japanese manufacturers had captured more than 60 percent of the small but rapidly expanding calculator market.

In the early seventies, a second technological breakthrough, the development of low-cost integrated microcircuits, allowed for the production of small hand-held calculators and enabled United States manufacturers to compete with Japanese manufacturers. Most of these small calculators had four or five functions (+, −, ×, ÷, and %), a floating decimal point, and an eight-digit display. The least expensive models had only four functions, a six-digit display, and a fixed decimal point. More expensive models contained a memory, while models for business and scientific purposes often contained a memory plus up to 15 engineering and mathematical functions and had 12-digit displays.

In 1971, Bowmar introduced a four-function pocket calculator which retailed for $240. By late summer, Rapid Data Systems and Equipment, Ltd., TI, and Commodore Business Machines, Inc., introduced competing machines. Many other firms soon entered the business, but Bowmar held its dominant market position through 1972. In mid-1972, Rapid Data introduced a calculator which retailed for under $100, and this began an industrywide downward trend in pricing. TI soon came out with its TI-2500 at $149 retail, $30 less than a competitive Bowmar model. Bowmar quickly matched TI's price, whereupon TI dropped its price another $30. By late 1974, the TI-2500 was retailing for $44.95. Such price erosion was prevalent throughout the industry.

As prices plummeted, unit sales skyrocketed. Total industry unit sales went from ½ million in 1971 to about 12 million in 1974. Industry estimates as to when the market would reach saturation were mixed. One source stated that saturation level would be 1 to 1.3 calculators per household, and that there were about 60 million households in the United States. He estimated the average life span of a calculator to be about 3 years, and he said the replacement rate for calculators would eventually level off at 20 to 25 million annually. The transistor radio industry, with which the calculator industry was frequently compared, had leveled off at about 35 million units annually. (See Exhibit 1 for historical and projected unit and dollar sales.)

The cost of producing calculators had also shown remarkable reductions. Semiconductor components for the early calculators which retailed for about $400 had cost about $170. In 1974 these components had been replaced by an

LSI chip which cost under $5, and it was thought that an integrated manufacturer with a volume output could save another dollar on these chips. Assembly time for calculators now ranged from a few minutes to half an hour. In fact, labor and manufacturing overhead had been driven down so far that the chip, the display, and the keyboard now normally represented 70 to 80 percent of a unit's cost.

By the end of 1974, an estimated 25 to 30 United States and Japanese calculator manufacturers had dropped out of the business, and less than a dozen were expected to survive through 1975. In addition to Rockwell, the dominant forces remaining in the business were TI, Bowmar, Hewlett Packard (HP), National Semiconductor, Commodore, Casio, and Litronix.

TI was the largest semiconductor and calculator manufacturer in the world. It also produced low-cost keyboards and LED displays, and it supplied chips to more than 20 other calculator manufacturers. It had one of the broadest product lines in the industry. In 1974, TI held almost 30 percent of the United States unit market and about 19 percent of the world unit market and had dollar sales of nearly $250 million worldwide. TI's strategy consisted of four elements: (1) aggressive pricing to follow learning-curve reductions in cost (25 to 35 percent for each doubling of accumulated production), (2) continuing efforts to improve products and reduce costs, (3) building on shared experience, and (4) keeping capacity growing ahead of demand. TI concentrated on high-growth markets that would allow both rapid increases in cumulative volume and increases in market share which did not seriously affect competitors' growth. Its 25-person sales force called on 250 to 400 accounts whose retail outlets totaled approximately 5,000.

Bowmar produced its own displays, and in 1974 it began producing its own keyboards. Its ICs were purchased from either TI, Rockwell, or MOS Technology. Lack of IC capacity prevented Bowmar from responding rapidly to changes in technology and design and thus limited its growth. Bowmar had made a $7 million investment in an IC production plant, but for the year ending September 30, 1974, it had shown a $13 million after-tax loss on sales of $83 million, and there was some speculation that it might soon be forced into bankruptcy. Bowmar relied on manufacturers representatives (reps)[1] to sell its products.

HP was a major manufacturer of electronic instrumentation, computers, calculators, components, and medical electronics. In the calculator industry, it had concentrated on the more complex, more expensive units for scientific and business use, though by the end of 1974 it had begun to market some medium-priced models. It was expected that competition from TI, Rockwell, and Bowmar

---

[1] Manufacturers representatives (reps) were independent business people who served as the sales force for several complementary but noncompeting products. Reps who sold calculators were usually known as consumer electronics reps. Their product lines often included radios, television sets, cameras, stereo equipment, and so forth. These reps usually sold directly to retailers, though some sold to distributors who in turn sold to retailers. Reps were paid a commission consisting of a specified percentage of sales. In the case of calculators, their commission was usually about 5 percent.

would force HP to lower its prices, but that they would still be $30 to $50 above competing models because of the products' recognized excellence and advanced design. HP calculators were sold by reps to major department stores and to over 250 college bookstores.

National Semiconductor's consumer products group, Novus Electronics, concentrated on lower-priced models which were often used as promotional items and on private labeling for mass merchandisers such as Montgomery Ward and W. T. Grant. It also marketed calculators through drug and grocery outlets. Its products were sold by reps. National was a sound, fully integrated, and highly competitive semiconductor manufacturer. It had low overhead, strict cost accountability, and a strong international base in both sales and marketing. It was expected to continue to hold a large unit share of the market but not a large dollar share unless it started producing more sophisticated, more costly calculators.

Commodore had been very aggressive in the world market but was not doing very well in the United States market. Some industry sources felt that Commodore had to offer a more reliable product and faster repair turnaround to attain a better position in the United States.

Other companies which were considered strong contenders in the United States calculator industry were Litronix, whose lower-priced calculators ($19.99 and $29.99) were said to be especially good values, and Casio, a company which imported most of its calculators from Japan. Casio's calculators were considered especially reliable, with a defect rate as low as ½ of 1 percent. Its $19.99 hand model and $99.95 printing calculator were especially successful products. Many considered its $129.95 C-100P to be the best printing calculator on the market. Another company which was strong in the low end of the market was Unisonic. As calculator prices dropped, Japanese manufacturers began to make a comeback. They were expected to sell three times as many calculators in 1975 as they had sold in 1974 and to capture as much as 35 to 40 percent of the market as measured in units. (See Exhibit 2 for 1974 United States unit sales and market share data by manufacturer, Exhibit 3 for calculator lines produced by major manufacturers, and Exhibit 4 for 1974 United States sales by product categories.)

PATTERNS OF DISTRIBUTION

In the early days of the calculator industry, the bulk and price of calculators resulted in their being used primarily in offices. Therefore, they were mainly sold through business equipment stores. In the early seventies, when scientists, engineers, architects, and business people began to get interested in calculators, manufacturers started selling them through department stores and direct mail and to credit card companies who resold them via advertisements in monthly statements. By 1973, mass merchandisers were becoming popular outlets, and they were expected to become even more important as the market matured.

The trend toward distribution of calculators through mass-merchandise outlets caused problems for both manufacturers and mass merchandisers.

Though mass merchandisers welcomed the high volume and profits offered by calculators, the products' price instability, the need for secure means to prevent counter-top theft, and lack of trained salespeople caused them problems. Department stores usually were not hurt so badly by a manufacturer's price cut because they usually purchased relatively small quantities per order which they could promote heavily and sell fairly quickly and because manufacturers offered them some degree of price protection. However, mass merchandisers usually ordered basic inventory for the first 5 months and the last 7 months of the year, and they could not react as quickly as could department stores to price decreases nor could manufacturers offer as good price protection on the larger inventories. Thus, mass merchandisers needed to know well in advance what the manufacturer planned to do with regard to pricing.

To try to solve the problem of theft, some mass merchandisers literally bolted, chained, or glued display models to counters. Manufacturers began supplying display cases with holes big enough for a customer to reach through to try the calculator but too small for the calculator to pass through.

The third problem mass merchandisers faced was finding personnel qualified to demonstrate the calculators or finding ways to get around demonstrating them. As had been the case earlier with cameras, consumers usually needed more explanation about calculators than about most of the products mass merchandisers sold. Many mass merchandisers did not have adequate personnel to handle this task, and those who did usually did not have time to train them, especially since calculator models changed so rapidly. Some manufacturers provided instructional services for the stores, but they had problems with rapid personnel turnover. "Training new people becomes a full time job with an item as technical as the calculator," one manufacturer commented. "We've started sending instructions on cassettes to salespeople so that they can listen to explanations of the products while keeping one hand on the calculator."

Traditionally, different manufacturers had concentrated on different distribution channels. Bowmar had focused primarily on office machine outlets, direct mail, and mass merchandisers, while HP's and TI's primary outlets had been major department stores and college bookstores. In 1973 TI had tried unsuccessfully to enter the mass-merchandiser market with its Exactra model which retailed for $20 to $30. The fact that Exactra was a TI line was not emphasized in its advertising. Novus sold its products primarily through mass-merchandiser, drug, and grocery outlets. Unisonic, the major supplier to K Mart, concentrated on mass merchandisers. (See Exhibit 5 for 1974 United States unit sales by distribution channel.)

THE ROCKWELL ENTRY

Rockwell executives decided in early 1974 to begin manufacturing calculators under the Rockwell brand. To handle the marketing of the calculators, they hired Mr. James Donaldson from a major consumer products company to be vice president of marketing for the Microelectronic Product Division. Mr. Donaldson joined Rockwell in April 1974. Rockwell's aim was to gain at least 12 percent penetration of the market within a year after entry.

Rockwell's initial marketing plan focused on department stores and calculator shops in 20 key markets. This plan would place Rockwell products in 548 outlets. Once this target was met, Rockwell would begin opening similar accounts in 20 secondary markets. This would add another 188 outlets. Rockwell management thought the prestige of department stores such as Bloomingdales and Neiman Marcus would help establish the company's reputation and that stores such as Macy's, Bamburger's, and Gimbels were essential to generate large sales volume. They also hoped to get supplemental distribution through premium accounts, hardware stores, and internal business within the company. (See Exhibit 6 for primary and secondary markets and the number of target accounts in each.)

Rockwell executives felt strongly that, to compete in a market where competition was so firmly entrenched, their support of the trade would have to be exceptionally strong. They decided to market a family of six calculators whose distinctive color styling and graphics would develop a strong brand identification so that Rockwell products could be easily recognized and each would help sell the others. Furthermore, they felt that having a complete line of calculators would allow for replacement and trade-up purchases among Rockwell consumers. The first line is shown in Table 1. (See Exhibit 7 for detailed descriptions and manufacturer's selling price of each model.)

Rockwell sold its calculators through a direct sales force consisting of Mr. Adam Thomas, national sales manager, five regional sales managers, and 17 district sales managers. This group met for the first time August 4–8, 1974. It began its sales efforts in Rockwell's 20 target markets during the week of August 12. Salespeople were assigned a product mix objective, and they were in turn responsible for the even distribution of products by models for each of their target accounts.

To decrease the problems which defective or unsatisfactory calculators

TABLE 1

Product		Manufacturer's suggested retail price
10R,	8-digit electronic calculator	$29.95
20R,	electronic calculator with memory and percent	49.95
30R,	slide rule memory electronic calculator	59.95
*51R,	universal converter electronic calculator	109.95
*61R,	advanced slide rule electronic calculator	119.95
*80R,	10-digit printer electronic calculator	169.95

* Rechargeable.

might cause retailers, Rockwell instituted a consumer satisfaction policy. Under this policy, if a consumer returned his Rockwell calculator within 30 days of purchase for refund or exchange, the retailer was authorized to accept the calculator and return it to the nearest Rockwell Customer Service Center. He would then be issued a credit for that product at the quantity price of his last order consistent with the current price sheet. (Other manufacturers usually issued the same or similar products for returned merchandise.) Moreover, each calculator carried a 1-year warranty under which Rockwell repaired or replaced free of charge any parts which became defective through normal use. If the defect became evident 30 days after the purchase, the owner sent the calculator to one of Rockwell's consumer Service Centers in New York, Chicago, Dallas, or Los Angeles, not to the retail outlet where he purchased it. Rockwell's goal was to complete each service request within 48 hours of the calculator's arrival at the service center. To maintain a consumer image for high quality and reliability, Rockwell's goal was to have less than 3 percent customer returns for warranty repairs.

In three out of five instances, Rockwell's regional sales offices, Consumer Service Centers, and distribution warehouses were located in one facility. The central distribution facility was in El Paso, near the source of most of Rockwell's calculator production. Weekly sales reports plus 6-month sales estimates by account and by model were sent from computer terminals in regional distribution warehouses to the central computer in El Paso where they were used for inventory control and sales projections. Efficient communication between sales, service, and distribution were essential, management felt, if Rockwell were to support adequately the trade and its consumers.

Another method by which Rockwell supported the trade was through liberal stock adjustment and price change policies. If a retailer found it necessary to adjust his inventory, Rockwell accepted up to 5 percent of the prior 6 months' purchases without restocking charge, provided the products returned were listed on the current price sheet, were new, unused, and in their original cartons, and were authorized by the account's district sales manager. Returns had to be prepaid to a Rockwell Customer Service Center, and an equal dollar-value order had to be placed at the same time as the return. In the event Rockwell reduced prices, dealers received a credit for the difference between the old and new price for shipments made in the prior 30 days. Dealers were advised of price changes 10 days before they occurred.

Rockwell management considered training retail salespeople to be an essential part of its program. Rockwell's salespeople were instructed to emphasize the company's in-store retail training programs in all sales presentations. Rockwell's salespeople were also expected to arrange formal group training meetings for retail salespeople whenever possible and to conduct ongoing over-the-counter training at each retail outlet.

The primary thrust of Rockwell's initial advertising campaign was a cooperative program under which Rockwell paid an advertising allowance of up to 3 percent of a retailer's net purchases. Rockwell made available prepared scripts, films, newspaper ads, specification sheets, mailers, and point-of-purchase displays to retailers who wished to use them. For retailers who preferred to prepare their own advertisements, Rockwell insisted that the name *Rockwell* appear in the headline, that the name be used as many times as the retailer's name, and that one or more Rockwell calculators be identified and described. Rockwell ads appeared in local newspapers, on local radio and television stations, in metro editions of *Time, Newsweek,* and *Sports Illustrated,* and on billboards. Moreover, in November and December, Rockwell ran a few national television commercials, and calculators were occasionally mentioned in some major corporate television ads. Industry sources estimated Rockwell's 1974 advertising expenditures to have been about $1.3 million. (See Exhibit 8 for samples of advertisements Rockwell supplied, and Exhibit 9 for advertising expenditures of different calculator manufacturers.)

Since TI was already well established in most of the accounts Rockwell wanted to enter, Rockwell management felt it should offer better retail and wholesale prices than TI offered. For example, the suggested retail price for its lowest-priced model, the 10R, eight-digit electronic calculator, was $29.95 as compared to $44.95 for TI's lowest-priced model, the TI-2500. Moreover, Rockwell offered retailer margins of from 28 to 40 percent. Industry sources reported that department store margins on calculators usually ranged from 30 to 35 percent, while mass-merchandiser margins on calculators were usually from 10 to 18 percent.

Rockwell delivered its first branded calculators in September 1974, and by the end of 1974, it had sold approximately 500,000 units. It had succeeded in opening most of its primary and secondary target accounts plus many others, and in all it had about 300 accounts which together had 2,500 outlets. In January 1975, it introduced five new models. The 12R, 21R, and 31R, which retailed for $29.95, $49.95, and $59.95 respectively, and all of which were rechargeable, then became the lower end of Rockwell's regular line, and the nonrechargeable 10R, 20R, and 30R became promotional items. (See Exhibit 10 for details of Rockwell's new product line.)

INDUSTRY AND MARKET DEVELOPMENTS, EARLY 1975

During the early part of 1975, the calculator industry was characterized by continuing price reductions and further manufacturer shakeouts. It was thought that the companies that had the marketing clout, the manufacturing ability, the component capability, and the cash on hand would force marginal companies out of business, and retailers were becoming increasingly conscious of the need to have a good solid company as their supplier. The distinction between products for mass merchandisers and products for department stores was increasingly blurred because of the drop in all prices. Many felt that, if general economic conditions were better, department stores might get out of the calculator business entirely. Most felt it was only a matter of time before mass merchandisers took over the vast majority of the calculator business.

The movement toward using distributors also appeared to be increasing, and some people thought that distributors would eventually handle as much as 80 percent of calculators sold. Moreover, more sophisticated marketing practices were expected to be introduced. "Calculator manufacturing companies have traditionally been run by engineers, and the only marketing tactic they've known is to cut price," one retailer commented.

Though there had been little consumer research done in the industry, that which had been done indicated that the average age of purchasers was decreasing, that male heads of households were the primary users, followed by female heads of households, and that usage by the latter group was increasing. Thirty-eight percent of the purchasers said they paid less for their calculators than they had expected to pay. Twenty-six percent said they bought TI products, and thirty-one percent of the people who said they were planning to purchase a calculator in the future said they would buy a TI product. Half said they knew what brand they wanted before they went into the store and that they did, in fact, buy that brand.

SURVEY BY *HOME FURNISHINGS DAILY*

Early in 1975, *Home Furnishings Daily* surveyed 50 retailers in 26 major markets to determine how the various calculator manufacturers were perceived by the trade. TI was carried by 88 percent of the retailers surveyed, Litronix by 50 percent, Rockwell by 48 percent, Bowmar by 38 percent, HP by 34 percent, and Casio by 30 percent. No other manufacturer was in more than 25 percent of the accounts.

In terms of brand awareness, TI was clearly the market leader, with 98 percent of the retailers saying that TI had the most consumer recognition of any of the brands. TI was followed by Bowmar, HP, Rockwell, Litronix, and Casio, in that order, while Canon, Commodore, Corvus, Craig, Lloyds, Novus, Sharp, and Unisonic received very limited mention. TI was especially well known in the moderate-priced segment of the market, while HP was more popular in the higher-priced, scientific segment. Bowmar received its highest brand recognition on the East Coast, while Commodore, Novus, and Litronix were better known on the West Coast.

In terms of profitability for retailers, TI ranked first, Bowmar second, and Casio third. However, retailers reported that calculators were so frequently used as promotional items to generate traffic that retailer margins were not very large on any line. Generally speaking, the higher-priced products had higher-percentage markups, usually around 40 percent. Litronix products, followed by Rockwell and TI, were said to represent the best value. TI held the number-one ranking for machine cosmetics, followed by HP and Rockwell. HP was said to offer the best training program for retail salespeople. TI ranked second and Rockwell third. Many retailers stated, however, that no manufacturer offered really good training, and they considered this a serious gap in manufacturers' services.

In overall advertising assistance, TI ranked first, followed by Litronix and

Rockwell. HP was said to offer the most attractive and instructional point-of-purchase aids. It was followed by Rockwell and TI. Retailers said that most manufacturers offered a "rolling" cooperative advertising plan under which they paid up to 3 percent of sales within a specified time period, usually 3 months. HP's cooperative advertising allowance was only 2 percent of sales.

The industry as a whole was given high marks for product reliability, with an average defect rate of only 2 to 3 percent. HP's defect rate was said to be less than 2 percent, and Litronix, Casio, and Rockwell were also rated very high in product reliability. No one emerged as the clear leader in offering price protection. Most offered 30-day price protection programs, though Lloyds offered a 90-day plan while Casio had a 60-day plan. In terms of growth potential, Rockwell ranked highest, followed by HP, Litronix, and Novus.

This survey indicated that TI was the undisputed industry leader. In nearly half the outlets surveyed, TI had at least a 50 percent market share. However, there was some indication that TI's dominance might be slipping. Some retailers said TI was losing market share in their outlets, and others said they were anxious to reduce their dependence on TI because of its dictatorial manner. One buyer said there was a lack of communication between TI's field salespeople and its headquarters staff, and that this resulted in the salespeople's inability to supply information to help retailers plan their product lines. Another said he got double shipments around Christmas and that it was very difficult to cancel an order from TI. The company was also criticized for its rapid price-cutting policies and for a price structure which many retailers considered far too high for the products offered. Another source of contention between TI and retailers was that TI had recently opened some retail units in Europe, one in Dallas, and one in San Francisco and was thought to be considering opening such outlets across the country to sell its calculators plus other consumer electronic products which it was expected to introduce soon.

The retailers stated that Bowmar was the only manufacturer to raise retail prices in 1974, and doing this yielded retailer profits as high as 40 percent even on lower-priced products. Nevertheless, Bowmar was known to be in a very weak financial position, and this made retailers cautious about reordering the line. They expected Bowmar to trim its line and concentrate more on low-end goods in an attempt to reestablish its position in the market.

While HP was widely praised for its product quality, it was criticized for not allowing for larger retail margins. One retailer said HP gave him only about a 25 percent markup. Furthermore, some retailers said they had problems getting orders on time, but they felt this was due to HP's only recently entering the consumer market. In February, HP began a new sales effort to build a broader retail base. Its lowest-price machine was the HP-21 which retailed for $125.

Rockwell was the only supplier mentioned by at least 4 percent of the retailers in all 15 rating categories. Many retailers said Rockwell's pricing had been extremely aggressive, especially since it had introduced its lower-price rechargeable units in January. However, retailers gave mixed reports about how well the products were moving. Some said the products had not moved well in the fall of 1974 because of delivery problems and because advertising support had been late. Other retailers thought Rockwell had tried to get into the market too late in the year, after a lot of retailers had placed their orders for Christmas. Many thought Rockwell would become a more attractive supplier as time went on because retailers were increasingly looking for a solid company to buy from. "Rockwell has the money behind it to survive in this business," one industry source said. "That's what's going to make the difference in the future."

THE DECISION

As Rockwell executives considered the company's future in the calculator industry, they felt sure that Rockwell could get substantially more volume from its current department store and specialty shop accounts. However, they thought the company could not afford to overlook mass merchandisers if, in fact, that was where the future of the market lay. To get into mass merchandisers, however, Rockwell's advertising and selling costs would increase substantially. For example, in February Rockwell's 1975 budget, assuming it remained with its current outlets, was about $2 million for advertising and about $3 million for selling and distribution. If Rockwell decided to pursue mass merchandisers, the executives felt the advertising budget would have to be increased to $5 million and the selling and distribution costs would probably rise to about $4 million.

They thought that Rockwell would probably focus on 50 major mass merchandisers who had a total of 2,000 outlets. Some thought that Rockwell might have trouble getting into a few mass merchandisers because relationships between retailers and suppliers were often stronger in the mass merchandiser market than in the department store market. They pointed out that Unisonic had a secure position as K Mart's supplier, and there was no way that Rockwell could get into K Mart outlets. Most thought, however, that Rockwell would be wise to try to get into mass-merchandise channels before TI established a foothold there, and they felt sure that mass merchandisers would prefer working with Rockwell to working with TI.

EXHIBIT 1
TOTAL UNITED STATES CALCULATOR SALES
Rockwell International: Microelectronic Product Division

	Units	Dollars
1971	500,000	$100,000,000
1972	2,500,000	350,000,000
1973	8,000,000	560,000,000
1974	12,000,000	680,000,000
1975 (est.)	15,000,000	630,000,000
1976 (est.)	18,000,000	600,000,000

Source: Various published sources.

EXHIBIT 2
1974 UNITED STATES UNIT SALES AND MARKET SHARE DATA, BY MANUFACTURER
Rockwell International: Microelectronic Product Division

	Unit sales, millions*	Market share, %
Texas Instruments	3.3 –3.5	29
National Semiconductor (Novus)	1.1 –1.3	10
Bowmar	1.1 –1.3	10
Rockwell	0.9 –1.1	8
Commodore	0.9 –1.1	8
Unisonic	0.7 –0.9	7
Litronix	0.5 –0.7	5
Casio	0.5 –0.7	5
APF	0.4 –0.6	4
Hewlett Packard	0.35–0.45	3
Remington	0.25–0.35	3
Corvus	0.2 –0.3	2
Unitrex	0.15–0.25	2
Other	0.5	4
Total	10.85–13.05	100

* Includes both branded- and private-label sales.
Source: Estimates of industry analysts.

EXHIBIT 3
CALCULATOR LINES PRODUCED BY MAJOR MANUFACTURERS
Rockwell International: Microelectronic Product Division

	Simple 4–5 functions	Simple, with memory	"Slide rule"	Scientific/professional
Texas Instruments	X	X	X	X
National (Novus)	X	X		
Bowmar	X	X	X	X
Rockwell	X	X	X	X
Commodore	X	X	X	
Unisonic	X	X	X	
Litronix	X	X	X	
Casio	X	X	X	X
APF		X	X	X
Hewlett Packard	X			
Remington	X	X		X
Corvus	X	X	X	
Unitrex	X	X	X	X

EXHIBIT 4
1974 UNITED STATES SALES BY PRODUCT CATEGORY
Rockwell International: Microelectronic Product Division

Product category	Unit sales, millions	Average retail selling price	Total retail sales, millions
Simple 4 or 5 functions	7.0– 8.0	$35	$245–280
Simple 4 or 5 functions, with memory	1.1– 1.3	65	72–85
"Slide rule", i.e., any unit with a square root or 1/x function	2.4– 2.6	75	180–195
Scientific/professional	0.6– 0.8	225	135–180
	11.1–12.7*		$632–740

* Total differs from unit totals in Exhibit 2 because numbers were derived from different sources. Industry analysts repeatedly emphasized the difficulty of gathering accurate market data.

Source: Estimates of industry analysts.

EXHIBIT 5
1974 UNITED STATES SALES BY DISTRIBUTION CHANNEL
Rockwell International: Microelectronic Product Division

	Est. unit sales, millions	Total industry sales, %
Department stores	5.4– 7.2	45–60
Mass merchandiser	3.0– 4.2	25–35
Others (drug, book, specialty, appliance, and office equipment stores; catalog houses; mail order)	1.8– 2.4	15–20
	10.2–13.8	

Source: Estimates of industry analysts.

EXHIBIT 6
ROCKWELL'S PRIMARY AND SECONDARY MARKETS
Rockwell International: Microelectronic Product Division

INTRODUCTORY TARGET MARKETS

■ *New York:* 3 key retailers with total of 39 stores

■ *Los Angeles:* 3 key retailers with total of 68 stores

■ *Chicago:* 3 key retailers with total of 66 stores

■ *Philadelphia:* 3 key retailers with total of 31 stores

■ *Boston:* 2 key retailers with total of 18 stores

■ *San Francisco/Oakland:* 4 key retailers with total of 44 stores

■ *Detroit:* 3 key retailers with total of 37 stores

■ *Cleveland:* 3 key retailers with total of 24 stores

■ *Washington:* 3 key retailers with total of 30 stores

■ *Pittsburgh:* 3 key retailers with total of 22 stores

■ *Dallas/Ft. Worth:* 4 key retailers with total of 24 stores

■ *St. Louis:* 1 key retailer with 9 stores

■ *Minneapolis/St. Paul:* 2 key retailers with total of 13 stores

■ *Houston:* 3 key retailers with total of 19 stores

■ *Miami:* 2 key retailers with total of 20 stores

■ *Seattle/Tacoma:* 2 key retailers with total of 16 stores

■ *Atlanta:* 2 key retailers with total of 19 stores

■ *Indianapolis:* 2 key retailers with total of 17 stores

■ *Baltimore:* 3 key retailers with total of 20 stores

■ *Tampa/St. Petersburgh:* 1 key retailer with 12 stores

SECONDARY INTRODUCTORY MARKETS AND DEALERS

■ *New Orleans:* 2 key retailers with total of 13 stores

■ *Tulsa:* 1 key retailer with 8 stores

■ *Phoenix:* 1 key retailer with 5 stores

■ *Portland:* 1 key retailer with 6 stores

■ *Richmond:* 1 key retailer with 16 stores

■ *Sacramento:* 1 key retailer with 6 stores

■ *Salt Lake City:* 2 key retailers with 8 stores

■ *San Antonio:* 2 key retailers with a total of 12 stores

■ *San Diego:* 1 key retailer with 10 stores

■ *Akron:* 1 key retailer with 9 stores

■ *Denver:* 2 key retailers with total of 15 stores

■ *Birmingham:* 1 key retailer with 7 stores

■ *Cincinnati:* 1 key retailer with 8 stores

■ *Columbus:* 1 key retailer with 9 stores

■ *Charlotte:* 1 key retailer with 6 stores

■ *Hartford:* 1 key retailer with 4 stores

■ *Jacksonville:* 1 key retailer with 3 stores

■ *Honolulu:* 1 key retailer with 8 stores

■ *Milwaukee:* 2 key retailers with a total of 16 stores

■ *Boise:* 1 key retailer with 19 stores

435

Source: Company records.

EXHIBIT 7
ROCKWELL'S INITIAL PRODUCT LINE
Rockwell International: Microelectronic Product Division

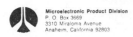

Microelectronic Product Division
P. O. Box 3669
3310 Miraloma Avenue
Anaheim, California 92803

CALCULATOR
PRICE LIST
EFFECTIVE: JULY 15, 1974
ISSUED: JULY 15, 1974

MODEL & DESCRIPTION	*MFR SUGGESTED RETAIL	STANDARD SHIPPING QUANTITY	APPROX WEIGHT LBS	96 TO 492	498 TO 990	996 TO 1998	2004 & UP
10R, 8-digit Electronic Calculator Basic Answer features: • 8 digits • 4 functions • Algebraic logic • Floating decimal • Repeat function • Battery operated, and included • AC jack	$29.95	12	12	21.75	21.75	21.75	21.75
20R, Electronic Calculator with Memory and Percent All Basic Answer features PLUS Full accumulating memory Automatic constants • % key Automatic mark-on and discount Battery operated, and included • AC jack	$49.95	12	12	35.00	34.50	34.00	33.50
30R, Slide Rule Memory Electronic Calculator All Basic Answer features PLUS Full accumulating memory Automatic constants • % key Automatic mark-on and discount Sign change • Register exchange Reciprocals • Square • Square roots Battery operated, and included	$59.95	12	12	42.00	41.50	40.75	40.00
51R, Universal Converter Electronic Calculator • All Basic Answer features PLUS • full accumulating memories • Two-place or floating decimal • Automatic constants • Fraction calculations • 224 fixed conversions plus programmable conversion • Extra-large display • Rechargeable batteries plus AC charger and case	$109.95	6	12	71.50	70.75	70.00	69.25
61R, Advanced Slide Rule Electronic Calculator • All Basic Answer features PLUS • Full accumulating memory • Automatic constants • Register exchange Sign change • Reciprocals • Sum of the squares • Square roots • Log functions • Trig function in degrees of radians • Extra-large display • Powers • Rechargeable batteries plus AC charger and case	$119.95	6	12	78.00	77.25	76.50	75.50
80R, 10-digit Printer Electronic Calculator • 4 functions Commercial logic • 10 digits plus 2 columns of symbols • Thermal printer • Floating decimal with override • Automatic constant and repeat • Subtotals, group totals and grand totals • Operates on AC • Easily obtainable additional tapes • U. L. Listed	$169.95	2	12	107.00	105.50	103.75	102.00

6-25-74

*Manufactures suggested retail price.
For shipment of less than 96 units, but 12 or more units to a location in standard shipping quantity, add 2% for each location.

436

A specific Answer.

Want to advertise a certain model? We'll help you do it with illustrations and copy for
each individual calculator in the line.

All The Answers at once.

We'll help you advertise the whole line together, too. Use both our copy and our artwork—
or just the artwork with your own copy.

437

EXHIBIT 8
Continued

TV and you?
Here's The Answer.

We've prepared a series of 20-second TV commercials with a 10-second close reserved especially for you—so you can tell your customers that you have The Answers.

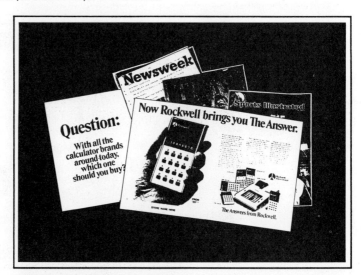

The Answer in October
magazine advertising.

This is our 3-page announcement ad—the opening gun in our arresting campaign in Metro editions of *Time*, *Newsweek* and *Sports Illustrated*. Our aim: to create customers who'll be Answerable to our brand—and ours alone. The body of this advertisement will remind readers who we are, tell them what we have and build awareness and preference. What's more, they'll leave the ad knowing exactly where to go to get an Answer . . . *because your name goes right on the bottom of the page.*

EXHIBIT 8
Continued

The Answer again and again.

In November and December, we'll follow our introductory advertisement—in the same magazines—with these two attention-getters: A full-color spread, plus a color page reminding people that The Answers make great Christmas gifts. Each advertisement will contain another round of informative, persuasive copy. And each will again show the dealer name at the bottom of the page . . . *a profitable place for your store name to be.*

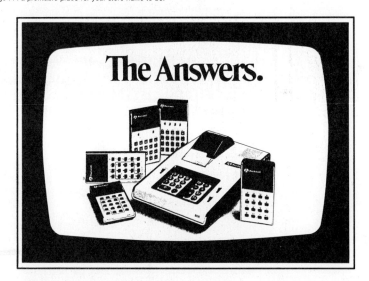

The Answer on TV.

We've scheduled a series of delightful, people-oriented commercials to run from the latter part of November to mid-December. Air time? During periods when large numbers of men and women will learn about our product. The content? Examples of ways people can use and benefit from our product. The goal? To get more people to look for The Answers.

EXHIBIT 8
Continued

The Answer in a leaflet.

This leaflet contains a picture of The Answer calculators, plus a list of the main features of each. Put it on your counter. Enclose it in your customer mailings. Let it remind. Inform. Tempt. Let it raise questions . . . to which you have The Answers.

EXHIBIT 9
1974 ADVERTISING EXPENDITURES ON CALCULATORS BY MANUFACTURERS
Rockwell International: Microelectronic Product Division

Texas Instruments	$4,575,800
National Semiconductor (Novus)	672,200
Bowmar	1,202,400
Rockwell	1,310,200
Commodore	2,300
Litronix	174,200
Casio	510,800
Hewlett Packard	297,700
Total	$8,745,600

Source: Leading National Advertisers, Inc., Multi-Media Survey, January–December 1974, pp. 70–73. This survey included magazines, newspaper supplements, network television, spot television, network radio, and outdoor advertising.

EXHIBIT 10
Rockwell International: Microelectronic Product Division

 Rockwell International
Business Equipment Division
950 De Guigne
Sunnyvale, California 94086
(408) 735-7000

CALCULATOR PRICE LIST
Page 1 of 2

EFFECTIVE DATE: 15 JAN 1975
ISSUE DATE: 5 JAN 1975

MODEL NUMBER AND DESCRIPTION	STD SHIP QTY	48-95	96-& UP
PROMOTIONAL ROCKWELL LINE			
10R, 8-digit Electronic Calculator			
Basic Answer features: • 8 digits • 4 functions • Algebraic logic • Floating decimal • Repeat function • Battery operated, and included • AC jack • Weight: 9 oz. **Mfr Suggested Retail: $24.88**	12	18.00	18.00
20R, Electronic Calculator with Memory and Percent			
All Basic Answer features PLUS: • Full accumulating memory • Automatic constants • % key • Automatic mark-on and discount • Battery operated, and included • AC jack • Weight: 10 oz. **Mfr Suggested Retail: $39.88**	12	28.75	28.75
30R, Slide Rule Memory Electronic Calculator			
All Basic Answer features PLUS: • Full accumulating memory • Automatic constants • % key • Automatic mark-on and discount • Sign change • Register exchange • Reciprocals • Square • Square roots • Battery operated, and included • Weight: 10 oz. **Mfr Suggested Retail: $49.88**	12	35.75	35.75
THE ANSWER-ROCKWELL LINE			
12R, 8-digit, Electronic Calculator with Square Root			
Basic 8 features: • 8 digits • 4 functions + square root • Algebraic logic • Floating decimal • Repeat function • Battery operated, and included • AC jack • AC adapter included • Weight: 9 oz. **Mfr Suggested Retail: $29.95**	12	21.75	21.75
21R, Rechargeable Electronic Calculator with Memory and Percent			
All Basic Answer features PLUS: • Full, addressable memory • Automatic constants • % key • Automatic mark-on and discount • Rechargeable batteries • AC charger jack • AC charger/adapter & case • Weight: 10 oz. **Mfr Suggested Retail: $49.95**	12	35.50	35.00
31R, Rechargeable Slide Rule Memory Electronic Calculator			
All Basic Answer features PLUS: • Full addressable memory • Automatic constants • % key • Automatic mark-on and discount • Sign change • Register exchange • Reciprocals • Square • Square roots • Rechargeable batteries • AC charger jack • AC charger/adapter & case • Weight: 10 oz. **Mfr Suggested Retail: $59.95**	12	42.50	42.00
61R, Advanced Slide Rule Electronic Calculator			
All Basic Answer features PLUS: • Full accumulating memory • Automatic constants • Register exchange • Sign change • Reciprocal • Sum of the squares • Square roots • Log functions • Trig function in degrees of radians • Extra-large display • Powers • Rechargeable batteries plus AC charger/adapter, and case • Weight: 1 lb 10 oz. **Mfr Suggested Retail: $79.95**	6	54.00	53.50

Shipments to one or more additional locations of 12 or more units in standard shipping cartons will be made for a 2% handling charge.

EXHIBIT 10
Continued

Rockwell International
Business Equipment Division
950 De Guigne
Sunnyvale, California 94086
(408) 735-7000

CALCULATOR PRICE LIST
Page 2 of 2
EFFECTIVE DATE: 15 JAN 1975
ISSUE DATE: 5 JAN 1975

MODEL NUMBER AND DESCRIPTION		STD SHIP QTY	48-95	96-& UP
63R, Scientific Slide Rule Electronic Calculator	All Basic Answer features PLUS: •Full addressable memory •Scientific notation •Two level parenthesis •Automatic constants •Register exchange •Sign change •Reciprocal •Square roots •Log functions •Trig functions in degrees or radians •Degree/radian conversion •Factorial •Extra-large display •Powers •Rechargeable batteries plus AC adapter and case •Weight: 1 lb 10 oz. **Mfr Suggested Retail: $99.95**	6	65.50	65.00
51R, Universal Converter Electronic Calculator	All Basic Answer features PLUS: •Full accumulating memories •Two-phase or floating decimal •Automatic constants •Fraction calculations •224 fixed conversions plus programmable conversion •Extra-large display •Rechargeable batteries plus AC charger and case •Weight: 1 lb 10 oz. **Mfr Suggested Retail: $99.95**	6	65.50	65.00
80R, 10-digit Printer Electronic Calculator	All Basic Answer features PLUS: •4 functions •Commercial logic •10 digits plus 2 columns of symbols •Thermal printer •Floating decimal with override •Automatic constant and repeat •Subtotals, group totals and grand totals •Operates on AC •Easily obtainable additional tapes •U.L. listed •Dust cover •Weight: 6 lbs **Mfr Suggested Retail: $139.95**	2	90.00	88.25
82R, 12-digit Printer Electronic Calculator	All Basic Answer features PLUS: •4 functions •Commercial logic •12 digits plus 2 columns of symbols •Thermal printer •Floating fixed monetary decimal selection •Automatic constant and repeat •Subtotals, group totals and grand totals •Operates on AC •Percent, 4-key memory, •Non-add key •Easily obtainable additional tapes •Dust cover •U.L. listed •Weight: 6 lbs **Mfr Suggested Retail: $169.95**	2	109.00	107.00

ACCESSORIES	STD QTY	DEALER COST		STD QTY	DEALER COST
01R AND 02R ACCESSORY KITS			**107R AND 108R AC ADAPTER/CHARGER**		
01R — Brown Vinyl Case, AC Adapter, for Models 10R, 20R, and 30R; Input 120V-60 Hz; Output 7.9 VDC. 50 Ma **Mfr Suggested Retail: $5.95**	6	$3.60	107R AC Adapter/Charger 120/60 for 51R, 61R, 63R, 21R, 31R **Mfr Suggested Retail: $4.95**	6	3.00
02R — Brown Vinyl Case, AC Adapter, for Models 10R, 20R, and 30R; Input Switchable between 120V-60Hz and 220V-50 Hz; Output7.9 VDC, 50 Ma **Mfr Suggested Retail: $8.95**	6	$5.40	108R AC Adapter/Charger Switchable 120/220 for international use **Mfr Suggested Retail: $6.95**	6	4.20
105R AND 106R AC Adapter			**205R CARRYING CASE**		
105R AC Adapter 120V-60 Hz for 10R, 20R, 30R, 12R **Mfr Suggested Retail: $4.95**	6	3.00	Carry case for 10R, 20R, 30R, 12R, 21R, 31R **Mfr Suggested Retail: $2.00**	12	1.20
106R AC Adapter Switchable 120V-60 Hz for international use **Mfr Suggested Retail: $6.95**	6	4.20	**207R CARRYING CASE** Carry case for 51R, 61R, 62R **Mfr Suggested Retail: $3.00**	12	1.80
			TT270 TAPES Three Tapes for Models 80R/82R 2¼'' x 164' Each	3	$1.95

Shipments to one or more additional locations of 12 or more units in standard shipping cartons will be made for a 2% handling charge.

LEVI STRAUSS & COMPANY

BENSON P. SHAPIRO
Associate Professor
Harvard Graduate School of Business Administration

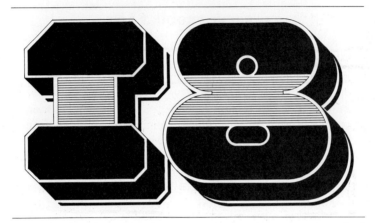

In February 1971 Mr. Mel Bacharach, vice president–marketing of Levi Strauss & Company, was considering what action the firm should take with regard to the manufacture and distribution of boys' wear. The company was the largest (by several times) manufacturer of nationally branded boys' wear of high quality and was the "Cadillac of the industry" with a strong brand reputation. While the production and sale of such merchandise had constituted a sizable portion of the total Levi's business over the years, the company had consciously limited the resources allocated to the Boys' Department because of its low profits, the demands of other parts of the business, and chain store dominance of the boys' market.

LEVI STRAUSS & COMPANY

In 1971, the company was one of the largest firms in the apparel industry with sales in 1970 of $327 million (see Exhibit 1 for financial data). It manufactured

Certain information in this case has been disguised.

a wide variety of jeans, slacks, shorts, and related apparel for men, boys, and women in the United States and overseas.

In the spring of 1971, Levi Strauss & Company was due to issue stock for public ownership. Of the proceeds of the stock sale, $32 million were to be spent for facility expansion, one-half in calendar 1971 and the remainder in calendar 1972.

CURRENT PRODUCT LINE

The product line and the marketplace had undergone substantial change in the years since World War II. Just after the war, Levi Strauss & Company manufactured a short product line of basic blue jeans and related items mainly for the working man. During World War II, however, jeans had begun to become popular for general wear. In the fashion revolution of the early fifties there had been a shift to more informality and diversity in wearing apparel. Manufacturers responded with cotton (chino) pants and later with men's slacks with a buckle in the back. Many of these casual pants were made like jeans (an inexpensive, durable construction), looked like sportswear, and were of washable fabrics. Levi's responded to the needs of the marketplace with a new department—Levi's Lighter Blue that offered faded-blue denim jeans which were an instant success.

During the late 1950s the fashion boom began to gain momentum. Among males, teen-agers led the way. At the end of the fifties white jeans caught on, and in 1961 Levi Strauss successfully introduced its White Levi's line and pastel jeans. In 1964, the first true permanent press slacks ever made were introduced by the firm under its Sta-Prest label, creating a revolution in the garment industry. With no initial competition, the company significantly increased its sportswear penetration and distribution.

Male dress became increasingly fashion-oriented throughout the 1960s. The marketplace demanded pants of new designs in an increased range of fabrics, patterns, and color. Style numbers became obsolete at an accelerated rate. Levi Strauss and its competitors were forced to offer a wider variety of faster changing styles.

By 1971, Levi Strauss & Company was selling a broad line of jeans, slacks, and shorts for men, women, and boys, and some related apparel such as shirts and jackets.

As Levi Strauss grew it also changed organizationally (see Exhibit 2 for an organization chart). There was a general move toward departmentalization and, later, adoption of the product manager concept. During the late 1960s more and more merchandising personnel had been added, and the line divided into finer and finer departments. In January 1968 the women's operation, Levi's For Gals, was made into a separate division, and in very early 1971 the men's sportswear operation had been made a division.

The new sportswear operation provided a typical example of a specific product line. It was divided into three segments: Mr. Levi's, Young Men's Casuals, and Rugged Sportswear. The sportswear line differed from the original

Levi's in that sportswear was manufactured by a more expensive process resulting in a more "finished" garment. In addition, sportswear was typically, but not always, made of more expensive and more colorful fabrics and was "dressier."

The Mr. Levi's line was designed to appeal to the "more mature man," with the major segment probably being sold to consumers in the mid-twenties to early forties age range. The pants were sized to accommodate the changes in body configuration which typically took place during the twenties. The young men's line was designed to appeal to the male from midteens to midtwenties and was sized for the trimmer build and styled for the younger taste.

The Mr. Levi's line consisted of four models. Exhibit 3 describes each model and shows the number of fabrics and colors for each model. Each model-fabric-color combination was manufactured in 55 different primary sizes.

THE PRODUCT MANAGER'S FUNCTION AND PRODUCT PLANNING

The company had adopted the product manager form of organization in the fall of 1969. Although the product manager had a wide range of responsibilities, he was not directly responsible for profits. He did not control the sales force or manufacturing facilities. He was a merchandising executive responsible for designing, pricing, and planning the production and distribution of a segment of the product line.

Models in the men's and boys' lines tended to change relatively infrequently. Most of the season-to-season product variation was in fabrics and colors whose choices were the responsibility of the product managers. Product managers actually purchased the piece goods (fabrics) and accessories (ornaments, etc.), prepared sales estimates, and determined the timing of product production. They set dates for the expected delivery of garments to retailers and were also responsible for designating merchandise for closeouts (merchandise left after a style went out of fashion) and seconds.

The complexity and timing of the product-planning function had changed rather abruptly over the preceding few years. While there were still two major seasonal lines—fall (or back-to-school) and spring—there were now more "sweeteners" introduced between the regular lines. These products were designed to exploit current fashion trends. In the past retailers had committed themselves to purchasing goods 5 months before the merchandise would be placed on sale in their stores. By 1971, retailers would commit themselves only 2 to 3 months in advance of retail sales, forcing a basic change in the product-planning function. While previously the sales force had gone into the field and received orders upon which the product manager relied in purchasing piece goods, this practice had changed over the years. By 1971 the product manager had to purchase piece goods and order the garments into production before the salespeople had called on the retailer. Thus, rather than producing upon receipt of orders, the firm was producing in anticipation of orders.

Because the style of piece goods was rapidly changing, the choice of fabrics was critical. The cost of the fabric, on the average, accounted for about 40 to 45 percent of the total cost of a garment. Since Levi Strauss considered itself a producer of mass fashion, it produced garments only in large quantities. Its normal minimum purchase of a fabric (in one color) was 75,000 yards, worth about $100,000. It was necessary to produce at least 15,000 pairs of a model-fabric-color combination to break even, since about 3,000 to 4,000 pairs per model-fabric-color combination would become closeouts sold at reduced prices.

ADVERTISING

As of 1971 Levi Strauss & Company's advertising program could be divided into five segments. The most important and largest advertising program was designed to change the consumer's image of the firm from that of a manufacturer of jeans to that of a manufacturer of a variety of fashion pants in addition to jeans. The primary media for the program were network TV and radio. Management believed that TV reached a wide range of prospective consumers and offered the opportunity for creative, action-oriented advertising. Radio was used to obtain additional teen-age impact in the metropolitan markets. Both media were used on a seasonal basis with peak advertising in the heavy retail selling periods of early spring, fall or back-to-school, and Christmas.

The second segment was cooperative advertising, which emphasized retail sales generation. The firm paid about 50 percent of media cost with the store paying the remainder. As part of the cooperative program the company provided advertising copy for all media.

The firm had a trade advertising program which was used primarily to develop more sales from existing retail accounts. It was directed at enhancing the retailer's image, and that of the firm as a manufacturer of fashion pants. Some executives believed that Levi Strauss & Company had a better, more fashion-oriented consumer image than retailer image and wished to enlarge the trade program.

The fourth segment of the firm's advertising was that run by the Levi's For Gals Division. This cooperative advertising effort was partly a print advertising program in the nation's major fashion magazines to support the brand image. However, the program was also designed to gain more extensive distribution for a relatively new line. An attempt was being made to get the division's salespeople to emphasize cooperative advertising with prestige accounts because it was believed that association with prestige stores could be used to improve the image of the firm.

The fifth segment of advertising activity consisted of dealer support, including point-of-purchase displays and other sales aids.

Management believed that the firm had an unusually large, well-established advertising program for an apparel manufacturer.

SALES FORCE

Levi Strauss & Company had a sales force of about 365 persons, 50 of whom were account executives. The account executives were very competent, experienced salespeople who managed the firm's relationship with between one and three large existing accounts, providing intensive sales contact with major accounts. The other salespeople covered geographic territories, on potential and existing accounts.

The Levi's For Gals sales force was separate from the rest. As of early February 1971, the sportswear sales force was in the process of being separated from the rest of the men's and boy's sales force. There was general feeling among management that many salespeople might emphasize the easy-to-sell basic jeans line to the detriment of the more fashion-oriented apparel which had great potential but took more time to sell. More importantly, sales management was concerned about the length of time it took a salesperson to present the whole line. The retail buyer was bound, some believed, to lose interest during a long sales presentation. A separate sportswear sales force was introduced in California in early 1970. In early 1971, the Eastern sales force was partially divided, with special sportswear salespeople being designated for the nine largest metropolitan areas. The sportswear salespeople sold both men's and boys' sportswear. All salespeople, except those just getting started, were compensated solely on commission, and paid their own expenses. Arrangements with account executives varied somewhat.

DISTRIBUTION

The company had approximately 15,000 retail accounts comprising more than 25,000 separate stores in the United States and Canada. These accounts could be classified in two groups: primary and secondary distribution. Included in primary distribution were department and specialty stores. In the secondary group were Army-Navy stores and basement divisions of department stores. These were solicited for basic jeans business but not for the more fashion-oriented business.

The distribution system used by the firm had changed over the past years to reflect changes in the product line. In 1964 when a decision had been made to upgrade the sportswear line to a maximum retail price of $25, a decision had also been made to upgrade distribution to stores more capable of selling such goods and more able to contribute to the firm's image. Some executives believed in 1971 that in spite of high total sales the firm was not selling enough to outlets which would lend an image of prestige and fashion to the company.

The company had an explicit policy of not selling to discounters or private label[1] chain operations such as Sears, Montgomery Ward, and J. C. Penney in the continental United States. Most executives of the firm believed that (1) more money could be made selling branded merchandise through department and specialty stores and (2) there was a significant risk in allocating a large share of the firm's business to any single retail organization. In 1971, no single customer accounted for as much as 4 percent of the company's sales.

The firm did not solicit business from discount stores because its executives

[1] These chains typically sold merchandise only under their own brand names.

Discounters

believed discounters would have a negative effect on the image of the Levi's brand and upon the support of established accounts.

Levi Strauss & Company management was aware of the interest which both the chain stores and the discount stores had in the firm's products.

PRICING

Prices of Levi Strauss & Company merchandise were based upon fabric and manufacturing costs. Most of the firm's merchandisers believed that company prices were exceptionally reasonable for the garments offered and that the consumer who purchased a Levi Strauss garment was not very price conscious. Some felt that Levi's prices were too low for the quality provided. On the other hand, several executives were concerned with the increasing competition. Many small new firms had recently entered the men's fashion pant market because of its rapid growth.

The more fashionable items in the line were typically priced higher than the staple goods for three reasons: ① higher fabric cost (more stylish fabric with more complex treatments), ② higher labor input because of more intricate construction and changeover costs as new models were introduced, and ③ higher inventory losses due to faster obsolescence and a higher percentage of clearance goods. The Levi's For Gals line was a good example of the relationship among prices. The basic jean in the line retailed for $6. The more fashionable women's jeans retailed from $10 to $20, and the women's sportswear pants retailed from $12 to $24. As more fashionable items had been added to the line, the upper price limit had been rising. The division's margins on the higher-priced items, furthermore, was greater than on the lower-priced items.

Exhibit 4 shows average wholesale prices and suggested retail markups for a variety of lines from 1965 to 1970.

PRODUCTION

The company supplemented its own production with that of contractors. In 1970 it had used more than 40 independent contractors who manufactured about 17 percent of its unit volume, a slightly higher proportion than the senior manufacturing executive would have preferred. Contractors were used to provide flexibility in capacity, although they had serious disadvantages (higher costs, greater difficulty in maintaining quality standards, and inaccurate delivery schedules).

In the late 1960s and in 1970 Levi Strauss & Company had consistently sold more goods than it could produce. The anticipated availability of funds from the public offering of stock was expected to alleviate that problem by providing increased production capacity.

PRODUCT INTEGRITY

Quality assurance was an exceedingly important function at Levi Strauss & Company. The director of product integrity reported to the president and was a director of the corporation. He had personnel working in all factories and had the authority to stop production or reject incoming raw materials. Typically, quality problems arose when the factories and textile mills were working at capacity. It was at these times that the product integrity department was most criticized by merchandising and production personnel who believed that the product quality standards were overly strict. Product integrity personnel, however, thought that the maintenance of a reputation for high quality was crucial to the long-term growth of the firm. Although some managers believed that the women's and boys' product lines did not require the stringent quality standards of the men's lines, the product integrity department enforced nearly the same high-quality standards for all product lines. Some managers felt that the quality standards were too high and resulted in overly high prices for the consumer and in overly low profits for the company.

THE BOYS' WEAR OPERATION

The question of what to do with the boys' wear operation had been discussed for several years prior to 1971. In 1966 a statement of policy (see Exhibit 5) ranked future market development in the following order: (1) slacks for young men, (2) women's jeans-type sportswear, and (3) boys' and juveniles' pants. By 1971 several of these policies had been implemented; the Levi's For Gals Division had been formed in 1968, and in very early 1971 the Sportswear Division had been created. In June 1970 a unified boys' wear merchandising group had been organized. A major marketing research and planning study had been prepared in 1970. Excerpts are in Appendix A. Appendix B includes general information available in 1971 on the apparel market.

Many executives thought that the boys' wear operation had been treated as an "orphan" or "afterthought." The most commonly stated examples were that when either textiles were hard to obtain or production facilities were in great demand, the boys' wear operation was neglected in favor of other areas. Other issues also concerned marketing management. Although sales of boys' wear were substantial (in the same range as the Levi's For Gal's Division) and contributed significant gross profit dollars to the company, the cost of goods sold averaged about 5 percent higher than the remainder of the firm. Thus, dollar gross margin per unit was significantly lower because of the combination of a relatively low unit price and lower percentage margins.

Several alternatives were open to management. First, the whole operation could be discontinued. Second, it could be made into a full-fledged division. Finally, the boys' operation could continue to be included in the men's basic, dress, and casual jean area and in the men's sportswear division. If the boys' wear operation were to be continued in any form, there were major decisions to be made concerning product line, advertising, and distribution.

With regard to the product line, some executives favored emphasizing only a few basic items, each of which would generate large volume and, they felt, higher profits. Other executives believed that if Levi Strauss & Company were to be in the business it should be committed to it with a full line which could fill all of a retailer's needs. The boys' line for spring 1971 retail sales is enumerated in Exhibit 6. A major innovation was to be introduced in the fall 1971 line. The garment looked like sportswear and was made of a fabric typically used for sportswear, but was of jeans-type construction so that it could retail for about $2 less than the same garment in sportswear-type construction.

The advertising issues were quite involved. One boys' wear merchandiser believed that because the Levi's line was known primarily as a teen-age line, substantial advertising was needed to convince both the retailer and the consumer that Levi Strauss was an important supplier of boys' wear. There was also concern about whether the major portion of the advertising budget should be devoted to consumer advertising or trade advertising. The most appropriate target for consumer advertising was not clearly evident. One group felt that the emphasis should be on advertising directed toward the child. If this were done, the reasoning went, the child could be made more aware of his clothing and would want to become involved in the choice of it. He could be interested in style and fashion and would be likely to follow the teen-agers in their loyalty to Levi's.

Other executives, on the other hand, stressed the importance of advertising to mothers. Since they were already the decision makers, it would be easier to convince them to buy Levi's than to stimulate young boys to take an interest in clothing. These executives reasoned furthermore that if mothers could be made more aware of Levi's they would tend to buy Levi's for their husbands. One theory regarding the teen-age strength of Levi's proposed that while males were aware of Levi's and purchased them during the teen-age years when they bought their own clothes, females were not as aware and did not tend to purchase Levi's for their children or husbands.

With regard to distribution, the key issue involved whether or not to solicit sales from chains and discounters. One group of executives was in favor of this approach because they believed it to be the only way to develop a large business in boys' wear. Other executives were categorically against the idea because it offered too much control to too limited a number of retailers, and might threaten the support of established outlets. These executives, were, furthermore, against selling goods under a private label. Finally, they doubted that Levi's could earn as high a margin as it desired by selling through these outlets.

Many of the executives believed that it was exceedingly difficult to obtain exposure and shelf space in boys' wear departments. They knew that many people in the department store trade believed that boys' wear departments were weak because top-level department store managers were not willing to invest heavily to meet the chains and discounters in a price-sensitive area.

EXHIBIT 1
CORPORATE FINANCIAL DATA
Levi Strauss & Company

Income statements, in millions of dollars

	Fiscal year ended				
	Nov. 27, 1966 (52 weeks)	Nov. 26, 1967 (52 weeks)	Nov. 24, 1968 (52 weeks)	Nov. 30, 1969 (52 weeks)	Nov. 29, 1970 (52 weeks)
Net sales	147.8	159.0	196.2	250.7	327.8
Cost of goods sold	106.1	112.9	133.3	171.0	222.4
Gross profit	41.7	46.1	62.9	79.7	105.4
Marketing, general, and administrative expenses	26.3	30.8	35.4	46.8	63.9
Operating income	15.4	15.3	27.5	32.9	41.5
Other income expenses and taxes	7.5	7.5	15.4	18.4	23.1
Net income after tax	7.9	7.8	12.1	14.5	18.4
Net income per share	0.81	0.80	1.24	1.50	1.92

Balance sheet, in millions of dollars

Current assets		Current liabilities and equity	
Cash	8.1	Payable to banks	32.5
Accounts receivable	47.2	Accounts payable	34.5
Inventories	95.6	Accrued liabilities	10.5
Others	5.5	Other	6.6
	156.4		84.1
		Long-term debt	25.2
Property plant and equipment (net)	27.5	Other	1.3
Other Assets	11.2	Stockholders' equity	84.5
	195.1		195.1

Notes: (1) Figures may not add because of rounding. (2) These are incomplete summaries, since they do not include the necessary notes.

EXHIBIT 2
CHART OF ORGANIZATION
Levi Strauss & Company

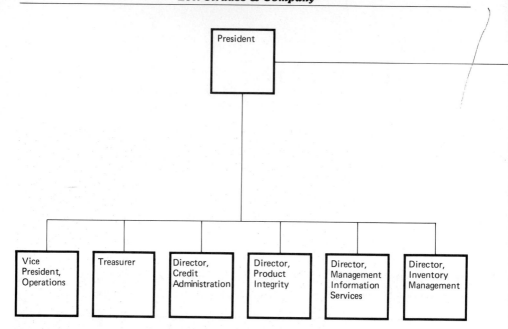

Note: This chart represents reporting relationships only, with no implication of relative importance of functions.
Source: Corporate Planning, July 1971.

452

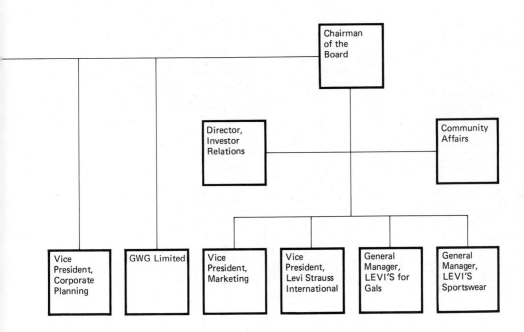

EXHIBIT 3
THE MR. LEVI'S LINE
Levi Strauss & Company

	Model name			
	Traditional/Classic	**Saville**	**Cavalero**	**Sportster**
Nature of styling	Ivy league (basic taper)	Ive league but sportier	Quite fashionable	Continental (no belt)
Active fabrics	3	6	11	5
Active fabric-color combinations	9	12	30	18
Range of suggested retail prices	$11–13	$12–15	$13–15	$13–15
Average suggested retail price	$11 +	$15 –	$14.50	$14.00

EXHIBIT 4
INDEX* OF AVERAGE WHOLESALE PRICES AND SUGGESTED RETAIL MARKUPS
Levi Strauss & Company

	1965	**1966**	**1967**	**1968**	**1969**	**1970**
Basic Blue Jeans:†						
Av. wholesale price	93	94	100	108	117	117
Retail markup, %	32	32	39	39	40	42
Boys' Double-Knee Jeans:						
Av. wholesale price	80	85	100	105	104	108
Retail markup, %	40	40	40	41	41	42
Stretch Jeans:†						
Av. wholesale price	97	95	100	108	108	108
Retail markup, %	44	44	44	44	44	44
Classic Fashion Jeans:†						
Av. wholesale Price		90	100	106	109	109
Retail markup, %		45	46	47	48	49
Young Men's Casual Sportswear:						
Av. wholesale price		99	100	106	120	124
Retail markup, %		46	46	47	48	49
Mr. Levi's:						
Av. wholesale price			100	107	109	116
Retail markup, %			47	48	50	50

* Note that 1967 prices = 100 percent.

† Includes boys' sizes.

EXHIBIT 5
Levi Strauss & Company

POLICY STATEMENT, 1966

Today Levi Strauss & Company stands as the largest manufacturer of our type of apparel in the world. We are recognized as leaders in our field. It is our desire to conduct our affairs as business statesmen, recognizing our obligations to our communities and to our country so that we will not only maintain but reinforce this position of leadership. We will remain an ethical manufacturer providing customers with full value and maintaining a reputation for fair and honest business practices. Our major objective in the next few years is to obtain an increasing share of the popular priced pants market both here and overseas.

We will strive to establish a solid base in most of the important areas of the pants apparel business. This will include expansion of present markets by age groups, sex, and price lines. There are tremendous opportunities for growth beckoning in several fields, but we must establish priorities so that the desired growth can be obtained without straining our resources, both financial and otherwise.

Regardless of new opportunities, it is our purpose and desire to maintain the distinctiveness of brand and company identity of Blue Levi's. The tradition and identity of the original Levi's jeans are a unique and invaluable asset and must not be diminished in importance. Levi's is one of the strongest brand names in the apparel and consumer products field.

Regarding new merchandising opportunities, our present view would rank them in the following order: (1) Mr. Levi's—slacks for the young men; (2) women's jeans-type sportswear (eventually as a separate division); and (3) a separate department to concentrate on boys' and juveniles' pants. Each of these fields will only be entered in turn after we have assurance that our objectives of superior quality and service have been established in our present lines and can be assured in the new merchandise.

Although as we expand individual ability and efficiency will be demanded and recognized, we must never lose sight of our basic philosophy of responsibility to our own personnel at all levels. We are aware of the need for any progressive business to be increasingly responsive to a wide range of social responsibilities in all areas in which it operates and we have long been considered a leader in these matters. We will continue to plan, insofar as possible, so as to provide steady employment throughout the year for our production workers. We must maintain relationships with everyone working for Levi Strauss & Company in a manner that will encourage the loyalty and interest which have been among our most unique and valuable assets. We want to provide a productive, satisfying, and challenging work environment for employees, regardless of position or department, so that anyone who applies himself will be assured of security as well as career opportunities for personal development and advancement.

EXHIBIT 6
BOYS' WEAR LINE—SPRING 1971
Levi Strauss & Company

Model	Description	Number of fabrics	Number of fabric-color combinations	Suggested retail price (price depends on size and fabric)
Hopster Flares*	Sportswear	10	37	$7.50–11.00
Cordova Flares*	Sportswear	7	25	8.00–11.00
Trimcuts*	Cuffed sportswear	2	11	5.50– 9.00
Trimcuts*	Cuffless sportswear	1	4	6.50– 7.50
Swinger Flares*	Sportswear	3	11	6.00– 9.00
Levi's Bell Bottoms*	Jeans	4	8	5.50– 7.50
Levi's Flares*	Jeans	4	15	6.00– 8.50
Levi's Dress Flares†	Jeans	3	6	10.00
Blue Levi's	Jeans	1	1	6.00
Saddleman Boot Jean	Jeans	1	1	6.00– 7.00
Super Slims	Jeans	1	1	5.50
Boys' Double-Knee Levi's	Jeans	2	6	4.50– 5.50
Authentic Levi's Jacket	Denim jacket	1	1	7.50
Stretch Levi's	Jeans	1	3	4.98
Levi's Slim Fits	Jeans	1	3	5.50
Sta-Prest Levi's	Jeans	1	4	6.50– 7.50
Sta-Prest Slim Fits*	Jeans	1	4	5.50
Nuvos	Jeans	1	3	6.50
Levi's Jeans Shorts	Shorts	2	5	4.00
Frayed Shorts	Shorts	1	2	4.00

* Available in boys' sizes (6–12) and students' sizes (25–30 waist).

† Available only in students' sizes (25–30 waist).

No designation means available only in boys' sizes.

This listing does not include the Little Levi's line which was available in juvenile sizes 2–7. There were seven models in that line, with 32 model-fabric-color combinations, and retail prices ranging from $3.98 to $6.00 for the pants.

Source: Spring 1971 catalog.

APPENDIX A
BOYS' WEAR MARKET REVIEW

BOYS' PANTS MARKET

The boys' pants market covers boys from ages 2 to 14, including juveniles (sizes 2–7), boys (sizes 6–14), and students or preps (waists 25–30). Primary consumers for Levi's boys' wear are wearers of boys' and students' sizes.

POPULATION

U.S. Department of Commerce population projections indicate that the primary market (5–14-year-olds) will decline slightly (−3.8 percent) from 1969 to 1975 because of the recent low birthrate. The 5–9-year-old segment will decline by nearly 1 million persons, while the 10–14 group will rise nominally (see Table 1).

TABLE 1
BOYS' POPULATION PROJECTIONS, UNITED STATES, Thousands

	1969	1970	1971	1972	1973	1974	1975
Age group:							
0–4	9,545	9,571	9,746	9,996	10,261	10,540	10,835
5–9	10,626	10,507	10,209	9,939	9,747	9,623	9,649
10–14	10,411	10,500	10,654	10,709	10,718	10,701	10,580
Total 0–14	30,582	30,578	30,609	30,644	30,726	30,864	31,064
Total 5–14	21,037	21,007	20,863	20,648	20,465	20,324	20,229
% change from 1969 5–14		−0.1	−0.8	−1.8	−2.7	−3.4	−3.8

BOYS' PANTS PRODUCTION

Projections of boys' pants production in the United States are shown in Table 2. Growth in total production of boys' pants (18.6 percent from 1969 to 1975) will result primarily from increased per capita purchases, since population will remain relatively stable.

TABLE 2
PROJECTED DOMESTIC BOYS' PANTS PRODUCTION, Millions of units

	1969	1970	1971	1972	1973	1974	1975	% change 1969–1975
Jeans	76.8	79.0	81.2	83.4	85.5	87.7	89.9	17.1
Slacks	67.4	69.6	71.8	74.0	76.1	78.3	80.5	19.4
Shorts	8.5	8.9	9.3	9.6	10.0	10.3	10.7	25.8
Total	152.7	157.5	162.3	167.0	171.6	176.3	181.1	18.6

DISTRIBUTION CHANNELS AND
AVAILABLE MARKET

Of the total boys' market, a substantial portion is sold through non-Levi's channels (chains, discount houses, and variety stores). Only the remaining portion is available to Levi's boys' wear, as represented in Table 3.

TABLE 3
TOTAL AND AVAILABLE MARKET—BOYS' SIZES, Millions of units

	Jeans		Slacks and shorts	
	1970	1975	1970	1975
Sold through chains and discount stores	54	65	38	45
Sold through department and specialty stores	$\frac{25}{79}$	$\frac{25}{90}$	$\frac{41}{79}$	$\frac{46}{91}$

COMPETITION

The chains (Penneys, Sears, and Wards) are the major forces in the boys' pants market. In 1968, these three chains accounted for 47 percent of total jeans unit sales and 33 percent of total slacks unit sales.

Table 4 details approximate 1968 market shares for the major boys' pants manufacturers. Penneys, Sears, Wards, the discounters, and variety outlets base their appeal largely on reasonable quality at attractive prices, and they emphasize special price promotions. Boys' wear retailers in leading department and specialty stores generally believe that they should not engage in direct price competition with the chains and discounters but rather should base their appeal on quality, fashion and brand strength.

TABLE 4
MARKET SHARES IN 1968, AGES 6–13

Jeans			Slacks		
Brand	% total units	% total dollars	Brand	% total units	% total dollars
Penney	21.4	20.7	Sears	17.7	16.5
Sears	19.8	18.9	Penney	10.9	10.7
Levi's	6.0	9.3	Brand B	5.0	6.8
Ward	6.0	5.8	Ward	3.9	3.4
Brand A	3.3	3.5	Levi's	2.7	3.4
Brand B	2.8	3.5	Brand D	2.4	3.1
Brand C	2.2	2.8	Brand E	2.4	NA
Brand D	1.8	2.2	Brand F	1.9	NA
Others	$\underline{36.7}$	$\underline{33.3}$	Brand A	1.5	1.7
Total	100.0	100.0	Others	$\underline{51.6}$	$\underline{54.4}$
			Total	100.0	100.0

CONSUMER PURCHASE DECISION

Consumer surveys indicate that 6–13-year-old boys buy less than 10 percent of the total pants purchased for their use, while over 75 percent are bought by the boys' mothers, and 15 percent by other family members or groups. A consumer study conducted for LS & Co. in 1968 indicated that the degree of influence exerted by the boy on his mother's purchase decisions is a product of two factors: (1) his age and (2) his interest in the product being purchased. The study concluded that until the boy reaches the age of 8–10, he has little interest in pants and exerts minimal influence on his mother's purchase decisions. Around the age of 10, a boy begins to show some interest in his appearance and the pants he wears. At this age, the boy's influence on his mother's pants purchase decisions becomes evident and increases thereafter with the boy's age.

APPENDIX B
DATA GATHERED BY THE
MARKETING PLANNING DEPARTMENT

STORE SHARES

	Age of wearer				
	6–13*	14–18	19–24	25–34	35 & over
Male $8–$15 permanent press slacks					
Department stores	31%	46%	39%	42%	39%
Specialty stores	16	42	45	37	32
Chains	31	7	9	16	18
Discount stores	14	4	2	2	4
All others	8	1	5	3	7
	100%	100%	100%	100%	100%
Male $5–$12 jeans					
Department stores	24%	48%	47%	40%	31%
Specialty stores	8	37	38	40	36
Chains	(45)	6	6	9	21
Discount stores	14	7	8	8	10
All others	9	2	1	3	2
	100%	100%	100%	100%	100%

* All prices

BRAND PREFERENCE FOR MALE PANTS, Based on a sample of United States males

	Age of wearer				
	6–13	14–18	19–24	25–34	35 & over
Levi's	8%*	21%	20%	13%	7%
Farah	7	10	12	11	7
Penney	16	9	8	12	11
Sears	16	8	5	11	10
Blue Bell	2	4	3	2	1
H.I.S.		3	3	1	1
Haggar		2	2	5	5
Don't know or other	51	43	47	45	58

* To be read: "8 percent of those respondents aged 6 to 13 preferred Levi's."

A GROWING MARKET: UNITED STATES POPULATION

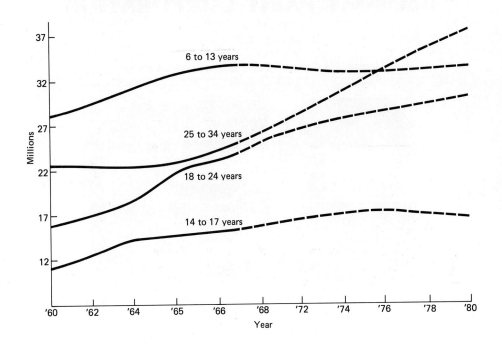

BELMONT PAINT CORPORATION

ULRICH E. WIECHMANN
Assistant Professor
Harvard Graduate School of Business Administration

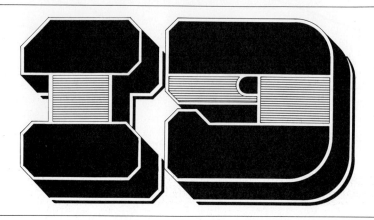

In March 1970, Mr. James Hilgers, vice president–marketing of the Belmont Paint Corporation,[1] met with Mr. Morton, the company's manager of branches, and with Mr. Oldman, manager of products,[2] to discuss what Belmont's future policy regarding franchised retail outlets should be.[3] Mr. Hilgers stated:

[1] All names, places, and other information that might identify the company have been disguised.

[2] See Exhibit 1 for a partial organization chart.

[3] Franchising originally referred to the practice of a manufacturer of granting to only a limited number of dealers or distributors the right to sell its products in a given territory, in exchange for dealers' or distributors' promise to promote the products in a specified manner. Many higher priced, infrequently purchased products, e.g., Magnavox radios, are sold this way.

More recently franchising has come to refer to the right and obligation of an individual to conduct a particular type of business according to a predetermined pattern. It is the practice under which marketers sell a product and/or service through a chain of retail outlets which are of similar appearance, follow uniform operating standards, and are owned and operated by legally independent businessmen. Fast-food outlets like Dunkin' Donuts or McDonald's are typical examples for this franchising of whole enterprises.

I think we would all agree that our network of controlled company-owned branches at the retail level is one of our main strengths in the market. In fact, most of our distribution problems come from the part of our business that doesn't go through our branches. However, it is quite clear that, unless we expand their number much faster, our branches cannot compensate for the many hardware store accounts we are losing each year. I wonder, therefore, whether we shouldn't make more extensive use of franchising to supplement our own branch network.

Mr. Morton observed:

Our experiment with franchising in Bridgeville, New Jersey, certainly looks quite encouraging so far. Of course, it is much too early to make an accurate judgment, but I know that Pat O'Brien, our District Sales Manager in the Bridgeville area, is seriously considering the possibility of setting up another franchised store pretty soon.

Mr. Oldman then remarked:

Frankly, I don't know why we should take franchising into consideration at all. If we go to all the trouble of searching out a promising location, negotiating a lease, setting up a store, and then turn the store over to an independent franchised dealer, then we no longer have control over the outlet. Why not simply put in a man as our employee?

Mr. Hilgers replied:

I can see your point. But don't forget the many current demands on our capital, which will not allow us to expand our branch network as much and as fast as we might want to. Besides, with franchising we may get market coverage in marginal locations which would not support a company-owned branch. I suggest that we investigate the pros and cons of franchising in detail to see whether the Bridgeville experiment should be repeated or not.

GENERAL INFORMATION ON THE PAINT INDUSTRY[1]

The paint industry was composed of roughly 1,600 companies operating about 1,875 plants and employing about 69,400 persons. Exhibit 2 shows, for 1968, the rank and estimated sales volume of the 20 largest paint manufacturers which together accounted for over 50 percent of total industry sales. Because of low capital requirements and readily available technology, paint manufacturing remained one of the industrial areas in which a large number of small local or regional companies were able to compete effectively against big national firms. Management of the Belmont Paint Corporation thought that among the multi-

[1] Based on *Marketing Guide to the Paint Industry*, Charles H. Kline & Co., Inc., Fairfield, N.J., 1969.

tude of paint brands there were about 15 well-known national brands. "The average consumer, however, probably couldn't name more than 3 or 4 different brands," one executive stated.

In 1968 total shipments of surface coatings by United States manufacturers amounted to 843 million gallons valued at $2,587 million. For the past 10 years industry gallon shipments had grown at 3.4 percent per year while dollar sales had increased at an annual rate of 4.7 percent. Compared with an annual growth of the gross national product of 6.3 percent over the same period, the paint industry thus had not kept pace with the expansion of the general economy.

One of the most serious problems affecting long-term industry growth was the increasing use of structural and surfacing materials requiring no paint or less paint, such as stainless steel, aluminum, glass, fiber glass, reinforced plastics, as well as wallpaper, wood panels, plastic films, and electroplated, phosphated, or oxidized metal films.

Finished-paint products fell into two general marketing categories: (1) industrial finishes, which were sold to manufacturers for the decoration and protection of their products as well as for industrial maintenance, like anticorrosion coating; and (2) trade sales paint products, which moved mainly to professional painters, contractors, and private households for home and building decoration and maintenance. Total industry shipments in 1968 split about evenly between industrial finishes (419 million gallons) and trade paints (425 million gallons).

Within the category of industrial finishes there were only a few standard product lines. Most industrial finishes were specially formulated for specific applications or even for individual customers. The bulk of industrial finishes moved through the manufacturers' sales forces directly to the industrial users; about 10 to 15 percent of industry volume was sold through distributors and jobbers.

Trade sales paints, in addition to a large variety of interior and exterior house paints, included special coatings for automotive and machinery refinishing, traffic paints for pavement marking, and other special-purpose paints. Approximately 20 percent of all manufacturers' shipments were sold directly to the end users, mainly to contractors. The remaining 80 percent of industry shipments moved through a complex distribution system including building and lumber wholesalers, hardware jobbers, paint distributors, department stores, drugstores, discounters, and paint specialty stores. A particular feature of this distribution system was that several manufacturers owned and operated their distribution outlets. Exhibit 3 shows the distribution channels used by the industry for the 425 million gallons of trade paints shipped in 1968.

As can be seen from Exhibit 3, the general public, i.e., private households, constituted the most important single customer group for trade sales paints. Although no exact figures were available, it was believed that a large and growing proportion of paints sold over the counter to the general public was applied by the householders themselves.

A consumer study conducted in 1968 by *Better Homes and Gardens* in cooperation with the National Paint, Varnish and Lacquer Association gave some indication of the magnitude of the do-it-yourself market: More than 80 percent of the respondents said that they had done their interior painting them-selves, and nearly 70 percent stated this for exterior paint jobs. Excerpts of the findings of the survey are included in the Appendix.

COMPANY BACKGROUND

The Belmont Paint Corporation in 1969 was one of the larger paint manufac-turers in the United States. Founded in 1897 as a small retail paint store, the company had experienced a rapid internal growth which had been supple-mented by a number of acquisitions of other paint manufacturers.

The basic philosophy to which the company had adhered through all the years of its history was described by management as earning and keeping public confidence through top-quality products and service. "In the future, as in the past, our main concern will be how to please the consumer," one executive stated, "how to cope with the great variety of products necessary to suit con-sumer needs, how to get the products to the dealers, and how to get the dealers to stock this variety of products."

In 1969 the Belmont Paint Corporation operated 15 plants in the United States and employed about 10,000 people. The organization comprised three divisions, formed by acquired paint companies and six consolidated subsidiaries.

Consolidated net sales had shown a steady growth ever since the company had been founded, amounting to roughly $250 million in 1969 with an after-tax net income of roughly $9.3 million. Net income had not kept pace with the in-crease in sales and had actually declined over the 5-year period from 1965 to 1969. Management attributed this development to the inflation of wages and salaries and other selling, general and administrative expenses and to increased costs related to the company's expansion and modernization program. Competi-tive conditions had not permitted price increases adequate to offset the impact of increased costs on profits. Exhibit 4 presents a 5-year comparison of financial data. Exhibits 5 and 6 show a consolidated balance sheet and income statement for the fiscal year ending August 31, 1969.

In 1969, aside from finished-paint products, the company's product line comprised pigments, colors, and chemicals; paint accessories, such as brushes, rollers, and trays; metal containers; as well as a wide array of paint-application and home-decorating products purchased from other manufacturers. Exhibit 7 shows a percentage breakdown of consolidated net sales by product groups in 1969.

Finished-paint products were sold under a number of different trademarks, reflecting in part the names of formerly independent paint manufacturers which had been acquired by the Belmont Paint Corporation. The company's brands had always enjoyed a very strong reputation in the market. Trade paints ac-counted for roughly $92 million of total company sales of paint products; indus-trial finishes accounted for about $62 million.

DISTRIBUTION OF TRADE PAINTS

Originally the company had distributed its trade paint products through drug-stores and lumberyards. In the 1920s and 1930s these outlets were gradually replaced by hardware stores. Until the end of World War II these hardware dealers, supplemented by some company branches, represented the backbone of Belmont's distribution system for trade paints.

It was not the company policy to officially grant territorial protection to its dealers.

Changes in the pattern of retailing after the war forced the company to revise its distribution system. The traditional hardware dealers, of which Belmont had supplied about 25,000 in 1945, found their existence increasingly threatened by the emergence and growth of discount-type mass merchandisers. Belmont's response to the decreasing number of hardware stores was (1) expansion of the network of company-owned branches and (2) distribution through mass merchandisers.

In 1969 there were 965 company-owned branches in operation, performing both wholesale and retail functions. As wholesalers the branches supplied the remaining 3,034 traditional retail accounts, like hardware stores and paint specialty stores, and they also sold a line of professional coatings to the so-called *bulk market*. The bulk market comprised professional painters, contractors, builders, and some industrial users. For many branches the dealer and bulk business combined accounted for the major part of their total sales volume. Traditionally the policy for the branches had been to take all the retail business that was readily available but to concentrate their sales effort on the bulk and dealer market. Many branch managers, therefore, spent the greatest part of their time contacting painters, contractors, and dealers. They were assisted in this effort by salespeople, who often worked for a number of branches simultaneously.

Branch managers typically received a fixed salary ranging from $7,200 to $8,400 annually, and they also were entitled to a certain percentage of the net profit before taxes they achieved in their branches. This percentage varied with local conditions, but a branch manager's profit share typically amounted to about 25 percent of the net profit of his branch.

The recruitment of qualified branch personnel was described by management as one of the most pressing problems which stood in the way of a more rapid expansion of the branch network.

As retailers, the branches sold paints, paint-application products, and other home-decorating products to private households. Paint products sold to private consumers were not always the same as the professional coatings supplied to the bulk market.

In the mid-1960s the Belmont Paint Corporation had started to upgrade its retail facilities by establishing what was called *modernized company stores.* These were company branches of modern design, larger than conventional branches, covering a sales area of at least 4,000 square feet and generating an average annual sales volume of about $250,000. They offered the consumer a broad selection of home-decorating articles, like carpeting, tiles, wallpaper, lighting fixtures, book shelves, and drapery, in addition to paints and painting tools. In 1969 the company had about 150 of these branches in operation. Most of the nonpaint products were purchased for resale by the Belmont Paint Corporation from other manufacturers. The relationship between the sales volume of paint products and the volume of nonpaint products in the branches was roughly 70:30. Management believed that the added variety and convenience these new outlets offered to the consumer made them attractive decorating centers. The modernized company stores relied to a somewhat greater extent on sales to the retail market than did the conventional branches. At most, however, half the volume of the modernized company stores came from the retail market.

Management had planned to open about 10 to 20 new branches each year. The establishment of a new branch required a sizable investment both in terms of management time and capital. New locations were normally sought out by the district sales managers (see Exhibit 1) and then went through a process of evaluation in the regional and home offices.

The capital investment for a new branch varied considerably, depending on local conditions, the size of the branches, and the merchandise carried. On the average, management expected an investment of $50,000 to $75,000 for each new branch which was opened. No rigid cutoff rate existed for the return on investment, but the company aimed at reaching a return of at least 12 percent after taxes by the end of the third year on the investment for a new branch. Management also tried to follow the rule of establishing a new branch only if it was reasonable to expect that the branch would at least break even after the first full fiscal year in operation.

Total operating expenses of company branches, inclusive of all salaries, rent, and overhead such as heat, electricity, utilities, local sales promotion, depreciation, and maintenance, amounted to roughly 26 percent of net sales on the average. Operating expenses of modernized company stores were somewhat higher, amounting to about 28 percent of net sales. Salaries accounted for about 62 percent of total operating expenses, rent for roughly 13 percent, and heat, electricity, and other overhead for the remaining 25 percent of all operating expenses.

In 1963 the company had begun to lease departments operated by its own employees in the newly emerging discount stores. "It was a major policy decision for us," one executive commented. "We realized that we had to be in these high volume outlets since they attract and will continue to attract a lot of our customers who formerly shopped in hardware stores." In 1969 Belmont operated 163 leased departments. In return for allowing Belmont to operate such a leased department, a discounter was usually paid a rent of 12 percent of the department's dollar volume. Total expenses, including rent, of the leased departments amounted to roughly 27 percent of their retail sales volume.

The Belmont Paint Corporation also sold to department stores and to discounters which operated their own paint departments. Some members in the organization strongly criticized this practice; they thought that selling to discount stores would disrupt the relationship between Belmont and the traditional dealers.

Recently a trend had become apparent which indicated that most of the company's leased departments might eventually be operated by the discount merchandisers themselves. Giant-Valu, a national chain of discount stores in which Belmont operated 124 leased departments, had already started to take over these departments on a broad scale. Management roughly estimated that 120 of its leased departments operated in a number of different discount chains might be taken over within the next 5 years and that about 20 new departments would be established over the same time period. Some executives of the Belmont Paint Corporation viewed this development with great concern.

"If the discounters take over the departments we lose control over that part of our business," one member of management stated. "I think the quality of customer service will deteriorate. We believe that the special sales effort and the service our people in the departments put in add greatly to the sales volume the departments make."

Mass merchandisers and leased departments relied for about 50 percent of their volume with Belmont products on brands which were also carried by company branches and traditional paint outlets. The remainder of their volume came either from private labels supplied by Belmont or from company brands not sold in branches or traditional outlets in a given market area. When a leased department was taken over, Belmont continued to supply the discount outlet with the brands which had been sold in the leased department before.

Aside from selling through mass merchandisers, leased departments, company branches, and traditional retailers, Belmont to a small extent marketed its products through distributors, who in turn sold to dealers and to the bulk market.

Exhibit 8 provides a graphical summary of the company's primary channels of distribution for trade paints and home-decorating products.

Exhibit 9 shows the development in the number of company branches and leased departments over the period from 1963 to 1969.

All retail outlets—company branches, traditional dealers, mass merchandisers, and leased departments—were charged the same prices by the company.[1] If resold at the normal retail prices, paint products provided these outlets with an average gross margin of 40 percent of the retail price. Nonpaint products, like wallpaper, carried higher margins, usually averaging 45 percent. Retail prices, and consequently retail margins, for Belmont's products tended to be lower in mass-merchandising outlets and in leased departments than in company branches and traditional paint outlets.

Distributors were given a functional discount averaging 15 percent of the dealers' price. If a branch sold to a dealer it was credited with a functional allowance of 12.5 percent of the dealers' price to cover the handling expenses incurred.

Sales to the bulk market gave branches an average gross margin of about 27 percent.

---

[1] Quantity and cash discounts not considered.

THE FRANCHISING EXPERIMENT

"If we want to maintain our widespread distribution and our dealer family we have got to find a replacement for the hardware stores that are going out of business," Mr. Morton said. "Franchising may offer a solution to this problem."

The franchising experiment in Bridgeville, New Jersey, that he was discussing with Mr. Hilgers and Mr. Oldman had been initiated by the district sales manager in the New Jersey area, Mr. Patrick O'Brien. When a new shopping center went under construction in Bridgeville, a place with 35,000 people, Mr. O'Brien had thought that it would be a suitable location for a home-decorating store. Bridgeville retail paint sales were about $300,000 a year.

Mr. O'Brien explained:

> We didn't think of establishing a company branch there, simply because we already had two branches in a radius of 10 to 15 miles from the shopping center, which provided sufficient coverage of the bulk market in that area. The shopping center looked like a good place, though, for a dealer who wanted to work just in the consumer market. So, we began looking for a man who had enough money plus the determination to set up and run a store for himself.
>
> We talked to a number of people, but they either didn't have the money or they didn't show the willingness to work as hard as you have to in the paint business. When John Kelley was finally found he looked to us like a very ideal person for the store. He had the $21,000 which was needed as the initial investment in fixed assets and working capital; he had the determination to work; he held a Master's degree in business; and he had been a very successful salesman for General Electric for a number of years. Plus, he had a father-in-law, Joe Gardner, who had long years of retail experience and who wanted to help him in the store. So, we went along with John.

No formal contract was concluded between Mr. Kelley and the Belmont Paint Corporation. The company assisted him in negotiating his lease with the landlord, and then the store was set up following closely the proven layout and merchandising pattern for the modernized company stores.

Since both Mr. Kelley and his father-in-law were inexperienced in the paint business, the Belmont Paint Corporation offered to train them before the opening of the store. Mr. Gardner spent 6 weeks working in one of the corporate branches of the district, and the company also provided them with a programmed course designed for the training of its branch managers.

For the opening day in July 1969, Belmont arranged the usual grand opening with local advertisements, balloons, and free samples. Suppliers of non-paint products were urged to supply some free merchandise as well.

Like all dealers, Mr. Kelley was granted the regular cooperative advertising allowance.

Other than the time it took the personnel of the district office to help and advise Mr. Kelley before and after the opening, the establishment of the store required no traceable investment from the Belmont Paint Corporation. In Mr. O'Brien's view the advisory work did not represent any considerable burden for his office.

Mr. Kelley's store was supplied by one of the company's branches in the area. It covered an area of 2,600 square feet and was identified as a Belmont store by a prominently displayed sign. Like the modernized company stores, it carried a broad line of home-decorating products other than paint.

Mr. O'Brien had made it clear to Mr. Kelley that he strongly preferred him not to cater to the professional painter market.

> The painter market is a high risk business which requires a lot of expertise. Well, John wouldn't listen. After the store was opened, he had all the painters coming into his store, and he soon found himself with bad debts. On the whole, John has been very successful, though. His store is well merchandised, and he will make a profit in his first year. Of course, we have no control over what he is doing and how he is actually doing.
>
> I am currently considering opening another franchised store between Milltown and Cedarbrook. We lost one of our dealers there because he switched to a competitor's line.

JOHN KELLEY

Mr. Kelley had started the venture because he wanted to be in business for himself. Before coming to the Belmont corporation, he had contacted a number of other paint companies. Mr. Kelley explained that:

> I decided to go with Belmont because they looked to me as the most professional and the most experienced.
>
> Also, Belmont has a good name. My customers don't come into the store because I am John Kelley, but because I represent the Belmont Paint Corporation. The brand name is very important.
>
> What I liked when I first talked to the Belmont people was that they clearly stated what the facts, what the profit potential, and what the pitfalls in paint retailing are. I knew nothing about the paint business, so I strictly followed their suggestions and their merchandising program. I get all the information I need from them. I just have to pick up the phone or tell the branch salesman, who comes here every Monday and Thursday.
>
> Another thing which makes a small business like this one profitable is that we need very little inventory. Belmont has a one-day delivery service.
>
> They also offered to help me with my bookkeeping, but I didn't want that. I don't want anybody breathing down my neck telling me to do that or do this. Why not become an employee then! Besides, they don't know and don't care what my particular situation requires, and so they can't tell me what to do and how to grow.

Mr. Kelley then went on to praise his relationship with the Belmont Paint Corporation.

> The Belmont corporation is great. There are no frictions and no real problems with them. There have only been minor nuisances in the past, and they could be quickly eliminated.
>
> What I would have liked is somewhat better assistance at the start. Joe, my father-in-law, didn't find the training particularly helpful, and once the store was opened we were practically on our own. They should have been in the store every

week to get us going. Also, they should use a more liberal credit policy. I put in $21,000 initially, of which $4,500 was for store fixtures, most of the rest for inventory. There should have been more working capital.

Another point, I think the company should be more scrutinizing in deciding who may carry their products. A few weeks ago, another dealer, 8 miles away, started price cutting on one of the Belmont lines. I had to follow suit because my customers came in and asked why I charged more for the same product.

The store sure needs a lot of work. Most of my customers here are in the $12,000 to $15,000 income bracket, and it is strictly a do-it-yourself market. They know something about painting, but not much. Most of them are disgusted with the discounters. They want the "old personal touch." Less than 1% just come in, grab a can, and pay—they want advice, suggestions. So I am in the store more than 10 hours a day, and so is Joe. We have a part-time assistant who comes in for the evening hours from 4 to 9. My wife also helps me regularly with the paper work. There is always something to do in the store, even if there are no customers. I make sure that every can of paint is dusted, and I don't accept dented cans. We have a lot of women coming in, and they just don't buy dusty or dented cans.

So far we can be very satisfied with the result of our work. The Belmont people figured that we wouldn't make a profit in the first year, but I am confident now that we will reach full payback of our initial investment of $21,000 in the first year and maybe even make 3% sales profit after tax on top of it. Our sales will run about $120,000 for the year; half of this is on paint and the other half in decorating products. Our expenses are reasonable since most of the people here are members of the family; total expenses are about $2,200 per month of which $1,500 is for rent, heat, electricity, and other overhead, and the rest for salaries. We achieved some savings by looking carefully for the best suppliers for the decorating items. For example, I didn't take the lighting items from Belmont; I got another line much cheaper direct from a small manufacturer.

Mr. Kelley then commented on his plans for the future:

This store is already getting too small. There is a chance that I can add the store next door. This would enable us to broaden our entire assortment, especially the decorating line. I also want to have more stores, and I already have some ideas where to put them. Once I have a chain of stores, one of them will be dealing principally with professional coatings. The painter business is tricky, and I got burned because I didn't listen to Pat O'Brien, who told me to stay out of it. I am more careful now. We are just setting up a special room in the back for the painters with a special entrance, so they don't have to walk through the store. Another idea for the future is that once there are four or five stores I may try to add my own house brand of paint. It cuts out a middleman and gives you more flexibility.

SUMMARY

It was against this background that Mr. Hilgers and his colleagues tried to determine what the company's future policy with regard to franchising should be. One of the questions that had to be answered in this context was whether the Bridgeville experiment could serve as a model for the establishment of other franchised stores.

EXHIBIT 1
PARTIAL ORGANIZATION CHART
Belmont Paint Corporation

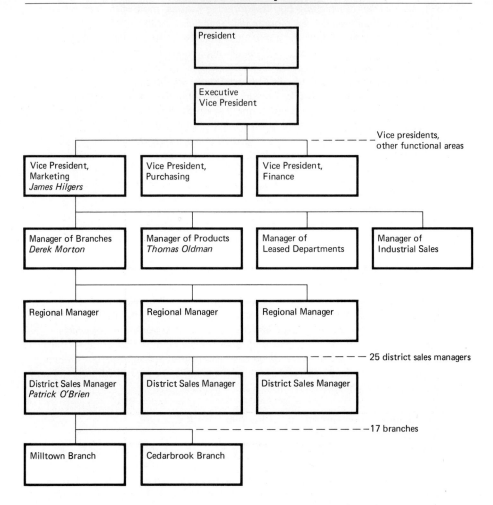

President

Executive Vice President

— — — — Vice presidents, other functional areas

Vice President, Marketing
James Hilgers

Vice President, Purchasing

Vice President, Finance

Manager of Branches
Derek Morton

Manager of Products
Thomas Oldman

Manager of Leased Departments

Manager of Industrial Sales

Regional Manager

Regional Manager

Regional Manager

— — — — 25 district sales managers

District Sales Manager
Patrick O'Brien

District Sales Manager

District Sales Manager

— — — — — — — — 17 branches

Milltown Branch

Cedarbrook Branch

EXHIBIT 2
MAJOR U.S. MANUFACTURERS OF PAINTS, LACQUERS, AND VARNISHES IN 1968
Belmont Paint Corporation

Company	Sales,* $ millions	Company	Sales,* $ millions
Sherwin Williams	200	Minnesota Paints	40
Belmont	154	Benjamin Moore	40
Du Pont	150	National Lead	40
PPG Industries	140	Conchemco	27
SCM (Glidden)	135	Grow Chemical	26
Celanese	80	Reliance Universal	25
Inmont	75	Textron	25
Mobil Chemical	75	Valspar	22
Cook Paint & Varnish	50	Armstrong	20
Pratt & Lambert	45	Total	1,414
O'Brien	45		

* Sales are rough estimates for sales of paints, lacquers, and varnishes at manufacturer's prices only.

Source: Company records.

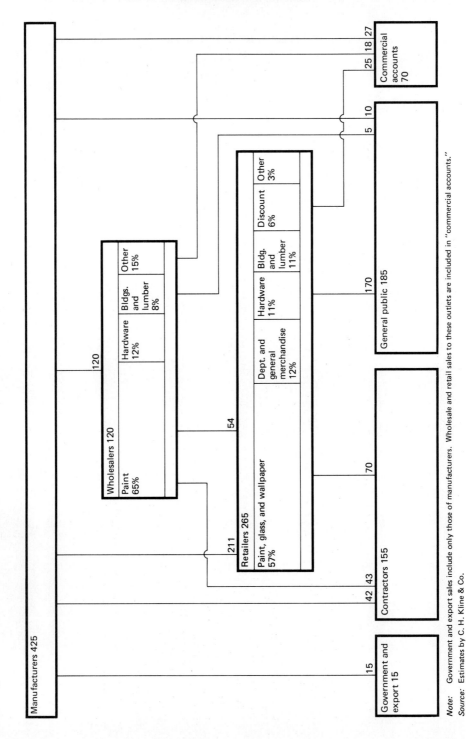

EXHIBIT 3

DISTRIBUTION CHANNELS FOR TRADE-SALES PAINTS, 1968, MILLION GALLONS

Belmont Paint Corporation

Manufacturers 425

Commercial accounts 70 — 25 18 27

General public 185 — 5 10

Wholesalers 120 — 120
Paint 65% | Hardware 12% | Bldgs. and lumber 8% | Other 15%

Retailers 265 — 211
Paint, glass, and wallpaper 57% | Dept. and general merchandise 12% | Hardware 11% | Bldg. and lumber 11% | Discount 6% | Other 3%

54 — 70 — 170

Contractors 155 — 42 43

Government and export 15 — 15

Note: Government and export sales include only those of manufacturers. Wholesale and retail sales to these outlets are included in "commercial accounts."

Source: Estimates by C. H. Kline & Co.

474

EXHIBIT 4
FIVE-YEAR COMPARISON OF FINANCIAL DATA, BELMONT PAINT CORPORATION AND CONSOLIDATED SUBSIDIARIES
Belmont Paint Corporation

Year ended August 31

	1969	1968	1967	1966	1965
Net sales	$247,569,567	$226,263,330	$208,704,610	$201,965,443	$186,005,794
Income before income taxes	15,235,865	18,135,549	18,263,457	20,906,667	20,187,825
Net income after income taxes	9,320,909	9,494,932	9,682,647	11,282,124	10,624,565
Earnings per share of common stock	2.96	3.02	3.10	3.66	3.36
Earnings as percent of sales	3.8%	4.2%	4.6%	5.6%	5.7%
Return on invested capital—common stock*	9.0%	9.6%	10.2%	12.9%	12.8%
Cash dividends declared:					
Preferred	$ 522,588	$ 149,722	$ 139,029	—0—	$ 189,565
Common	5,325,432	5,308,255	5,292,979	$ 4,930,216	4,377,098
Preferred and common shareholders' equity	114,233,475	110,474,893	106,633,369	102,607,544	100,191,932
Common shareholders' equity	101,291,276	97,323,094	93,470,169	89,456,344	83,004,404
Capital expenditures	15,360,859	15,651,699	13,499,128	6,234,831	3,834,894
Provisions for depreciation	4,632,559	3,942,635	3,289,004	2,758,358	2,527,615
Working capital	84,837,742	81,459,324	72,110,757	64,993,657	65,696,925
Ratio of current assets to current liabilities	4.8:1	4.9:1	4.8:1	4.6:1	4.7:1
Total assets	$178,687,248	$162,216,050	$154,436,897	$124,037,217	$120,191,925
Number of employees	10,121	9,702	9,316	9,129	8,580

* Based on common shareholders' equity at beginning of year.

Source: Company records.

475

EXHIBIT 5
CONSOLIDATED BALANCE SHEET, AUGUST 31, 1969
Belmont Paint Corporation

Assets

Current assets:	
Cash	$ 5,700,258
Short-term investments, at cost	—0—
Trade accounts receivable, less allowances	28,377,945
Inventories, at lower of cost or market:	
Finished merchandise	47,664,218
Work in process, raw materials, and supplies	20,333,042
Total current assets	$ 67,997,260
Prepaid expenses	2,977,739
Recoverable federal income taxes	1,094,374
Deferred federal income taxes	1,104,593
Total current assets	$107,252,169
Investments and other assets:	
Common shares of other companies, at cost	2,091,383
Receivables, advances, and miscellaneous assets	1,949,960
	$ 4,041,343
Property, plant and equipment— on the basis of cost:	
Land	2,570,839
Buildings	31,031,080
Machinery and equipment	75,175,042
	$108,776,961
Less allowances for depreciation	41,383,225
	$ 67,393,736
	$178,687,248

Liabilities

Current liabilities:	
Notes payable	$ 1,408,515
Trade accounts payable	6,791,195
Payrolls, compensation, and other accruals	12,523,274
Dividends payable on preferred stock	138,662
Taxes other than income taxes	1,552,781
Income taxes	—0—
Total current liabilities	$ 22,414,427
Long-term debt:	
5.50% debentures with annual payments of $1,000,000 commencing in 1973	25,000,000
Revolving credit notes payable*	12,500,000
	$ 37,500,000
Deferred federal income taxes	3,201,879
Reserves	1,337,467
Shareholders' equity:	
Capital stock:	
Preferred	4,597,719
Common	16,671,078
Other capital	623,921
Retained earnings	92,389,656
	$114,282,374
Less cost of common shares in treasury	48,899
	$114,233,475
	$178,687,248

* A group of banks had made available to the company until December 31, 1970, a revolving credit aggregating $12.5 million at an interest rate equivalent to the prime commercial rate (8.5 percent in March 1970).

Source: Company records.

EXHIBIT 6
STATEMENT OF CONSOLIDATED INCOME
FOR YEAR ENDED AUGUST 31, 1969
Belmont Paint Corporation

Net sales	$247,569,567
Other income—net	659,321
	$248,228,888
Costs and expenses (including depreciation of $4,632,559):	
Cost of products sold	155,426,149
Selling, general, and administrative expenses	72,314,624
Pensions	2,370,156
Interest	2,882,094
	$232,993,023
Income before income taxes	15,235,865
Income taxes	5,914,956
Net income	$ 9,320,909

Source: Company records.

EXHIBIT 7
PERCENTAGE BREAKDOWN OF CONSOLIDATED
NET SALES BY PRODUCT GROUPS IN 1969
Belmont Paint Corporation

Consolidated net sales	100
Finished paint products	62.3
Pigments, colors, and chemicals	13.8
Paint accessories and decoration products*	19.4
Metal containers	4.5

* Mostly purchased from other manufacturers for resale.
Source: Company records.

EXHIBIT 8
CHANNELS OF DISTRIBUTION FOR TRADE PAINTS, PAINT ACCESSORIES, AND HOME-DECORATING PRODUCTS AND SALES VOLUME BREAKDOWN (ROUNDED FIGURES) BY CHANNELS, FISCAL YEAR 1969
Belmont Paint Corporation

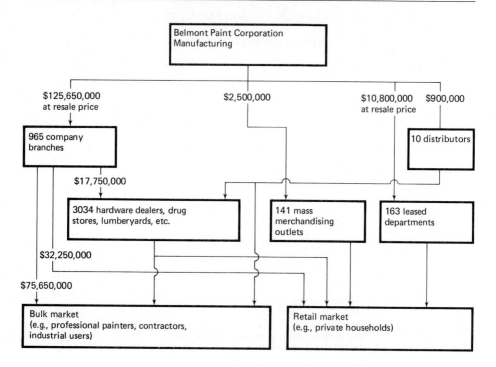

EXHIBIT 9
DEVELOPMENT IN THE NUMBER OF BELMONT RETAIL OUTLETS BY TYPE OF OUTLET, END OF FISCAL YEARS 1963–1969
Belmont Paint Corporation

Year	Company branches	Leased departments
1963	850	2
1964	855	21
1965	857	43
1966	877	64
1967	885	105
1968	906*	131
1969	965†	163

* Includes addition of 14 branches from the consolidation of an acquired paint company.

† Includes addition of 73 branches from the consolidation of an acquired paint company.

Source: Company records.

APPENDIX
EXCERPTS FROM A CONSUMER SURVEY
ON PAINTING, 1968[1]
For the 12-month Period—1967

METHOD

The study was conducted by National Family Opinion, Inc., of Toledo, Ohio, under the supervision of *Better Homes and Gardens*. Respondents were not aware of the identity of the sponsor.

On January 19, 1968, a one-page questionnaire was mailed to a national cross section of 10,000 families. The questionnaire included questions on interior painting, exterior painting, and remodeling. The paint questions were asked in only half the sample, or a total of 5,000 questionnaires, which provided 4,218 returns.

A seven-page follow-up questionnaire was then sent to a sample of 1,239 families who indicated on the first questionnaire that they had done some interior painting in 1967. Ninety-two percent (1,137) of these follow-up questionnaires were completed, returned, and tabulated.

A similar questionnaire was sent to 1,202 families who indicated on the one-page questionnaire that they had done some exterior painting in 1967. Of these follow-up questionnaires 92 percent (1,106) were completed.

RESULTS

The results in the report are presented separately for interior and exterior painting. They are based in part on the respondents to the first questionnaire and in part on the respondents to the follow-up questionnaires.

I. PAINTING ACTIVITY

A. INTERIOR PAINTING

	Total U.S. households, thousands*	Percent†
Did any	27,407	47
Areas painted:		
Walls or ceilings	24,392	89
Basement walls or floors	2,467	9
Woodwork	11,237	41
Cabinets	5,481	20
Other	548	2

* Number is projected to total United States households from percent of sample.

† Percent who did any interior painting is based on the 4,218 total returns. Other percentages are based on the 1,998 respondents in the sample who reported doing some interior painting.

480

[1] *Residential Paint Markets, 1968,* a study of consumers conducted by *Better Homes and Gardens* in cooperation with the National Paint, Varnish and Lacquer Association, Washington, July 1968.

B. EXTERIOR PAINTING

	Total U.S. households, thousands*	Percent†
Did any	16,911	29
Areas painted:		
House (sides & trim)	6,595	39
House (trim only)	7,272	43
Garage	4,397	26
Floors, steps	507	3
Garage trim	676	4
Porches, carports	1,184	7
Fences, railings	507	3
Other buildings	676	4

* Number is projected to total United States households from percent of sample.

† Percent who did any is based on the 4,218 total returns. All other percentages are based on the 1,211 respondents in the sample who reported doing some exterior painting.

II. BRAND OF PAINT

A. INTERIOR PAINTING

Question. Suppose you have decided to paint a room in your house and you have to buy paint. . . .

B. EXTERIOR PAINTING

Question. Suppose you have decided to paint the house this summer; it'll be a do-it-yourself job and you need to buy some paint. . . .

	Interior painting, %*			Exterior painting, %†		
	Yes	No	Did not answer	Yes	No	Did not answer
Are you concerned about whether you buy Brand A or Brand B; that is, are you particular about what brand you buy?	70	26	4	80	15	5
If a brand is suggested to you will it make a difference if it is a "known brand" (or a name with which you are familiar)?	67	27	5	74	21	5
Will you decide ahead of time (before you go to the store) what brand you will buy?	65	30	5	73	21	6
Will you discuss various brands of paint?	57	36	7	64	29	7
Will you think about paint advertising that you've seen previously?	56	38	6	55	38	7

* Percentages are based on the 1,137 total returns.
† Percentages are based on the 1,106 total returns.

III. PURCHASE OF PAINT

A. INTERIOR PAINTING

Question. Who actually purchased the paint?

	Percent*
Husband	36
Homemaker	37
Both	14
Contractor	7
Landlord	2
Other relatives	3
All others	1
Did not answer	1

    * Percentages are based on the 1,137 total returns.

B. EXTERIOR PAINTING

Question. Who actually purchased the paint?

	Percent*
Husband	53
Homemaker	14
Both	10
Contractor	13
Other	3
Don't know	1
Did not answer	6

    * Percentages are based on the 1,106 total returns.

IV. STORE SELECTION

A. INTERIOR PAINTING

Question. Who decided at which store to buy the paint?

	Percent*
Husband	33
Homemaker	28
Both	26
Contractor	7
Landlord	3
Other relatives	2
All others	1
Did not answer	1

    * Percentages are based on the 1,137 total returns.

Question. At what *type* of store did you buy the paint?

	Percent*
Paint store	39
Department store	20
Hardware store	15
Discount store	9
Lumberyard	7
Mail order	3
All others	4
Don't know	2
Did not answer	2

* Percentages are based on the 1,137 total returns.

B. EXTERIOR PAINTING

Question. Who decided what store to go to in order to buy the paint?

	Percent*
Husband	53
Homemaker	7
Both	17
Contractor	14
Other	2
Don't know	1
Did not answer	6

* Percentages are based on the 1,106 total returns.

Question. At what type of store did you purchase this paint?

	Percent*
Paint store	35
Department store	16
Hardware store	16
Lumberyard	9
Discount store	6
Mail order	5
Other	3
Don't know	4
Did not answer	6

* Percentages are based on the 1,106 total returns.

V. INFORMATION REQUIRED—INTERIOR PAINTING

Question. What kind of advice or information about inside painting do you like to have available? (Check three of the following.)

	Percent*
Information on washability	84
How to determine amount of paint needed	71
Cost information	69
How best to apply paint	62
Color information; advice on color schemes	60
How to prepare surfaces	56
Types of paint available; qualities of each	44
Other	2
Did not answer	3

* Percentages are based on the 1,137 total returns and add to more than 100 percent because of multiple responses.

VI. SOURCES OF INFORMATION

Question. If you were looking for information regarding various brands of indoor (or outdoor) paint and the qualities or colors that each have, where would you most likely go for this information?

	Indoor paint, Percent*	Outdoor paint, Percent†
Magazines	37	29
Newspapers	12	18
TV	5	5
Radio		1
Other (where?):	56	62
Dealer	52	53
Another person	4	8
Other	1	1
Did not answer	26	2

* Percentages are based on the 1,137 total returns and add to more than 100 percent because of multiple responses.

† Percentages are based on the 1,106 total returns and add to more than 100 percent because of multiple responses.

VII. PAINT APPLICATION

A. INTERIOR PAINTING

Question. Who actually did the painting?

	Percent*
We did our own painting	87
We let a contract for paint and labor	7
We bought the paint and hired a painter to apply it	5
Did not answer	1

* Percentages are based on 1,137 total returns.

Question. If you did your own painting, who applied the paint?

	Percent*
Husband	33
Homemaker	29
Both	33
Other	10

* Percentages are based on the 989 respondents who did their own painting and add to more than 100 percent because of multiple responses.

B. EXTERIOR PAINTING

Question. When you painted your house, how was the painting done?

	Percent*
Bought paint and applied it myself or with family help	68
Bought paint and hired a painter to apply all of it	8
Bought paint . . . applied part myself; hired a painter to apply part	5
Let a contract for both paint and labor	11
Did not answer	8

* Percentages are based on the 1,106 total returns.

POLYCAST TECHNOLOGY CORPORATION

NANCY J. DAVIS
Research Associate
Harvard Graduate School of Business Administration

STEVEN H. STAR
Associate Professor
Harvard Graduate School of Business Administration

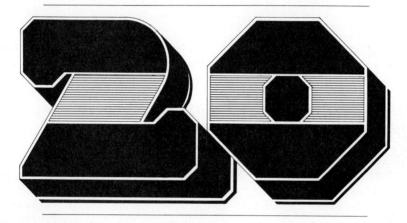

In March 1976, Herbert Engelhardt, president of Polycast Technology Corporation, a manufacturer of cell-cast acrylic sheet, was considering what steps Polycast should take to increase its business both with distributors and with original equipment manufacturers (OEMs). With regard to distributors, there were essentially two problems. First, Polycast's major domestic competitors, Rohm and Haas, which had heavily promoted its brand of acrylic and sheet under the brand name Plexiglas, and, to a lesser degree, American Cyanamid, had both developed very strong relationships with many distributors. It was extremely difficult for another manufacturer to break into this distribution system unless it offered some significant competitive advantage. Second, before 1973, when Herbert Stein, a Boston financier, brought Engelhardt in as president, Polycast had gone through a period of instability during which product quality and marketing practices deteriorated considerably. Though by 1976 most of these problems had been solved, the negative image still lingered in the marketplace. Similar problems hampered Polycast's efforts with OEMs, though most of them tended not to be as tied to manufacturers as were most distributors. However, OEMS posed another problem—they were difficult to identify and to locate. Engelhardt felt it essential that Polycast face these problems head on and begin to build a more solid customer base of both distributor and large OEM accounts.

THE PRODUCT

Polycast manufactured cell-cast acrylic sheet, a product which served primarily as a substitute for glass. Except for the fact that it scratched more easily and was more expensive than normal plate glass, its advantages were substantial. It weighed only half as much as glass, but it was 5 to 17 times more impact-resistant. It could be sawed, filed, shaped, routed, tapped, sanded, cemented, machined, polished, and painted—all with conventional tools. When heated, it could be bent, molded, or drawn. Compared to other substitutes for glass, acrylic sheet was highly resistant to normal chemicals in the atmosphere and to industrial fumes, and it did not become brittle or discolor easily when exposed to the outdoors or to direct sunlight. It could be made in transparent, translucent, opaque, colorless, or colored forms. The colorless sheet was equal in clarity to the finest optical glass and had a light transmission rate greater than 92 percent. Moreover, it was nonconductive and therefore was an excellent electrical and thermal insulator.

Polycast acrylic sheet was used for a multitude of end products. For example, the colorless product was used for windows and doors, transparent tints were used for glare and solar heat control, and patterned surfaces were used for panels when privacy was desired. In addition, it was used for chair mats, signs, lighting fixtures, safety shields for manufacturing, decorating panels, furniture, sky-domes, telephone booths, vending machine covers, and home furnishings such as wine racks, picture frames, trays, fish tanks, shelves, planters, and cutting boards. A bullet-resistant, thicker acrylic sheet was used for banks, payroll offices, and other facilities which required a combination of protection and architectural beauty.

COMPANY HISTORY

Polycast Technology Corporation traced its origins to The Polycast Corporation which was founded in 1955 in Stamford, Connecticut. By the midsixties, The Polycast Corporation was in serious financial trouble, and in 1968, it was reorganized under the provisions of Chapter X of the Federal Bankruptcy Act and the name was changed to Polycast Technology Corporation. The new management, in 1968, was able to secure financing primarily because of a new manufacturing process which had been developed by previous management. This process required a lower capital investment than the more conventional processes used by other manfacturers. In late 1968, Cast Optics Corporation in Hackensack, New Jersey, another cast acrylic sheet manufacturer in financial trouble, was offered for sale and in early 1969, was acquired by Polycast. In 1968 and 1969, Polycast reported sales of $1,407,814 and $3,351,225 and pretax incomes of $422,243 and $789,546, respectively.

Between 1968 and 1972, the new management tried to transform Polycast from a small company relying heavily on government business to a larger company serving the commercial market. However, it had been extremely difficult to open distributor accounts, partly because of inconsistencies in Polycast's products and sales policies and partly because most distributors were loath to endanger the long-term relationships that had been built with Rohm and Haas or American Cyanamid. In an attempt to solve these problems, the then president of Polycast established a separate company which set up about 20 distributor locations. Of Polycast's $5.224 million net sales in 1972, approximately $1.5 million went to miscellaneous distributors and OEMs, and the remainder to the new distributor network. Between 1969 and 1972, however, Polycast encountered problems involving a strike by factory employees, high management turnover, lost records, inadequate controls, and shortage of working capital. By 1972, the company was again in serious financial trouble, and for the years from 1969 to 1972 showed losses every year, totaling almost $4.7 million pretax.

Toward the end of 1972, Herbert Stein agreed to help the company borrow money but only if new management assumed the major role in Polycast's operations. On January 1, 1973, Engelhardt, a 47-year-old businessman who had considerable expertise in dealing with problem companies, became president of Polycast. The situation he inherited was chaotic. There were no internal controls; the books and records were in such disarray that Price Waterhouse and Company refused to give an opinion on them for Polycast's financial reports to the public and the SEC; product quality and sales practices were so inconsistent that the company had a bad reputation with the trade; and almost no one on the management team seemed to know what was going on. Engelhardt began to assemble a new management team. He cabled for help to Ben Danziger, a former business associate who was then the UN's specialist on small-industry development in Liberia. Danziger, who joined Polycast in March 1973, eventually held temporarily every top management job from finance to marketing to production control. Engelhardt also hired a new controller, a new sales manager, a new manufacturing director, and a new personnel manager and appointed a technical director. He also closed the distributorships, since they had consistently lost money since their inception and made relationships with Rohm and Haas or American Cyanamid distributors very difficult to establish.

During the first 9 months of 1973, Polycast encountered severe price competition from other manufacturers. That situation changed drastically in October 1973, however, when the worldwide energy crisis caused raw material shortages, higher costs, and more stable prices. Polycast was fortunate in that its chief supplier of methyl methacrylate monomer (MMA), its major raw material, honored its allocation to Polycast. Polycast, in turn, had to allocate its shipments, as did other acrylic sheet manufacturers, but since it had a steady supply of MMA, it used this opportunity to help establish itself as a reliable supplier. By the end of 1973, Engelhardt and Danziger had upgraded personnel at all levels, improved record keeping and internal controls, cleared out old inventories, established relationships with new customers, resumed normal credit terms with suppliers, and published audited financial statements for the first time in 4 years. They had also repaid debts, resolved lawsuits, set new highs in production and sales, established positive shareholders' equity, and generated $1 million in working capital. On 1973 sales of $9.2 million, Polycast showed pretax earnings of $571,000.

The raw material shortage continued into 1974. Engelhardt remembered, "Every morning I looked at myself in the mirror and said, 'Methyl methacrylate monomer, methyl methacrylate monomer. Where can I get methyl methacrylate monomer?'" Other manufacturers were scouring the globe, making short- and long-term commitments and paying premiums, Engelhardt recalled. "With a turn-around on my hands I couldn't risk expensive commitments. And then we got lucky!" "Luck" came in the form of a decision by Engelhardt to settle out of court a suit in which Polycast was a litigant against a major supplier of MMA. The settlement included an agreement for the supplier to deliver to Polycast a significant amount of MMA during the shortage. Since Polycast had a better relative supply of MMA than did most other manufacturers, it was in a better position to supply acrylic sheets during the 6 months the shortage lasted after the settlement. On 1974 sales of $12.8 million, Polycast's pretax earnings were $2.4 million.

By late 1974, the raw material shortage had ended and the marketplace again became quite price competitive. Again, there was some turnover at high managerial levels, as Engelhardt and his team continued the slow, methodical process of trying to build a new company. Polycast finished 1975 with sales of $10.3 million and pretax earnings of $400,000.

THE MARKET AND COMPETITION

TECHNOLOGY

The process by which Polycast made acrylic sheet was known as *cell casting*. In this process, methyl methacrylate monomer (MMA) and various catalysts were pumped into a plate-glass cell mold of the desired size and thickness. Acrylic sheet was produced when the monomer polymerized due to the action of the catalysts and, depending on the type of cell-cast process, hot air or hot water and steam circulating around the cell.

Acrylic sheet could also be made by two other major processes: extrusion and continuous casting. Extruded sheets were made by feeding already polymerized, granulated MMA into a machine where it was heated to a liquid and forced through a flat orifice. This process was fast, simple, and required relatively low capital investment. Extruded sheet could be manufactured economically only in thicknesses of ⅛ inch and below, and normally sold for 20 percent to 30 percent less than cell-cast sheet. Optical properties, strength, and heat and weather resistance of extruded sheets were inferior to those of cell-cast sheet. Major uses of extruded sheet were ceiling panels and windows.

In continuous casting, MMA was poured between two continuously moving stainless steel belts. Continuous-cast products were of more uniform thicknesses, were easier to handle, and required less labor. However, capital costs were higher, optical qualities were inferior to those of cell-cast sheet, and thicknesses were limited to the range between ⅛ and ⅜ inch. Major end uses of continuous-cast sheet included sanitary ware (e.g., bathtubs, showers, and bathroom bowls), large signs, and other applications where optical qualities were not critical. (See Exhibit 1 for consumption of acrylic sheet by process type, 1965—1980; Exhibit 2 for consumption of acrylic sheet by end use, 1965–1980; Exhibit 3 for consumption of acrylic sheet by end use and process, 1974; Exhibit 4 for estimated consumption and average price of acrylic sheet, 1960—1980; and Exhibit 5 for estimated profitability ranges for acrylic sheet by process type.)

In addition to acrylic sheet (cell-cast, extruded, and continuous-cast), a new polycarbonate-extruded sheet known as Lexan had been introduced into the market by General Electric. Polycarbonate had some properties similar to acrylic; its biggest advantage was even greater break resistance than acrylic sheet, and, therefore, it was especially useful for school and office windows in areas where vandalism was high. However, it was not as clear as acrylic, it discolored more easily, it was softer, and it was more expensive. It was made by a process comparable to extruded acrylic sheet, and it was relatively easy for a manufacturer to switch from making one of these products to the other. (See Exhibit 6 for estimated United States consumption and sales by producers of polycarbonate sheet, and Exhibit 7 for a comparison of acrylic and polycarbonate sheets.)

MANUFACTURERS

In the cell-cast acrylic sheet business, there were four major United States companies—Rohm and Haas, American Cyanamid, Swedlow, and Polycast—plus numerous small companies with annual sales under $1 million. Japanese firms were playing an increasingly important role as their practice of selling at prices substantially below those of United States manufacturers touched off a price war in the industry.

Rohm and Haas, which had been producing acrylic sheet since the thirties, dominated the industry primarily because of its long-standing position of prominence, its well-known Plexiglas brand name, its ownership of the largest facilities in the world for producing MMA raw material which it not only used for its own sheet and other products but also sold to other manufacturers, and its exceptionally strong distribution network. In 1975, over 200 distributors offered Plexiglas as their major acrylic sheet line. One means by which Rohm and Haas had recently strengthened its position with its distributors was its *profit incentive plan.* Under this plan, it set annual quotas for each of its accounts. On any products bought over quota, a distributor received a 20 percent discount in addition to the standard industry discounts.

Rohm and Haas also offered the broadest assortment of colors, sizes, and thicknesses of acrylic sheet and the most comprehensive technical service program. It regularly held seminars for end users such as architects and contractors, it shared its customers' advertising expenses if the Plexiglas name was used, and it supplied its salespeople and distributors with a multitude of promotional pieces. It manufactured both cell-cast and continuous-cast acrylic sheet, and it had recently purchased a small company which had the second largest polycarbonate sheet production facility in the United States. While it was considered a very good company, it was also viewed as conservative, slow moving, and inflexible in its marketing practices. It had been gradually losing market share, especially in its continuous-sheet segment. It had approximately 50 salespeople. In 1975, its total corporate sales were just over $1 billion, about $70 million of which was thought to be in acrylic sheet.

American Cyanamid began manufacturing cell-cast acrylic sheet in 1960 primarily as an outlet for the MMA monomer which was made from by-products of its fiber operations. Its acrylic sheet operation was believed to have been unprofitable for many years due to high overhead, poor plant location, high inventories, and a limited product line. For the most part, it manufactured products of only ⅛- to ½-inch thickness and purchased thicker products from Rohm and Haas. It had managed to break into Rohm and Haas' distribution network by offering an alternative and some degree of flexibility, though it had captured few of Rohm and Haas' really strong distributors. As with the rest of the industry, it also sold directly to some end users. There were reports that it might introduce a continuous-casting facility in the near future. Total corporate sales for 1975 were about $2 billion, about $20 million of which was thought to be in acrylic sheet.

Swedlow was the leading supplier of cell-cast acrylic sheet for windows and canopies of commercial and military jets and helicopters. It had a proprietary stretching process which provided improved toughness and shatter resistance. In the late 1960s, Swedlow pioneered the development of continuous-cast acrylic sheet, and this product had come to account for over 60 percent of Swedlow sales. Its sales force numbered only 15 people, and its marketing policies and product quality were, at least in the beginning, erratic. In 1974, it experienced a sharp profit decline due to the adverse effects of the energy crisis on the sign and recreational vehicle businesses and its inability to obtain sufficient MMA. Total corporate sales for 1975 were $30 million, about $25 million of which was acrylic sheet.

In 1975, Swedlow sold its entire continuous operation for $25 million to Montedison U.S.A., a subsidiary of the multibillion-dollar Italian chemical company which previously produced only cell-cast and extruded sheet in Europe. Exactly what role Montedison would play in the United States acrylic sheet business was not clear. Its purchase of Swedlow's continous-sheet operation surprised many industry observers because of the high price paid, the growing overcapacity in continuous-cast sheet, and the seemingly precarious competitive position in the United States of the Swedlow continuous-cast operation. (See Exhibit 8 for a competitive profile of the various manufacturers and the estimated cell-cast sheet capacity of each.)

DISTRIBUTORS

In 1975, approximately 45 percent of the industry's total acrylic sheet sales, and a larger portion of cell-cast sheet sales, were through plastics distributors. The balance was partly through sign supply or glass distributors directly to fabricators and OEMs, or to the U.S. government via bidding procedures. For an OEM to buy direct, Rohm and Haas normally required that the order be for about $6,000 to $10,000 of merchandise at a time. American Cyanamid's and Polycast's minimum order quantities for OEMs were stated similarly, but in practice were somewhat more flexible.

There were three major chains of plastics distributors[1]—Continental Plastic and Chemical Company and United Plastics and Supply Corporation, both of which had branches throughout the United States, and American Plastics, whose operations were concentrated in the Northeast. In addition, there were about 350 independent plastics distributors.

With over 60 branches, Continental was the largest plastics distributor. It distributed products such as nylon, Teflon, delrin, and manufactured acrylic tubing and rods; moreover, it distributed and sometimes fabricated (cut, polished, and shaped) products such as acrylic sheet, polycarbonates, polyethylene, polypropylene, acetate, and vinyl. In all, Continental distributed over 500 types of products, most of which came in many sizes and variations. Continental sales were estimated to be about $60 million, about 30 percent of which was thought to be in acrylic sheet. Over the years, Rohm and Haas and Continental had developed a very strong relationship, but Polycast had secured approval for its products from Continental headquarters and did sell small amounts of material to some Continental branches. However, the branch manager for the New England region stated that Rohm and Haas had always supplied his acrylic sheet needs quite adequately, and he had no reason to look to other manufacturers. He stated, further, that since acrylic sheet was basically a commodity item, it was among Continental's lower-margin items. Four salespeople reported to this district manager. Each had about 1,000 accounts in his territory, of which about 500 were considered "active," i.e., they purchased more often than two or three times a year. The salespeople averaged about seven calls a day.

[1] Names of all distributors have been disguised.

With over 50 branches, United was the second largest plastics distributor. Like Continental, it both fabricated and manufactured products. Its total sales were estimated to be about $50 million, about $15 million of which was in acrylic sheet. Rohm and Haas was United's chief acrylic sheet supplier, but Polycast had recently been approved as a supplier by United. This meant that branch managers could now purchase from Polycast if they needed or wanted to.

American fabricated and distributed products. Its five branches accounted for sales of about $15 million. Its acrylic sheet sales were about $8 million. American carried primarily Rohm and Haas' acrylic sheet, but occasionally it bought from Polycast.

The operations of the 350 United States independent plastics distributors varied greatly. Some merely bought and resold materials. Many did some fabricating. A few were essentially distributors' distributors in that they inventoried unusual colors and sizes which they resold to other distributors or to OEMs. Still others not only distributed but also manufactured products such as skylights and hockey rink enclosures. Distributors within a given area frequently swapped materials, and they generally knew a lot about each other's operations. "Customers don't hesitate to tell us who we're bidding against and what their offers are," commented one independent distributor. Acrylic sheet often accounted for an important percentage of an independent distributor's sales.

There were about 75 sign supply distributors throughout the United States. Their product lines included virtually everything necessary to make signs— acrylics, polycarbonates, ballasts, frames, electrical wire, paint, letters, some plastics, and so forth. The amount of acrylic sheet purchased by a sign distributor was small when compared to that purchased by most plastics distributors. In fact, many sign supply distributors purchased acrylic sheet from plastics distributors rather than from manufacturers. Acrylic sheet manufacturers seldom tried to sell direct, except to the very large sign manufacturers. Sign supply distributors sold usually to custom sign makers, a far more specialized and homogeneous customer group than that served by plastics distributors.

Since acrylic sheet was rapidly becoming widely used as a glass substitute, many glass distributors now carried it. The largest glass distributor, which had about 150 branches, was owned by a large manufacturer. In addition, there were about 200 independent glass distributors. Acrylic sheet generally accounted for 10 to 20 percent of a glass distributor's sales and was a relatively high-margin item. Glass distributors normally sold to glaziers and contractors.

END USERS

There were essentially three categories of acrylic sheet end users. The first included companies, schools, and other institutions which used the sheet to replace glass windows or for some other functional purpose for their own physical facilities. The second consisted of a wide range of OEMs who used it to manufacture everything from napkin holders to sky-domes. The third consisted of general consumers who bought acrylic sheet to replace glass windows and storm doors or to use in various hobbies. Most end users purchased acrylic sheet from distributors, though some large OEMs and institutions bought direct from the manufacturer.

THE SITUATION AT POLYCAST, MARCH 1976

By early 1976, Engelhardt had assembled what he considered to be a top-notch management team. It was still relatively new, with only Danziger and the heads of manufacturing and technical services at the company for more than 2 years. The controller and the vice president of sales had been with Polycast less than 6 months. All of Polycast's seven top executives received annual salaries over $30,000. "These people are good enough to run a company five times our current size, but they have to be flexible and hard working enough to meet the outrageous demands of a small enterprise struggling for its very existence," Engelhardt said. In all, Polycast employed about 210 people. (See Exhibit 8 for an organization chart.)

In March 1976, Engelhardt stated that Polycast's financial outlook for 1976 was not at all certain. At that time, the price of MMA was high, while the price of acrylic sheet was very depressed due to Japanese firms'[1] dumping of acrylic sheet on the market at very low prices and Rohm and Haas' decision to meet those prices. Engelhardt stated that "at current prices, no one's making money converting MMA to sheet," but that if pricing returned to normal, Polycast should make a reasonable profit. He also said:

> If we made a million dollars, that's one half million after taxes, and our stockholders' equity is about $3.5 million, so that would be about 14 percent return on stockholders' equity, which is not bad. And I think we could even do better with reasonably improved prices. This is a small company where the leverage is high: if anything goes wrong, there's usually a tragedy; and if everything goes right, it's considered all in a day's work.

(See Exhibit 10 for Polycast's operating statements for 1973–1975.)

PRODUCT LINE

In 1976, Polycast made acrylic sheets in 17 thicknesses ranging from 0.060 to 2.00 inches, and 29 sizes ranging from 36 × 48 to 84 × 120 inches. Its opaque sheets came in 21 colors, its transparent sheets in 57 colors, and its translucent sheets in 102 colors. Its standard line consisted of 77 sizes and thicknesses of

---

[1] In early 1976, an antidumping action instituted by Polycast, in the face of widespread industry resignation, led to a preliminary finding that the Japanese had been engaging in dumping. As an apparent result of this action, the Japanese began to substitute equally low-price Taiwanese-manufactured products for products they had previously exported from Japan.

colorless sheets, 110 colors, and 19 textured sheets. Delivery time on standard items was normally 1 week. It also offered a great variety of nonstandard items. Delivery time on these was normally 2 weeks (as compared to 4 to 5 weeks for Rohm and Haas' specialty items), though Polycast could sometimes deliver specialty items in less than 1 week. In addition, Polycast occasionally took orders for products meeting certain specifications set forth by OEMs. Polycast management thought that Rohm and Haas offered about 5 to 10 percent more acrylic sheet items than Polycast, but that other companies offered considerably shorter lines than did Polycast.

About half of Polycast's business consisted of "bread and butter" products (4 × 6 and 4 × 8 feet; in thicknesses of ⅛, ³/₁₆, and ¼ inch; in clear, white, and a few popular colors) which were ordered in standard quantities. All manufacturers made these products, and Engelhardt described price competition for them as "brutal." The other half of Polycast's sales consisted of "service business," i.e., orders which required fast turnaround, small quantities, special colors, and special sizes. The larger sheet manufacturers were not especially interested in "service business" because it disrupted their production-cost-oriented tight scheduling of long production runs of standard items. Engelhardt stated that Polycast was definitely tending toward the service business. During normal times, Polycast's gross margins on standard items were about 20 percent while its gross margin on service items was about 30 percent.

Polycast's list prices and discount policies were standard for the industry under normal conditions. (See Exhibit 11 for Polycast's standard product line and price list as of September 1975.) During normal times, distributors' margins on acrylic sheet ranged from 15 to 25 percent, as compared to 25 to 30 percent on their total product lines. However, with the current industrywide price war, manufacturers' list prices meant very little, and distributors' margins on acrylic sheet often had been reduced to 10 percent or less.

Engelhardt thought Polycast's competitive position, especially with distributors, would be stronger if it offered a wider variety of sizes of regular acrylic sheet or some new product lines. He also thought that delivery from stock and manufacturing orders against a 2-week delivery schedule would strengthen Polycast's position with all distributors. Regarding the regular acrylic sheet line, Engelhardt pointed out that Rohm and Haas made sheet up to 4 inches thick, while Polycast had recently been able to increase its products to 2 inches. He estimated the market for thicker sheets to be only about $5 million, annually, but he thought Polycast could get a good share of this business. He also thought the company could generate an additional $1 to $1.5 million in sheets of larger dimensions if it had adequate capacity. Making any additional sizes, or more of the existing sizes, would necessitate the construction of several new casting machines, estimated to cost about $200,000 each.

One new product line being considered was extruded polycarbonate, the most familiar product being General Electric's Lexan. Getting into this business would cost about $500,000 in equipment and other developmental expenses, $500,000 in start-up expenses, and another $500,000 for working capital to support the business once it started operating. The same equipment would also give Polycast the capacity to extrude acrylic sheet, a fast-growing but low-margin business.

Another product being considered was copolymer biaxially oriented sheet, a stretchable product used primarily for military aircraft. To get into this business could cost Polycast about $200,000. The total annual United States market was estimated to be about $5 million.

ADVERTISING AND PROMOTION

Unlike Rohm and Haas, which had spent large sums of money to establish the Plexiglas name, Polycast did virtually no advertising and promotion. Sales management thought it was unlikely that Polycast would begin to do much consumer advertising but that it would probably start attending trade shows and perhaps do some trade advertising. "Trade advertising is useful to establish an image as a reputable company with our distributors," a Polycast manager commented. "But most of our money will go into personal selling—working with architects and other end users, for example."

CHANNELS OF DISTRIBUTION

In 1975, about 65 percent of Polycast's sales went through distributors, while the remaining 35 percent was sold directly to OEMs. In about 20 of Polycast's distributor accounts, Polycast was responsible for about half the acrylic sheet volume. These tended to be smaller, newer, shorter-line distributors. With the larger, full-line distributors, which were still quite loyal to Rohm and Haas or American Cyanamid, Polycast seldom accounted for more than a very small part of their acrylic sheet sales. Polycast usually sold only fill-in products or specialty items to them.

While Polycast sold to about 20 sign supply distributors, it had as much as half the acrylic sheet business of only one or two. Some of Polycast's earliest customers had been glass distributors and glaziers, who bought small quantities, usually at fairly low prices. By 1975, it had about 10 glass distributors, but it was the major supplier to none of those accounts. (See Exhibit 12 for a breakdown of total industry sales and Polycast's sales by type of channel in 1975.)

THE SALES ORGANIZATION

Polycast's sales organization was headed by Mr. Walter Schneider, who had left a position as national sales manager for one of the major plastic distributors in early 1976. Seven field salespeople reported to him and he was looking for an eighth. The sales force covered the entire United States, and top management handled a few accounts directly. Sales territories were organized geographically, with consideration given to the amount of business available in any given area. On the average, a salesperson had about 100 accounts, which included both distributors and OEMs. He usually visited an important account once or twice a month. Salespeople received a salary plus a bonus based on a sales quota with existing accounts and on opening new accounts. On the average, a salesperson's total income was over $20,000, 10 to 20 percent of which was usually bonus. In addition, Polycast furnished salespeople with a company car, paid all their travel and entertainment expenses, and offered other normal fringe benefits such as health insurance. Engelhardt stated that it cost about $50,000 annually to keep one salesperson on the road.

The salespeople ranged in age from the midtwenties to the midforties. Most had college degrees, though not necessarily in technical areas. Since there had been very high turnover in the sales force, most of the salespeople were new to the acrylic sheet business. Schneider stated that he expected the high turnover to continue for another year as he tried to assemble a force which could do the job Polycast needed. When a new salesperson was hired, he usually spent 2 weeks at company headquarters where he learned about the products, the way orders were processed, the way problems were handled, and generally the way the organization worked. Then he spent "a few days to a couple of weeks" visiting customers with other salespeople.

Schneider stated that there were some "morale" problems among the salespeople, mainly, he thought, because they had not received consistent supervision and guidance. (Schneider was Polycast's fourth sales vice president in less than 4 years.) He said that communication between headquarters and the field sales force had been poor in the past and that the salespeople had not recognized the company's problems, especially with regard to pricing. He felt this problem would be alleviated now that the company had closer supervision of the sales force and had a specific price list. However, with the current intense price competition, salespeople frequently called him to ask if they could sell below list to meet competition.

Schneider felt that sales could approximately double without increasing the size of the sales force. "Ben and Herb have done a lot to establish Polycast as a reliable supplier," he commented. "We have proven to the industry that we are a supplier who can turn out competitive quality products. Our real plus is our service."

In addition to the seven field salespeople, three other people reported to Schneider. A sales assistant handled much of the sales paperwork, customer complaints, and miscellaneous sales-related and secretarial tasks. A marketing assistant followed up sales leads, gathered information for trade shows, and did other marketing-oriented tasks. Polycast also had a customer service group which quoted prices to customers, took and processed orders, and pursued problems related to orders.

Since Polycast had been approved by headquarters or regional offices of the major distributor chains, selling to those chains now involved essentially the same process as did selling to independents. A Polycast salesperson described the selling task as "visiting major accounts regularly, usually every four to six weeks, supplemented by more frequent telephone contact with many accounts."

Polycast salespeople sometimes took orders during visits, but often they only talked with purchasing agents of chain branches or principals of independent distributors, discussed their problems and concerns, and tried to convince them to call Polycast the next time they needed acrylic sheet. Most orders were actually taken by Polycast's customer service group which the distributor telephoned when he needed to purchase material. The salespeople had, in recent months, been instructed to place major emphasis in their calls on convincing distributors of their critical need for a second source.

Visits to four distributors provided some insights into their concerns and the nature of Polycast's selling process:

(1) Carlson Plastics was a family-owned, full-line distributor. The Polycast salesperson estimated its annual sales to be $1 million, about 20 percent of which was in acrylic sheet. Carlson's chief supplier was American Cyanamid, but it also bought a lot of material from Polycast. Moreover, American (a chain distributor) had recently been offering Carlson lower prices than either manufacturer. The salesperson speculated that American was buying material at very low prices from Rohm and Haas, marking it up by 12 or 13 percent, and still selling at prices substantially below Polycast's. The owner of Carlson told the Polycast salesperson, "I'd rather buy from you, but I've gotta go where the dollars are." He stated further than in the past Carlson had "gotten stuck with some bad material from Polycast" and had stopped buying from Polycast for a while. "We started buying from Polycast again primarily because its quality improved and the Polycast representative has been in a lot and has helped us out with problems and special orders whenever he could." Regarding the acrylic sheet business generally, he said, "Many years ago it was the backbone of the industry; now it's like quicksand. Our margins on it are ridiculously low."

When asked what new products he would like to see Polycast develop, he said that products with better abrasion resistance would be attractive to the entire industry and that he was getting a lot of calls for nonglare acrylic sheet, a product which only Rohm and Haas now produced. Concerning polycarbonates, he said that the market was small and that margins were often lower than acrylic sheet margins. He stated further that polycarbonates' chief competition had formerly been extruded acrylic sheet, but prices of imported cast acrylic sheet were now often as cheap as the extruded acrylic. Carlson had four outside salespeople who visited OEMs, and five inside salespeople who took orders from OEMs and other distributors. Each of his four outside salespeople regularly called on 75 to 100 accounts, but there might be as many as 1,000 accounts in any given territory.

(2) The purchasing agent for United's branch was not aware that his regional manager had recently approved Polycast. He estimated that acrylic sheet accounted for 15 to 20 percent of his branch's business. He stated that, at the present time, his chief concern with regard to acrylic sheet was price, but that distributors were also interested in manufacturers' support. "We want manufacturers to sell to distributors only, and not to bypass us and go directly to OEMs," he said. United's branch had three outside salespeople and three inside salespeople. "Most of our orders are still taken by the inside people, but cus-

tomers are increasingly asking our outside people if they can deliver products to them immediately," he said. "They're not inventorying anything! Why should they buy a lot today when they can buy it cheaper tomorrow?"

(3) The Central Plastic Company was both a distributor and an OEM. Its industrial division sold products to industrial customers, and its architectural division manufactured products such as skylights and domes for hockey rinks and handled all orders for anything that had to do with a building. Fourteen salespeople and five representative organizations sold for both divisions. Central's purchasing agent, who bought material for both divisions, stated that he would like to buy a lot more from Polycast than he currently purchased but that Rohm and Haas had a very strong relationship with Central's top management and with architects, and that the architects usually specified Plexiglas in their orders. He estimated that acrylic sheet accounted for 12 to 15 percent of Central's total sales and that the company's gross profit margin on it was now less than 10 percent. While the Polycast representative was visiting the company, he was asked to get price quotations on a particular order. He called headquarters and found that the lowest price he could offer was $1.25 as compared to $1.05 which a competitor was offering. The purchasing agent decided to order from Polycast despite the price difference. The Polycast representative doubted that he would have gotten this order if he had not been at Central at that moment.

(4) Wizard Plastics was a full-line, family-owned fabricator and distributor. Polycast was its chief supplier of acrylic sheet. It usually bought anywhere from $100,000 to $225,000 worth of acrylic sheet annually. It had three outside and three inside salespeople. When visited, the owner said he was bidding for a job against Carlson and asked what prices Polycast could offer on that particular order. The order was very complex in that it required a variety of sizes, some of which could be derived from cutting larger sheets. Wizard had to submit its bid the next morning, so the Polycast representative called Polycast's customer service personnel and requested that they determine the optimum mix of products that would satisfy Wizard's requirements, get the lowest prices possible, and notify him first thing the next morning as to what they could offer. He promised Wizard's owner that he would telephone him early the next morning. Carlson management had not mentioned this order to the Polycast representative when he visited that company earlier in the day.

According to Schneider, most distributor salespeople tended not to be technically oriented, and he preferred that Polycast's salespeople deal directly with OEMs when a technical problem arose. He said that a lot of distributor "selling" was done via the telephone. He estimated that the average annual income of a distributor salesperson, who was compensated by a straight salary, was between $10,000 and $15,000, while some who worked on commission might make $30,000 or more annually.

A Polycast salesman stated that the most difficult task in selling to commercial OEMs was finding them in the first place. He had searched through various industrial directories, but 95 percent of the leads generated in this manner had been dead ends. He said that distributors usually would not tell him who their major OEMs were because they were afraid of losing accounts, but they would tell him about OEMs who were buying direct from Rohm and Haas or American Cyanamid. Once he found an OEM account, he encountered a new set of problems in that larger OEMs often had purchasing agents, engineers, and other technical people involved in the decision-making process, and relationships had to be maintained with all these people. Moreover, the task of selling to OEMs usually involved bidding on a certain piece of business, and OEMs often played off manufacturers and distributors against each other in an attempt to get a low price. OEMs sometimes ordered products according to specifications regarding shape, dimensions, and various tolerances, and on such orders they often needed technical advice from the acrylic manufacturer.

Continental's district manager said that with large OEMs his salespeople usually began with the purchasing agents, but they also often dealt with maintenance supervisors, safety coordinators, and engineers. He said that, for the more complicated sales, a single call might last from 1½ to 3 hours and several such calls might be required. According to his salespeople, their customers currently bought acrylic sheet on the basis of price, service, and quality, in that order.

The owner of Carlson said that, in addition to servicing their regular OEMs, his salespeople spent a lot of time looking for new customers. "A salesperson can canvass a whole industrial park in an afternoon," he said. "We consider anyone who might be thinking about switching from glass to acrylic to be a potential customer." He went on to say that his regular customers demanded a lot of "maintenance selling" because they would call whomever they thought of first when they needed something. Only one distributor said that price was relatively insignificant to his customers. He said that they looked for a distributor who was dependable, gave them good service, and sold top-quality products.

Various branches of the government were considered OEMs. However, selling to them differed from selling to commercial OEMs in that manufacturers were required to submit sealed bids on specific jobs and thus had no idea what prices they were bidding against.

CONCLUSION

As Engelhardt reviewed Polycast's current situation, he enumerated several strengths. He thought the company management team was getting into good shape and that it had a clear, comprehensive view of the market. He thought further that Polycast now manufactured an extensive line of high-quality products, even though he wanted to expand the line more in the direction of specialty products.

The major factor restricting Polycast's growth, Engelhardt thought, was its distribution system. He said:

> We're being held back by the difficulty of convincing the distributors of their need for a second source, by our inability to find OEMs, and by our inability to compete in this price war. To a significant extent, we're selling the orders our competitors can't supply or can't supply quickly. We've got to find a way to break into the normal distribution channels.

EXHIBIT 1

CONSUMPTION OF ACRYLIC SHEET
BY PROCESS TYPE, 1965–1980 (Millions of pounds)
Polycast Technology Corporation

Year	Cell cast	Continuous cast	Extruded	Total
1965	125	*	5	130
1970	170	10	10	190
1974	163	57	35	255
1975	155	47	23	225
1980 (est.)	185	90	60	335

* In development.

Source: Butcher and Singer, *The Outlook for Acrylic Sheet,* Oct. 6, 1975; and R. M. Kossoff & Associates, Inc. (Reprinted by permission.)

EXHIBIT 2
ESTIMATED CONSUMPTION OF ACRYLIC SHEET
BY END USE, 1965–1980 (Millions of pounds)
Polycast Technology Corporation

End use	1965	1970	1974	1980 (est.)	Compounded growth rate, % 1965–1974	1974–1980
Signs	70	95	100	120	3.3	3.1
Glazing	15	25	45	80	10.4	9.6
Lighting	15	25	35	40	9.6	2.2
Floor mats	5	20	20	25	12.8	3.8
Sanitary ware			10	20	NA	13.0
Architectural	5	10	20	25	14.3	4.6
Military/gov't	2	3	4	5	7.2	7.1
Other OEM*	14	12	20	25	4.0	4.0
Total	130	190	255	335	7.8	5.0

* Indicates aircraft, furniture, safety, display, etc.

Source: Butcher and Singer, *The Outlook for Acrylic Sheet,* Oct. 6, 1975; and R. M. Kossoff & Associates, Inc. (Reprinted by permission.)

EXHIBIT 3
CONSUMPTION OF ACRYLIC SHEET BY END USE AND PROCESS, 1974 (Millions of pounds)
Polycast Technology Corporation

End use	Cell cast	Continuous cast	Extruded	Total	%
Signs	70	29	1	100	39.3
Glazing	27	8	10	45	17.7
Lighting	13		22	35	13.7
Floor mats	17	3		20	7.8
Sanitary ware		16	1	17	6.6
Architectural*	18	1	1	20	7.8
Military/gov't.	5			5	1.9
Other OEM†	13			13	5.2
Total	163	57	35	255	100.0

* Includes skylights, building facings, and facades.

† Includes furniture.

Source: Butcher and Singer, *The Outlook for Acrylic Sheet,* Oct. 6, 1975; and R. M. Kossoff & Associates, Inc. (Reprinted by permission.)

EXHIBIT 4
ESTIMATED CONSUMPTION AND AVERAGE PRICE OF ACRYLIC SHEET, 1960–1980
Polycast Technology Corporation

Year	Overall sheet consumption, million lb	Average price, $/lb	Total value, $ million
1960	70	0.77	54
1965	130	0.72	94
1970	190	0.65	123
1974	255	0.88	224
1975	225	0.85	190
1980 (est.)	335	1.10*	369*

* Polycast estimate.

Source: Butcher and Singer, *The Outlook for Acrylic Sheet,* Oct. 6, 1975; and R. M. Kossoff & Associates, Inc. (Reprinted by permission.)

EXHIBIT 5
ESTIMATED PROFITABILITY RANGES FOR ACRYLIC
SHEET BY PROCESS TYPE (Cents per pound)
Polycast Technology Corporation

	Cell cast	Continuous	Extruded
Selling price	90–95	80–85	75–85
Costs			
Monomer or other	28–36	28–36	50–55*
Labor	8–12	5–6	2–3
Plant overhead (including depreciation)	8–12	16–25	5–7
Administrative	10–12	10–12	5–6
Selling expenses	10–15	8–12	5–6
Miscellaneous	5–6	5–6	3–4
Total	71–93	72–97	70–80
Pretax profit (loss)	26–2	8–(12)	15–5

* Cost of molding powder.

Source: Butcher and Singer, *The Outlook for Acrylic Sheet,* Oct. 6, 1975;
and R. M. Kossoff & Associates, Inc. (Reprinted by permission.)

EXHIBIT 6
ESTIMATED CONSUMPTION OF
POLYCARBONATE SHEET, 1965–1980
Polycast Technology Corporation

	Consumption	
Year	Million lb	$ million
1965	2	3
1970	4	6
1974	20	30
1975	15	25
1976 (est.)	20	34
1977 (est.)	45	60–65

Current producers of polycarbonate sheet

	Estimated PC sales, 1974	
Company	$ million	%
General Electric (Lexan)	20	67
Rohm and Haas	6	20
Others	4	13
	30	100

Source: Butcher and Singer, *The Outlook for Acrylic Sheet,* Oct. 6, 1975; and R. M. Kossoff & Associates, Inc. (Reprinted by permission.)

EXHIBIT 7
COMPARISON OF ACRYLIC AND POLYCARBONATE SHEET
Polycast Technology Corporation

	Acrylic sheet	**Polycarbonate sheet**
Est. sales volume, 1975	$185 million	$20–$25 million
Proj. growth rate, 1975–1980	12.5%	22%
Major production methods	Casting and extrusion	Continuous extrusion
Proprietary techniques	Continuous casting, stretching	Press polishing, use of additives
Price, $/lb	$0.85–$1.00	$1.60–$1.70
Marketing	Mostly distributors	Mostly distributors
Advantages	Better optics, better weather resistance, lower price	Better impact resistance, thinner sheets give equal properties
Disadvantages	Poor chemical and abrasion resistance	Poor chemical abrasion and weather resistance, higher price

Source: Butcher and Singer, *The Outlook for Acrylic Sheet,* Oct. 6, 1975; and R. M. Kossoff & Associates, Inc. (Reprinted by permission.)

EXHIBIT 8
COMPETITIVE PROFILE OF ACRYLIC SHEET MANUFACTURERS AND ESTIMATED CELL-CAST SHEET CAPACITY OF EACH
Polycast Technology Corporation

Company	1974 est. sales		Types produced	Strengths	Weaknesses	Estimated cell-cast sheet capacity, 1974	
	$ million	%				Million lb	%
Rohm and Haas	125	54	Cell casting and continuous	Plexiglas trademark, distribution, largest in MMA monomer	Conservative, slow moving, losing market share	115	58
American Cyanamid*	30	13	Cell casting	Monomer	Uneconomical plant size, weak distribution	40	20
Polycast	13	6	Cell casting	Efficient casting process	Distribution, no monomer	25	12
Swedcast (Montedison)	15	7	Continuous	Good continuous process	No monomer in U.S., distribution		
Swedlow	5	2	Stretched (cell casting)	Good process	Distribution, no monomer	5	2
Other	12	5	Cell casting			15	8
Extruded sheet producers	30	13	Extruded	Simplicity, low cost	Ease of entry, no monomer		
Total	230	100				185	100
Estimated 1975 sales of cell-cast sheet						155	
Excess capacity						30	

* Joint venture with Rohm GmbH (a large European acrylic specialist) was announced in June 1976.

Source: Butcher and Singer, *The Outlook for Acrylic Sheet,* Oct. 6, 1975; and R. M. Kossoff & Associates, Inc. (Reprinted by permission.)

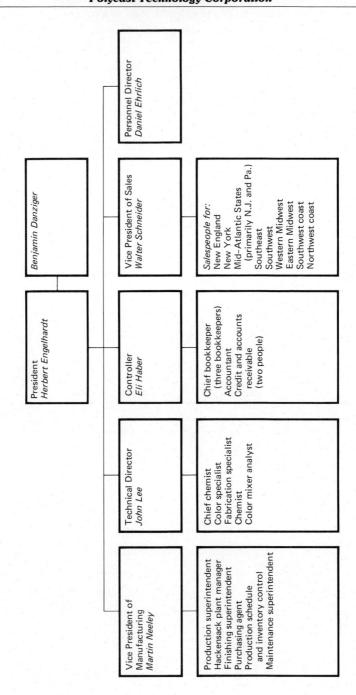

Benjamin Danziger

President
Herbert Engelhardt

Personnel Director
Daniel Ehrlich

Vice President of
Manufacturing
Martin Neeley

Technical Director
John Lee

Controller
Eli Haber

Vice President of Sales
Walter Schneider

Production superintendent
Hackensack plant manager
Finishing superintendent
Purchasing agent
Production schedule
and inventory control
Maintenance superintendent

Chief chemist
Color specialist
Fabrication specialist
Chemist
Color mixer analyst

Chief bookkeeper
  (three bookkeepers)
Accountant
Credit and accounts
  receivable
  (two people)

Salespeople for:
New England
New York
Mid–Atlantic States
  (primarily N.J. and Pa.)
Southeast
Southwest
Western Midwest
Eastern Midwest
Southwest coast
Northwest coast

EXHIBIT 10
OPERATING STATEMENTS, 1973–1975
(Thousands of dollars, except earnings per share)
Polycast Technology Corporation

	1973	1974	1975
Net sales	$9,206	$12,821	$10,318
Cost and expenses:			
Cost of goods sold	5,770	7,762	7,772
Selling, general, and administrative expenses	2,536	2,579	2,166
Interest (net)	302	101	(34)
	8,608	10,442	9,905
Earnings (loss) before income taxes and extraordinary items	598	2,379	413
Taxes on income:			
Federal	268	1,073	188
State	27	103	21
	295	1,176	209
Earnings (loss) before extraordinary items	303	1,203	204
Extraordinary items:			
Benefit of tax loss carry-forward	268	1,073	390
Income from settlement with former management			222
Net earnings (loss)	$ 571	$ 2,276	$ 816
Earnings (loss) per share:			
Before extraordinary items	$0.27	$1.04	$0.16
Extraordinary items	0.24	0.92	0.49
Net earnings (loss)	$0.51	$1.96	$0.65

EXHIBIT 11
PRICE LIST, EFFECTIVE SEPTEMBER 2, 1975
(Prices per square foot in standard packages for standard sizes)
Polycast Technology Corporation

Thickness, inches	Colorless sheet		White translucent sheet		Color sheet	
	Unmasked	Masked	Unmasked	Masked	Unmasked	Masked
0.060	$0.92	$1.02	$ 1.13	$ 1.23	$ 1.25	$ 1.35
0.080	0.92	1.02	1.13	1.23	1.25	1.35
0.100	0.91	1.01	1.12	1.22	1.25	1.35
0.125	0.94	1.04	1.13	1.23	1.23	1.33
0.150	1.11	1.21	1.28	1.38	1.37	1.47
0.187	1.22	1.32	1.40	1.50	1.50	1.60
0.220	1.36	1.46	1.53	1.63	1.66	1.76
0.250	1.49	1.59	1.65	1.75	1.80	1.90
0.312	2.24	2.34	2.53	2.63	2.78	2.88
0.375	2.76	2.86	3.40	3.50	3.40	3.50
0.500	3.76	3.88	4.57	4.69	4.57	4.69
0.625	4.68	4.80	5.72	5.84	5.72	5.84
0.750	5.63	5.75	6.86	6.98	6.86	6.98
0.875	6.59	6.71	7.98	8.10	7.98	8.10
1.000	7.52	7.64	9.11	9.23	9.11	9.23
1.125	8.47	8.59	11.23	11.35	11.23	11.35
1.250	9.42	9.54	13.34	13.46	13.34	13.46

Thickness, inches	Colorless sheet, unmasked	White translucent and color sheet, unmasked
Textured DP-30; Textured P-30		
0.125	$1.03	$1.29
0.187	1.29	1.57
0.220	1.42	1.72
0.250	1.54	1.87
Textured DP-32 Silhouette **Textured P-32 Silhouette**		
0.125	$1.11	$1.29
0.187	1.35	1.57
0.220	1.49	1.72
0.250	1.63	1.87
Textured P-4		
0.125	$1.16	$1.29
0.187	1.43	1.57
0.220	1.55	1.72
0.250	1.66	1.87

POLY II UVA, MILITARY PRICE LIST

Thickness, inches	Colorless sheet, masked
0.060	$1.62
0.080	1.78
0.100	1.90
0.125	2.04
0.150	2.19
0.187	2.43
0.220	2.64
0.250	2.85
0.312	3.69
0.375	4.42
0.500	5.90

POLYCAST MP 1.25

Thickness, inches	Bullet-resisting sheet
1.25	$9.54

EXHIBIT 12
TOTAL INDUSTRY SALES AND POLYCAST'S SALES BY CHANNEL TYPE, 1975 (Millions of dollars)
Polycast Technology Corporation

	Total industry sales (est.)	Polycast's sales
Plastics distributors	130	$ 2.9
Sign supply distributors	39	0.8
Glass distributors	39	0.8
Commercial OEMs	52	3.7
U.S. government	5	2.1
Total	265	$10.3

PRICING POLICY

The determination of price strategies and of individual product prices is of major importance to marketing managers. Through pricing, management attempts to recover the costs of the separate elements in the marketing mix—the product itself, associated advertising and personal selling expenses, and the various services provided to consumers by the channels of distribution—as well as to generate residual profits for the firm.

From a consumer viewpoint, the price of a product is the amount payable for the benefits offered by the "bundle" of attributes represented by the "extended" product and its supporting services. Changes in the nature of this bundle may increase or reduce not only the marketer's costs but also the price that the consumer is willing to pay. One of the marketing manager's tasks, therefore, is to determine the optimal trade-off position for the firm.

Consequently, pricing policy should be seen in perspective as one of several interdependent elements in the marketing mix. Economic theorists have historically tended to exaggerate the role of price as a determinant of demand at the expense of such nonprice variables as promotion and distribution. The economic concept of pricing generally emphasizes the level of price charged, overlooking such important marketing considerations as how prices are paid by consumers. "Can I charge it?" or "What terms can you give me?" may be equally or more important to consumer purchase decisions than the basic "How much is it?"

An organization's pricing objectives are normally derived from its overall marketing strategy and may change over time in response to changing conditions, both in the marketplace and in the firm's own resources. A common trade-off conflict is between short-run profits versus sales and market share targets which may enhance profits in the long run.

Pricing policies must take into account not only the response of the ultimate consumer or industrial buyer but also the needs and characteristics of intermediaries in the channels of distribution. Sufficient margins must be offered at each level of distribution to make it financially attractive for the distributor to carry the product.

Finally, pricing policies may reflect a communications objective. Many firms cultivate a "value for money" image and are anxious to ensure that each item in the line reflects this image, even if some are only marginally profitable as a result. Taking this policy a step further, some firms may offer one or more "loss leaders"—perhaps on just a temporary basis—to attract attention to the entire product line. At the other end of the spectrum are situations in which the marketer seeks to enhance the quality image of the product by deliberately charging a relatively high price.

Apart from organizational goals, a number of other factors also serve to influence prices and pricing policies. These include the cost structure of the firm, the price elasticity of both primary and selective demand, the competitive structure of the industry in which the firm is competing, product characteristics and the availability of supply relative to demand, and also legal considerations.

COST STRUCTURE

Several aspects of an organization's cost structure need to be considered: (1) the level of variable costs per unit and the extent to which these are likely to form a high proportion of selling price, (2) the level of fixed costs, (3) the potential for economies of scale, and (4) a firm's costs relative to those of its competitors.

When an organization is operating with high fixed costs and relatively low costs per unit, such as a hotel or airline operating below capacity, the incremental cost of accommodating new guests or passengers is comparatively little in relation to the prices charged. Under such circumstances, earnings may rise sharply if sales increase. Capital-intensive organizations such as this are termed volume-sensitive.

Alternatively, the reverse may be true: Fixed costs may be comparatively low and variable costs per unit fairly high. Clothing products and certain foodstuffs are examples of products with a substantial material and/or labor content. Since competition tends to force prices down, unit contribution is often low and even substantial increases in sales volume may not improve earnings by a large dollar amount. On the other hand, an increase in price may have a significant impact on dollar earnings. In such instances, profitability is said to be price-sensitive.

A simple example (Table 1) will illustrate these two situations. Imagine two products: A, where variable costs amount to 90 percent of the selling price, and B, where they only amount to 10 percent. For convenience, let us say that the manufacturer's selling price is $1 in both instances and that current sales of each are 1,000 units.

For product A, increasing price by 10 percent doubles unit contribution, whereas for B it only rises by 11 percent. However, increasing sales by 20 percent only adds $20 to the gross contribution of product A versus $180 for product B.

The first set of calculations assumes no price elasticity, but if demand were to fall by 10 percent as a result of a 10 percent increase in price, product A would still show an 80 percent increase in gross contribution whereas product B's gross contribution would be unchanged. If we assume that some incremental marketing expenses would be required to increase sales by 20 percent—say, an

TABLE 1

	Present situation		Increase price 10%		Increase sales 20%	
	A	B	A	B	A	B
Price	$1.00	$1.00	$1.10	$1.10	$1.00	$1.00
Less	0.90	0.10	0.90	0.10	0.90	0.10
Unit contribution	$0.10	$0.90	$0.20	$1.00	$0.10	$0.90
Gross contribution:						
× 1,000 units	$100	$900	$200	$1,000		
× 1,200 units					$120	$1,080
× 900 units			$180	$ 900		

extra $100 on advertising—then the incremental *effect on contribution for* A *would be (+ $20 − 100) = − $80; for* B *it would be (+ $180 − 100) = + $80.*

This example illustrates not only the impact of variable cost structure on pricing decisions, but also the need for marketing managers to evaluate the price elasticity of demand (discussed below) and the extent to which sales volume is a function of marketing effort.

The potential for economies of scale presents opportunities for some firms, since manufacturing, marketing, or administrative efficiencies as the scale of operations increases may result in reduced costs per unit, thus providing an opportunity to enhance both profits and unit market share.

PRICE ELASTICITY OF DEMAND

A key factor influencing pricing decisions is the sensitivity of demand for the product in question to changes in selling prices. If demand rises (falls) sharply when prices are lowered (increased), then demand is said to be highly elastic. Conversely, if demand is little affected by price changes, it is said to be inelastic.

The price sensitivity of demand for a particular product category reflects the importance of the product for consumers, the income level of present consumers, the existence of substitute products, the extent to which potential exists for increasing consumption (i.e., is demand close to saturation?), and whether or not the product in question is merely a small component in a much larger entity.

The price sensitivity of demand for a given product category is not necessarily the same as that for an individual brand within that category. The less differentiated individual brands are in the eyes of the consumer, the more difficult it is for one marketer to charge a premium price without losing substantial market share. Conversely, a small price cut by one firm may lead to substantial increases in selective demand. Since such situations tend to lead to destructive price competition, one of the industry's larger firms may emerge as a price leader.

It is important to recognize that price elasticity for a particular product category is not necessarily constant but may vary between different price levels and also over time. For instance, the demand for air travel between two cities might change relatively little between (say) $20 and $30 but prove to be highly price-elastic between $13 and $20. This could reflect the presence of two different market segments: one consisting of consumers who are not price-sensitive and see no viable alternative to flying, and a second of consumers with limited funds who are willing to travel by more time-consuming modes such as cars or buses which cost (say) $12 per trip.

The marketing manager may also find that, although some price changes have little immediate effect on demand, clear trends become apparent later. For instance, a sharp increase in electricity prices might not result in an immediate decline in consumption. However, usage behavior and living habits could change over time, and eventually many consumers might choose to purchase more efficient electrical appliances. Likewise a long-term reduction in the cost of an industrial chemical could gradually stimulate development of new applications.

COMPETITIVE STRUCTURE OF THE INDUSTRY

The number of firms in an industry often has a direct effect on pricing policy. When many competitors are selling an undifferentiated product, such as an agricultural commodity, individual marketers have little discretionary power to influence the prices at which they sell. In the absence of government regulation or the presence of a cartel, price is set by free market conditions and the marketer has little option but to accept it.

At the other extreme are those marketers who have no direct competition for a needed product. In theory, monopolists have complete discretionary power to establish their own selling prices. However, in practice, government regulatory bodies (as in the case of public utility commissions overseeing electricity and telephone companies) often set the rate structure which the company has to accept. Even where no regulations exist, many monopolists choose not to set prices which will maximize profits, either for ethical reasons or for fear of attracting new regulatory controls or new competitors.

In oligopolistic situations, where there are relatively few competitors, as in the steel or heavy electrical industries, it is common to find one or two of the principal firms acting as price leaders. Other firms are often content to follow this lead, settling for a stable market share in return for an acceptable margin of profits. Although the industry leaders have some discretionary influence over selling prices in such situations, they risk losing this role if their own prices stray too far from those dictated by underlying supply and demand forces in the industry.

As well as evaluating the nature and extent of existing competition, the marketing manager must also appraise potential entrants to the industry before establishing a pricing policy. If barriers to entry are high—due to the need for substantial capital investments and/or access to scarce resources or expertise—then the prospect of new entrants may be remote. However, high prices and high earnings within an industry may attract new competitors who are prepared to make the necessary investment for entry. Recognizing this, many firms in oligopolistic industries adopt low, "keep out" prices, preferring lower earnings now to the prospect of additional competitors in the future.

Typically, a firm attempts to escape from the constraints that industry structure imposes on pricing policy by differentiating other elements of the marketing mix. Analysis of competitive offerings, distribution channels, and consumer needs will provide insights into the extent to which such differentiation is both realistic and operationally feasible.

A final consideration concerns the level of the firm's costs relative to those of the competition. A low-cost situation makes it possible to choose between enjoying extra profits, allocating more resources to marketing activities in an effort to build sales, or initiating an aggressive, low-price strategy. A firm with relatively high costs lacks this flexibility and will probably seek to avoid a low-price strategy because this will put it at a financial disadvantage relative to competitors with similar or larger sales volumes.

LEGAL CONSIDERATIONS

In formulating price strategy, the marketing manager must also take into account governmental legislation and policy relating to pricing practices in the business community. Both state and federal laws may impact on pricing decisions, but the discussion here will be confined to a brief look at federal legislation.

The most significant laws in the United States relating to pricing are the Sherman Act of 1890, the Clayton Act of 1914, and the Robinson-Patman Act of 1936 which amended the Clayton Act and created the Federal Trade Commission. The Sherman Act was passed to control the activities of the giant trusts of the late nineteenth century and made it explicit that collusive activities by companies to fix prices, or to attempt to fix prices, were illegal.

The Clayton Act and its amendment, the Robinson-Patman Act, speak to the issue of price discrimination but their provisions are subject to interpretation. The basic thrust of these acts is to make it unlawful for any person or firm in interstate commerce "to discriminate in price between different purchasers . . . where the effect of such discrimination may be substantially to lessen competition or tend to create a monopoly in any line of commerce."

Pricing policies are said to be discriminatory when a firm sells the same product at different prices to different buyers who are competing with one another. Hence it is not discriminatory for a marketer to sell to wholesalers and retailers at different prices, since the two are not in direct competition. The law only allows price discrimination in certain circumstances, such as meeting the price of a competitor in good faith or when the price differential is cost-justified (e.g., volume discounts where it can be demonstrated that there are economies of scale in production runs, order processing, and handling).

In recent years, the Federal Trade Commission has taken an active role in proceeding against pricing practices which are alleged to be unfair to consumers. Examples include limiting the extent and duration of "sale" prices and preventing firms from advertising discounts from so-called "list prices" for goods in product categories where consumers are never, in fact, required to pay the full list price.

PRICING POLICIES FOR NEW PRODUCTS

In establishing the price for a new product, the characteristics of the product itself play a central role. If it is merely a "me-too" item, not strongly differentiated from competitive offerings, then the level of existing prices may prove the crucial determinant. However, greater price discretion may be available to the marketer of a distinctively different product which has no close substitutes and is unlikely to be imitated in the short term.

Other inputs to the pricing decision include an analysis of the market, prospective consumer segments, existing or potential competitors, and the needs of the trade. Management must estimate the potential volume of demand in each major segment and the speed with which this demand will develop. These may be sensitive to changes in both the price and the level of marketing effort. Sometimes a new product may be test-marketed at different prices in matched cities in order to obtain a better feel for the sensitivity of demand to these variables.

An evaluation of competitive activity, if any, will provide details of the competitors' price range and the terms they offer the trade. It may also help the marketer evaluate the possibility of price retaliation by firms marketing products likely to be displaced by the newcomer.

Communications and distribution decisions likewise have implications for pricing. The larger the communications budget, the higher fixed costs will be, while the margin requirements of different distribution channels may impact upon the ex-factory selling price and/or the recommended retail selling price.

By reviewing all these factors and undertaking a sensitivity analysis of the economic implications of alternative strategies, the marketing manager may be able to resolve the question of whether to adopt a skim or penetration policy.

Skimming is usually limited to distinctively different products. It involves setting a high initial price which skims the cream of demand at the outset, yielding high profits during the period before competition enters the market and prices start to fall. High initial prices are sometimes employed as a means of restricting demand at the outset when supplies of the product are limited. Market penetration is the opposite approach. It involves use of a low price to stimulate market growth and enable the firm to gain a dominant position, hopefully preempting competition and ensuring long-run profitability.

As the product matures and competitive activity increases, periodic evaluations will be necessary to ensure that the pricing policy is realistic in the light of market conditions and the objectives of the firm.

SUMMARY

Pricing policy should be seen in perspective as one of several interdependent elements in the marketing mix, relating not only to economic goals but also to the needs and characteristics of distributors, as well as being congruent with product positioning and communications objectives.

Other factors influencing pricing policies include the cost structure of the firm, the price elasticity of demand, the competitive structure of the industry, and legal considerations. When introducing new products, greater flexibility in setting prices is available when the product is distinctively different from existing market offerings.

SOUTHWEST AIRLINES: II

CHRISTOPHER H. LOVELOCK
Assistant Professor
Harvard Graduate School of Business Administration

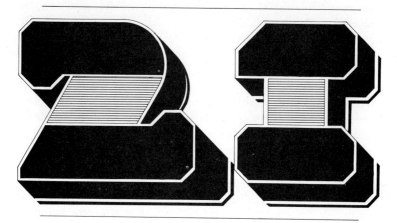

BRANIFF'S "GET ACQUAINTED SALE": HALF PRICE TO HOUSTON'S HOBBY AIRPORT trumpeted the headlines on the full-page advertisement in the February 1, 1973, edition of *The Dallas Morning News*.

M. Lamar Muse, president of Southwest Airlines, held up the advertisement for members of the airline's management team and advertising agency executives to see, commenting as he did so:

> *OK, gentlemen, at least we now know what Braniff's response to our San Antonio promotion will be. They are hitting us hard in our only really profitable market. Every decision they have made to date has been the wrong decision, so how can we turn this one to our advantage?*

SOUTHWEST AND ITS COMPETITION

Southwest Airlines Co. had been organized as a Texas corporation in March 1967 with the objective of providing improved quality air service between the cities of Dallas, Houston, and San Antonio. These cities, each 190 to 230 miles apart, formed a triangular route structure in eastern Texas. Southwest had been certified as an intrastate carrier on these routes by the Texas Aeronautics Commission in February 1968, but lawsuits by Braniff International Airways and Texas International Airlines (TI) had delayed initiation of service until June 1971.

The Dallas–Houston market, the largest of the three, was dominated by Braniff, which carried some 75 percent of the local traffic on that route during the first half of 1971 (Exhibit 1). A major international carrier with an all-jet fleet of 74 aircraft, Braniff's systemwide revenues in 1970 were $325.6 million, and it carried 5.8 million passengers. Southwest's other principal competitor, Texas International, served the Southern and Southwestern United States and Mexico. In 1970 TI had a fleet of 45 aircraft, carried 2.2 million passengers, and generated $77.8 million in total revenues.

There was considerable public discontent with the quality of service provided by these two carriers on intrastate routes within Texas—a fact which Southwest hoped to exploit. Among other things, their local flights typically represented segments of longer, interstate flights, and it was often hard for local passengers to get seats.

After carefully assessing costs, Southwest settled on a $20 fare for each route. This compared with existing Braniff and TI coach fares of $27 from Dallas to Houston and $28 from Dallas to San Antonio. Management hoped that Southwest could anticipate an initial price advantage, although Braniff and TI would probably reduce their own fares promptly.

Southwest executives had calculated that an average of 39 passengers per flight would be required to break even. They considered this level of business (and better) a reasonable expectation in light of the market's estimated potential for growth and the frequency of flights which Southwest planned to offer. Nevertheless, they predicted a period of deficit operations before this break-even point was reached.

OPERATING EXPERIENCE

Southwest finally inaugurated scheduled revenue service with a blaze of publicity on June 18, 1971. The airline offered all coach class flights and introduced a number of innovations and attractions, including new Boeing 737 twin-jet aircraft, fast ticketing, glamorous hostesses, and inexpensive, exotically named drinks. Service was initially confined to the Dallas–Houston and Dallas–San Antonio routes, although Southwest also had authority to fly between Houston and San Antonio.

Despite extensive promotion, initial results were hardly spectacular. Between June 18–30, 1971, Southwest had an average of 13.1 passengers per flight on its Dallas–Houston service and 12.9 passengers on the Dallas–San Antonio route; passenger loads during the month of July showed only marginal improvement (Exhibit 3). Both competitors had met Southwest's lower fares immediately, as well as improving the frequency and quality of their services on the two routes served by the new airline, and heavily promoting these changes.

Management concluded that it was essential to improve schedule frequencies to compete more effectively with those of Braniff and TI. This became possible with the delivery of the company's fourth Boeing 737 in late September 1971, and on October 1, hourly service was introduced between Dallas and Houston and flights every 2 hours between Dallas and San Antonio.

Surveys of Southwest passengers departing from Houston showed that a substantial percentage would prefer service from the William P. Hobby Airport, 12 miles southwest of downtown Houston, rather than from the new Houston Intercontinental Airport, 26 miles north of the city. Accordingly, arrangements were completed in mid-November for 7 of Southwest's 14 round-trip flights between Dallas and Houston to be transferred to Hobby Airport (thus reopening this old airport to scheduled commercial passenger traffic). Additional schedule revisions made at the same time included a reduction in the number of Dallas–San Antonio flights to four round trips each weekday, inauguration of three round trips daily on the third leg of the route triangle between Houston (Hobby) and San Antonio, and elimination of the extremely unprofitable Saturday operation on all routes.

These actions contributed to an increase in transportation revenues in the final quarter of 1971 over those achieved in the third quarter, but Southwest's operating losses in the fourth quarter fell only slightly, from $1,006,000 to $921,000 (Exhibit 4). At year's end 1971, Southwest's accumulated deficit stood at $3.75 million (Exhibit 2).

Although the majority of ticket sales were made over the counter at the airport terminals, sales were also made through travel agents and to corporate accounts (Exhibit 6). Travel agents received a 7 percent commission on credit card sales and 10 percent on cash sales. Corporate accounts—companies whose personnel made regular use of Southwest Airlines—received no discount but benefited from the convenience of having their own supply of ticket stock (which they issued themselves) and of receiving a single monthly billing. The vice president–marketing was responsible for a force of six sales representatives whose job was to develop and service both travel agents and corporate accounts, encouraging maximum use of Southwest through distribution of point-of-sale materials and pocket timetables, development of package arrangements, etc. Sales representatives also promoted Southwest's air freight business, which featured a special rush delivery service for packages.

Between October 1971 and April 1972, average passenger loads system-wide increased from 18.4 passengers per flight to 26.7 passengers. However, this was still substantially below the number necessary to cover total costs per trip flown, which had been tending to rise (Exhibits 4 and 5).

It had become evident that the volume of traffic during the late morning and early afternoon could not realistically support flights at hourly intervals. It was also clear that most Houston passengers preferred Hobby Airport to Houston Intercontinental, and the decision was made to abandon the latter airport altogether.

On May 14, 1972, Southwest Airlines introduced a new schedule which reduced the total number of daily flights between Dallas and Houston from 29 to 22, primarily by cutting service in the 9:30 A.M. to 3:30 P.M. period from hourly to every 2 hours. Eleven flights daily continued to be offered on the Dallas–San Antonio route and six between San Antonio and Houston (Hobby). Braniff quickly retaliated by introducing its own service from Dallas to Hobby and undertook an extensive publicity program promoting this airport.

From a financial viewpoint, the most significant aspect of Southwest's actions was that the new schedule made it possible for the company to dispose of its fourth Boeing 737. Experience had shown that the 737s could be turned around (i.e., loaded and unloaded) at the gate in as little as 10 minutes. This meant that an hourly schedule on the Dallas–Houston run could be maintained with only two aircraft, instead of three. With the slack provided by the reduced midday frequencies and a schedule which involved periodically flying an aircraft around all three legs of the route triangle, management concluded that a total of three aircraft would suffice and that the fourth could be sold. Southwest had no trouble finding a ready buyer for this aircraft and made a profit of $533,000 on reselling it. The combination of capital gain, lower operating costs, and a continued increase in revenues resulted in a reduction of the quarterly net loss from $804,000 to $131,000 between the first and second quarters in 1972 (Exhibit 4).

CHANGES IN PRICING STRATEGY

For some months, Southwest had been experimenting with a $10 fare on Friday evening flights after 9:00 P.M. In May this reduced fare was extended to post-9:00 P.M. flights on a daily basis. The result was sharply higher load factors on these discount flights relative to the average achieved on full-fare flights (Exhibit 3).

June 1972 saw Southwest Airlines celebrating its first birthday. This provided an opportunity for more of the publicity stunts for which the airline was already becoming renowned. Posters were hung inside the aircraft and in the waiting lounges, the aircraft cabins were decorated, and there was an on-board party every day for a week. This activity, promoted by newspaper advertising, generated considerable publicity for the airline and, in management's view, reinforced Southwest's image as the plucky, friendly little underdog which had now survived an entire year against powerful, entrenched competition.

At this point, Southwest management decided it was time to take a hard look at the fare structure and its relationship to costs and revenues. They soon concluded that the airline could no longer afford a $20 fare on daytime flights. New tariffs were therefore filed with the Texas Aeronautics Commission, effective July 9, 1972; these raised Southwest's basic one-way fare from $20 to $26, established a round-trip fare of $50, and offered a $225 Commuter Club Card, entitling the purchaser to unlimited transportation on all routes for 30 days.

The key consideration was how the competition would react. "For a few days," admitted the vice president–marketing, "we were really sweating."

Braniff's initial response was to devote an additional aircraft to its Dallas–Hobby Airport flights on July 11, thus permitting them to offer on-the-hour service most hours of the business day. However, on July 17, Texas International increased their fares to the same level as Southwest's; then on July 21 Braniff met all aspects of the fare and on-board service changes, also adding a $10 Sundowner flight to Hobby at 7:30 P.M. As a result of Braniff's increased service and the higher fares, Southwest's patronage fell back by 2 percent between the second and third quarters of 1972, but transportation revenues increased.

During September new advertising was launched, based on the slogan "Remember What It Was Like Before Southwest Airlines?" which Southwest's advertising agency saw as a war cry to rally consumers. The principal media used in this campaign were billboards and television. TV commercials cited the advantages of flying Southwest, notably its dependable schedules.

At the end of October, another major change was made in pricing strategy. The $10 discount fares, which had never been advertised, were replaced by half-fare flights ($13 one way, $25 round trip) on the two major routes each weekday night after 8 P.M. Saturday flights were reintroduced, and *all* weekend flights were offered at half fare. An intensive 3 week advertising campaign accompanied these new schedules and price changes, using 1-minute radio commercials on country and western, top forty, and similar type stations[1] (Exhibit 10). The response was immediate, and November 1972 traffic levels were 12 percent higher than those in October—historically the best month of the year in Southwest's commuter markets.

In the new year, management turned its attention to its largest single remaining problem. The company was now actually making money on its Dallas–Houston flights but still incurring substantial losses in the Dallas–San Antonio market. Southwest offered only 8 flights a day on this route versus 34 by its major competitor (Exhibits 8 and 9) and in January was averaging a mere 17 passengers on each full-fare flight. The Dallas–San Antonio market had not grown as rapidly as had Dallas–Houston, and Southwest held a smaller market share (Exhibit 7).

Management concluded that unless a dramatic improvement in patronage was quickly achieved on this route, they would have to abandon it. They decided to make one last attempt to obtain the needed increase and on January 22, 1973, announced a "60-Day Half-Price Sale" on *all* Southwest Airlines flights between Dallas and San Antonio. This sale was promoted by TV and radio advertising. If successful, it was Lamar Muse's intention to make this reduced fare permanent, but he felt that by announcing it as a limited period offer, it would stimulate consumer interest even more effectively while also reducing the likelihood of competitive response. Exhibit 11 shows a sample radio script.

The impact of these half-price fares was even faster and more dramatic than the results of the evening and weekend half-price fares introduced the previous fall. By the end of the first week, average loads on Southwest's

---

[1] A top forty station is one which specializes in playing currently popular rock music recordings.

Dallas–San Antonio service had risen to 48 passengers per flight and continued to rise sharply at the beginning of the following week.

On Thursday, February 1, however, Braniff employed full-page newspaper advertisements to announce a half-price "Get Acquainted Sale" between Dallas and Hobby on all flights, lasting until April 1 (Exhibit 12). However, fares on Braniff's flights between Dallas and Houston Intercontinental remained at the existing levels.

Lamar Muse immediately called an urgent management meeting to decide what action Southwest should take in response to Braniff's move.

EXHIBIT 1
SOUTHWEST AIRLINES AND COMPETITORS: AVERAGE DAILY LOCAL PASSENGERS CARRIED IN EACH DIRECTION, DALLAS-HOUSTON MARKET
Southwest Airlines: II

	Braniff*		Texas Int.*		Southwest		Total local market† (one direction)
	Psgrs.	% of mkt.	Psgrs.	% of mkt.	Psgrs.	% of mkt.	passengers
1967	416	86.1	67	13.9			483
1968	381	70.2	162	29.8			543
1969	427	75.4	139	24.6			566
1970							
1st half	449	79.0	119	21.0			568
2d half	380	76.0	120	24.0			500
Year	414	77.5	120	22.5			534
1971:							
1st half	402	74.7	126	23.4	10	1.9	538
2d half	338	50.7	120	18.0	209	31.3	667
Year	370	61.4	123	20.4	110	18.2	603
1972:							
Jan.	341	48.3	105	14.9	260	36.8	706
Feb.	343	47.6	100	13.9	277	38.5	720
Mar.	357	47.5	100	13.3	295	39.2	752
Apr.	367	48.3	97	12.8	296	38.9	760
May	362	48.5	84	11.3	300	40.2	746
June	362	46.8	81	10.5	330	42.7	773
1st half	356	48.0	93	12.5	293	39.5	742
July	332	48.1	74	10.7	284	41.2	690
Aug.	432	53.7	56	6.9	317	39.4	805
Sept.	422	54.9	55	7.2	291	37.9	768
Oct.	443	53.1	56	6.7	335	40.2	834
Nov.	439	50.6	55	6.3	374	43.1	868
Dec.	396	52.1	56	7.4	308	40.5	760
2d half	411	52.1	59	7.5	318	40.4	788
Year	384	50.1	77	10.0	306	39.9	767
1973:							
Jan.‡	443	51.5	62	7.3	354	41.2	859

* These figures were calculated by Mr. Muse from passenger data which Braniff and TI were required to supply to the Civil Aeronautics Board. He multiplied the original figures by a correction factor to eliminate interline traffic and arrive at net totals for local traffic.

† Excludes figures for another carrier which had about 1 percent of the local market in 1969 and 1970.

‡ Projected figures from terminal counts by Southwest personnel.

Source: Company records.

EXHIBIT 2
BALANCE SHEET AT DECEMBER 31, 1972, 1971, AND 1970
Southwest Airlines: II

	1972	1971	1970
Assets			
Current assets:			
Cash	$ 133,839	$ 231,530	$ 183
Certificates of deposit	1,250,000	2,850,000	
Accounts receivable:			
Trade	397,664	300,545	
Interest	14,691	35,013	
Other	67,086	32,569	100
	479,441	368,127	100
Less allowance for doubtful accounts	86,363	30,283	
	393,078	337,844	100
Inventories of parts and supplies, at cost	154,121	171,665	
Prepaid insurance and other	75,625	156,494	31
Total current assets	2,006,663	3,747,533	314
Property and equipment, at cost:			
Boeing 737-200 jet aircraft	12,409,772	16,263,250	
Support flight equipment	2,423,480	2,378,581	
Ground equipment	346,377	313,072	9,249
	15,179,629	18,954,903	9,249
Less accumulated depreciation and overhaul allowance	2,521,646	1,096,177	
	12,657,983	17,858,726	9,249
Deferred certification costs less amortization	371,095	477,122	530,136
	$15,035,741	$22,083,381	$539,699
Liabilities and stockholders' equity			
Current liabilities:			
Notes payable to banks (secured)	$ 950,000	$	$
Accounts payable	124,890	355,539	30,819
Accrued salaries and wages	55,293	54,713	79,000
Other accrued liabilities	136,437	301,244	
Long-term debt due within 1 year	1,226,457	1,500,000	
Total current liabilities	2,493,077	2,211,496	109,819
Long-term debt due after 1 year:			
7% convertible promissory notes		1,250,000	
Conditional purchase agreements—Boeing Financial Corp. (1½% over prime rate)	11,942,056	16,803,645	
	11,942,056	18,053,645	
Less amounts due within 1 year	1,226,457	1,500,000	
	10,715,599	16,553,645	
Contingencies:			
Stockholders' equity			
Common stock, $1.00 par value, 2,000,000 shares authorized, 1,108,758 issued (1,058,758 at Dec. 31, 1971)	1,108,758	1,058,758	372,404
Capital in excess of par value	6,062,105	6,012,105	57,476
Deficit	(5,343,798)	(3,752,623)	
	1,827,065	3,318,240	429,880
	$15,035,741	$22,083,381	$539,699

Notes to financial statement not shown here.
Source: Southwest Airlines Co. *Annual Reports,* 1971 and 1972.

EXHIBIT 3
MONTHLY FLIGHTS AND PASSENGER COUNTS
ON EACH ROUTE BY TYPE OF FARE
Southwest Airlines: II

| | Dallas–Houston | | | | Dallas–San Antonio | | | |
| | Full fare | | Discount | | Full fare | | Discount | |
Month	Psgrs.*	Flights	Psgrs.*	Flights	Psgrs.*	Flights	Psgrs.*	Flights
June 1971†	3.6	276			1.9	148		
July	10.3	642			5.2	346		
Aug.	11.3	672			4.8	354		
Sept.	11.7	612			4.8	327		
Oct.	14.6	764			6.5	382		
Nov.	14.0	651	0.1	3	4.2	240		
Dec.	14.5	682	0.2	5	4.0	165		
1971 total	80.0	4,299	0.3	8	31.4	1,962		
Jan. 1972	16.0	630	0.2	4	2.8	141		
Feb.	15.9	636	0.2	4	2.8	142		
Mar.	17.9	664	0.4	5	3.9	204	0.3	5
Apr.	17.4	601	0.3	4	4.3	185	0.3	4
May	17.1	554	1.5	30	3.5	177	0.7	21
June	16.5	474	3.3	47	3.8	170	1.4	31
July	13.6	447	4.0	47	3.3	162	1.8	31
Aug.	15.7	496	4.0	50	3.2	177	1.8	31
Sept.	13.7	436	3.8	53	3.1	154	1.6	30
Oct.	16.0	474	4.8	71	3.4	173	1.8	27
Nov.	15.1	403	7.4	104	2.4	122	4.2	77
Dec.	12.8	377	6.3	91	2.4	117	3.9	69
1972 total	187.7	6,192	36.2	510	38.9	1,924	17.8	326
Jan. 1973‡	15.1	404	6.8	101	1.4	75	6.3	122

* In thousands.
† Part-month only.
‡ Estimated figures.

EXHIBIT 3
Continued

San Antonio–Houston

Month	Full fare Psgrs.*	Flights	Discount Psgrs.*	Flights	Total: all routes Psgrs.*	Flights
June 1971†					5.5	424
July					15.5	988
Aug.					16.1	1,026
Sept.					16.4	939
Oct.					21.0	1,146
Nov.	0.9	72			19.1	966
Dec.	1.7	134			20.4	986
1971 total	2.6	206			114.0	6,475
Jan. 1972	2.0	128			20.9	903
Feb.	2.1	134			20.9	916
Mar.	2.8	146			25.4	1,024
Apr.	2.3	130			24.7	924
May	2.5	138			25.3	1,020
June	2.6	140			27.6	862
July	2.1	131			24.7	818
Aug.	2.4	146			27.0	900
Sept.	2.2	127			24.4	800
Oct.	2.5	139			28.5	884
Nov.	2.3	123	0.5	16	32.0	845
Dec.	2.0	110	0.5	16	27.8	780
1972 total	27.8	1,592	1.0	32	309.2	10,676
Jan. 1973‡	2.4	120	0.5	16	32.5	838

* In thousands.
† Part-month only.
‡ Estimated figures.
Source: Company records.

EXHIBIT 4
QUARTERLY INCOME STATEMENTS*
Southwest Airlines: II

	1971		1972			
	Q3	**Q4**	**Q1**	**Q2**	**Q3**	**Q4**
Transportation revenues†	887	1,138	1,273	1,401	1,493	1,745
Operating expenses:						
Operations & maintenance	1,211	1,280	1,192	1,145	1,153	1,156
Marketing & gen. admin.	371	368	334	366	313	351
Depreciation & amortiz.	311	411	333	334	335	335
Total	1,893	2,059	1,859	1,845	1,801	1,842
Operating profit (loss)	(1,006)	(921)	(586)	(444)	(308)	(97)
Net interest revenues (costs)	(254)	(253)	(218)	(220)	(194)	(204)
Net income (loss) before extraordinary items	(1,260)	(1,174)	(804)	(664)	(502)	(301)
Extraordinary items	(571)‡	(469)‡		533§		
Net income (loss)	(1,831)	(1,643)	(804)	(131)	(502)	(301)

* In thousands of dollars.

† Includes both passenger and freight business. Freight sales represented 2 percent of revenues in 1972.

‡ Write-off of preoperating costs.

§Capital gain on sale of one aircraft.

Source: Company records.

528

EXHIBIT 5
INCREMENTAL COSTS PER FLIGHT
AND PER PASSENGER, 1971–1972*
Southwest Airlines: II

Category	Last half 1971	First half 1972	Last half 1972
Incremental costs per flight			
Crew pay	$ 46.62	$ 50.61	$ 56.82
Crew expenses and overnight	5.28	4.24	4.93
Fuel	93.50	93.35	94.91
Airport landing fees	10.44	12.87	12.37
Aircraft maintenance	69.98	69.51	75.19
	$225.82	$230.58	$244.22
Variable costs per passenger			
Passenger-handling personnel	$1.09	$0.88	$0.80
Reservation costs†	0.92	0.11	0.10
Ramp, provisioning, and baggage handling‡	0.98	0.40	0.29
Baggage claims and interrupted-trip expenses	0.01	0.01	0.01
Passenger beverage and supplies	0.25	0.13	0.43
Traffic commissions and bad debts	0.61	0.62	0.74
Passenger liability and insurance§	0.90	0.38	0.43
	$4.76¶	$2.53	$2.80

* Includes all costs treated as variable by Southwest management for the purposes of planning and analysis.

† Initially, Southwest contracted out its reservation service to American Airlines; after October 1, 1972, Southwest's own employees handled this task.

‡ Initially contracted on a minimum cost-per-flight basis, subsequently used own employees on a phased schedule as facilities permitted.

§ During the last half of 1971, Southwest paid a minimum total premium for passenger liability insurance due to the low number of passengers carried.

¶ Comment by management: "The high figure for costs per passenger during the last half of 1971 represents the effect of minimum staffing with very few passengers. The minimum-staffing effect declines substantially in later periods, and begins to represent a true variable."

EXHIBIT 6
TICKET SALES BY OUTLETS, JULY 1971–JANUARY 1973
Southwest Airlines: II

Month	Counter	Travel agents*	Corporate accounts*	Total
July 1971	$245,177		$28,193	$273,370
Aug.	238,780		48,111	286,891
Sept.	260,511		40,105	300,616
Oct.	328,578		46,828	375,406
Nov.	293,507		54,432	347,939
Dec.	308,510		57,902	366,412
Jan. 1972	325,495	$46,923	$16,020	388,438
Feb.	318,604	43,211	16,335	378,150
Mar.	378,508	53,520	17,005	449,033
Apr.	375,120	49,434	17,560	442,114
May	364,327	55,240	20,125	439,692
June	399,235	52,337	16,110	467,682
July	384,336	44,590	14,390	443,316
Aug.	439,712	49,423	19,477	508,612
Sept.	409,743	45,263	11,746	466,752
Oct.	467,847	64,303	22,399	554,549
Nov.	491,227	80,086	22,111	593,424
Dec.	461,751	50,516	14,472	511,739
Jan. 1973 (est.)	516,355	63,317	16,013	595,685

* Noncounter sales were not broken out separately for travel agents and corporate accounts until January 1972.

Source: Company records.

530

EXHIBIT 7

ESTIMATED MARKET SIZE, DALLAS–HOUSTON AND DALLAS–SAN ANTONIO ROUTES*

Southwest Airlines: II

	Local passengers carried annually (both directions)			
	1969	**1970**	**1971**	**1972**
Dallas–Houston:				
Braniff	268,630	265,910	246,170	300,780
Texas Intl.	91,690	70,950	69,790	51,010
Other	4,390	4,790	1,830	1,910
Southwest			80,187	223,581
	364,710	341,650	397,977	577,281
Dallas–San Antonio:				
Braniff	144,010	124,690	135,660	177,020
Texas Intl.	10,400	15,040	5,290	1,800
American	4,100	4,120	3,600	2,580
Other	520	560	380	330
Southwest			31,302	56,653
	159,030	144,410	176,232	238,383

* These estimates were made by Southwest Airlines' economic consultant in New York.

    Source: Company records.

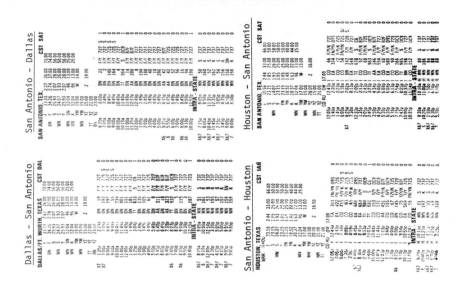

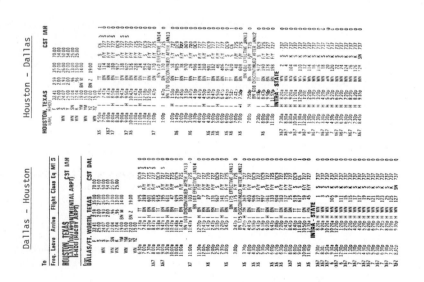

EXHIBIT 8
Continued

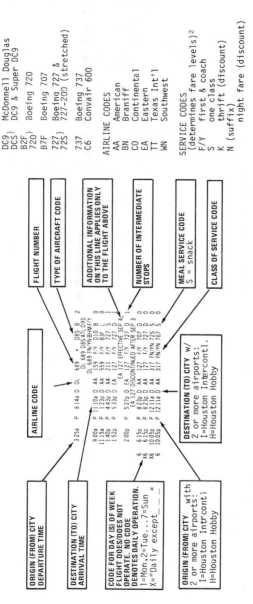

AIRCRAFT CODES[1]

DC9} McDonnell Douglas
DCS} DC9 & Super DC9
B2F}
720} Boeing 720
B7F} Boeing 707
727} Boeing 727 &
72S} 727-200 (stretched)
737 Boeing 737
C6 Convair 600

AIRLINE CODES
AA American
BN Braniff
CO Continental
EA Eastern
TT Texas Int'l
WN Southwest

SERVICE CODES
(determines fare levels)[2]
F/Y first & coach
S one class
K thrift (discount)
N (suffix)
night fare (discount)

ORIGIN (FROM) CITY DEPARTURE TIME

DESTINATION (TO) CITY ARRIVAL TIME

CODE FOR DAY (S) OF WEEK FLIGHT DOES/DOES NOT OPERATE. NO CODE DENOTES DAILY OPERATION.
1=Mon, 2=Tue...7=Sun
X="Daily except____"

ORIGIN (FROM) CITY with 2 or more airports:
I=Houston Intrcontl
H=Houston Hobby

AIRLINE CODE

FLIGHT NUMBER

TYPE OF AIRCRAFT CODE

ADDITIONAL INFORMATION ON THIS LINE APPLIES ONLY TO THE FLIGHT ABOVE

NUMBER OF INTERMEDIATE STOPS

MEAL SERVICE CODE
S = snack

CLASS OF SERVICE CODE

DESTINATION (TO) CITY w/ 2 or more airports.
I=Houston Intercontl.
H=Houston Hobby.

[1] Although the type of aircraft on each flight was known to Southwest, it was not possible to calculate the total capacity offered on each route since an unknown number of seats on other airlines' flights were blocked for interstate (as opposed to local) passengers. All aircraft were jets except for the Convair 600 turboprop. Column 3 indicates the one-way fare (including tax) and column 4 the round-trip fare.

[2] Fares for each service class on each route appear at the top of each route listing.

Source: World Airline Guide, North American edition, January 1973.

533

EXHIBIT 9
ANALYSIS OF WEEKLY FLIGHT SCHEDULES BY
SOUTHWEST AND COMPETING CARRIERS, JANUARY 1973
Southwest Airlines: II

Dallas–Houston*

	Mon-Fri total I	Mon-Fri total H	Sat I	Sat H	Sun I	Sun H	Total week
Braniff	80	35	8	5	12	7	147
Texas Intl.	45		6		9		60
Southwest		55		2		5	62
Total	125	90	14	7	21	12	269

Houston*–Dallas

	Mon-Fri total I	Mon-Fri total H	Sat I	Sat H	Sun I	Sun H	Total week	Full fare	Discount
Braniff	70	45	9	7	12	7	150	297	
Texas Intl.	49		6		10		65	125	
Southwest		55		3		4	62	100	24
Total	119	100	15	10	22	11	277		

Dallas–San Antonio

	Mon-Fri total	Sat	Sun	Total week
Braniff	85	16	15	116
Texas Intl.	10	1	2	13
American	10	2	2	14
Southwest	20	1	3	24
Total	125	20	22	167

San Antonio–Dallas

	Mon-Fri total	Sat	Sun	Total week	Full fare	Discount
Braniff	85	14	17	116	232	
Texas Intl.	5	1	1	7	20	
American	10	2	2	14	28	
Southwest	20	2	2	24	30	18
Total	120	19	22	161		

San Antonio–Houston†

	Mon-Fri total	Sat	Sun	Total week
Braniff	5		1	6
Texas Intl.	10	2	2	14
American	5	1	1	7
Continental	45	9	9	63
Eastern	20	4	4	28
Southwest	15	1	1	17
Total	100	17	18	135

Houston†–San Antonio

	Mon-Fri total	Sat	Sun	Total week	Full fare	Discount
Braniff	10	2	1	13	19	
Texas Intl.	15	3	3	21	35	
American	5	1	1	7	14‡	
Continental	45	9	9	63	126‡	
Eastern	20	4	4	28	56‡	
Southwest	15	1	1	17	30	4
Total	110	20	19	149		

* I = flights to/from Houston Intercontinental; H = Houston/Hobby.
† Southwest flights on this route used Houston-Hobby Airport; all other airlines used Houston Intercontinental.
‡ Some flights offered thrift or night fares with savings of $3–$5 over regular fare.
Source: Exhibit 8.

EXHIBIT 10
SAMPLE RADIO COMMERCIAL FOR HALF-FARE, OFF-PEAK FLIGHTS, FALL 1972
Southwest Airlines: II

NUMBER: **98-23-2**   *Length:* **60 sec (Dallas version)**   *Date:* **10/13/72**

- MUSIC: Fanfare
- ANNCR: Southwest Airlines introduces the Half-Fare Frivolity flights.
- HOSTESS: Now you can afford to fly for the fun of it.
- SFX: LAUGHTER OF ONE PERSON BUILDING FROM UNDER, WITH MUSIC
- ANNCR: Now you can take any Southwest Airlines flights any week night at eight o'clock and all flights on Saturday or Sunday for half-fare. Just $13 or $25 round trip.
- SFX: LAUGHTER, MUSIC OUT. STREET SOUNDS UNDER.
- MAN: You mean I can visit my uncle in Houston for only $13?
- ANNCR: Right.
- MAN: That's weird. My uncle lives in St. Louis.
- MUSIC: MEXICAN FIESTA SOUND
- CHICANO: Take your wife or lover on a Southwest Airlines Half-Fare Frivolity Flight to San Antonio this weekend. Float down the river while lovely senoritas strum their enchiladas and sing the beautiful, traditional guacamoles.
- SFX: ROCKET BLASTING OFF
- ANNCR: Take a Southwest Airlines Half-Fare Frivolity Flight to Houston and watch astronauts mow their lawns.
- SFX: FOOTBALL CROWD NOISES
- ANNCR: Take a Southwest Airlines Frivolity Flight to Dallas and watch Cowboys hurt themselves.
- SXF: OTHERS OUT. RINKY-TINK MUSIC UP.
- HOSTESS: Half-Fare Frivolity Flights, every week night at eight o'clock and *all* weekend flights. Only $13. Almost as cheap as the bus. Cheaper than your own car. So relax with me, and stop driving yourself.
- ANNCR: Southwest Airlines' Half-Fare Frivolity Flights.
- HOSTESS: Fly for the fun of it.

NUMBER: 118-23-2   *Length:* 60 sec (Dallas version)   *Date:* 12/21/72

■ **WOMAN:** Harold, this is your mother in San Antonio talking to you from the radio, Harold. I want you to know that Southwest Airlines is having a half-price sale, Harold. For 60 days you can fly between San Antonio and Dallas for half price. Only $13, Harold. I expect to see a lot of you for those 60 days. Are you listening, Harold? Harold! (STATION WIND) I'm talking to you!

■ **MUSIC:** LIGHT, HAPPY

■ **HOSTESS:** Southwest Airlines half-fare flights. Every flight between San Antonio and Dallas every day. Only $13.

■ **SFX:** STREET NOISES

■ **IRATE MALE VOICE:** Hey! You people fly Southwest Airlines during this half-price sale, you're gonna have a lonely bus driver on your conscience. Take the bus. It only costs a little more, but it's four hours longer! You'll have a lot more time with me, won't you? (FADE) Well, won't you?

■ **SFX:** STREET NOISES

■ **MAN:** There is a cheaper way than Southwest Airlines. Put on roller skates, tie yourself to a trailer truck . . .

■ **MUSIC:** LIGHT, HAPPY

■ **HOSTESSES:** Fly Southwest Airlines. Half price between Dallas and San Antonio on every flight every day. Why pay more?

■ **VOICE:** Half price? Can they do that?

■ **SECOND VOICE:** They did it!

536

537

OPTICAL DISTORTION, INC.

DARRAL G. CLARKE
Associate Professor
Graduate School of Management
Brigham Young University

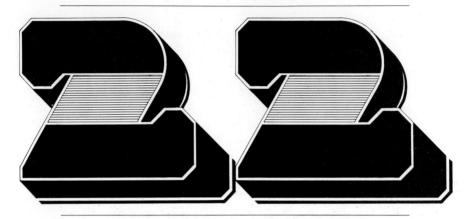

Late in the fall of 1974, Mr. Daniel Garrison, president and chief executive officer of Optical Distortion, Inc. (ODI), had asked Mr. Ronald Olson, marketing vice president of ODI, to develop a marketing plan for ODI's new (and only) product—a contact lens for chickens.[1] While contact lenses served the purpose of improving human eyesight, the purpose of the lens developed by ODI was partially to blind the chickens.

Mr. Garrison explained:

> *Like so many other great discoveries, our product concept was discovered quite by accident. In 1962 a chicken farmer in Arizona had a flock of chickens that developed a severe cataract problem. When he became aware of the problem, he separated the afflicted birds from the rest of the flock and subsequently observed that the afflicted birds seemed to eat less and were much easier to handle. So dramatic was the difference that a poultry medical detailman visiting the farm, rather than being asked for a cure, was asked if there was any way to similarly afflict the rest of the*

---

[1] Throughout the case *chicken* is used as a technical term to describe the female bird (3 months old or older) raised for the purpose of egg production. Male birds are referred to as *friers* or *broilers*.

flock. It has not proved possible chemically or genetically to duplicate the reduced vision of the chickens resulting from the cataracts, but a chicken wearing the ODI lenses has its vision reduced enough to obtain the good behavior the Arizona farmer observed. This behavior has important economic implications for the chicken farmer.

By late 1974, the ODI lens had been tested on a number of farms in California and Oregon with satisfactory results, and Mr. Garrison was convinced that "the time has come to stop worrying about the product and get this show off the ground." While his timetable was "tentative," he hoped that the ODI lens could be introduced in at least one region during the spring of 1975 and that national distribution would be achieved by the end of 1977 (at the latest). As he explained:

Our patent and license protection [see below] should hold off competition for at least three years, but—if we have the success I believe we will—I would expect the large agricultural supply firms to find a way around our patent by the late 1970's. By 1980, I would expect the big boys to have come in, and competition to be fierce. If we are to gain the fruits of our development work, we will have to be strong enough to fight them on their own terms. To do this, we will have to be a multi-product multi-market company which can provide effective service anywhere in the country.

COMPANY BACKGROUND

The ODI lens had been invented in 1965 by Robert D. Garrison (Daniel Garrison's father), working with Mr. Ronald Olson, the owner of a large chicken farm in Oregon. Mr. Robert Garrison had conceptualized and designed the original product and had then worked with Olson to test and refine the lenses on Olson's chicken farm. In 1966, their efforts attracted the attention of Mr. James Arnold, a local businessman, who invested approximately $5,000 in the venture. By late 1966, the three men had formed a corporation to exploit Garrison's invention.

Further testing of the lens in Olson's chicken farm during 1967 had, however, identified several technical difficulties with the product. In particular, the early prototypes did not always remain in the chicken's eyes after insertion, and frequently caused severe irritation by the later months of the chicken's 12-month laying life. Both problems had been quite serious because, as Daniel Garrison explained, "No farmer is going to spend time looking into the eyes of his chickens to make sure the lenses are still there and the eyes are not bloodshot."

By 1968, ODI had solved the retention problem by modifying the size of the lens and was issued a United States patent on the lens in December 1969. ODI found that the irritation problem could be essentially eliminated by making the lenses of a soft plastic called a *hydrophilic polymer*. The patents for hydrophilic polymer, the same material used by Bausch and Lomb to produce soft contact lenses for human use, were controlled by New World Plastics of Baltimore, Maryland. The New World Plastics' hydrophilic polymer could not be injection-molded, however, and manufacturing costs using alternative production processes were far too high for the chicken market. Since New World Plastics' hydrophilic polymer was the only such material known at the time, ODI had reached an impasse, and the company became dormant.

In 1973, Robert Garrison asked his son Daniel Garrison, a second-year student at the Harvard Business School, to contact New World Plastics and see if any progress had been made in the hydrophilic polymer. Daniel Garrison found that the hydrophilic polymer could now be injection-molded and became enthusiastic about the potential of the product. With the approval of the owners, Daniel Garrison obtained a long-term license from New World Plastics for the exclusive use of hydrophilic polymer for nonhuman applications.

Under the terms of the license, New World agreed not to produce the polymer for other firms seeking nonhuman markets and not to carry out development work on related polymers for such firms. ODI, in turn, agreed to pay New World Plastics $50,000 ($25,000 per year for the first 2 years) and to purchase its lenses exclusively from New World. New World would manufacture the lenses and sell them to ODI at a price of $0.032 per pair (in bulk), regardless of quantity. ODI was to supply New World with injection molds (at a cost of $12,000 each). Each injection mold had an annual capacity of 7.2 million pairs and an expected life of 15 million pairs.

During the negotiations with New World Plastics, Daniel Garrison purchased 25 percent of the stock of ODI from the previous owners and was elected president and chief executive officer of the firm. Having completed the license agreement with New World, he was able to raise $200,000 in the venture capital markets. About this time, Mr. Ronald Olson became vice president–marketing, and the two men began devoting a substantial portion of their time to ODI. As of late 1974, Daniel Garrison and Olson were the only reasonably full-time employees of the firm, although Robert Garrison and James Arnold remained active as stockholders and board members.

THE POULTRY INDUSTRY

Poultry and egg production had its beginnings in the family barnyard. As late as 1900, it was not unusual for a family to have its own chickens or to buy eggs fresh from a small local farmer, even in urban areas. In 1921, the largest commercial egg farm in the United States was in Petaluma, California, and boasted a flock of about 2,000 hens. The hens were not housed, but ran loose in a large pasture with small roosting and laying houses nearby. The eggs were picked up twice daily and loaded into a horse-drawn wagon.

In an effort to increase the efficiency of egg production, some California farmers began confining the birds in large henhouses during the 1930s and 1940s. In other parts of the United States, eggs were still being collected from haystacks until the 1940s when henhouses became common in other areas of the country. Continuing their innovation, California poultrymen began to increase the utilization of henhouse space by further confining the birds in groups of three or four within multitiered wire cages of 18 × 12 inch size. By the 1950s, these innovations had spread widely throughout the United States and had led to considerable concentration in the poultry industry (see Exhibit 1).

In 1974, the largest commercial flock of laying hens in the United States was 2.5 million birds, and 80 percent of the 440 million laying hens in the United States were housed on 3 percent of the known chicken farms. California, North Carolina, and Georgia accounted for 25 percent of the nation's chickens, while nine additional states (mostly in the South and Northeast) accounted for an additional 36 percent of the chicken population. Two counties in southern California contained 20 farms which housed 21 million chickens. Further details on the distribution of chicken farms in the United States are given in Exhibits 2 and 3; data on the economics of chicken farming are shown in Exhibits 4 and 5.

As might be expected from the changes in the size and number of chicken farms, the business of running a large chicken farm had changed a great deal since the 1920s. Daniel Garrison characterized the problem of managing chicken farms of various sizes as follows:

> **1** Small farms (10,000 or fewer birds). *These small farms are usually family operated. They could possibly contract their production to a larger producer, but more probably, they sell their eggs locally through small grocery or milk and egg stores or at their own farm. A farmer of this size probably purchases starter pullets only once or twice a year. The birds would be housed in hen houses of about 1,000–2,000 birds. The number of such farms has recently been declining at a rate of about 25% per year.*

> **2** Medium farms (10,000–50,000 birds). *A chicken farm of this size is typically operated professionally. Such farms are usually still owned and managed by the farmer. The farmer-owner performs administrative tasks and makes most decisions regarding the operation of the farm himself. A farm of this size requires considerable business as well as agricultural skill. Such an owner would have yearly cash flows on the order of $375,000 to manage. He would deal with large corporate suppliers such as hatcheries, feed companies, and equipment manufacturers. He most probably also negotiates with a large corporate purchaser of his egg production. Individual cash transactions can be as large as $35,000.*

> **3** Large farms (over 50,000 birds). *A chicken farm of this size is, in many ways, like a small manufacturing firm. Administration of the farm is sufficiently complex to require the skills and efforts of several people. The farm could employ 100 or more people and have an annual cash flow of $12 million. Such farms may mix their own feed in facilities costing up to $500,000. Their egg production may be sold through complex negotiated contracts with regional offices of large grocery chains. Some may convert waste into fertilizer in their own conversion plants as a byproduct. The farmer would purchase starter pullets (or grow their own) at least 4 times a year in order to smooth labor demands on the farm. On a farm of this size, a hen house would typically house from 5,000–10,000 birds.*

On the basis of various government surveys. Garrison estimated that the United States chicken population would grow very slowly between 1975 and 1979:

1975	457.0 million birds
1976	461.6 million birds
1977	466.2 million birds
1978	470.8 million birds
1979	475.6 million birds

Eighty percent of these chickens would be on the three percent of United States chicken farms having 10,000 or more chickens. Garrison believed that a farm would have to have at least 10,000 birds to be sold profitably by ODI, but that 50 percent penetration of such farms within 5 years was a realistic projection.

CANNIBALISM AMONG CHICKENS

Like many other fowl, chickens were social birds and chicken societies had a definite social structure. A self-selected ranking of chickens began when chickens were about 8 to 10 weeks of age and resulted in a complete peck order by the time the birds reached sexual maturity. According to Mark O. North,[1] a poultry consultant, "This order is the result of the birds being able to identify other birds in the group, and through fighting and pecking, establish a hierarchical type of social organization."

Mr. North believed that the recognition of the comb on the head of the chicken was a means of preserving the peck order, as was the position of the head. Dominant-type chickens carried their heads high, while submissive birds maintained a low head level. If a submissive bird raised her head too high, she was immediately pecked by one or more of her superiors until the head was lowered. Pecking could increase until the birds became cannibalistic. Submissive birds were also pecked if they entered the "territory" of a cage claimed by a more dominant bird. Thus cannibalism was a greater problem when more birds were confined in cages. Cannibalism also varied with the breed of the chicken, and, unfortunately, the more productive strains tended to be more cannibalistic. According to Daniel Garrison, a major United States breeder had developed an extremely productive chicken, but "you had to put a sack over her head to keep her from killing her penmates."

Besides the obvious loss to the farmer when a bird was killed by her pen mates, submissive birds got less time at the feeding trough and thus produced fewer eggs than the more dominant birds. Also, once the peck order was established, replacing a dead bird seriously disturbed the peck order.

Debeaking had been the major means of combating cannibalism for nearly 50 years. The debeaking process did not interfere with the formation of the peck order but reduced the efficiency of the beak as a weapon. The debeaking operation was simple in concept: Through the use of a hot knife and an anvil, the upper and lower mandibles of the chicken's beak were cut off at different lengths. The beak was then pressed against the hot knife to cauterize the wound and prevent excess bleeding. In the debeaking operation, the chickens were

[1] *Poultry Digest,* December 1973.

subjected to considerable trauma which resulted in a temporary weight loss and the retardation of egg production for at least a week; at this age, the loss was only one egg. If the beak were cut too short, the chicken would often enter a permanent regression; if left too long, the beak would grow back and become a deadly weapon again. The establishment of the peck order among debeaked chickens took a longer time and involved greater social stress than it did among chickens with their full beaks since clear victories were rare.

Experience had shown that debeaking reduced mortality due to cannibalism from as high as 25 percent for flocks of birds with full beaks to about 9 percent for debeaked flocks.

Debeaking was usually done during the first few weeks after the 20-week-old hens were purchased. The farmer's own employees or a service company could be hired to provide the debeaking crews, depending on the size of the farm. The cost of the debeaking operation was almost entirely labor. An experienced crew of three men, each earning about $2.50 per hour, could debeak approximately 220 birds per hour.

THE ODI LENS

Daniel Garrison felt that the ODI contact lens was the first product to actually confront the cause of cannibalization rather than just minimize its effects. A bird wearing the ODI lens had its depth of perception reduced to about 12 inches and its visual acuity greatly reduced through an induced case of astigmatism. Thus, the ability of one bird to recognize the comb of another was seriously impaired, and in order to feed, the chickens had to walk around with their heads lowered. Thus the main visual cues for the peck order were removed, no peck order emerged, and cannibalism was reduced significantly.

The ODI lens was much like the soft contact lenses worn by humans except that it was slightly larger, had a red tint, and had a distortion built into the crown. When asked why the lenses were colored, Daniel Garrison responded:

> It may sound like rubbish to many people but chickens, like humans, respond psychologically to the color of their environment. We have found that changing the color of the birds' environment will affect the birds in many different ways such as altering their appetites or rate of sexual maturity, as well as affecting their cannibalistic tendencies. When birds are placed in a red colored environment, deaths due to cannibalism are reduced. This red color, together with the distortion of the lenses, affects the chicken's ability to act out her aggressions. Our tests have shown that flock mortality is reduced to an average of 4.5% when contact lenses are used instead of debeaking.

The lens was larger than the eye opening so that, when in place, the rim of the eye opening and the outer eyelid acted as retainers keeping the lens in place. The inner eyelid, or nicitating membrane, a semitransparent membrane that flicked back and forth across the eyeball keeping it moist and clean, was under the lens and thus could perform its natural function.

Daniel Garrison estimated that a trained crew of three men, similar to the debeaking crews, could install the lenses in about 225 chickens per hour. The insertion of the lenses did not result in great trauma to the birds as debeaking did. The chickens were up and about within a few hours, and neither weight loss nor reduction in egg production were noticeable.

Daniel Garrison doubted that the lenses could be reused.

The lenses are harder to take out than they are to put in, and a further problem in reusing them is the fact that the melting point of the hydrophilic polymer is very close to the sterilization temperature. You could end up with a mass of hydrophilic polymer rather than a pot full of contact lenses very easily.

Besides reducing chicken mortality due to cannibalism and egg production loss due to trauma, the ODI lens had the potential of reducing a farmer's feed cost. A debeaked chicken could only eat if the feed in her trough was at least ⅜ inch deep (the difference in length between the upper and lower mandibles of her remaining beak). Presumably, therefore, a farmer using ODI lenses instead of debeaking his chickens would be able to reduce the depth of the feed in his troughs by approximately ⅜ inch or more. Mr. Gil Jaeger, a University of Maine poultry extension specialist, had conducted a study which suggested that food disappearance per 100 birds per day was reduced from 24.46 pounds when the feed in the trough was 2 inches deep to 23.68 pounds when the feed in the trough was only 1 inch deep. In other words, a farmer with a 20,000-bird flock could save 156 pounds of feed per day if he could reduce the depth of feed in his trough from 2 inches to 1 inch. At $158 per ton for chicken feed, this would represent considerable annual savings, especially for large flocks. According to Mr. Garrison, ODI lenses would permit a farmer to reduce the depth of feed in his troughs by at least ⅜ inch (probably to a depth of 1 inch) and would result in further savings because "a bird with a full beak *and* the ODI lenses can't see well enough to be fussy so she doesn't bill much at all [billing throws feed out of the trough], and she doesn't drool in her food as debeaked birds do."

Although he was unaware of any broad-scale research that measured the loss of feed due to billing, Daniel Garrison felt that a farmer would find that maintaining a 1- or 1½-inch food level for debeaked birds would be impractical due to more frequent trough refilling.

DEVELOPING A MARKETING PROBLEM

As he began to develop the marketing plan requested by Daniel Garrison, Olson was acutely conscious of "the need to think big while recognizing that our assets are, after all, rather limited. There's no question this product has a whale of a future," he explained. "The problem is to achieve that potential as rapidly as is practical without too much strain on our limited managerial and financial resources." (See Exhibit 6 for ODI's balance sheet as of September 30, 1974.)

In discussions with Mr. Garrison, Olson had come to a number of tentative conclusions. First, it was virtually certain that ODI would enter the market via a region-by-region roll-out, beginning in California. On a rough basis, he estimated that the annual costs of a West Coast regional office and warehouse would be about $196,000 per year (see Exhibit 7), plus about $40,000 for each salesperson (including expenses) and $35,000 for each technical representative. He felt that, initially at least, each salesperson should cover no more than about 80 farms, and that there should be one technical representative for each five salespeople. The technical representatives would follow up all major sales to make sure that the lenses were being used in such a way as to maximize benefits to the farmer.

Second, he and Mr. Garrison had agreed that the minimum price which they should consider was $20 per box[1] of 250 pair, or $0.08 per pair. While this price would represent an incremental cost for the farmer (the labor cost for de-beaking and insertion of lenses was approximately the same), the farmer would presumably obtain benefits much greater than $0.08 per chicken because of reduced cannibalization, less trauma, and greater feeding efficiency. Such benefits would justify a price much higher than $0.08 per pair, Olson felt, but he wasn't sure it would be possible to convince farmers of such benefits until after they had had considerable experience with the lenses. It was probable, he thought, that a higher price would require more intensive sales and technical coverage, which would considerably increase ODI's fixed costs. Nevertheless, he was hesitant to introduce the lenses at a low price initially in the hope of raising it later because (1) "Chicken farmers, even the big ones, are an independent-minded breed of men, who might react very unfavorably if they get the idea that they have been taken," and (2) "Because of our limited resources, we have to try to obtain maximum contribution as soon as possible."

High contribution, Olson reasoned, was critical to support the headquarters, regional office, and advertising and promotional costs inherent in a "think big" strategy. He and Daniel Garrison had agreed that ODI should be marketing on a national basis within 2 to 3 years, which would require four to five regional offices. Monthly advertising in the eight leading poultry industry publications would cost approximately $100,000 per year, as would participation in the most important industry trade shows. Headquarters expenses, Mr. Garrison had forecast, would rise from $184,000 per year at a volume of 20 million pair to $614,000 at 60 million pair and $1.2 million at 120 million pair. Moreover, Mr. Garrison's strategy of becoming "much more than a one product company" called for an investment of at least $250,000 per year in research and development as soon as the company could generate the funds or become large and profitable enough to be able to obtain additional capital on favorable terms from the equity market.

---

[1] The plastic boxes would cost $0.10 each and could be filled by ODI at $0.14 per box. Order processing and shipping were estimated at $0.18 per box.

As he sat down at the already cluttered desk in the corner of his den, Olson thought:

> It's really a tough problem. There's a lot at stake here; more than enough potential for a big company to put fifty people on the project. There are only four of us, and none of us can yet put full time into the company, although Daniel and I are each spending at least 50 hours per week on ODI. Still, we've got to do as good a job as a big company would, and I think we can. . . . If we pull it off, we will have revolutionized the business of animal behavior in much the same way as IBM revolutionized the processing of data.

EXHIBIT 1
CHICKEN CENSUS, 1880–1969
Optical Distortion, Inc.

Year	Number of farms raising chickens commercially	% of all farms	Number of chickens
1880	NA	NA	102,272,135
1890	NA	NA	258,871,125
1900	NA	NA	233,598,085
1910	5,580,758	NA	280,410,531
1920	5,839,489	NA	359,607,148
1925	5,505,617	NA	409,290,849
1930	5,375,559	NA	379,159,783
1935	5,833,079	NA	371,603,136
1940	5,152,354	84.4	338,240,109
1945	4,900,948	83.4	433,110,674
1950	4,218,857	78.3	342,956,055
1954	3,418,204	71.5	375,800,447
1959	2,172,264	58.6	351,029,294
1964	1,210,669	38.3	343,167,807
1969	471,284	17.3	371,008,459

EXHIBIT 2
DENSITY OF UNITED STATES CHICKEN POPULATION, 1969
Optical Distortion, Inc.

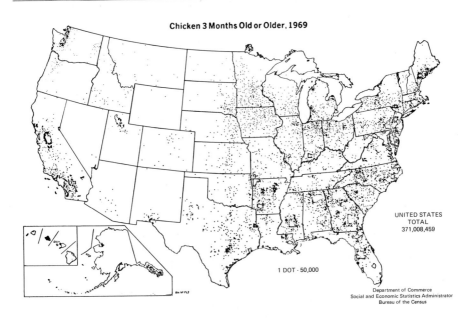

Chicken 3 Months Old or Older, 1969

UNITED STATES TOTAL
371,008,459

1 DOT · 50,000

Department of Commerce
Social and Economic Statistics Administrator
Bureau of the Census

547

EXHIBIT 3
CHARACTERISTICS OF U.S. CHICKEN FARMS, 1969*
Optical Distortion, Inc.

State	Total farms (sales over $2,500)	Chickens on total farms	Flock size 20,000–49,999			50,000–99,999			100,000 and over		
			# of farms	# of farms reporting flock size	# of chickens†	# of farms	# of farms reporting flock size	# of chickens†	# of farms	# of farms reporting flock size	# of chickens†
Pacific:											
Washington	1,929	5,230,575	40	20	1,090,102	11	11	663,378	10	10	2,085,936
Oregon	1,825	2,249,752	13	13	414,220	3	3	229,000	6	6	848,705
California	3,023	46,203,988	320	320	9,517,453	114	114	7,459,944	87	87	22,952,283
Alaska	25	25,617	0	0	‡	0	0	‡	0	0	‡
Hawaii	90	1,069,618	8	8	255,000	4	0	‡	12	0	‡
	6,892	54,779,550	381	381	11,276,775	132	128	8,352,322	105	103	25,886,924
New England	2,621	17,265,305	135	128	3,660,578	31	20	1,320,796	15	13	2,974,242
Middle Atlantic	12,867	31,036,554	240	240	6,969,792	55	55	3,419,870	29	29	5,239,990
East North Central	54,429	46,650,039	339	339	9,267,919	57	39	2,631,736	22	20	3,461,252
West North Central	112,119	41,213,868	158	156	4,372,320	34	27	1,808,508	21	16	2,480,555
South Atlantic	29,971	82,176,127	860	860	24,221,265	168	155	10,085,341	70	66	12,065,486
East South Central	29,045	36,617,712	317	317	8,854,258	62	58	3,795,730	27	25	5,661,485
West South Central	31,101	46,450,783	412	412	11,876,032	77	75	5,111,151	42	39	11,264,948
Mountain	14,295	7,018,828	28	23	682,444	15	0	‡	14	3	806,350
Total U.S.	293,340	363,208,766	2,870	2,856	81,547,775	631	557	41,566,445	345	314	74,856,267
Percent of total	100%	100%	1%		22.4%	0.2%		11.4%	0.1%		20.6%

* The data in Exhibit 3 are not fully consistent with those in Exhibits 1 and 4 because of differences in sources and definitions.

† The number of chickens for which flock size was reported.

‡ Not reported to preserve the confidentiality of individual farm flock sizes.

EXHIBIT 4
CHICKEN FARM TRENDS, 1964–1969*
Optical Distortion Inc.

Flock size	Number of farms			Chickens		
	1964, %	1969, %	% change	1964, %	1969, %	% change
Under 3,200	98.5	93.8	−61	22.9	13.0	−61
3,200–9,999	1.1	3.2	−28.9	21.0	14.9	−23.4
10,000–19,999	0.3	1.7	+35.6	14.1	18.0	+38.2
20,000–49,000	0.1	1.0	+82	18.1	22.4	+81.2
50,000–99,999	0.001	0.2	+83	6.4	11.2	+89.7
100,000 and over	0.05	0.1	+50	7.5	20.6	+189.7
Total			−61			+6.1

* The data in Exhibit 4 are not fully consistent with those in Exhibits 1 and 3 because of differences in sources and definitions.

EXHIBIT 5
AVERAGE COST PER DOZEN EGGS PRODUCED, 1974
Optical Distortion, Inc.

		Cost/dozen eggs*
Laying stock:		
Purchase cost per hen	$2.40	
Allocation for replacing dead birds	0.21	
	$2.61	11.9¢
Annual feed costs per hen	$7.04	32.0¢
Labor		2.4¢
Supplies, taxes, utilities, etc.		1.8¢
Miscellaneous adjustments:		
Cull sales per dozen (credit)		(0.3¢)
Laying stock value adjustment (credit)		(1.7¢)
Net cash and labor cost per dozen		46.1¢
Depreciation (15% average value of buildings and equipment)		1.2¢
Interest (8% on land, laying stock, and average value of buildings and equipment)		1.4¢
Management per dozen		1.3¢
Total costs per dozen		50.0¢
Average price per dozen		53.0¢
Average profit per dozen		3.0¢

* Assuming 22 dozen eggs per hen-year.

EXHIBIT 6
BALANCE SHEET, SEPTEMBER 30, 1974
Optical Distortion, Inc.

Current assets:		
Cash		$200,025
Patent*	$103,000	
Less accumulated depreciation	28,000	
		75,000
Total assets		$275,025
Current liabilities		$ 0
Long-term debt		0
Stockholders' equity		275,025
Total liabilities and equity		$275,025

* ODI, at incorporation, valued the contact lens for chickens patent at $103,000 and depreciated it over its 17-year life.

EXHIBIT 7
PROJECTED COSTS OF CALIFORNIA REGIONAL OFFICE AND WAREHOUSE
Optical Distortion, Inc.

Office expense:		
Rent, utilities, etc.		$ 36,000
Personnel:		
Regional manager	$30,000	
Administrative assistant	15,000	
Regional technical manager	22,000	
3 secretaries (@ $10,000)	30,000	
Shipping clerk	10,000	
		107,000
Other expenses		53,000
Total projected annual costs		$196,000

THE INFORMATION BANK

NANCY J. DAVIS
Research Associate
Harvard Graduate School of Business Administration

STEVEN H. STAR
Associate Professor
Harvard Graduate School of Business Administration

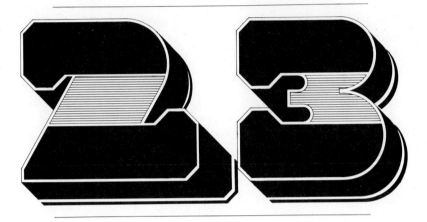

In February 1975, Mr. Carl Keil, director of marketing, was formulating a pricing strategy for The Information Bank, a computerized system for the storage and retrieval of general information drawn from about 60 publications. Since joining The Information Bank in December 1974, Keil had reorganized sales territories, changed the compensation system for salespeople, and begun to concentrate on specific geographic areas and vertical selling within industries. He had also taken significant steps toward securing less costly hardware and telecommunications systems. Now, however, he had to construct a consistent pricing policy which would allow the company to improve its financial position. "We currently have rate structures ranging from no charge at all to a flat rate of $1,350 per month for unlimited usage," he thought. "Our average per hour access revenue is about $20. If we retain this structure, we will never have a manageable billing system."

DESCRIPTION OF THE SERVICE

The Information Bank, a subsidiary of The New York Times Company, maintained and marketed a fully automated system for the storage and retrieval of general information. The computer in which the information was stored was located in the Times Building in New York City. It contained about 1 million abstracts of articles, 60 percent of which was from 6 years of *The New York Times* material and 40 percent from 3 years of 60 other publications. Approximately 20,000 abstracts were added per month, half from *The New York Times* and half from the other publications. New entries were usually added within 72 to 96 hours of receipt of the source publications. (See Exhibit 1 for list of publications abstracted.)

The abstracts were tersely written summaries, headed by bibliographic citations that gave the journal titles, dates, pages, and, when applicable, the columns. The abstracts were "manufactured" by a highly skilled group of editors and writers. Editors who specialized in particular areas—the United States economy, for example—read all the incoming articles about this subject and marked critical passages. The articles then went to a writer who also specialized in that particular area, and he or she wrote the abstract. Abstracts ranged in length from one or two sentences up to 300 or 400 words.

A customer of The Information Bank received information from the Bank's computer by means of a cathode-ray-tube (CRT) video terminal located at his office. Connections between the CRT and the computer were made through regular telephone lines or through other telecommunications channels. Customers could also purchase a high-speed printer which operated at up to 165 characters per second. The auxiliary printer provided a hard-copy capability to the customer. If the customer did not have a printer but wanted printed abstracts, he could request that The Information Bank print them and mail them to him. It normally took several days to receive the abstracts.

The Information Bank's system was designed so that the user need not be an information scientist, a computer specialist, or a librarian. Each step was conducted in plain English. Messages to and from the computer could be spelled out completely, though a set of abbreviations had been developed which an experienced researcher could use to save time. If the researcher became confused about what was going on with the system, he could press a special key which flashed an explanatory message on the CRT screen. If the explanation was not adequate or if the system malfunctioned, he could telephone a specially trained person at the New York office. To use the system, the researcher typed in descriptors—i.e., subject headings or index terms comparable to subject headings in a card catalog—and the computer scanned the Bank and printed the relevant abstracts onto the CRT. On the average, an abstract had about 10 descriptors. If the researcher typed in a very general descriptor, the computer suggested more specific terms and asked if he would like to use any of them instead of or in addition to the one he first entered. If the descriptor entered matched two or more terms in the Bank, the computer displayed all the terms so the researcher could select the one most appropriate for his search. If the descriptor entered had a widely used synonym which Information Bank editors had chosen for filing entries, the computer usually automatically switched to the synonym. The system was designed to allow the combining of terms through boolean logic for more complex searches. For example, the terms *Great Britain* and *labor contracts* could be entered and combined, and only those abstracts about both Great Britain and labor contracts would be retrieved.

Because of the volume of material available on many subjects, the computer could conceivably provide hundreds of abstracts if the researcher did not somehow restrict the search. To do this, he used modifiers, words which directed the search in a highly specific fashion. Only one modifier could be used or several could be used simultaneously. The principal modifiers were:

- *Byline.* A term which limited material to that *by* a given person. If the researcher did not use the byline, he got both material *by* and *about* the person.
- *Sketch material.* A term which selected material primarily of biographical interest.
- *Date of publication.* A term which limited material to that which appeared on a single date, several dates, or during any given time period(s) such as a month or a year.
- *Journal.* A term which limited material to that published in one or more of the newspapers and magazines the Bank contained.
- *Source.* A term which limited the material to that received from a specific wire service or other credited source.
- *Type of material.* A term which limited the abstracts to specific types such as editorial, letters to the editor, news analysis, obituary, or critical review.
- *Graphics.* A term which limited the abstracts to those accompanied by specific illustrations such as maps, charts, and photographs.

In addition to the regular storage and retrieval system, The Information Bank offered *The New York Times* on microfiche. Microfiche was similar to conventional-roll microfilm, but it was easier to use and could be produced more frequently. A fiche consisted of a 4 × 6 inch negative which contained 98 frames. Each frame was a microphotograph of a 9 × 12 inch sheet on which The Information Bank personnel had mounted clippings. The contents of a daily *Times* could be printed on a single fiche, while Sunday editions required four fiche. Except for items of no discernable research value, *Times* fiche contained virtually all the news and editorial material published in the paper. Advertisements of potential research value were included. A clipping on fiche was located by the regular procedure of entering descriptors and modifiers into the CRT terminal. The fiche file number and the specific frame number for the clipping were included in the abstract's bibliographic citation. Fiche of current material were mailed to customers twice a week, and customers could obtain fiche of back issues of the *Times*. Keil thought that, as copyright agreements were made with other publishers, material from their publications could also be issued on microfiche. While 80 percent of The Information Bank's customers said they were satisfied with the abstracts, 50 percent still subscribed to the microfiche service. To use the microfiche, a customer had to have a microfiche reader. Readers available ranged from very inexpensive, small units to large readers with printers which produced printed copies of any article on the fiche.

THE MARKET AND COMPETITION

In February 1975, a few companies in addition to The Information Bank offered computerized information storage and retrieval systems. However, most of these concentrated on highly specialized information such as that needed by lawyers or doctors. Four of the major companies in this business were Mead Data Central, Inc., System Development Corporation (SDC), Predicasts, Inc., and Bunker Ramo. Mead's system, known as LEXIS, supplied legal information for law offices. SDC offered a system for 10 different fields—life sciences, engineering, geosciences, business management, chemistry, government research and development, agriculture, education, medicine, and petroleum. While SDC's system contained almost 4 million citations, it did not provide abstracts of the periodicals covered. Predicasts specialized in domestic and international statistics and major indexing services. Bunker Ramo's information base went back only 90 days, and the information was categorized into only 10 general areas. None of these companies supplied the wide variety of general information which The Information Bank supplied.

Eight companies, some of which were small businesses that needed information but had limited financial resources, had begun to subscribe to The Information Bank and to resell it at retail. The Information Bank had made only short-term arrangements with these companies.

Keil had no idea what the sales volume of Mead, SDC, Predicasts, Bunker Ramo, and other companies in the field might be, but industry sources estimated that by 1980 the information storage and retrieval business would be a billion-dollar industry. Keil expected numerous companies to enter the field in the next few years, but he thought that they might concentrate on one specific area of the information process. Publishing companies, for example, might develop indexing and abstracting organizations, and RCA, Xerox, Western Union, and ATT had indicated interest in the computer area and telecommunications aspects of the business. Satellite transmission was lowering communication costs to the point that worldwide access to data bases would soon be both technically and economically feasible.

Keil stated that, in the United States, federal, state, and local government agencies probably accounted for about 30 percent of the potential market for The Information Bank's services. He noted, for example, that in Washington the Library of Congress was trying to make its services more readily accessible to the Senate and House of Representatives, and that it had been instrumental in installing several terminals at the Senate and the House, as well as in its own buildings. Keil thought college, university, and public libraries probably constituted another 25 percent of the total potential market. He felt this market segment would be difficult to develop because its funding was very erratic and locating the appropriate decision makers was difficult. Another 25 percent of the potential market consisted of corporations, Keil thought. He said that large corporations such as those included on the *Fortune 500* list were setting up information centers which should be a prime market for The Information Bank. The final 20 percent of the potential market, Keil thought, comprised the intelligence community and foreign embassies.

HISTORY OF THE INFORMATION BANK

The development of The Information Bank began in 1966. Initially, management thought it would be used as a service for *The New York Times'* news and editorial department with future commercial development to follow after a thorough test period. Issues of the *Times* going back to the turn of the century would be abstracted and included in the Bank, so writers would have quick, easy access to any historical data they needed when writing a story. Not until the early seventies, however, did management try to market the system to organizations outside the *Times*. Though various salespeople were hired and the information base was expanded to include publications other than the *Times,* a major unified marketing program did not get underway until Mr. Carl Keil joined the company in December 1974.

The 33-year-old Keil brought to the job an extremely varied background. While studying for his undergraduate degree in math and civil engineering at Bucknell University, he ran food concessions, worked as an electrician, and did a variety of other jobs. After graduating, he worked for a year at Mobil Oil where, at the age of 23, he was the company's youngest district manager. He then spent 2 years in the Army, during which time he also ran a personnel service for people who were being discharged. In 1966, he joined IBM's new interactive time-sharing operation. During his 5 years at IBM, he did virtually everything from selling to programming to tinkering with technical aspects of the system. He next was hired by the United States Postal Service's marketing organization. There he was responsible for marketing plans and for a national sales force consisting of about 700 salespeople. Meanwhile, he had taken graduate courses in business at the University of North Carolina, Temple University, Columbia University, and the Harvard Business School.

The situation Keil inherited offered significant opportunities for improvement. The 1974 annual report of The New York Times Company stated: "A full-scale marketing program, and the continuing costs of expanding the data base, caused The Information Bank to incur larger expenses than in prior years." To be more specific, the company had spent about $3 million on the system in

1974, while total revenues had been about $240,000. About $1 million had been spent to abstract data, $600,000 to rent the IBM computer, and $200,000 on trade shows and media advertising, primarily newspaper ads. The remaining $1.2 million had been spent on administrative costs, systems supports, and trainers' and salespeople's salaries and expenses. Since 1966, The New York Times Company had spent about $9 million developing the system.

The sales organization Keil inherited consisted of four salespeople and two trainers who taught customers to use the system. One salesperson had previously been a broker, one had been an administrative assistant in a large company, the third had just finished a masters degree in information science, and the fourth had been a time-sharing salesperson for a computer company. Only the last had any related selling experience before joining The Information Bank. The salespeople were paid a straight salary of about $21,000. No commissions or other special incentives were offered, but the company did pay all their selling expenses. This constituted a very large sum because the salespeople all operated out of the New York office, and there was no clear geographic definition to their territories. Consequently, a salesperson could make a presentation in Pittsburgh one day, move on to Houston the next, to Los Angeles the following day, and finally back to New York. There was some specialization by industry, but for the most part, the salesperson who answered the telephone when a response to an advertisement came in got that account. In addition to the sales staff, Keil had one secretary and one billing clerk. All billing was done manually.

In February 1975, The Information Bank had 38 customers. They were scattered all over the United States and one was located in Canada. (See Exhibit 2 for a list of customers as of February 1975.)

According to the company's records, a customer currently used the system an average of about 15 hours per month, and this figure was reached about 3 months after the system was installed. Keil felt that, as a larger customer base was built, average usage would increase because the system would be enhanced with material geared to specific customers. For example, more pertinent material and new index terms peculiar to the banking or oil industries would be added. Keil also planned for salespeople and trainers to visit customers more frequently to show them how to use the system more effectively and to encourage them to disseminate information about it. He said that "in a couple of years," average monthly usage should be up to 30 hours, but he warned that this was a highly subjective estimate.

Usage of The Information Bank closely paralleled the usage pattern typical of an interactive time-sharing operation. People began using the system around 9 A.M., and the number of users increased steadily until about 11:30 A.M. A slight lull occurred during lunchtime, then usage increased more rapidly until it reached a peak between 2 and 2:30 P.M. From then until 5 P.M., it dropped steadily and then leveled off. Keil hoped that eventually The Information Bank would have customers in selected markets in each time zone, which would give the system an effective capacity of 375 users (terminals). While The Information Bank's computer could, theoretically, handle as many as 400 terminals, Keil's experience suggested that response time would be slow and customers would lose interest if more than approximately 300 terminals were in use at one time. By spreading usage across the various time zones, he reasoned, it would be possible to increase capacity by 25 percent (i.e., from 300 to 375 terminals), since it would be unlikely that all terminals would be in use at the same time.

Keil decided to visit several customers to try to arrive at a "typical" customer format. In the industrial segment, he visited a major oil company and a major bank. He called the oil company an "ideal user." The Information Bank's terminal was located in the company's "public affairs secretariat" which serviced the top level of the organization. In addition to The Information Bank, this department subscribed to UPI, API, Reuters, and a data base oriented to the oil industry. It had four video-tape recorders, three television monitors, and a large file of clippings. It was run by two people who had Ph.D.s in philosophy. They said they used The Information Bank to find out what various people had said about issues affecting the oil industry, to determine what other oil companies were doing, to determine what was being said about their company, to provide material for executives' speeches, to anticipate questions executives were likely to be asked, and to determine how to position the company's advertising. It took these researchers 5 to 10 minutes to do a typical search, and they normally used the Bank 10 to 20 hours a month. Records were not kept of who requested what information, and the people in charge said they were not called upon to justify their expenses. They suspected that other oil companies had comparable departments.

At the bank which Keil visited, he found what he called "an excellent example of a bad placement." The Information Bank's terminal was located in and charged to the bank's library, though it was used primarily for credit checks on companies which approached the bank for loans. The credit officer sent his request to the librarian who actually did the search. A logbook was kept, but usage of the system was not charged back to the credit department. The librarian was not anxious for other people to learn about the system because additional requests would mean additional expenses for her department, and this might soon necessitate the hiring of another librarian. This bank used the system between 17 and 18 hours a month. Keil thought usage would be much higher if the system were placed in the commercial loan department and credit officers were trained to use it, or in the international and investment departments.

Keil visited three government agencies which subscribed to The Information Bank. At the State Department, The Information Bank's terminal was located in the library, but a large number of employees had been trained to use it, and it was extremely accessible. There was a logbook for the user to register his or her name, department, and request, but usage of the Bank was not charged back to specific departments. The average search here took at least 10 minutes, and the system was used approximately 25 hours a month. Someone apparently considered this usage to be rather high because the librarian had recently been requested to do searches for untrained people rather than training new people to use it. However, the librarian stated that she was not under substantial pressure to decrease usage of the system or overall costs in her department.

At the office of the Secretary of the Air Force, The Information Bank's terminal was located in the library and was used by four very skilled librarians, normally for information regarding military and foreign affairs. Though they maintained several files on a wide variety of topics, they said they went first to The Information Bank when requested to research a subject. The average time of a search was 5 minutes, and the Bank was used about 15 hours per month. One librarian said she had been asked to supply a copy of a speech, but the person making the request gave an incorrect date for the speech. She said she located the speech in about 15 minutes using The Information Bank, but that it would probably have taken 1½ days for her to find it through regular research methods. This was the closest anyone came to quantifying the benefits of the Bank.

The Environmental Protection Agency (EPA) initially had a terminal located in Washington and another in North Carolina. However, the head librarian, who kept the terminal in her office and was its sole user, said she was not getting many requests for information she thought the Bank was likely to contain, and so she had eliminated one terminal. Keil said she was generally negative about the system and that she felt the EPA didn't need it. She said she used it about once a week.

In the library segment, Keil visited both publicly funded libraries as well as college and university libraries. The Philadelphia Free Library, a public library system consisting of a main library and 55 branches, offered The Information Bank to the general public. About 50 percent of its inquiries came from the business community (about half of which were from news media), about 30 percent from the educational community, and about 20 percent from miscellaneous sources. Fifteen to twenty percent of the users were referred to the Bank by library personnel. The system was operated by two highly skilled librarians whose average search lasted 6 to 8 minutes. The librarians averaged about 250 searches which amounted to 25 to 35 hours on-line per month. This number seemed to be increasing as word of the system spread throughout the greater Philadelphia area as a result of newspaper articles and talk show appearances by the librarians who ran the system. On any given inquiry, the library would do 15 minutes of searching for free, but after that, it charged $1 per minute. Most of the searches which lasted more than 15 minutes were done for the business community. The librarian in charge of the Bank said it was quite expensive but that it had generated so much good will within the local business and academic communities that there would be a tremendous uproar if the city tried to cut it out of the library's budget. He said further that comparisons could not be made between the cost of the Bank versus the cost of a skilled researcher doing the task manually because the Bank was infinitely faster and generated far more data than a person using printed indexes ever could.

The Connecticut State Library used The Information Bank in a manner similar to the Philadelphia Free Library. The terminal was located in a special department which had been set up in 1973 to function as a free telephone information service for anyone in Connecticut. It was staffed by six full-time and three part-time librarians. The head librarian said they had been unable to categorize their customers. Their average search took 3.4 minutes, and they averaged 245 searches a month. September, December, and January were their heaviest months, and the number of searches per month appeared to be increasing. There was no charge for the first 10 minutes of a search, but the department charged 75 cents per minute after that. The librarians usually would not handle large research projects, but they did inform callers of other library resources available. The department was financed by federal funds distributed by the New England Library Board. Each library which received these funds decided how to use them.

College and university libraries usually faced more budgetary restraints than did public libraries who had the system. Adelphi University had an Information Bank terminal located in its reference department, and it was operated by seven reference librarians. For anyone affiliated with Adelphi the library charged $3 per search for the first 30 citations, then 25 cents for each additional citation. Adelphi also offered the system to businesses on Long Island. By paying $100 a year, a company gained access to the service and got two free searches. After that, the subscribing company paid $25 for the next 20 abstracts, and 50 cents for each additional abstract. A typical search at Adelphi took about 6 minutes. One librarian estimated that she and the other six librarians together might do anywhere from 8 to 80 searches a month. She said further that the library had publicized the Bank heavily within the university, and that it was used by students, faculty, and administrators alike. This library also offered SDC's systems.

At the University of California at Berkeley, the head librarian said that, during the first 6 months when the library offered The Information Bank free of charge, students made most of the inquiries. In order to cover out-of-pocket costs, however, the library had begun to charge for the system, and the chief users now were faculty and graduate students, especially those from departments such as the graduate school of public policy which subsidized the program. The charge was $25 for the first 15 minutes, and $25 for each 15 minutes thereafter. In addition to the 15 minutes of search time, the user received up to 50 abstracts by deferred print. Four librarians operated the system, and their typical search took between 10 and 15 minutes. They now used the system between 3 and 5 hours a month. The head librarian said that most of their searches were for people who were doing extensive research on topical issues. Most already had a file of articles from scholarly publications, but they also wanted to cover everything that had been written in general news media. The library no longer advertised the Bank for the total community because management felt it was too expensive for most students. When requests came in, the librarians tried to steer students to other resources which could satisfactorily satisfy their needs. The head librarian said that originally their communications costs had been very high, but that The Information Bank personnel had made an arrangement with the telephone company in California whereby the library was now charged $20 per hour for a minimum of 5 hours per month. This library also had systems by Lockheed, SDC, and Medline.

Keil did not visit customers in the intelligence community, but he thought these customers used the Bank in their training programs and in the normal course of their intelligence work. Most of their searches, he thought, were simple name checks which probably took no more than 3 or 4 minutes. He thought a typical customer in this segment would probably do 350 to 400 searches a month. He suspected that the Bank's usage for training purposes was probably controlled but that its usage for normal intelligence work probably was not monitored.

KEIL'S OBJECTIVES FOR THE INFORMATION BANK AND CHANGES INSTITUTED AS OF FEBRUARY 1975

In the business plan which Keil presented to top management in January 1975, he listed the following business and marketing objectives:

■ *Business objectives*

1 Within the next 24 months have The Information Bank operating as a profitable business.

2 Establish a dominant marketing position over the next 24 months in general data base retrieval companies who are marketing on a commercial basis.

3 Organize and develop a professional marketing team capable of carrying out objectives one and two.

4 Insure that both EDP systems and communications are capable of supporting an expandable and reliable service consistent with the high standards of The New York Times Company.

5 Establishment of measurement system which will track usage of the base and produce statistics that will be used in evaluating journal entries and chronological use, as well as producing marketing information. This system will be used to determine system performance, billing, and commission information.

■ *Marketing objectives*

1 Formulate a pricing policy which will hit a breakeven point at 60 percent of system capacity.

2 Formulate a compensation plan for the sales staff that will motivate them to higher productivity levels.

3 Establish revenue benchmarks on a monthly basis which total an annual revenue of $1.1 million.

4 Hire in 1975 a sales manager and trainer for the Washington office.

5 Hire two new salespeople and a trainer for the New York office.

6 Create and establish an identity for The Information Bank.

7 *Formulate a sales strategy through industry penetration, application selling and geographical concentration that will optimize our sales resources.*

8 *Through development of a professional marketing team, newsletters and promotional pieces, demonstrate to our customers and prospects that The Bank is a sound, viable business.*

9 *Have a flexible promotion program which, when needed, may be used to create a demand for the service consistent with the ability to meet that demand.*

10 *Through a better understanding of the market and evaluation of marketing feedback, formulate a technical priority list for communications and systems.*

11 *Minimize expenses through sound management decisions and practices.*

Keil first addressed the issue of the geographic spread of customers. Geographic concentration would enable the company to take advantage of wide-band leased telephone lines which provided better quality communication with less line noise than did regular lines and which could accommodate several users at one time, thereby lowering costs. Furthermore, it would allow the company to build a local staff of salespeople and trainers and to concentrate its advertising and promotional activities. Keil's first target market was the Northeast. However, he did not want to neglect opportunities beyond this area. Therefore, in drawing up new sales responsibilities, he assigned salespeople specific geographic areas in the Northeast plus specific industries in other parts of the United States. He thought that, once the salespeople developed expertise in selling to specific industries, they could probably sell to most major companies within that industry. (See Exhibit 3 for the new sales responsibilities.)

Within the Northeast, the lucrative Washington market was selected for maximum attention. Keil leased office space there and hired a sales manager and a trainer. He thought the Washington office would serve to test the viability of a local office and staff.

To strengthen the sales force, Keil began instructing his salespeople in professional selling techniques. He personally critiqued many of their sales calls and demonstrations, circulated pertinent literature, and provided cassette-tape presentations on sales techniques. He held several sales meetings and scheduled additional meetings at frequent intervals during the rest of the year.

Keil also changed the compensation system by formalizing a commission plan for the salespeople. The plan emphasized the generation of net new revenue from both existing accounts and new accounts. However, a $100 bonus for opening a new account was also offered. Keil estimated salespeople's salaries and commissions would amount to about 15 percent of total revenue generated, an amount typical of the data-processing industry. His goal, which he thought would be reached by June 1976, was to have each salesperson handling 20 to 25 customers, each of whom would spend between $900 and $1,000 a month on The Information Bank. The salespeople should eventually be earning between $25,000 and $30,000 annually, Keil thought.

The selling task for The Information Bank consisted of personal sales calls at high management levels in the prospect company, library, or agency.

"Ideally, we like to talk to the chief executive officer or someone else who is high enough to see the overall information needs of the company," Keil commented. "Often we begin with the vice presidents of advertising or public relations, who may or may not be high level officials." Ms. Sally Bachelder, who specialized in library accounts, said she always met with the director of a library, though she might give a demonstration of the system to several librarians. With all types of customers, multiple sales calls were necessary to close an account.

To support the personal sales effort and build product awareness, Keil did a limited amount of media advertising and direct mail. He hired Mr. William Saxon to create cartoons for the ads, and he ran a few ads in *The Washington Post, The Wall Street Journal, The New York Times,* and some association magazines aimed at the Washington market. He sent direct-mail pieces to the chief executive officers, advertising vice presidents, and marketing vice presidents of *Fortune* magazine's 1,000 largest corporations, to association executives, and to people designated by the Bank's salespeople as potential customers. He budgeted approximately $50,000 for the advertising and direct-mail campaign for 1975. (See Exhibit 4 for sample advertisements.)

Once the initial sale was made and a terminal installed, a good training program was necessary to teach the various users the most effective research methods. Keil stated that the Bank's training program was "pretty strong." Less than 1 hour of instruction would get the researcher started. However, at the present time, several different types of terminals were used by the Bank's subscribers because, in the past, they had purchased or leased their hardware from whomever they wished. While the terminals all performed the same functions, they differed slightly in the keyboard arrangement and certain keys included, in the appearance and dimensions of the screen, and in some phases of operation. New operators often became confused if their terminals did not contain the exact keys and terms mentioned in The Information Bank's user's guide, and they frequently called in the Bank's trainers.

THE PRICING ISSUE

As Keil examined The Information Bank's financial situation, he found himself in a morass of pricing strategies. The official price schedule had been published in June 1973, but another set of rates had been drawn up early in 1974. (See Exhibits 5 and 6 for these two price schedules.) Salespeople might use either of these, and they were accustomed to making all kinds of unusual promotional deals so that, in reality, there was a wide variety of pricing schemes. Some customers were getting the system free. The amount a customer paid was seldom based on the amount of time he spent using the system. In some cases, the customer paid telephone charges, while in others they were paid by The Information Bank. Most communication was done via regular telephone lines, rather than the less costly types of lines which were increasingly becoming available.

Keil broke the price the customer had to pay into three components—the CRT terminal and other equipment, lines of communication between the terminal and the central computer, and usage of the system. With regard to the hardware, he found that the average customer was paying about $400 a month for a CRT terminal, a modem,[1] and an abstract printer. Some customers were using an Incoterm CRT, a very expensive terminal which had been customized for The Information Bank. From his experience in the data-processing industry, Keil knew that terminals not customized for the Bank could perform the necessary functions perfectly adequately at substantially less cost and that, if all the equipment were purchased or leased from one source, the total cost would probably be less. Therefore, he arranged for a computer hardware company to supply customers with a CRT terminal, a modem, and a high-speed abstract printer for only $280 a month. The company billed The Information Bank, not the Bank's individual customers, for the hardware. Keil thought the Bank would probably charge customers the amount it paid for the hardware, rather than marking it up by any amount. If a customer wanted a microfiche reader or reader-printer, he could purchase it from several sources. Prices ranged from $20 to $2,000.

To communicate with The Information Bank's computer, most customers used either regular direct-dial connections or WATS lines which the company already leased. On the average, customers located outside the greater New York City metropolitan area who did not have access to a company-leased WATS line paid $15 to $30 per hour in communications charges. Not only were these the most expensive communication methods, but line noise often interrupted the communication, and messages to and from the computer were interspersed with unwanted signals. Customers usually thought something was wrong with the computer when this happened.

Keil thought The Information Bank should begin to rely more heavily on leased lines which provided higher-grade communication with virtually no noise bursts. Once it secured an adequate number of customers within a city for a leased line to be cost effective, The Information Bank would most likely use a time-division multiplexing line, i.e., a line which could be split into different channels to handle more than one customer simultaneously. The point-to-point connection of such a line would be between an eight-channel multiplexer attached to The Information Bank's computer in New York and an eight-channel multiplexer in another city, Washington, D.C., for example. If a customer in Washington wanted to sign onto the computer, he would call the multiplexer in Washington, and it would transmit the communication to New York via one of the channels of the line. The cost of an eight-channel line between Washington and New York was $315 per month, while the cost of a comparable line between New York and San Francisco was $2,300 per month. Each multiplexer cost $4,500. Keil had to decide whether the cost of the lines and the multiplexers would be covered by the customer or The Information Bank.

---

[1] The type of signal produced and processed by the computer and the CRT terminals was known as a *digital* signal, while the signals transmitted over telephone lines were *analog* signals. To convert one type of signal into the other, a modem (*modulator-dem*odulator) was used. Therefore, The Information Bank's computer would generate messages using digital signals which would pass through a modem before entering the telephone lines. At the customer's office, the signals would again be processed through a modem which converted them from analog to digital signals for use by the CRT.

With regard to usage of the system, Keil had to decide whether The Information Bank should charge a fixed monthly fee or a fee tied to hourly usage. If he chose the latter option, he had to decide whether the fee would be determined by the volume used (for example, X amount for the first 50 hours and Y amount for every hour over 50), by the time of the day the system was used, or by some combination of the two. For whatever alternative he chose, he had to decide exactly what the prices would be.

Unfortunately, he had very few guidelines as to which choice and what prices would be most acceptable in the marketplace. He noted that the Bank currently had some customers paying more than $50 per hour who apparently did not consider the price exorbitant. Other customers, however, were paying flat monthly rates for unlimited usage, while still others were paying virtually no usage fee at all. He had spoken with staff members of a commercial time-sharing service who marketed similar interactive computer time for $100 per hour. Since they used time-division multiplexing lines, their customers did not have to pay large communications charges. Keil also had the pricing schedules of LEXIS, SDC, and Predicasts, but since they were not really direct competitors, he was not sure how applicable their pricing schemes were to The Information Bank's situation. (See Exhibit 7 for LEXIS', SDC's, and Predicasts' price lists.)

In deciding how to price the microfiche, Keil noted that only half the Bank's current customers subscribed to microfiche, probably, he thought, because of its high cost—$900 per year—and the widespread availability of less costly microfilm. He wanted to lower the cost considerably to get more customers and to lessen the likelihood that customers would arbitrarily cancel their fiche subscriptions. Furthermore, he thought reduction in microfiche prices would be a good marketing tactic if he decided to raise usage prices of the total system. It cost The Information Bank about $4.80 to produce a master of a fiche, and it produced about 500 masters per year. To produce a copy of a master cost about 21 cents, and the cost of handling and mailing a copy was about 75 cents. The copies (i.e., the items that were sent to the customers) were sent out 110 times a year.

Keil estimated that, in 1975, total operating costs to be incurred by The Information Bank would be about $2.5 million:

Computer lease (flat rate)	$600,000
Marketing expenses	$925,000
System improvements	$150,000
Indexing and abstracting	$700,000
Miscellaneous office expenses	$125,000

These expenses did not include the cost of any terminals, customers' modems, or other equipment, because Keil assumed these equipment costs would be passed through to customers. The $150,000 budgeted for system improvement included provisions for modifications or additions to the system's hardware and software which would be required as additional customers were brought onto the system.

PLANS FOR THE FUTURE

Keil felt that the future of The Information Bank was extremely bright. He mentioned several products which the Bank could furnish at minimal cost. It already offered a daily news summary which an editor wrote from the earliest edition of the *Times*. A customer could simply call up the summary on his CRT and scan the major news events. Keil had not tracked usage of the news summary, but one day the editor who wrote it was sick, the summary was not written, and Keil's office was flooded with calls. Keil thought the Bank would soon also offer a summary of each day's business news. Another possible spin-off product was books of abstracts on particular subjects. It would cost very little to print the abstracts, and another subsidiary of The New York Times Company would actually publish the book. Finally, Keil thought the Bank might also start providing corporate profiles which gave names, titles, and addresses of leading officers of major corporations and that it would eventually offer proprietary data to various customers.

EXHIBIT 1
PERIODICALS INCLUDED IN THE BANK
The Information Bank

THE INFORMATION BANK®

Data Base

 A SUBSIDIARY OF THE NEW YORK TIMES COMPANY

I. THE NEW YORK TIMES

Input into the data base comprises virtually all news and editorial matter from the final Late City Edition, including Sunday feature sections and daily and Sunday regional material not distributed within New York City. Current issues are normally processed four or five working days after publication. At present, New York Times material extends back to January 1, 1969.

II. OTHER PUBLICATIONS

General Circulation Newspapers:

Atlanta Constitution
Chicago Tribune
Christian Science Monitor
Houston Chronicle
Los Angeles Times
Miami Herald
National Observer
New York Times
San Francisco Chronicle
Washington Post

Foreign Affairs:

Atlas
Economist of London
Far Eastern Economic Review
Foreign Affairs
Foreign Policy
Latin America
Latin America Economic Report
Manchester Guardian
Middle East
Times of London

Newsweeklies, Monthlies, Quarterlies:

American Scholar
Atlantic
Black Scholar
Commentary
Commonweal
Consumer Reports
Current Biography
Ebony
Harpers
Nation (The)
National Journal
National Review
New Republic
New York
New York Review of Books
New Yorker
Newsweek
Psychology Today
Saturday Review
Sports Illustrated
Time
US News and World Report
Variety
Village Voice
Washington Monthly

Business Publications:

Advertising Age
American Banker
Automotive News
Barron's
Business Week
Editor and Publisher
Forbes
Fortune
Harvard Business Review
Journal of Commerce
Wall Street Journal

Science Publications:

Astronautics
Bulletin of Atomic Scientists
Industrial Research
Science
Scientific American

Material selected from the magazines and newspapers listed above is being processed at varying rates according to priorities established in consultation with subscribers. At present, top priority is being given to Business Week, Los Angeles Times, The Wall Street Journal and The Washington Post. However, current selections from most of these periodicals are now available. Back files for most of these publications extend back to January 1, 1973, and for many to early 1972.

Selection Criteria

Normally **included** are:

Significant news items, interpretive articles, and articles of opinion or commentary originating with or exclusive to the source periodicals.

Biographical material.

Business and financial news and interpretive items on business and financial subjects unless of interest only on a very short-term basis or only to a narrow, highly specialized group.

Editorials.

Surveys, background or chronological reviews, and similar descriptive material on subjects of general interest.

Items by or about people of substantial general interest, regardless of content.

Commercial and political advertising when of research value.

EXHIBIT 2
INFORMATION BANK SUBSCRIBERS
The Information Bank

	Location
Royal Canadian Mounted Police	Canada
Library of Congress	Washington, D.C.
U.S. Army War College	Carlisle, Pa.
State Department	Washington, D.C.
Gruner & Jahr	New York City
Army Library	Washington, D.C.
National Broadcasting Company	New York City
Enoch Pratt Memorial Library	Baltimore, Md.
Kansas City Public Library	Kansas City, Mo.
Brooklyn Public Library	New York City
New York State Library	Albany, N.Y.
United Nations	New York City
Connecticut State Library	Hartford, Conn.
IBM	White Plains, N.Y.
Hill & Knowlton	New York City
Mobil Oil	New York City
General Foods	White Plains, N.Y.
Exxon	Linden, N.J.
Detroit Free Press	Detroit, Mich.
Shell	Houston, Tex.
B. F. Goodrich	Akron, Ohio
General Mills	Chicago, Ill.
Reuters	New York City
Chase Manhattan	New York City
New York Public Library	New York City
Philip Morris Incorporated	Richmond, Va.
Gulf	Houston, Tex.
Dentsu	New York City
U.S. Academy at West Point	West Point, N.Y.
Voice of America	Washington, D.C.
University of Pennsylvania	Philadelphia, Pa.
Time Incorporated	New York City
Louisville Courier Journal	Louisville, Ky.
Adelphi University	Garden City, N.Y.
Philadelphia Free Library	Philadelphia, Pa.
Secretary of Air Force	Washington, D.C.
Environmental Protection Agency	Raleigh, Durham, N.C.
University of California at Berkeley Library	Berkeley, Calif.

EXHIBIT 3
INFOBANK TERRITORY ASSIGNMENTS
The Information Bank

■ *Smith*

1 Geography: Northern New Jersey
2 Colleges and universities: West
3 Banking, accounting, diversified financial services, brokers, law firms, law enforcement agencies, New York City government, ethical drugs, automobiles, trucks and farm implements, oil, gas, coal and other energy companies.

■ *Jones*

1 Geography: Philadelphia
2 Colleges and universities: Midwest
3 Broadcast and print media, advertising and public relations agencies, consumer personal products and services, consumer durables and household products, leisure time products and services, apparel, textiles, transportation products and services.

■ *Randolph*

1 Geography: Boston
2 Insurance, real estate, utilities, metals, mining (noncoal), chemicals, electronics, office products and services, rubber, machinery, construction and construction products, consultants, think tanks and research organizations, foundations.

■ *Bachelder*

1 Geography: Pittsburgh
2 Colleges and universities: East
3 Municipal public libraries, state, county, and regional library systems, colleges and universities.

■ *Franke*

Washington, D.C., area

EXHIBIT 4
SAMPLE ADVERTISING
The Information Bank

SPARKLE WITH STATISTICS!

■ Business and industrial management groups use the system as a "barometer" of consumer and political opinion…in economic and public-affairs work…as an updating service for executives.

■ Full source of economic, financial and appropriations data — useful in forecasting, planning, analysis and review of budgets.

■ In presentations to regulatory agencies, trade association legal and management groups use Information Bank as source of supporting data.

The Information Bank: your personal source of comprehensive, accurate data on thousands of subjects.

 Computerized information retrieval has come of age with The Information Bank. This on-line, interactive system gives you the opportunity of searching for the specific data you need — from 60 worldwide sources at the same time! No need to check through individual indexes or reference files. No need to set up special research projects. No need to learn a computer language. The Information Bank is designed to serve you, the end-user… with speed and accuracy on a routine day-to-day basis. In response to inquiries you type in, fully informative "abstracts" appear on your terminal screen *in seconds*. Using an optional printer, you can also obtain printed copies of whatever material you've retrieved.

A proven system — based on years of testing, development, and the refinement of an unmatched data base.

At the heart of The Information Bank's data base is material from The New York Times — daily and Sunday editions

dating back to 1969. Supplementing this vast resource are "abstracts" from 59 other journals — published in this country and abroad. The scope is extensive, ranging from the Los Angeles Times to The Times of London. You can look into every conceivable subject, requesting specific material as indicated in this chart:

Elections		News articles
Legislation		Forecasts
Litigation	**20K**	Analyses
Labor/	**ABSTRACTS**	
Management	**ADDED**	
Energy	**MONTHLY**	Surveys
World trade		Summaries
Finance		Biographies
Science		
		By-line pieces
Companies		Features
Organizations	Maps	Columns
Foundations	Charts	Editorials
Industries	Diagrams	

Here are just a few ways The Information Bank can help you in fulfilling objectives.

■ Provides current (and historical) background material for those involved in Congressional liaison work.

■ Managers and directors of associations utilize the system in compiling reports and articles for membership; also in preparing speeches and panel-discussion data.

■ Helps you stay responsive to status of legislative hearings, budgets, committee action — affecting your own department and others.

A simple-to-operate system: key factor in The Information Bank's wide acceptance in government, industry, libraries.

New subscribers, under our start-up plan, get comprehensive on-site training plus 200 hours of computer time for the first 60 days. This usage is charged at our flat rate. Thus, you have a unique opportunity to discover the full potential of this system.

THE INFORMATION BANK
The New York Times Company

Mr. Carl Keil, Director of Marketing
The New York Times Information Bank
229 West 43rd Street
New York, N.Y. 10036
(212) 556-1111

Please have your Washington office contact us regarding:
□ description of system; □ demonstration.

Name_____

Title_____ Phone_____

Agency or Organization_____

_____

Address_____

City, State, Zip_____

□ Send literature only

569

EXHIBIT 4
Continued

Presenting a computerized information-retrieval system that brings you the specific data you need...from over 60 worldwide sources.

THE INFORMATION BANK

The Information Bank represents computerized information-retrieval at its most productive. Designed to serve the end-user directly—this on-line, interactive system "guides" you to the specific data you need on virtually *any* subject of current or historical interest. The Information Bank pinpoints your desired data by searching through its *entire* data base in a matter of seconds. System is fully operational across the U.S., following almost a decade of testing, development and the refinement of an unmatched data base.

The Information Bank is a service of The New York Times Company. **NYT**

Designed for routine, day-to-day use:

At long last, the time-consuming process of checking through individual indexes, reference files and clippings is eliminated. So is the need for special task-force research. In response to inquiries you type in, fully informative "abstracts" appear almost instantly on your terminal screen. Thus, you can scan and bypass unwanted pieces quickly. Selected material can be arranged in chronological (or reverse-chronological) order at the touch of a button. As you'll see in chart "A" the system allows you to select material by publication, date, type of article, etc. Further, an optional printer can provide hard-copy of whatever data you've retrieved. All steps are in plain English, no computer language to learn.

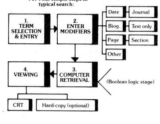

A. Four simple steps in typical search:

Data base grows at rate of 20,000 items monthly:

No other computerized system—anywhere in the world—can match the remarkable scope and size of this data base. Over one million abstracts are "stored" in The Information Bank's disk memory, and the expansion process constantly enriches this data base. Prime source of Information Bank material is The New York Times, daily and Sunday editions dating back to 1969. Additionally, the system contains items from more than 60 other leading journals—published in this country and abroad. The following chart breaks down the data base by *type* of article...

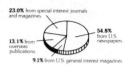

As the next chart demonstrates, when you access The Information Bank for data on a desired subject—you can request almost *any* type of article...

Subscriber list covers many fields:

- University libraries
- State and local libraries
- Government agencies/departments
- Law enforcement
- Research centers
- Foundations
- Communications/Publishing
- Advertising/PR
- Industrial companies
- Consumer-products firms

- Conglomerates
- Plus subscribers in Canada, Mexico

Generally speaking, The Information Bank's basic computer-usage charge to such subscribers averages between $45/50 per hour.

Communications charges and equipment rental are additional and separate. Most new subscribers now make their own arrangements for communications and "hardware," through direct contacts with suppliers. In certain cases, however, The Information Bank will assist in such matters.

A few technical details:

- Subscribers receive comprehensive on-site training at no charge for designated individuals and groups.
- New subscribers, under our start-up plan, get comprehensive on-site training plus 200 hours of computer time for the first 60 days. This usage is charged at our flat rate. Thus, you have a unique opportunity to discover the full potential of this system.
- Subscribers with existing compatible CRTs simply access our computer on a telephone "dial-up" basis.
- With multiple CRTs available, the system can readily function on a multi-department basis, as a central-library tool, *and* for individual searches.
- Microfiche reader-printer available as an option—for viewing or copying the full New York Times article from which an "abstract" is taken.
- To assure continuous, smooth performance of system, subscribers can reach the "Systems Monitor Office" in New York by using a special toll-free number.
- Information Bank supplies an informative Newsletter for its subscribers—covers latest developments in the system, new "descriptor" terms, tips and advice for

gaining optimum performance. We try to share with you the experiences gained over our *entire* subscriber network.

How the system helps you fulfill objectives...

Provides current (and historical) background material for those involved in Congressional liaison work.

Managers and directors of associations utilize the system in compiling reports and articles for membership; also in preparing speeches and panel-discussion data for meetings.

In communications or media-liaison work, The Information Bank gives overview of public and press reactions to current situations.

Helps you stay responsive to status of legislative hearings, budgets, committee action—affecting your own department and others.

Provides comparative benchmarks with the private sector, in such matters as recruiting, employment, transfers, job benefits, etc.

Full source of economic, financial and appropriations data—useful in forecasting, planning, analysis and review of budgets.

In dealing with regulatory agencies, trade association legal and management groups find Information Bank an invaluable source of supporting data.

Serves the needs of agencies whose overseas bureaus and personnel need up-dating from key U.S. sources.

THE
INFORMATION
BANK
A service of The New York Times Company **NYT**

The New York Times Information Bank
229 West 43rd Street
New York, N.Y. 10036
(212) 556-1111

EXHIBIT 4
Continued

DAZZLE THEM WITH YOUR DATA

Saxon

The Information Bank: your personal source of comprehensive, accurate data on thousands of subjects.

 Computerized information retrieval has come of age with The Information Bank. This on-line, interactive system gives you the opportunity of searching for the specific data you need — from 60 worldwide sources at the same time! No need to check through individual indexes or reference files. No need to set up special research projects. No need to learn a computer language. The Information Bank is designed to serve you, the end-user… with speed and accuracy on a routine day-to-day basis. In response to inquiries you type in, fully informative "abstracts" appear on your terminal screen *in seconds.* Using an optional printer, you can also obtain printed copies of whatever material you've retrieved.

A proven system — based on years of testing, development, and the refinement of an unmatched data base.

The Information Bank is currently operating for subscribers across the U.S. — and in Canada and Mexico as well. Among these are government agencies, libraries, universities and research centers, communications firms and leading companies on the Fortune 500 list. In many cases, subscribers use their existing CRTs and access our computer on a telephone "dial-up" basis. Others lease CRTs from major suppliers (or through The Information Bank) to receive the service.

Data base almost one million items; continues to grow at the rate of over 20,000 items monthly.

At the heart of The Information Bank's data base is material from The New York Times — daily and Sunday editions dating back to 1969. Supplementing this vast resource are "abstracts" from 59 other journals — published in this country and abroad. The scope is extensive, ranging from the Los Angeles Times to The Times of London. You can look into every conceivable subject, requesting news articles, columns, editorials, analyses, surveys, biographies, illustrated items (maps, charts, diagrams, etc.), and reviews.

DATA-BASE BREAKDOWN BY
INPUT OF ARTICLES (1974)

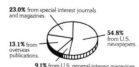

23.0% from special-interest journals and magazines.

54.8% from U.S. newspapers.

13.1% from overseas publications.

9.1% from U.S. general-interest magazines.

Functions on a multi-department basis, as a central-library tool, for individual searches.

Here are just a few ways The Information Bank can help you…

■ Provides current (and historical) background material for those involved in Congressional liaison work.
■ In communications or media-liaison work, The Information Bank gives overview of public and press reactions to current situations.
■ Helps you stay responsive to status of legislative hearings, budgets, committee action — affecting your own department and others.
■ Provides comparative benchmarks with the private sector, in such matters as plant and operations, management training and services, employee benefits, etc.
■ Full source of economic, financial and appropriations data — useful in forecasting, planning, analysis and review of budgets.

You get comprehensive on-site training, plus unlimited computer time for the first two months to help you discover the full potential of this system. Next step: for complete descriptive material, or better yet, a private demonstration — use the coupon below.

THE INFORMATION BANK The New York Times Company

Mr. Carl Keil, Director of Marketing
The New York Times Information Bank
229 West 43rd Street
New York, N.Y. 10036
(212) 556-1111

Please have your Washington office contact us regarding:
☐ description of system; ☐ demonstration.

Name_____
Title_____ Phone_____
Agency or Organization_____

Address_____
City, State, Zip_____
☐ Send literature only

EXHIBIT 5
PRICE SCHEDULE, JUNE 15, 1973
The Information Bank

The following price schedule has been formulated to provide several classes of service to suit the varying needs of our customers most economically. For example, a corporate library which uses The Information Bank to produce a large volume of current awareness searches for corporate divisions and departments could achieve the lowest per-search costs by subscribing to a Class IV subscription giving unlimited use during morning hours. Conversely, a medium-sized newspaper requiring only a few searches per day, but needing the availability of the system throughout the day, would best be served by a Class I or II subscription providing limits on total hours used but fewer restrictions on when this use is made.

1 Minimum subscription duration is 4 months. Subsequent service is sold on a monthly basis. Service may be canceled following 1 month's prior written notice.

2 Training period. During the first 2 months of service, while a subscriber's staff is learning to use The Information Bank, service will be supplied on an unlimited basis during all hours of system operation for the minimum monthly subscription rate of $675. Following this period the subscriber may choose the class of service best suited to his needs.

3 Equipment and communications. Prices shown in the following list do not include CRT terminals, printers, microfiche readers, or communications services or equipment.

However, CRT terminals and printers may be leased for up to a year on a monthly basis from The Information Bank at the rate of $163 per month for one CRT terminal plus $30 monthly maintenance and $120 per month for one hard-copy printer plus $30 maintenance. At the end of the year, the equipment may be purchased, with partial credit given for lease payments, or the lease continued with the equipment manufacturer. If the service subscription is canceled before the lease has run, The Information Bank will terminate the equipment lease at return freight cost only.

Communications services are normally obtained for subscribers by *The Times* Communications Department and billed to them at cost.

4 Use of Information Bank data by third parties. Use of The Information Bank is normally limited to a subscriber's own organization. However, special arrangements may be made to use service in Classes I and II to supply searches to nonsubscribers. An extra charge of $250 per month is made under such arrangements.

EXHIBIT 5
Continued

CLASSES OF SERVICE

I

- Hours of availability: 9 A.M. to 6 P.M. Monday through Friday.
- Type of access: up to a total of 25 hours of on-line use per month.
- Price: $675 per month (extra access is available at $20 per hour).

II

- Hours of availability: 8 A.M. until system shutdown Monday through Sunday.
- Type of access: up to a total of 25 hours of on-line use per month.
- Price: $775 per month (extra access is available at $20 per hour).

III

- Hours of accessibility: 8 A.M. until system shutdown Monday through Sunday.
- Type of access: unlimited.
- Price: $1,350 per month.

IV

- Hours of accessibility: 8 A.M. to 1 P.M. Monday through Friday.
- Type of access: unlimited during hours specified.
- Price: $675 per month (emergency service in afternoons is available on a spot basis at $50 per afternoon).

V

- Hours of accessibility: 1 to 6 P.M. Monday through Friday.
- Type of access: unlimited during hours specified.
- Price: $850 per month (emergency service in mornings is available on a spot basis at $50 per morning).

THE NEW YORK TIMES ON MICROFICHE

Microfiche of the news and editorial contents of *The New York Times* on 4 × 6 inch fiche, 25× reduction. Mailed to subscribers on a weekly (Wednesday to Tuesday) basis on the Friday after the last Tuesday of each week's group. $900/year.

(Written agreements will be entered into with *The New York Times* Sales, Inc.)

EXHIBIT 6
SUBSCRIPTION RATES AND OTHER TERMS, EARLY 1974
The Information Bank

I. TERM

If subscriber provides his own terminal, the subscription is for a minimum of 6 months. After 6 months, the subscription continues automatically unless canceled. Thirty days' prior written notice is required for cancellation.

If subscriber has *The Times* lease the terminal for him, the subscription must be for a minimum of 1 year. Renewals will be automatic, and also for a period of 1 year, unless 30 days' prior written notice of cancellation is given.

II. START-UP PERIOD

The start-up period is defined as the first 2 months of a subscription, starting when the installation is certified to be operational.

Unlimited access is permitted during the days and hours of normal operation (Monday through Friday, 8 A.M. to 12 midnight, eastern time, major holidays excepted; also most Saturdays, 9 A.M. to 5 P.M.).

A flat amount of $625 per month is charged to cover costs of installation, start-up, and training.

III. TERMINALS AND OTHER EQUIPMENT

Terminals may be selected from among the models specified by *The Times* as compatible with The Information Bank system.

Terminals may be purchased or leased by subscriber, or leased by *The Times* on behalf of subscriber.

■ *Typical costs are:*

Incoterm CRT terminal SPD 10/20 monthly rental	$163.00
Centronics printer monthly	133.00
Maintenance for each of the above monthly	30.00

■ *Telephone data sets (modems):*

For leased-line connections monthly	55.00
For dial-up connections monthly (approx. figure)	115.00

Microfiche readers or reader-printers are not marketed by *The Times*. A variety of models ranging in price from $100 to over $2,000 are available.

EXHIBIT 6
Continued

IV. COMMUNICATIONS

■ May be provided by subscriber

■ May be arranged with a common carrier through *The Times*

■ May be provided by The Information Bank through its network as part of the service. However, *The Times* reserves the right not to provide network service to a given location, or to discontinue service to a given location upon adequate notice. Network communications are available only in the continental United States.

V. SUBSCRIPTION RATES

Rates are effective at the start of the third month of subscriptions (see Section II) and do not include costs of terminals and other equipment (see Section III), communications costs (unless communications are provided through The Information Bank network as part of the service), and the costs of microfiche.

Rates for service including communications vary with the subscriber's distance from New York City, as follows:

■ Zone I: 0–   75 miles

■ Zone II: 75–   250 miles

■ Zone III: 250–   500 miles

■ Zone IV: 500–1,000 miles

■ Zone V: 1,000–1,500 miles

■ Zone VI: 1,500–3,000 miles

Rates vary with the number of hours of usage (connect time) according to Table 1. Future communications rates may be adjusted downward if warranted by increased use of the system.

TABLE 1

Without communications, per minute		With communications, per minute					
Hours per month	All zones	Zone I	Zone II	Zone III	Zone IV	Zone V	Zone VI
First 10	$0.75						
Second 10	0.68						
Third 10	0.63		*To Be Determined*				
Fourth 10	0.58						
Fifth 10	0.54						
Over 50	0.50						

EXHIBIT 6
Continued

TABLE 2

Without communications	With communications	
$875.00	Zone I:	$1,025.00
	Zone II:	1,175.00
	Zone III:	1,325.00
	Zone IV:	1,475.00
	Zone V:	1,625.00
	Zone VI:	1,775.00

Access is at any time that the system is in operation.

Subscribers will be billed a minimum of 4 hours of service per month.

FLAT-RATE OPTION. Subscribers may contract for up to 25 hours of service per month at a flat rate, as shown in Table 2. Additional hours may be purchased on a connect-time basis in accordance with the rate schedule shown in Table 1.

VI. MULTIPLE SUBSCRIPTIONS

On second and subsequent subscriptions by the same subscriber, whether or not for the same locations, hours logged on all terminals will be pooled for billing purposes.

VII. RE-SALE OF SERVICE

Special terms may be arranged for subscribers wishing to resell Information Bank materials.

VIII. MICROFICHE

Microfiche of *The New York Times* is available to subscribers at $75 a month. Sets for past years (1969–1973) are available at $600 a year.

EXHIBIT 7
PRICING SCHEDULES OF THREE MAJOR INFORMATION STORAGE AND RETRIEVAL COMPANIES
The Information Bank

	LEXIS (Mead Data Central, Inc.)	Systems Development Corporation	Predicasts
Equipment	$500/mo for the initial research terminal (i.e., a video display unit, a printer, and communications equipment) and all communications costs between that terminal and Mead Data Central's computer in Dayton, Ohio.* $375/mo for each additional terminal installed in same city.* $450/mo for each additional terminal installed in another city.*	Charges not available in company promotional literature.	Charges not available in company promotional literature.
Communications	Included in equipment charges.	$10/hr via TYM-share communications plus any locally incurred charges to the nearest TYM-share city.†	$10/hr via TYM-share communications in N. America. $15/hr in Europe. WATS lines and regular direct dial to Palo Alto could also be used.

Usage

LEXIS (Mead Data Central, Inc.):

There are two classes of subscription. Schedule A has a minimum monthly use commitment of $1,000; schedule B has a minimum monthly use commitment of $2,500. Use charges in each class are divided into three categories:

1. Research time (peak hours)
2. Research time (off-peak hours)
3. Search time

Research time is the total time a user is in contact with MDC's central computer, from the time he transmits his identification number until he terminates communications with the computer.

Systems Development Corporation:

Data base	Hourly rate	Off-line printing per citation
Life Science	$90	$.25
Engineering	90	.20
Geosciences	60	.15
Business mgt.	45	.10
Chemistry	45	.08
Govt. R & D	45	.10
Agriculture	30	.10
Education	25	.08
Petroleum	35	.05

Predicasts:

$90/hr of connect time
$425 annual access fee for market abstracts
$360 annual access fee for F & S indexes
$500 annual access fee for domestic statistics
$500 annual access fee for international statistics

EXHIBIT 7
Continued

Peak hours are the following:

Monday through Friday
9 A.M. to 7:30 P.M., Eastern time
8 A.M. to 7:30 P.M., rest of U.S.

Off-peak hours are the following:
Monday through Friday

7:30 P.M. to 12 P.M., Eastern time
7:30 P.M. to 11 P.M., Central time
7:00 A.M. to 8 A.M.
7:30 P.M. to 10 P.M., Mountain time
6:00 A.M. to 8 A.M., Pacific time
7:30 P.M. to 9 P.M.

Saturday

10 A.M. to 4 P.M., Eastern time
9 A.M. to 3 P.M., Central time
8 A.M. to 2 P.M., Mountain time
7 A.M. to 1 P.M., Pacific time

Search time is that small portion of research time beginning with the transmission of a search request to the central computer and ending with the appearance on the research terminal of a statement that a certain number of documents (e.g., cases) satisfy the request. Search time does not include the time when messages, replies, or documents are displayed on the terminal screen; when the user is typing requests or instructions, or reading or thinking; and when the hard-copy printer is operating.

Use charges in each category are measured to the nearest second as follows:

EXHIBIT 7
Continued

LEXIS (Mead Data Central, Inc.)	Systems Development Corporation	Predicasts

Schedule A

Research time (peak hours)	$97/hr
Research time (off-peak hours)	48/hr
Surcharge for search time	195/hr

Schedule B

Research time (peak hours)	$77/hr
Research time (off-peak hours)	48/hr
Surcharge for search time	195/hr

To eliminate inequities, any unused portion of the minimum monthly use commitment or any use above the minimum monthly commitment is accumulated and carried forward within each calendar quarter. There is no carryforward from one calendar to the next.

There is no additional use commitment for additional terminals.

Installation and training

LEXIS (Mead Data Central, Inc.)	Systems Development Corporation	Predicasts
$2,500 for the first terminal installed. $200 for each additional terminal installed. (Covers training of all users plus written instructional and reference materials.)	Charges not available in company promotional literature.	Private instruction at customer's site = $200 plus expenses Scheduled seminar = $50/person or $100/company

* These charges apply to terminals installed in the states of Illinois, Missouri, New York, Ohio, and Texas, the District of Columbia, and some other large metropolitan areas, a list of which can be obtained from an MDC representative. Installation of LEXIS research terminals elsewhere must be by special arrangement and possibly at a special charge.

† SDC had TYM-share-entry points in 50 United States cities and three European cities.

UNITED STATES POSTAL SERVICE

CHRISTOPHER H. LOVELOCK
Assistant Professor
Harvard Graduate School of Business Administration

L. FRANK DEMMLER
Formerly, Research Assistant
Harvard Graduate School of Business Administration

In mid-November 1974, Robert F. Jordan, Director of Product Management at the United States Postal Service (USPS), was reviewing a proposal from the Retail Products Division to standardize the fee for Postal Service money orders at 35 cents.

On the basis of the proposal before him, as well as the dissenting views of the Finance Department, Mr. Jordan had to prepare a marketing recommendation for transmittal to the Assistant Postmaster General for Customer Services, William D. Dunlap. In making his evaluation, he was mindful of the fact that the money order business, a profitable one for the Postal Service, not only faced direct competition from several sources but had also been plagued in recent years by a steadily shrinking market (Exhibit 1).

The Office of Product Management was one of eight marketing-related organizational groupings in the Department of Customer Services. As Director of Product Management, Mr. Jordan was responsible for five product-related divisions (including Retail Products) and also for the Market Research Division.

The U.S. Postal Service (USPS) was one of the oldest, largest and most visible federal agencies in the United States. In 1973–1974, the USPS operated some 31,000 post offices (including contract stations) and had 710,000 employees. Total revenues that year were $9.0 billion, and total operating expenses $11.3 billion.

Services offered by the USPS included several distinct categories of mail service, postal money orders, and Mailgrams (a joint venture with Western Union). First-class mail was the principal service offered, and the 51 billion pieces sent in 1973–1974 yielded revenues of $5.0 billion.

THE MONEY ORDER MARKET

Postal money orders, which came under the Retail Products Division, had a long history. The Post Office had first started selling them in 1864, at which point it had a near monopoly of the money order business. Over time, the size of the market grew rapidly. However, many competitors, notably banks and express companies, entered the field and gradually obtained a sizable market share for themselves.

While industry data were not available, postal officials estimated that the money order market totaled in excess of 500 million transactions in fiscal year 1972. At an estimated average service fee of 30 cents, this transaction level would generate over $150 million in fee revenues.

The market was thought to be divided into three segments of roughly equal size. USPS controlled one segment, national money order brands and major banks a second, and other financial institutions (such as savings and loans) a third. The total market was believed to be declining at a 2 percent annual rate. This was ascribed primarily to the growing use of personal checks, reflecting lower charges, greater convenience, and a more sophisticated attitude toward personal money management among the population at large.

The most significant competition to the USPS came from national money order companies, of which the two leading firms were Travelers Express (a subsidiary of Greyhound Corporation) and American Express. The value limit of their individual money orders was typically $200, while the fee varied according to the market involved. By contrast, the third market segment—sales through local financial institutions—was seen as rather disorganized. Institutions in this segment typically charged a flat fee for all values of money order, but these fees varied widely from place to place, ranging from free to 50 cents each. Value limits were at least $200 and often higher.

USPS MONEY ORDERS

Prior to fiscal year (FY) 1973–1974, USPS money orders were issued nationally in denominations up to $100. Fees were 25 cents for orders with a face value under $10, 35 cents for orders from $10.00 to $49.99, and 40 cents for $50 to

TABLE 1

FY	Transactions		Fee revenue	
	Thousands	%	Thousands	%
1970	181,750	−3.6	$56,174	−5.8
1971	179,439	−1.3	55,074	−2.0
1972	176,089	−1.9	54,672	−0.7
1973	170,776	−3.0	54,037	−1.2
1974	164,491	−3.7	51,655	−4.4

$100. Exhibit 2 details changes in postal money order fees since their inception in 1864. The most recent fee increase had been in March 1966.

The USPS money order business was divided into three basic categories: domestic (96.8 percent of total volume), military (3.0 percent), and international (0.2 percent). While the number of transactions, 165 million per year, paled in comparison with the volume of first class mail, money orders were still a very significant business. In addition to the revenues derived from fees, the high face value of money orders, averaging $30 each, provided a daily cash flow estimated at over $100 million. In FY 1974, the income from fees and float interest generated $57 million in revenues. By postal accounting standards, the money order business was a very profitable one for the Postal Service, with attributable costs[1] of only $2.6 million annually. Consequently, postal executives were concerned at the falling volume of business, which in the past 5 years had continued the steady decline begun in the early 1950s (see Table 1).

The weak market performance of postal money orders was ascribed to several factors, notably aggressive marketing by competitors. Brands such as American Express and Travelers Express had achieved good distribution, particularly in retail outlets situated in high-traffic areas and offering lengthy business hours (for example, 7-11 Stores, supermarkets, and drugstores). Many banking institutions were offering money orders "fee free" for the purpose of attracting new savings, checking, and loan accounts.

Postal Service executives speculated that certain actions taken in recent years by the USPS might also have contributed to the decline of its money order business. Such actions included shorter weekly hours (due to Saturday closings of post offices) and allowing contract stations (commercial retail outlets which provided post office services on a contractual basis for the USPS) to sell competitive money orders. Compounding the postal money order's competitive difficulties was the stipulation, in most instances, that USPS money orders only be sold in contract stations during the local post office's standard opening hours.

---

[1] The Postal Service differentiated between the costs of running the system and those which were directly traceable to providing a specific product or service. The former were termed *institutional costs;* the latter *attributable costs.* This procedure was an outgrowth of recommendations made by the Kappel Commission. In the case of money orders, the variable costs of paper, printing, processing, and the like plus direct overhead were charged as attributable costs. However, lobby facilities and the window clerk were charged as institutional costs. Postal products and services were expected to cover their attributable costs and also make a contribution to institutional costs.

MARKETING ACTIVITIES ON USPS MONEY ORDERS[1]

Concern among USPS executives over declining postal money order sales and fee revenues led to a series of actions designed to counteract this trend.

Starting in FY 1972, the product and its market were carefully analyzed by the Office of Product Management to identify opportunities for expansion over a 2-year period. Additionally, market research studies and test markets were conducted to upgrade the money order form itself and to ascertain the best advertising and promotional mix to use in merchandising the line to customers.

After several years of study and research, originally initiated by the old Post Office Department, a new money order form was introduced nationally in October 1973. The Postal Service completely revised both the aesthetics and function of the form. The new one included (1) a full-size four-color receipt, (2) a full-information money order, and (3) a voucher for increased internal control. It was felt by Product Management that this new form was competitively superior to any form in the industry and would contribute to greater customer acceptance, as well as improving the efficiency and security of USPS money order operations (see Exhibit 3). Posters were hung in post offices (Exhibit 4) to announce the change.

PROMOTIONAL TESTS

The effectiveness of advertising and promotional activity directed at USPS money orders was tested, with three cities being selected as test markets and each matched against a control city. The money order market development plan was highlighted by the following promotional elements:

1   *Media advertising.* A television advertising campaign was aired in each city beginning in November 1972. Thirty-second commercials featured a construction worker going about his dangerous job and stressed the safety of USPS money orders as a method of sending money (Exhibit 5).

2   *Sales promotion.* Three unique, direct-mail sales promotion efforts were developed and targeted at high-potential, money order–using households in each test market. The basic format was a color-printed self-mailer offering a coupon with one of the following purchase incentives:

■*Promotional incentive*	■*Purchase requirement*
1 free stamped envelope	1 money order[2]
1 fee-free money order	4 money orders
2 free stamped envelopes	2 money orders

---

[1] Some of the market research data on money orders has been disguised.

[2] This promotion is shown in Exhibit 6.

Special materials were developed to communicate the promotion to key field personnel, from management to window clerks. Field execution of the promotion was held to be very satisfactory, and excellent cooperation was obtained from local post offices.

The results of the test showed a modest increase in money order sales volume for each of the promotions, with free stamped envelopes generating a larger sales increase than the offer of four money orders for the price of three. However, it was decided not to expand the program nationally at this point, since the sales increases resulting fell slightly short of the level needed to make such a program economically viable. It was concluded that further testing should be undertaken.

TEST OF ALTERNATIVE USPS MONEY ORDER FEES

Another area of analysis and planning concerned the fees charged for different denominations of postal money orders. These fees had remained unchanged since March 1966, despite steadily rising costs in overall Postal Service operations. In FY 1972, it was felt by USPS product management that an opportunity existed to revise and improve the existing money order pricing structure.

Related to this issue was the decision to raise the maximum face value in which the money orders could be sold from $100 to $300. It was recognized that initially this would lead to a reduction in unit volume (and therefore in fee revenues), since sums of $100.01 to $300.00 would henceforth require only one money order instead of two or three. However, the change was expected to provide a competitive advantage and lead to a long-run sales increase.

A market test of alternative value-fee combinations was initiated in January 1972. The primary objective of this test was to determine the impact of alternative fee structures on both postal revenues and money order purchasers. A secondary objective was to develop a price for money orders in the $100 to $300 range, the higher-value ceiling established for the new money order system.

Three different value-fee combinations were tested. In all cases, the value ceiling was raised from $200. This was felt to be responsive to the needs of customers for higher-value money orders; it also eliminated the pricing disadvantages associated with having to buy two money orders for a value between $100 and $200, and placed the USPS ceiling at parity with key competition. It was not feasible to test the higher $300 limit for the new money order system at that time due to the mechanical limitations of existing hardware.

Two flat-fee schedules, one at 35 cents and the second at 25 cents, were tested along with the higher-value ceiling. The flat-fee approach was expected to eliminate many customer communications and operations disadvantages. The 35-cent price was close to current pricing and at parity with national competition. The more aggressive 25-cent price would, it was anticipated, yield a competitive price advantage.

A third alternative was also tested. This kept the then-current variable-fee schedule and added a 50-cent fee for values in the $100 to $200 range.

TABLE 2

Test area	Fee	Ceiling
City A ⎱ City B ⎰	25¢ (all values)	$200
City C ⎱ City D ⎰	35¢ (all values)	$200
City E ⎱ City F ⎰	Current to $100 50¢ for $100–$200	$200

Each alternative value-fee combination was tested in two cities (Table 2). Sales trends in the remainder of the country served as the control for these test markets.

The result of these tests, shown in Exhibit 7, suggested that the 35-cent flat fee was the best revenue-producing alternative of the three tested. Meantime, money orders in the $100.01–$200.00 range were found to account for approximately 5 percent of all sales transactions, as shown in Table 3.

CUSTOMER SURVEY FINDINGS

The Market Research Division initiated a study in October 1973 which identified consumer attitudes toward money orders. A nationally projectable quota sample was employed. Individual interviews were conducted to screen for money order or cash users in 13 towns and cities, including several of the test cities where the alternative fee structures were being test-marketed.

The objectives of this study were to:

1   Identify consumer behavior patterns in buying and using money orders.
2   Assess attitudes toward money orders in general and the USPS brand in particular.
3   Determine attitudes toward a flat-fee structure versus a variable-fee structure. (A small survey of postal clerks was also undertaken on this topic.)

Each respondent was exposed to only a fixed-fee concept (35 cents) or a variable-fee concept (either 25 cents–40 cents or 25 cents–50 cents). Respondents were asked a number of open-ended questions designed to discover per-

TABLE 3

	Percent of sales transactions (before/after introduction of $200 value ceiling)	
Money order value	Before	After
$0–$10.00	30	30
$10.01–$50.00	50	50
$50.01–$100.00	20	15
$100.01–$200.00		5

ceived likes and dislikes for the specific fee concept presented and to evaluate perceived cost-value relationships for different-valued money orders.

By those who used them, money orders were seen as a safe, practical, and easy method of giving and sending money and as value for what they cost. Postal money orders tended to be viewed as better than money orders in general, reflecting the fact that they were sold by one of the largest and most conspicuous institutions of the federal government.

Cash users were somewhat less anxious about postal money orders than about other brands, but not enough to change their primarily cash-using behavior. This group appeared to view the idea of using money orders as strange and somewhat disconcerting, regarding them as hard to find, handle, fill out, and cash. However, despite a preference for cash transactions, one-third of this group had checking accounts and half had savings accounts.

The survey found that the principal purposes for which respondents purchased money orders were for payment of bills (including rent, mortgage, and insurance), repayment of loans, mail-order purchases, and sending money to friends and relatives. Compared with the general population, money order users tended to have below-average incomes and were somewhat more likely to reside in either rural areas or central cities.

Not surprisingly, most respondents buying USPS money orders reported doing so in a post office, whereas users of other money orders tended to buy theirs in a grocery or drugstore or in a bank. The main reasons given among other money order users for not buying the USPS brand related to the relative inconvenience of post office hours and location. Some also cited the cost of USPS orders.

Concerning the different fee alternatives, a higher percentage of those who were exposed to the fixed-fee concept made positive comments concerning the fee structure than were made by those in the variable-fee groups. On the other hand, when asked what fee they expected to pay for various values of money order, respondents in both variable- and fixed-fee groups clearly expected to pay more for higher-value orders. They also indicated that higher-value money orders would be worth a higher fee to them.

RECOMMENDATIONS FOR ACTION

After examining the results of the market test and consumer survey, Mr. Mac-Innes, Product Manager for Money Orders, drafted a proposal for his superior, Mr. Vandegrift, recommending adoption of a flat 35-cent fee for all USPS money orders. This recommendation was based on the following conclusions:

1   The flat-fee structure was preferred by customers, principally because of its simplicity. This was confirmed both by the survey findings and the fact that not one complaint had been received in the 18-month test market.

2   On the basis of the market test results, the flat fee was expected to result in an increase in money order revenue of at least 5 percent.

3   It would strengthen the Postal Service's competitive position as the flat fee was preferred by competitive users as well as postal users. Additionally, the 35-cent fee would, on average, be lower than many current competitive rates.

4   A flat-fee structure would streamline postal operations by cutting back on clerk errors and increasing productivity. Additionally, a small survey of postal clerks had shown that they preferred the convenience and simplicity of a flat-fee structure.

THE FINANCE DEPARTMENT'S POSITION

Mr. Vandegrift had then circulated the proposal for a flat 35-cent fee to a number of other organizations within the Postal Service, both at Headquarters and in the field, for their review. A number of these had made comments and asked questions. Concurrence was eventually received from, among others, the Law Department, Government Relations, the Consumer Advocate, Retail Operations, and all the regions. One important organization, however, did not agree—the USPS Finance Department.

The Finance Department was responsible for the financial policies, practices, and operations of the Postal Service. This Department had a separate Money Order Branch and had been the only organization within the Postal Service with a major interest in money orders before the marketing function was established. In fact, many of the functions and interests normally associated exclusively with marketing in other organizations had fallen historically to the Finance Department.

Much internal correspondence passed between Product Management and Finance. A number of meetings were held and additional research and testing undertaken. Nevertheless, the differences between the two groups on this issue remained unresolved.

The Finance Department's final position included the following points.

1   While conceding that a flat fee was admittedly simpler, it was argued that customers would have to pay too high a price for simplicity. The proposal was unfair to those purchasing money orders for less than $10 in that they would have to pay 10 cents more than at present.

2   It was pointed out that many competitors in the money order business, notably banks, already charged lower fees than the Postal Service. An increase in USPS fees would, therefore, please the competitors. However, the Postal Service's chief function was to service its customers, not raise a price umbrella over the competition.

3   There was no evidence that a flat fee would build business for USPS. In fact, American Express, which presumably watched the market closely, had recently returned to a variable-fee structure. Sales were more likely to be decided on the basis of factors such as convenience of location and service hours, and whether or not the customer felt "at home" on the premises.

4   The Finance Department emphasized that money order users typically included the less-well-educated, less-prosperous elements of society, such as minority groups and blue-collar workers.

MR. VANDEGRIFT'S MEMORANDUM

Mr. Vandegrift felt that the Finance Department's objections to the memorandum were not sufficient to withdraw the recommendation. He summarized his division's viewpoint in a covering memo to Mr. Jordan accompanying the formal proposal.

In his memo, Mr. Vandegrift emphasized that most purchasers bought money orders of varying amounts, so that the proposed change would be essentially a wash for these people. Research showed that a small minority bought exclusively low-value orders. He also pointed out that a majority of this group, when surveyed, had indicated a preference for the flat-fee concept. Particularly significant, in his view, was the fact that not one complaint had been received from the test markets during the 18-month period when the fixed fee was being tested. Indeed, survey results showed that the majority of consumers had not even noticed any change in the fee structure.

Finally, he included data on fees charged by USPS and competitive brands (Exhibit 8). He indicated that there was good evidence for believing that American Express's return to a variable-fee structure was intended to provide flexibility for pricing their money orders in response to local market conditions.

A DECISION TO BE MADE

Mr. Jordan finished reading all the materials in the folder which Mr. Vandegrift had sent him and leaned back in his chair. What action should he recommend at this point to Assistant Postmaster General Dunlap, he wondered. As he saw it, there were basically three options open to him. One was a recommendation to go ahead, carefully documenting the arguments in favor of this move and countering as many as possible of the Finance Department's objections. A second was to specify an additional program of research and testing; while a third was to recommend retaining a variable-fee structure, in which case a decision still had to be taken on what fee to charge for the new $300 money order. Whichever of these alternatives he selected would have to be accompanied by a general marketing proposal for improving the Postal Service's share of the money order business.

EXHIBIT 1
POSTAL MONEY ORDER SALES, 1930–1974
(DOMESTIC TRANSACTIONS ONLY)
U.S. Postal Service

FY	Transactions, thousands	Average fee	Value of sales, millions	Average value per transaction to nearest $0.10
1930	203,307	8.4¢	$1,735	$ 8.50
1935	213,351	9.3	1,829	8.60
1940	255,502	9.4	2,103	8.20
1945	282,421	14.0	4,827	17.10
1950	302,848	17.7	4,641	15.30
1951	321,797	18.4	5,236	16.30
1952	375,215	18.1	5,946	15.80
1953	368,762	18.3	6,032	16.40
1954	359,685	18.6	6,049	16.80
1955	349,273	18.6	5,865	16.80
1956	346,505	18.6	5,926	17.10
1957	334,882	18.9	5,880	17.60
1958	311,025	22.6	5,442	17.50
1959	286,647	23.2	5,158	18.00
1960	273,633	23.4	5,031	18.40
1961	264,267	23.5	4,958	18.80
1962	251,842	25.3	4,787	19.00
1963	242,871	25.4	4,709	19.40
1964	235,414	25.6	4,719	20.00
1965	220,045	25.8	4,551	20.70
1966	215,361	27.5	4,734	22.00
1967	204,950	31.2	4,724	23.00
1968	196,763	31.3	4,707	23.90
1969	188,569	31.6	4,733	25.10
1970	181,750	30.9	4,723	26.00
1971	179,439	30.3	4,268	23.50
1972	176,089	31.0	4,340	24.60
1973	170,776	31.4	4,400 (est.)	25.70
1974	164,491	31.5	NA	NA

EXHIBIT 2
POSTAL MONEY ORDERS: DOMESTIC FEES SINCE 1864
U.S. Postal Service

Money order value	Nov. 1 1864	July 1 1866	Sept. 1 1868	July 15 1872	July 1 1875	July 2 1883	July 26 1886	July 1 1894
$0–$2.50	10¢	10¢	10¢	5¢	10¢	8¢	5¢	3¢
$2.51–$5.00	10	10	10	5	10	8	5	5
$5.01–$10.00	10	10	10	5	10	8	8	8
$10.01–$15.00	15	10	10	10	10	10	10	10
$15.01–$20.00	15	10	15	10	15	15	15	10
$20.01–$30.00	20	25	15	15	15	15	20	12
$30.01–$40.00		25	20	20	20	25	25	15
$40.01–$50.00		25	25	25	25	25	25	18
$50.01–$60.00						30	30	20
$60.01–$70.00						35	35	25
$70.01–$75.00						40	40	25
$75.01–$80.00						40	40	30
$80.01–$100.00						45	45	30

Money order value	Apr. 15 1925	July 20 1932	Mar. 26 1944*	Nov. 1 1944	Jan. 1 1949	July 1 1957	July 1 1961	Mar. 26 1966
$0–$2.50	5¢	6¢	10¢	6¢	10¢	15¢	20¢	25¢
$2.51–$5.00	7	8	14	8	10	15	20	25
$5.01–$10.00	10	11	19	11	15	20	20	25
$10.01–$15.00	12	13	22	13	25	30	30	35
$15.01–$20.00	12	13	22	13	25	30	30	35
$20.01–$30.00	15	15	25	15	25	30	30	35
$30.01–$40.00	15	15	25	15	25	30	30	35
$40.01–$50.00	18	18	30	18	25	30	30	35
$50.01–$60.00	18	18	30	18	35	30	35	40
$60.01–$70.00	20	20	34	20	35	30	35	40
$70.01–$75.00	20	20	34	20	35	30	35	40
$75.01–$80.00	20	20	34	20	35	30	35	40
$80.01–$100.00	22	22	37	22	35	35	35	40

* The 66⅔ percent increase prescribed in 1944 was to apply until 6 months after the termination of hostilities of World War II; however, the act was repealed and on November 11, 1944, the previous rates were restored.

591

EXHIBIT 3
OLD AND NEW POSTAL MONEY ORDER DESIGNS
(REDUCED SIZE)
U.S. Postal Service

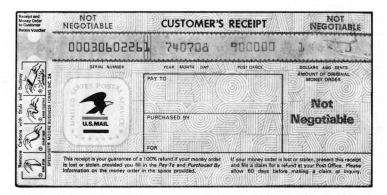

Old design: This order was off-white in color with black lettering. It contained the words "U.S. Postal Money Order" in place of "Invalid-Training Purposes Only" shown on this training copy.

New design: The customer's receipt was predominantly pale blue in color, with red, yellow, and black lettering. It carboned through to a separate post office receipt and a money order form. The latter, sent to the recipient, was yellow and buff with black lettering.

592

EXHIBIT 5
TV COMMERCIAL FOR USPS MONEY ORDERS
U.S. Postal Service

Needham, Harper & Steers, Inc.
909 Third Avenue, New York, New York 10022
(212) 758-7600

CLIENT: U.S. POSTAL SERVICE
PRODUCT: U.S. POSTAL SERVICE
AS FILMED TV COMM'L NO: UPMO2083
TITLE: "MALE RISK"

DATE: 12/8/72
LENGTH: 30 SEC.

1. MAN: Me and Marge ... the way we feel,

2. there's too many risks in life as it is.

3. Now, when it comes to paying bills,

4. me and Marge, we pay by safe Postal Money Orders.

5. You lose them or they get stolen from you,

6. you get a refund and nobody can say you didn't pay a bill when you did.

7. Because with U.S. Postal Money Orders,

8. you get a receipt from Uncle Sam to prove you did.

9. I get them down at the Post Office, or Marge does.

10. Postal Money Orders,

11. they're safer than money.

594

POSTAL MONEY ORDERS—GUARANTEED 100% SAFE

Mail a money order FREE

"Me and Marge, we always pay our bills with Postal Money Orders—the kind you buy at the Post Office.

"They're safer than money.

"And now—something extra—something FREE.

"You can get a stamped envelope FREE when you buy a Postal Money Order and give the clerk the special certificate below.

"Do it today. It's the safest way to send money through the mail."

OFFER ENDS MARCH 31, 1973

Tear off here

Safety First

UNITED STATES POSTAL SERVICE
U.S. MAIL

Postal Money Order

10¢ VALUE

BRING TO POST OFFICE

10¢ VALUE

FREE STAMPED ENVELOPE

U.S. Postal Money

FREE stamped envelope

Buy a Money Order at your Post Office

Get a stamped envelope FREE

Hurry! Offer expires March 31, 1973

10¢ VALUE

BRING TO POST OFFICE

10¢ VALUE

EXHIBIT 7
MONEY ORDER TEST MARKETS: PERCENTAGE CHANGE IN TRANSACTION VOLUME AND DOLLAR REVENUE VERSUS PREVIOUS YEAR
U.S. Postal Service

Period	25¢ flat-fee test (cities A and B)		35¢ flat-fee test (cities C and D)		Old pricing to $100, 50¢ fee for $100–$200 (cities E and F)		Control (rest of U.S.)	
	Transactions	$ revenue	Transactions	$ revenue	Transactions	$ revenue	Transactions	$ revenue
1972:								
Qtr. 3	−2.1%	−21.3%	−4.2%	+6.0%	−0.1%	+0.9%	−1.4%	−1.2%
Qtr. 4	+11.2%	−12.6%	+0.4%	+10.1%	+1.1%	+0.7%	+3.0%	+4.1%
1973:								
Qtr. 1	+17.6%	−14.1%	+0.7%	+2.3%	+0.8%	+0.4%	−2.3%	−1.9%
Qtr. 2	+11.3%	−17.5%	−1.1%	+4.1%	NA	NA	−1.7%	−1.1%
12-month total	+10.4%	−15.2%	−0.9%	+5.1%	NA	NA	−0.7%	−0.1%

Source: USPS records.

EXHIBIT 8
USPS AND COMPETING MONEY ORDER FEE
STRUCTURES, NOVEMBER 1974
U.S. Postal Service

Money order face value	USPS fees	
	Actual	Proposed
$ 0–$10.00	25¢	35¢
$10.01–$50.00	35¢	35¢
$50.01–$300.00	40¢	35¢

Average fees for competitive brands*

Money order face value	American Express		Travelers Express		Minor brands	
	Range	Average	Range	Average	Range	Average
$ 5.00	35–50¢	42.5¢	25–45¢	34.2¢	15–50¢	30.6¢
$ 25.00	35–50¢	43.1¢	35–45¢	41.9¢	15–50¢	36.2¢
$100.00	35–50¢	47.2¢	35–50¢	43.9¢	35–100¢	38.8¢

* Fees charged varied by market. Minor brands often offered fee-free money orders as a promotional incentive to account holders.

Source: USPS Office of Product Management.

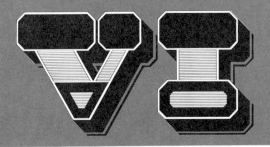

MARKETING RESEARCH

Marketing research is one of several systematic procedures for gathering information needed by management for decision making. Some marketing decisions are based almost entirely on intuition derived from managerial experience. However, in most instances, attempts are made to gather together quantitative data and qualitative information which, after analysis, will help management to:

1   *Identify marketing problems and opportunities*

2   *Determine the magnitude and dimensions of a specific situation*

3   *Provide a forecast of future conditions*

4   *Evaluate alternative marketing strategies and select the most appropriate course of action*

5   *Monitor subsequent performance in the marketplace and indicate any need for changes in strategy*

It is useful to group marketing information into two categories, primary and secondary data. Primary data is new information which has to be specially collected through market research activities. Secondary data is information which already exists in some form. It may need to be reorganized and reanalyzed, but the basic data have previously been collected.

The advantages of researching secondary data include potential economies of both time and money, since the needed information may already be available either in-house or in a library. Even where secondary data prove insufficient to permit management to make an informed decision, they may constitute an important input into design of a new marketing research survey, helping to shape the survey design and define the nature of additional data to be collected.

This note will focus on marketing research activities for collection of primary data, while Sources of Marketing Information, one of the Appendixes at the end of this book, discusses collection of secondary data.

MANAGEMENT'S ROLE IN MARKETING RESEARCH

Marketing research is not an element in the marketing mix, but rather a tool used for gathering information to help make decisions about the marketing mix. Although the conduct of research is often delegated to specialists, marketing managers do need to become involved in the research process and to develop some understanding of both its potential and limitations. Among the managerial tasks relating to the research process are:

1   *Deciding when to initiate research and identifying the need for specialized help*

2   *Working with the specialists to define the problem to be studied and clarifying for them how the resulting data will be used in decision making*

3   *Deciding how much to spend on the research*

4   *Reviewing the proposed research design*

5   *Ensuring that the data collected are analyzed in such a way that they will be relevant to the decisions to be made*

6   *Selecting the most appropriate format for presenting the research findings to other members of the management team*

In deciding whether to use low-cost techniques providing crude estimates of trends and relationships or costly and sophisticated techniques yielding highly refined estimates, the manager should be guided by several considerations.

The key factor should be the payoff expected from the additional information generated by the research—obviously a function of the purpose for which it is being conducted. The larger the amounts at stake in a particular situation and the greater the degree of uncertainty, then the more worthwhile it becomes for management to invest substantial sums in obtaining information which can reduce the associated risks.

It may therefore be appropriate to look at several alternative research approaches and relate their costs to the anticipated value of the respective results. Other considerations in selecting research procedures include time and budgetary constraints, the nature of the problem, and the risk of tipping off a competitor about the organization's interest in a particular issue.

DEFINING THE PROBLEM AND RESEARCH OBJECTIVES

The problem definition stage is perhaps the most critical in the research process. Unless the marketing manager is clear about why the research is being done and what he or she hopes to obtain from the results, there is a real risk that the resulting study will not generate meaningful data for managerial decision making. The manager must therefore define the problem precisely for the market research specialists, discussing it within the context of the decision to be made.

By way of defining research problems more clearly, it is often useful to undertake some exploratory research. In addition to researching secondary data sources, this may also take the form of discussions with knowledgeable persons (other managers, trade representatives, or outside experts) and pilot surveys of small groups of consumers.

The information thus gained, often at modest expense of both time and money, can then be used to help clarify and refine the research problem under consideration. Sometimes it may lead management to close off one avenue of exploration entirely and focus on other alternatives.

Two of the most common types of marketing research projects are consumer surveys and test marketing. The balance of this introductory text will be devoted to a brief review of some of the issues raised by each.

CONSUMER SURVEYS

Three fundamental issues face the marketing researcher in designing a consumer survey. The first is sample design—deciding which people to interview and how many of them to include in the survey. The second concerns selection of the most appropriate method of communicating with members of the sample population; the third relates to design of the questionnaire itself. As will be seen, these three issues are interrelated.

SAMPLE DESIGN

Whereas industrial marketers often sell to a limited number of buyers, each of whom is known to management, consumer marketers are only rarely in such a situation. In most instances, the market for consumer products is a large one, and management typically does not know the identity of those who purchase its products.

Time and cost considerations typically make it impossible for a marketer to survey all existing or potential consumers. Instead, a sample of consumers is surveyed in the expectation that their opinions will be representative of the larger group from whom they are drawn.

Problems for the researcher include deciding how large the sample should be and how to ensure that it is, indeed, representative. A nonrepresentative sample is likely to yield biased results. For instance, it would be unwise for a marketer of pocket calculators to generalize about market reaction to an inexpensive new model, based on the results of a survey in which most respondents were middle-aged, upper-income men. A key task for the researcher is to employ sampling procedures which will maximize the likelihood that the people included in the sample are a representative cross section of the consumers in whom management is interested.

The size of sample that is needed will be determined by several considerations: the number of people in the total "population" from which the sample is to be drawn[1], the degree of confidence which management needs to be able to place in the results; the proportion of those in the sample who are expected to respond to the survey; and the nature of the analysis which will be performed on the resulting data. Statistical formulas can be used to determine the optimal sample size for a particular research project.

One of the problems facing researchers is that a carefully designed sample may prove of little value if the response rate to the survey is low. When a significant number of those sampled do not respond to a survey, there is a risk of nonresponse bias in that those who make the effort to respond may have different characteristics from those who do not. It is often the case that respondents are more interested in the topic of the survey or have stronger feelings than do nonrespondents. While many researchers believe that a low response rate may sometimes lead to seriously biased findings, it is well to recognize that poor sample design in the first place may be just as significant a cause of bias.

---

[1] *Not an important consideration when the population size is large.*

CHOICE OF SURVEY METHOD

There are three basic ways for marketing researchers to obtain information in a survey, namely, personal interviews, telephone interviews, and questionnaires designed for unsupervised completion by respondents.

The major criteria usually employed in selecting between these alternatives include cost per completed response, the length and nature of the questions to be posed, the characteristics of the sample, the time frame available for completion of the research, and the nature of the research topic.

PERSONAL INTERVIEWS. Personal interviews tend to be expensive. When in-depth interviews are conducted in respondents' homes by skilled interviewers, costs per response of $20 to $50 and higher are quite common. Other problems are that such surveys bias the nature of the responses. On the other hand, personal interviews usually result in very high response rates, can go into a topic in great depth, and provide the researcher with greater flexibility than do other survey methods.

TELEPHONE INTERVIEWS. Telephone interviews are attractive to many marketing researchers, since they allow for personal contact but are much faster and cheaper to implement. Response rates are generally high. However, there are limits as to the amount of information which can be obtained in a telephone survey. Costs per completed response depend on the duration of the interview, being typically in the range of $3 to $8 when conducted by a professional research firm; they are, of course, more expensive when calls are being made long distance.

If telephone directories are used, then unlisted numbers may produce a biased sample, since 19 percent of all United States households have unlisted numbers. Studies indicate that the ratio for unlisted numbers is particularly high among certain groups, notably nonwhite subscribers (32 percent), women aged 18 to 34 (27 percent), and subscribers in the five largest metropolitan areas (29 percent)[1]. Contrary to popular belief, subscribers in the highest and lowest income brackets have a much lower incidence of nonlistings than do those with incomes in the range $5,000 to $9,000 (25 percent). One way of getting around the nonlistings problem is through use of random-digit dialing, but this increases costs, since many numbers dialed at random prove to be disconnected or else are institutional or commercial listings.

SELF-COMPLETION QUESTIONNAIRES. Many surveys involve distributing a questionnaire which respondents then complete themselves. While it is sometimes possible to gather consumers together in a central location to fill out a questionnaire, the most common approach is for questionnaires to be distributed and returned through the mail.

Mail surveys are very versatile and still relatively inexpensive, despite recent increases in postage. Costs per completed response generally range from $1 to $2

---

[1] Gerald J. Glasser and Gale D. Metzger, "National Estimates of Nonlisted Telephone Households and Their Characteristics," Journal of Marketing Research, vol. 12, pp. 359—361, August 1975.

after all preparation and mailing expenses have been taken into account; they vary according to the length (and weight) of the questionnaire and the percentage response rate. The most serious problem in mail questionnaires is low response rates, typically in the 20 to 40 percent range for large-scale consumer surveys. However, use of preliminary contacts (through phone calls or postcards), monetary inducements and reminder letters has often served to increase response rates significantly, although adding to total costs in the process.

QUESTIONNAIRE DESIGN

Designing questionnaires which will obtain the information needed by management quickly, accurately, and from as large a percentage of the sample as possible is a surprisingly difficult task.

Among the issues involved in questionnaire design are the following: First, what information is needed? *The acid test here is to ask, How will the answers to these questions help management make better decisions? There is no sense in cluttering up the questionnaire with questions which might yield "interesting" answers but are irrelevant to decision making. However, sometimes it may be desirable to include "warm-up" questions on peripheral issues to help put a respondent at ease or to provide a broader context in which very specific or somewhat personal questions can be asked.*

Second, how should the questions be asked? *The wording or phrasing of questions deserves careful attention. It is important to avoid ambiguity or needless complexity so that the respondent doesn't ask himself/herself: What does this question mean? A common mistake is to address two issues in the same question; e.g., "Does this razor give you a close, comfortable shave?" Obviously there are two issues here, closeness and comfort, each of which needs to be addressed separately if useful answers are to be obtained.*

Third, what response categories should be used? *In exploratory research, especially when using small samples, it is often appropriate to allow "open-ended" responses to get the full flavor of how people feel about particular topics, as expressed in their own words. However, in large-scale surveys which ask fairly specific questions, it's generally necessary to structure responses into categories which can be coded for computer analysis. (This holds true whether the actual questionnaire is completed by the respondent or filled in by an interviewer.) Rating scales or importance rankings are often a useful device to discover how strongly people feel about particular issues, what priorities they set, etc.*

Lastly, in what order should the questions be asked? *To make the process of answering questionnaires simpler and more interesting (especially if it is a long questionnaire), it may be necessary to begin with some warm-up questions which put the survey in context and enable respondents to make speedy progress at the outset. It is important to recognize that some questions may not be appropriate for all respondents. For instance, if someone has never used a particular type of product, then that respondent should be instructed to skip* questions dealing with specifics of usage behavior for that product. Questions should normally be grouped in logical sequence, so that the questionnaire focuses in on one issue for a while, then moves to another. This usually allows for more thoughtful responses than would jumping rapidly from one topic to another and back again. A final consideration is to leave possibly sensitive questions, such as the respondent's age or income, until the end of the questionnaire.

It is always advisable to pretest questionnaires on a small representative sample before moving to the full-scale survey. In this way, any "bugs" in the design can be identified and corrected. Even minor changes in phrasing, ordering of questions, or instructions to interviewers may have a significant effect on the accuracy and completeness of the responses.

TEST MARKETING

The idea behind test marketing is to see how consumers actually respond to a product when it is placed on the market. Just as researchers may choose to survey a limited sample of consumers, so test marketing allows a firm to assess a product's performance in a limited but representative market area.

Objectives behind test marketing include the following. First, it can help to improve knowledge of a product's sales potential in advance of a decision on whether to proceed to a national introduction, with its attendant costs and risks. Second, a firm may wish to pretest two or more alternative marketing plans to determine which is optimal. These might include differences in such marketing mix elements as product features or packaging; advertising copy, expenditure levels, or media usage; price; promotional activities and expenditures; and the type of distribution channels used.

Test marketing may also provide opportunities to observe channel reactions, monitor the ways in which consumers buy and use the product (possibly providing new insights into the way the market is segmented), and also serve to identify any resulting product shortcomings or strategic problems.

Decisions facing the marketer include selection of test cities and duration of the test market program. If the objective is simply to pretest a particular marketing program, then a single city may suffice, providing it is considered representative of the larger market in which the firm intends to sell. However, if the objective is to test alternative marketing mixes, then two or more carefully matched cities may be required to provide an appropriate basis for comparison, depending on the number of variables under review. The nature of the product will serve to influence the duration of the test, which must be long enough to allow for repeat purchases if the product is a frequently purchased consumer good. However, the longer the test lasts, the more risk there is of outside "contamination." For instance, a competitor may seek to disrupt the test by engaging in a major promotion, or the product may come to be sold to retailers and consumers outside the test market area, thus making it hard to assess actual performance.

MONITORING TEST MARKETS

To maximize the usefulness of a test market, management should draw up a detailed plan of the information it intends to collect. Since product shipments from the factory cannot necessarily be equated with retail sales (not least on account of the need to stock the distribution "pipeline"), it may be necessary to conduct retail store audits. The firm can use its own personnel, or engage a professional retail auditing firm such as A. C. Nielsen, to collect data for both its own and competing products concerning the level and type of distribution achieved, as well as deals, displays, and sales volume.

This information may usefully be supplemented by surveys of both consumers and the trade. In addition to identifying purchase behavior patterns among different consumer segments, it may also be useful to ask questions about brand awareness, advertising recall, product trial, and future intentions concerning repurchase.

Interviews with the trade, probably conducted by the marketer's own sales force, may yield valuable insights into how retailers and wholesalers feel about the product's performance, consumer reactions, and future prospects. Distributors may also have useful suggestions to make in such areas as pricing strategy, advertising, promotions, and point-of-sale display materials.

CONCLUSION

The field of marketing research is a complex and detailed one. Although actual implementation of such research is often left to specialist researchers, the marketing manager cannot afford to remain totally uninvolved. In particular, he or she needs to be an active participant in defining the objectives of the research to ensure that the resulting information is relevant to the decisions which management has to take.

While it is not necessary to possess detailed knowledge of research procedures, the marketing manager should have sufficient understanding to be able to interpret the resulting findings intelligently and to recognize possible sources of bias.

DAISY: I
THE WOMEN'S SHAVING MARKET

NANCY J. DAVIS
Research Associate
Harvard Graduate School of Business Administration

STEVEN H. STAR
Associate Professor
Harvard Graduate School of Business Administration

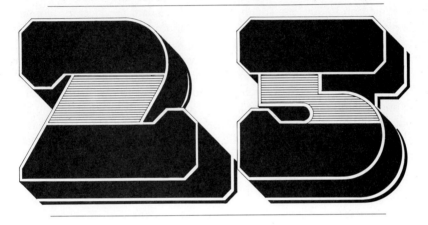

In January 1974, top executives of the Gillette Safety Razor Division (SRD) met to discuss the division's position and possible courses of action with regard to the women's "wet" shaving market. Since the introduction of Lady Gillette in 1931, SRD had held a dominant share of this market. For the most part, its products for women had been essentially style variations of men's razors. Attempts had been made to design shaving products exclusively for women, but these had performed no better than existing products when tested. Nonetheless, in the late sixties and early seventies, SRD executives had become increasingly convinced that a substantial market existed for a shaving product designed especially for women. Their belief was strengthened by the performance of Flicker, a shaver designed specifically for women and introduced in mid-1972 by the American Safety Razor Company. Over the last year and a half, Flicker's sales had grown steadily, and it had consistently increased its market share.

Demographic information regarding the women's shaving market was generally gathered by SRD's Marketing Research Department in nationwide triennial surveys. In addition, infrequent ad hoc consumer studies were conducted to test advertising concepts or product performance. Although this information constituted a good base of data, the SRD executives agreed that they needed more thorough current data about the women's shaving market than they currently had if they were going to make a major effort in that market. Therefore, they asked Mr. Bryan Dwyer, who was then responsible for Lady Trac II and had earlier worked on Lady Sure Touch, both SRD shaving products for women, to coordinate a task force to develop a new shaving product for women. This task force consisted of two components. The technical component had the responsibility to develop and test a variety of new product concepts. It included representatives from SRD's Research and Development, Engineering, Manufacturing, and Finance departments. The second component was to develop data for positioning and advertising the product in the marketplace. Representatives included members of the Marketing Research Department, the Sales Department, and the advertising agency which would handle the product, the J. Walter Thompson Company. In late January 1974, this second group met to determine what they needed to know about the women's shaving market and to develop a consumer survey intended to give them this information.

THE COMPANY

The Gillette Company was founded in 1903 to manufacture and market a safety razor and blade invented by King C. Gillette. Until 1948, the company's product line was limited to safety razors, double-edge blades, and shaving cream. In 1948, Gillette acquired the Toni Company, a leading manufacturer of women's hair preparations. This acquisition was followed by acquisitions of the Paper Mate Corporation (1955), Harris Research Laboratories (1956), the Sterilon Corporation (1962), the Braun Company (1967), Buxton, Incorporated (1971), Welcome Wagon International, Inc. (1971), S. T. Dupont (1972), Jafra Cosmetics (1973), and Hydroponic Chemical Company, Inc. (1973). Each of these acquired companies was operated independently of the Safety Razor Division.

Although Gillette had marketed a brushless shaving cream in a tube for many years, the company's first major thrust in the toiletries business occurred when SRD introduced Foamy Shave Cream (1954) and Right Guard Deodorant for men (1960). This deodorant soon came to be positioned as a product for the entire family and quickly gained a substantial share of the deodorant market. Also during the 1960s, SRD introduced an aftershave lotion, a men's cologne, and several hair-grooming products for men. These toiletries grew so rapidly that a considerable amount of management time had to be diverted from the highly profitable razor and blade business. Therefore, in 1967, a separate Toiletries Di-

TABLE 1

	Net sales, %	Contribution to profits, %
Blades and razors	31	66
Toiletries and grooming aids	32	21
Braun products	22	7
Writing instruments	7	5
All others	8	1
	100	100

vision with its own headquarters, manufacturing plant, and sales force was established.

In 1973 Gillette's worldwide corporate net sales exceeded the billion dollar mark for the first time, reaching $1,064,427,000. Income before taxes totalled $149,965,000, the highest in the company's history. The approximate contributions of Gillette's most important lines to its worldwide total sales and profits are shown in Table 1. During 1973, net sales of $519,876,000 and net income of $53,051,000 were attributed to sources outside the United States and Canada. The company had approximately 31,500 employees, 9,400 of whom were located in the United States. Over 7 million individual purchases of Gillette products in more than 200 countries and territories were made daily.

THE SAFETY RAZOR DIVISION

SRD was responsible for manufacturing and marketing blades and razors in the United States. Throughout its history, SRD had been a leader in shaving technology. Among its most revolutionary innovations were the Super Blue Blade that had a plastic coating applied to the blade edge which significantly reduced the force required to cut beard hair (1958), the super stainless steel blade introduced in 1965, and the Techmatic shaving system introduced in 1966. The super stainless steel blade differed from the regular stainless steel blade in that its metallurgy and plastic coating were marked technological improvements which provided a smoother shave. The Techmatic shaving system consisted of a razor and a replaceable cartridge which contained a tightly wound steel band of continuous shaving edges. When one edge became dull, the user wound a new one into place. When all edges were used up, the user simply clicked on a new Techmatic cartridge. In 1970, partly in response to a bonded blade developed by Wilkinson,[1] SRD test-marketed a shaver[2] which it called Sure Touch. Sure

[1] Wilkinson's bonded system consisted of a single blade permanently encased in a plastic shaving cartridge. It was a significant improvement over existing systems in that the angle of the blade was preset at the factory and the plastic casing kept the blade properly aligned. (With existing systems, if the razor were dropped or if the blade were not screwed in tightly, the result was often an uneven shave with frequent nicks and cuts.) Once a Wilkinson bonded blade became dull, the cartridge, but not the entire shaver, was thrown away and a new cartridge was attached.

[2] SRD management used the term *razor* to refer to a shaving instrument which employed replaceable blades or cartridges and the term *shaver* to refer to a shaving instrument whose razor and blade were sealed together in a single unit. Shavers did not employ replaceable blades or cartridges. When the cutting edge became dull, the whole unit had to be replaced.

Touch was a plastic, disposable shaver which had the Techmatic shaving head permanently attached to the handle. Each head contained a band of five stainless steel shaving edges, and when all five edges became dull, the user simply threw the shaver away. Sure Touch was initially positioned as a razor for men. However, SRD's other products for men continued to be more popular than Sure Touch, so SRD decided to turn Sure Touch into a woman's product by putting a colored handle on it. Lady Sure Touch proved to be only marginally successful, however, and SRD ceased to expect significant volume gains from the brand.

In 1971, SRD's research and development group explored the possibility of developing for women a reciprocal shaving razor (i.e., where two cutting edges faced each other). This concept was called Atra. To shave with Atra, one used a scrubbing action—the shaver could be moved both upward and downward without the user's changing her grip on it. While Atra apparently gave a close, comfortable shave, in user tests, it, Lady Sure Touch, and virtually any other shaving product lost to another instrument SRD developed in 1971, the Trac II twin-blade shaving system. This was a razor which featured two recessed blades locked in a parallel position and encased in a plastic cartridge for extra shaving protection. Lightweight and easy to handle, Trac II was said to have "established a whole new standard in shaving ease and comfort." By 1973 the Atra project had been abandoned, and SRD introduced Lady Trac II, a man's Trac II with a colored handle.

In 1973 SRD, whose products were marketed only in the United States, accounted for about one-sixth of Gillette's worldwide sales and one-third of profits. Its product line included 10 razors, 22 blades, and Cricket, a disposable lighter originated by a French subsidiary of Gillette. SRD had begun marketing Cricket in the United States in 1972. (See Exhibit 1 for product line.)

SRD's distribution system was one of the most extensive in the United States. In 1973 Gillette razors and blades were sold by more than 450,000 retail outlets in the United States, including 103,000 chain and independent drugstores, 193,000 food stores (of which 20 percent were classified as supermarkets), and 8,200 discount and variety stores. Convenience stores, liquor stores, tobacco shops, and automotive outlets made up the balance of its distribution outlets.

While SRD sold directly to large drug, food, and discount chains, most of its retail accounts were served by 2,100 independent wholesalers. The latter group included 400 drug wholesalers, 400 food wholesalers, 900 tobacco wholesalers, and 400 toiletry merchandisers. Toiletry merchandisers usually distributed to food and/or discount stores, often on a rack-jobbing[1] basis. SRD management estimated that these wholesalers and toiletry merchandisers together

---

[1] Rack jobbers were essentially wholesalers who set up retail displays and kept them stocked with merchandise. They visited retail outlets frequently to replace defective or worn merchandise, add new items, and set up promotional displays. The retailers usually retained formal authority to determine which products and brands they would carry and how they would be priced, but in practice these functions were often delegated to the rack jobber.

employed approximately 13,200 salespeople and were responsible for about 50 percent of SRD sales. Gillette exercised no direct control over wholesaler salespeople, but it did offer the wholesalers a variety of incentives such as advertising allowances, off-invoice allowances, and placement money for putting up special displays.

The SRD sales force consisted of a national accounts manager (who was responsible for about 20 large accounts), 4 regional managers, 18 district managers, 90 territory representatives, and 20 sales merchandisers. The territory representatives generally called on buyers at wholesale firms and at the headquarters of small chain and independent retail accounts. They also visited the top 10 to 20 percent of the retail outlets served by their wholesaler accounts as well as virtually all the retail outlets of their own accounts. Sales merchandisers called only on retail outlets where they made sure displays were well stocked, tried to obtain special displays and promotions, and left suggested orders for store managers. SRD's sales force was supplemented by about 80 part-time corporate retail merchandisers who performed these functions for all of Gillette's products. The total cost of the sales organization normally ran about 5 percent of sales.

SRD's sales promotion and media advertising were considered exceptionally strong. In working with the trade, SRD often offered 10 percent off invoice allowances for purchases above a certain level, 5 percent cooperative advertising allowances, and placement money for special displays. Consumer promotions might consist of premium offers, coupons, cents-off deals, on-pack premiums such as a free razor with a cartridge of blades, and so forth. SRD normally ran eight promotional cycles annually. Five or six products were usually promoted in each cycle; four of the cycles usually contained consumer promotions. About 90 percent of SRD's advertising consisted of sponsorship of prime time television programs and various sports events. It did some limited print advertising, primarily in men's magazines. It had done a small amount of television and magazine advertising for Lady Sure Touch, but by and large its advertising was oriented to the men's market. In 1973 SRD's total advertising expenditures were estimated to be $17 million.

The standard SRD display consisted of razors and blades in blister packs hanging from hooks on a pegboard. These were almost always located near a cash register or checkout lane, though whenever possible, SRD had multiple displays in a single outlet. For example, in large drugstores or mass-merchandise outlets, razors were frequently displayed in the health and beauty aids department, while a limited supply of the best-selling razors was also displayed along with blades at checkout lanes. In food stores, razors and blades were almost always displayed only at checkout lanes.

THE MARKET

In 1973, total United States retail sales of blades were about $416 million, or 2.372 billion units. The total retail sales of razors were about $52 million. At the manufacturer level, blade sales totalled about $266,240,000 and razor sales about $33,280,000. In addition to SRD, three companies—Schick, Wilkinson, and American Safety Razor—accounted for the major share of the wet shaving market. With about a 1 percent share, private labels were not considered a major factor.

Schick Safety Razor Company, a division of Warner-Lambert Company, was especially strong in the injector[1] segment of the wet shaving market. (Schick electric shavers were sold by Schick Electric Company, a totally separate company which was not connected with Warner-Lambert.) Schick's share of the injector market was about 78 percent, and injector blades and razors represented about 17 percent of the combined markets. Schick's major products for women were Lady Eversharp (an injector razor), Lady Schick Band Razor (a Techmatic-type razor), and Lady Super II. These were all essentially adaptations of men's razors, with the Lady Super II containing Schick's version of the Trac II shaving system. Schick's share of the wet shaving market was about 21 percent.

Wilkinson was a division of the British Match Company located in England. Its products were sold and distributed in the United States by the Colgate-Palmolive Company. It was especially strong in the bonded-razor segment of the market. It marketed a nondisposable plastic razor for women in England which it was rumored to be considering marketing in the United States. Its share of the United States wet shaving market was about 6 percent.

American Safety Razor Company (ASR), a division of Philip Morris, marketed its products under the brand names Personna, Gem, and Flicker. It held about a 12 percent share of the wet shaving market. With Flicker, it had become the market leader in products designed especially for women. Flicker was thought to account for about 41 percent of ASR's dollar sales. ASR also manufactured about 80 percent of the private label blades sold.

In 1974, in addition to injector, band, and bonded razors, the more conventional double-edge and single-edge razors were still on the market. Double-edge razors, the oldest shaving instruments still being sold in any quantity, used replaceable double-edge blades. The standard double-edge razor held the blade at only one angle, while the adjustable product had a dial with which the user could alter the blade angle and exposure to suit his own preferences. Single-edge razors were those which used replaceable blades with only one shaving edge. Except for injector razors, very few single-edge razors were still on the market in 1974. (See Exhibit 2 for a list of competitive razors in each category.)

Over 20 types of blades were marketed in 1974. Many of these were double-edge blades that were differentiated according to the metal from which they were made. Blades bonded in replaceable plastic cartridges were consid-

---

[1] The injector razor was distinguished primarily by the method by which it was loaded. First, the user inserted a stem attached to a small case of blades into a slot on the razor. Next, he pulled a blade-loader device back to the end of the case and a blade moved into a position so that, when the device was pushed toward the razor, the new blade pushed out the old blade. The new blade was then locked into position until removed by the injector. Almost all injector razors used single-edge blades.

ered part of this market, as were disposable shavers. (See Exhibit 3 for the major manufacturers' blade lines, and Exhibit 4 for illustrations of various shaving products.)

THE WOMEN'S SHAVING MARKET

According to SRD's Marketing Research Department, the following women's razors had been introduced since the early sixties:

1962	Lady Gillette (Gillette)[1]
1963	Lady Eversharp (Schick)
1966	Lady Techmatic (Gillette)
1967	Lady Schick Band Razor (Schick)
1971	Lady Sure Touch (Gillette)
1972	Flicker (American Safety Razor)
1973	Lady Trac II (Gillette)
1973	Lady Super II (Schick)

With the exception of Flicker, these razors were colored-handle versions of men's razors, blister-mounted on a card. (See Exhibit 5 for pictures of these razors.)

Flicker was obviously not a colored-handled version of a man's razor. It was a disposable band razor with a circular shape, except for the even cutting edge. When one cutting edge became dull, the user rotated another into place. Each shaver contained five cutting edges. Using newspaper advertising only, ASR introduced Flicker into seven Midwestern markets between June and September 1972. During the fourth quarter of 1972, ASR extended Flicker's distribution to 23 markets, again using only newspaper advertising. In the first quarter of 1973, eight more markets were opened, and ASR added spot television ads and ads in magazines and newspaper supplements to Flicker's regular newspaper advertising. During the second quarter of 1973, Flicker's distribution was further extended to 34 more markets, bringing the total to 65. These 65 markets accounted for about 67 percent of the total United States population. In addition to the three types of advertising ASR had been using, it added both day and night network television. In each of its markets, it offered liberal terms to the trade.

The SRD market researchers estimated that in 1974 women would purchase for their own use about $75,400,000 in "wet" razors and blades, and that in 1975 the total would reach $83,330,000. They thought these expenditures would break down as shown in Table 2.

---

[1] While the first razor to carry the name *Lady Gillette* was introduced in 1931, the name was used for almost every new product for women SRD introduced up through the early 1960s.

TABLE 2

	1974	1975
Regular razors	$11,340,000	$12,350,000
Disposable razors (Flicker and Lady Sure Touch)	7,280,000	12,740,000
Blades (excluding Flicker and Lady Sure Touch)	56,810,000	58,240,000
Total	$75,430,000	$83,330,000

TABLE 3

Gillette		
Lady Trac II	$ 3,770,000	20.1%
Lady Gillette	650,000	3.5
Lady Sure Touch	520,000	2.8
Lady Techmatic	390,000	2.1
"Male" razors	3,120,000	16.6
	$ 8,450,000	45.1%

Competitors		
Flicker	$ 6,110,000	32.6%
All other disposables*	650,000	3.5
Lady Super II (Schick)	780,000	4.2
Lady Eversharp Injector		
by Schick	520,000	2.8
"Male" razors	2,110,000	11.8
	$10,170,000	54.9%
Total	$18,620,000	100 %

* Several small companies manufactured a wide variety of inexpensive disposable shavers. These were usually convenience items sold in places such as airports. Their retail price was often two or three shavers for about $1. They were not considered a major factor in the women's shaving market.

In 1972 women had spent $68,250,000 on "wet" shaving products for their own use, while in 1973 the comparable total had been $70,460,000. The dollar sales of wet shaving equipment for women were substantially larger than sales of other health and beauty aids. For example, it was estimated that, in 1974, women would spend $63 million on eyebrow pencil and eye shadow, $59 million on hair color rinses, $55 million on mascara, and $14 million on rouge. Moreover, it was estimated that women would spend about $42 million on electric shavers in 1974.

SRD products were expected to account for about $8,450,000 of the total $18,620,000 spent solely on wet razors in 1974 (Table 3). Researchers noted that nearly 40 percent of this $18,620,000 would be spent for disposable razors.

According to SRD's Marketing Research Department, there were 83.6 million women over 13 years old in the United States, about 18.7 million of whom did not remove hair from their legs or underarms. Of the 64.9 million remaining, 15.8 million used electric shavers and 2.6 million used depilatories. Thus, there were 49.8 million women who used "wet" shavers; 30 million of these currently used Gillette products.

In calculating share of the total markets which the leading women's products held, SRD researchers felt that Lady Trac II, Schick's Super II for Women, Lady Gillette, and Lady Techmatic should be considered part of the razor market because they were individual units for which new blades or cartridges

TABLE 4[*]

	Gillette Lady Trac II	Schick Super II for Women	Lady Gillette	Gillette Lady Techmatic	Lady Sure Touch	Flicker
		% of total razor market dollars			**% of total blade market dollars**	
June '72			2.5	2.5		0.4
Jan. '73			1.1	1.2	0.2	1.8
June '73	3.7	1.2	0.9	1.3	0.9	2.1
Jan. '74	4.6	0.9	0.8	1.4	0.5	2.0
		% of total razor market units			**% of total blade market units**	
June '72			2.9	2.5		0.2
Jan. '73			1.3	1.2	0.1	1.0
June '73	2.6	1.0	0.9	1.1	0.6	1.2
Jan. '74	3.5	0.7	0.9	1.1	0.3	1.3

[*] The market share data are based on the *total* razor and blade markets, not on the market for women's products alone.

could be purchased. They felt, however, that since Lady Sure Touch and Flicker were disposable items, they were more comparable to blades and cartridges. Therefore, they felt that Lady Sure Touch and Flicker should be evaluated as part of the blade market. SRD researchers followed the performance of various products in representative food and drug stores in the United States. They were unable to monitor product movement in mass-merchandise outlets, so they felt their data should be considered only a general indicator of product performance. Nevertheless, using SRD data, recent market shares of the different products in their respective markets are shown in Table 4.

SRD researchers felt that Flicker's success in gaining distribution indicated that the market would, in fact, welcome a razor distinctively designed for women. Table 5 provides a summary of the percentages of food and drug stores through which the major women's shaving products were distributed.

In addition to these general market data, SRD's research and development department had information about the differences between hair removed by women and that removed by men. Women's hair was generally finer (0.0040 inch thick) than men's beard hairs (0.0065), and it was fairly uniform, while

TABLE 5

	Gillette Lady Trac II		Schick Super II for Women		Lady Gillette		Gillette Lady Techmatic		Lady Sure Touch		Flicker	
	Drug	Food	Drug	Food	Drug	Food	Drug	Food	Drug	Food	Drug	Food
June '72					37%	6%	21%	6%			10%	3%
Jan. '73					35	2	21	10	8%	8%	29	25
June '73	22%	10%	8%	7%	36	2	23	6	32	15	46	35
Jan. '74	25	13	11	5	33	2	19	4	29	14	54	45

men's beard hair was very irregular in shape. While the average man's beard shaving area was about 48 square inches, the total average shaving area for a woman was approximately 412 square inches: 400 for legs and 12 for underarms. There were approximately 210 hairs per square inch for underarms and 28 for legs, as opposed to approximately 310 hairs per square inch on a man's face. Thus, on the average, men cut approximtely 15,000 hairs during a shave; women cut about 14,000. Both men's and women's hair grew at a rate of about $1/_{60}$ inch a day. On the leg, hairs generally grew downward, with some growing sideways, and under the arms they grew both up and down. Moreover, the researchers had determined that the amount of force required to produce pain on a woman's leg and underarms was 25 to 40 percent higher than the force needed to produce pain on a man's face.

FURTHER RESEARCH

In late January 1974, SRD's task force met with Mr. Michael Lindroth and Ms. Alison Yancy of the J. Walter Thompson Company, the advertising agency which SRD planned to work with if it decided to make a major effort in the women's shaving market. The purpose of this meeting was to determine exactly what further information SRD needed to know about the women's shaving market and to develop a marketing research program which would provide this information.

The group's working assumption was that it would be necessary to use a large-scale (about 2,000 respondents) questionnaire survey to elicit the types of information they thought they would need. Personal interviews rather than a mail survey were considered necessary to ensure effective communication on a subject likely to be considered "sensitive" by the respondents. Based on previous experience with such surveys, the group estimated that each consumer interview should take no longer than 60 minutes to be completed. As was SRD's usual practice, an outside contract research supplier would be responsible for the actual implementation of the survey, at a cost of approximately $15 per interview.

EXHIBIT 1
SRD PRODUCT LINE, JANUARY 1974
Daisy: I

■ *Blades:*

Trac II (5- or 9-cartridge packages)

Standard Techmatic Band (10 shaving edges)

Adjustable Techmatic Band (packages contained 5, 10, or 15 shaving edges)

Platinum Plus Double Edge (packages contained 5, 10, or 15 blades)

Super Stainless Double Edge (packages contained 5, 10, or 15 blades)

Platinum Plus Injector (7- or 11-blade packages)

Super Blue (10- or 15-blade packages)

Regular Blue Blade (5- or 10-blade packages)

Thin (4- or 10-blade packages)

Valet (10-blade package)

■ *Razors:*

Trac II

Lady Trac II

Techmatic

Lady Techmatic

Trac II Twinjector

Super Adjustable Double Edge

Knack

Lady Gillette Double Edge

Super Speed Double Edge

Three Piece Double Edge

Lady Sure Touch

■ *Disposable Lighters:*

Cricket Lighters

Cricket Table Lighters

EXHIBIT 2
MAJOR RAZORS ON THE MARKET, JANUARY 1974
Daisy: I

■ *Double edge:*

Gillette Standard Double Edge

Gillette Super Adjustable

Lady Gillette

Gillette's Super Speed

Gillette Three Piece

Wilkinson Double Edge, nonadjustable

Schick, nonadjustable double edge

Assorted private label

■ *Single edge:*

Gem Contour II Razor (ASR)

Assorted private label

■ *Injector:*

Schick Standard Injector

Schick Adjustable Injector

Lady Schick Injector

■ *Band:*

Gillette Techmatic

Gillette Lady Techmatic

Schick Instamatic

Lady Schick Instamatic

■ *Bonded:*

Gillette Trac II

Gillette Lady Trac II

Schick Super II

Wilkinson Bonded

Personna, Double II (ASR)

EXHIBIT 3
BLADE LINES BY MANUFACTURER, JANUARY 1974
Daisy: I

■ *Gillette:*

Platinum-Plus, double-edge
Stainless Steel, double-edge
Premium, double-edge
Super Blue Blades, double-edge
Blue Blades, double-edge
Thin Blades, double-edge
Carbon Blades, double-edge
Regular Techmatic Band
Adjustable Techmatic Band
Gillette Platinum-Plus Injector
Trac II Cartridges
Lady Sure Touch

■ *Schick:*

Platinum/Stainless, double-edge
Plus Platinum, double-edge
Plus Platinum, Injector
Super Chromium, double-edge
Super Chromium Injector
Super II Cartridges
Instamatic Band

■ *Wilkinson:*

Wilkinson Sword, double-edge
Stainless Steel, double-edge
Bonded Cartridges
Sword Master, double-edge

■ *American Safety Razor:*

Personna Stainless/Chrome, double-edge
Personna Tungsten, double-edge
Personna Face Guard, double-edge
Personna Double II
Flicker
Gem Super Stainless Steel Blade,
    single-edge
Personna Injector

EXHIBIT 4
RAZOR AND BLADE ILLUSTRATIONS
Daisy: I

TYPICAL <u>DOUBLE EDGE</u> RAZORS AND BLADE

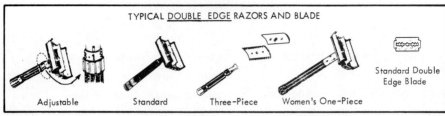

Adjustable Standard Three-Piece Women's One-Piece Standard Double Edge Blade

TYPICAL <u>INJECTOR</u> RAZORS AND BLADE

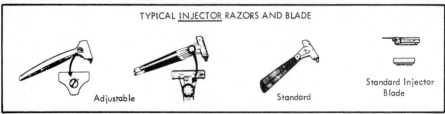

Adjustable Standard Standard Injector Blade

TYPICAL RAZORS WITH BLADES <u>SEALED IN PLASTIC</u>

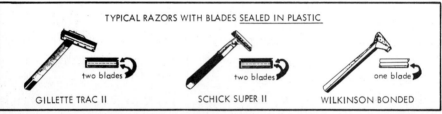

two blades two blades one blade

GILLETTE TRAC II SCHICK SUPER II WILKINSON BONDED

TYPICAL <u>CONTINUOUS BAND</u> RAZORS AND CARTRIDGES

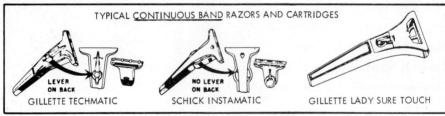

LEVER ON BACK NO LEVER ON BACK

GILLETTE TECHMATIC SCHICK INSTAMATIC GILLETTE LADY SURE TOUCH

TYPICAL <u>ELECTRIC</u> RAZORS TYPICAL <u>SINGLE EDGE</u> RAZOR AND BLADE PERSONNA FLICKER

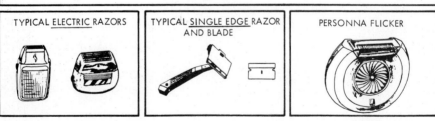

EXHIBIT 5
SHAVING PRODUCTS MARKETED FOR WOMEN, JANUARY 1974
Daisy: I

Lady Gillette

Lady Eversharp Injector Razor by Schick

Lady Techmatic by Gillette

Schick Super II for Women

Lady Trac II by Gillette

Lady Sure Touch by Gillette

REVOLUTIONARY NEW BLADE FOR LEGS AND UNDERARMS DESIGNED NOT TO CUT YOU!

Flicker by American Safety Razor

DAISY: II
RESEARCHING THE WOMEN'S SHAVING MARKET

NANCY J. DAVIS
Research Associate
Harvard Graduate School of Business Administration

STEVEN H. STAR
Associate Professor
Harvard Graduate School of Business Administration

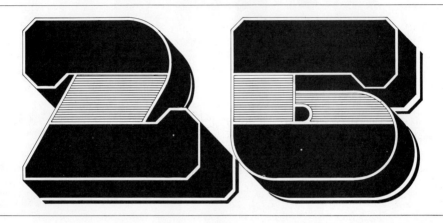

Shortly after SRD's top executives decided that SRD should further pursue the women's shaving market, the newly created task force of SRD's Marketing Research Department and the J. Walter Thompson Company's Research and Planning Department convened. Following the recommendation of SRD's market researchers, it was decided that they would gather objective data regarding blade and razor usage and consumer demographics, while the J. Walter Thompson group would focus more on the subjective aspects of why women shaved and how they felt about it.

THE SRD MARKETING RESEARCH DEPARTMENT'S SURVEY

For their survey, SRD's market researchers selected a sample of 2,500 women, 13 years of age or older, which was representative of the total female shaving population in the continental United States. Of these women, about 75 percent had removed hair from their legs and/or underarms during the past month. The interviews were conducted in person at the respondents' homes during the last week of January 1974. In the interview, the woman was shown illustrations of razors and blades and was asked what brand and type of razor and blade she was then using. (See Exhibit 1 for illustrations.) After giving her response, she was offered 25 cents for the actual blade, and two-thirds of the women who shaved with "wet" razors complied. The purpose of this was to measure the comparison between the blades women thought they were using and the blades they actually were using. About one-third of those who provided their blades either said they didn't know what blade they were using or said they were using a blade other than those they were actually using. Therefore, the statistics were not as precise as SRD researchers would have liked.

From the data gathered, the researchers determined that slightly over 75 percent of the women interviewed, or 65 million women on a national basis, removed hair from their underarms and/or legs either by shaving or by using depilatories and waxes. In 1967, the comparable percentage had been about 70 percent. The respondents who showed the least incidence of hair removal were women over 55 years of age, nonwhites, and women in lower socioeconomic groups. On the average, the respondents shaved their underarms about 85 times per year and their legs about 90 times per year. During the summer months, the frequency with which the women shaved increased by about 50 percent.

Of the women in the study who shaved their legs and/or underarms, about four-fifths said they used a wet razor for their last shave and one-fourth said they used an electric razor for their last shave. The total exceeded 100 percent because some used different razors for their underarms and their legs. Of the wet shavers, about half used a double-edge razor, less than one-fifth used a Trac II, a Schick Super II, or a Wilkinson Bonded Razor, and about one-fifth used an injector razor. Continuous-band razors, disposable razors, and single-edge razors were used by almost 20 percent. Double-edge razors were especially strong among older, lower socioeconomic, nonmetropolitan, nonwhite, and Southern women. Trac II and the bonded systems were stronger among younger, up-scale, metropolitan, white, and Eastern demographic groups. Injector usage was highest among whites and in the South, while band usage was higher among up-scale, white, and younger (18–34) groups. Disposable razors were weakest among older women, and depilatory usage was predominant among nonwhite and lower-income women.

Of the 1,344 women who shaved with a wet razor, more than half or, on a national basis, about 30 million women had used Gillette blades for their last shave. Gillette double-edge blades were used by about a third of these women and by about 70 percent of all double-edge blade users. About 10 percent of all wet shavers used Trac II blades.

When SRD's researchers questioned the women about the quality of the shave they received from the various systems, new systems such as Trac II, Lady Sure Touch, and Flicker all received higher ratings than older double- or single-edge systems. Among these women, Trac II had by far the highest "conversion level": about two-thirds of those who tried it had converted to it from their previous system. Flicker and Wilkinson Bonded both had a conversion level somewhat lower, while Lady Sure Touch had the lowest conversion level of about one-third.

About half the women who shaved with wet razors shaved with a new blade which they did not share with someone else. Of the remaining about one-fourth said they shaved with a used blade which someone else had cast off. Lady Sure Touch and Flicker were most often purchased by the women who intended to use them, and they were used almost exclusively by those women. Trac II and Schick Super II were shared the most. More than a third of the women who used these systems were using a blade that had first been used by someone else. The women who did not share a blade thought that, on the average, they used about 10 blades a year. (See Exhibit 2 for a sample page from the SRD questionnaire, Exhibit 3 for the categories of information gathered, and Exhibit 4 for selected data derived from the survey.)

THE J. WALTER THOMPSON COMPANY'S SURVEY

In February 1974, Ms. Alison Yancy of the J. Walter Thompson Company began gathering information about how women felt about shaving and what their shaving habits were. Her major source of information was a series of six "creative development" sessions, each of which was attended by nine or ten women who had agreed to participate in the research. In all, 57 women attended. The criteria for selection were (1) that the woman normally shaved at least twice a month and (2) that she usually used a regular wet razor, not an electric one. Yancy accepted all brands of razors except the Gillette Trac II. Trac II users were disqualified because Yancy thought she might use these women to test the new product if SRD did in fact develop one, and she was sure that such a product would contain the Trac II system. The groups she recruited are shown in Table 1. The women did not know the study was being done for Gillette.

TABLE 1

Under age 25	Ages 25–34
1 group of working women	1 group of working women
1 group of housewives	1 group of housewives
1 group of college students	
1 group of high school students	

Each creative development session consisted of three phases of inter-viewing: a self-administered questionnaire, a personal interview with Yancy, and a focus group session. Yancy stated that it was essential to have the self-administered questionnaire and the personal interview precede the group session so that the women being interviewed would have their own ideas and opinions regarding shaving firmly planted in their minds. Otherwise, once in a group session, one or more particularly strong, vocal respondents often swayed others to their position, and the dissenting voices were not heard. The self-administered questionnaire which Yancy used is shown in Exhibit 5. In the personal interview, Yancy questioned the women in depth on their responses to this questionnaire.

From the 57 women interviewed, Yancy learned that while the women tended to perceive shaving products and the act of shaving as masculine, they considered the end results to be feminine. Most said that shaving made them feel cleaner and more feminine, but they did not view it as a glamorous or pleasant task. Most considered it a necessary evil, comparable to eyebrow plucking. They felt that the dictates of modern American society were such that, in order for a woman to be considered well groomed, feminine, and appealing to men, her skin should be smooth and almost totally void of hairy stubble. Thus, they said, young girls were conditioned at an early age via romantic stories, mass consumer advertising campaigns, and peer groups to believe that removing hair, particularly from the legs, was necessary for social acceptance. Many said that they began shaving their underarms partly for social grooming and partly for personal hygiene, but that they began shaving their legs almost solely for personal grooming. They said that once they started shaving they had to keep it up because hair growing out caused their legs to itch. The women surveyed felt that shaving did not add to their appearance in a positive sense, but that it prevented potential "detraction" from their appearance by removing unsightly hair.

Fifty-four of the women said they preferred a blade razor to an electric razor, even though shaving with a blade razor was time-consuming, tedious, messy, and involved a number of steps. They said further that cutting and nicking were constant problems, especially on the back of the ankles, knees, and thighs and under the arms. Cutting apparently produced negative feelings, not so much because of the pain but because of the time and bother required to stop the bleeding and because of the unsightly appearance of scabs and/or Band-Aids. Skin irritations were also a problem, especially when deodorant was applied immediately after shaving the underarms. In spite of these complaints, however, when asked what they would do if it were socially acceptable not to shave, 29 said they would continue to shave as usual and only 13 said they would not shave at all.

Most of the women said they shaved in the evening during the latter part of the week, and that for special occasions they would shave more frequently, more carefully, and more thoroughly. Moreover, they were more likely to use toiletry products such as shaving cream for special occasions. Fifty-one said they shaved before, during, or after a bath.

Yancy learned that on the average the women interviewed spent about 10

TABLE 2

	Characteristics/benefit rating	
	Importance, average	Own razor, average
No nicks or cuts	9.54	6.51
Close shave	9.28	7.95
Easy to control	7.86	6.68
Adjustable to underarms/legs	7.58	3.81
Convenient to use	7.42	7.54
Economical	7.14	6.82
Safe to dispose of blades	6.88	7.53
Fast shave	6.40	6.54
Feminine razor	3.56	4.54
Attractive razor	2.96	4.84
Total: 57 respondents		

minutes shaving their legs and about 5 minutes shaving their underarms. Concerning preshaving preparations, 65 percent used soap and water, 10 percent shaved dry, and 25 percent used shaving cream. Most women held the razor in the same hand throughout the shaving process. They shaved their legs in an upward direction, beginning with the front then proceeding to the backs and the thighs. The latter procedure required considerable bending, twisting, and stretching, they said.

The final item on the personal questionnaire consisted of a list of characteristics associated with shaving. The women were first asked to rate each characteristic on a 10-point scale, where 1 point meant "extremely unimportant" and 10 points meant "extremely important." Then they were asked to rate their own razors' performance on each characteristic. The results are shown in Table 2. (See Exhibit 6 for selected data produced by this study.)

EXHIBIT 1
RAZOR AND BLADE ILLUSTRATIONS
Daisy: II

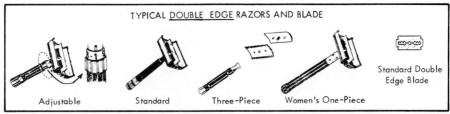

TYPICAL <u>DOUBLE EDGE</u> RAZORS AND BLADE

Adjustable Standard Three-Piece Women's One-Piece Standard Double Edge Blade

TYPICAL <u>INJECTOR</u> RAZORS AND BLADE

Adjustable Standard Standard Injector Blade

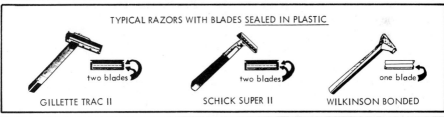

TYPICAL RAZORS WITH BLADES <u>SEALED IN PLASTIC</u>

two blades two blades one blade

GILLETTE TRAC II SCHICK SUPER II WILKINSON BONDED

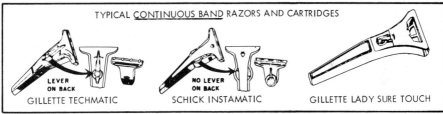

TYPICAL <u>CONTINUOUS BAND</u> RAZORS AND CARTRIDGES

LEVER ON BACK NO LEVER ON BACK

GILLETTE TECHMATIC SCHICK INSTAMATIC GILLETTE LADY SURE TOUCH

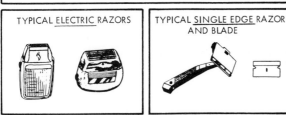

TYPICAL <u>ELECTRIC</u> RAZORS

TYPICAL <u>SINGLE EDGE</u> RAZOR AND BLADE

PERSONNA FLICKER

EXHIBIT 2
SAMPLE PAGE FROM THE SRD QUESTIONNAIRE
Daisy: II

1. First of all, I would like to ask you some questions about shaving and other methods of hair removal. Some women remove hair from their underarms or legs, while others do not.

   During the past year have you removed hair from either your underarms or legs?

   Yes 20- 1
   No 2

   SKIP TO QUESTION 170

2. The last time you removed hair from your underarms or legs, did you remove hair both from your underarms and legs, just your underarms or just your legs?

   **Underarms and legs .... 21- . 1
   **Just underarms 2
   Just legs 3

   SKIP TO QUESTION 4

3. During the past year, have you removed hair from your underarms?

   **Yes 22- 1
   No 2

   SKIP TO QUESTION 39

4. During the past month have you removed hair from your underarms?

   Yes 23- 1
   No 2

5. Would you please pick out the method you used the last time you removed hair from your underarms?

   INTERVIEWER: HAND RESPONDENT THE "HAIR REMOVAL METHOD" CARD.

   * Razor that uses blades 24- 1
   * Electric razor 2
   Depilatory cream 3
   Wax 4
   Abrasive.................... 5
   Other (SPECIFY)_____ 6

   5a. What brand was that?   25-
                                               26-

   SKIP TO QUESTION 29

6. Now would you pick out the type of razor you used?

   INTERVIEWER: HAND RESPONDENT THE RAZOR ILLUSTRATION CARD.

   Adjustable Double Edge 27- 1
   Standard Double Edge 2
   Three Piece Double Edge 3
   Women's Double Edge 4
   Adjustable Injector.................. 5
   Standard Injector 6
   Gillette Trac II 7
   Schick Super II 8
   Wilkinson Bonded 9
   Gillette Techmatic 28- 1
   Schick Instamatic 2
   Gillette Lady Sure Touch........... 3
   Single Edge 4
   Personna Flicker 5
   Electric 6
   Other (SPECIFY)_____ 7

7. Thinking about the shave you got the very last time you shaved your underarms, would you say that this shave was very good, good, fair or poor?

   Very Good 29- 1
   Good 2
   Fair 3
   Poor 4

8. How long have you been using a
   _____ type of razor
   INSERT RAZOR CIRCLED ABOVE
   to shave your underarms?
                                   30-
                                   31-
   SPECIFY WEEKS, MONTHS OR YEARS

9. How long have you been using the particular razor that you shaved your underarms with the last time?

   SPECIFY WEEKS, MONTHS OR YEARS

                                   32-
                                   33-

EXHIBIT 3
TYPE OF INFORMATION GATHERED
BY THE SRD SURVEY
Daisy: II

1   *Incidence of hair removal*
Past-year hair removal
     Underarms
     Legs
Past-month hair removal
     Underarms
     Legs

2   *Last hair removal method*
Wet/dry/other
Type/brand of razor used last (if any)
Brand of blade used (if any)
Length of time using last-used razor

3   *Facts about razor ownership*
Self-ownership/borrow
New or used
Method of acquisition (self-purchase, gift, etc.)
Sharing of razor

4   *Last-used blade*
Brand and type
Number of shaves per blade
Was last-used blade new or used before?
Sharing of blade
Who purchased blades?

5   *Shave preparation and time of shave*
Method of preparation
     Shave-cream type (if any)
     Brand of shave cream
     Sharing of shave cream
     Who purchased shave cream?
     Who decided on brand?
Aftershave lotion or cream (if any)
     Type
     Brand
Proximity time of hair removal to bath or shower

6   *Frequency of hair removal for both underarms and legs*
Past 24 hours
Past month
Summer
Winter

EXHIBIT 3

Continued

7 *History of respondents hair removal*
Age when first removed hair
Previous blade
Purchase intention
All razors ever tried

8 *Razor and blade I.D.*
Interviewer records type brand and color
Purchase of blade in razor
Interviewer records brand of package seen

9 *Trial and satisfaction with new systems* (Lady Sure Touch, Flicker, Trac II)
Method of acquisition
Sharing—Who shared
Shaving frequency
Repurchase
Satisfaction overall and on specific shaving attributes

10 *Difficulties in shaving certain areas (knees, ankles, etc.)*
Incidence of problem
Area of problem
Problem always present when shaving?
Any razor-ease problem?
Any razor make problem more difficult?

11 *Corporate image*
Rating of
      Gillette Co.
      Schick Co.
      Personna (ASR) Co.
      Wilkinson Co.

12 *Attitudes toward shaving*
Rating on scale of pleasant users
Importance of various shaving attributes
      Closeness
      Nicks and cuts
      Shaves per blade
      Comfort

13 *Demographics*

Skin condition (dry, oily, average)	Education
Age	Family income
Marital status	Socioeconomic status
Occupation	Race
Telephone	

EXHIBIT 4
SELECTED RESPONSES TO THE SRD QUESTIONNAIRE[1]
Daisy: II

TABLE 1
INCIDENCE OF HAIR REMOVAL AMONG WOMEN IN PAST MONTH (Razors and/or depilatories)

	% of women interviewed
Removed hair from:	
Both underarms and legs*	59
Underarms only	17
Legs only	8
Underarms and/or legs	84
Total underarms	76
Total legs	67
Did not remove hair	16
Total sample: 2,500 women	

* To be read: 59 percent of the women surveyed removed hair from both their underarms and legs in the past month.

TABLE 2
FREQUENCY OF HAIR REMOVAL AMONG WOMEN WHO SHAVED IN THE PAST MONTH

	Underarms	Legs
Winter frequency rate*	50	55
Summer frequency rate	80	85
Winter/summer average	62	65

* To be read: The women who shaved in the past month shave their underarms 50 times during the winter (October–March) and 80 times during the summer (April–September).

[1] All data in Exhibit 4 have been disguised and are not useful for research purposes.

EXHIBIT 4
Continued

TABLE 3
INDEX OF INCIDENCE OF HAIR REMOVAL AMONG WOMEN DURING THE PAST MONTH (Razors and/or depilatories)

	Both under-arms and legs	Under-arms only	Legs only	Under-arms and/or legs	Total under-arms	Total legs	Did not remove hair
Sales region:							
East	93*	109	125	97	96	96	109
South	99	82	100	96	96	99	114
Central	106	100	75	104	105	104	86
West	97	100	125	99	97	99	105
Age:							
13–17	105	73	200	105	100	110	82
18–24	132	55	50	117	120	127	40
25–34	137	55	75	122	124	133	23
35–44	119	73	100	112	112	118	59
45–54	100	155	150	110	108	103	64
55+	33	164	125	56	53	39	318
Residential location:							
Major metro	97	109	100	99	99	97	105
Minor metro	105	91	125	104	103	106	86
Other urban	93	127	100	99	99	94	105
Nonmetro	99	82	100	97	96	99	114
Urban	95	100	100	97	96	96	114
Suburban	111	91	150	110	108	113	64
Rural	93	100	100	95	95	94	118
Marital status:							
Married	110	100	100	108	108	109	73
Single	81	100	125	86	84	84	150
Race:							
White	108	82	100	104	104	107	86
Nonwhite	30	227	50	59	59	31	309
Education:							
College	117	100	75	113	115	115	55
Noncollege	92	100	125	95	93	94	118
Occupation:							
Housewife, employed	111	109	50	108	111	107	73
Housewife, not employed	95	100	100	95	95	96	118
Other, employed	105	145	100	110	111	104	64
Other, not employed	79	100	25	79	82	76	173
Student	111	64	150	106	104	113	77
Household income:							
Under $7,000	57	118	125	69	66	61	218
$7,000–$9,999	108	100	75	105	107	106	82
$10,000–$14,999	117	91	150	115	114	119	45
$15,000 and over	125	82	50	115	119	121	45

* The formula to be used to interpret the data in Tables 3 through 8 is $(Y - X)/X =$ ____%, where X and Y are values in the same column and row Y is being compared to row X. Comparisons cannot be made *across* columns. For example, Table 3 is to be read: On the average, women in the East remove hair from both their underarms and legs 6.1 percent less frequently than do women in the South. The calculation is as follows: $(93 - 99)/99 = -6.1\%$

EXHIBIT 4
Continued

TABLE 4
TYPE OF RAZOR LAST USED AMONG WOMEN
(Underarms and/or legs past month)

	% all past-month shavers	% past-month blade shavers
Multiple mention		
Total double-edge	42*	54
Total injector	8	11
Trac II	11	14
Super II	2	3
Wilkinson Bonded	4	5
Total plastic sealed	17	22
Total Band	6	7
Lady Sure Touch	1	1
Flicker	3	4
Total disposable	4	5
Single-edge	1	1
Total Blade Razors	77	100
Electric	23	
Sample size	1,794	1,344

* To be read: **42** percent of all past-month shavers used a double-edge razor for their last shave.

EXHIBIT 4
Continued

TABLE 5
BLADE USED FOR LAST SHAVE IN PAST
MONTH (Underarms and/or legs)

	% past-month blade shavers
Multiple mention	
Gillette Premium Double Edge	22*
Gillette Carbon Double Edge	15
Total Gillette Double Edge	37
Techmatic	6
Trac II	14
Gillette Injector	4
Lady Sure Touch	1
Total Gillette	62
Gillette Import Double Edge	1
Schick Double Edge	7
Personna Double Edge	4
Wilkinson Double Edge	6
Total competitive major brand double-edge	17
Competitive injector	7
Wilkinson Bonded	5
Schick Super II	3
Schick Instamatic	1
Personna Flicker	4
Single-edge	1
Other blade	2
Sample size	1,344

* To be read: 22 percent of the women who shaved with a blade during the past month used a Gillette Premium Double Edge Blade for their last shave.

EXHIBIT 4
Continued

TABLE 6
WHO DECIDED ON BRAND OF BLADES PURCHASED

	Respondent, %	Husband, %	Other, %
Gillette Platinum-Plus, double-edge	70*	18	12
Gillette Stainless, double-edge	66	18	16
Gillette Carbon, double-edge	77	5	18
Techmatic	77	9	14
Trac II	57	24	19
Gillette Injector	49	40	11
Lady Sure Touch	90	5	5
Import, double-edge	71	12	17
Schick, double-edge	75	15	11
Personna, double-edge	71	18	11
Wilkinson, double-edge	55	20	15
Competitive injector	73	16	11
Wilkinson Bonded	57	14	29
Schick Super II	74	11	15
Schick Instamatic	74	10	16
Personna Flicker	91	4	6
Other blade	69		19
Total	70	15	15

* To be read: Of the women who used Gillette Platinum-Plus blades and who had shaved within the last month, 70 percent decided which brand of blades they would purchase.

TABLE 7
WHO BOUGHT LAST SHAVE-BLADE PACKAGE
(Past-month wet shavers—underarms and/or legs)

	Respondent bought, %	Husband bought, %	Someone else bought, %
Gillette Platinum-Plus, double-edge	76*	16	8
Gillette Stainless, double-edge	75	12	13
Gillette Carbon, double-edge	83	6	11
Techmatic	78	9	13
Trac II	67	16	17
Gillette Injector	64	28	9
Lady Sure Touch	82	12	6
Import, double-edge	77	12	11
Schick, double-edge	71	23	6
Personna, double-edge	82	12	6
Wilkinson, double-edge	69	21	10
Competitive Injector	75	17	8
Wilkinson Bonded	65	11	24
Schick Super II	71	7	22
Schick Instamatic	74	15	11
Personna Flicker	90		10
Other Blade	73	15	11
Total	75	13	12

* To be read: Of the women who used Gillette Platinum-Plus blades and who had shaved within the last month, 76 percent actually purchased the blades themselves.

EXHIBIT 4
Continued

TABLE 8
OWNERSHIP OF LAST-SHAVE RAZOR
(Past-month shavers)

	Self-owned, not shared,
Adjustable double-edge	48*
Standard double-edge	55
Three-piece double-edge	67
Women's double-edge	80
Adjustable injector	48
Standard injector	58
Trac II	41
Super II	49
Wilkinson Bonded	59
Techmatic	54
Instamatic	60
Sure Touch	98
Flicker	95
Electric	70
Total double-edge	56
Total injector	54
Total bonded	46
Total band	55
Total disposable	96

* To be read: Of the women who had shaved in the past month with an adjustable double-edge razor, 48 percent owned the razor themselves and did not share it with anyone else.

TABLE 9
AGE BEGAN SHAVING
(Among all women who shaved)

Age	Underarms, %	Legs, %
10–13	33*	36
14–15	35	34
16–17	13	12
18–19	10	9
20+	9	9
Totals 100%	100	100

* To be read: 33 percent of the women who shaved said they began shaving between the ages of 10 and 13.

636

EXHIBIT 4

Continued

TABLE 10
SHAVING PREPARATION LAST USED
(Among wet shavers)

Shaving preparation	Underarms, %	Legs, %
Shaving cream	31*	34
Shave dry	8	5
Water only	10	8
Soap and water	50	52
Preshave	1	1
Totals 100%	(1,323)	(1,127)

* To be read: 31 percent of the wet shavers said they used shaving cream when they shaved their underarms.

EXHIBIT 5
THE J. WALTER THOMPSON COMPANY QUESTIONNAIRE
Daisy: II

NAME _____ ADDRESS _____ CITY _____

TELEPHONE # _____ AGE _____ SCHOOL/YEAR IN SCHOOL_____

(If applicable)

1 At approximately what age did you first begin to shave?

_____

2 Why did you first start shaving? What were the reasons?

_____

_____

_____

3 When you first began to shave, what type of razor did you use (electric, double-edge, single-edge, injector, etc.)?

_____

4 Which of the following statements best describes your *current* shaving habits? (CHECK ONE)

_____**A** I use a blade razor all the time.

_____**B** I use a blade razor most of the time, and occasionally use an electric shaver.

_____**C** I use an electric shaver most of the time, and occasionally use a blade razor.

_____**D** I use an electric shaver all the time.

5 Is your current razor a men's razor or one that is specifically made for women? (CHECK ONE)

_____Men's razor

_____Women's razor

_____Don't know

6 Which of the following types of blade razors do you use *most often*? (CHECK ONE)

_____Double-edge razor (blades on both sides of razor)

_____Single-edge or injector (one blade only)

_____Continuous band (Techmatic, Instamatic, etc.)

_____Twin-bladed razor (two blades on *one* side)

_____Disposable razor (Flicker, Lady Sure Touch)

7 What *brand* of blade razor are you currently using?

_____

8 How did you obtain your current razor? (CHECK ONE)

_____Purchased it

_____Was given to me as a gift

_____Someone else's castoff, other family member gave it to me

_____Borrowed, share it with someone else

9 How long have you used this current razor? (CHECK ONE)

_____Less than 1 month

_____Less than 6 months

_____6 months–1 year

_____1–2 years

_____2–5 years

_____More than 5 years

10 What do you particularly like about the blade razor you are currently using? Please list everything that you like about it.

_____

_____

_____

_____

11 What, if anything, do you dislike about the blade razor you are currently using?

_____

_____

_____

_____

638

EXHIBIT 5

Continued

12 Do you use a blade razor that requires the blade to be changed? In other words, to change blades, do you have to remove one and replace it with another?

_____No _____Yes

12a If you answered Yes to question 12, do you load and unload the razor yourself, or do you have someone else do it for you? (CHECK ONE BELOW)

_____Load and unload it myself

_____Have someone else do it for me

If someone else changes your blades, please explain why you don't do this yourself. Give all reasons.

_____

_____

_____

13 Which of the following types of razor *blades* do you use?

_____Double-edge (edges on both sides of large blade)

_____Single-edge/injector (one edge on small blade)

_____Continuous band (many edges on one band)

_____Twin-bladed (two edges on one side of blade)

_____Use disposable razor, don't buy blades

_____Other _____
Please describe

14 Which of the following brands of razor *blades* do you buy or use *most often?*

_____Gillette   _____Schick

_____Personna   _____Wilkinson

_____Other _____
Please specify brand

15 Which of the following statements best describes how you obtain the *blades* you use? (CHECK ONE)

_____I buy them myself

_____Other family member buys/roommate buys

_____Whole family uses same brand, so anyone buys

16 How often do you usually shave? (CHECK ONE)

_____Every day

_____Every 2–3 days

_____At least once a week

_____Less than once a week

17 Approximately how many shaves do you get from each razor blade? (Consider shaving both legs and underarms as *one* shave.)

_____

18 What qualities or characteristics are important to you in shaving? In other words, what do you expect or want a shaver to do for you? List everything that you consider important and *number* them in the order of their importance to you.

_____

_____

_____

_____

_____

_____

19 If you were going to go out and buy a new blade razor today, what would you look for? What would this razor look like and what would you expect it to do? List everything that would enter into your final decision.

_____

_____

_____

_____

20 Think about your feelings and attitudes toward shaving. Then look at the grooming functions listed below. Consider your feelings toward each of these and compare them to your feelings about shaving. Which one is most similar to your feelings about shaving? Check one of these and then explain why your

639

EXHIBIT 5
Continued

feelings toward shaving and this other grooming function are similar.

_____Applying make-up

_____Bathing

_____Pedicures

_____Manicures

_____Eyebrow plucking

_____Brushing teeth

_____Hair care

They are similar because _____

_____

_____

_____

21 Which is the most difficult area of the body for you to shave, your underarms or your legs?

_____Underarms   _____Legs

Why? _____

_____

_____

_____

22 Other than possibly nicking or cutting yourself, what other problems do you have with the actual act of shaving? What problems or difficulties of any kind do you have while shaving?

_____

_____

23 Do you feel that a woman's shaving needs differ from those of a man? In other words, does the shaving of underarms and legs require something of a razor that a man's razor simply can't do very well?

_____Yes

_____No

What? _____

_____

_____

24 What do you feel could be improved

on current razors that would be more helpful to a woman's shaving needs?

_____

_____

_____

25 Following are a list of incomplete sentences. Please read each one and complete the sentence to reflect your feelings on each idea.

A I think that body hair on a woman is _____

_____

B The primary motive for a woman shaving is _____

_____

C When I need a shave, I feel _____

_____

D After shaving, I feel _____

_____

E The best things about shaving are _____

_____

F The worst things about shaving are _____

_____

G After I have used my razor, I usually put it _____

_____

H The specific place where I am most likely to shave my legs is

_____

(Tub, shower, sink, etc.)

26 Following is a list of multiple choice statements. For each of these statements, read all choices and check the one which most closely describes your own feelings. For several of these statements, it is possible that you may want to check more than one of the choices.

A When I shave, I cut or nick myself . . .

EXHIBIT 5
Continued

_____ almost every time

_____ occasionally

_____ hardly ever

B When I shave, I get a rash or skin irritation . . .

_____ almost every time

_____ occasionally

_____ hardly ever

C During the summer months, I usually shave my legs . . .

_____ more frequently than during winter months

_____ less frequently

_____ about the same

D When I shave my legs, I usually use . . .

_____ shaving cream

_____ soap

_____ just water

_____ something else

_____ nothing

E After I shave my legs, I usually use . . .

_____ a cream or lotion

_____ something else

_____ nothing

F Once you start shaving hair it . . .

_____ hastens hair growth

_____ makes hair coarser

_____ makes hair darker

_____ doesn't affect hair

G If it were socially acceptable *not* to shave, I would . . .

_____ continue to shave my underarms and legs

_____ shave only my underarms

_____ shave only my legs

_____ not shave at all

STOP. DO NOT TURN PAGE

EXHIBIT 5
Continued

1   Earlier in this questionnaire, you were asked to compare shaving with one of a number of other grooming functions. Think about all these functions again, including shaving (READ LIST BELOW). Now, rate all these functions in the order of their importance to you.

_____Applying make-up   _____Hair care

_____Bathing   _____Manicures

_____Brushing teeth   _____Pedicures

_____Eyebrow plucking   _____Shaving

2a   (HAND RESPONDENT ATTRIBUTE LIST A) Here are a list of attributes or characteristics which you may or may not consider to be important to you in your normal shaving routine. Above this list is a scale which rates these attributes on their importance—from extremely important to extremely unimportant. Using this scale, tell me how important each of these benefits or characteristics is to you. (RECORD BELOW)[1]

2b   (HAND RESPONDENT LIST B) Now think about your current razor and how it performs or relates to each of these descriptions. Using the scale at the top of the page, rate your own razor. For instance, on "no nicks or cuts"—if you *never* have any trouble with your razor cutting you, you might choose "10"—"excellent description." If you cut yourself *almost* every time you shave, you might consider this a "poor description."[1]

	Q2a	Q2b
No nicks or cuts	_____	_____
Fast shave	_____	_____
Convenient to use	_____	_____
Easy to control	_____	_____
Safe to dispose of blades	_____	_____
Close shave	_____	_____
Attractive razor	_____	_____
Feminine	_____	_____
Adjustable to legs/underarms	_____	_____
Economical	_____	_____

[1] For reasons of space, the scales themselves are not reproduced here.

EXHIBIT 6
RESPONSES TO THE J. WALTER THOMPSON COMPANY QUESTIONNAIRE[1]
Daisy: II

TABLE 1

Age first began to shave	No. of respondents
12	18
13	19
14	11
15	6
16	1
17	2
	57

TABLE 2

Brand of razor currently using	No. of respondents
Gillette	24
Schick	17
Personna Flicker	7
Wilkinson	5
Don't know	4
	57

TABLE 3

Current razor being used	No. of respondents
Men's	30
Women's	22
Don't know	5
	57

TABLE 4

How current razor was obtained	No. of respondents
Purchased it for self use	33
Received as gift	6
Someone's castoff	10
Share with someone else	8
	57

[1] These data have been disguised and are not useful for research purposes.

EXHIBIT 6

Continued

TABLE 5

Type of razor used most often	No. of respondents
Double-edge	24
Injector	16
Band	6
Twin-bladed	3
Disposable	8
	57

TABLE 6

Length of time current razor has been used	No. of respondents
Less than 1 month	2
1–6 months	6
6 months–1 year	10
1–2 years	17
2–5 years	14
More than 5 years	8
	57

TABLE 7

Frequency of shaving	No. of respondents
Every day	2
Every 2–3 days	14
At least once a week	30
Less than once a week	11
	57
More in summer	49
Less in summer	0
About the same	8
	57

TABLE 8

Blades bought and/or used most often	No. of respondents
Gillette	25
Schick	18
Wilkinson	9
Personna	4
Other	1
	57

TABLE 9

How blades are obtained	No. of respondents
Purchased by respondent	35
Purchased by other family member/roommate	14
Whole family uses same brand, so anyone buys	8
	57

TABLE 10

No. of shavings per blade	No. of respondents
1	3
2	3
3	5
4	3
5	12
6	5
7	6
10	8
15	2
18	1
20	1
40	1
Don't know	7
	57

DAISY: III
POSITIONING

NANCY J. DAVIS
Research Associate
Harvard Graduate School of Business Administration

STEVEN H. STAR
Associate Professor
Harvard Graduate School of Business Administration

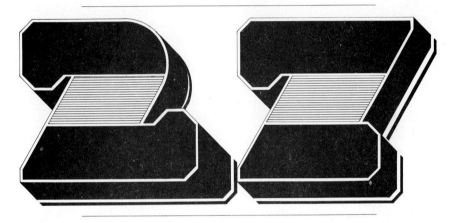

By March 1974, the task force researchers had developed considerable information on the women's shaving market, and the task force product development group had designed Daisy, a disposable shaver designed specifically for women. At this point, Mr. Bryan Dwyer, now product manager for Daisy, and the task force had to determine exactly how Daisy should be positioned. After considering Daisy's various attributes, the J. Walter Thompson Creative Department had developed audio-visual material for seven basic advertising concepts, each of which emphasized one specific attribute of Daisy. The J. Walter Thompson Research Department then tested these concepts with a group of women. From the women's responses, Dwyer and his task force would determine which features of Daisy should be emphasized and which would be played down.

Confidential company and industry data have been disguised, and while useful for purposes of case analysis, they are not useful for research purposes.

THE DEVELOPMENT OF DAISY

Over the last decade the members of SRD's product development group had conducted periodic studies to determine the characteristics women preferred in shaving products. In recent years, they had made films of women shaving to see how women grasped razors, the angle at which they approached the skin, and so forth. As talk of a major effort in the women's market increased, they began to do both in-plant and out-of-plant tests of handles of various lengths, plus tests of a handleless stubby shaving unit somewhat comparable to Flicker. The women preferred a unit with a handle slightly longer than that of Lady Sure Touch, about the same length as that of Lady Trac II.

The product development group also tested shaving units of different weights. The heaviest was a double-edge unit weighing about 64 grams; the lightest weighed about 5 grams. Generally speaking, the lighter units were more often preferred, though units weighing 10 grams or less were usually considered too light. It was almost certain that the Trac II system would be used in the new product, but the group still tested several configurations—a unit with a Trac II system on both sides, a unit with single blades on each side, different angles of the Trac II system, and a "guarded edge" blade that had been dulled slightly with a metallurgical coating.

After carefully reviewing the results of the product development group's studies and the consumer research done by Dwyer's task force and the J. Walter Thompson Research Department, SRD managers identified five features which they considered necessary for a successful product for women. The first requirement, they thought, was that the Trac II system be used. They estimated that the twin-bladed shaving system would account for 25 to 30 percent of the total 1974 blade market in the United States, and they expected continued rapid expansion in 1975. Women would increasingly be interested in twin-bladed shaving, they thought, as male shaving attitudes and word of mouth concerning the system's superiority increased. They felt that Lady Trac II represented the ultimate in a close, safe shave, but since it was merely a colored-handle version of the men's Trac II, it was not obviously designed especially for women.

A second requirement for success, management thought, was that a woman would purchase and use the product herself, without sharing it with anyone. Consumer research had indicated that this would most likely happen if the product was disposable. Though Lady Sure Touch had never enjoyed much success, Flicker had been quite successful. SRD management had interpreted this as meaning that indeed there was a potential market for a disposable shaver. Management also pointed out that disposability would strengthen the product's position with the trade because, if the product used replaceable cartridges, retailers would have to carry separate cartridges for it, and SRD's salespeople would have to obtain pegboard space for them. These cartridges would probably not differ from regular brown Trac II cartridges except they would be colored, and SRD already had trouble getting retailers to carry enough of the brown cartridges. In fact, even though SRD had nearly a 60 percent share of blade sales, it had been able to maintain only slightly more than 40 percent of available pegboard space. The final key factor in favor of a disposable product was that it would generate more contribution per user than did SRD's other systems.

SRD's third requirement for a successful product, according to SRD management, was that the product must provide the highest retail turnover of any female shaving product to maximize trade interest. The fourth requirement was that the product be featured in a uniquely feminine package to maximize consumer interest. And the fifth requirement was that SRD's design staff create a completely unique display system, whose aim would be to generate consumer trial.

The product which SRD's development group had now designed especially for women was Daisy, a lightweight (13 grams), disposable shaver with a permanently locked-on, nonreplaceable Trac II cartridge. The handle was curved near the head of the shaver to provide better visibility and easier access to hard-to-reach areas such as behind knees. Daisy was molded out of high-impact polystyrene. Around the handle were indented Daisy designs which acted as grips and provided aesthetic appeal. The name *Gillette* was also molded into the handle. Each shaver had its own clear safety cap which protected the shaver's cutting edges during shipment and which was especially convenient when the consumer packed the shaver for traveling. (See Exhibit 1 for a picture of Daisy.)

CONSUMER RESPONSES TO PRODUCT-POSITIONING CONCEPTS

To determine the relative emphasis which should be given to Daisy's different features, the J. Walter Thompson Company's Creative Department produced seven possible positioning concepts, each of which emphasized a particular feature or benefit of the shaver. These are shown in Table 1.

The research team's task now was to obtain reactions of women currently using a wet shaving system to these various approaches to Daisy's introduction.

TABLE 1

Positioning concept	Major feature/benefit
Blind spots	Curved handle for closeness and safety
Daisy loves me	Product name, safer than older razor
Twin-bladed shave	Hysteresis* demonstration showing closeness
Bows to a woman's needs	Shaver designed specifically for a woman's needs, a new design
A girl shouldn't have to	Disposability, convenience of not changing blade
Wouldn't hurt a thigh	Safety, no nicks or cuts
Under 50¢/a dollar	Low price

* A hysteresis demonstration illustrated how the Trac II system worked. It showed the first blade lifting the hair, cutting off part of it, and holding it up while the second blade cut the rest of the hair very close to the skin surface. This type of illustration was used heavily in the early advertisement for the men's Trac II.

TABLE 2

Under age 25	Age 25–34
1 group of working women	1 group of working women
1 group of housewives	1 group of housewives
1 group of high school students	
1 group of college students	

In all, six sessions were conducted, and the same 57 women who had participated in the survey Ms. Alison Yancy conducted in February also participated in this study. All respondents shaved at least twice a month, usually with a wet razor. The specific groups are shown in Table 2. Each group of nine or ten women again arrived at the J. Walter Thompson Company at an appointed time. About a week before the sessions, the women had been sent a sample Daisy shaver and had been asked to use it before coming to the sessions. Before the women screened the position concepts, Yancy spent about 30 minutes chatting with them about their experiences shaving with Daisy.

The creative material for each of the seven position concepts consisted of an idea board (a graphic representation of what one might see in a commercial) and an audio track that included the general message about the product which would appear in a commercial. The respondents were shown the idea boards and listened to the audio tracks of each concept. The order in which the concepts were presented varied from one group to the next. Immediately after each presentation, the women were asked for their reactions. The concepts, audio tracks, and responses were as follows:

CONCEPT 1: BLIND SPOTS

AUDIO TRACK

Announcing the end of blind spots. Introducing the Daisy disposable shaver.

The Daisy's curved head makes it easier to see what you're shaving . . . especially underarms, calves and ankles.

And the Daisy's twin blades give you the closest, safest shave possible. The blades are recessed and permanently locked in. You never have to change them. So, after weeks of shaving, throw the whole thing away.

Gillette's new disposable Daisy . . . designed to shed some light on the blind spots.

CONSUMER RESPONSES TO THE "BLIND SPOTS" CONCEPT

I think the blind spot is a good point because you can't see under your arms unless if you're in the shower or in the tub and you go crosswise.

I like this idea because I think that in order to get at the blind spots and everything . . . you'd get a good shave that way because there are a lot of places that are hard to reach.

I have a real hard time getting behind my knees and I shave up over my knees because of the short skirts. It does seem to get in there. I like the shape because of that.

I really like the shape of it . . . you've got a secure feeling in your hand with this. It's a nice shape. It fits right in the palm of your hand and I like the curve on it better than a straight edge razor.

The thing is, I noticed with this razor—and it hasn't been said—but with my razor, my Lady Sure Touch, I never know the angle to hold it at, 'cause if I hold it too far this way, I don't get any hair, and if I hold it too far this way all I get is skin. And on this one, it's the end is like it's flat, so there's only one angle you can hold it at and so you kind of just have to get the right angle and that would be important to me.

I interpreted it as being like there are certain spots around your leg that it's difficult to see, and I thought that they were saying that this razor was going to make you be able to see those spots you can't see.

It did say that you get to the blind areas that you do have difficulty shaving if you shave . . .

Well, the idea of the blind spots is appealing to me because I have trouble getting to the blind spots.

I think with the straight handle you're right there on your leg and you want to see what you're doing and either you take it away or you lift it up. At least this way, with the curve there, there's some type of space that you can see what you're doing, without having to take it off and putting it back down.

In other words, you could take this either way, if your blind spots are where the regular razor misses or where you can't happen to see, this will cover both.

When you can see what you're doing, you won't miss patches of hair and have to go back over it again.

It gets into it on the basis of you can see better rather than on the basis of you won't nick yourself. It's more credible in a way.

Well, it says that you could see what you're doing so you won't get cut . . . it was a lot better . . . it brought out the point a little more.

My immediate reaction to that one, without having held it up to my leg and out to see that it did do that—let you see around—was, well, that's silly, the curved handle. It doesn't make any bit of difference. This one, unless it like actually showed on TV like better than just those pictures that it really did curve out, there would be no way for me to tell that it really did.

It says so many good things at the beginning of the commercial and then at the end they just say about throwing it away. I don't feel so guilty.

CONCEPT 2: DAISY LOVES ME

AUDIO TRACK

My new Daisy loves me. My old razor loves me not.

Daisy shaves me smooth, cuts me not . . . because its twin blades shave me closely and they're recessed for safety.

Daisy shaves me easy, worries me not . . . because its new curved head makes it easier for me to see what I'm doing.

And Daisy lasts for weeks . . . bothers me not because I never change a blade. I just throw the whole thing away.

Gillette's new disposable shaver. Daisy loves me.

CONSUMER RESPONSES TO THE "DAISY LOVES ME" CONCEPT

It hits the eye. It teases the imagination. What's it going to do, you want to try it.

To get people's attention. I think by hearing some type thing a lot of people pay more attention to something like that than getting facts. You know, a lot of times you hear things, if it has a rhyme to it, your ear pays more attention to it than a regular talking type thing.

It's an original, stupid commercial. It will stick in your mind.

When I first heard the ad, I thought it was cute and liked it and then I was trying to think of where I heard it . . . the other Gillette Soft and Dri commercial has the same idea to it.

Of course, you could get confused with, you know, Daisy in your tank.

It sounds like the toilet bowl thing.

It must remind me too much of the Soft 'N Dri commercial. I don't like the way they just keep saying, loves me, they just kept repeating that too much.

It's a good commercial, but I don't think it says enough about the razor. I think more force is put on the name rather than what the blade does. I'd rather have a commercial that just told me what something does, without that loves me, loves me not. I just prefer straight facts.

It said a lot, but it was really all hidden in the loves me, loves me not.

I said I didn't like it . . . if the daisies would be in the commercial that's not what we're advertising. You're not advertising flowers, you're advertising a shaver. And I don't think flowers have anything to do with it except the name.

I like what they do on the premise of the Daisy, daisy loves me, loves me not. I thought it was very cute advertising. If I was looking through a magazine, that was being advertised, I would look at it twice.

I think if it were in a magazine it would be a good advertisement, because you could stop and you could look at it . . . but for on TV it would probably be another one where you'd get up and get yourself a cup of coffee.

I also do not like a commercial where it degrades the intelligence of a person and I think this daisy business is very juvenile.

I get to the point where this loves me, loves me not is, like adding sugar on top of frosting.

It's too cute, I mean, to the point of yuck!

I think the cliche is sort of childish. I mean, I don't disapprove of cliches, but that one is just that's already bordering on the hackneyed. The approach is a little bit too childish and too flippant.

It's so degrading, it talks down to you so much.

CONCEPT 3: TWIN-BLADED SHAVE

AUDIO TRACK

Introducing the disposable Daisy. The first twin-bladed shaver you use for weeks and then throw away without ever changing blades.

Watch how the twin blades work. The first blade shaves close and then before that stubborn hair snaps back, the second blade shaves it clean away.

And because Daisy's twin blades are recessed and locked in place, there's no safer shave.

The new disposable razor from Gillette . . . don't let a close shave pass you by.

CONSUMER RESPONSES TO THE "TWIN-BLADE SHAVE" CONCEPT

The only part I like is the hair part, where it misses the one and then it catches the second one which tells me it's better than a regular shaver.

This one shows exactly what it will do, to the point. I think the idea of getting the second hair, you know, 'cause a lot of times when I shave, as I'm shaving, I watch closely and I have to keep going back.

I sort of liked that one . . . it's a real graphic description, I think and I can relate to that a whole lot better . . . it presents it in a more like factual manner instead of a real frivolous.

Two blades should be a closer shave.

This is good . . . a lot of times I'll start shaving and feel like I've gone right over and it didn't take that much hair off. And I've had to go over again.

This one says to me that you're getting a smooth, close shave with a double edge razor that will pick up what's left from the first cut and will pick up the stubble after the first blade cuts the hair.

Where does the hair go, when you're cutting your hair now, where does it go. It's going into the blade of the razor, in here. Now how can you use it over and over again without removing the razor to clean it . . . it's like accumulating and accumulating. That's the way to dull a razor.

It's going to get clogged up.

A lot of times I have to open up my razor to take the blade out, and there is hair clogging.

They have other women's razors out that are twin blades, but this isn't emphasizing the shape of it . . . or that it doesn't cut you and they've had other twin blade razors out for women that say the same thing . . . I think the shape is the most appealing thing to me.

I don't really think that that's the most important thing. There's other razors out that have them too, so I don't think that's most important.

I don't believe that it actually pulls up the hair and goes over it again. I just can't see how it's physically possible that a razor could actually pull up a hair.

I would just wonder if that second blade is gonna take the skin with it . . . it's funny 'cause when I saw it (demo) for the men's razors, I guess I just don't worry about my husband chopping his face up, you know. But I do worry about me chopping my legs up.

I don't find it offensive, but I don't find it believable either.

I wondered about that. I've never really looked at one follicle of hair. It should shave it the first time.

I don't care if the razor has one or two blades, as long as it's clean, close, comfortable, and I'm not gonna get nicked or cut. These are the important things to me.

To me you're not getting across what you really want to get across about the new shape. It's a safer shave, cleaner shave, for hard to reach areas, and the fact that that's really a totally new shape in a razor.

The reason I don't like it is because they all stress that they'll give you a close shave. Of course, they indicate because it's got a twin blade, it will get the one behind it, but I think they should stress more the fact that it's curved in such a position that it can get to the parts that we usually chop. To me that would hit home quicker.

Well, it doesn't show the difficult areas that you think about shaving, like underarms or by your ankles or under the legs.

I wouldn't sit through it 'cause I know this whole spiel already about pulls the hair and this and that.

I don't like, if it's a repeat of that same commercial . . . sometimes I'll be marking papers and watching television and if something is interesting, I'll put my head up and if I turn my head up and see hairs being cut off twice, I'll put my head back down. The shape would be more important, just one shot of the shape.

It reminds me of a man's commercial.

They're copying and we've already been through all this with the previous commercials showing the diagram of the hair being done, so that's just repetitive.

It's just like the men's razor—the Trac II.

CONCEPT 4: BOWS TO A WOMAN'S NEEDS

AUDIO TRACK

Introducing the Daisy . . . the first shaving instrument that bows to a woman's needs.

Gillette curved the handle so you can see around your own curves.

And locked in two blades so you never have to change them . . . and made the Daisy disposable so after weeks of clean, safe shaving, you toss the whole thing away.

The Daisy from Gillette . . . the company smart enough to see the difference between men and women's shaving needs.

CONSUMER RESPONSES TO THE "BOWS TO A WOMAN'S NEEDS" CONCEPT

I'm becoming sensitive to different advertisements that have to discriminate.

I don't like the way she says for a woman's needs. I mean, I feel like they're advertising a feminine hygiene deodorant.

On the other hand, the more liberated you want to be distinct from a man, you don't have to use the same thing a man uses in the beginning.

I resented the emphasis put on women. The razor made for a woman, because it seems to be that that's what they're doing in the advertising business, is they're using the whole idea of women's liberation to push their products when a lot of them are not at all liberated . . . as soon as I hear any kind of commercial like that, I automatically turn it off.

It just says, they shape the handle. It's made so you can see around your curves. I mean, it doesn't say anything to me. It doesn't say anything about the safety of it, the closeness of it.

It does say a lot, but it doesn't emphasize the things I think are important like safety. I mean, it mentions it, but not really, and closeness, alright it kind of mentions it but . . .

We have different problems than a man does. We have problems getting around the ankle and the back of the leg.

It told me that you can move it around your curves which is what a woman needs. I mean, our leg doesn't look like a man's face, you know. My leg is curved and I need it to curve around that bump.

It sounded good, real good, cause it expressed a lot about the shaver itself. It says that they know the difference that a man's razor should be something different than a woman's razor and that they're not putting them both on the same level, but that it is geared to a woman's needs and not a man's needs.

> . . . *you do need a different kind of razor cause you're not shaving your face. What could be more appropriate for a woman than a woman's razor? Like even Women's Lib would have to say yeah.*
>
> *I think it's telling you what you want to know exactly about the curved razor and that's what we want to know, that the razor is curved and it will be easy for us to get the back of our legs and the shins, and that's exactly what this tells you.*
>
> *I like that commercial because it's more direct than the others. It tells you right out and it's not so much of the art work involved. It shows the blade and that's the thing, and it explains the razor in full detail and that's it, explaining why it's built the way it is and what its purposes are, which is what we want to know.*
>
> *I like the curvature of the handle, the head on it. It looks like it would be easy to hold, it's light and I think women would be prone to get it cause of the shape.*
>
> *What my particular problem is with shaving is reaching the back of my thighs and reaching the back of my ankles. That one hits it to a tee, that's what it told me.*
>
> *I think the idea of the curve is terrific. It's easier to see, especially when you're shaving your underarms.*
>
> . . . *because I know myself when I shave under my arms especially it's rather difficult for us to see what you're doing and you have to get around areas where* . . .
>
> *The first thing I thought when I saw that was that it was flexible, it moved* . . . *I thought, gee, maybe it's like those dolls that have wire in them that bends in different ways.*
>
> *I also felt it looked like it was moveable.*
>
> *The particular picture makes it look as if it's bendable.*

CONCEPT 5: A GIRL SHOULDN'T HAVE TO

AUDIO TRACK

> *There are some things a girl just shouldn't have to do* . . . *and changing blades is one of them.*
>
> *So, Gillette created Daisy, the new disposable shaver.*
>
> *The Daisy with Gillette's famous twin blades permanently locked in for week after week of close, safe shaves.*
>
> *But Daisy's priced so low you won't mind throwing it away. New disposable Daisy, two for about a dollar.*
>
> *Great new throw-away idea.*

CONSUMER RESPONSES TO THE "A GIRL SHOULDN'T HAVE TO" CONCEPT

> . . . *what do they mean by weeks, three or ten?*
>
> *Why shouldn't a girl have to throw away a razor blade? It's as though we're real delicate, can't touch a blade at all.*
>
> *I mean, 16 year old boys do it all the time, why can't 16 year old girls change blades* . . . *it's like underrating them, because you know, like for heaven's sake, you touched the razor, you'll kill yourself.*
>
> *It seems silly to me that they say there are some things a girl shouldn't have to do. I mean, I can think of a few things a girl shouldn't have to do, but changing my blades isn't one of them.*
>
> *I don't like it either, it just annoys me this business about a woman, a girl*

shouldn't have to change a razor blade . . . why shouldn't a woman have to change a razor blade, she changes a tire.

It doesn't say anything about the product other than it's disposable and my biggest complaint on this I think it's a waste of natural resources.

Now we're in the energy crisis and this and that, and about plastic, you know, and then you figure they make them and then it's gonna be thrown away, and it's just a waste of money to me.

I hate razor blades laying around with little kids.

Well, I think it's not as important stressing that you don't have to change the blade. I think it's more important to stress that it's safer and it's closer.

There were a lot of good ideas expressed in this one that weren't expressed in the first one, but they put the emphasis on the wrong thing, changing the blade.

I think it was a nice idea of not having to change the blade, but it . . . doesn't say much about the product. It just says you know, you don't have to change the blades.

. . . it doesn't stress . . . they didn't really say why it will give you a close shave, because of the contour of it, the recessed blades, because of double blades, all it says it's something a woman shouldn't have to do. It's patronizing.

There's so much to this razor that it's really a good idea that makes me want to buy it. But this commercial told me that it's disposable, that it's cheap and it said once that it was a safe shave . . . but it didn't tell me enough. I'd never, I wouldn't buy it.

I mean, I know this product is gonna come out anyway. It's just a matter of which commercial. But my opinion is that it shouldn't emphasize disposability for people who can't stand disposable stuff.

The only thing that bothers me about this is this one in particular is emphasizing the one thing that I really don't like about it and that's its disposability.

I think it's a waste of natural resources. I do, I mean, here we are trying to conserve whatever resources we have and you are given two products, you know, that you use one and you throw it away and you have this perfectly good case that you can never use again. It just goes into the wastebasket. I think there should be a way of maybe changing the top where you don't have to dispose of the whole thing at once.

I think that's very important. I think that's good. I like just using things and throwing them away, buying new things.

CONCEPT 6: WOULDN'T HURT A THIGH

AUDIO TRACK

Introducing the Daisy from Gillette. The first woman's shaver that wouldn't hurt a thigh . . . or ankle or knee or shin or underarm.

The Daisy's twin blades are recessed and permanently locked in at a safe angle, so there's no way to hurt yourself.

Then, after weeks of close, safe shaving, throw the whole thing away and pick the other Daisy.

The Daisy . . . it wouldn't hurt a thigh.

CONSUMER RESPONSES TO THE "WOULDN'T HURT A THIGH" CONCEPT

I like it because it was cute and it's catchy when you see it.

I agree, I think this is the best one. It's got a tingle to it.

I think it's cute. It's real attention getting. It won't hurt a thigh. I like that.

It says a big thing about it not cutting you and trying to make it a little bit funny. I think they're trying to make it a little amusing to you . . . I think they're making fun of it themselves a little bit too, the company is making fun of it, but they're trying to get across to you that it will work.

There's no way to hurt yourself. I like it better and it won't hurt a thigh. Well, you know, a lot of catchy ads like the Alka Seltzer always has an ad that you remember or something. I won't hurt a thigh. I don't know, but no way you can hurt yourself, I would remember that.

The fact that it doesn't cut you is the most impressive thing to me. So it's the most important thing to stress.

It's recessed, it's not gonna dig into you.

Well, it states what you want to know about the razor itself. That it's curved and so you can't hurt yourself . . . and it's a recessed blade so that right there means that it's gonna be difficult to cut or nick yourself.

I like the idea of not having to change the blade, but then I don't like the idea of after a couple uses having to throw it away. It doesn't say how long you're going to be able to use it before you're going to be able to throw it away. It says a couple of weeks, but it depends on how long you're going to shave, how many times a week you shave, and how dull that blade is going to be.

CONCEPT 7: UNDER 50¢/A DOLLAR

AUDIO TRACK

Gillette introduces the new disposable shaver for under 50¢ (under a dollar). The Daisy . . .

Two blades . . . one to shave you close, the other to shave you closer. Permanently locked in at a safe angle so you never change blades. The Daisy . . . weeks of close, safe shaving before you throw the whole thing away.

Two Daisy shavers for 99¢ and that's less than 50¢ apiece.

The new Daisy disposable shaver. Don't let a good shave or a good deal pass you by.

CONSUMER RESPONSES TO THE "UNDER 50¢/A DOLLAR" CONCEPT

When I think of it for under 50¢, I think of some cheap little thing.

. . . if they say it's under 50¢, it sounds like you're getting a good deal . . . but the first thing that will come into my mind is gee, that's too cheap.

I just want to say that the Daisy, first disposable shaver under a dollar leads me to believe there's only one for under a dollar.

The one thing that really bothers me about this is that it's misleading as far as I'm concerned about the price.

Very misleading, because originally it's telling you 50¢ and then it's coming back and saying you have to get two for 99¢. You can't get it for 50¢, you have to buy it for 99¢.

I think the emphasis should be on what it does. I mean you do want the cost, but . . .

Price is important, but I don't think it's the major thing. Most of us are more concerned with the safety factor, the ease of use, than the price. The price enters into it, but I think the other considerations are more important. Is it going to do the job?

I don't think that money should be the main thing because a lot of people will say, yeah, under a dollar, but how long is it gonna last.

All they do is tell you that it's cheap and disposable.

The only thing I don't like, you keep saying after weeks. It depends how much you're going to shave and how thick your hair is, how coarse your hair is, and everyone is going to get more or less shaves.

I just don't believe all this business of weeks and weeks. That this one blade is going to last for weeks and weeks.

THE DECISION

As the SRD task force and the J. Walter Thompson researchers reviewed these comments about Daisy, they were well aware that the women surveyed had expressed both positive and negative feelings about virtually every one of Daisy's attributes. Whether the feature being emphasized was Daisy's curved handle, its name, the Trac II shaving system, the convenience of not having to change blades, the closeness of the shave, or the product's price, some women thought it was great while others were at best skeptical. The SRD and J. Walter Thompson groups now had to weigh the relative importance of these responses and generalize as best they could about how well they probably reflected the opinions of most women in the 15-to-34-year age group. Specifically, they had to assign some priorities to the various features so that the Creative Department would know exactly what the thrust of their advertisements should be. (See Exhibits 2 and 3 for samples of Flicker's advertising.)

EXHIBIT 1
PICTURE OF DAISY
Daisy: III

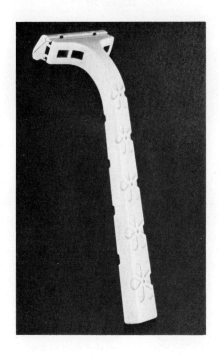

1. WOMAN: Think of all the nicks and cuts you've had from shaving with a man's razor.

2. Now, there's Flicker, specially designed just for you.

3. To cut hair, not skin.

4. Flicker's five unique wire-wrap blades

5. give you a smooth, safer shave.

6. It's like flicking hair away.

7. You may never nick your knees or scrape your shins again.

8. Try Flicker, the first disposable ladies' safety shaver

9. designed to cut hair, and that's all.

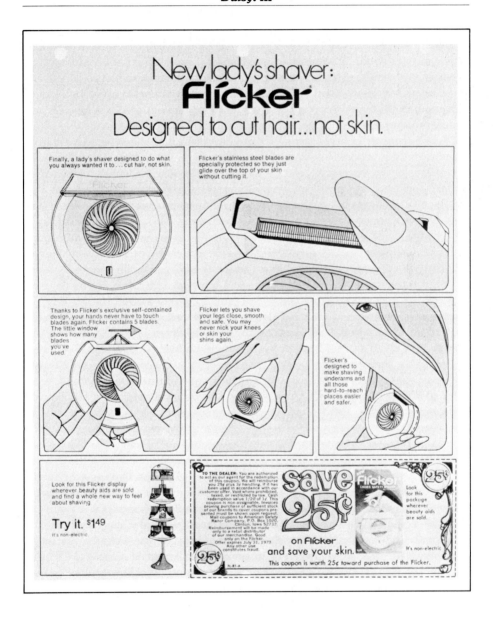

DAISY: IV
DESIGNING A TEST MARKET

NANCY J. DAVIS
Research Associate
Harvard Graduate School of Business Administration

STEVEN H. STAR
Associate Professor
Harvard Graduate School of Business Administration

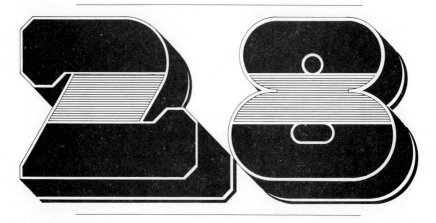

By May 1974, the Gillette Safety Razor Division had, according to Mr. Bryan Dwyer, product manager for Daisy, "a great product, a super package, great displays, and fabulous advertising." The product was Daisy, a lightweight, disposable shaver with a permanently locked-on Trac II cartridge. The polystyrene handle was curved near the shaver's head to provide better visibility and easier access to hard-to-reach areas. Daisy was produced in two colors—lavender and rose. (See Exhibit 1 for a picture of Daisy.)

Daisy was packaged in what looked like two cups placed together. The top cup was transparent, exposing the two shavers inside. In designing the package, the task force had worked on several concepts, and in consultation with some consumers, narrowed the choices to the cup package and a blister package.

About 250 women were then interviewed in a shopping center and asked which package they preferred. Seventy-nine percent chose the cup. According to Dwyer, the Daisy package looked very feminine, provided good visibility of the shavers, provided easy and safe disposability, and was reusable. (See Exhibit 2 for a picture of the Daisy package.)

The Daisy package did not fit onto a regular pegboard display as did most SRD packages, but it was designed to be displayed in health and beauty aids departments. (Flicker had initially been displayed in health and beauty aids departments along with other feminine grooming products, and it had made the transition to regular pegboard displays without any serious decline in sales.) Three systems were designed for Daisy—a floor boutique display which held 72 Daisy packages, a counter carousel display which held 36 Daisy packages, and a shelf extender which held 12 Daisy packages. (See Exhibit 3 for pictures of the various displays.)

The Daisy task force felt that selling two disposable shavers at a retail price around $1 would generate high consumer interest, and that consumer interest would produce enthusiastic trade support because of the sales potential associated with a fast-selling product. They estimated that, on the average, a woman would buy five Daisy packages a year, substantially more than any other woman's wet shaver or razor on the market. The theme "Wouldn't Hurt a Thigh" had been adopted, and the J. Walter Thompson Company had created advertisements for television, magazines, and newspapers. (See Exhibits 4 and 5 for sample advertisements.)

SRD's management concurred with the task force's recommendation to test-market Daisy to determine its real sales and profit potential prior to launching the product nationally. They felt that the test should continue for a full year so that the product's seasonality could be adequately assessed, but they also pointed out that, if after 6 months the test market was proving successful, SRD could proceed with a national roll-out while the test market was still running. They were especially concerned with the following questions:

1   How should Daisy be priced?
2   What would be the effect of different advertising levels on sales and total market?
3   Exactly what sales and market share levels could Daisy expect?
4   How much and what type of both consumer and trade promotions were needed?
5   What would the trade's reaction to Daisy be? Would they buy it? Would they give it the display it needed? Would they keep the displays stocked?
6   What would be the reaction of the SRD sales force?

In discussions with SRD's Marketing Research and Sales Departments, the Daisy task force decided that testing Daisy in four markets in different geographic regions would allow them to test different variables and to average out

TABLE 1

Designated marketing area	Population	% of total U.S. population
Memphis	2,435,100	1.18
Dayton	1,521,300	0.74
Seattle	1,723,400	0.84
Milwaukee	2,641,500	1.28
	8,321,300	4.04

regional idiosyncrasies but would keep the test small enough for the team to carefully monitor exactly what was going on in each market. The designated marketing areas (DMAs)[1] they selected were Memphis, Tennessee, Dayton, Ohio, Seattle, Washington, and Milwaukee, Wisconsin. These metro areas had a combined population of 8,321,300, or 4.04 percent of the total United States population. The population by DMA is shown in Table 1. (See Exhibits 6 and 7 for data about each of these cities.)

After selecting the test market cities, the members of the task force had to determine exactly what they were going to test and where they were going to test it. One member argued that, since they had four cities, they should test four key variables: price, advertising levels, consumer and trade promotions, and support and incentives required by the SRD sales force. Another member thought they should pair the cities somehow and test one or two key variables in each pair. Still another member felt they should hold all variables constant in all four markets. She said:

> The more we start tinkering with different pricing structures or offering different terms to the trade in different cities, the less conclusive our data is going to be because it will be based on too small a sample. We'd be better off to hold everything constant and try to generalize from 4.04% of the population rather than to try to test a lot of different variables and generalize from less than 1% of the population.

"Obviously we can't test everything we'd like to," Dwyer said. "Let's look carefully at each of our questions and see what trade-offs we're going to have to make."

PRICE

In an attempt to determine the appropriate price point for Daisy, the members of the task forces were considering two retail prices, $0.99 and $1.19. SRD's pricing structure for direct-buying retailers and wholesalers would then be as

---

[1] A designated marketing area (DMA) was defined in terms of the reach of television stations. That is, a DMA consisted of an area within which the local stations achieved the largest share of the 9 A.M. to 12 midnight of average quarter-hour household audience or within which one station achieved a larger share of the 9 A.M. to 12 midnight average quarter-hour household audience than any station outside the DMA.

TABLE 2

	I	II
Retail price per package[a]	$0.99	$1.19
Regular invoice price to direct-buying retailers and wholesalers[b]	0.594	0.714
Introductory-special-deal invoice price to direct-buying retailers and wholesalers[c]	f	f
Regular invoice price to retail accounts being serviced by wholesalers[d]	0.713	0.857
Introductory-special-deal invoice price to retail accounts being serviced by wholesalers[e]	f	f

[a] The price at which SRD *recommended* retailers sell the product. In reality, SRD had no control over this price, and large retail outlets frequently discounted the price.
[b] The price SRD charged its immediate customers.
[c] The price SRD charged its immediate customers after various trade allowances were deducted.
[d] The price at which wholesalers sold the product to their customers.
[e] This price took into account any special offers wholesalers wished to make to their customers. SRD had no control over this price.
[f] To be decided.

shown in Table 2. The task force suspected that some discounting would probably occur, especially in the markets where Daisy retailed for $1.19. Nevertheless, they thought these prices, once introductory trade allowances were taken into account, would be very helpful in gaining distribution for Daisy in health and beauty aids departments of supermarkets, mass-merchandise outlets, and large drugstores where gross margins averaged about 40 percent. At that time, Lady Sure Touch, Lady Trac II, and Flicker were retailing for the prices shown in Table 3.

MEDIA ADVERTISING LEVEL

In developing a television commerical for Daisy, the J. Walter Thompson researchers created three different commericals, which they showed to about 500 women over a 3-day period. Each day, about 165 women were shown what they were told was a pilot program for a new television series. A Daisy commerical was inserted at an appropriate point in the program. After the viewing, focus groups were held in which the women were asked their opinions of the

TABLE 3

	Manufacturer's suggested retail price	Actual retail price range
Lady Sure Touch	$1.29	$1.10–$1.50
Lady Trac II	2.95	2.59– 3.25
Flicker	1.49	1.29– 1.69

Daisy commerical as well as their opinions of the program which was the professed object of the survey.

To test the effects of different levels of advertising, Dwyer and the task force thought they might test at least two levels. Some markets would receive relatively low expenditures, while others would receive relatively high expenditures. The data with which they would determine exactly what "high" and "low" would be were sketchy. They knew that in 1973 Flicker had spent $1,450,500 on media advertising in the 65 markets where it was distributed throughout the United States, and that Memphis, Seattle, Dayton, and Milwaukee were included in these markets. (See Exhibit 8 for Flicker's media advertising expenditures.) On Lady Sure Touch, SRD had spent approximately $846,000 nationally in 1973, mainly on national television and magazines. It had not done any media advertising of Lady Trac II. In contrast to the small amount spent on the products for women, SRD had spent about $9 million on media advertising plus another $4.5 million on samples for launching the man's Trac II in 1972.

SALES AND MARKET SHARE

The product manager and his team suspected that the sales and market share Daisy could get would largely be a function of the amount of advertising and promotion with which SRD supported it. Nevertheless, they had to establish some realistic, profitable objectives based on the current size of the markets, their projections about how these markets might expand as a result of increased advertising and promotion by SRD, the position of competitive products, Daisy's performance in shave tests, and some estimates of what trial and repurchases Daisy could get. Earlier they had estimated that, on the average, a woman would buy five Daisy packages a year, substantially more than any other woman's wet shaver or razor on the market.

Since Daisy was a disposable product more comparable to blades than to razors, the members of the task force planned to base their estimates on the total blade market (i.e., blades purchased for both men and women), which they thought would consist of approximately 2.372 billion blades throughout the United States in 1974. To estimate the size of the markets in each of their test cities, they multiplied the total blade market by the percentage of the United States population in each DMA. Since they had fairly accurate estimates of the sales of Lady Sure Touch and Flicker, they could calculate market share data. However, they could not compare the position of Lady Trac II with that of Flicker and Lady Sure Touch because Lady Trac II was considered part of the razor market. (See Exhibit 9 for market shares of these products.)

In "shave tests" where SRD researchers asked several people to compare the performance of Daisy with that of Flicker, Lady Sure Touch, and Lady Trac II, Daisy ranked well above the other products. On a scale where 100 was the highest possible score, Daisy scored 92 points, Lady Trac II scored 84 points,

Lady Sure Touch scored 73 points, and Flicker scored 68 points. Moreover, Dwyer knew that, even with limited marketing support, Lady Sure Touch had been tried by about 6 percent of the women who shaved in the United States, and 55 percent of those who tried it had repurchased it.

TRADE PROMOTIONS

To get strong support at the retail level and to achieve desired levels of distribution, the task force felt SRD had to offer the trade very substantial promotional deals. American Safety Razor (ASR) had used four types of trade promotions to introduce Flicker and to secure display space in health and beauty aids departments. The first trade promotion was an 8⅓ percent off-invoice allowance; that is, the manufacturer's invoice price was reduced by 8⅓ percent, regardless of the amount of the product the customer ordered.[1] ASR's second type of trade promotion was the cooperative advertising allowance. After a retailer ran an advertisement which included a picture of Flicker, he sent a tear sheet of the ad to ASR, and ASR paid him $1.50 for every counter display and $3.25 for every floor stand he had purchased. (Sometimes wholesalers ran ads for several of their customers, in which case they too were eligible for cooperative advertising allowances.) ASR's third program was the display allowance. Under it, ASR paid its direct-buying retail customers $0.50 for every counter display and $1.25 for every floor stand they purchased. ASR's final introductory trade promotion consisted of placement money. In this program, ASR paid $1 to wholesaler salespeople for every 24-unit counter display they sold and $2 for every 54-unit floor stand they sold.

When SRD first introduced Lady Sure Touch, it offered a 16⅔ percent off-invoice allowance and a $0.30 display allowance for every 12-unit display placed in retail outlets. When it began to sell Lady Sure Touch nationally, its trade promotions consisted of a 10 percent off-invoice allowance, a cooperative advertising allowance which consisted of $0.50 per 12-unit carton purchased, and a $0.75 display allowance for each special display set up in a retail outlet. By May 1974, SRD was offering no trade promotions on Lady Sure Touch. The introductory trade promotions for Lady Trac II had consisted of a 16⅔ percent off-invoice allowance plus 3.5 million samples distributed to the trade. By May 1974, SRD offered only a 10 percent off-invoice allowance.

For Daisy's introduction, the task force was considering a 16⅔ percent off-invoice allowance, an 8 percent cooperative advertising allowance, and 4 percent placement money. When the task force's representative from SRD's

---

[1] Off-invoice allowances were sometimes escalated—a manufacturer might offer 2.5 percent off each case if a retailer purchased, say, 25 cases, 5 percent off if he purchased 50 cases, and so on. While the escalated buying allowance usually did increase the initial orders of a product, many retailers opposed it because they felt it constituted unusual and unwarranted pressure from a supplier.

sales department asked the district managers their opinions of this trade promotion structure, most agreed it would probably be adequate. However, the manager of the Dayton district thought it might be better to reduce the cooperative advertising allowance and add an additional display allowance for chains. He stated further that placement money should be $1 per counter display because wholesaler salespeople would not be interested in anything less. The manager of the Milwaukee district felt strongly that a larger off-invoice allowance would be more effective. He thought a 25 percent off-invoice coupled with a 5 percent cooperative advertising allowance would be the optimum trade promotion. He felt that placement money was not a useful promotion because, while it did increase the initial sell-in, it sometimes led to overloading the trade. Since SRD accepted merchandise returns, he thought placement money might simply result in customers' ordering large quantities initially but returning a lot if it did not move very quickly.

CONSUMER PROMOTIONS

When ASR introduced Flicker, it did not run any consumer promotions. On one occasion since the introduction, it had run a self-liquidating promotion whereby a customer could purchase two pair of pantyhose for $1.50 if she mailed in a coupon which was printed on the Flicker package. Coupons were also often included in newspaper ads.

SRD had run only one consumer promotion with Lady Sure Touch. It consisted of a coupon on the Lady Sure Touch package which allowed the customer to purchase 10 pieces of elegant stationery for $1.

SRD had run three consumer promotions with Lady Trac II. The first was a coupon placed in Lady Trac II packages for 50 cents off on the purchase of Soft and Dry antiperspirant. The second and most successful was a coupon in Lady Trac II packages for a free pair of pantyhose. This promotion doubled Lady Trac II's market share. The third was a vial of Sea and Ski Sun Cream placed on each Lady Trac II package. The total cost of these promotions, including the premium item, trade discounts, and various other expenses, generally ranged between 15 and 30 percent of sales.

Daisy's task force members were considering two types of consumer promotions for Daisy. First, they wanted to distribute samples to as many women in the 18-to-34 age group as they could afford. These samples would consist of a single Daisy shaver in a blister pack with a 10-cents-off coupon which could be applied to the purchase of a regular Daisy package. Two relatively inexpensive ways were found to distribute these samples. The first was through a company which had arrangements with various movie theaters whereby women who attended one of those theaters during a specified time period received a free sample of a particular product. The theaters often ran special ads stating that the product was being given away, gave passes to the manufacturer's salespeople and their major accounts, and displayed posters promoting the product in their

TABLE 4

	Movie theaters	Superboxes
Memphis	94,000	18,000
Seattle	59,000	11,000
Dayton	67,000	13,000
Milwaukee	102,000	19,000
	322,000	61,000

lobbies. It was felt that up to 8 million women (throughout the United States) could be reached through this program, at a cost (not including the samples themselves) of approximately $78 per thousand samples distributed. It was estimated that each sample would cost about $0.17.

Another method by which Daisy might be sampled was the Superbox program, a program whereby various manufacturers gave samples of their products to a company which then assembled "Superboxes" containing the products and sold them to university book stores. These stores in turn either sold or gave away the Superboxes to their customers. SRD might be able to reach as many as 1.5 million women (throughout the United States) via this program, at a cost of $55 per thousand women, not including the samples themselves.

Both programs were available in all four test cities, and the task force estimated that through them SRD would be able to reach approximately the number of women in each city as shown in Table 4.

The second type of consumer promotion Daisy's team wanted to consider was widescale couponing. The coupons would be placed inside sample packages of Daisy and in print ads in newspapers and magazines. When presented for redemption at a retail store, a coupon would entitle the bearer to 10 cents off the listed retail price of Daisy. The retailer would then send the coupon to the manufacturer for reimbursement plus handling fee, usually about $0.05 for each redeemed coupon.

DISTRIBUTION

One of the task force's most difficult problems was determining distribution objectives for Daisy. The members wanted to make projections for Daisy's initial sell-in before the advertising programs started and for 3 and 6 months after the program had been inaugurated. They had substantial data on the number of accounts, number of stores, and SRD's sales by different types of customers. (See Exhibit 10.) Moreover, the Marketing Research Department had supplied national trends in food and drug stores for the major women's shaving products, and they were fairly certain the same distribution patterns would be applicable to Daisy's four test market cities. They felt that these data should be used only as general indicators, however, because the sample of stores checked was relatively small and because the Research Department did not generate data on distribution of specific Gillette products in mass-merchandise outlets. (See Exhibit 11.)

In assessing what the reactions of different types of customers probably would be, the task force relied heavily on its representative from the sales department, Mr. Steve Tandy. Now SRD's director of sales planning, Tandy had considerable experience in field sales and now served as liaison between sales and marketing. Tandy stated that about half of SRD's blade business went through food stores, where the blades were purchased by women for their husbands. However, food stores had never been good outlets for razors, and only about 18 percent of SRD's razor sales went through food stores. (The men's Trac II had achieved over 75 percent distribution in food stores, but this was considered highly unusual.) While SRD considered Daisy as part of the blade market, food stores would view it more as a razor because of the amount of space it required. If it did not generate substantially more purchases than did most razors, it would be unprofitable for a food store to carry it. Tandy suspected, however, that the favorable experience many food stores recently had with Flicker would actually make these customers more willing to try Daisy.

Tandy felt Daisy would be more readily accepted in drugstores than in food stores. Small drugstores and drug chains accounted for a substantial amount of SRD's razor sales, and these outlets usually reacted favorably to products for women. The only problem might be that drug wholesalers, who were responsible for selling and servicing small drugstores, were often skeptical about new products for women.

Mass merchandisers, Tandy felt, would be Daisy's most avid customers. SRD enjoyed very favorable relations with most of them, and they usually were not averse to trying new products for women, especially when the products offered them good margins. Toiletry merchandisers ran such diverse businesses that Tandy could not readily assess their probable acceptance of Daisy. Moreover, he thought SRD should count on virtually no business for Daisy from food wholesalers and tobacco jobbers.

Tandy also pointed out significant features of each of the test market cities. Memphis, he thought, would be a tough test town. It had five food chains, three of which were not headquartered in Memphis. He described SRD's relationships with two of these chains as "touchy," and he said a third chain was not interested in nonfood items. He also foresaw a couple of problems with drug chains. Again, very few of them were headquartered in Memphis. In one drug chain, the relationship between SRD's headquarters salesperson and the chain headquarters, where the decision about Daisy would be made, was very strong, but the SRD salesperson who handled the Memphis stores would not get credit for selling Daisy, and he was expected to react quite adversely since he would be expected to service the stores that carried the product. In another chain, the district manager for Memphis had considerable influence over product selection, and the salesperson who dealt with him was quite certain he would not be interested in Daisy. SRD's relation with local mass merchandisers was excellent, but those headquartered elsewhere posed problems. Tandy stated that Memphis' major strengths as a test market were (1) it was an "average" American city in income levels, family size, cars per family, television viewing, and so forth; (2) it was fairly isolated geographically so that the people who composed the market were pretty clearly defined; (3) the reach of the local media was fairly well defined, and television stations and newspapers from outlying areas were not major factors in the market; and (4) most of the stores of SRD's major accounts were located within Memphis' DMA.

Tandy stated that Seattle had all the strengths of Memphis as a test market, plus it was located in SRD's smallest district. The district manager, who had been in the area for about 8 years, supervised only four or five men, so that he himself had excellent rapport with SRD's major accounts. Since SRD's district office was located in Seattle, the district manager knew all the relevant people in the Seattle area.

Tandy felt that the Milwaukee area was an excellent test market because it had virtually no outside influence except for Zayre's and the Walgreen drugstore chain. The Zayre influence consisted of five Shopper City stores which Zayre had acquired but which still retained their old name and which had a fair degree of autonomy. Another plus for Milwaukee was that the district manager was considered an exceptionally competent administrator who could easily handle the thousands of details necessary to make the test market work.

Tandy stated that Dayton was a fairly good test market for SRD in that SRD had a career salesperson with about 15 years' experience selling SRD products who could practically guarantee distribution in all his major accounts. However, Dayton posed some problems in that it was not as isolated geographically as were the three other markets. The influence of Cincinnati and Columbus were felt in both television and print media.

REACTION OF THE SRD SALES FORCE

In all, about 15 SRD salespeople would be involved in the test market. They were considered to be highly motivated, professional salespeople, most of whom enjoyed good relations with their customers. While they had had substantial experience with new products, products for women had always posed special problems for them. Both they and their customers knew that SRD had never before made a serious commitment to the women's shaving market.

Test markets also posed special problems for the sales force. In addition to convincing customers to buy the new product, the salespeople had to make extra calls on retail outlets to be sure the product was adequately stocked and properly displayed. In the case of Daisy, they even had to convince customers to put the product in health and beauty aids departments and therefore increase the total space they were devoting to SRD products.

To generate enthusiasm for the Daisy test market, the task force members thought they would hold a 2-day sales meeting at the Nordic Hills Inn in Chicago. At this meeting, extensive promotional material about Daisy which the salespeople would later use with their customers was to be distributed. The total cost of this material would be about $22,000. In addition, Dwyer thought he

TABLE 5

	Temporary, per unit	Permanent, per unit
Floor boutiques (72 Daisy packages)	$7.00	$17.00
Counter carousels (36 Daisy packages)	2.25	4.50
Shelf extenders (12 Daisy packages)	1.10	2.50

would offer an AM-FM radio to all salespeople who met their quotas, but he thought the cost of this sales promotion would not exceed $2,000. He did not want to offer special monetary incentives to the salesperson, but some members of his team thought that would be the only way to get the salespeople to give Daisy the support it needed.

MERCHANDISING VEHICLES

While special merchandising vehicles had been designed for Daisy, the task force had not yet decided whether to order permanent metal displays or temporary cardboard displays for the test markets. As was the custom in the trade, SRD would cover the cost of these displays. The initial cost of permanent displays was substantially greater than that of temporary displays (Table 5). However, Dwyer was certain that all the temporary displays would be thrown away, probably as soon as they became stocked out, and he knew that retailers also often threw away "permanent" displays. He estimated that, under optimum conditions, retailers would retain about 75 percent of the permanent displays after the test market. "Not only do we have to consider the initial cost of the displays," he told his team, "we also have to estimate what we think the retention rate of the permanent displays will be."

Some of these merchandising vehicles were obviously more suitable for certain retail outlets than for others. To determine the number of each type of display that was needed, the task force had to rely on the estimates of the four regional managers involved. Their early estimates are shown in Table 6.

TABLE 6

	Floor boutiques		Counter carousels		Shelf extenders	
	Permanent	Temporary	Permanent	Temporary	Permanent	Temporary
Memphis	150–200	263	250–300	525	60–75	130
Seattle	120	187–300	60	75–200	15	40–50
Dayton	155	250	130	350	30	80
Milwaukee	100–150	225	195	375	50	90
Total	525–625	925–1,038	635–685	1,325–1,450	155–170	340–350

MISCELLANEOUS FINANCIAL CONSIDERATIONS

Gillette's cost accounting department estimated that capital equipment expenditures for Daisy's test market would be about $525,000. This would include the handle mold, packaging tooling, developmental costs, and assembly line setup. If the decision was made not to go national with Daisy, the total capital equipment of $525,000 would have to be written off.

The cost accounting department had also determined that manufacturing costs for the test market would be $0.308 per package. Adding freight costs resulted in an estimated cost of $0.338 per package. The direct costs of the sample packages which contained only one shaver and which were blister-packed on cardboard amounted to $0.17 per package, including freight.

EXHIBIT 1
PICTURE OF DAISY
Daisy: IV

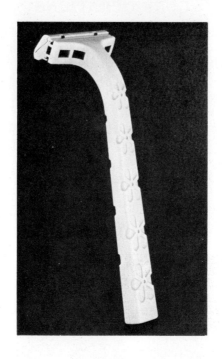

EXHIBIT 2
THE DAISY PACKAGE
Daisy: IV

EXHIBIT 3
THE DISPLAY VEHICLES
Daisy: IV

FLOOR BOUTIQUE

COUNTER CAROUSEL

SHELF EXTENDER

EXHIBIT 4
SAMPLE DAISY ADVERTISEMENT:
MAGAZINE ADVERTISEMENT
Daisy: IV

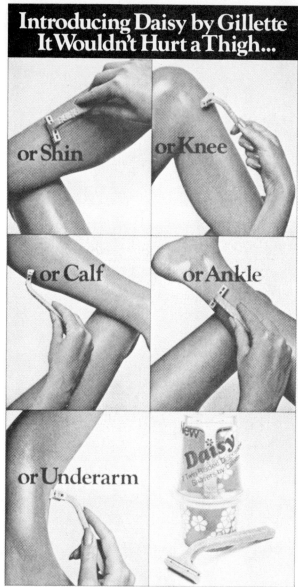

674

EXHIBIT 5
SAMPLE DAISY ADVERTISEMENT:
TELEVISION STORYBOARD
Daisy: IV

The Daisy Shaver by Gillette

"Wouldn't Hurt A Thigh" Commercial

ANNCR (VO): Introducing Daisy by Gillette.

The new woman's shaver that's curved,

so it wouldn't hurt a thigh.

Or ankle.

Or shin.

Or knee.

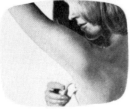

Or underarm.

The Daisy has twin blades, recessed and permanently locked in at a safe angle.

so you won't hurt yourself.

Then after weeks of close, safe shaving it's disposable. Throw it away and pick the other Daisy.

Two for only a $1.19.

The Daisy Shaver. It wouldn't hurt a thigh.

675

EXHIBIT 6
DATA REGARDING THE FOUR TEST MARKET CITIES
Daisy: IV

City	Memphis	Seattle	Dayton	Milwaukee
Time zone	Central	Pacific	Eastern	Central
Rank by households	16	26	32	14

Population and households, 1972

	Memphis	Seattle	Dayton	Milwaukee
Total population	2,435,100	1,723,400	1,521,300	2,641,500
% of United States	1.18	0.84	0.74	1.28
Total households	777,900	600,600	490,900	840,100
% of United States	1.16	0.89	0.73	1.25
TV households	753,680	571,990	480,390	813,974
% of United States	1.16	0.88	0.74	1.25
Effective buying income	$8,248,367,000	$5,942,930,000	$5,210,313,000	$8,908,236,000
Effective buying income per household	$10,603	$9,895	$10,614	$10,608

Television market profile, % household, February–March 1973

	Memphis	Seattle	Dayton	Milwaukee
UHF penetration	68	NA	59	65
Color TV ownership	59	67	68	69
Multiset households	44	37	48	38
CATV penetration	7	11	7	8

Daypart average quarter-hour households reached by total local stations, thousands, February–March 1973

	Memphis	Seattle	Dayton	Milwaukee
Mon.–Fri.:				
9 A.M. –noon	130	108	111	113
Noon –4:30 P.M.	210	129	150	175
4:30 P.M.–7:30 P.M.	390	305	242	340
11 P.M. –11:30 P.M.	260	134	197	280
11:30 P.M.–1 A.M.	95	61	102	100
Sat.–Sun.:				
9 A.M. –midnight	280	202	202	285
7:30 –11 P.M.	458	334	327	425

EXHIBIT 7
ADVERTISING COSTS BY MEDIUM
IN TEST MARKET CITIES
Daisy: IV

Television spot advertising
(1 spot is a 30-second commercial)

Prime time (7–11 P.M. EST or 7–10 P.M. CST)		Daytime and fringe evening	
Memphis	$803/spot	Memphis	$80/spot
Dayton	416/spot	Dayton	80/spot
Milwaukee	597/spot	Milwaukee	87/spot
Seattle	491/spot	Seattle	58/spot

Insertions in newspaper supplements, per insertion

Memphis	$3,600
Dayton	3,850
Milwaukee	3,850
Seattle	3,600

Regional issues of magazines, per insertion

Family Circle		McCalls	
Memphis region	$ 975	Memphis region	$1,520
Dayton region	1,151	Dayton region	1,066
Milwaukee region	2,175	Milwaukee region	2,304
Seattle region	1,750	Seattle region	1,095
Good Housekeeping		**Woman's Day**	
Memphis region	$ 747	Memphis region	$ 540
Dayton region	550	Dayton region	666
Milwaukee region	1,024	Milwaukee region	1,090
Seattle region	576	Seattle region	665

EXHIBIT 8
FLICKER ADVERTISING EXPENDITURES BY MEDIUM
Daisy: IV

| | 1972 | | 1973 | | | | 1974, |
	3d qtr.	4th qtr.	1st qtr.	2d qtr.	3d qtr.	4th qtr.	1st qtr.
Day network TV				$ 42,000	$148,000		$309,000
Night network TV				112,000	321,000	$171,000	
Spot TV			$ 9,000	10,000			
Magazines and supplements			115,000	244,000			
Newspaper	$33,000	$147,000	126,000	150,000			
Network radio							
Total	$33,000	$147,000	$250,000	$558,000	$469,000	$171,000	$309,000
Total 1972	$180,000						
Total 1973				$1,448,000			

EXHIBIT 9
1973 UNIT SALES AND UNIT SHARE OF LADY SURE TOUCH, LADY TRAC II, AND FLICKER IN DAISY'S TEST MARKETS
Daisy: IV

	Lady Sure Touch		Flicker		Total blade sales in units
Memphis	26,098	0.09%	307,950	1.1%	27,995,000
Seattle	22,323	0.11	358,722	1.8	19,929,000
Dayton	21,746	0.12	438,912	2.5	17,556,000
Milwaukee	51,682	0.17	576,992	1.9	30,368,000

	Lady Trac II	Total razor sales in units
Memphis	15,038	375,960
Seattle	16,692	417,300
Dayton	13,195	329,810
Milwaukee	25,147	628,680

678

EXHIBIT 10
SRD BUSINESS IN TEST MARKET CITIES, 1973
Daisy: IV

	Number of head-quarters	Number of retail outlets	1973 sales of Lady Sure Touch	1973 sales of Lady Trac II
Milwaukee				
Drug chains	5	51	$ 8,715	$ 9,570
Food chains	2	92	912	
Discount merchandisers	12	124	10,331	17,769
Toiletry merchandisers	11	1,440	3,623	2,896
Drug wholesalers	8	982	11,190	9,523
Food wholesalers	3	280	913	
Misc. other wholesalers	10	2,680	929	592
Total	51	5,649	$36,613	$40,350
Dayton				
Drug chains	2	64	$ 6,357	$ 6,903
Food chains	3	163	652	
Discount merchandisers	2	13	2,941	2,873
Toiletry merchandisers	2	273	434	2,273
Drug wholesalers	3	300	2,688	4,777
Food wholesalers	3	1,300	1,956	3,562
Misc. other wholesalers	5	675	377	800
Total	20	2,788	$15,405	$21,188
Memphis				
Drug chains	7	25	$ 4,165	$ 5,415
Food chains	5	203	2,095	2,725
Discount merchandisers	1	60	9,235	12,055
Toiletry merchandisers	8	675	1,100	1,430
Drug wholesalers	4	1,170	900	1,170
Food wholesalers	11	960	800	973
Misc. other wholesalers	11	3,000	200	354
Total	47	6,093	$18,495	$24,122
Seattle				
Drug chains	3	37	$ 8,884	$17,517
Food chains	2	109	552	1,201
Discount merchandisers	1	36	464	
Toiletry merchandisers	7	73	3,723	5,205
Drug wholesalers	3	425	1,856	2,852
Food wholesalers	0	0		
Misc. other wholesalers	2	67	221	
Total	18	747	$15,700	$26,775

EXHIBIT 11
DISTRIBUTION OF WOMEN'S SHAVING PRODUCTS IN FOOD AND DRUG STORES*
Daisy: IV

	Gillette Lady Trac II		Schick Super II for Women		Lady Gillette		Gillette Lady Techmatic		Lady Sure Touch		Flicker	
	Drug	Food	Drug	Food	Drug	Food	Drug	Food	Drug	Food	Drug	Food
June '72					37%	6%	21%	6%			10%	3%
Jan. '73					35	2	21	10	8%	8%	29	25
June '73	22%	10%	8%	7%	36	2	23	6	32	15	46	35
Jan. '74	25	13	11	5	33	2	19	4	29	14	54	45

* The numbers indicate the percentage distribution in the drug and food stores which SRD researchers monitored regularly.

DAISY: V
DESIGNING A NATIONAL MARKETING PROGRAM

NANCY J. DAVIS
Research Associate
Harvard Graduate School of Business Administration

STEVEN H. STAR
Associate Professor
Harvard Graduate School of Business Administration

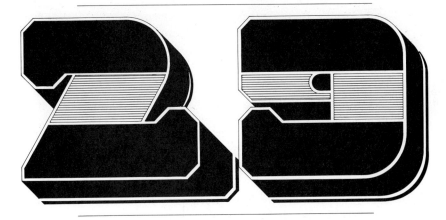

By January 1975, SRD's test market of Daisy had been running for 6 months, and SRD had gathered considerable data about the product's performance in the four test market cities. SRD management had decided to keep the test running through June 1975, but it was generally felt that SRD should proceed with its national roll-out while the test was going on. If SRD did not do so, many executives felt, competitors would copy the product and distribute it nationally immediately.

DAISY'S TEST MARKET

The Daisy task force had established the following general marketing objectives for Daisy:

1   To generate incremental profit for SRD by aggressively marketing Daisy to the potential 65 million women shavers in the United States.

2   To expand the current $75-million female wet shaving market by informing women that Daisy will provide the ultimate in a close, safe shave.

3   To establish SRD as the leader in the women's wet shaving market by drawing more women into the Gillette wet shaving franchise by trading women up to the Daisy shaving system.

4   To convince women of the advantages of using a disposable twin-bladed shaving system exclusively designed to satisfy a woman's shaving needs.

5   To preempt competition from further inroads into the women's disposable wet shaving market, thereby protecting SRD's current position in the twin-bladed shaving field.

6   To generate enthusiastic trade support by introducing a female shaver which will generate a high level of profitability due to its rapid turnover.

In designing the test market, the task force members had decided to pair the cities and to test what they considered the most important variable, i.e., different advertising levels. By putting Memphis and Seattle together and Dayton and Milwaukee together, they had two units, each of which represented 2.02 percent of the total United States population. They had settled on a suggested retail price of $1.10 per package. Trying to test for other items such as different promotion strategies would only complicate the test to the point that the results might be inconclusive, they thought.

The specific objectives which the team had established for Daisy's test market were as follows:

1   To achieve a 1.4 percent share of the entire blade market in the Dayton and Milwaukee DMAs and a 2.0 percent share of the blade market in the Memphis and Seattle DMAs within Daisy's first product year.

2   To test the impact of two different advertising levels upon the share development in each pair of the test markets. Milwaukee and Dayton would receive relatively low expenditures, while Memphis and Seattle would receive relatively high expenditures.

3   To generate the equivalent of $686,268 in full revenue sales (i.e., revenue before trade discounts) by selling 2,079,600 shavers (i.e., 1,039,800 packages) in Daisy's first product year in the test markets.

4   To achieve a 9 to 11 percent trial rate among the potential women shavers in the test market areas.

TABLE 1

	Start of advertising, Sept. 9, 1974	By Jan. 1, 1975	By July 1, 1975
Food	25%	40%	50%
Drug	40	65	70
Mass merchandiser	50	75	80

5 To achieve at least a 15 percent conversion rate among sample recipients.

6 To achieve an initial repurchase rate of 65 percent, followed by subsequent repurchase rates of 80 percent, then 90 percent, ad infinitum.

7 To achieve the levels of distribution shown in Table 1.

8 To obtain permanent placement of the Daisy displays in female-oriented shopping areas of the store, away from the traditional pegboard locations.

9 To determine the impact of Daisy share growth on Lady Trac II share levels as well as determine reaction of "one-time" Daisy purchasers.

The task force had established market share objectives by looking at the position of Lady Sure Touch, Lady Trac II, and Flicker in the various markets, considering Daisy's outstanding performance in shave tests, and estimating what the impact of the different advertising levels would be. They then calculated the sales requirements as shown in Table 2.

The test market officially got underway on July 1 and 2, 1974, when the Daisy task force met with the salespeople from the Memphis, Seattle, Dayton, and Milwaukee markets. These salespeople had already been told that a test market of a new product for women was scheduled for their areas, and many had been consulted about specific accounts as district managers and regional managers worked with the task force in setting distribution objectives. The salespeople began selling Daisy on July 8, and initial orders were shipped on July 15.

To guarantee that a substantial number of women would at least try Daisy, between 350,000 and 400,000 samples were distributed between August 26

TABLE 2

	Dayton and Milwaukee (low-media expenditures)	Memphis and Seattle (high-media expenditures)
Total U.S. blade market for 1974	2.372 billion	2.372 billion
× % U.S. population in test city DMAs	× 2.02%	× 2.02%
= Total blades sold in DMAs in 1 year	= 47.9 million	= 47.9 million
× Anticipated share levels	× 1.4%	× 2.0%
= Total consumer sales	= 670,600	= 958,000
+ Pipeline coverage @ 3 months	+ 191,000	+ 260,000
Total shipments	= 861,600 shavers (430,000 packages)	= 1,218,000 shavers (609,000 packages)

and September 9. About 325,000 of these were distributed via movie theaters and 25,000 through the Superbox program on college campuses. The remainder were sent to beauty editors, various cosmeticians, stewardesses, and other women selected by the salespeople. Each sample package, which consisted of a single shaver blister-packed on cardboard, contained a 10-cents-off coupon to be applied to the purchase of a regular Daisy package.

To further stimulate trial and repurchases, SRD relied heavily on its advertising campaigns. Daisy's television advertising began on September 9, its newspaper advertising on September 29, and its magazine advertising in November issues. The advertisements were targeted toward the 15-to-34-year age group, and they emphasized that Daisy would give a better, safer shave than other products because (1) its curved handle provided maximum visibility and control while the user shaved areas which were hard to see and reach; (2) it had the most advanced shaving head on the market—twin blades, set at precise angles to give a closer, safer shave than single-bladed razors provided; (3) the twin-blade cartridge was permanently locked into place to eliminate any need for blade handling, and that, when the blade was finally used up, the entire shaver was discarded; (4) recessed grips in the shape of daisies were molded into the handle to facilitate steady handling of the shaver; and (5) a transparent safety cap provided protection for both travel and storage. The tone of Daisy's advertising was described as "exciting and of news value, implying this is a significant new product in female shaving." The product was presented in a contemporary, light manner, conveying that it was an impulse item easy to use, inexpensive to buy, and available everywhere. (See Exhibits 1 to 3 for sample advertisements.)

Daisy's introductory advertising used both television and print media. In Memphis and Seattle, SRD's media expenditures for Daisy were equivalent to an annual national level of $5.5 million while in Dayton and Milwaukee the comparable figure was $3.5 million. The actual expenditures in Memphis and Seattle totaled $133,320 for the first year, while those in Dayton and Milwaukee amounted to $84,840. If these numbers were extrapolated nationally in direct proportion to the percentage of the national population contained in the cities, the national expenditures would have been substantially higher than they actually were because media costs per thousand people reached were substantially higher on a local or regional basis than on a national basis.

The specific objectives of the advertising programs are shown in Table 3. (See Exhibit 4 for summaries of the media plans for the test markets.)

The task force had worked very closely with SRD headquarters and field salespeople in establishing distribution objectives. "We looked at each of our accounts individually, determined which ones we could count on from the very beginning, which would probably purchase Daisy once it got established in other outlets and our advertising program got underway, and which would probably never touch Daisy," Tandy said later. The trade terms which the task force decided upon consisted of a 16⅔ percent off-invoice allowance, 4 percent placement money, and an 8 percent cooperative advertising allowance. Daisy's cost structure with these terms is shown in Table 4. The Daisy task force was confi-

TABLE 3

Vehicle	Objective	Dayton and Milwaukee	Memphis and Seattle	Cost per thousand	
				Target (15–34 years old)	Women
Prime network	Maximize reach	38%	49%	$8.25	$2.80
Late fringe network	Obtain frequency against working women and upper-income groups	35%	35%	$5.80	$1.80
Selective magazines	Maximize exposure in beauty/grooming environment	19%	11%	$4.75	$2.00
Sunday supplements	Maximize trial and coupon response	8%	5%	$8.35	$3.25
		100%	100%		
Summary					
Total TV		73%	84%		
Print		27%	16%		
Reach and frequency*					
Introduction		87%/3.9	90%/4.7		
Sustaining		32%/1.4	63%/2.6		

* This meant that, under its introductory advertising plans, SRD would reach 87 percent of the women in Dayton and Milwaukee an average of 3.9 times, while in Memphis and Seattle, it would reach 90 percent of the women an average of 4.7 times.

dent that these terms, plus the selling expertise of SRD's sales force, would enable Daisy to achieve desired distribution objectives, even in health and beauty aids departments.

TEST MARKET RESULTS

When SRD's salespeople initially started selling Daisy, most buyers responded with "Oh no, another lady's razor." However, once the salespeople completed their presentation, the buyers generally were impressed by the Daisy program and SRD's commitment to the product. They commented positively on the

TABLE 4

	Per unit	72-unit floor boutique	36-unit counter carousel	12-unit shelf extender
Suggested retail	$1.10	$79.20	$39.60	$13.20
Regular invoice	0.66	47.52	23.76	7.92
Deal invoice	0.55	39.60	19.80	6.60
Regular wholesale	0.79	57.02	28.51	9.48
Deal wholesale	0.66	47.52	23.76	7.92

package, the shaver itself, the display concepts, and the promotional support. The salespeople used portable Fairchild Projector audio-visual aids to tell the Daisy story, and this, many felt, greatly increased the professionalism of the presentation.

As had been anticipated, customers in some cities responded more favorably and more quickly than those in other cities. In Milwaukee, all the local mass merchandisers, all the drug wholesalers, one of the two major food chains, and over half the toiletry merchandisers had ordered Daisy by the end of July. In Dayton the major mass merchandisers, three of the four drug wholesalers, and all the tobacco jobbers ordered Daisy immediately. However, only one of the two major drug chains had placed an order by the end of July. Moreover, none of the food chains, toiletry merchandisers, or food wholesalers ordered Daisy during July though several had indicated that they were interested in the product and that their orders would soon be forthcoming. In Memphis, all drug chains, all drug wholesalers, half the food wholesalers, and half the tobacco jobbers placed orders during the first month. However, none of the five food chains and only five of the fifteen mass merchandisers ordered Daisy in July. The buyer for the largest mass merchandiser ordered only token quantities, but said that if Daisy moved well initially without advertising, he would purchase large quantities and run a two-packages-for-$1 special. In Seattle, all drug chains and drug wholesalers ordered Daisy immediately, as did two of the three food chains. Seattle mass merchandisers proved to be reluctant to purchase Daisy, as were food wholesalers and tobacco jobbers. In many instances throughout the test market cities, salespeople stated that many orders were expected to come through soon, but were being delayed because chain headquarters or wholesalers had to carefully survey the retail outlets they serviced to know better what quantities they could move.

As the test market progressed, several additional accounts were opened. Milwaukee attained the highest overall distribution and display, while Memphis still proved to be the most difficult market in spite of intensive efforts by SRD's sales force. By the end of August, 10 of SRD's 11 national accounts (two drug chains, eight mass merchandisers, and one drug wholesaler) had ordered generous quantities of Daisy for their stores in the four test cities. Also by this time, a few accounts had begun to reorder Daisy. Daisy's management team felt this was especially encouraging because it indicated that retail movement was good even before the sampling and media advertising programs began.

Over the next few months, SRD salespeople periodically held intensive retail campaigns to secure display space for Daisy and keep the displays stocked. On the whole, they found that Daisy moved well if it was displayed well but that there were frequent delays in getting the product from an account's warehouse into its retail stores. The 36-package counter carousel proved to be the most popular display vehicle, and Dwyer ordered 500 additional units. He was also considering ordering more boutiques because many were being discarded when their stock was depleted, and reorders were draining SRD's supply.

As Dwyer had expected, Daisy was heavily promoted by many retailers. In

TABLE 5

Seattle	172,288	
Memphis	160,634	
Milwaukee	220,685	
Dayton	199,307	
National accounts	8,978	
	761,892	(1,523,784 shavers)

fact, only a few independent food and drug stores charged the full suggested retail price of $1.10. Pricing in food and drug chains and mass-merchandise outlets was usually under $1, often in the 88 to 99 cents range. When retailers advertised special price promotions, the results were often impressive. For example, Raleigh Drug Stores in Memphis sold virtually all their stock the first day of a heavily advertised promotion in which they sold Daisy for 59 cents per package, and Super Discount Stores in Memphis sold 375 packages in the first 3 days of their two-packages-for-$1 promotion.

By January 1, 1975, SRD had shipped Daisy packages as shown in Table 5. Dwyer was quite pleased with these sales, especially since most had occurred during winter months which were traditionally slow periods for women's shaving products.

The percentages of the different types of accounts which had purchased Daisy are shown in Table 6.

Throughout the months of the test, Daisy attained the unit share[1] levels shown in Table 7. Daisy's product management team noted that if Daisy could attain a 4.1 percent share nationally as it did in the Memphis/Seattle markets, it would be SRD's fourth best-selling blade, just behind Trac II 5s, Trac II 9s, and Super Stainless Steel 5s.

Since Flicker was currently the leading shaving product for women, Dwyer and his associates were extremely interested in Daisy's performance in relation to Flicker. Distribution of the two products in the drug and food stores which SRD monitored is shown in Table 8.

[1] The unit share data in Table 7 are based on the *total* blade markets in the DMAs, not on the markets for women's products alone.

TABLE 6

	Memphis	Seattle	Dayton	Milwaukee
Drug chains	66%	100%	100%	100%
Food chains	80	100	100	100
Mass merchandisers	73	100	100	100
Toiletry merchandisers	100	80	100	91
Drug wholesalers	100	100	100	100
Food wholesalers	70	0	50	66
Misc. wholesalers, mainly tobacco jobbers	91	0	100	70

TABLE 7

	Sept.	Oct.	Nov.	Dec.
Memphis/Seattle	0.75%	3.0%	3.8%	4.1%
Dayton/Milwaukee	1.7	3.0	2.3	1.8

In addition to showing that Daisy was achieving high levels of distribution, the test market results indicated that on a unit basis Daisy outsold Flicker by the ratios shown in Table 9. Moreover, when Daisy and Flicker were promoted simultaneously, Daisy invariably outsold Flicker by a substantial margin. For example, a leading discount chain in Milwaukee promoted both products in October. During this period, Daisy's sales per store were 402 packages, while Flicker's were 231 packages. In November and December, when neither product was promoted, Daisy's and Flicker's per store sales for this account were as shown in Table 10. Dwyer's group felt Daisy's sales were especially impressive since Daisy had been on the market only 6 months while Flicker had been on the market 2 years. Dwyer thought that Daisy's sampling program had probably

TABLE 8

			Aug., %	Sept., %	Oct., %	Nov., %	Dec., %
		High advertising					
Drug	*Memphis*						
		Daisy	32	47	55	63	68
		Flicker	49	46	44	47	53
	Seattle						
		Daisy	17	22	43	48	52
		Flicker	88	82	80	75	70
Food	*Memphis*						
		Daisy			42	38	50
		Flicker	21	20	19	19	25
	Seattle						
		Daisy		11	37	37	31
		Flicker	49	53	46	63	67
		Low advertising					
Drug	*Dayton*						
		Daisy	33	53	87	93	93
		Flicker	78	83	80	87	87
	Milwaukee						
		Daisy	21	92	92	92	92
		Flicker	95	98	100	92	92
Food	*Dayton*						
		Daisy		21	21	17	18
		Flicker	49	53	57	50	50
	Milwaukee						
		Daisy	10	41	45	48	45
		Flicker	61	62	64	62	64

	TABLE 9	
	Memphis/Seattle	**Dayton/Milwaukee**
Food	4.2 to 1	1.5 to 1
Drug	3.4 to 1	1.2 to 1

	TABLE 10	
	Daisy	**Flicker**
November	146	76
December	145	65

contributed substantially to the successful sales. The test results indicated that at least one of every three sample recipients later purchased a Daisy shaver.

The chief problems the test market had revealed centered on the merchandising vehicles. Especially, it was extremely difficult to keep them adequately stocked, and when they became stocked out, many retailers threw them away. Moreover, some retailers did not use the top card on the Daisy counter carousel either because it had been lost in original packing or because they thought it made the display too high. Some cosmeticians (i.e., saleswomen, usually in drug stores and mass-merchandise outlets) felt the Daisy floor boutique was not very feminine and they took it down. Particularly during the Christmas season, when retailers needed space for Christmas displays, many Daisy displays were removed, especially in food stores. Several retailers said that neither the boutique nor the carousel was durable, and they doubted the vehicles would last as permanent display systems. Many felt the boutique had too much open space and that it should be redesigned to hold larger quantities. In the first 6 months of the test market, SRD had sold 210 floor boutiques, 274 counter carousels, and 68 shelf extenders.

As a result of these complaints, Daisy's display vehicles were redesigned and two new ones were created. The counter carousel, which originally had consisted of four tiers, each containing nine packages, was converted to a three-tier, 12-packages-per-tier display. This vehicle was considered most appropriate for drug wholesalers, some drug chains, some toiletry merchandisers, and some tobacco jobbers. The floor boutique, which originally consisted of six tiers, each holding 12 packages, was converted to a five-tier display with each tier holding 18 packages. It was thought that products in this vehicle would be sold primarily to food chains, some drug chains, some toiletry merchandisers, and food wholesalers. Daisy's product management team thought that ideally the boutique would be located near the L'eggs pantyhose boutique or in the feminine care section in health and beauty aids departments.

Two new display vehicles, the Omni display and cut-case displays, were designed primarily for discount chains. The Omni was a six-tier display, each tier containing 30 packages. The cut-case display was simply a cardboard carton in which 72 packages were shipped. Directions on the top and sides of the carton indicated how it should be cut open so that it could be used as a display vehicle. Finally, for toiletry merchandisers and tobacco jobbers who called on small accounts, the Adapta display was created. This unit contained 12 Daisy packages, and it could be fastened to pegboard, clamped to a shelf, or hooked onto any other display vehicle SRD would need for the national program. It was essentially a more versatile version of, and a replacement for, the shelf extender used in the test market. The unit cost, including freight, of each display vehicle was as follows:

- ■ Carousel $ 4.50
- ■ Boutique   17.00
- ■ Omni   28.60
- ■ Adapta   2.60
- ■ Cut case   1.40

(See Exhibit 5 for SRD accounts by headquarters and number of retail outlets.)

The test market had also revealed that, while consumer "pick up" of Daisy was strong, no permanent "home" had been established for the brand. Exactly how SRD could establish Daisy in the health and beauty aids sections of retail outlets was still a matter of much discussion. Dwyer noted that Towne-Oller, an organization that measured movement of about 6,100 items from warehouses into retail outlets, had reported that in 1974 United States blade and razor sales in a representative sample of food stores had totaled $29,063,074. If Daisy could capture a 4.1 percent unit share of this market, its dollar sales in food stores would be $1,598,470, and it would rank number 42 on the Towne-Oller list, behind such blade items as Trac II 5s (number 8) and Trac II 9s (number 12). It would also generate more dollars than all individual sizes of body talcs, hand lotions, and all leading depilatories.

Since the conversion rate of Daisy's sample recipients had been exceptionally high during the test markets, Dwyer felt that widespread sampling would be an important part of Daisy's national launch. He was "fairly certain" that product managers in Gillette's Personal Care Division were interested in a joint promotion of Daisy and Earthborn Shampoo, a "natural scent" shampoo which was considered very strong among women in the 18-to-34 age group. Introduced nationally in May 1974, Earthborn had captured a substantial share of the market and was then the fourth best-selling shampoo on the market. It was distributed through 75 percent of the food stores and 80 percent of the drugstores in the United States. Its advertising budget for 1975 was $9.7 million. Under the program currently being discussed, the Personal Care Division would pay SRD 17 cents per shaver, and a 10-cent in-pack coupon to be applied to the purchase of a regular Daisy package would be included. It was thought approximately 6 million shavers would be distributed through this program. Dwyer was also considering distributing 2 to 3 million samples via the theater sampling program, 1 million through the college Superbox program, and 500,000 to 750,000 through the mail. Moreover, he was discussing a tie-in promotion whereby 1 to 2 million Daisy shavers would be distributed in conjunction with L'eggs pantyhose.

FINANCIAL IMPLICATIONS

The task force was sure Daisy would cannibalize sales of Lady Sure Touch, and the test market proved that this did, in fact, occur. It was not a matter of serious concern, however, because SRD was in the process of phasing out Lady Sure Touch. The group was concerned, however, about Daisy's effect on Lady Trac II. The test alleviated these concerns because it indicated that Daisy hardly affected Lady Trac II at all. It appeared that most of Daisy's customers were drawn from competitors or from women who normally shaved with their husbands' used blades. Even if Daisy did cannibalize Lady Trac II's sales somewhat, its estimated profitability was greater than that of Lady Trac II.

The controller had calculated Daisy's cost per sample to be about 17 cents and its cost per package to be 33.8 cents. He thought the full selling price before any promotional offers would be 66 cents per package. An additional $350,000 would be required for capital tooling for the national launch.

CONCLUSION

As Dwyer and his associates reviewed Daisy's performance during the first 6 months of the test market, they were quite pleased with the results. They were anxious to get the national launch underway quickly so that Daisy would be well established in time for the busy summer selling season. In planning the national roll-out, they first had to determine exactly what their sales objective would be. Next, they had to decide what mixture of samples, advertising, and trade terms would most likely guarantee that they meet their objective. Finally, they had to estimate the probable demand for each of the different types of merchandising vehicles, and they had to formulate a plan whereby the sales force would be more successful than they were during the test market in getting retailers to keep the displays well stocked.

EXHIBIT 1
SAMPLE DAISY ADVERTISEMENT:
MAGAZINE ADVERTISEMENT
Daisy: V

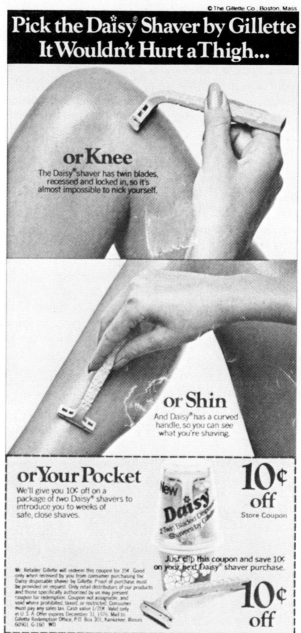

Look for the Daisy Disposable Shaver in the
Health & Beauty Aids Section.

EXHIBIT 2
SAMPLE DAISY ADVERTISEMENT:
TELEVISION STORYBOARD
Daisy: V

The Daisy Shaver by **Gillette**

"Wouldn't Hurt A Thigh" Commercial

ANNCR (VO): Introducing Daisy by Gillette.

The new woman's shaver that's curved,

so it wouldn't hurt a thigh.

Or ankle.

Or shin.

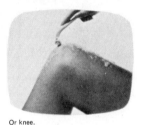

Or knee.

Or underarm.

The Daisy has twin blades, recessed and permanently locked in at a safe angle.

so you won't hurt yourself.

Then after weeks of close, safe shaving it's disposable. Throw it away and pick the other Daisy.

Two for only $1.10.

The Daisy Shaver. It wouldn't hurt a thigh.

693

EXHIBIT 3
SAMPLE DAISY ADVERTISEMENT:
NEWSPAPER ADVERTISEMENT
Daisy: V

EXHIBIT 4

THE DAISY ADVERTISING PROGRAMS
Daisy: V

LOW-EXPENDITURE CITIES: DAYTON/MILWAUKEE

MEDIA PLAN SUMMARY. Equivalent national cost $1.75 million (6 months).

TELEVISION

A. NETWORK PRIME

1   Duration: 9 weeks of network prime time beginning in September 1974.

2   Impact: Averaging 44 G.R.P.'s[1] per week

3   Frequency: Equivalent to three commercials per week

4   Scheduling: Shows like:

ABC Sunday Night Movie	NBC Emergency
ABC Tuesday Night Movie	NBC Friday Night Movie
ABC Marcus Welby	NBC Adam 12
NBC Sunday Night Movie	NBC Police Story
NBC Sanford and Son	

B. LATE FRINGE (AFTER 11:30 P.M. EST, 10:30 CST)

1   Duration: 14 weeks of late fringe television beginning in September 1974

2   Impact: Averaging 33 G.R.P.'s per week

3   Frequency: Equivalent to four commercials per week

4   Scheduling: Shows like:

ABC Wide World of Entertainment
CBS Late Movies
Tonight Show

---

[1] A rating point is the percentage of TV or radio households which a station reaches with a program. The term *gross rating point* refers to the number of rating points a program bearing a commercial has on each station in an area, multiplied by the number of times it is run within a specified period, such as a week.

EXHIBIT 4
Continued

PRINT

A. NEWSPAPERS

- Sunday supplements
- Four-color advertisements
- 10-cent in-store coupon advertisement

B. MAGAZINES

- Four-color advertisements in:
  Woman's Day
  McCall's
  Family Circle
  Ladies' Home Journal

(Two to three insertions per month)

HIGH-EXPENDITURE CITIES: MEMPHIS/SEATTLE

MEDIA PLAN SUMMARY. Equivalent national cost $2.75 million (6 months).

TELEVISION

A. NETWORK PRIME

1   Duration: 12 weeks of network prime time beginning in September 1974
2   Impact: Averaging 66 G.R.P.'s per week
3   Frequency: Equivalent to four commercials per week, total of 48 commercials
4   Scheduling: Shows like:

ABC Sunday Night Movie	NBC Emergency
ABC Tuesday Night Movie	NBC Friday Night Movie
ABC Marcus Welby	NBC Adam 12
NBC Sunday Night Movie	NBC Police Story
NBC Sanford and Son	

EXHIBIT 4

Continued

B. LATE FRINGE (AFTER 11:30 P.M. EST, 10:30 CST)

1   Duration: 22 weeks of late fringe television beginning in September 1974

2   Impact: Averaging 40 G.R.P.'s per week

3   Frequency: Equivalent to five commercials per week, total of 110 commercials

4   Scheduling: Shows like:

ABC Wide World of Entertainment

CBS Late Movies

Tonight Show

PRINT

A. NEWSPAPERS

- Sunday supplements
- Four-color advertisements
- 10-cent in-store coupon advertisement

B. MAGAZINES

- Four-color advertisements in:
  Woman's Day
  McCall's
  Family Circle
  Ladies' Home Journal

(Two to three insertions per month)

EXHIBIT 5

SRD CUSTOMERS AND APPROXIMATE NUMBER OF
RETAIL OUTLETS SERVICED BY EACH

Daisy: V

	No. of headquarter accounts	Approx. no. of retail outlets
Drug chains	760	8,700
Food chains	230	17,100
Discount chains	510	8,200
Toiletry merchandisers	370	100,700
Drug wholesalers	430	64,300
Food wholesalers	470	99,100
Misc. other wholesalers	850	177,900
Total	3,620	476,000

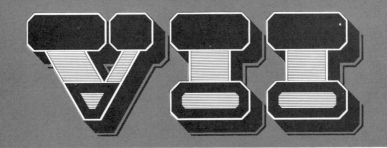

MARKETING PROGRAMS

A total marketing program is an effort on the part of the marketer to satisfy the desires or interests of consumers in the purchase of products or services. Such a marketing program is a combination or "mix" of all the various tools at the marketer's disposal—personal selling, advertising, distribution, pricing, and attendant services—to meet the desires or interests of consumers. By formulating an explicit marketing program, the marketer determines whether it has a reasonable opportunity to obtain an adequate share of market and, over the life of the product or service, at least satisfactory profits.

To communicate in more detail what is meant by a total marketing program, the first section of this introductory text describes consumers' interests. The succeeding section takes up the marketing tools which may satisfy these interests. The third section discusses the division of responsibility among marketing institutions for implementing a marketing strategy. How these consumer interests, marketing tools, and institutions are integrated in the formulation of a strategy is the subject of the fourth section. Finally, the fifth section concludes by examining both the implications of the interrelated nature of the various elements in the resulting marketing systems and the dynamic environment in which these systems operate.

CONSUMERS' INTERESTS

Consumers' interests may be described in many different ways; one way is to divide such interests into five categories, as follows:

1   *Consumers' interest in various features of the product or service itself, such as its performance, its appearance, the variety of styles or sizes in which it is available, and its prestige or "snob appeal"*

2   *Consumers' interest in information about the performance, appearance, variety, accessibility, repair service, and price of the product*

3   *Consumers' interest in physical accessibility (convenience) when shopping for and purchasing a product*

4   *Consumers' interest in attendant services associated with the sales of a product such as installation, delivery, credit, and repair service*

5   *Consumers' interest in the price which must be paid for a product.*

These consumer interests have all been previously described. Earlier text has described how the pattern of interests which must be satisfied varies in particular situations. In the purchase of staple food items, for example, most consumers are likely to be more concerned with accessibility and low price and less interested in attendant services. On the other hand, in the purchase of washing machines, most consumers are likely to be more concerned with product performance and repair service and less interested in accessibility and in variety and appearance of the product. Such differences in consumers' interest patterns suggest that different marketing strategies are appropriate for these two types of products.

Even within a given product category, however, consumers may vary in their patterns of interests. Consumer interests are hardly homogeneous. As an example, consider the market for desserts. Some consumers, who view themselves as gourmet cooks, may be quite interested in the taste, texture, and appearance of a dessert. In addition, they may want a wide variety of dessert alternatives, and they may actively seek information about both new desserts and new recipes for established products. Such consumers may be willing to pay a relatively high price to satisfy their interests. Conversely, there are other consumers who are less concerned with meal preparation and serving, who may be less interested in performance, appearance, variety, and information about desserts. These consumers may be less willing to pay a premium price for a dessert product unless it provides unusual ease of preparation.

The existence of heterogeneous patterns of consumers' interests suggests that different marketing programs are appropriate to attract different groups of consumers. In the preceding examples, a fancy dessert product which required more-than-average preparation time and which allowed the consumer considerable freedom to vary the appearance of the dessert might be appropriate for the first group of consumers. Advertising copy for such a product could be relatively detailed, and the product could command a premium price. For the second group of consumers, the marketer would probably offer a very easy-to-prepare product, employ a limited advertising budget with fairly short copy, and set a relatively low price.

There can also be important qualitative differences among offerings in the manner in which they endeavor to fulfill particular consumer interests. Without varying the proportion of the consumer's dollar spent on the satisfaction of particular interests, two offerings can appeal to entirely different need profiles of consumers. For example, one marketer of floor wax may stress durability in its marketing offering, whereas another floor wax marketer who allocates the same proportion of the consumer's dollar to the intrinsic product may stress the non-yellowing characteristics of its wax. Beer provides another example of this phenomenon. Among brands of beer the advertising to sales ratio may not vary, but one brand may communicate a low-calorie message to consumers whereas another communicates entirely different images to consumers by emphasizing robust social occasions in its advertising. Obviously such qualitative differences among products are as important as differences in the proportion of the consumer's dollar used for the satisfaction of particular informational interests.

INTEGRATION OF CONSUMER INTERESTS

Although analytically it is useful to categorize the various consumer interests which may have to be satisfied to make a particular marketing offering profitable, it is a mistake to conclude that the consumer necessarily recognizes the separate interests which the brand he or she prefers satisfies. To the formulator of a marketing program, for example, the distinction between the product offered to the consumer and the information conveyed may be perfectly clear. The consumer, however, may see these two aspects of the offering only as a

*totality. For example, it may be difficult for a buyer of men's clothing to distin-
guish between what the product does for his appearance and what the advertising does for his self-confidence.*

*The tendency of consumers to view offerings as totalities emphasizes the
importance of formulating complete marketing programs to satisfy the array of
interests of particular consumer segments. Too frequently, marketing offerings
have failed, even though they admirably fulfilled most consumer interests. By
slighting one particular consumer interest, the marketing manager may keep a
particular consumer segment from viewing the offering as an acceptable totality.*

SELECTION OF MARKETING TOOLS

*Diagnosing the consumer interests which a particular offering should satisfy is
only part of the task of formulating a marketing program. Next come the
tasks of selecting the marketing tools to fulfill those interests and possibly the
enlistment of other marketing institutions to bring those tools to bear upon the program. The marketing tools employed to fulfill consumer interests are the traditional elements of the "marketing mix," including such decision variables as
packaging, brand, advertising, personal selling, pricing, and physical distribution.
Although in practice the selection of marketing tools and the allocation of tasks
among institutions are interrelated, for analytical purposes they will be discussed
separately.*

*Typically marketers have a variety of tools which, at least in theory, they
can use to fulfill any particular consumer interest. For example, publicity stimulated by public relations efforts, advertising, personal selling, packaging, display,
distribution through prestigious channels, and the stimulation of interest in an
offering among those who have a strong influence on consumers (such as
architects in the construction of homes) are all means of communicating information to consumers. In practice, of course, the marketer may be confined to a
much narrower array of available tools. The nature of the product and the
monopolization of certain tools (such as prestigious channels) by competition
may limit the tools available.*

*Nevertheless, in particular situations marketers may not need or perhaps
cannot afford to use all the tools available to them to fulfill any one consumer
interest. They do, however, frequently use several of the available tools. For example, packaged-goods manufacturers frequently use both the package itself and
advertising to convey information to consumers. The use of more than one tool
to fill a single consumer interest demands, of course, that the marketer indicate
how the task of fulfilling this interest is to be partitioned and then allocated
among the various tools which might be used.*

*Sometimes marketers find that, in addition to using several tools to fulfill
one consumer interest, one tool has a role in filling several consumer interests.
Packaging, for example, may not only fulfill informational interests but may also
represent an essential part of the product itself. Consider, for example, the packaging of cookies or salt. In the first instance, the packaging frequently conveys*

large amounts of information about the reputation of the manufacturer, the type of cookies inside, and the uses to which they may be put. In addition, the package is essential to maintaining the freshness of the product, a key attribute of cookies. In the case of salt, the container governs how the product is dispensed, which is of much concern to consumers when using salt. Thus in selecting a package for these products, marketers must consider how such packages will fulfill product interests as well as informational interests.

The selection of marketing tools is frequently a compromise. Not only may the most-wanted tools be unavailable to the marketer, but the choice of tools to fulfill one consumer interest may severely constrain use of these tools in fulfilling other consumer interests.

THE DIVISION OF MARKETING RESPONSIBILITY

A complete marketing program specifies more than how the various marketing tools will be used and combined to meet the interests of particular groups of consumers. A complete program also states which of the various institutions in the marketing system—the manufacturer, the trade association, wholesalers, manufacturers' representatives, and retailers of all sizes and categories—will satisfy particular consumer interests, and what portion of the price paid by the consumer will accrue to each institution as compensation. As discussed earlier, the marketing manager in a manufacturing company must decide what activities his or her own firm will perform and what activities it will delegate to wholesalers and to retailers, i.e., to "the trade." The marketer must also determine the margins these various institutions are to receive for the activities they perform.

Some consumers' interests may be satisfied directly by the manufacturer; others, indirectly by the manufacturer working through wholesalers and retailers. Some interests may be met both directly and indirectly. For example, informational interests may be satisfied both directly by the manufacturer (e.g., national advertising) and indirectly through retailers (e.g., cooperative advertising). Through vertical integration (e.g., a retailer with wholly owned manufacturing facilities or a manufacturer with a door-to-door consumer sales force) a firm may provide all the satisfactions which consumers receive from the marketing system for a particular purchase.

The total price paid by consumers to satisfy their interests is divided among the institutions which satisfy those interests. In a competitive marketing system, revenue from consumers will be distributed among institutions in proportion to the perceived value of the various activities these institutions perform. For example, if a manufacturer fills most of the consumers' informational interests through national advertising, it will tend to price its product so that it receives a larger share of total revenue than would be the case if it decided that retailers, through local advertising at their own expense, should provide consumers with most of the information about this product.

FORMULATING MARKETING STRATEGIES

The phrase marketing mix *is often applied to the specific selection of tools a marketer employs to fulfill consumer interests in the sale of its offering, and to the division of responsibility among various marketing institutions for the use of those tools.*

A study of the marketing mixes that have been successfully implemented in the contemporary economy reveals a tremendous variation in patterns. To illustrate, proprietary remedy manufacturers often have no sales force at all. Advertising is used to sell the product to consumers, and advertising "pulls" the product through the channels of distribution. At the retail level little or no effort is made to secure selling support. In contrast, manufacturers of other types of products, e.g., heavy machinery, often rely primarily on the "push" of personal selling by either a direct sales force or the sales force of distributors, and put relatively little of the information burden upon advertising.

The part played in marketing programs by the distributive trade varies markedly. Sometimes the trade plays a considerable part in the sales program, and the close support and cooperation of the trade is sought, as has generally been true with heavy appliances. In other instances the part played by the trade is not highly important, and little effort is devoted to securing trade support, as is true among the proprietary medicine companies cited above. Likewise, the employment of promotional devices and of point-of-purchase effort in marketing programs varies widely.

In the matter of pricing policy, wide variation is likely to be found. In some instances competition is carried out largely on the basis of price, and margins are narrow. In other instances prices are established which allow wide margins, and competition is carried out on a nonprice basis through product quality or service or advertising. In some instances resale prices are maintained; in others they are not.

In short, the elements of marketing programs designed to meet consumer interests can be combined in many ways. Or, stated another way, the marketing mixes for different types of products vary widely, and even for the same class of product, competing companies may employ different mixes. The only indisputable generalization is that the various elements in a marketing program have to be combined in a logically integrated manner to conform to market forces bearing on the individual product, and to be consistent with the needs and interests of the program's target market segment.

INTERRELATED AND DYNAMIC NATURE OF THE MARKETING ENVIRONMENT

Although consumer interests, the offerings of individual manufacturers, marketing tools, and the division of responsibility among marketing institutions for implementing a marketing program have previously been discussed separately, they are, of course, influenced enormously by the marketing environment.

Changes in any one of these components—consumer interests, marketing tools, institutional responsibility, or environment—may have an effect on all the other components. Moreover, the competitive nature of most advanced economies necessitates constant review and frequent modification in these components, as manufacturers, wholesalers, and retailers seek to improve their offerings to consumers, improve their competitive positions, and obtain greater sales and profits.

In addition to these internally stimulated changes, there are also other forces which keep the marketing environment in a constant state of flux. The social, economic, and technological environment is undergoing continuous modification. Consumers become better educated and more affluent, the margins of labor-intensive wholesalers and retailers are eroded by increasing labor costs, and technology provides marketers with the ability to create new products. Inevitably, such environmental changes affect various components of the marketing system and require changes in their interrelationships.

There is still another dynamic dimension to the environment in which marketing operates. Changes in the legal and political climate generate new opportunities, such as in the construction of low-cost housing, and impose new constraints on the marketing system, such as more limited control by manufacturers over their channels of distribution. Inevitably, these changes force adoption and modification in marketing systems. The result, of course, is that what was a logically integrated marketing program which fulfilled consumer needs effectively and profitably in the past must be constantly scrutinized and frequently modified if it is not to become obsolete in the future.

SUMMARY

A total marketing program uses each of the principal elements in the marketing mix—the product itself, packaging, pricing, advertising, personal selling, distribution, and attendant services—to meet consumer needs. The consumer interests which such a program should attempt to satisfy may relate to product characteristics, information about pricing and product performance, the availability of the product in the marketplace, and details of attendant services offered. It is important that no significant consumer interest be overlooked. The fact that different consumer segments may vary in their needs may require the marketer to develop separate programs for different segments.

One of the tasks facing the marketing manager is to identify the role of the different institutions in the marketing system in satisfying specific consumer interests. Some interests may be satisfied by the manufacturer alone, others by intermediaries alone, and still others by the combined actions of both parties. To ensure the necessary cooperation of such intermediaries, the marketing program must also be designed with the needs of marketing intermediaries in mind.

THE H. J. HEINZ COMPANY: I

RONALD KURTZ
Formerly, Research Assistant
Harvard Graduate School of Business Administration

MARTIN V. MARSHALL
Professor
Harvard Graduate School of Business Administration

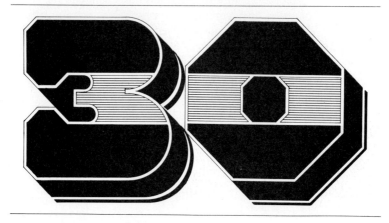

In May 1964 Mr. Thomas Smith[1] was given responsibility as product manager for Heinz Ketchup. Mr. Smith had just joined Heinz from another consumer–packaged-goods company where he had served as a product manager. Mr. Smith's initial assignment was to identify and seek to correct the factors that had contributed to the decline in Heinz Ketchup's market share since 1962. As a first step, he reviewed the Heinz Ketchup situation as of May 1964.

THE HEINZ COMPANY

Henry J. Heinz established the company bearing his name in Pittsburgh in 1869 as a marketer of horseradish. In 1880 the company began to produce and sell

---

[1] Disguised name.

tomato ketchup; it subsequently extended its product line to over 300 food items, including baby foods, Worcestershire sauce, mustard, condensed and ready-to-serve soups, beans, pickles, vinegar, relish, tomato juice, spaghetti, and macaroni. In 1963 Heinz purchased the Star-Kist Company, a marketer of tuna and other fish products, and in 1964 it was planning to purchase the Ore-Ida Foods Company, a marketer of prepared potato products.

Heinz' sales and profits for the previous 5 fiscal years are given in Exhibit 1. Approximately half the company's sales income and about 85 percent of its profits came from operations in 150 foreign countries.

HEINZ' MARKETING ORGANIZATION AND OPERATION

Upon joining Heinz in May 1964, Mr. Smith found himself in what was essentially a totally new management organization. As background, in late 1963 a new executive vice president for Heinz United States had taken office and given special attention to reorganizing and restaffing the company's marketing and sales department. A partial organization chart is given in Exhibit 2.

A new vice president of marketing, who had come from Procter & Gamble in January 1964, immediately sought to correct the weaknesses he saw in Heinz' product management system. Although Heinz had established a product management system in 1955, it had committed what were later considered to be several "classic and common" mistakes in implementation. The first product managers were selected from among the company's best salesmen. They were given responsibility for both grocery and institutional sales of their products, but the product management function had a rather narrow scope; their primary operating emphasis was on detail work concerned with the implementation of promotions and the design of promotion materials.

The new vice president of marketing sought to institute a product management system wherein the product managers were given real responsibility for the first time for the sales and profits of their brands. He established two groups of product managers, with one group reporting to a general manager of grocery marketing and the other to a general manager of institutional food marketing. In addition, he created a marketing services department to provide proper staff support to the product groups. A number of experienced marketing men, including Mr. Smith, were attracted from outside the company to fill various new positions.

Once the product management groups were staffed, emphasis was, for the first time, placed upon the preparation of documented annual marketing plans for each product for the review of senior management. In the proposed marketing planning process, the product managers were to recommend sales and profit goals for their products. In addition, they were to specify anticipated action and expenditures in the areas of advertising, sales promotion, market research, and product innovations. Support for the product manager's recommendations was to be provided by a review of competitive conditions within the particular product category.

Once senior management concurred with the marketing plans, the product managers were to be responsible for executing the plans. As a continuing review of the implementation of the marketing plans, product managers were to submit separate appropriation requests for all major expenditures. These documents were expected to contain support for the recommended action and the sales and profit goals as well as periodic evaluations of achievement. Usually the planning process was to begin in September, preceding the company's fiscal year, May 1 through April 30.

At the same time as changes were being made in the marketing department, changes were undertaken in the company's sales department. It was reorganized into two separate sales forces, one for grocery sales and the other for institutional food sales. Seven new sales managers were recruited from outside the company. Because the sales force contained relatively few college graduates, management planned to upgrade the quality of the sales force over the longer term by active recruitment of college graduates. The company also planned to substantially reduce the size of the sales force from its existing level of about 1,100 salespeople.

In early 1964 the Heinz grocery sales force sold all Heinz items to chains and major wholesalers with about 50,000 retail outlets (accounting for 85 to 90 percent of all United States food sales) and to local wholesalers serving the remaining 150,000 food stores. Heinz had organized its grocery sales force by six zones containing a total of 30 districts. Reporting to each district manager were account representatives, who called on the local outlets of the major chains, and sales supervisors, who were responsible for the salespeople calling on the more important independent stores. No direct deliveries to retail stores were made. Shipments to major chains were processed through chain warehouses. Shipments to independents were processed through local wholesalers.

THE PRODUCT

In undertaking his new responsibilities, Mr. Smith found that ketchup[1] contained tomatoes, sugar, distilled vinegar, salt, onions, and various spices, depending on the brand. Tomatoes served as a "carrier" of the other ingredients, and other carriers could be substituted without significantly changing the flavor of ketchup.

The production of ketchup was not a particularly complex process. Any company already engaged in vegetable processing could enter the ketchup business by doing little more than adding a bottling line. However, to build a modern, efficient ketchup plant would require an investment as large as $10 million.

For Heinz, the production of ketchup began in January when the tomato plants were cultivated in Georgia. By March or April the plants were ready to be

---

[1] Ketchup, catsup, and catchup are differences in spelling arising from the traditions of various brands.

TABLE 1

	Cost per case
Tomatoes	$0.50
Bottles and caps	1.00
Labor and spices	1.25
Total	$2.75

transplanted in various locations in the East, where Heinz had several facilities for manufacturing ketchup. In July harvesting of the tomatoes was begun. The first frost, usually in October, ended the harvest period. This process differed somewhat in California where the plants could be cultivated and there was no need for transplanting. In contrast to an earlier time when Heinz grew its own tomatoes, the company in the 1960s primarily relied on contracting for the purchase of a given quantity of tomatoes according to its estimated needs.

Heinz had seven facilities for producing ketchup: one in New Jersey, one in Pennsylvania, two in Ohio, one in Iowa, and two in California. Tomatoes delivered to these plants in "lugs" or baskets were first carefully washed. The tomatoes were then inspected to assure they met contract requirements for the exact degree of ripeness and red color. Bruises or imperfections were trimmed out, and the tomatoes were washed again. After cutting the tomatoes into several pieces, they were cooked to a pulp. Various spices and ingredients were added prior to a second period of cooking. The ketchup was then bottled and packed in shipping cartons.

The costs to produce a case of 24 fourteen-ounce bottles of ketchup were considered to be fairly standard throughout the industry. With a ton of tomatoes yielding 40 cases of ketchup, the costs were only slightly affected by usual fluctuations in the price of tomatoes. In 1964 the variable costs (all expenses other than general overhead) were as shown in Table 1.

THE KETCHUP MARKET

Mr. Smith had found that since 1958 the total ketchup market had grown from 4 to 7 percent annually, somewhat greater than the growth in population. In 1964 the market was expected to total 24.5 million equivalent cases (one case equaled 24 bottles of 14-ounce size). This would be a 6 percent increase over 1963 sales. Annual case sales are shown in Exhibit 3. Heinz was one of three brands accounting for around 70 percent of the total ketchup market. Although still the number-one brand, Heinz had been losing market share to the Hunt and Del Monte brands since late 1962. These losses had become particularly serious in the previous 18 months as competition had greatly expanded its marketing efforts. This was in contrast to the period from 1958 to 1961 when Heinz had achieved at least moderate gains in its share each year. Market share trends are presented in Exhibits 4 and 5.

As a result of examining consumer data, Mr. Smith concluded that, although there were some variations among brands, differences in consumer income did not seem to appreciably affect ketchup usage. The major prospect was the housewife with a large family. Heavy users of ketchup would consume a 20-ounce bottle in as few as 3 days. Flavor and thickness, to a certain degree, were the major product characteristics of importance to the consumer (odor and color were much less important). Differences in preference for sweetness or spiciness were not evident when examining consumer data by the usual demographic classifications. There were no apparent differences in ketchup usage on a regional or seasonal basis.

Mr. Smith noted that because ketchup was considered an important staple by the trade, it was frequently featured as a "traffic builder." Market share data indicated consumer sensitivity to price differences between Hunt and Del Monte and between those two brands and Heinz. Although ketchup was believed to be a planned purchase by most shoppers, special displays usually generated significant increases in volume (from multiple-unit purchases) even in the absence of price reductions.

COMPETITION

The Hunt-Wesson Division of Hunt Foods and Industries Inc. produced canned fruits and vegetables, cooking oils, matches, and tomato sauce, paste, and ketchup. Hunt was the result of a merger in 1943 of the Hunt Brothers Company and the Val Vita Company, two California food processors with combined sales of around $10 million. Hunt Industries Inc. (a diversified producer of foods, glass containers, and paint) had total sales of around $400 million. The Hunt-Wesson Division, which resulted from the acquisition (1961) and eventual integration (1964) of the Wesson Company, contributed 68 percent of total revenue. Almost half the division's sales were in canned fruits and vegetables and the various tomato products.

Hunt marketed three brands of ketchup: Hunt's, Pride of the Farm, and Snider's (a spicy, hot ketchup). Snider's had been purchased from the General Foods Corporation in 1953. Until the early 1960's, Hunt had placed most of its promotional effort behind Snider's, then its largest selling brand. At that time, emphasis was switched to the Hunt brand, and an aggressive marketing effort was initiated. The division of Hunt's sales by brand is shown in Exhibit 6.

The Hunt-Wesson Division produced the number-one brands of tomato sauce and tomato paste, and Heinz had learned that Hunt also wanted to become the market leader in ketchup. After making substantial gains in market share, in late 1963 Hunt apparently concluded it was rapidly approaching a resistance point at which it would be difficult to attract additional switchers from Heinz. Recognizing that Heinz had a strong flavor preference among consumers, Hunt apparently developed a strategy to disrupt traditional flavor standards and to confuse the consumer in the belief that this strategy would facilitate share gains after the ketchup market reconsolidated. This was believed to be the essential thinking behind Hunt's decision to begin test-marketing two flavored ketchups (hickory and pizza) in February 1964.

Five brands with limited distribution accounted for most of the remaining business. Brooks (limited to the Midwest) and Ritter (confined to the East) at one time represented as much as 6 percent of the national market. The two brands, owned by one company, had shares of 15 to 20 percent in their home areas. Libby's (primarily in Chicago) and Stokely (mostly in the South) were major brands in other segments of the food business, but together they had little more than 2 percent of the national ketchup market. Finally, Kuner's, which was distributed only around Denver where it was once the leading brand, held around 1 percent of the national market. In previous years, several major food companies (Campbell, Welch, and Dole) had been unsuccessful in their attempts to enter the ketchup market. (See Exhibit 7 for market share by region of the various companies.)

Although Heinz had not done extensive research, Mr. Smith concluded there was evidence that consumers evaluated different brands of regular ketchup on the basis of flavor (in terms of spiciness or "in general") and thickness. Color and odor were of secondary importance. From its laboratory tests, it was known that the Heinz product was much thicker than Del Monte and somewhat thicker than Hunt. From blind tests (brand concealed) among Pittsburgh women's clubs and organizations, it was concluded that Heinz' flavor was significantly preferred over Hunt but only slightly preferred over Del Monte. Otherwise, there were no major product or flavor variations among the various brands of ketchup. Heinz and several other brands did offer a "hot" ketchup which was considerably spicier than regular ketchup. However, these hot ketchups represented only a small portion of the total market.

Packaging also was fairly standard throughout the industry. All brands used heavy glass bottles with a tapered neck and broadened body and base. The tall, long-necked bottle had first been used because of ketchup's tendency to oxidize (creating a black ring and thickening across the surface) when exposed to air. The small neck reduced the surface of ketchup that could turn or discolor while on the shelf. Despite the advent of the airproof cap that eliminated this problem, manufacturers continued to use the traditional bottle design.

Regular ketchup was available in 14- and 20-ounce sizes, while hot ketchup was generally offered only in a 12-ounce size. There had been no successful packaging innovations since the introduction of the 20-ounce size in 1956. Several companies including Heinz had unsuccessfully attempted to market ketchup in widemouthed jars that would facilitate spooning out the product.

PRICING

The Heinz wholesale and retail prices had traditionally been at a slight premium over competition. During the previous 6 years, however, Heinz had maintained its wholesale prices while competition had been steadily reducing their prices and using monthly price changes as a promotion tool. Competitive price cuts, facilitated by bumper crops that greatly reduced tomato prices, were particularly severe in 1962 and 1963.

By early 1964, Heinz' wholesale prices were $1.50 or more higher per case of 24 bottles (14-ounce size) than the competition's (see Exhibits 8 to 11). At the retail level, competition was about 6 cents under the Heinz price (see Exhibit 12). In addition, "competition had broken the decile"; i.e., it was selling at less than 20 cents per 14-ounce bottle. Mr. Smith considered this an important psychological factor in consumer purchasing behavior.

Just before Mr. Smith had become product manager, Heinz' management had reviewed the historical share performance of Heinz Ketchup as related to its premium price (see Exhibit 13). From this study management concluded that the Heinz share was being unfavorably affected by the extent to which its price premium had increased. To correct this situation, in March 1964 management initiated wholesale-price reductions of about 40 cents a case on the 14-ounce size. As competition raised its prices by 15 cents a case at about the same time, a reduction of 55 cents a case in the Heinz cost premium was achieved. On the 20-ounce size, for which a 50-cent-a-case price reduction had been made in June 1963, the price was also lowered about 40 cents a case. This cut the Heinz premium on this size to less than $1 per case. In total, these price reductions lowered the Heinz gross margin by "about 20% on a per case base."

Mr. Smith could not yet determine the effect of these price reductions on market share. He expected that it would take 2 or 3 months before the trade would begin to reflect the price cuts in lower retail prices. He hoped that the retail price of the 14-ounce size would be reduced 2 cents a bottle.

PROMOTIONS

Heinz had traditionally run two trade promotions a year, one in the spring and one in the fall. These promotions offered the trade a special 25-cent-a-case price reduction (on all three sizes) in about a 12-week period. The deduction was made from the invoice as the merchandise was shipped. Promotions were run nationally, and special deals in specific areas were uncommon.

In return for the case allowance, the trade was encouraged to cut its retail price, advertise Heinz, and/or give a special display to Heinz. To facilitate this, Heinz usually furnished the trade with advertising and display materials. In practice, it was considered fortunate if the trade featured Heinz once in the 12-week period. Usually the promotions appeared to do little more than build trade inventories. Heinz' shipments typically increased at the first of the promotion period, substantially contracted during the middle, and then "boomed" at the end of the promotion period.

These two traditional promotion periods were essentially the extent of Heinz' past promotional efforts. Recently Heinz had tried 5- and 7-cent coupons placed in newspapers and magazines. According to Mr. Smith, coupons were not characteristic of the product category, as ketchup prices did not leave sufficient room for a coupon whose absolute size would seem "meaningful to the consumer and profitable to the company."

The promotional efforts of Hunt and Del Monte did not appear to differ substantially from those of Heinz. These competitors did, however, fluctuate their prices from month to month as an added promotional tool. In addition, they would generally guarantee trade inventories (reimburse in the amount of the price reduction for stock already held by the trade), whereas Heinz did not. As a result of their aggressive marketing efforts, Hunt and Del Monte had begun to be featured by the trade substantially more (and Heinz somewhat less). Trends in the retail advertising for each brand are given in Exhibit 14. Heinz' share of trade inventories, which closely approximated share of shelf space, had also been falling (Exhibit 15).

Competitive promotional allowances were usually around 50 cents a case on the 14-ounce size. In December, Del Monte had traditionally used a consumer offer of a 25- to 50-cent refund or self-liquidating premium. The three major brands had occasionally used newspaper or magazine coupons worth 5 to 7 cents off regular prices (a redemption of about 5 percent was average). Coupons mailed directly to the consumer had not been used prior to the test introduction of Hunt's flavors in March 1964. Price-off label packs (reduction shown on label) were not used because of the problems in production and because the 2-cent saving that could be offered would not mean much to the consumer. Contests and sweepstakes were sometimes used to provide a theme for store displays and national advertising and to create general activity for the brand. A cost of $10,000 was average for point-of-purchase material used to support major promotions.

ADVERTISING

Until January 1964 Clyde Maxon had been the exclusive Heinz advertising agency for 30 years. In early 1964 Doyle Dane Bernbach was given responsibility for Heinz' soup advertising. At about the same time, Clyde Maxon initiated basic changes in the copy for ketchup advertising.

For many years, according to Mr. Smith, Heinz' advertising had utilized "traditional approaches of mood and appetite appeal." In early 1964 copy was switched to the theme that the best-tasting ketchup was thick and rich and Heinz was the thickest and richest of all ketchups. This emphasis on flavor through thickness and richness was based on the belief that these attributes were important to the consumer. There were some doubts, however, that the theme had been executed as well as it could have been. The first commercial in this series, "The Youngsters," is reproduced in Exhibit 16.

Mr. Smith described the ketchup advertising as "passive." Although he felt there was nothing really wrong with it, he did not believe it was very effective in "gaining the attention of consumers." A big part of the problem, in his opinion, was a lack of originality. He wanted "something fresh and original that would persuade consumers that Heinz was the only superior ketchup brand—not just a good product or a fun product, but the only superior brand."

Heinz had concentrated its advertising in women's magazines and network television, where it hoped to reach housewives with large families, considered to be the heavy users of ketchup. Heinz had not allocated its media weight in proportion to its own sales volume; rather, weight fell in proportion to the geographic distribution of population.

In reviewing Heinz' advertising efforts Mr. Smith found that in 1961 and 1962 the Heinz advertising expenditures of slightly less than $2 million accounted for 60 percent of total ketchup advertising. In 1963 when Heinz cut its expenditures and Hunt greatly increased its budget, Heinz' share of ketchup advertising was cut in half (Exhibit 17 contains annual advertising expenditures). In 1964, Hunt was expected to spend $6 million, based on its current rate (Exhibit 18 presents recent bimonthly advertising expenditures).

Whereas the media used by Hunt and Del Monte had once resembled the Heinz pattern, Hunt had begun to show a change in 1964. Its advertising at that time was being shifted to large-audience magazines (every issue of *Life, McCall's,* and *Redbook*) and evening network television. Del Monte's pattern indicated little change in its media usage or budget, although it had substantially increased its advertising expenditures in 1963.

EXHIBIT 1
HEINZ' SALES AND NET INCOME, 1960–1964
The H. J. Heinz Company: I

Fiscal year ending	Net sales	Net income
Apr. 27, 1960	$340,223,700	$12,287,815
May 3, 1961	365,989,576	13,614,681
May 2, 1962	375,810,168	14,165,806
May 1, 1963	464,215,226	12,364,429
Apr. 29, 1964	488,211,364	14,548,838

Source: Annual Report.

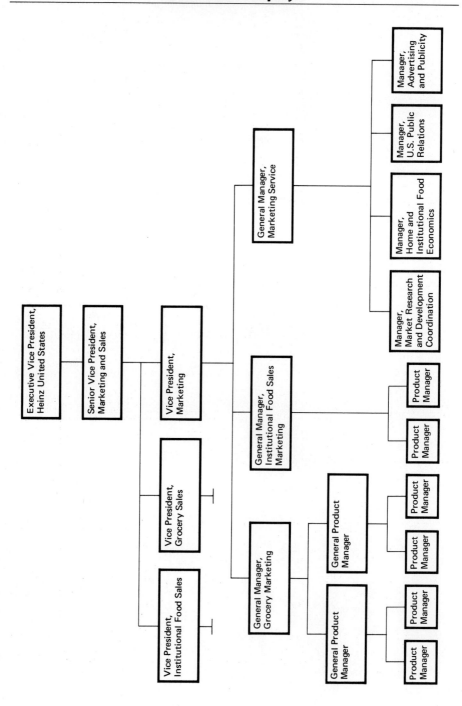

EXHIBIT 3
TOTAL KETCHUP MARKET, MILLIONS OF CASES
The H. J. Heinz Company: I

Calendar year	Regular size*	Large size	Total Number	% change
1957			16.81	
1958	15.63	1.83	17.46	4
1959	15.28	3.01	18.29	5
1960	15.38	3.87	19.25	5
1961	15.64	4.75	20.39	6
1962	15.55	5.98	21.53	6
1963	16.45	6.67	23.12	7
1964 (est.)	16.67	7.91	24.58	6

* Including Heinz Hot Ketchup.
Source: Company records.

EXHIBIT 4
SALES AND MARKET SHARE BY BRAND
The H. J. Heinz Company: I

	Heinz		Hunt*		Del Monte		All other	
	Cases, millions	Market share	Cases, millions	Market share	Cases, millions	Market share	Cases, millions	Market share
Calendar year:								
1959	4.65	24.5	NA	NA	3.47	19.0	NA	NA
1960	5.09	26.5	3.52	18.3	3.66	19.0	6.97	36.2
1961	5.69	27.9	3.21	15.7	3.68	18.1	7.81	38.3
1962	6.01	27.9	3.28	15.2	4.05	18.8	8.20	38.1
1963	6.15	26.6	4.33	18.7	4.48	19.4	8.16	35.3
1964 (est.)	6.19	25.2	5.05	20.5	5.10	20.8	8.24	38.5
Heinz fiscal year:								
1963	6.05	27.3	3.51	15.9	4.26	19.3	8.26	37.4
1964	6.04	25.6	4.77	20.3	4.64	19.7	8.13	34.6

* Includes all three Hunt brands.

Source: Company records.

EXHIBIT 5
BIMONTHLY SALES AND MARKET SHARE BY BRAND
The H. J. Heinz Company: I

	Total market, million cases	Heinz % share	Heinz Thousand cases	Hunt* % share	Hunt* Thousand cases	Del Monte % share	Del Monte Thousand cases	All other % share
Apr./May 1962	3.56	26.9	958	16.1	573	19.1	680	37.9
June/July	3.67	28.1	1,028†	14.8	542	18.3	671	38.8
Aug./Sept.	3.50	29.8	1,045†	15.6	545	18.8	658	35.8
Oct./Nov.	3.67	25.1	922	14.0	513	20.0	733	40.9
Dec./Jan. 1963	3.82	27.0	1,032†	16.6	634	21.4	815	35.0
Feb./Mar.	3.86	27.5	1,062†	18.3	703	18.1	701	36.1
Fiscal 1963	22.08	27.3	6,047	15.9	3,510	19.3	4,258	37.4
Apr./May	3.86	24.8	958	21.5	831	18.7	719	35.0
June/July	3.92	25.7	1,006†	19.5	766	18.7	730	36.1
Aug./Sept.	3.74	27.9	1,044†	18.7	698	18.2	681	35.2
Oct./Nov.	3.93	26.7	1,048†	17.7	698	21.3	836	34.3
Dec./Jan. 1964	3.85	25.2	973	20.1	774	21.5	827	33.2
Feb./Mar.	4.29	23.6	1,012†	23.4	1,002	19.8	850	33.2
Fiscal 1964	23.59	25.6	6,041	20.3	4,769	19.7	4,643	34.5
Apr./May	4.10	23.9	981	21.8	894	20.9	857	33.4

* Includes all three Hunt brands.
† Special promotion during this period.
Source: Company records.

EXHIBIT 6

HUNT'S MARKET SHARE BY BRAND
The H. J. Heinz Company: I

Calendar year	Hunt's	Snider's and Pride of the Farm	Total
1961	8.7	7.0	15.7
1962	7.7	7.5	15.2
1963	10.7	8.0	18.7
1964 (est.)	15.8	4.7	20.5

Source: Heinz Company records.

EXHIBIT 7
MARKET SHARE BY REGION (CALENDAR YEAR)
The H. J. Heinz Company: I

	Heinz				Hunt*				Del Monte				All other			
	1960	1961	1962	1963	1960	1961	1962	1963	1960	1961	1962	1963	1960	1961	1962	1963
New England	35.2	38.6	38.9	40.1	10.8	7.8	7.8	9.3	4.1	4.4	5.7	7.1	49.9	49.2	47.6	43.5
Metro New York	44.2	46.3	46.9	46.4	31.8	26.0	24.3	25.6	11.2	11.1	10.4	11.9	12.8	16.6	18.4	16.1
Mid-Atlantic	36.6	38.5	40.9	40.5	14.9	12.4	11.2	12.1	11.3	10.0	9.4	10.0	37.2	39.1	38.5	37.4
East central	28.2	30.0	28.7	28.3	14.7	11.3	12.1	17.7	15.5	14.1	15.1	16.0	41.6	44.6	44.1	38.0
West central	28.5	29.5	28.2	25.9	13.6	10.4	8.8	13.2	18.6	18.4	19.8	20.5	39.3	41.7	43.2	40.4
Southeast	12.9	13.9	13.6	13.8	21.3	20.8	20.4	20.1	21.8	20.4	20.7	21.2	44.0	44.9	45.3	44.9
Southwest	12.1	11.3	12.3	11.4	23.5	21.1	19.7	23.4	33.6	31.9	34.7	34.1	30.8	35.7	33.3	31.1
Pacific	20.6	22.5	23.1	20.6	19.8	20.4	20.9	27.3	29.7	28.4	28.7	26.6	29.9	28.7	27.3	25.5

	Heinz		Hunt*		Del Monte		All other	
	1963	1964†	1963	1964†	1963	1964†	1963	1964†
Northeast	44.8	42.1	NA	20.1	10.3	11.6	NA	26.2
East	32.8	30.8	NA	15.9	14.1	15.4	NA	37.9
North central	26.0	24.9	NA	7.5	19.8	21.6	NA	36.0
South	12.8	12.8	NA	25.6	25.9	26.3	NA	35.3
West	19.9	18.4	NA	27.4	26.3	28.1	NA	26.1

* Includes all three Hunt brands.
† Estimate.
Source: Company records.

721

EXHIBIT 8
DIRECT-BUYER'S LIST PRICES, HEINZ AND COMPETITION (CASE OF 24, FOURTEEN-OUNCE SIZE)
The H. J. Heinz Company: I

	Heinz*				Del Monte,* N.J.†	Hunt,* N.J.‡
	East	South	West Coast	Northwest		
Sept. 24, 1962	$5.19		$4.76	$4.99	$3.80	$3.80
Oct. 19	5.19		4.76	4.99	3.60	3.60
Mar. 9, 1963	5.19		4.76	4.99	3.60	3.30
June 18	5.19		4.76	4.99	3.90	3.30
June 28	5.19		4.76	4.99	3.90	3.60
Sept. 25	5.19		4.76	4.99	3.60	3.60
Sept. 27	5.19		4.76	4.99	3.60	3.40
Oct. 5	5.19		4.76	4.99	3.50	3.40
Oct. 17	5.19	$4.80	4.76	4.99	3.50	3.40
Nov. 22	5.19	4.80	4.76	4.99	3.90	3.40
Dec. 16	5.19	4.80	4.76	4.99	3.55	3.40
Jan. 14, 1964	5.19	4.80	4.76	4.99	3.55	3.10
Jan. 20	5.19	4.80	4.76	4.99	3.40	3.10
Mar. 9	5.19	4.80	4.76	4.99	3.25	3.10
Mar. 25	5.19	4.42	4.38	4.59	3.25	3.10
Apr. 28	5.19	4.42	4.38	4.59	3.40	3.25
June 1 (expected)	4.77	4.42	4.38	4.59	3.40	3.25

* Heinz' prices included delivery whereas Hunt's and Del Monte's did not.

† Prices at the California plant were 40 cents per case less and at the Indiana plant 20 cents per case less.

‡ Prices at the California plant were 40 cents per case less and at the Ohio plant 20 cents per case less.

Source: Company records.

EXHIBIT 9
DIRECT-BUYER'S LIST PRICES, HEINZ AND COMPETITION (20-OUNCE SIZE)
The H. J. Heinz Company: I

	Heinz* (case of 24)			Del Monte* (case of 12), N.J.†	Hunt* (case of 12), Ohio‡
	East	West Coast	Northwest		
Apr. 24, 1962	$7.29	$6.68	$7.02	$3.00	$2.90
July 11	7.29	6.68	7.02	2.75	2.65
Sept. 24	7.29	6.68	7.02	2.55	2.45
Oct. 19	7.29	6.68	7.02	2.40	2.30
Mar. 19, 1963	7.29	6.68	7.02	2.40	2.05
Apr. 19	7.29	6.68	7.02	2.40	2.20
June 18	7.29	6.68	7.02	2.55	2.20
June 27	6.79	6.30	6.62	2.55	2.20
June 28	6.79	6.30	6.62	2.55	2.35
Nov. 12	6.79	6.30	6.62	2.45	2.25
Nov. 18	6.79	6.30	6.62	2.35	2.20
Mar. 25, 1964	6.40	5.94	6.25	2.35	2.20

* Heinz' prices included delivery whereas Hunt's and Del Monte's did not.
† Prices at the California plant were 20 cents per case less.
‡ Prices at the California plant were 10 cents per case less.
Source: Company records.

EXHIBIT 10
TYPICAL CARLOAD FREIGHT CHARGES
The H. J. Heinz Company: I

To	14-ounce size (per case of 24)			20-ounce size (per case of 12)		
	N.J.	Calif.	Ohio-Ind.	N.J.	Calif.	Ohio-Ind.
Jacksonville	$0.28			$0.22		
Boston	0.13			0.10		
Philadelphia	0.06			0.05		
Atlanta		$0.62			$0.48	
Kansas City		0.54			0.41	
Salt Lake City		0.24			0.18	
Dallas			$0.32			$0.25
St. Louis			0.16			0.12
Detroit			0.07			0.05

Source: Company records.

EXHIBIT 11
INDEPENDENT-DEALER BUYING PRICES
The H. J. Heinz Company: I

	14-ounce size (case of 24)				20-ounce size (case of 24)			
	Heinz	Hunt	Del Monte	All other	Heinz	Hunt	Del Monte	All other
Apr./May 1962	$5.28	$4.42	$4.30	$4.18	$7.42	$6.19	$6.07	$5.76
June/July	5.23	4.34	4.25	4.15	7.32	6.19	5.98	5.78
Aug./Sept.	5.11	4.30	4.20	4.10	7.18	5.86	5.81	5.71
Oct./Nov.	5.23	4.01	3.89	3.91	7.34	5.45	5.35	5.33
Dec./Jan. 1963	4.99	3.79	3.74	3.72	6.98	5.04	4.97	5.23
Feb./Mar.	4.90	3.74	3.74	3.72	6.79	4.82	5.11	5.14
Apr./May	5.14	3.50	3.74	3.67	7.18	4.58	5.11	5.16
June/July	5.18	3.43	3.70	3.70	7.22	4.85	5.23	5.14
Aug./Sept.	5.09	3.64	3.91	3.82	6.91	5.18	5.38	5.16
Oct./Nov.	5.16	3.53	3.60	3.79	6.86	5.28	5.33	5.30
Dec./Jan. 1964	5.23	3.53	3.60	3.82	6.91	4.85	4.90	5.16
Feb./Mar.	5.09	3.36	3.46	3.84	6.82	4.82	5.02	5.30
Apr./May	5.11	3.36	3.38	3.72	6.58	4.82	5.00	5.24

Weighted average includes promotion allowances and delivery charges.
Source: Company records.

EXHIBIT 12
AVERAGE RETAIL PRICES (CENTS PER BOTTLE)
The H. J. Heinz Company: I

	14-ounce size				20-ounce size			
	Heinz	Hunt	Del Monte	All other	Heinz	Hunt	Del Monte	All other
June 1962	25.6	NA	22.2	22.7	36.9	NA	32.3	33.0
Aug.	25.6	NA	21.9	22.7	36.6	NA	32.2	32.9
Oct.	25.5	22.4	22.1	22.8	36.8	31.4	32.1	32.8
Dec.	25.8	21.5	21.3	22.0	36.8	30.5	30.2	32.2
Feb. 1963	25.2	20.9	20.8	21.5	36.0	29.8	28.9	31.5
Apr.	25.0	20.8	20.7	21.3	35.7	28.7	29.0	30.7
June	25.2	20.3	20.6	21.0	36.2	27.6	28.8	30.6
Aug.	25.1	20.1	20.3	21.1	35.8	28.0	29.0	30.4
Oct.	25.0	20.0	21.0	21.3	35.4	28.7	29.4	30.9
Dec.	25.1	19.9	20.4	21.3	35.3	28.9	29.1	31.1
Feb. 1964	25.3	19.9	20.3	21.4	35.3	27.6	28.5	30.4
Apr.	25.2	18.8	19.9	21.0	35.1	27.7	28.6	30.1

Source: Company records.

EXHIBIT 13
HEINZ' MARKET SHARE AND RETAIL PRICE PREMIUM
The H. J. Heinz Company: I

	Total share*	14-ounce size†		20-ounce size	
		Share	**Cents more**	**Share**	**Cents more**
1957	20.0	20.0	6.6		
1958	22.8	18.2	5.8	4.6	
1959	25.5	17.7	5.1	5.8	8.9
June/July 1960	26.6	17.8	5.0	7.2	8.3
Aug./Sept.	26.6	17.6	5.0	7.3	8.3
Oct./Nov.	25.5	16.6	4.8	7.3	7.8
Dec./Jan. 1961	29.4	19.4	4.0	8.2	7.0
Feb./Mar.	29.9	19.9	4.1	8.1	6.7
Apr./May	27.4	17.4	4.2	8.2	6.8
June/July	26.5	16.4	4.6	8.4	6.7
Aug./Sept.	27.3	17.3	4.5	8.4	6.8
Oct./Nov.	27.0	17.2	4.3	8.2	6.6
Dec./Jan. 1962	29.4	18.7	3.8	9.1	5.9
Feb./Mar.	28.2	18.0	3.8	8.5	6.1
Apr./May	26.9	16.3	3.9	9.1	6.1
June/July	28.1	17.4	4.0	9.1	5.9
Aug./Sept.	29.8	19.2	3.9	9.1	6.4
Oct./Nov.	25.1	14.9	5.0	8.8	7.6
Dec./Jan. 1963	27.0	16.5	5.0	9.1	7.7
Feb./Mar.	27.5	16.5	5.0	8.6	7.8
Apr./May	24.8	14.7	5.5	8.8	8.6
June/July	25.7	15.3	5.4	9.1	8.2
Aug./Sept.	27.9	17.1	4.9	9.5	7.3
Oct./Nov.	26.7	15.6	5.1	9.8	7.0
Dec./Jan. 1964	25.2	14.2	5.3	9.7	7.5
Feb./Mar.	23.6	13.4	5.6	8.9	7.5
Apr./May	23.9	12.7	5.7	9.9	6.7

* Includes hot ketchup.
† Excludes Heinz Hot Ketchup.
Source: Company records.

EXHIBIT 14
RETAIL ADVERTISING BY BRAND
The H. J. Heinz Company: I

	All-commodity importance of stores advertising, %		
	Heinz	**Hunt***	**Del Monte**
Dec./Jan. 1962	32	10	21
Feb./Mar.	37	23	26
Apr./May	23	11	24
June/July	31	9	23
Aug./Sept.	35	14	31
Oct./Nov.	18	11	31
Dec./Jan. 1963	35	13	32
Feb./Mar.	37	25	20
Apr./May	27	31	23
June/July	35	24	32
Aug./Sept.	40	25	22
Oct./Nov.	35	24	34
Dec./Jan. 1964	30	31	38
Feb./Mar.	32	36	31
Apr./May	27	27	30

* Includes all three brands.
Source: Company records.

EXHIBIT 15
HEINZ' SHARE OF TRADE INVENTORIES, PERCENT
The H. J. Heinz Company: I

	All stores	**Chain stores**	**Super independents**	**Large independents**	**Medium and small independents**
Feb. 1963	31.3	30.0	31.2	37.6	28.1
Apr.	33.4	31.2	34.2	40.4	30.1
June	29.6	26.5	31.9	36.8	26.5
Aug.	27.9	31.0	30.7	35.1	25.9
Oct.	31.5	28.7	33.1	39.1	28.4
Dec.	28.8	28.2	27.1	33.7	27.9
Feb. 1964	26.6	24.6	25.7	32.2	27.3
Apr.	28.1	24.2	29.0	36.5	28.0

Source: Company records.

▪ *Video*	▪ *Audio*
1 Open on scene at home. Youngsters are around table eagerly watching mother come through door with tray of hamburgers and a bottle of Heinz Ketchup.	SOUND EFFECTS: Natural sounds.
2 Cut to closeup of unidentified ketchup bottle on tray which mother is bringing to table. Super audio.	ANNOUNCER (voice over): The best-tasting ketchup is *thick* and *rich*.
3 Cut to closeup of table as ketchup bottle is set down to reveal it is Heinz Ketchup.	SOUND EFFECTS: Bottle coming down on table
4 Move into extreme closeup of label on left screen. Super audio.	ANNOUNCER (voice over): It even *pours* thick and rich!
4a Boy about 11 years old reaches for bottle and tips it to pour on his hamburger. No ketchup comes out. He continues to shake bottle gently, a look of anticipation on his face.	SOUND EFFECTS: Drum roll begins and builds, under.
5 Cut to his sister, about 12, who is watching him with expectation.	Drum roll continues.
6 Cut to younger sister, who watches with a look of fascinated interest.	Drum roll continues.
7 Cut to younger brother, about 5, who also looks on, wide-eyed.	Drum roll continues.
8 Cut back to boy with ketchup, as he still shakes it gently. No ketchup yet.	Drum roll continues.
9 Cut to extreme closeup of hamburger and ketchup bottle. The Ketchup pours out, thick, and rich.	Music hits triumphantly: "Pomp and Circumstance"—full, and majestic.
10 Cut to older sister. A look of delight is on her face.	Music continues.
11 Cut to younger sister. Her eyes dance and she grins with glee.	Music continues.

EXHIBIT 16
Continued

■ *Video*	■ *Audio*
12 Cut to face of younger brother. He giggles and smiles with pleasure.	Music continues.
12a Cut back to boy with ketchup as he completes his pour.	Music continues.
13 Dissolve to Heinz Ketchup on left screen, begin title crawl of audio. Music holds under.	ANNOUNCER (voice over): Heinz Ketchup is the thickest, richest . . .
14 Hold bottle. Continue crawl. Music holds under.	ANNOUNCER (voice over): . . . best-tasting, best-selling ketchup in the world . . .
15 Hold bottle. Continue crawl. Music holds under.	ANNOUNCER (voice over): . . . because . . .
16 Hold bottle. Continue crawl. Music holds under.	ANNOUNCER (voice over): . . . Heinz puts more better-tasting things in its ketchup . . .
17 Rolling titles continue.	ANNOUNCER (voice over): . . . Than anyone else in the world!
18 Dissolve back to group at table as they enjoy their hamburgers with ketchup.	Music up full!
19 Pull back from action and bring up Heinz Ketchup label full screen.	ANNOUNCER (voice over): Heinz—it pours *thick* and *rich!* (Music rises magnificently and ends)

Source: Company records.

EXHIBIT 17
ANNUAL ADVERTISING EXPENDITURES BY BRAND (CALENDAR YEAR)
The H. J. Heinz Company: I

	Heinz				Hunt*			
	1960	1961	1962	1963	1960	1961	1962	1963
Newspapers, thousands	$ 261	$ 207	$ 216	$ 2	$ 28			
Magazines, thousands	720	899	970	588	1,722	$301	$243	$2,216
Radio, thousands								
Network TV, thousands	827	815	678	844				865
Spot TV, thousands								
Total, thousands	$1,808	$1,921	$1,864	$1,434	$1,751	$301	$243	$3,081
Market share	26.5	27.9	27.9	26.6	18.3	15.7	15.2	18.7
Cases, millions	5.09	5.69	6.01	6.15	3.52	3.21	3.28	4.33

	Del Monte			
	1960	1961	1962	1963
Newspapers, thousands	$192	$ 99	$142	$ 11
Magazines, thousands	682	568	561	491
Radio, thousands				
Network TV, thousands			257	511
Spot TV, thousands				
Total, thousands	$874	$667	$960	$1,013
Market share	19.0	18.1	18.8	19.4
Cases, millions	3.66	3.68	4.05	4.48

* Includes all three Hunt brands.
Source: Company records.

EXHIBIT 18
BIMONTHLY ADVERTISING EXPENDITURES
(THOUSANDS OF DOLLARS) BY BRAND
The H. J. Heinz Company: I

Heinz fiscal 1964	Heinz	Hunt	Del Monte
May/June 1963	23	89	195
July/Aug.	68	681	186
Sept./Oct.	814	1,086	224
Nov./Dec.	24	1,167	188
Jan./Feb. 1964	783	1,409	94
Mar./Apr.	82	1,025	39
	1,794	5,457	926

Source: Company records.

THE H. J. HEINZ COMPANY: II

RONALD KURTZ
Formerly, Research Assistant
Harvard Graduate School of Business Administration

MARTIN V. MARSHALL
Professor
Harvard Graduate School of Business Administration

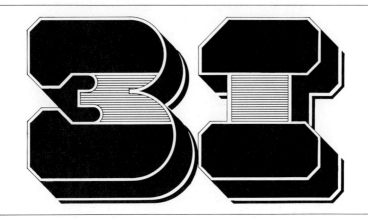

After 4 months in his new position as product manager for Heinz Ketchup, in September 1964 Mr. Thomas Smith[1] began the preparation of a marketing plan for the remainder of the 1965 fiscal year (through April 30, 1965) and for the 1966 fiscal year (May 1, 1965, through April 30, 1966). After reviewing his budgetary situation, Mr. Smith gave his attention to four areas which he believed to be important: (1) additions to the product line, (2) changes in the implementation of promotions, (3) new advertising copy, and (4) new media allocations. These were the areas he identified as requiring special consideration after reviewing the brand's activities during the previous 2 years.

---

[1] Disguised name.

THE BUDGETING SITUATION

Mr. Smith thought there were several factors to be considered before proposing a marketing budget for the remainder of fiscal 1965 and for fiscal 1966. Since April the Heinz retail price had been reduced by only 0.6 cent on the 14-ounce size and 1.3 cents on the 20-ounce size (see Exhibit 1). Although this was less than management had hoped for, Heinz' market share had reversed its trend downward (see Exhibit 2). In addition, retail trade support (advertising and inventories) had apparently improved (see Exhibit 3).

In previous years Heinz' marketing expenditures had been well above those of Hunt and Del Monte. In fiscal 1964, however, Heinz' $2.2 million in advertising was only twice that of Del Monte and less than half of Hunt's $5.5 million advertising expenditure (Exhibit 4). Heinz' promotional expenditures of around $1.2 million in fiscal 1964 were unusually high and reflected an effort to lower its price premium without a formal price reduction. This promotional budget could not be accurately compared with the approximately $200,000 being spent on promotion by Hunt and Del Monte because of their frequent price changes.

Thus far in fiscal 1965, Heinz' advertising expenditure had been at an annual rate in excess of $3 million. This compared to a rate of about $1 million for Del Monte and over $6 million for Hunt. The Hunt expenditure was expected to go as high as $7 million when it began the introductory advertising for the national expansion of flavors. Because of the recent Heinz price reduction and its expected effect on sales and profits, Mr. Smith concluded he probably would have to cut back on Heinz' marketing expenditures.

For fiscal 1965, he estimated Heinz would have consumer sales of 6.7 million cases and trade inventory increases of 300,000 cases for total shipments of 7 million cases (excluding institutional sales). This was based on the expectation that the total market would grow to around 25 million cases (fiscal 1963 and 1964 sales had been $22.1 million and $23.6 million, respectively).

With an estimated 70 cents a case available for advertising, promotions, and profit, he hoped to approximate the same dollar profit obtained in fiscal 1964. To achieve this profit goal, he felt he could recommend a marketing budget of $3 million, or 44 cents a case (as opposed to 59 cents a case in fiscal 1964), for fiscal 1965. He proposed tentatively to allocate approximately $2 million of this to advertising and $900,000 to promotions.

At approximately 30 cents a case, the Heinz advertising allocation would be considerably less than the estimated $1.35 a case being spent by Hunt and about 50 percent greater than the Del Monte expenditure (21 cents a case). Mr. Smith knew, however, that he could not match the Hunt effort. Hunt, in sustaining apparently large losses, was willing to do "investment spending" to increase its market share.

For fiscal 1966, he was considering a sales goal of 8 million cases (assuming a total market of around 26.5 million cases). To achieve this goal, he had tentatively concluded that a $4.1 million marketing budget would be required. This budget could be split with about $2.8 million for advertising and $1.3 million for promotions. In total this tentative budget would amount to around 51 cents a case.

ADDITIONS TO THE PRODUCT LINE

Mr. Smith perceived two tentative alternatives for expanding the Heinz Ketchup line. The first was to add flavored ketchups as Hunt appeared to be doing. In analyzing this alternative, he considered several factors. He knew from field reports that Hunt was expected to stop test-marketing and begin national distribution in February 1965. If Hunt did go national, his own senior management would be inclined to introduce flavored ketchups into the Heinz line in order to be competitive. He knew that the Heinz organization could have flavored ketchups on the market within about a month. Just as Hunt was doing, Heinz probably would use 14-ounce bottles and price the flavored ketchups at the same level as regular ketchup.

Mr. Smith had ordered special research to monitor the results of Hunt's test-marketing. From this he learned that in the first 4 months of test-marketing, Hunt's flavored ketchups had sold very well. As favorable trade response had led to rapid distribution, Hunt's flavored ketchups were able to gain up to 8 percent of the market. However, despite heavy promotion and advertising expenditures, the combined share of the two flavored ketchups had declined to around 2 or 3 percent by September 1964 (Exhibit 5).

A second possibility was to add new sizes and/or shapes of ketchup bottles. Mr. Smith was especially interested in the possibilities of a 26-ounce size and of a widemouthed jar.

As the growth in the ketchup market in recent years had come in the 20-ounce-size bottle (see Exhibit 6), Mr. Smith believed that a 26-ounce "household size" bottle would appeal to many families because of its convenience for heavy ketchup users. For the 26-ounce size, he was considering a base wholesale price of $4.07 per case of 12 (delivered in the East). Where the 20-ounce size was being retailed at 31, 33, or 35 cents, he expected the 26-ounce size to be priced at 39, 41, and 43 cents, respectively (so that the trade would have the same markup on both sizes). This would result in about a 5 percent saving an ounce at wholesale and a 3 to 6 percent saving an ounce at retail. Whether the trade would react favorably to an additional size was a moot question. Because of the low cost of glass, the manufacturing cost (per ounce) for the 26-ounce size would not differ from those for other sizes.

As indicated, Mr. Smith was also considering the possibilities of a widemouthed jar, which could be easier to use and more convenient for storage than the usual ketchup bottle and thus might provide real consumer benefits. However, in the past Heinz had unsuccessfully test-marked such containers five times. As he reviewed those tests, Mr. Smith noted that sales volume, in the absence of advertising or promotional support, had been very high initially and then fell off rapidly. Because there was little research data, he hypothesized that the tests were unsuccessful for two reasons. First, the diameter of the openings was 60 millimeters or more (versus 30 millimeters for regular ketchup bottles) in each case. This forced consumers to spoon the ketchup out of the jar at all times, rather than giving them the option, which they probably wanted, of pouring or spooning. Second, despite being offered in small sizes, in each test the wide-mouthed jar was priced higher than the regular 14-ounce bottle, resulting in a price premium which consumers probably considered to be excessive.

Mr. Smith believed the first problem could be overcome by using a wide-mouthed jar of 12 ounces with an opening of 48 millimeters. This opening would be small enough to allow pouring and just large enough to allow spooning. In addition, a 12-ounce jar could be priced about 1 cent below the retail price of the regular 14-ounce bottle, and he had tentatively concluded that the widemouthed bottle might do well at this relative price level. To achieve this retail price, he would need a wholesale base price of about $4.56 a case of 24 delivered in the East. Because a larger and thus more expensive cap would be required, manufacturing costs (per ounce) would be 10 percent greater than for a 14-ounce bottle.

On the one hand, Mr. Smith leaned toward the addition of at least one new item to the Heinz Ketchup line. An additional item or items might enable Heinz to obtain a larger share of shelf facings, and greater shelf facings could lead to increased sales. Further, as he believed that the trade responded less and less to successive promotions on the same item, he viewed additional items as providing more promotion opportunities. Also, he thought a broader product line might help to segment the ketchup market to Heinz' advantage. On the other hand, he was quite conscious of the possibility that any of the new items he was considering would be short-lived novelties.

CHANGES IN IMPLEMENTATION OF PROMOTIONS

In August Mr. Smith had run a promotion on the 14-ounce size that differed in several ways from past Heinz practice. Based on his evaluation of the promotion results, he was considering several changes for future promotions.

In August Heinz had offered an allowance of 40 cents a case in one area where its share was low, 15 cents in an area where its share was high, and 25 cents in three areas where its share varied from low to high. To receive this allowance, the trade was required to furnish proof of compliance with a per-formance contract. This contract called for a Heinz ketchup display, featuring Heinz in a newspaper ad, and/or a price reduction. To complement the contract, the allowance was to be credited on a later statement rather than on the invoice accompanying the original shipment. The promotion ran for 5 weeks, with sales limited to an 8-week supply. As additional incentives, 5 cents a case (any size) was allowed on railcar purchases, and dealers were permitted to pay for one-third of their order each 30 days while maintaining the 2 percent cash discount.

TABLE 1

	1964	1963
Number of weeks	5	12
Average weekly case sales, thousands	146.6	144.8
Cost/case sold	24.5¢*	85.4¢†

* Case allowance only.
† Case allowance plus special advertising.

As little information was available by September, it was difficult to compare the results of this promotion with one run at about the same time of the year in 1963. The 1963 promotion, a 25-cent allowance throughout the United States, ran from July through September for 12 weeks. It had been heavily supported with special advertising. Based on the data in Table 1, Mr. Smith concluded the results of the current promotion were favorable, because "the higher average weekly sales were achieved at a much lower cost per case."

In further trying to assess the profitability of the current promotion, he examined the computation of incremental gross profit, shown in Table 2.

As the cost of the promotion was $178,400, an incremental gross profit of $107,800 was achieved.

Mr. Smith also had the information shown in Table 3 on market share and shipments of the 14-ounce size.

From these data he concluded that the promotion had generated incremental business profitably. Further, he believed three generalizations could be made about the promotion. First, substantial brand activity (average weekly volume) could be achieved at a lower absolute promotional cost by reducing the length of the promotion period. Second, different allowances in various regions could be used to improve both cost efficiency and sales effectiveness. Third, no particular problems were caused by limiting the supply available for purchases, restricting the promotion to one size, or enforcing the performance contracts (thus delaying payment of the allowance until proof was furnished).

Tentatively, Mr. Smith was planning two additional promotions for the remainder of fiscal 1965. In November he expected to offer a 25-cent allowance on the 12-ounce hot ketchup and a 40-cent allowance on the 20-ounce size, repeating a June/July 1964 promotion (the only other promotion run thus far in

TABLE 2

	14-ounce size						
	Promotion period (5 wks) est. sales			Postpromotion period (5 wks) est. sales			Total diff.
	Actual	No. prom.	Diff.	Actual	No. prom.	Diff.	
Cases, thousands	728	360	368	158	360	(202)	166
Gross profit, thousands of dollars	1,255.0	620.6	634.4	272.4	620.6	(348.2)	286.2

TABLE 3

	Base period, 20 weeks	Promo. period, 4 weeks	Postpromo.* 8 weeks	Promo. & postpromo. comb., 12 weeks
		Market share		
Area 1 (15¢)	21.8	24.8	24.3	24.5
Area 2 (25¢)	17.0	17.6	16.3	17.0
Area 3 (25¢)	13.0	15.0	14.5	14.8
Area 4 (25¢)	7.2	7.6	7.2	7.4
Area 5 (40¢)	10.9	10.9	10.7	10.8
U.S.	13.6	14.8	14.3	14.5
		Average week shipments, thousand cases		
Area 1	16.6	40.5	8.3	19.0
Area 2	15.5	35.3	7.6	16.8
Area 3	18.6	47.8	8.0	21.3
Area 4	7.7	15.5	4.9	8.4
Area 5	7.1	17.3	4.0	8.6
U.S.	65.5	156.4†	32.8	74.1

* Estimate.

† Differs from 146.6 shown in Table 1 because first week (when promotion was introduced to trade) is not included.

fiscal 1965). For January he was planning a 25-cent allowance on the 14-ounce size and a 40-cent allowance on the 20-ounce size. He planned to continue these promotions for 5 weeks, while allowing purchases up to an 8-week supply.

For fiscal 1966 promotions, he had developed one possible schedule (Table 4). With a total of six separate promotion periods, this schedule would result in each product being featured three times. In this way, Mr. Smith believed he could stimulate considerable Heinz activity without losing trade support.

ADVERTISING COPY

In August 1964, Doyle Dane Bernbach assumed responsibility for ketchup advertising. At about this time, research was completed on the "Youngsters" com-

TABLE 4

	Case allowance		
	12-ounce hot	14-ounce regular	20-ounce regular
May	25¢	5¢ for carload 15¢	40¢
August			
October			40¢
November	25	25	
January			25
March	25	25	

mercial, which had been initiated by Clyne Maxon only 3 or 4 months earlier. This commercial had been based on the following copy strategy:

The objective will be to convince the consumer (primarily housewives) that Heinz ketchup tastes better than any other ketchup. As proof of this, it will be shown that Heinz puts more, better tasting things (spices, vinegar, and tomatoes) in its ketchup than other brands; thus making Heinz thicker and richer.

The research on the "Youngsters" commercial included recall of copy points and verbatim responses from members of the sample. Based on his study of the data, Mr. Smith concluded that the commercial was successful in attracting and holding an audience. However, he had reservations about the commercial's effectiveness because there was little evidence that the viewers associated thickness with superior flavor, the primary objective (Exhibit 7).

Doyle Dane Bernbach had proposed replacing "Youngsters" with two new commercials for which no research was available. These new commercials had been inspired by actual laboratory tests which the agency personnel saw while touring the Heinz facilities. After viewing the Heinz tests[1] for thickness and consistency, the agency believed the tests could be effectively adapted to familiar home situations.

The new commercials were described by agency personnel as being "distinct breaks from traditional approaches in food advertising." Both emphasized product quality as evidenced by demonstrations that were similar to actual laboratory tests. A "Plate Test" commercial (Exhibit 8) involved putting portions of Heinz and a competitive brand on an ordinary dinner plate. When the plate was tilted, liquid ran from the ketchup of the competitive brand but not from Heinz. The objective of this commercial was to show that Heinz was thicker and richer and thus worth a slightly higher price.

A "Ketchup Race," the second of the proposed commercials, involved inverting two ketchup bottles (one Heinz and the other a competitive brand) to see which brand was thin enough to run out of the bottle first (Exhibit 9). The purpose of the commercial was to show that Heinz was too thick and rich to run.

Although he was not particularly concerned about the rather standard-copy approach used by Del Monte ("the livelier flavor"), Mr. Smith did want something to try to counter the Hunt commercials that had begun within the past year. These commercials emphasized that Hunt was the ketchup with "the big tomato taste." To convey this message, a large tomato was shown resting on

---

[1] To control quality, Heinz conducted frequent samples of batches in the final stage of cooking. To test for thickness, a measured amount of ketchup was placed in a cube on an inclined plane. One side of the cube was then removed, and a measurement was made of the distance which the ketchup moved down the plane in a specified period of time. To test for consistency or "weepage," portions of ketchup were placed on a blotter marked with concentric circles. The liquid (which looked like water but was actually vinegar) that separated from the product in a given period of time might not go past a certain distance for the batch to be approved.

TABLE 5

	Fiscal 1963	Fiscal 1964
Gross home impressions	781,420,000	399,311,000
Media expenditures	$2,305,000	$2,180,000
Cost/1,000 home impressions	$2.95	$5.46

the top of an empty bottle. The tomato "popped" into the bottle, followed by a shot of a full bottle of Hunt's Catsup.

ADVERTISING MEDIA

In previous years almost all Heinz ketchup advertising was placed in magazines and network television. It was not until early 1964 that spot television was used. For fiscal 1963 and 1964, the Heinz media obtained the results shown in Table 5.

In September, Doyle Dane Bernbach recommended a new media schedule for the remainder of fiscal 1965 and for fiscal 1966. The agency proposed to drop magazines and to concentrate in daytime network television and spot television. While agreeing with the recent practice of allocating Heinz expenditures according to Heinz sales volume rather than population concentration, the new agency felt its proposal could do this more efficiently. Whereas the cost of major magazines (full-color page) and prime time television (1 minute) was around $4 per thousand, daytime television could be purchased for around $1.25 per thousand and spot television for $2 per thousand for a commercial minute.

In support of its proposal, the agency emphasized two considerations. First, Heinz had a good base, in terms of market share, throughout the country. The agency felt this business could be supported by daytime television without excessive coverage. Second, Heinz market share showed sizable regional variations. The agency proposed to give extra weight to the stronger markets through spot

TABLE 6

District	Sales volume contribution, %	Total media allocation %	Total media allocation $ thousand	Network charge, $ thousand	Remainder for spot TV, $ thousand
1	5.37	5.37	79.4	27.0	52.4
2	5.03	5.03	74.3	21.9	52.4
. . .					
15	4.84	4.84	71.5	39.6	31.9
Total top 15	72.10	72.10	1,065.0	429.4	635.6
Total bottom 15	27.90	27.90	412.5	412.5	
Total 30 districts	100.00	100.00	1,477.5	841.9	635.6

TABLE 7

Average 4-week period	Network TV only	Spot TV only	Combined (adjus. to total U.S.)
Net reach*	41.0%	46.0%	52.0%
Average frequency	2.9	3.1	3.8
Net homes reached, thousands	20,862.1	12,860.3	26,652.7
Gross home impressions, thousands	62,141.5	39,850.0	101,991.5
Cost/1,000 gross home impressions	$1.31	$1.63	$1.44

* Based on an estimated 50 million homes with television sets.

television. This was essentially a strategy of trying to recover lost business where Heinz was traditionally strong rather than trying to develop new business in weaker markets. It was further emphasized that concentration in one medium would provide the benefits of dominance, discounts, and greater impact of the theme.

For a hypothetical situation, the agency gave the following example of how its proposal would be implemented. First, the top 15 of Heinz' 30 districts were identified. It was then determined that they contributed 72 percent of the Heinz volume. Second, the cost for a support level of daytime network television was determined. From this it was calculated that the network charges (based on geographic concentration of the audience and local station charges) for the bottom 15 districts were $412,500, or 49 percent of the total $841,900 network expenditure. Third, the supplemental expenditure for spot television in each of the top 15 districts was computed as shown in Table 6.

For the remainder of fiscal 1965, the agency recommended the use of four programs on daytime television. These were "Concentration" and "Match Game" (two game programs featuring famous personalities), the "Loretta Young Show" (reruns of a family situation show), and the "NBC News" (see Exhibit 10). Each of these shows was selected for its concentration of women in larger, younger families (considered the prime ketchup users). Table 7 shows the objectives the agency established for its proposed media schedule.

Although Mr. Smith recognized his budget was considerably smaller than the $6 million or more being spent by Hunt, he was concerned that the reach of the proposed schedule was too narrow. On the other hand, as Hunt was using *Life, McCall's,* and "My 3 Sons" (a prime time television program), the Heinz cost efficiency would be much better. The schedules of Del Monte (which was

TABLE 8

Average 4-week period	Hunt	Del Monte
Net reach	77%	40%
Frequency	3.5	2.2
Gross rating points	268	87
Cost/1,000 impressions	$2.73	$1.65

TABLE 9

Average 4-week period	Network TV only	Spot TV only	Combined (adjus. to total U.S.)
Net reach	45.0%	55.0%	58.0%
Average frequency	4.1	4.5	5.5
Net homes reached, thousands	22,915.5	15,148.3	29,730.0
Gross home impressions, thousands	95,279.2	68,809.6	164,088.8
Cost/1,000 gross home impressions	$0.99	$1.42	$1.16

beginning to cut its magazine expenditures and concentrate in network television) and Hunt were estimated to be achieving the results shown in Table 8.

For fiscal 1966, the agency proposed the use of 10 shows in daytime television (Exhibit 11). The expected results of the media schedule are shown in Table 9.

Direct-buyer's prices, dollars*

	Heinz				Del Monte, N.J.†	Hunt, N.J.†
	East	South	West Coast	Northwest		
Case of 24, 14-oz size						
June 1, 1964	4.77	4.42	4.38	4.59	3.40	3.25
July 16	4.77	4.42	4.38	4.59	3.25	3.25
Sept.	4.77	4.42	4.38	4.59	3.40	3.40
Case of 24/12, 20-oz size						
July 16, 1964	6.40		5.94	6.25	2.25	2.25
Sept.	6.40		5.94	6.25	2.40	2.40

Independent-dealer buying price, dollars‡

	14-ounce size (case of 24)				20-ounce size (case of 12)			
	Heinz	Hunt	Del Monte	All other	Heinz	Hunt	Del Monte	All other
Apr. 1/May 1964	5.11	3.36	3.38	3.72	3.29	2.41	2.50	2.62
June/July	4.92	3.36	3.43	3.70	3.23	2.45	2.50	2.62
Aug./Sept.	4.80	3.36	3.29	3.62	3.25	2.44	2.40	2.62

Average retail price, cents

	14-ounce size (case of 24)				20-ounce size (case of 12)			
	Heinz	Hunt	Del Monte	All other	Heinz	Hunt	Del Monte	All other
Apr. 1964	25.2	18.8	19.9	21.0	35.1	27.7	28.6	30.4
June	25.0	18.6	19.8	NA	34.0	28.0	28.2	NA
Aug.	24.6	19.1	19.8	NA	33.8	27.9	28.0	NA

* Manufacturer's list prices. Heinz prices include delivery whereas Hunt's and Del Monte's do not.
† Prices were 40 cents per case (14 oz) and 15 cents per case (20 oz) lower at the California plants. Prices were 20 cents per case (14 oz) lower at the Midwest plants.
‡ Delivered price including special promotions.
Source: Company records.

EXHIBIT 2
BIMONTHLY SALES AND SHARE BY BRAND
The H. J. Heinz Company: II

	Total market, million cases	Heinz		Hunt*		Del Monte		All other, % share
		% share	Thousand cases	% share	Thousand cases	% share	Thousand cases	
Apr./May 1964	4.10	23.9	981	21.8	894	20.9	857	33.4
June/July	4.11	27.1†	1,111	19.6	807	18.7	766	34.6
Aug./Sept.	4.10	25.3†	1,037	19.4	798	22.4	917	32.9

* Includes all three Hunt brands.
† Special promotion run during this period.

EXHIBIT 3
HEINZ' TRADE SUPPORT
The H. J. Heinz Company: II

Retail advertising

All-commodity importance of stores advertising

	Heinz	Hunt*	Del Monte
Apr./May 1964	27%	27%	30%
June/July	40	22	24
Aug./Sept.	33	22	34

Heinz' share of inventories

	All stores	Chains	Super independents	Large independents	Medium & small independents
April 1964	28.1	24.2	29.0	36.5	28.0
June	27.3	24.4	26.7	36.0	NA
Aug.	29.5	24.0	34.8	36.0	NA

* Includes all three Hunt brands.
Source: Company records.

EXHIBIT 4
BIMONTHLY ADVERTISING EXPENDITURES (THOUSANDS OF DOLLARS) BY BRAND
The H. J. Heinz Company: II

	Heinz	Hunt*	Del Monte
Heinz fiscal 1964			
May/June 1963	23	89	195
July/Aug.	68	681	186
Sept./Oct.	814	1,086	224
Nov./Dec.	24	1,167	188
Jan./Feb. 1964	783	1,409	94
Mar./Apr.	82	1,025	39
	1,794†	5,457	926
Heinz fiscal 1965			
May/June	501	945	339
July/Aug.	579	832	260

* Includes all three brands.
† Production and other charges increased total expenditures to $2.2 million.
Source: Company records.

EXHIBIT 5
DATA USED TO MONITOR HUNT'S TEST-MARKETING OF FLAVORED KETCHUPS
The H. J. Heinz Company: II

Total Hunt data

	Sales zone 1*				Sales zone 2*			
	Test area		Entire zone		Test area		Entire zone	
Market share	**20-oz**	**14-oz†**	**20-oz**	**14-oz†**	**20-oz**	**14-oz†**	**20-oz**	**14-oz†**
Aug./Sept. 1963	4.2	9.5	3.9	9.7	6.1	16.8	5.5	20.8
Oct./Nov.	3.8	10.1	3.7	9.7	6.5	14.9	6.1	18.7
Dec./Jan. 1964	5.5	11.7	4.4	10.3	6.3	17.6	8.1	19.6
Feb./Mar.‡	3.7	20.6	3.9	13.9	7.3	20.1	6.7	25.1
Apr./May	4.9	14.4	4.6	11.6	9.1	22.2	7.9	22.4
June/July	4.3	13.2	4.1	11.1	8.1	20.8	7.0	17.2
Aug./Sept.	3.6	14.3	4.4	10.9	5.9	15.4	6.7	17.1

Aug.-Sept. '64 special breakout, Hunt flavors§

	Sales zone 1			Sales zone 2		
	Pizza	**Hickory**	**Total**	**Pizza**	**Hickory**	**Total**
Zone distribution, %	5	9	9	45	51	51
Share of market, total zone, %	0.1	0.1	0.2	0.4	1.0	1.4

* Sales in test areas represented about 25 percent of sales in zone 1 and 15 percent of sales in zone 2. Data includes all three Hunt brands.

† Includes regular and flavored ketchups.

‡ First full period of distribution of flavored ketchups.

§ Ordered in midsummer, thus allowing time to track only one bimonthly period of movement.

Source: Company records.

EXHIBIT 6
SALES GROWTH OF LARGE-SIZE (20-OZ) KETCHUP
The H. J. Heinz Company: II

	1958	1959	1960	1961	1962	1963	1964*
Share of total ketchup sales, %	10.4	16.5	20.1	23.3	25.5	28.9	32.2

	Millions of cases			% change vs. year ago		
	14 oz	20 oz	Total	14 oz	20 oz	Total
June/July 1961	2.66	0.83	3.49	2	23	6
Aug./Sept.	2.53	0.77	3.30	3	24	7
Oct./Nov.	2.65	0.81	3.46	3	18	6
Dec./Jan. 1962	2.59	0.89	3.48	3	18	6
Feb./Mar.	2.78	0.87	3.65	6	13	7
Apr./May	2.64	0.92	3.56		13	3
June/July	2.72	0.95	3.67	2	15	5
Aug./Sept.	2.60	0.90	3.50	3	17	6
Oct./Nov.	2.72	0.95	3.67	3	17	6
Dec./Jan. 1963	2.71	1.11	3.82	5	25	10
Feb./Mar.	2.76	1.10	3.86	(1)	26	6
Apr./May	2.73	1.13	3.86	3	23	8
June/July	2.77	1.15	3.92	2	21	7
Aug./Sept.	2.68	1.05	3.74	3	18	7
Oct./Nov.	2.81	1.12	3.93	3	18	7
Dec./Jan. 1964	2.54	1.31	3.85	(6)	18	1
Feb./Mar.	3.00	1.29	4.29	9	17	11
Apr./May	2.78	1.32	4.10	2	17	6
June/July	2.75	6.36	4.11	(1)	18	5
Aug./Sept.	2.86	1.24	4.10	7	16	10

* Estimated.

Source: Company records.

745

EXHIBIT 7
RECALL OF "YOUNGSTERS" COMMERCIAL
The H. J. Heinz Company: II

METHOD. Housewives in Texas, Ohio, and Iowa were called on the day the show carried the commercial and asked to watch the program. The following day the women (who had been selected so as to be representative of the families listed in the telephone book of the three cities) were questioned about the commercial. The completed sample method included 195 housewives.

In the commercial audience	80%
Not in the commercial audience	20
	100%

Of those in the commercial audience:

Gave recall related to specific commercial	42%
Gave incorrect recall only	7
Remember song on commercial but did not recall anything about it	3
Did not remember seeing commercial	48
	100%

Of those who gave recall related to specific commercial:

Children eating hamburgers/mother serving/misc. correct situation video recall	88%
Recall of music ("Pomp and Circumstance")	41
Thick/thickest/thicker than others	43
Rich/richest	19
Shows ketchup pouring out	33
Tastes good/best taste	17
Shows bottle of ketchup	14

Source: Company records.

DOYLE · DANE · BERNBACH · INC. ADVERTISING

20 WEST 43RD STREET, NEW YORK, N. Y. 10036 LO 4–1234

RADIO · TELEVISION

program	TELEVISION	air date	AS RECORDED
client	H. J. Heinz	length	60 SECONDS HKTV 400
product	KETCHUP	job no.	"PLATE" HK189 6

VIDEO

1. HANDS SLIDE IN 2 BOTTLES OF KETCHUP ONE LABELED "TOMOTO KETCHUP", THEN WITH LABEL AWAY FROM CAMERA

2. TURN HEINZ TO SHOW LABEL
3. POUR HEINZ ON TILTED PLATE
4. POUR COMPETITIVE BRAND BESIDE HEINZ

5. OBSERVE BOTH KETCHUPS: COMPETITIVE BRAND SEPARATES AND WATER RUNS DOWN PLATE. CAMERA FOLLOWS TRICKLING WATER.
6. WATER RUNS INTO FRENCH FRIED POTATOES AT BOTTOM OF PLATE. FORM HOLDS UP SOGGY FRENCH FRY.
7. DIP UNTOUCHED FRENCH FRY INTO HEINZ WHICH IS STILL INTACT. HOLD IT UP.

8. MOVE IN TO ECU HEINZ LABEL

AUDIO

1. V.O.: Tsk, tsk. They'll never learn. They took our tomatoes. They use a lot of our spices. They even copied our bottle. But they still can't make ketchup--

2. like Heinz.
3. Put a little Heinz on a plate.
4. Do the same with another ketchup-- any leading ketchup.
5. Now watch. That's water running out of the other ketchup.

6. Is that what what you like on your French fries?
7. Or is this more like it. Thick, clingy, ketchuppy Heinz Ketchup- Without the runny water those other ketchups have. With Heinz, you get every drop of taste.
8. It's one of the reasons you may pay a little more for Heinz.

EXHIBIT 9
STORYBOARD FOR "KETCHUP RACE" COMMERCIAL
The H. J. Heinz Company: II

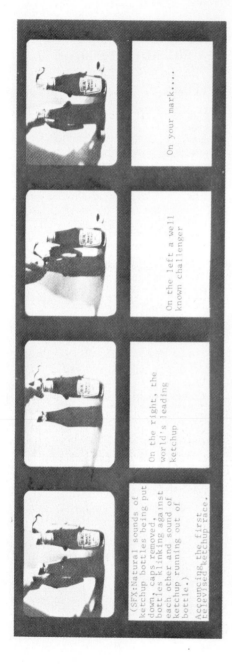

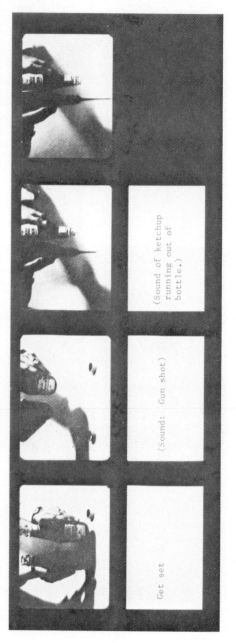

748

EXHIBIT 9
Continued

EXHIBIT 10
PROPOSED FISCAL 1965 MEDIA
The H. J. Heinz Company: II

	Concentration*	Match Game*	Loretta Young†	NBC News†
Cost/minute	$ 4,958	$ 4,958	$ 3,086	$ 2,855
Total minutes (39 weeks)	60	57	39	39
Est. av nat'l. rating	7.3	7.5	4.6	3.9
Est. share	41%	30%	20%	17%
Home impressions/commer. min	3,805,000	3,910,000	2,398,000	2,033,000
Total home impressions, thousands	228,300	222,870	93,522	79,287
Cost/1,000 home impressions/commer. min.	$1.30	$1.27	$1.29	$1.40

* Alternate-week quarter-hour sponsorship (3 minutes plus billboards).
† Every-week participation (1 minute).
Source: Company records.

EXHIBIT 11
PROPOSED FISCAL 1966 MEDIA
The H. J. Heinz Company: II

	Cost/ min, $	Tot. min (52 wk)	Est. nat'l. rating	Home impress./ commer. min, thousands	Tot. home impress., thousands	Cost/1,000 impress./min, $
NBC						
The Doctors	5,323	78	6.9	3,546.7	276,642.6	1.50
Jeopardy	5,296	52	7.1	3,649.5	189,774.0	1.45
Moment of Truth	3,785	26	5.0	2,570.1	68,822.6	1.47
ABC						
American Bandstand	3,539	23	6.7	3,443.9	79,209.7	1.03
Father Knows Best	3,406	64	4.7	2,415.9	154,617.6	1.41
Flame in the Wind	2,828	57	3.3	1,696.2	96,683.4	1.67
Trailmaster	3,297	78	6.3	3,238.3	252,587.4	1.02
Rebus	2,600	6	3.5	1,799.1	10,794.6	1.45
Day in Court	3,165	22	4.2	2,158.9	47,495.8	1.47
The Young Marrieds	3,800	15	4.1	2,107.5	31,612.5	1.80

Source: Company records.

THE H. J. HEINZ COMPANY: III

RONALD KURTZ
Formerly, Research Assistant
Harvard Graduate School of Business Administration

MARTIN V. MARSHALL
Professor
Harvard Graduate School of Business Administration

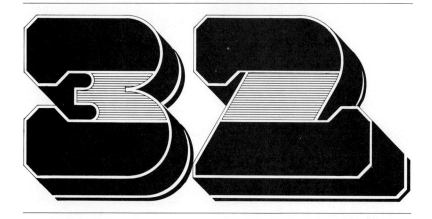

In May 1964 when Mr. Thomas Smith[1] became product manager for Heinz Ketchup, the brand had been experiencing a market share decline for about 18 months. During the following 16 months that Mr. Smith had managed the brand, its market share had been increased, so that in September 1965 it was back to about its 1962 level. Before preparing the brand's marketing plan for fiscal 1967 (May 1, 1966, to April 30, 1967), Mr. Smith believed it would be helpful to review both the action he had taken and competitive activity during this period.

---

[1] Disguised name.

STEPS TAKEN TO IMPROVE
THE BRAND'S SHARE

In March 1964, after reviewing data that indicated Heinz' retail-price premium of over 5 cents a bottle (14-ounce size) was an unfavorable influence on its share, management had initiated a wholesale-price reduction aimed at lowering Heinz' retail price by 2 cents a bottle. Similar action was taken to reduce the price premium of the 20-ounce size. Although Heinz' retail prices had not varied significantly, Heinz' price premium had been reduced about 2 cents a bottle (see Exhibit 1 for average wholesale and retail prices). This was the result of competitors having raised their prices three times while Heinz had only recently (June 1965) raised its prices (see Exhibits 2 and 3 for direct-buyers' base prices).

Where it had once been the dominant ketchup advertiser, Heinz' expenditures per case had become only a third of Hunt's and about twice those of Del Monte because of their substantial increases in advertising effort. Believing that he could not afford to match this increased competitive advertising, Mr. Smith had sought ways to improve the efficiency of Heinz' advertising efforts.

Beginning September 1964 Mr. Smith had initiated changes in the advertising media and copy employed by the brand. Media expenditures, which were allocated by sales districts according to their contribution to Heinz' volume, were concentrated in daytime television and spot television, in contrast to the previous practice of allocating the budget about equally between print and television on a national basis that resulted in a cost per 1,000 homes which he believed to be excessive. In addition, during the previous 6 months Heinz had begun very limited use of 30-second commercials (only 60s had been used previously) in an effort to achieve greater reach and frequency at an efficient cost. Using approximately the same budget as in 1964 (Exhibit 4), Mr. Smith expected to achieve three times the number of gross home impressions in 1965 (1,140 million versus 399 million).

This tripling of relative media weight was accompanied by a new copy approach which research showed to have increased stopping power and improved delivery of the sales message. In October 1964 Mr. Smith began to use two commercials, "Ketchup Race" and "Plate Test," which had been prepared by the new agency he had selected a month earlier. While the brand's previous commercial, "Youngsters," had high recall, it did not appear effective in conveying the desired message of Heinz' superior flavor and thickness. Thus Mr. Smith substituted the new commercials, which employed demonstrations adopted from actual laboratory tests, in an effort to overcome this problem. Based on research conducted in May 1965 (see Exhibits 5 and 6 for data on commercial and copy point recall), he believed the two commercials were successfully communicating a more competitive selling story.

Mr. Smith had also made changes aimed at improving the effectiveness and cost efficiency of Heinz' promotional activities. Previously Heinz had run two promotions annually (for periods of 12 weeks each) with allowances of 25 cents per case on all sizes. Because the trade rarely merchandised these pro-grams, the promotions generally resulted in building trade inventories rather than consumer sales.

To overcome these problems, Mr. Smith had acted in four areas. First, promotions were run for shorter periods (4 or 5 weeks) but more frequently. In seven out of the eight bimonthly periods that Mr. Smith had managed the brand, he had offered promotions on one or more sizes. Second, before the trade was credited with the allowance, it had to supply proof that it had dis-played, advertised, and/or reduced the price of the item. Previously credits had been issued without proof of performance. Third, Mr. Smith had varied the amount of the allowance regionally (to allow for differences in competitive con-ditions) and by item. Finally, he had increased promotional expenditures in 1965 to about twice those of 1964.

In the first 9 months of 1965, Heinz' market share had reversed its down-ward trend and begun to increase (see Exhibit 7). In addition, Heinz was re-ceiving favorable trade response relative to competition (see Exhibit 8 for Heinz' retail advertising and share of inventories), and was often promoted even in the absence of special allowances. If this improvement could be sustained, Mr. Smith expected Heinz' market share to be around 29 percent in 1965 (as com-pared to 25 percent in 1964).

NEW PRODUCT TEST MARKETS

Mr. Smith had been prompted to explore the possibilities of adding to the ketchup line for three basic reasons. First, he believed that new items might seg-ment the consumer market to Heinz' advantage. Second, he concluded that new items could provide additional promotion opportunities, thus avoiding the apparent reductions in trade and consumer enthusiasm that resulted from fre-quent promotions for the same item. Finally, he knew that management was concerned about the possible need for responding to Hunt's addition of flavored ketchups to its line.

Mr. Smith had delayed adding flavored ketchups to Heinz' line. From spe-cial research obtained on Hunt's test markets, where the market share gained by flavored ketchups had fallen rapidly after initial popularity among the trade and consumers, he concluded that flavored ketchups offered little or no opportunity. Although he continued to watch Hunt's progress in national distribution, he con-centrated his own efforts on innovation in package size. A 26-ounce size, aimed at heavy users, and a 12-ounce widemouthed jar, providing the option of spooning or pouring the ketchup for easier use, were developed.

Mr. Smith had placed the 26-ounce size in a test market in Baltimore in November 1964 and the 12-ounce wide mouth in Kansas City–Omaha in De-cember 1964. He had delayed national introduction in order to test whether the products could maintain trade and consumer interest as opposed to being short-lived novelties. In addition to the sales data from the two test districts, the product manager had information on these products from three other sources. These were a product concept study, general research on the ketchup market, and a study of purchasers of the widemouthed jar.

Sales data for 1965 (see Exhibit 9) indicated that large sizes would account for around 37 percent of total industry volume, thus continuing a growth trend begun in 1957 with the introduction of the 20-ounce size. Additional information indicating a market for even larger sizes was revealed in the ketchup market study (see Exhibit 10) completed by Heinz in February 1965. Research showed that (1) 10 percent of the sample purchased ketchup at least once a week, (2) over half the respondents purchased more than one bottle their last time, and (3) two-thirds of the sample had more than one bottle in their pantry. Mr. Smith also had information from a concept study in which people were asked the likelihood of their purchasing different ketchup flavors, types of containers, and container sizes. The research, completed in July 1965, indicated that consumers were more interested in the packaging innovations and confirmed Mr. Smith's previous hypothesis that flavored ketchups offered less opportunity.

With this information as a background material, Mr. Smith had more insight for evaluating the Baltimore test market results. The 26-ounce size, at a retail price 8 cents above the 20-ounce size, had obtained better than a 3 percent share of the market (see Exhibit 11) despite an inability to obtain distribution in stores accounting for more than about one-third of grocery sales. Compared to the rest of the sales zone in which Baltimore was located, the 26-ounce size had apparently contributed to a greater increase in Heinz' share of the total market for large sizes (see Exhibit 12 for computation of incremental sales).

These results had been obtained with an incremental marketing expense of only $6,000 ($4,000 of which was a 40-cent-a-case introductory allowance on 10,000 cases, or about 11 weeks' supply). With an estimated 660 incremental cases a week, this expense was recovered in about 6½ weeks of sales (priced at $4.02 a case). The effect of special defensive efforts by Hunt during the first 3 months of the test was not known.

Data from the ketchup market study had indicated that most consumer suggestions for changes in ketchup products were in the area of packaging. Particularly for Heinz, there was a desire for a more convenient way to get the ketchup out of the bottle (Exhibit 13). This was confirmed in the concept test, where consumers appeared very interested in a widemouthed jar. Special research (among purchasers of the widemouthed jar who took advantage of a 25-cent refund offer) revealed that consumers perceived other benefits. The respondents commented favorably on the bottle's greater convenience for storage and nicer appearance. There was negligible comment on the wide mouth's price, which at retail was about 1 cent below the 14-ounce size to avoid an excessive premium for the new size.

The trade, viewing the wide mouth as a "true innovation," had responded favorably to the new product. As a result, Heinz obtained over 50 percent distribution with only an $8,000 expenditure for promotion. There was no incremental advertising expense to support the wide mouth. Since its introduction,

TABLE 1

	Total zone		Omaha–Kansas City			
	Total Heinz	14-oz size	Total Heinz	12- and 14-oz sizes*		
				Total	14 oz	12 oz†
June/July 1964	26.7	13.6	29.3	16.3	16.3	
Aug./Sept.	25.2	15.0	26.6	16.4	16.4	
Oct./Nov.	25.6	14.5	27.4	15.7	15.7	
Dec./Jan. 1965	28.1	15.3	30.1	15.4	13.6	1.8
Feb./Mar.	27.2	14.9	30.6	16.9	15.3	1.6
Apr./May	28.0	15.1	31.3	15.4	13.3	2.1
June/July			31.6	15.4	13.7	1.7

* Excludes hot ketchup.
† Distribution for Dec./Jan. through June/July was 37, 53, 60, and 58 percent, respectively.

the wide mouth had accounted for around 1.8 percent of the Omaha–Kansas City market. The market share information in Table 1 was collected to compare the test market results with total sales data for the zone in which Omaha and Kansas City were located.

The test market results were just in the range of the 1½ to 2 percent share which Mr. Smith considered as a minimum for maintaining the product on the market. However, there was some evidence that sales had been unduly depressed in Kansas City, where the sales force had not been as aggressive in its efforts to gain trade support. In addition, Mr. Smith felt the special research data had indicated greater potential for the widemouthed jar than it was achieving.

With a wholesale price of $4.56 a case (21 cents a case below the price of the 14-ounce size), the widemouthed jar provided Heinz with a gross margin (net of delivery expense) of $1.26 a case. However, if either the 26-ounce or widemouthed jars were to be introduced nationally, Mr. Smith expected to raise their wholesale prices to bring them in line with June price changes on the 14- and 20-ounce sizes. National introduction would also require plant conversion costs of around $100,000 per item to facilitate increased production.

Hunt had introduced its flavored ketchups nationally in February 1965. These products were supported with heavy advertising expenditures and a mailing of 25 million coupons good for a free bottle. Within a relatively short time, the flavored ketchups were being stocked in stores accounting for around 85 percent of grocery volume. In addition, the trade gave about 10 percent of ketchup shelf space to the new flavors.

Together, the two flavors initially gained 6.5 percent share of the market. By September, however, their combined share was 4.7 percent and falling, as it had in the test market (see Exhibit 14). In addition, the trade was featuring and advertising the Hunt brand considerably less than in the preceding months. Hunt had just begun test-marketing a "steak house" ketchup, but there was no evidence that it would be more or less successful than the other Hunt flavors. Research on Del Monte's distribution of a barbecue ketchup in the Southwest and West and on Campbell's test-marketing of a V-8 sauce was also unavailable.

EXHIBIT 1
AVERAGE WHOLESALE AND RETAIL PRICES
The H. J. Heinz Company: III

Independent-dealer buying price, dollars*

	14-ounce size (case of 24)				20-ounce size (case of 12)			
	Heinz	Hunt	Del Monte	Others	Heinz	Hunt	Del Monte	Others
Aug./Sept.1964	4.80	3.36	3.29	3.62	3.25	2.44	2.40	2.62
Oct./Nov.	4.80	3.43	3.38	3.62	3.23	2.39	2.39	2.59
Dec./Jan. 1965	4.80	3.72	3.60	3.70	3.24	2.60	2.54	2.62
Feb./Mar.	4.75	3.84	3.79	3.77	3.23	2.66	2.59	2.63
Apr./May	4.75	4.01	3.96	3.86	3.25	2.80	2.75	2.76
June/July	4.82	4.15	4.10	4.01	3.23	2.90	2.83	2.76
Aug./Sept.	4.87	4.27	4.18	4.10	3.32	2.80	2.89	2.78

Average retail price, cents

	14-ounce size			20-ounce size		
	Heinz	Hunt	Del Monte	Heinz	Hunt	Del Monte
Aug. 1964	24.6	19.1	19.8	33.8	27.9	28.0
Oct.	24.3	19.1	19.0	34.0	27.5	27.4
Dec.	24.5	19.2	19.5	33.5	27.1	27.3
Feb. 1965	24.2	19.9	19.6	33.7	28.1	27.8
Apr.	24.1	19.9	19.8	33.3	28.5	28.0
June	24.1	20.5	20.4	33.2	28.8	28.6
Aug.	24.2	21.1	21.0	33.3	29.9	29.7

* Delivered price including special promotions.
Source: Company records.

EXHIBIT 2

DIRECT-BUYERS' BASE PRICES
(CASE OF 24, FOURTEEN-OUNCE SIZE)
The H. J. Heinz Company: III

	Heinz*					Del Monte,* N.J.†	Hunt,* N.J.†
	East	South	Southwest	West Coast	North-west		
June 1, 1964	4.77	4.42		4.38	4.59	3.40	3.25
July 16	4.77	4.42		4.38	4.59	3.25	3.25
Sept.	4.77	4.42		4.38	4.59	3.40	3.40
Nov. 13	4.77	4.42		4.38	4.59	3.40	3.65
Nov. 16	4.77	4.42		4.38	4.59	3.65	3.65
Feb. 15, 1965	4.77	4.42		4.38	4.59	3.90	3.65
Feb. 17	4.77	4.42		4.38	4.59	3.90	3.90
May 28	4.77	4.42		4.38	4.59	4.15	4.15

	Northeast and East	Midwest	South-west	Southeast, South, and Calif.	North-west	Del Monte	Hunt
June 14	5.02	4.77	4.42	4.50	4.69	4.15	4.15
July 9	5.02	4.77	4.29	4.50	4.69	4.15	4.15

* Heinz' prices included delivery whereas Hunt's and Del Monte's did not.
† Prices were 40 cents per case lower at California plants and 20 cents per case lower at Midwest plants.
Source: Company records.

EXHIBIT 3
DIRECT-BUYERS' BASE PRICES
(CASE OF 24 OR 12, TWENTY-OUNCE SIZE)
The H. J. Heinz Company: III

	Heinz*			Del Monte,* N.J.†	Hunt,* N.J.‡
	East	West Coast	North-west		
Sept. 1964	6.40	5.94	6.25	2.40	2.40
Nov. 13	6.40	5.94	6.25	2.40	2.55
Nov. 16	6.40	5.94	6.25	2.55	2.55
Feb. 15, 1965	6.40	5.94	6.25	2.65	2.55
Feb. 17	6.40	5.94	6.25	2.65	2.65
May 28	6.40	5.94	6.25	2.80	2.80

	Heinz*						Del Monte,* N.J.†	Hunt,* N.J.‡
	Northeast and East	Mid-west	South-west	South-east and South	Calif.	North-west		
June 14	6.70	6.65	6.40	6.40	6.09	6.40	2.80	2.80
July 9	6.70	6.65	5.98	6.25	6.09	6.40	2.80	2.80

* Heinz' prices included delivery whereas Hunt's and Del Monte's did not.
† Prices are 20 cents per case lower at California plant.
‡ Prices are 5 cents per case lower at Ohio plant and 15 cents per case lower at California plant.
Source: Company records.

EXHIBIT 4
COMPETITIVE MARKETING EXPENDITURES
The H. J. Heinz Company: III

	Calendar 1964			Calendar 1965 (est.)		
	Heinz	Hunt*	Del Monte	Heinz	Hunt*	Del Monte
Advertising, thousand	2,921	5,925	1,120	2,483	6,760	814
Promotion, thousand	651	163	130	1,297	1,711	316
	3,572	6,088	1,250	3,780	8,471	1,130
Spending/case, $	0.57	1.19	0.25	0.50	1.51	0.24

Monthly advertising, thousand

	Heinz	Hunt*	Del Monte
May/June 1964	501	945	339
July/Aug.	579	832	260
Sept./Oct.	488	1,009	126
Nov./Dec.	488	705	262
Jan./Feb. 1965	330	1,511	72
Mar./Apr.	335	1,891	4
Fiscal 1965	2,721	6,893	1,063
May/June	436	1,271	66
July/Aug.	472	475	135

* Includes all three brands.
Source: Company records.

EXHIBIT 5
COMMERCIAL RESEARCH
The H. J. Heinz Company: III

METHOD. Housewives in Omaha ("Ketchup Race") and Cincinnati, Minneapolis, and Cleveland ("Plate Test") were called the day the show carried the commercial and asked to watch the program. The following day the women (who had been selected so as to be representative of the families listed in their city's telephone book) were questioned about the commercial. Samples of 215 ("Plate Test") and 210 ("Ketchup Race") were obtained.

	Plate test, 60 sec	Ketchup race, 30 sec
In the commercial audience	86%	81%
Not in commercial audience	14	19
	100%	100%
Of those in the commercial audience:		
Gave recall related to test commercial	62%	59%
Gave incorrect recall	2	3
Remember seeing commercial but recall nothing about it	5	1
Did not remember seeing commercial	31	37
	100%	100%

Source: Company records.

EXHIBIT 6

COPY POINT RECALL AMONG THOSE WHO GAVE
RECALL RELATED TO COMMERCIAL
The H. J. Heinz Company: III

Plate test

Heinz isn't water, others are/Heinz is thicker	61%
You don't want water on French fries	31
Heinz can stand without getting watery/other brand got watery	24
The best tomatoes are in Heinz	11
Others copy the bottle, but not the ketchup	19
Two kinds of ketchup shown on plate	71
Heinz did not run	58
Showed ketchup on French fries	40
Showed two bottles	22
More spicy/richer	21
Good product/superior	15

Ketchup race

Heinz is thicker/thick	80%
Richer/more flavor	29
Not watery	19
Not contain water/doesn't separate	14
Other product watery	25
Better flavor/spicier	14
Made of good quality tomatoes	15
The race/contest between two ketchups	17
Heinz lost the race/ran out slower	78
Showed two bottles	29

Source: Company records.

EXHIBIT 7
BIMONTHLY SALES AND SHARE BY BRAND
The H. J. Heinz Company: III

	Total market, million cases	Heinz		Hunt*		Del Monte		All other, % share
		% share	Thous. cases	% share	Thous. cases	% share	Thous. cases	
Apr./May 1964	4.10	23.9	981	21.8	894	20.9	857	33.4
June/July	4.11	27.1†	1,111	19.6	807	18.7	766	34.6
Aug./Sept.	4.10	25.3†	1,037	19.4	798	22.4	917	32.9
Oct./Nov.	4.12	26.1	1,075	18.8	773	21.5	886	33.6
Dec./Jan. 1965	4.04	28.2†	1,140	19.1	772	21.2	857	31.5
Feb./Mar.	4.39	27.2†	1,195	23.7	1,041‡	18.6	816	30.5
Fiscal 1965	24.86	26.2	6,539	20.2	5,085	20.3	5,099	32.6
Apr./May	4.28	28.5†	1,222	23.3	999	18.1	775	30.1
June/July	4.39	30.5†	1,341	22.0	965	17.3	759	30.2
Aug./Sept.	4.18	29.8†	1,247	21.6	902§	18.6	780	30.0

* Includes all three Hunt brands.
† Promotion run during this period.
‡ 25 million coupons mailed direct to consumers.
§ One free case (20-ounce size) with purchase of seven cases.
Source: Company records.

EXHIBIT 8
HEINZ' RETAIL ADVERTISING AND
SHARE OF INVENTORIES
The H. J. Heinz Company: III

All-commodity importance of stores advertising

	Heinz	Hunt*	Del Monte
June/July 1964	40	22	24
Aug./Sept.	33	22	34
Oct./Nov.	29	20	32
Dec./Jan. 1965	28	20	25
Feb./Mar.	37	30	29
Apr./May	33	26	19
June/July	35	22	20
Aug./Sept.	22	20	28

Heinz share of inventories

	All stores	Chains	Super independents	Large independents
Aug. 1964	29.5	24.0	34.8	36.0
Oct.	30.6	27.5	36.3	32.8
Dec.	27.2	23.3	28.9	32.8
Feb. 1965	28.9	24.6	32.1	34.3
Apr.	28.1	24.7	30.0	33.6
June	27.3	24.8	27.6	32.4
Aug.	27.6	22.9	29.2	35.7

* Includes all three brands.
Source: Company records.

EXHIBIT 9
TOTAL KETCHUP MARKET
The H. J. Heinz Company: III

	Millions of cases			% change vs. year ago		
	14 oz	20 oz	Total	14 oz	20 oz	Total
Apr./May 1964	2.78	1.32	4.10	2	17	6
June/July	2.75	1.36	4.11	(1)	18	5
Aug./Sept.	2.86	1.24	4.10	7	16	10
Oct./Nov.	2.72	1.40	4.12	(3)	25	5
Dec./Jan. 1965	2.55	1.49	4.04		14	5
Feb./Mar.	2.77	1.62	4.39	(8)	26	2
Apr./May	2.72	1.56	4.28	(2)	18	4
June/July	2.71	1.68	4.39	(2)	24	7
Aug./Sept.	2.63	1.55	4.18	(8)	25	2

Source: Company records.

763

EXHIBIT 10
PATTERN OF CONSUMER KETCHUP PURCHASES
The H. J. Heinz Company: III

	Age of housewife			Family income		
	Under 35	35–54	Over 54	Under $4,000	$4,000–$7,000	Over $7,000
Last purchased ketchup:						
In past week	34	31	19	25	34	27
1 week–1 month ago	52	47	36	41	48	48
Frequency of purchase:						
Once a week or more	12	9	7	9	10	9
Every 2 weeks	23	14	7	16	19	11
Every 3–5 weeks	34	36	24	26	33	37
Brand purchased last:						
Heinz	25	36	38	28	29	41
Hunt*	29	21	23	22	26	20
Del Monte	22	25	18	20	22	23
No. of bottles bought last:						
1	43	41	45	44	40	43
2	36	37	27	31	36	35
3	4	6	6	6	4	6
Size purchased last:						
14 oz	69	77	80	79	74	73
20 oz	32	26	17	20	27	29
Brands on hand:						
Heinz	26	35	41	27	31	42
Hunt*	23	26	22	27	30	35
Del Monte	24	27	18	19	26	26
No. of bottles on hand:						
1	36	33	43	42	36	32
2	33	35	28	30	32	35
3	13	11	10	9	11	15

* Includes all three Hunt brands.

Source: Company records.

EXHIBIT 11
BALTIMORE MARKET SHARE AND DISTRIBUTION TRENDS FOR 26-OUNCE SIZE
The H. J. Heinz Company: III

| | Total Heinz share | 26-ounce size | | | (20 & 26 oz) share of total ketchup sales |
| | | Market share | Distribution | | |
			In stock	Out of stock	
Aug./Sept. 1964	30.8				27.2
Oct./Nov.	31.9	1.3	32	4	31.7
Dec./Jan. 1965	33.8	3.1	31	3	32.0
Feb./Mar.	31.7	3.4	50		33.2
Apr./May	32.4	2.8	38	17	31.9
June/July	33.4	3.9	35	6	
Aug./Sept.	36.1	3.5			32.2

Source: Company records.

EXHIBIT 12
ANALYSIS OF INCREMENTAL SALES FROM 26-OUNCE SIZE
The H. J. Heinz Company: III

| | Baltimore | | | | Remainder of zone | | | |
| | Before 26 oz | After 26 oz | Differ. | | Before 26 oz | After 26 oz | Differ. | |
			No.	%			No.	%
Average weekly shipments, thousands of cases								
20 oz	2,060	2,015	(45)	(2)	9,600	10,200	600	6
26 oz		850	850					
Total	2,060	2,865	805	39	9,600	10,200	600	6
Market share								
20 oz	12.1	12.0	(0.1)	(2)	15.0	16.6	1.6	11
26 oz		3.0	3.0					
Total	12.1	15.0	2.9	(24)	15.0	16.6	1.6	11

| **Incremental sales from 26 ounce** | | |
	Cases	Market share
Actual Baltimore sales	2,865,000	15.0
Est. sales without 26 oz	2,185,000 (+6%)	13.4 (+11%)
Gain	680,000	1.6

Source: Company records.

765

EXHIBIT 13
IMPROVEMENTS DESIRED IN USUAL BRAND
The H. J. Heinz Company: III

	Own usual brand				
	Total	Heinz	Hunt	Del Monte	Other
Hard to pour/need better way to get it out of bottle	4%	5%	1%	5%	3%
Put it in plastic container	1	2		4	1
Need better container	2	4		2	3
Make it sweeter		1			
Make it spicier	3	1	7	2	3
Make it less spicy					1
Make it less sweet					1
Improve the flavor	1	2	1	1	2
Make it thicker/not so watery	2		2	2	4
Make it thinner		1			
Make it easier to find in stores					1
Make it less expensive		1		1	
Miscellaneous		2		4	1
	13%	19%	11%	21%	20%

Note: Remainder of sample did not suggest improvements.
Source: Company records.

EXHIBIT 14
HUNT'S MARKET SHARE AND DISTRIBUTION BY PRODUCT
The H. J. Heinz Company: III

	14-ounce size only							
	Hunt regular		Hickory		Pizza		Snider and Pride of the Farm	
	Share	Dist.	Share	Dist.	Share	Dist.	Share	Dist.
Dec./Jan. 1965	12.5	68					3.2	42
Feb./Mar.	10.3	68	3.6	72	2.9	70	2.4	42
Apr./May	10.0	67	3.9	81	2.8	79	2.5	39
June/July	10.2	67	3.3	83	2.4	81	2.8	38
Aug./Sept.	7.3	67	2.8	83	1.9	81	2.0	37

Source: Company records.

THE UNITED STATES AUTOMOBILE INDUSTRY, EARLY 1975

NANCY J. DAVIS
Research Associate
Harvard Graduate School of Business Administration

STEVEN H. STAR
Associate Professor
Harvard Graduate School of Business Administration

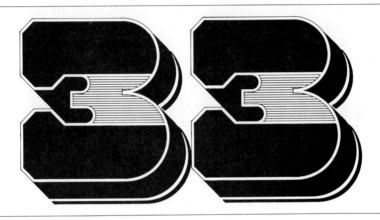

In late February 1975, top executives of General Motors Corporation, Ford Motor Company, Chrysler Corporation, and American Motors Corporation were trying to decide whether their respective companies should extend their program of consumer cash rebates which they had been running since mid-January. The rebate programs had become what *Time* magazine called "one of Detroit's rare full-dress fire sales." While most executives agreed that the program had been successful in reducing the industry's huge inventories, many felt that their cost did not justify their continuance. "We've spent a fortune on advertising alone and rebates have completely wiped out profits on some models," commented one executive. "If we keep that up, we'll be bankrupt, no matter how many cars we sell." "The rebate program has moved cars like no other program ever has," another executive countered. "If we don't continue it, we've got to come up with some equally effective sales tools. If we don't sell cars, there's obviously no way we can stay in business."

BACKGROUND

At the beginning of 1975, the United States economy was experiencing its most tumultuous state since the 1930s. The official jobless rate stood at 7.1 percent in December 1974, and it was expected to reach 8 percent in January. During 1974, inflation had wiped out more than 5 percent of the public's purchasing power. In the fourth quarter of 1974, real gross national product declined at an annual rate of 9.1 percent, and for calendar year 1974 it was 2.2 percent below its 1973 level, the sharpest drop in 28 years.

Probably no other industry contributed more to, and was more affected by, the troubled economy than the automobile industry. One out of every six United States workers depended on the industry for a living, either being employed directly by an auto manufacturer or by one of the thousands of firms that supplied auto parts, or working in the steel, glass, rubber, aluminum, copper, and plastics industries, all of which were closely tied to the auto industry. The industry had been responsible for half the fourth quarter's decline in GNP and was the major factor in the high unemployment rate. In Detroit's inner city areas, unemployment had skyrocketed to 23 percent, while in the city as a whole it was 9.1 percent. Pontiac, Michigan, 35 miles north of Detroit, had a 20.9 percent unemployment rate as a result of layoffs at three GM plants.

Statistics within the auto industry were grim. The 7.3 million cars sold at retail by the four United States automakers in 1974 represented a 25 percent drop from 1973's all-time high of 9.8 million units. Even imports, which had survived past slumps in relatively good shape, were off 20 percent. Compared with the poor final quarter of 1973, when the Arab oil embargo scared shoppers away from auto showrooms, United States auto sales for the fourth quarter of 1974 were down 30 percent. With almost a 3-month supply of new cars (i.e., approximately 1.7 million units) in dealer lots or in transit to them, the industry had been forced to shut 14 plants. Of the 750,000 people employed by the industry at the beginning of 1974, 100,000 hourly and 20,000 white-collar employees had been temporarily laid off, and another 100,000 had been permanently laid off. In sum, 1974 proved to be the worst year for the automakers since the recession year of 1958, when only 4.3 million cars were sold. (See Exhibit 1 for United States new car retail sales by corporation and make, 1965–1974, and Exhibit 2 for United States retail sales of imported cars by make, 1973 and 1974.)

Several reasons for the auto industry's problems were advanced. According to *Time* magazine, auto manufacturers, who in the past had been rightly vaunted for their marketing skills, had in recent years failed "to grasp and react swiftly enough to the changes taking place in their market." If the companies had taken more seriously the apparent desire for greater car safety and less polluting engines, *Time* said, they might have avoided the strict standards imposed by the government. According to industry estimates, meeting these standards added $499 to $600 to the price of a car.

Another problem, *Time* asserted, was that Detroit had not responded fast enough to the public's growing preference for small cars. Between 1965 and 1973, sales of small imported cars jumped 200 percent to 1.7 million units, and domestic subcompacts (described later) such as the Ford Pinto, the Chevrolet Vega, and the American Motors Gremlin increased in popularity. Nevertheless, Detroit continued increasing the size and power of the majority of its cars. Not until January 1974, in the midst of the "energy crisis" when small cars accounted for about 52 percent of sales, did United States auto manufacturers begin to switch their production to more moderate-size vehicles. By summer, small-car production was up, but the urgency was out of the energy crisis. Nevertheless, sales of big, high-profit cars were still lagging, while material costs were soaring, so manufacturers again stepped up production of small cars, frequently loading them with expensive equipment such as power seats and windows which formerly had been optional. With this price boost, the average list price of 1975 small models was about $1,000 above the comparable 1974 models. This represented about a 25 percent increase over 1974, while the average price of full-size models went up "only" 15 percent. The theory behind these increases was that consumers were more interested in fuel economy than sticker price. This theory proved to be fallacious, however, and small-car sales began to lag also. Manufacturers who had a glut of big cars during the energy crisis, wound up with an oversupply of small cars too.[1] (See Exhibit 3 for 1974 models' factory list prices or point-of-entry prices by general market classifications and make, and Exhibit 4 for 1975 models' factory list prices or point-of-entry prices by general market class and make.)

The federal government, dealers, and consumer groups repeatedly pointed to the higher prices of cars as the main reason for consumer apathy, and they pressed manufacturers to cut prices. Manufacturers countered with several arguments against price cuts. Industry analysts, they said, believed automobile sales would not respond to cuts or boosts because consumers, concerned about the economy, simply weren't buying. To support this point they cited Subaru,[2] whose December sales decreased 57 percent despite a $300 price cut, and Mazda,[2] whose December sales decreased 60 percent despite a $400 price cut.

[1] "Detroit's Gamble to Get Rolling Again," *Time*, Feb. 10, 1975, pp. 68–73.

[2] Subaru and Mazda were both Japanese subcompacts which had been introduced in the United States in the late sixties and had experienced considerable difficulty. Subaru's problems began when it initially introduced very lightweight models that did not meet United States safety standards, and they got worse when Japanese distributors failed to provide heavier cars for United States dealers as they had promised. Though Subaru's products and services were apparently improving, the company was having trouble changing the negative image it received as a result of these earlier problems. Mazda's problems had been due to its revolutionary rotary engine being far less efficient than had been predicted and to the car initially being marketed as a subcompact though its actual selling price was above the normal subcompact range.

The manufacturers also felt that a price cut could actually have a negative effect on sales because consumers would wonder what the companies did to cheapen their products, they would wait to see if prices would go still lower, and they would suspect that dealers really were not passing on the savings. They stated further that, once the sticker price was cut, it would be hard to raise it again, and virtually impossible to do so if federal price controls were again imposed.[1] Finally, some pointed out that, if the price cut did not work, it would be embarrassing to rescind it. The auto manufacturers were supported by Leonard Woodcock, president of the United Auto Workers Union, who asserted that auto profits were "razor thin" because of the sharp rise in materials costs and that there was "no basis [upon which] they can make any substantial downward movement in price."

Mr. Joseph M. Callahan, editor of *Automotive Industries*, cited uncertain future fuel availability and confusion about the 1975 cars as major factors contributing to consumers' reluctance to purchase cars. To support his argument, Callahan pointed to the question of whether catalytic converters[2] were good or bad and to Congress' cancellation of the ignition interlock system.[3] He thought that people assumed that, since Congress had backed down on this, it might do likewise with its requirements for costly pollution control and safety equipment.

Not only did the industry have problems as a result of its failure to satisfy consumers, but it was also faced with some very difficult production economics. With a total annual production capacity of 12 million units, it needed an annual "standard volume" of production of 9.6 million units to recover fixed costs, materials, and labor. Once it reached that goal, only variable costs were charged against each additional car, and profits soared disproportionately. Below that goal, profits dropped just as disproportionately. In early 1975, production was at an annual rate of only 6.5 million cars.[4]

Automakers cited other causes of their problem—high car-loan interest

---

[1] In August 1971, the federal government imposed a freeze on all salaries, wages, prices, and rents throughout the United States for 90 days. These sweeping controls were removed on November 13, but partial controls were maintained for a while, and to raise prices on many items, a company had to go through a lengthy process of petitioning the government's Price Commission and waiting for its approval.

[2] Catalytic converters were pollution control devices placed on many 1975 models. By late 1974, controversy had arisen about the converters' utility and safety as there was some evidence that the emissions produced by cars with converters were more dangerous to the environment than the emissions produced by cars without converters. Moreover, overheated particles from some catalytic converters were thought to have been responsible for some roadside brush fires.

[3] The ignition interlock system was a safety device which had been required for all 1974 cars. A car equipped with this device could not be started unless all passengers' seat belts were fastened, and if a seat belt were unfastened after the car was started, a loud buzzer sounded. Consumer reaction to the ignition interlock system was so negative that Congress had removed the requirement for the 1975 models.

[4] "Auto Rebates: A Financial Disaster for Detroit," *Business Week,* Mar. 10, 1975, pp. 72–73.

rates, costlier gasoline, and a shattering of consumer confidence by anti-inflation pronouncements from the Ford administration. Chrysler Chairman Lynn Townsend stated that since mid-1974 when President Ford advised Americans to buy less in an attempt to curb inflation, sales of automobiles had trended downward. "I would like to see something to counteract the 'don't buy' philosophy," Townsend commented. "I would like to see the President come out with a major program encouraging automotive sales."[1]

DEALERS

Not only were automobile dealers confronted with problems produced by the severe sales slump, but their problems were compounded by the high cost of financing inventories and by the overall tightening of money for new-car loans. The National Automobile Dealers Association (NADA) counseled dealers to whittle inventories to 30 days, to save where they could on financing, and to count on diversification into service, parts, and leasing to pull them through. Unfortunately, few took this advice, and by the end of the year they were saddled with very heavy inventories. (See Exhibit 5 for dealer inventories, January 1975 and February 1974 and 1975.) Soon after the 1975 models came out, dealers began pressuring manufacturers to cut prices. "The auto companies are pleading with everyone to do something for them—the government, the dealers, the public," commented Mr. Ed Mullane, head of the Ford Dealer Alliance. "Why don't they do something for themselves? The prices just aren't credible."[2]

As of January 1, 1975, there were 24,981 dealers handling new United States cars, a drop of 368 from January 1, 1974. This was substantially lower than the 5 percent dealer mortality rate which had been predicted in early 1974.

GENERAL MARKET CLASSIFICATIONS

In 1975 cars were divided into essentially four size categories—subcompact, compact, intermediate, and full—plus a separate category known as specialty/sports. Subcompacts were small cars which were especially convenient for around-town driving, short trips, and as second cars. Two adults were usually all subcompacts could carry comfortably. While the ride in subcompacts was usually rough and noisy, they normally cost less to run than larger cars. Imports had traditionally dominated this class, but in recent years United States manufacturers had begun to pursue it more aggressively. Imports held a 57.1 percent share in 1974, but this was down from 88.2 percent in 1970. By 1971 GM and Ford substantially increased their activity in this area, and by 1974 they held 17.9 and 19.4 percent of the category, respectively. AMC had concentrated a great deal of its efforts in this class, but by 1974 it still had only a 5.5 percent share.

[1] "The Recession Hits Hardest in Detroit," *Fortune*, December 1974, p. 33.

[2] "The Dealers Grab at Gimmicks," *Business Week*, Dec. 21, 1974, p. 24.

Most compacts could accommodate four adults reasonably comfortably, even though they were up to 3 feet shorter and 1 foot narrower than intermediates. Compacts were generally easy to maneuver, and they were considered a practical choice for a small family's only car. Imported compacts were generally much more expensive than domestic compacts. Chrysler Corporation took an early lead in the compact class with its Dodge Dart and Plymouth Valiant. With a 37.2 percent share, it maintained this lead in 1974. GM was second with 28.3 percent, Ford third with 19.2 percent, imports fourth with 8.3 percent, and AMC fifth with 7.0 percent. Since 1970 Ford's position in this category had steadily decreased while GM's had steadily increased.

On the average, intermediate-size cars were 1 foot shorter than full-size cars but only 1 or 2 inches narrower. Unlike compacts, intermediate four-door sedans were viable six-passenger cars, and intermediates usually had gas mileage comparable to similarly equipped compacts of the same make. There had been very little fluctuation in shares in the intermediate category since 1970. The most significant percentage change had been AMC's jump from a 2.5 percent share in 1973 to a 4.4 percent share in 1974. GM still held over half this market, as it had for several years. Ford was second with 26.6 percent and Chrysler third with 14.8 percent. Imports were not a factor in this category.

Full-size cars seated six adults and handled long trips with comparative ease. However, their bulk made them unwieldy in heavy traffic, and they usually consumed more fuel than intermediates. This category was subdivided into high-price cars (1975 retail price: $8,197–$21,307), medium-priced cars ($4,625–$6,529), and standard-price cars ($3,243–$5,465). GM was the undisputed market leader in full-size cars, with 70.0 percent of the high-price class, 69.5 percent of the medium-price class, and 50.8 percent of the standard-price class. Ford and Chrysler had gradually been losing share in the latter category over the last 5 years, and AMC was considered a minor contender with only a 1.6 percent market share in 1974. The only import in the full-size category was Mercedes-Benz with 11.2 percent of the high-price class.

The specialty/sports classification consisted primarily of subcompact- and compact-size cars with racy designs and larger engines. Though widely considered to be attractive in appearance, specialty/sports cars often gave noisy, rough rides and poor fuel economy. Since 1970, GM had held almost half the specialty/sports market. Ford appeared to be challenging GM in this area, however, as its share jumped from 25.1 percent in 1973 to 37.5 percent in 1974, while GM's dropped from 54.3 to 47.2 percent in the same period. Chrysler had never been very strong in the category, and by 1974 its share was only 2.4 percent, down from 9.8 percent in 1970. Similarly, AMC's share had dropped from 3.0 percent in 1970 to only 1.3 percent in 1974. In 1974 imports held an 11.6 percent share. (See Exhibit 6 for sales by general market class and make, 1970–1974, and Exhibit 7 for market shares by manufacturers and general market class, 1970–1974.)

Over the last 5 years, the market share held by full-size medium- and standard-price cars had dropped sharply, while the shares held by compacts, subcompacts, and foreign cars (most of which were compacts or subcompacts) climbed steadily. Intermediate-car shares had fallen somewhat, while shares held by full-size, high-price, and specialty/sports dropped somewhat in the early seventies but were increasing by 1973–1974. In 1974 the industry introduced eight new makes of specialty/sports cars.

In the sixties and early seventies, car prices closely paralleled car sizes, and to an extent that was still the case in 1975. However, because of the proliferation of models for any given make of car, there was a good deal of price overlap among the categories. For example, a subcompact loaded with expensive options might cost as much as a stripped-down model of a full-size, standard-price car.

GENERAL MOTORS CORPORATION

According to *Fortune* magazine, General Motors Corporation (GM) was the second largest firm in the United States in 1974. Factory unit sales of its five automotive divisions were 3,695,532, a 27.2 percent drop from 1973 levels. Its 1974 earnings of $950 million were 60 percent below 1973 earnings, and in January 1975 its board voted to reduce the quarterly dividend from 85 to 60 cents. It was rumored that top GM executives did not receive bonuses for 1974. In January 1975, out of a work force of 420,000 people, 92,000 employees were on indefinite layoff and another 40,000 were expected to be placed on temporary layoff sometime during the first quarter.

GM President Elliott M. (Pete) Estes stated that GM's major problems had been with its small car lines. He said that the company had made major investments in designing and producing small cars, but that it did not know how to sell them. The resulting oversupply of small cars had been responsible for most of GM's layoffs, Estes said. Estes further described GM's situation as of early January 1975 as follows:

> We're selling to dealers at the same rate we're building, which is about 16,000 cars and trucks a day now as opposed to our normal capacity of about 25,000 a day. Our dealers have about a 90-day supply of cars on hand, whereas our competitors are as high as 140 days. In some larger car lines, we actually have shortages. For example, Cadillac dealers only have about a 15-day supply of cars.[1]

At the beginning of 1974, GM products were sold by 11,860 dealers through a total of 17,320 franchises. The total number of franchises by GM division was as follows:

Chevrolet	6,060
Pontiac	3,275
Oldsmobile	3,325
Buick	3,040
Cadillac	1,620
Total franchises	17,320

[1] "The View from the GM Building," *Forbes*, Feb. 1, 1975, p. 13.

In 1974 GM averaged 213 sales per franchise and 310 sales per dealer versus 291 sales per franchise and 421 sales per dealer in 1973. In terms of sales per dealer, Chevrolet led the individual makes in the industry for the fourth consecutive year with 332 sales per outlet. Oldsmobile was fifth with 158, Pontiac sixth with 151, Buick eighth with 141, and Cadillac ninth with 138.

FORD MOTOR COMPANY

Ford Motor Company, the nation's second largest automobile manufacturer, had 1974 factory sales of 2,214,658 units, down 17.1 percent from 1973 levels. Profits for 1974 were $36 million, 60 percent below 1973 profits. Thanks to some tax credits, Ford showed a $22-million profit in the fourth quarter of 1974, but on a pretax basis, it lost $46 million during that quarter. By early January, 87,000 of its 178,000 employees had been laid off, and it had closed 10 of its 14 car assembly plants, 7 of its 9 truck assembly plants, and 5 of its 46 parts plants.

Like GM, Ford was experiencing major difficulty with its small-car lines. On January 10, its inventory of small cars stood at 144 days, and its total dealer inventories were about 700,000 units. It was thought that Ford executives did not receive bonuses for 1974.[1] Chairman Henry Ford II had warned back in November that the nation was headed for a depression, and in early January he announced flatly, "This year is going to be terrible."[2]

In 1974 the Ford Motor Company had 6,706 dealers and 10,089 franchises. The number of franchises by division were as follows:

Ford	5,620
Lincoln	1,565
Mercury	2,904
Total franchises	10,089

In 1974 Ford averaged 220 sales per franchise and 330 sales per dealer as opposed to 266 sales per franchise and 399 sales per dealer in 1973. The Ford Division ranked second in the industry with 318 sales per outlet; the Mercury Division was tenth with 117 sales per outlet; and the Lincoln Division was eleventh with 56 sales per outlet.

CHRYSLER CORPORATION

With 1974 sales of $11 billion, Chrysler was the eleventh largest United States manufacturer. In 1973, it had earnings of $255 million, and it had been the country's fourth largest company, but in 1974, it reported a shocking $52 mil-

[1] *Wall Street Journal,* Jan. 13, 1975.

[2] "Detroit's Gamble to Get Rolling Again," *Time,* Feb. 10, 1975, pp. 68–73.

lion loss, by far the biggest in its 50-year history. The worst damage hit in the fourth quarter when sales and production were running far under the company's break-even level of 275,000 cars per quarter. During this quarter, the company lost $73.5 million. For the first time since 1938, the board voted to omit the 35-cent quarterly dividend. Top executives took pay cuts, and cost-of-living allowances and employee stock savings programs for middle-level managers were suspended.

Chrysler's difficulties stemmed in part from the fact that it had only six auto assembly plants in the United States and therefore could not tune its production as closely to actual sales as could GM (which had 23 assembly plants) and Ford (14 plants). The company had to build relatively larger inventories than its rivals early in each new-model year so that dealers would have enough cars to sell. If its market projections were wrong, the results could be disastrous. Early in 1974, Chrysler, like other automakers, planned production according to the widespread forecasts of a year-end economic upturn. But the economy turned down, and Chrysler was caught with a massive 135-day backlog (i.e., 340,000 units) of unsold cars by the year's end. In an attempt to reduce that inventory, which was costing Chrysler dealers $2 million a week to finance, Chrysler substantially slowed production by temporarily closing three of its six plants and laying off 77,300 of its 155,000 employees.

Chrysler was also thought to have some fundamental problems with market strategy. For example, in the 1960s, it almost matched GM in sheer model proliferation, but in the 1970s it was slow to meet the growing small-car market. Its Valiant and Dart together had the largest share of compact-car sales, but in 1974 the company's biggest product investment was in a costly redesign of its full-size cars. It had also invested heavily in designing three new compacts which were scheduled to be introduced in the fall of 1975.

In 1974 Chrysler had 5,143 dealers and a total of 9,873 franchises. Its franchises broke down by division as follows:

Chrysler Division	3,359
Dodge Division	3,123
Plymouth Division	3,391
Total franchises	9,873

In 1974 Chrysler averaged 120 sales per franchise and 229 sales per dealer versus 151 sales per franchise and 284 sales per dealer in 1973. The Plymouth Division ranked third in the industry with 176 sales per outlet, the Dodge Division seventh with 149, and the Chrysler Division ranked last in the industry with only 36 sales per outlet. There were virtually no exclusive Chrysler Division dealerships. Rather, the division's products were almost always sold by dealers who also had a Plymouth Division franchise.

AMERICAN MOTORS CORPORATION

Because of its emphasis on the small, economy-car market, American Motors Corporation (AMC) suffered less during 1974 than did other United States manufacturers. During the first half of the year, when consumers were scrambling for small cars, its unit sales increased 15 percent while total domestic car sales dropped 21 percent. However, in September, the company was hit by a 3-week strike, and when full production resumed in October, AMC's inventory of unsold cars ballooned from a 47-day supply to a 115-day supply, or 72,000 vehicles, by December 1. According to an AMC executive, all but "several thousand" were on dealer lots. For 1974 AMC's sales were 15 percent below its 1973 sales. In early January, dealers were selling at an annual rate of only 200,000 units, though the company had to move an estimated 300,000 units annually just to break even.

To work off the inventories, AMC planned to shut down its plants for a week in January. Commenting on AMC's position, Chairman Roy D. Chapin, Jr., said, "A year ago this time, the small-car market was beyond all bounds of comprehension. We're suffering by comparison with the fact that we were selling everything we could churn out the door."[1]

In 1974, AMC's best-selling line was its compact, the Hornet. AMC's 1975 line consisted of the Gremlin in the subcompact category, the Hornet and Pacer in the compact category, and the Matador in the intermediate-size category. In all there were 17 models of these cars. During 1974, AMC had spent $60 million developing the Pacer. The Pacer was unveiled in mid-January 1975 and was scheduled to be in dealer showrooms by March 1. Designed with a sloping front that cut aerodynamic drag, the four-passenger vehicle had more headroom in back than a Continental Mark IV. The door on the passenger side was 4 inches longer than the driver's, an innovation aimed at facilitating entry to the back seat. The car's most striking feature was an abundance of glass—5,600 square inches versus the 3,300 of most compacts, and more than the Cadillac Eldorado. The Pacer claimed a 23-mile-per-gallon performance, and was priced at $3,299. AMC's projected 1975 sales of the Pacer were 70,000 units.

For the future, AMC executives were predicting that federal action to limit gasoline consumption would spur renewed interest in small cars and that this would again boost AMC sales. However, GM, Ford, and Chrysler were also stepping up their efforts in this market and were expected to pose serious competition for AMC. *Business Week* magazine speculated that "a weakened Chrysler may decide, as AMC has, to concentrate all its efforts on small cars," and it stated that GM and Ford were pouring a lot of money into programs to make larger cars more economical.[2]

In 1974 AMC had 1,862 dealers. Since these dealers handled all AMC lines, sales per franchise and sales per dealer were the same. AMC averaged

[1] "AMC Gambles $60 million on a New Compact," *Business Week,* Jan. 20, 1975, pp. 76–78.

[2] Ibid.

176 sales per outlet in 1974 versus 205 in 1973. At 176, it was tied with Plymouth for the third position in the industry.

FOREIGN CARS

At the beginning of the year, it looked as if 1974 would be a prosperous year for importers, with buyers flocking to showrooms when gasoline became scarce. However, the demand was so great that importers, with their car sources thousands of miles away, could not meet it. "In the midst of the buying mania, distribution fell apart, and by the time cars arrived, the market psychology was to buy nothing," one importer commented.[1] By the end of one year, sales of imported cars had dropped to a 4 year low. The total for the year was 1,389,323, down 20.39 percent from 1973 sales. However, market penetration for imports climbed to an all-time high of 16 percent. As in 1973, Volkswagen, Toyota, and Datsun held the top three positions.

Volkswagen's United States sales were about 30 percent below the 1973 level, and it was said to be losing money on each United States sale, even though it had boosted the price of the Beetle by nearly 50 percent in 2 years. (In January 1975, the Beetle sold for $2,895.) Over the last few years, VW had spent $2 billion on a major overhaul of its line. As a part of the process of changing to front-engine, front-wheel-drive autos, VW had dropped several older, rear-engine models and added three new models—the $4,295 Dasher, the $4,450 Scirocco, and the $2,995 Rabbit. Despite these new models, VW expected its 1975 sales in the United States to be down another 5 percent partly because of price increases of 7.9 to 10.3 percent on 1975 models, even though these increases were in line with other importers and United States manufacturers. In 1974, the United States had accounted for about 33 percent of VW's total sales. During that year, the company lost over $200 million, the first deficit it had shown since World War II. In recent months, VW's six West German plants had been operating at 60 percent of capacity, and nearly 80 percent of its 109,000 West German work force had been laid off.[2]

Japanese manufacturers were looking to export markets to help them survive the recession in Japan, where domestic car sales had decreased 30 percent in 1974. In 1974 total Japanese auto production had decreased only 10 percent, and there was talk of keeping it at that level in 1975 and of increasing exports from the 1974 level of one-third of production to one-half of production in 1975. Some felt that this was not an especially wise decision, however, because in the first 7 months of 1974, shipments of Japanese cars to the United States were 40 percent ahead of sales. Total Japanese exports to the United States were 999,577 in 1974, up 21.4 percent over 1973. Most Japanese manufacturers had increased prices several times during 1974.

Toyota, which sold 238,135 cars in the United States in 1974, 17.7 per-

---

[1] "Imports Shift to the Hard Sell," *Business Week,* Sept. 7, 1974, pp. 19–20.

[2] "Germany: VW Moves to Stem Its Overseas Losses," *Business Week,* Dec. 21, 1974, p. 25.

cent less than in 1973, had decided to deemphasize sales of its popular Corona model and to begin pushing the Corolla, which competed more directly with Chevrolet's Vega and Ford's Pinto. The Corolla sold for about $2,300, but Toyota management was planning a new lower-powered model which would sell for less.

Nissan Motor Corporation, manufacturer of Datsun, sold 185,162 cars in the United States in 1974, 19.9 percent less than in 1973. During 1974, there had been some problems between Datsun dealers in the United States and distributors in Japan. Dealers alleged that Nissan was using the United States as a dumping ground for automobiles unsalable in Japan, and they offered documented proof of severe maldistribution in eastern parts of the United States and within the New York area. They stated that Datsun dealers had been suffering from continuously inadequate supplies of certain models and that they had repeatedly been shipped unwanted models. They said that Nissan had never been able to supply non-West Coast dealers with enough cars to fulfill its commitments to them. Early in 1975, however, there was an oversupply of Datsuns in the United States, and Nissan was considering appointing new dealers. Retail prices on 1975 Datsuns ranged from $2,849 to $6,465, about 14 percent higher than 1974 prices.

The auto manufacturer which was weathering the recession better than any other was West Germany's Daimler-Benz, manufacturer of Mercedes-Benz. In 1974 it closed no plants and put no employees on short time. Rather, it recorded a 7 percent sales gain, to $5.4 billion, its earnings fell only a bit below 1973's $111.4 million, and its 1975 output was expected to equal 1974. Its return on stockholder's equity was 14 percent, down from the 20 percent in the late sixties but considerably higher than any other auto manufacturer. Daimler-Benz executives stated that their success was due to their taking a longer-range view than was customary in the automobile industry. They said they had not believed the world auto boom of the late sixties could last forever, and they simply refused to expand as fast as demand would have permitted, in spite of pressure from their dealers. "We did not want to make Mercedes-Benz into a mass producer," one executive commented.

In 1974 Daimler-Benz produced 340,000 cars, about 40,000 of which were shipped to the United States where they retailed for from $9,357 to $21,307. Recognizing that their cars were becoming extremely costly, Mercedes executives had begun speaking of them as "an investment." For the future, the company was concentrating on diesel engines rather than on model changes. It expected that the compact exterior, large interior, distinctive image, and economy of operation would keep demand high. It was widely held that Mercedes had replaced Cadillac as the "most desirable" car, and when Ford President Lee Iacocca introduced the Granada and the Monarch, he told the press, "This is a Mercedes."[1]

---

[1] "The Realist," *Forbes,* Jan. 15, 1975, pp. 22–23.

INDUSTRY ACTIONS BEFORE
THE REBATE PROGRAM

By the fall of 1974, it was apparent that the 1975 models had elicited very little enthusiasm from American consumers. Auto manufacturers began to try a wide variety of tactics which they hoped would stimulate sales. "Buy-a-car" buttons and bumper stickers suddenly appeared all over Detroit. In early November, Richard C. Gerstenberg, then chairman of GM, put his name to a series of ads that ran in more than 300 newspapers, appealing to Americans to buy cars to help the economy. Also in November, Ford cut the price of the Pinto $150 by lowering the base price and substituting lower-priced tires for the radial tires it had previously put on the car.

In early December, 13 San Diego Ford dealers received 150 specially ordered Pintos in red, white, or blue, put on "inflation fighter" decals, and dressed their salespeople in red blazers and blue slacks. By mid-December, not many of the cars had been sold, but dealers had increased their floor traffic, and the morale of their salespeople was said to be higher. An Atlanta Toyota dealer began to give away Christmas trees to people who came in for a demonstration drive, and one Lansing Chrysler dealer sent out thousands of mailings to past customers and had his salespeople telephone people selected randomly from the telephone book.

On December 12, the governor of Michigan, top executives of Ford, GM, AMC, and Chrysler, plus Leonard Woodcock, president of the United Auto Workers, met for 90 minutes with President Ford. During this meeting, they asked the President to jolt the public into buying cars by cutting taxes, to grant a one-shot investment tax credit, to freeze present auto antipollution and safety standards for 5 years, to come up with some "highly visible" innovations to restore public confidence in the economy, to remove federal excise tax from trucks, to encourage the Federal Reserve Board to loosen credit, to provide more public service jobs, and to extend unemployment benefits to auto workers who had been laid off.[1]

Early in January, GM and Ford instituted similar sales incentive programs. GM's program covered Chevrolet Vegas and Novas, Buick Apollos and Skylarks, Pontiac Venturas and Astres, and Oldsmobile Omegas. A salesperson had to sell one of any of these models to qualify, and thereafter he got $75 for the second and third sales and $100 for every sale beginning with the fourth. Where two lines were involved, sales could not be combined. Thus, a Chevrolet salesperson had to sell four Novas to qualify for $100 per Nova and four Vegas to earn $100 per Vega. Under Ford's program, salespeople received $50 for selling two Pintos or Mustang IIs, $125 for selling three or four, $250 for selling five or six, $500 for selling up to ten, and $1,000 plus a watch for selling fifteen. The only catch was the first four or five cars had to be 1974 leftovers. Both GM and Ford were also said to be considering lower-priced, stripped-down versions of their smaller cars.[2]

---

[1] *Wall Street Journal,* Dec. 13, 1974.

[2] *Wall Street Journal,* Jan. 7, 1975.

THE REBATE PROGRAMS

On Sunday, January 12, Chrysler Corporation announced its Car Clearance Carnival in television commercials during the Super Bowl game. The Car Clearance Carnival worked as follows: Each week, certain Chrysler cars and/or trucks were designated for a rebate. After negotiating the showroom price with a dealer, a customer buying or leasing an eligible smaller car such as the Dodge Dart received a $200 rebate directly from Chrysler. If he purchased or leased a designated larger car such as a New Yorker, he received a $300 rebate. In addition, if he traded in a specified model he received another $100.

New and used cars changed continually during the program, which was initially scheduled to run until February 16. Order dates, not delivery dates, determined eligibility. The Chrysler cars and their rebates were announced each Sunday to the public via the electronic media and to dealers by Mailgram. The trade-in model for which the customer could receive the extra $100 changed twice weekly. "The weekly specials are not predetermined," said Peter Dow, Chrysler's director of advertising. "We expect as we go along to answer the customers' desires in the marketplace."[1] For the first week, Chrysler's specials were the Plymouth Duster, the Dodge Dart Swinger, and the 1974 Colt, and the trade-in models through Wednesday, January 15, were the Ford Pinto and Chevrolet Vega. (See Exhibit 8 for details of rebated cars throughout Chrysler's program.)

The 5-week program was expected to cost $10 million for both rebates and advertising. Joe Garagiola, former baseball player and current television sports newscaster, appeared in ads in a carnival setting and urged viewers to "hurry, hurry, hurry to the nearest Chrysler dealer." (See Exhibit 9 for storyboards of Chrysler's TV ads, and Exhibit 10 for print ads run by various manufacturers during the rebate period.) Chrysler Chairman Lynn Townsend predicted the Carnival "will be a most effective stimulus to an automotive market which is so important to the economic well-being of this nation." He also called for the federal government to provide an immediate income tax cut, a 5-year hold on safety and emission standards, and car-financing credit to commercial banks and finance companies.[2]

As soon as Chrysler announced its rebate plan, companies which supplied Chrysler with auto parts also started offering rebates. For example, Warner Electric Brake and Clutch Company announced it would give $100 to any of its employees who bought a Chrysler product before May 1. Robert McInnis, vice president of Imerman Screw Products Company, announced a similar program and commented, "If this thing gets started, we can turn this economy right around."[3] By the end of the first week, at least 23 firms doing business with Chrysler were offering rebates.

During the first 10 days of the Carnival, all the Big Four registered gains,

---

[1] *Automotive News,* Jan. 13, 1975.

[2] Ibid.

[3] "Autos: A Bold Bid for Sales," *Newsweek,* Jan. 20, 1975, p. 63.

and their combined sales were up 41 percent over the January 1–10 period. Sales were down 15.4 percent from the comparable period in 1973, a substantial improvement from recent months when they had lagged by 25 to 35 percent. Chrysler's jump was the most dramatic. According to Townsend, Chrysler dealers sold 3,200 units the first day. For the January 11–20 period, Chrysler reported 23,608 new cars sold, up 89.35 percent from its January 1–10 sales. Sales of its Valiant and Dart models set an all-time record for the period. Late in the second week of the Carnival, Chrysler announced that during the third week, all but one of its six United States assembly plants would be open for the first time in 3 months. Shortly thereafter, Chrysler executives announced that Chrysler's inventories had dropped from 350,000 to 300,000 units and that it was extending its Carnival through February 28.[1]

Ford's immediate reaction to Chrysler's announcement was a newspaper ad on January 14 which said:

> You've probably heard about the weekly specials—with limited time discounts— being announced by Chrysler on some compacts. Ford offers a compact with a low price that doesn't end this week. Maverick. Sticker price at least $303 less than a comparably equipped Plymouth Duster. $250 less than a Dodge Dart Swinger. That's sticker price value . . . even before you talk to your Ford dealer.

Ford continued promoting sales through its dealer cash-incentive program instituted earlier.

In spite of this initial stance, on January 16, Ford announced that it too was instituting a rebate program which would run from January 18 through February 28. Under this program, Ford paid the rebates shown in Table 1.

According to Ford ad manager Ray Ablondi, the Ford Division alone would match or top Chrysler's $10 million advertising and promotion expenditures. As was the case with Chrysler, television was Ford's major advertising vehicle, though newspapers, weekly news magazines, and radio were also used heavily. Celebrities like Green Bay Packer coach Bart Starr often appeared in

---

[1] *Automotive News,* Jan. 27, 1975.

TABLE 1

Cars	1974 model final price	1975 model list price	Rebate
1975 Pinto	$2,579	$2,919	$200
1975 Maverick	2,790	3,025	200
1975 Comet	2,849	3,113	200
1975 Mustang II hardtop	3,134	3,529	300
1975 Mach I	3,674	4,265	500
1975 Ghia	3,481	3,938	500
1974 Capri	3,900	4,450	500
1975 Supercab pickup trucks	NA	4,010	350

TABLE 2

Cars	1974 model final price	1975 model list price	Rebates
Chevrolet Vega	$2,505	$2,799	$200
Chevrolet Nova	2,811	3,218	200
Pontiac Astre	NA	3,092	200
Pontiac Ventura	2,892	3,306	200
Oldsmobile Omega	3,043	3,435	200
Buick Apollo	3,037	3,476	200
Buick Skylark	3,037	3,476	200
Chevrolet Monza	3,371	3,966	500
Oldsmobile Starfire	3,533	4,157	500
Buick Skyhawk	3,558	4,186	500

Ford's ads. Ford's theme was "Ford breaks things wide open with no-nonsense cash rebates, no complicated deals."

GM's initial response to Chrysler's Car Carnival was to announce that GM was not considering reductions or rebates but that customers who took delivery of a 1975 GM vehicle between January 13 and March 1 would be protected in the event that any future price reductions occurred. It continued promoting cars through its dealer incentive plan instituted earlier in January. Moreover, Chevrolet ads proclaimed that it already had low-priced cars. Nevertheless, on Monday, January 20, with approximately a 90-day inventory on hand, GM announced that it would pay the rebates shown in Table 2, retroactive to January 13 and running through February 28.

AMC held out the longest, asserting that its new Pacer would generate so much showroom traffic that it would not have to roll back prices or offer other incentives and that by offering a second year of its warranty, the Buyer Protection Plan, free, it had in effect given a $100 price cut. Nevertheless, on Tuesday, January 21, AMC announced that, until February 28, it would offer the rebates listed in Table 3. The AMC customer could take the full refund in cash or in combination with the $99 Buyer Protection Plan.[1] Buyers of cars not included in the rebate program continued to receive the 12-month warranty without cost.

[1] AMC's Buyer Protection Plan was a warranty which covered virtually everything on an AMC car. The warranty was given to the customer free for the first 12 months, and he had the option to purchase it for the second 12 months for $99.

TABLE 3

Cars	1974 model final price	1975 model list price	Rebates
Gremlin	$2,481	$2,798	$200
Hornet	2,774	3,074	200
Hornet X	2,794	3,212	400
Hornet DL	3,055	3,512	400
Matador	2,850	3,276	300
Matador Cassini*	3,212	3,692	600

* The Matador Cassini carried a $300 option.

None of the foreign car manufacturers participated in the rebate program. "We feel that as soon as the price of gasoline is increased or we have rationing, a hard-hitting Datsun ad campaign will give us pretty good business," said one Datsun executive early in February. He said that Datsun's B-210 model had placed first in the Environmental Protection Agency's fuel ratings, with 27 miles per gallon in city driving and 39 on the highway. At that time, Datsun dealers had a 4-month supply of cars.

When a VW executive was asked if his company might offer rebates, he replied, "We have two all-new models, the Rabbit and Scirocco, with a built-in rebate of thirty-eight miles to the gallon." Fiat and Mercedes-Benz both said that they had been enjoying good sales right along and felt no need to offer special incentives or rebates. Honda was running a dealer incentive whereby 50 of its 350 United States dealers would win trips to Japan, and Volvo was sponsoring a program under which dealers could earn anywhere from $25 to $300 per unit.

Toyota was offering more incentives than any other importer. Its January–February "Get It On" program offered a $200 cash rebate to dealers on every 1975 Corolla they sold. The dealer could use the $200 in any way he saw fit. Toyota's second program also covered the Corolla. Under it, Toyota paid $15 for every $25 the dealer put up to pay salespeople cash or merchandise of up to $40 per Corolla sold. Toyota's third program, which was scheduled to run until March 31, offered 171 trips to Japan, Rio de Janeiro, or Copenhagen to Toyota's 950 dealers.[1] Commenting on the rebate program, Mr. Norman D. Lean, vice president and general operations manager of Toyota, said, "We've taken a good look at what success Pinto, Mazda, and Subaru have had, and none of them have had much luck in the marketplace. It didn't work for them, so I don't see any reason why Toyota should try the same thing."[2]

DEALERS' REACTION TO THE REBATE PROGRAM

During the first week of the Chrysler Car Carnival, Chrysler dealers were generally enthusiastic. "The showroom is like a circus, and the phone doesn't stop ringing," one New York dealer commented.[3] At a dealer meeting in Chicago, Al Wagner, Chrysler's Chicago zone manager, said the Chicago zone had been selling about 100 cars a day, but that the zone had sold 300 a day the first two days of the Carnival. One dealer said the Carnival had "helped traffic all up and down my street. People will leave my dealership and stop at the Chevy place across the street." Another said, "It has gotten people thinking about buying cars again, which they had not been doing." One of the most positive responses came from a Detroit dealer:

Spectacular would be an understatement. It's working. People are buying half specials and half other cars. We're making them offers they can't refuse—like, we'll

[1] *Automotive News,* Feb. 10, 1975.

[2] *Advertising Age,* Jan. 20, 1975.

[3] "Autos: A Bold Bid for Sales," *Newsweek,* Jan. 20, 1975, p. 63.

throw another $100 into the pot on any compact sold during the program. These buyers have been sitting on the fence for a while. They've been waiting for something to happen.

A more cautious dealer stated that his showroom traffic was up, but that "you have to be careful when you get a bunch of auto dealers together. What they say and what they do can be two different things. They certainly aren't going to say their traffic is down." One disgruntled dealer commented, "Sure, it's going to help traffic. It can't get worse."[1]

During the second week of the Carnival, January 19–25, the annual NADA convention was held in San Francisco. Attendance at this meeting was 3,200, off from 4,500 in 1974, and a tour to Mexico and a golf tournament planned in Hawaii were canceled for lack of applicants. Dealers interviewed at this meeting showed mixed opinions about the rebates. On the surface, there was plenty of enthusiasm. But many dealers voiced concern that the rebate schemes were too small to stimulate sales substantially, that they would have only a very brief impact on sales, and that they might simply be borrowing ahead on sales they would make in the spring anyway. "I just don't think rebates of $200 will change the course of the automotive history this year," commented one dealer.[2]

As the programs progressed, dealers expressed a wide variety of complaints about them. Some Chrysler dealers felt the fact that Chrysler's rebate models changed weekly made potential buyers postpone purchases, hoping their favorite model would be the next rebate special. Some dealers felt that rebated cars actually hurt sales of more-profitable, nonrebated cars, and they pointed to the fact that sales of their nonrebated lines were still running behind 1974 figures. Another problem, according to some dealers, was that rebates had been so successful in the beginning in cleaning out inventories that they were now causing aggravation because cars weren't there when people wanted them. Though some dealers were glad they did not have to get involved directly with rebates, others complained that it looked like the company didn't trust them. Still other dealers criticized the plans because they primarily covered small cars. (Only Chrysler's plan included full-size cars.) Some dealers complained that the rebates had not been large enough and that they had been forced to increase customer discounts by cutting into their own profits. Other dealers, however, had stiffened up prices, sold at full list, and increased per-car profits by $50 to $100.[3]

---

[1] *Advertising Age,* Jan. 20, 1975.

[2] "Mixed Reviews for Price Rebates," *Business Week,* Feb. 3, 1975, pp. 14–15.

[3] "Auto Rebates: A Financial Disaster for Detroit," *Business Week,* Mar. 10, 1975.

RESULTS OF THE REBATE PROGRAMS
AS OF FEBRUARY 24, 1975

By mid-February, questions about the effectiveness of the rebate programs and what should be done on March 1 when the programs were scheduled to end were widely discussed. Data for the four reporting periods thus far affected by rebates showed that sales had been quite volatile. During the January 11–20 period when only Chrysler and Ford were offering rebates, total industry sales were up 40 percent over the previous period. During the January 21–31 period, the first period during which all four United States manufacturers offered rebates, sales skyrocketed to 238,324 units, 82 percent higher than during the previous period. However, during the February 1–10 reporting period, sales dropped 42 percent below the January 21–31 level. For the February 11–20 period, sales went back up, reaching 193,683 units, only 210 units below the comparable total in 1974. 1975 sales still trailed comparable 1974 sales by about 10 percent, but that was an improvement from the 30 to 50 percent declines reported for most periods since the 1975 models were introduced in September 1974. Industry analysts estimated that the rebates had boosted showroom traffic by at least 50 percent and had whittled the industry's mountainous inventory of unsold cars by 8 or 9 percent. (See Exhibit 11 for sales by manufacturer and make by reporting period, Exhibit 12 for sales by general market class and make by reporting period, and Exhibit 13 for sales by model for each reporting period.)

Balanced against the program's success in moving cars was its considerable cost. Industry executives refused to be exact about these costs, often claiming that they really did not know them. But industry analysts estimated that the Big Four spent about $100 million in total advertising, rebate, and other expenses. During the February 11–20 period, rebates had boosted sales to 7.6 million units on an annual basis. However, many industry analysts did not expect this rate to continue, and they felt that it was still not adequate to result in higher production and more efficiencies as the manufacturers had hoped it would be. According to Arjay Miller, dean of the Stanford Business School and former president of Ford, at mid-February operating levels, a 10 percent price cut would require a 50 percent sales increase just for the auto companies to break even. Throughout the industry, there was widespread suspicion that rebated sales were only borrowing from sales that would have been made later in the year. In a spot check of 300 Vega purchasers, 34 percent said they would have bought later in the year and moved up purchases because of rebates, and only 23 percent said they had not planned to buy a car in 1975 before the rebate program.[1]

At Ford, February 11–20 sales were down 10.04 percent from comparable 1974 sales but up 51.82 percent from the January 11–20, 1975, sales period. Mr. John B. Naughton, Ford's vice president of sales, stated that Ford's massive

[1] Ibid.

rebate program had been very effective in getting people into showrooms, and that reduction in dealer inventory had been so great that Ford would boost production in March about 65 percent over its February production. The sales data which Naughton cited were dramatic—more Capris sold at wholesale in 72 hours than in the previous 30 days and Mustang stocks falling from 160 to 58 days.

However, Naughton did not favor extending the rebate program. "Rebates are like dope. You've got to get off it," he commented. One reason for not extending the program was cost, Naughton said, but he went on to say that Ford did not know the cost. "Even though it has been very successful in getting our stocks down, it has cost us a ton of money to do it," he said. He claimed that Ford made an average pretax profit of only $150 per car: "You can't stay in business long giving away $200 a car when you're only making $150 a car." He thought Ford might extend its Ford Close Look Value Check which it had tested in January in three cities. This was a traffic-building promotion offering Ford purchasers a chance at prizes up to $3,000.[1]

Chrysler's February 11–20 sales were 13.47 percent below comparable 1974 sales. However, they were 30.29 percent above January 11–20, 1975 sales, and Chrysler executives were confident that, by the beginning of March, the company could recall about 8,000 workers and reopen all its plants. They estimated that the company's factory float would be reduced from 80,000 in mid-January to 20,000 by March 1. On 80,000 cars worth roughly $270 million, carrying costs had been running nearly $2.2 million per month, based on short-term interest rates of 8 to 10 percent. So by moving 60,000 cars out to dealers, Chrysler saved about $1.7 million. Chrysler executives also thought that their dealers' inventories would stand at the industry average of about 90 days by March 1.[2]

Industry analysts estimated that when Chrysler's advertising campaign was combined with the rebates and other expenses, the total cost of its Carnival would approximate $25 million.[3] They thought further that Chrysler's current quarterly production rate was about 140,000 cars, substantially below the company's break-even level of 275,000 cars.[4]

At AMC, Executive Sales Director Eugene V. Amoroso noted that rebates had touched off a sales upswing and said, "Our dealers are most pleased. If there's a second round we'll be in it. We'll keep our dealers competitive."[5] However, Chapin admitted that AMC was not making any money on rebated cars, and AMC President William Luneburg expressed concern that the rebates were destroying the industry's credibility with the public. "Last fall the industry

---

[1] *Automotive News*, Feb. 17, 1975.

[2] "Auto Rebates: A Financial Disaster for Detroit," *Business Week*, Mar. 10, 1975.

[3] Ibid.

[4] "Another Chrysler Crunch," *Time*, Mar. 3, 1975, pp. 29–30.

[5] *Automotive News*, Feb. 3, 1975.

said it needed a price increase because of rising costs, and this is still true," he said. "People must think we're crazy, incompetent, or that we keep two sets of books."[1]

During the three periods GM had been participating in the program, its sales had shown consistent increases over the previous year. This had not been the case during the first two periods of 1975, and some GM executives felt that the company should continue rebates to keep sales up. "The steady improvement in new-car sales levels is matched by dealer reports of continuing resurgence in buyer interest," said Mack Worden, GM marketing vice president.

Mr. Robert Lund, general manager of GM's Chevrolet Division, freely expressed his distaste for rebates:

> Chrysler was the first with the five-year, 50,000-mile warranty, and it took a long time to come out of the disruptions caused by that. Then they initiated fleet leasing discounts. Now it's rebates. I hope the rebates aren't long term because they disrupt our relationship with the dealer and his with the consumer.[2]

[1] *Ward's Automotive World,* March 1975.

[2] Ibid.

EXHIBIT 1
UNITED STATES NEW CAR RETAIL SALES BY CORPORATION AND MAKE, 1965–1974
The United States Automobile Industry, Early 1975

	1965 Units	1965 %	1966 Units	1966 %	1967 Units	1967 %	1968 Units	1968 %	1969 Units	1969 %
General Motors Corp.										
Chevrolet	2,424,358	26.0	2,158,811	23.9	1,978,758	23.6	2,060,249	21.9	2,060,202	21.8
Pontiac	831,448	8.9	830,856	9.2	834,146	9.9	877,382	9.3	795,605	8.4
Oldsmobile	608,930	6.5	580,550	6.4	551,274	6.5	624,262	6.6	642,889	6.8
Buick	608,620	6.5	569,131	6.3	565,313	6.8	627,159	6.7	677,319	7.2
Cadillac	189,661	2.0	196,498	2.2	209,546	2.5	205,593	2.2	243,905	2.6
Total	4,663,017	49.9	4,335,846	48.0	4,139,037	49.3	4,394,645	46.7	4,419,920	46.8
Ford Motor Co.										
Ford	1,998,385	21.5	1,991,520	22.1	1,520,711	18.2	1,803,271	19.2	1,880,384	19.9
Mercury	331,367	3.6	308,049	3.4	295,511	3.5	367,515	3.9	352,137	3.7
Lincoln	42,636	.5	49,324	.5	35,218	.4	57,486	.6	58,835	.6
Total	2,372,388	25.6	2,348,893	26.0	1,851,440	22.1	2,228,272	23.7	2,291,356	24.2
Chrysler Corp.										
Chrysler-Imperial	219,773	2.4	244,791	2.7	222,300	2.7	236,564	2.5	230,587	2.4
Dodge	521,783	5.5	543,560	6.0	491,919	5.9	581,476	6.2	538,381	5.7
Plymouth	624,779	6.7	598,160	6.6	627,173	7.5	709,823	7.5	658,987	6.9
Total	1,366,335	14.6	1,386,511	15.3	1,341,392	16.1	1,527,863	16.2	1,427,955	15.0
American Motors Corp.	324,669	3.5	265,712	2.9	237,785	2.8	259,346	2.8	239,937	2.5
Imports	569,415	6.1	658,123	7.3	779,220	9.3	985,767	10.5	1,061,617	11.2
Other	18,088	1.0	13,403	.5	8,547	.4	7,969	.1	5,739	.3
Grand Total	9,313,912	100.0	9,008,488	100.0	8,357,421	100.0	9,403,862	100.0	9,446,524	100.0

EXHIBIT 1
Continued

	1970 Units	1970 %	1971 Units	1971 %	1972 Units	1972 %	1973 Units	1973 %	1974 Units	1974 %
General Motors Corp.										
Chevrolet	1,668,288	19.8	2,195,345	21.7	2,289,407	21.5	2,524,861	21.8	1,973,706	22.6
Pontiac	544,715	6.5	680,097	6.8	712,775	6.7	807,546	6.9	504,081	5.8
Oldsmobile	461,732	5.5	666,958	6.6	729,153	6.8	808,889	6.9	519,082	5.9
Buick	493,207	5.9	640,024	6.3	646,526	6.0	696,333	6.0	428,194	4.9
Cadillac	165,042	1.9	253,002	2.5	257,795	2.4	285,709	2.5	219,993	2.5
Total	3,332,984	39.6	4,435,426	43.9	4,635,656	43.4	5,123,338	44.1	3,645,056	41.7
Ford Motor Co.										
Ford	1,848,669	22.0	1,913,033	18.9	2,058,676	19.3	2,137,123	18.4	1,756,811	20.1
Mercury	310,375	3.7	450,224	4.5	578,424	5.4	530,345	4.6	330,513	3.8
Lincoln	56,654	.7	66,092	.6	94,434	.8	116,115	1.0	84,693	1.0
Total	2,215,698	26.4	2,429,349	24.1	2,731,534	25.5	2,783,583	24.0	2,172,017	24.9
Chrysler Corp.										
Chrysler-Imperial	163,921	1.9	168,284	1.6	193,272	1.8	175,884	1.5	120,054	1.4
Dodge	504,097	6.0	519,039	5.1	562,985	5.3	622,967	5.4	462,872	5.3
Plymouth	681,760	8.1	660,472	6.5	709,884	6.7	752,746	6.5	597,276	6.8
Total	1,349,778	16.0	1,347,795	13.3	1,466,141	13.8	1,551,597	13.4	1,180,202	13.5
American Motors Corp.	254,327	3.0	385,065	3.9	305,891	2.9	392,105	3.4	329,431	3.8
Imports	1,230,961	14.7	1,487,613	14.8	1,529,402	14.4	1,732,572	15.1	1,389,323	16.0
Other	4,456	.3	0	0	0	0	0	0	5,240	.1
Grand Total	8,388,204	100.0	10,085,248	100.0	10,668,624	100.0	11,583,195	100.0	8,721,269	100.0

Source: Ward's Automotive Yearbook, 1974 and 1975.

EXHIBIT 2
IMPORT NEW CAR SALES IN THE UNITED STATES, 1973 AND 1974
The United States Automobile Industry, Early 1975

	1973 sales	Share of imports, %	Share of total U.S. market, %	1974 sales	Share of imports, %	Share of total U.S. market, %
Volkswagen	476,048	27.5	4.1	334,423	24.0	3.8
Toyota	289,378	16.7	2.5	238,135	17.1	2.7
Datsun	231,191	13.3	1.9	185,162	13.3	2.1
Capri	113,069	6.5	1.0	75,260	5.4	0.9
Fiat	56,938	3.3	0.5	70,611	5.1	0.8
Mazda	104,960	6.0	0.9	61,192	4.7	0.7
Opel	68,225	3.9	0.6	59,279	4.3	0.7
British Leyland*	65,025	3.8	0.6	54,161	3.9	0.6
Volvo	59,026	3.4	0.5	52,167	3.7	0.6
Audi	46,136	2.7	0.4	50,435	3.6	0.6
Honda	38,957	2.2	0.3	41,719	3.0	0.5
Colt	35,523	2.1	0.3	42,925	3.1	0.5
Mercedes-Benz	37,683	2.2	0.3	35,294	2.5	0.4
Subaru	37,793	2.2	0.3	22,980	1.6	0.3
Porsche	23,771	1.4	0.2	21,029	1.5	0.2
BMW	13,629	0.8	0.1	14,693	1.0	0.2
Saab	17,018	1.0	0.1	13,425	1.0	0.2
Peugeot	4,010	0.2	0.1	7,948	0.6	0.1
Renault	7,542	0.4	0.2	7,255	0.5	0.1
Pantera	1,831	0.1	0.1	1,230	0.1	0.0
Cricket	4,891	0.3	0.1	0	0.0	0.0
Total	1,732,572	100.0	15.1	1,389,323	100.0	16.0

* Included Austin, MG, Jaguar, and Triumph.
Source: Ward's Automotive Yearbook, 1975, p. 40.

EXHIBIT 3
UNITED STATES RETAIL AUTOMOBILE SALES
BY GENERAL MARKET CLASS, 1974
The United States Automobile Industry, Early 1975

Corporation	Make	Model	No. of models	Factory-list-price range or point-of-entry-price range		1974 U.S. sales in units
Subcompact-size class						
GM	Chevrolet	Vega	4	$2,237–	$2,701	326,307
Ford	Ford	Pinto	3	2,292–	2,543	360,688
AMC		Gremlin	2	2,159–	2,312	102,648
GM*	Pontiac	Astre	4	3,092–	3,699	4,925
Volkswagen			9	2,625–	5,274	334,423
Toyota			7	2,199–	3,949	192,661
Datsun			10	2,455–	5,125	185,162
Fiat			9	2,465–	4,395	70,611
Honda			4	2,600–	2,700	41,719
Opel	Buick		4	3,274–	3,511	59,279
Mazda			9	2,995–	4,295	61,192
Colt	Dodge		6			42,925
Subaru			4			22,980
Saab			13	4,698–	5,198	13,425
Audi		Fox	1	3,975		26,457
Renault			10			7,255
Class total						1,852,657
% industry total						21.2%
Compact-size class						
GM	Buick	Apollo	3	$2,755–	$2,904	47,413
GM	Oldsmobile	Omega	3	2,763–	2,912	41,979
GM	Pontiac	Ventura	6	2,602–	2,911	59,280
GM	Chevrolet	Nova	12	2,527–	2,960	322,821
Ford	Ford	Maverick/Club Wgn. & Grabber	6	2,441–	2,742	237,519
Ford	Mercury	Comet	4	2,496–	2,654	82,565
Chrysler	Plymouth	Valiant	2	2,621–	2,768	349,122
Chrysler	Dodge	Dart/Spt.	4	2,559–	2,786	272,546
AMC		Hornet	7	2,359–	2,837	118,006
Toyota			2	2,839–	4,104	45,474
Volvo			4			52,167
Audi			1	4,975		23,978
BMW						14,693
Class total						1,667,563
% industry total						19.1%

* Indicates a 1975 model introduced in September 1974.

EXHIBIT 3
Continued

Corporation	Make	Model	No. of models	Factory-list-price range or point-of-entry-price range	1974 U.S. sales in units
Intermediate-size class					
GM	Chevrolet	Chevelle/Malibu	17	$2,960– $3,993	333,405
GM	Pontiac	LeMans	7	2,961– 4,434	129,922
GM	Oldsmobile	Cutlass	7	3,454– 4,084	271,324
GM	Buick	Century	8	3,482– 4,160	152,101
Ford	Ford	Torino	9	2,811– 3,673	354,115
Ford	Mercury	Montego	6	2,939– 3,942	77,421
Chrysler	Dodge	Coronet/Charger	14	2,823– 3,991	110,981
Chrysler	Plymouth	Fury/Satellite	12	2,768– 4,132	132,875
AMC		Matador	8	2,952– 3,559	72,233
Class total					1,634,377
% industry total					18.7%
Specialty/sports class					
GM	Chevrolet	Camaro	3	$2,828– $3,381	130,446
GM	Chevrolet	Corvette	2	5,499– 5,735	29,114
GM	Chevrolet	Monte Carlo	2	3,668– 3,912	275,450
GM*	Chevrolet	Monza	2	3,966– 4,164	4,112
GM	Pontiac	Firebird	4	3,055– 4,231	65,303
GM	Pontiac	Grand Prix	1	4,669	81,547
GM	Oldsmobile	Toronado	1	5,560	23,582
GM*	Oldsmobile	Starfire	1	4,157	2,900
GM	Buick	Riviera	1	5,305	18,310
GM*	Buick	Skyhawk	1	4,186	2,976
GM	Cadillac	Eldorado	2	7,491– 7,812	36,360
Ford	Ford	Mustang II	3	2,895– 3,325	277,075
Ford	Ford	Thunderbird	1	6,542	46,365
Ford*	Ford	Granada	8	3,698– 4,326	47,265
Ford*	Ford	Elite	1	4,721	25,592
Ford	Mercury	Cougar	1	4,301	71,640
Ford*	Mercury	Monarch	8	3,764– 4,393	16,878
Ford	Lincoln	Cont. Mark IV, & Mark III	1	9,198	47,643
Chrysler*	Chrysler	Cordoba	1	5,072	12,590
Chrysler	Plymouth	Barracuda	2	2,947– 3,132	6,648
Chrysler	Dodge	Challenger	1	3,023	9,672

* Indicates a 1975 model introduced in September 1974.

EXHIBIT 3
Continued

Corporation	Make	Model	No. of Models	Factory-list-price range or point-of-entry-price range	1974 U.S. sales in units
Specialty/sports class (*continued*)					
Chrysler	Dodge	Charger SE	1	3,388	6,143
AMC		Javelin	2	$2,999– 3,299	18,975
Mercedes-Benz			1		5,940
Porsche			5	5,400– 13,575	21,029
Triumph					19,086
Peugeot			6	4,830– 6,300	7,948
Jaguar					5,299
Austin					4,761
Capri					75,260
Pantera					1,230
MG					25,015
Class total					1,422,154
% industry total					16.3%
Full-size class: high-price cars					
GM	Cadillac	Calais, De Ville, Fleetwood	7	$5,997– 12,211	183,633
Ford	Lincoln	Lincoln V-8	2	7,417– 7,637	37,050
Chrysler	Chrysler	Imperial	2	7,062– 7,192	12,252
Mercedes-Benz			9		29,354
Class total					262,289
% total industry sales					3%
Full-size class: medium-price cars					
GM	Pontiac	Catalina, Bonneville, Safari, Grand Ville, Grand Safari	13	$3,855–$ 4,914	163,104
GM	Oldsmobile	Delta, Cruiser, Ninety Eight	19	4,064– 5,497	179,297
GM	Buick	Regal, LeSabre, Estate Wagon, Electra	17	3,888– 5,549	207,394

* Indicates a 1975 model introduced in September 1974.

EXHIBIT 3
Continued

Corporation	Make	Model	No. of models	Factory-list-price range or point-of-entry-price range	1974 U.S. sales in units
Full-size class: medium-price cars (*continued*)					
Ford	Mercury	Brougham, Monterey, Marquis, Colony Park	15	$3,189– $5,294	82,009
Chrysler	Chrysler	Newport, New Yorker, Town & Country	13	4,181– 5,625	95,212
Chrysler	Dodge	Swinger, Custom, Monaco	19	2,597– 5,126	63,530
Total class					790,546
% total industry sales					9.1%
Full-size class: standard-price cars					
GM	Chevrolet	Bel Air, Impala, Caprice	15	$3,620– $4,543	552,051
Ford	Ford	Mach 1 4, Custom, Galaxie, Squire, LTD	15	3,518– 4,615	408,192
Chrysler	Plymouth	Duster, Scamp, Custom, Sebring, Road Runner, Suburban, Regent	20	2,511– 4,621	108,631
AMC		Ambassador	2	4,599– 4,960	17,569
Total class					1,086,443
% total industry sales					12.5%
Miscellaneous U.S. cars					5,240
% total industry sales					1%
Grand total					8,721,269

EXHIBIT 4
1975 MODEL UNITED STATES CAR FACTORY LIST PRICES BY GENERAL MARKET CLASSES AND BRAND
The United States Automobile Industry, Early 1975

Brand	Factory-list-price range or point-of-entry price range
Subcompact-size class	
Chevrolet	$2,799–$ 3,257
Pontiac	3,092– 3,699
Ford	2,919– 3,431
AMC	2,798– 2,952
Volkswagen	2,895– 4,800
Toyota	2,711– 3,949
Datsun	2,849– 6,284
Fiat	2,741– 4,687
Audi	4,450
Mazda	2,997– 4,597
Opel	3,274
Honda	2,798
Colt	2,945
Subaru	2,999
Saab	5,198
Renault	3,295– 5,795
Compact-size class	
Chevrolet	$3,218–$ 3,883
Pontiac	3,306– 4,052
Oldsmobile	3,435– 4,389
Buick	3,449– 4,292
Ford	3,025– 3,346
Mercury	3,113– 3,513
Plymouth	3,247– 4,328
Dodge	3,269– 4,014
AMC	3,074– 3,512
Audi	5,695
Volvo	5,295– 7,495
Intermediate-size class	
Chevrolet	$3,415–$ 4,906
Pontiac	3,603– 4,895
Oldsmobile	3,756– 4,791
Buick	3,828– 4,930
Ford	3,954– 4,791
Mercury	4,092– 4,910
Dodge	3,591– 4,918
Plymouth	3,542– 5,573
AMC	3,276– 3,692

Brand	Factory-list-price range or point-of-entry price range
Specialty/sports class	
Chevrolet	$3,553–$ 6,810
Pontiac	3,726– 5,309
Oldsmobile	4,157– 6,766
Buick	4,186– 6,433
Cadillac	9,948– 10,367
Ford	3,529– 7,701
Mercury	3,764– 5,153
Lincoln	11,082
Chrysler	5,072
Capri	3,566
Porsche	6,300– 13,475
British Leyland	3,549– 13,100
Mercedes-Benz	17,056
Peugeot	5,610– 6,630
Full-size class: high-price cars	
Cadillac	$8,197–$14,570
Lincoln	9,214– 9,656
Chrysler	8,698– 8,844
Mercedes-Benz	8,862– 21,307
Full-size class: medium-price cars	
Pontiac	$4,625–$ 5,909
Oldsmobile	4,787– 6,366
Buick	4,784– 6,529
Mercury	4,950– 6,341
Chrysler	4,854– 6,424
Dodge	3,341– 5,905
Full-size class: standard-price cars	
Chevrolet	$4,358–$ 5,364
Ford	4,656– 5,465
Plymouth	3,243– 3,973

795

EXHIBIT 5
UNITED STATES DEALERS NEW CAR STOCK, DAYS-SUPPLY FIGURES
The United States Automobile Industry, Early 1975

	Jan. 1, 1975	Feb. 1, 1974	Feb. 1, 1975
American Motors	102	46	75
Hornet	104	34	61
Gremlin	132	27	85
Matador	79	50	85
Chrysler Corporation	136	81	107
Plymouth total	139	75	109
Valiant	155	57	108
Fury/Satellite	101	74	85
Gran Fury/Fury	147	122	166
Chrysler total	82	109	69
Chrysler	106	115	62
Cordoba	52		69
Imperial	119	76	158
Dodge total	157	81	123
Dart	153	56	122
Coronet	199	112	138
Charger SE	124		132
Monaco	143	124	96
Ford Motor	100	67	90
Ford total	108	65	87
Torino	86	69	108
Elite	137		158
Ford	80	126	102
Mustang II	160	42	90
Thunderbird	82	109	113
Maverick	126	42	90
Granada	88		100
Pinto	139	31	65
Lincoln total	49	98	86
Lincoln	50	115	88
Mark IV	47	85	84
Mercury total	83	71	109
Montego	85	77	115
Mercury	62	115	95
Cougar	86	49	123
Monarch	75		117
Comet	135	40	98

EXHIBIT 5
Continued

	Jan. 1, 1975	Feb. 1, 1974	Feb. 1, 1975
General Motors	84	94	91
Buick total	70	140	75
Buick	53	138	77
Riviera	83	110	111
Century	81	147	91
Apollo	106	138	64
Skyhawk	86		28
Cadillac total	30	70	66
Cadillac	31	70	69
Eldorado	25	66	56
Chevrolet total	94	74	99
Chevelle	88	82	119
Nova	154	67	93
Chevrolet	81	132	120
Camaro	67	49	95
Monte Carlo	49	91	88
Vega	140	21	81
Monza 2+2	177		66
Oldsmobile total	75	118	81
Cutlass	79	91	91
Oldsmobile	53	158	76
Toronado	60	208	93
Omega	198	87	99
Starfire	121		34
Pontiac total	105	131	99
Pontiac	107	178	120
LeMans	114	126	121
Firebird	44	50	64
Grand Prix	62	146	75
Ventura II	201	90	106
Astre	219		87
Total cars, U.S.	96	80	92

EXHIBIT 6
UNITED STATES AUTOMOBILE SALES BY GENERAL MARKET CLASSES AND MAKE, 1970–1974
The United States Automobile Industry, Early 1975

Brand	1970 Units	%	1971 Units	%	1972 Units	%	1973 Units	%	1974 Units	%
Subcompact-size class										
Chevrolet	22,520	1.9	327,701	16.8	329,568	15.9	451,654	18.0	326,307	17.6
Pontiac									4,925	0.3
Ford	76,038	6.5	331,955	17.0	434,875	20.9	481,106	20.0	360,688	19.5
AMC		3.4	70,470	3.6	100,183	4.8	133,018	5.5	102,648	5.5
Imports	1,034,377	88.2	1,222,502	62.6	1,211,878	58.4	1,337,847	56.5	1,058,089	57.1
Class total	1,172,636	100.0	1,952,628	100.0	2,076,504	100.0	2,403,625	100.0	1,852,657	100.0
% industry total	14.0%		19.4%		19.5%		20.8%		21.2%	
Compact-size class										
Chevrolet	246,553	20.1	253,790	19.9	336,157	22.8	349,297	19.3	322,821	19.4
Pontiac			48,633	3.8	66,178	4.5	75,719	4.2	59,280	3.6
Oldsmobile					9,854	0.7	50,826	2.8	41,979	2.5
Buick							36,679	2.0	47,413	2.8
Ford	377,794	30.9	269,799	21.1	249,692	17.0	301,194	16.6	237,519	14.2
Mercury			63,151	4.9	66,577	4.5	79,039	4.4	82,565	5.0
Plymouth	246,013	20.0	249,982	19.6	295,574	20.1	339,732	18.7	349,122	20.9
Dodge	202,890	16.6	234,745	18.4	257,116	17.5	293,045	16.2	272,546	16.3
AMC	84,000	6.8	68,091	5.4	89,019	6.0	138,740	7.6	118,006	7.0
Imports	66,788	5.6	88,652	6.9	102,151	6.9	149,336	8.2	136,312	8.3
Class total	1,224,038	100.0	1,276,843	100.0	1,472,318	100.0	1,813,607	100.0	1,667,563	100.0
% industry total	14.6%		12.7%		13.8%		15.7%		19.1%	

EXHIBIT 6
Continued

Intermediate-size class

	Units	%	Units	%	Units	%	Units	%	Units	%
Chevrolet	381,054	21.6	384,740	21.6	370,394	18.3	364,883	16.8	333,405	20.4
Pontiac	188,263	10.7	176,556	9.9	187,128	9.3	222,070	10.2	129,922	7.9
Oldsmobile	237,418	13.5	293,820	16.5	317,565	15.7	368,505	17.0	271,324	16.6
Buick	172,161	9.8	200,346	11.3	217,817	10.8	259,838	12.0	152,101	9.3
Ford	351,304	20.0	331,128	18.6	451,789	22.3	436,693	10.1	354,115	21.8
Mercury	98,848	5.6	64,529	3.6	121,496	6.0	130,138	5.9	77,421	4.8
Dodge	147,235	8.4	145,641	8.2	158,457	7.8	157,844	7.3	110,981	6.8
Plymouth	139,007	7.9	137,146	7.7	159,300	7.4	179,118	8.2	132,875	8.0
AMC	45,186	2.5	44,703	2.6	46,828	2.4	53,960	2.5	72,233	4.4
Class total	1,760,476	100.0	1,778,609	100.0	2,021,774	100.0	2,173,049	100.0	1,634,377	100.0
% industry total	21.0%		17.6%		19.0%		18.8%		18.7%	

Specialty/sports class

	Units	%	Units	%	Units	%	Units	%	Units	%
Chevrolet	286,157	29.4	293,090	29.6	275,396	26.7	432,025	31.3	439,122	30.9
Pontiac	106,613	11.0	124,404	12.6	118,580	11.5	195,459	14.1	146,850	10.3
Oldsmobile	16,554	1.7	39,029	3.9	46,463	4.5	45,931	3.3	26,482	1.9
Buick	24,862	2.6	37,021	3.7	33,912	3.3	27,911	2.0	21,286	1.5
Cadillac	16,085	1.7	35,903	3.6	40,082	3.9	50,205	3.6	36,360	2.6
Ford	205,167	21.0	162,855	16.4	171,412	16.6	224,506	16.2	396,297	27.9
Mercury	65,564	6.7	50,395	5.1	48,178	4.7	57,572	4.2	88,518	6.2
Lincoln	22,101	2.3	30,024	3.0	49,634	4.8	65,470	4.7	47,643	3.4
Chrysler									12,590	0.9
Plymouth	39,366	4.0	19,435	2.0	17,155	1.7	17,746	1.3	6,648	0.5
Dodge	56,571	5.8	29,566	3.0	26,165	2.5	24,242	1.8	15,815	1.0
AMC	29,407	3.0	23,329	2.4	26,152	2.5	26,894	1.9	18,975	1.3
Imports	104,741	10.8	145,238	14.7	178,795	17.3	213,940	15.6	165,568	11.6
Class total	973,188	100.0	990,289	100.0	1,031,924	100.0	1,381,901	100.0	1,422,154	100.0
% industry total	11.6%		9.8%		9.7%		11.9%		16.3%	

EXHIBIT 6
Continued

Brand	1970 Units	1970 %	1971 Units	1971 %	1972 Units	1972 %	1973 Units	1973 %	1974 Units	1974 %
Full-size class: high-price cars										
Cadillac	148,957	67.9	217,099	73.2	217,713	69.5	235,504	71.3	183,633	70.0
Lincoln	34,553	15.8	36,068	12.2	44,800	14.3	50,645	15.3	37,050	14.1
Chrysler	10,753	4.9	12,089	4.1	14,321	4.6	12,809	3.9	12,252	4.7
Imports	25,055	11.4	31,221	10.5	36,578	11.6	31,449	9.5	29,354	11.2
Total	219,318	100.0	296,477	100.0	313,412	100.0	330,407	100.0	262,289	100.0
% industry total	2.6%		2.9%		2.9%		2.9%		3.0%	
Full-size class: medium-price cars										
Pontiac	249,839	21.7	330,504	22.3	340,889	22.6	314,298	21.6	163,104	20.6
Oldsmobile	207,760	18.1	334,109	22.6	355,271	23.6	343,627	23.6	179,297	22.7
Buick	296,184	25.8	402,657	27.2	394,797	26.2	371,905	25.6	207,394	26.2
Mercury	144,963	12.6	152,114	10.3	159,936	10.6	147,468	10.1	82,009	10.4
Chrysler	153,168	13.3	156,195	10.6	178,951	11.9	163,075	11.3	95,212	12.1
Dodge	97,401	8.5	104,516	7.0	77,317	5.1	112,806	7.8	63,530	8.0
Total	1,149,315	100.0	1,480,095	100.0	1,507,161	100.0	1,453,179	100.0	790,546	100.0
% industry total	13.7%		14.7%		14.1%		12.5%		9.1%	
Full-size class: standard-price cars										
Chevrolet	732,004	38.9	936,024	45.7	977,892	44.1	857,204	47.6	552,051	50.8
Ford	838,366	44.5	817,296	39.9	950,908	42.9	693,084	38.5	408,192	37.6
Plymouth	257,374	13.6	253,909	12.4	246,855	11.1	212,103	11.8	108,631	10.0
AMC	56,033	2.9	38,868	2.0	39,791	1.9	39,493	2.1	17,569	1.6
Total	1,883,777	100.0	2,046,097	100.0	2,215,446	100.0	1,801,884	100.0	1,086,443	100.0
% industry total	22.4%		20.3%		20.8%		15.6%		12.5%	
Not classified	5,456	263	263,866		30,085		225,543		5,240	
% industry total	0.1%		2.6%		0.2 %		1.8%		0.1%	
Grand total	8,388,204		10,085,248		10,668,624		11,583,195		8,721,269	

EXHIBIT 7
MARKET SHARES BY MANUFACTURER AND GENERAL MARKET CLASS, 1970–1974
The United States Automobile Industry, Early 1975

Manufacturer	1970	1971	1972	1973	1974
Subcompact-size class					
General Motors	1.9%	16.8%	15.9%	18.0%	17.9%
Ford	6.5	17.0	20.9	20.0	19.5
American Motors	3.4	3.6	4.8	5.5	5.5
Imports	88.2	62.6	58.4	56.5	57.1
Total	100.0%	100.0%	100.0%	100.0%	100.0%
Compact-size class					
General Motors	20.1%	23.7%	28.0%	28.3%	28.3%
Ford	30.9	26.0	21.5	21.0	19.2
Chrysler	36.6	38.0	37.6	34.9	37.2
American Motors	6.8	5.4	6.0	7.6	7.0
Imports	5.6	6.9	6.9	8.2	8.3
Total	100.0%	100.0%	100.0%	100.0%	100.0%
Intermediate-size class					
General Motors	55.6%	59.3%	54.1%	56.0%	54.2%
Ford	25.6%	22.2	28.3	26.0	26.6
Chrysler	16.3	15.9	15.2	15.5	14.8
American Motors	2.5	2.6	2.4	2.5	4.4
Total	100.0%	100.0%	100.0%	100.0%	100.0%
Specialty/sports class					
General Motors	46.4%	53.4%	49.9%	54.3%	47.2%
Ford	30.0	24.5	26.1	25.1	37.5
Chrysler	9.8	5.0	4.2	3.1	2.4
American Motors	3.0	2.4	2.5	1.9	1.3
Imports	10.8	14.7	17.3	15.6	11.6
Total	100.0%	100.0%	100.0%	100.0%	100.0%
Full-size class: high-price cars					
General Motors	67.9%	73.2%	69.5%	71.3%	70.0%
Ford	15.8	12.2	14.3	15.3	14.1
Chrysler	4.9	4.1	4.6	3.9	4.7
Imports	11.4	10.5	11.6	9.5	11.2
Total	100.0%	100.0%	100.0%	100.0%	100.0%
Full-size class: medium-price cars					
General Motors	65.6%	72.1%	72.4%	70.8%	69.5%
Ford	12.6	10.3	10.6	10.1	10.4
Chrysler	21.8	17.6	17.0	19.1	20.1
Total	100.0%	100.0%	100.0%	100.0%	100.0%
Full-size class: standard-price cars					
General Motors	38.9%	45.7%	44.1%	47.6%	50.8%
Ford	44.6	39.9	42.9	38.5	37.6
Chrysler	13.6	12.4	11.1	11.8	10.0
American Motors	2.9	2.0	1.9	2.1	1.6
Total	100.0%	100.0%	100.0%	100.0%	100.0%

EXHIBIT 8
DETAILS OF CHRYSLER'S REBATE PROGRAM
The United States Automobile Industry, Early 1975

Car clearance carnival special offer	Rebate	Bonus trade	Bonus rebate
January 12–18:			
1975 Duster	$200	Any Ford Pinto, any Chevrolet Vega, 1971 or 1972	$100
1975 Dart Swinger		Plymouth Valiant, 1971 or 1972 Dodge Dart	
1974 Colt			
January 19–25:			
1974 Colt	$200	Any Buick	$200
Dodge Truck Special	200	Any Oldsmobile	200
Dodge Monaco	300	1972 or 1973 Dodge Monaco	100
Chrysler	300	1972 or 1973 Chrysler	100
January 26–February 1:			
Fury	$200	Any Torino	$100
Coronet	200	Any Chevelle	100
Colt	200	1971 or 1972 Satellite or Charger	100
February 2–8:			
Valiant (in stock)	$200	Any Chevrolet Nova	$100
Duster (in stock)	200	Any Ford Maverick	100
Dart (in stock)	200	1971 or 1972 Satellite	100
Colt		1971 or 1972 Coronet	100
February 9–15:			
Colt	$300	Any 1970 or 1971 Chrysler, Plymouth, or Dodge	$200
Any wagons	300	Any full-size Ford or Chevrolet	200
February 16–22:			
Fury	$200		
Coronet	200		
February 23–March 1:			
Colt, Valiant, Duster, Dart	$200	Any 1969 or 1970 Chrysler, Plymouth, or Dodge	$200
		Any Buick, Oldsmobile, or Pontiac	200

EXHIBIT 9

STORYBOARDS OF CHRYSLER'S CAR CLEARANCE CARNIVAL TELEVISION ADVERTISEMENTS
The United States Automobile Industry, Early 1975

1. JOE GARAGIOLA: If you own any Buick, Olds or Pontiac,

2. we want you in one of our cars now.

3. So listen.

4. This week Chrysler Corporation is giving back $200.00

5. on every new Dodge Dart and Plymouth Valiant Duster your dealers have in sight.

6. Now bring that Buick,

7. Olds or Pontiac

8. to one of these by the end of the week

9. and get back another $200.00

10. or a total of $400.00.

11. Man, you'll love that money.

12. Man, you'll love these cars.

EXHIBIT 9
Continued

1. JOE GARAGIOLA: Folks, we're busting things wide open

2. here at the Car Clearance Carnival.

3. This week's special is on

4. every new Plymouth Valiant,

Duster

6. and Dodge Dart your dealers have in stock.

7. Two doors, four doors, coupes,

8. buy or lease any one of them.

9. Make your best deal with the dealer

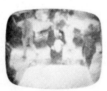

10. and Chrysler Corporation will send you

11. $200.00 on top of that.

12. So come on down. Get a great car. Get immediate delivery. And get that $200.00

"Don't dilly dally or delay, today is opening day."

Folks, Chrysler Corporation's Car Clearance Carnival is underway!

I'm Joe Garagiola, and for the next few weeks, I'll be your ringmaster bringing you all kinds of great values on Chryslers, Plymouths and Dodges.

We've got a lot of cars to move, and we're gonna move 'em, so be sure to watch for my carnival announcements on TV and radio.

I'll be announcing cash back deals on new model cars; 72 hour trade-in bonuses on certain used cars (one of 'em may be yours); and there'll be all kinds of free offers and surprises. And to kick off the carnival with a big bang, announcing:

The Colossal Carnival Sweepstakes.

Folks, this is your chance to win the use of a brand new Chrysler, Plymouth or Dodge *free* for a year. We'll be picking 48 winners, one for every day of the carnival. So hurry up, there's nothing to buy, just get down to your Chrysler Plymouth or Dodge dealer's and enter!

$200 Cash Back Deal.

Folks, the Plymouth Duster and Dodge Dart Swinger are great cars. They're roomy, easy on gas, and they look great, too. And now 'til Sunday, we've got a fantastic special on them! Buy or lease a new '75 Duster or Swinger — make your best deal with the dealer, and then Chrysler Corporation will send you a check for $200*!" on top of that!

And that's just one of a whole carnival of deals that'll be coming your way over the next few weeks.

$100 Trade-In Bonus.

Hey friend, if you own a Pinto or Vega – any year, any model – now 'til Wednesday is bonus time for you!

Get down to your Chrysler Plymouth or Dodge dealer's, trade for a new Plymouth Duster or Dodge Dart Swinger, make your best deal with the dealer, and then Chrysler Corporation will send you a bonus check for $100. That's $100 on top of the $200 we told you about before! But don't forget, this offer is only good 'til Wednesday, so get a move on!

UNLIMITED MILEAGE WARRANTY

"For the first twelve months of use, any Chrysler Motors Corporation dealer will fix, without charge for parts or labor, any part of our 1975 passenger cars we supply (except tires†) which proves defective in normal passenger use, regardless of mileage."

†Tires are covered by their own manufacturer.

The deals are fantastic here at Chrysler Corporation's Car Clearance Carnival. But folks, there's one deal that's fantastic all year 'round: Chrysler Corporation's new 12 month Unlimited Mileage Warranty on all their '75 cars. Go ahead, read it for yourself.

That's right, folks, no matter how many miles you drive in the first year, you're covered — and that includes parts *and* labor. All you have to take care of is normal maintenance like changing filters and wiper blades.

So make plans to come to Chrysler Corporation's Car Clearance Carnival going on at your Dodge and Chrysler Plymouth dealers.

It's a carnival of values!

Sweepstakes ends 2/26/75. Void in states of Georgia, Idaho, Missouri and Wisconsin and where prohibited by law. Contest limited to licensed drivers 18 years and over. No purchase necessary.
Limit one per customer. Retail customers only.
Entry blanks and complete details available at your Dodge and Chrysler Plymouth dealers.

CHRYSLER CORPORATION   CHRYSLER Dodge Plymouth Dodge Trucks

EXHIBIT 10
Continued

EXHIBIT 10
Continued

Ford breaks things wide open...

No-nonsense cash rebates up to $500

on America's best-selling line-up of small cars:

$500 on '75 Mustang II Ghia
$500 on '75 Mustang II Mach I
$300 on '75 Mustang II hardtop
$300 on '75 Mustang II 2+2
$200 on any '75 Pinto
$200 on any '75 Maverick
$350 on '75 SuperCab Pickup

NO NONSENSE. • No weekly cut offs. • No trade-in requirements. • No complicated details. • Just pick the one you want to buy or lease. • Get your Ford Dealer's best deal. • Then get your cash rebate directly from Ford Motor Company. • This rebate covers new '75's sold and delivered between now and February 28. So don't wait. • See your local Ford Dealer now.

FORD

FORD MEANS VALUE. NOW MORE THAN EVER.   FORD DIVISION

EXHIBIT 10
Continued

A $600 Cadillac option free with every Beetle.

One of the many improvements on the '75 Beetle is fuel injection. The same type of fuel injection you'll find on a Cadillac.

Only on a Cadillac, it's a $600 option.

On the Beetle, it's standard equipment.

Even more amazing, with a Beetle you can use both leaded and unleaded fuel.* Whichever fuel you use, the Beetle's fuel injection meters it precisely so that the engine runs more efficiently.   *California, unleaded only.

To help insure that the entire Beetle runs more efficiently, you also get a free computer analysis at the first 15,000 miles.

And every Beetle is covered by the Owner's Security Blanket, the most advanced car coverage in the world.

So now you don't have to be rich to own fuel injection.

Just smart.

The fuel injected '75 Beetle. Only $2,895.†

© Volkswagen of America, Inc. †Beetle Suggested Retail Price P.O.E., local taxes and any other dealer delivery charges additional

EXHIBIT 10
Continued

EXHIBIT 10
Continued

1975 Datsun.
3 Models at 39 MPG.

Other auto makers would be ecstatic if they could claim one model with mileage like that. We have three: The B-210 Hatchback, 2- and 4- Door Sedans.

In the U.S. Environmental Protection Agency tests of 1975 cars sold in the U.S. our B-210 got 39 miles per gallon on the highway, 27 in town. In today's economy, that's the kind of economy you need.

But the fantastic mileage is just one Datsun virtue. Good old-fashioned value is another. Every B-210 comes with these features included in its base price: 1400cc engine, power-assist front disc brakes, reclining bucket seats, carpeting, tinted glass, electric rear window defogger, trip odometer, whitewalls, full wheel covers and much more.

Datsun B-210. Drive one today, and see for yourself how much Datsun Saves!

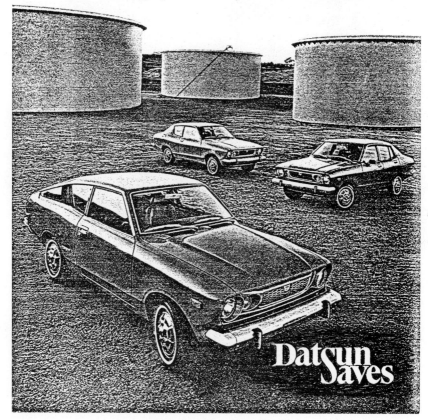

Datsun Saves

EXHIBIT 10
Continued

Mercedes-Benz:
The Nation's Number One
European Delivery Program.

Why did Mercedes-Benz sell more cars last year on its European Delivery Plan than VW, Renault, Volvo, Jaguar —more than any other manufacturer? The reasons are basic. Factors like cost savings and product quality, and hundreds of experienced and dedicated European Delivery specialists all over the country have helped Mercedes-Benz to the top.

And, take a look at the money you can save. Depending upon the Mercedes-Benz model you choose, our European Delivery Program can save you from about $800 to over $1,800, after paying for shipping and duty.

Want to know more? Our European Delivery Portfolio gives you full details. Send for it with this coupon today.

Mr. W. Peter Grassl,
Mercedes-Benz
of North America, Inc.,
One Mercedes Drive,
Montvale, New Jersey 07645
Please send me the Mercedes-Benz European Delivery Portfolio.

Name_____

Address_____

City_____

State_____Zip_____

TI15

EXHIBIT 10
Continued

A Cadillac is no stranger to hard work.

The operating efficiency of a Cadillac makes as much sense today as it did for the businessman in the days of the 1933 five-passenger Cadillac Phaeton. Perhaps even more. And in these times, it's good to know that Cadillac for 1975 offers improved efficiency that results in reduced overall operating costs. Plus Cadillac resale . . . traditionally one of the highest of all U.S. cars. It's all part of Total Cadillac Value. And that goes with you wherever your business takes you. Cadillac. **Then and Now . . . an American Standard for the World.**

EXHIBIT 11
SALES DATA BY MANUFACTURER AND MAKE, BY REPORTING PERIOD, JANUARY 1–FEBRUARY 20, 1975
The United States Automobile Industry, Early 1975

	Jan. 1-10		Jan. 11-20		Jan. 21-31		Total Jan.		Feb. 1-10		Feb. 11-20	
	Units	%	Units	%	Units	%	Units	%	Units	%	Units	%
General Motors Co.												
Chevrolet	17,157	40.3	35,707	54.6	65,637	53.0	118,501	51.1	36,387	52.7	50,866	51.4
Pontiac	8,126	19.1	8,403	12.8	15,302	12.4	31,831	13.7	10,589	15.3	14,113	14.3
Oldsmobile	7,980	18.7	9,138	14.0	18,529	15.0	35,647	15.4	10,763	15.6	14,359	14.5
Buick	5,881	13.8	7,703	11.8	17,858	14.4	31,442	13.6	8,921	12.9	11,676	11.8
Cadillac	3,482	8.1	4,505	6.8	6,574	5.2	14,561	6.2	2,405	3.5	7,915	8.0
Total	42,626	100.0	65,456	100.0	123,900	100.0	231,982	100.0	69,065	100.0	98,929	100.0
Ford Motor Co.												
Ford	27,663	81.1	29,463	80.5	58,638	84.9	115,764	82.8	32,106	82.0	46,012	82.8
Mercury	4,753	13.9	5,406	14.8	8,297	12.0	18,456	13.2	5,706	14.6	7,811	14.1
Lincoln	1,676	5.0	1,743	4.7	2,142	3.1	5,561	4.0	1,346	3.4	1,761	3.1
Total	34,092	100.0	36,612	100.0	69,077	100.0	139,781	100.0	39,158	100.0	55,584	100.0
Chrysler Corp.												
Chrysler	1,989	16.0	3,616	15.3	7,777	22.5	13,382	18.9	2,915	12.3	5,461	17.8
Plymouth	5,844	46.9	11,148	47.2	13,805	40.0	30,797	43.6	11,848	49.9	13,493	43.9
Dodge	4,635	37.1	8,844	37.5	12,961	37.5	26,440	37.5	8,968	37.8	11,804	38.3
Total	12,468	100.0	23,608	100.0	34,543	100.0	70,619	100.0	23,731	100.0	30,758	100.0
American Motors Co.	4,049	100.0	5,456	100.0	10,804	100.0	20,309	100.0	6,154	100.0	8,412	100.0
Total U.S. cars	93,235		131,132		238,324		462,691		138,108		193,683	
Imports							100,730					
Others							6,971					
Grand total							570,392					

813

EXHIBIT 12
SALES DATA BY MANUFACTURER AND MAKE, BY REPORTING PERIOD, JANUARY 1–FEBRUARY 20, 1975[1]
The United States Automobile Industry, Early 1975

Brand	Jan. 1–10 Units	%	Jan. 11–20 Units	%	Jan. 21–31 Units	%	Feb. 1–10 Units	%	Feb. 11–20 Units	%
Subcompact-size class										
Chevrolet	2,759	32.1	5,933	45.0	13,800	42.0	6,709	43.0	10,248	43.6
Pontiac	773	9.0	949	7.2	3,163	9.6	2,182	14.0	2,814	12.0
Ford	5,073	58.9	6,290	47.8	15,920	48.4	6,723	43.0	10,436	44.4
AMC	NA		NA		NA		NA		NA	
Imports	NA		NA		NA		NA		NA	
Total	8,605	100.0	13,172	100.0	32,883	100.0	15,614	100.0	23,498	100.0
Compact-size class										
Chevrolet	2,464	17.6	5,518	21.7	13,003	31.0	6,956	21.7	10,338	27.3
Pontiac	683	4.9	842	3.3	2,471	5.8	1,564	4.9	2,078	5.5
Oldsmobile	568	4.1	657	2.6	2,164	5.0	1,097	3.4	1,542	4.1
Buick	635	4.5	899	3.5	3,109	7.3	1,509	4.7	1,925	5.1
Ford	2,485	17.7	2,370	9.3	6,278	14.8	4,245	13.3	6,077	16.0
Mercury	703	5.0	739	2.9	2,079	4.9	1,308	4.0	2,009	5.3
Plymouth	3,762	26.8	8,522	33.5	7,413	17.5	8,781	27.4	7,379	19.5
Dodge	2,722	19.4	5,862	23.2	5,851	13.7	6,559	20.6	6,565	17.2
AMC	NA		NA		NA		NA		NA	
Imports	NA		NA		NA		NA		NA	
Total	14,022	100.0	25,409	100.0	42,368	100.0	32,019	100.0	37,913	100.0
Intermediate-size class										
Chevrolet	2,733	15.3	5,676	25.1	8,229	21.4	4,784	21.6	6,293	19.3
Pontiac	1,730	9.6	1,690	7.5	2,332	6.1	1,877	8.5	2,321	7.2
Oldsmobile	3,756	21.0	4,283	19.0	7,714	20.1	4,823	21.8	6,353	19.5
Buick	2,041	11.4	2,525	11.2	4,895	12.7	2,639	11.9	3,981	12.2
Ford	3,660	20.5	3,425	15.2	4,034	10.5	2,737	12.3	3,852	11.8
Mercury	953	5.3	1,050	4.6	1,340	3.5	799	3.6	1,223	3.8
Dodge	935	5.3	1,315	5.8	3,518	9.1	1,437	6.5	2,401	7.4
Plymouth	2,082	11.6	2,626	11.6	6,392	16.6	3,067	13.8	6,114	18.8
AMC	NA		NA		NA		NA		NA	
Total	17,890	100.0	22,590	100.0	38,454	100.0	22,163	100.0	32,538	100.0

EXHIBIT 12
Continued

Specialty/sports class

Chevrolet	4,683	19.4	9,313	29.3	17,107	27.5	10,458	30.2	13,804	28.3
Pontiac	2,651	11.0	2,623	8.3	3,907	6.3	2,726	7.9	3,781	7.8
Oldsmobile	790	3.3	946	3.0	3,389	5.4	1,642	4.7	2,130	4.4
Buick	657	2.7	873	2.7	3,302	5.3	1,399	4.0	1,608	3.3
Cadillac	683	2.8	857	2.7	1,278	2.1	411	1.2	1,382	2.8
Ford	10,355	42.9	11,317	35.6	25,162	40.4	12,935	37.3	18,619	38.2
Mercury	1,968	8.2	2,241	7.1	3,097	5.0	2,308	6.7	3,018	6.2
Lincoln	891	3.7	801	2.5	1,060	1.7	550	1.6	795	1.6
Chrysler	1,001	4.2	1,983	6.2	2,779	4.5	1,828	5.3	2,854	5.9
Dodge	439	1.8	820	2.6	1,154	1.8	427	1.1	745	1.5
AMC	NA		NA		NA		NA		NA	
Imports	NA		NA		NA		NA		NA	
Total	24,118	100.0	31,744	100.0	62,235	100.0	34,684	100.0	48,736	100.0

Full-size class: high-price cars

Cadillac	2,799	75.8	3,648	76.7	5,296	80.0	1,994	68.8	6,533	84.7
Lincoln	785	21.2	942	19.8	1,082	16.0	796	27.5	966	12.5
Chrysler	111	3.0	171	3.5	271	4.0	108	3.7	211	2.8
Imports	NA		NA		NA		NA		NA	
Total	3,695	100.0	4,761	100.0	6,649	100.0	2,898	100.0	7,710	100.0

Full-size class: medium-price cars

Pontiac	2,289	22.3	2,299	18.2	3,429	14.2	2,240	19.3	3,119	17.7
Oldsmobile	2,866	28.0	3,252	25.7	5,262	21.8	3,201	27.5	4,334	24.5
Buick	2,548	24.9	3,406	26.9	6,552	27.1	3,374	29.0	4,162	23.6
Mercury	1,129	11.0	1,376	10.9	1,781	7.4	1,291	11.1	1,561	8.8
Chrysler	877	8.6	1,462	11.6	4,727	19.5	979	8.4	2,396	13.6
Dodge	539	5.2	847	6.7	2,438	10.0	545	4.7	2,093	11.8
Total	10,248	100.0	12,642	100.0	24,189	100.0	11,630	100.0	17,665	100.0

Full-size class: standard-price cars

Chevrolet	4,249	41.1	8,766	59.1	12,541	63.4	7,152	56.7	9,518	57.5
Ford	6,090	58.9	6,061	40.9	7,244	36.6	5,466	43.3	7,028	42.5
Total	10,339	100.0	14,827	100.0	19,785	100.0	12,618	100.0	16,546	100.0

[1] Excludes imports.
Source: Ward's Automotive Reports.

EXHIBIT 13
UNITED STATES NEW CAR RETAIL SALES BY MODEL BY REPORTING PERIOD DURING REBATE PROGRAM
The United States Automobile Industry, Early 1975

	Jan. 1-10		Jan. 11-20		Jan. 21-31		Feb. 1-10		Feb. 11-20	
	1974	1975	1974	1975	1974	1975	1974	1975	1974	1975
Chevrolet	6,966	4,249	10,063	8,766	16,079	12,541	10,726	7,152	12,898	9,518
Corvette	364	488	522	864	1,192	1,242	740	735	953	1,112
Chevelle	4,784	2,733	6,377	5,676	10,014	8,229	6,231	4,784	7,473	6,293
Nova*	4,901	2,464	6,627	5,518	9,936	13,003	5,996	6,956	6,764	10,338
Sportsvan	245	269	375	501	750	957	343	328	532	665
Monte Carlo	2,860	2,438	4,744	5,011	8,064	7,000	4,444	4,157	5,722	5,232
Camaro	2,158	1,266	2,463	2,494	4,166	3,638	2,476	2,281	2,742	3,217
Vega*	9,741	2,759	11,826	5,933	16,888	13,800	9,448	6,709	13,624	10,248
Monza		491		944		5,227		3,285		4,243
Total Chevrolet	32,019	17,157	42,997	35,707	67,089	65,637	40,404	36,387	50,708	50,866
Pontiac	2,710	2,289	2,594	2,299	4,866	3,429	2,907	2,240	3,500	1,119
Grand Prix	1,153	1,565	1,200	1,376	1,689	1,837	1,490	1,292	1,530	1,913
LeMans	2,043	1,730	2,101	1,690	2,784	2,332	2,523	1,877	2,630	2,321
Firebird	930	1,086	969	1,247	1,767	2,070	1,302	1,434	1,396	1,868
Ventura*	1,281	683	1,370	842	2,239	2,471	1,580	1,564	1,587	2,078
Astre		773		949		3,163		2,182		2,814
Total Pontiac	8,117	8,126	8,234	8,403	14,345	15,302	9,802	10,589	10,643	14,113
Oldsmobile 98	797	1,176	974	1,410	1,786	2,174	942	1,363	1,282	1,717
Oldsmobile 88	1,453	1,690	1,898	1,842	3,625	3,088	1,660	1,838	2,348	2,617
Toronado	356	431	430	426	748	604	376	371	509	556
Cutlass	3,315	3,756	4,399	4,283	8,213	7,714	3,801	4,823	5,398	6,353
Omega*	777	568	1,015	657	1,859	2,164	830	1,097	1,204	1,542
Starfire*		359		520		2,785		1,271		1,574
Total Oldsmobile	6,698	7,980	8,716	9,138	16,231	18,529	7,609	10,763	10,741	14,359

EXHIBIT 13
Continued

Electra 225	1,795	1,426	1,598	1,660	2,827	2,895	1,259	1,591	1,796	2,058
LaSabre/Centurion	2,478	1,122	1,847	1,746	3,098	3,657	1,684	1,783	2,461	2,104
Riviera	510	252	430	285	759	536	373	231	471	329
Century	2,576	2,041	2,489	2,525	4,856	4,895	2,138	2,639	2,964	3,981
Apollo*	888	635	824	899	1,630	3,109	854	1,509	1,350	1,925
Skyhawk*		405		588		2,766		1,168		1,279
Total Buick	8,247	5,881	7,188	7,703	13,170	17,858	6,308	8,921	9,042	11,676
Cadillac	2,570	2,799	2,769	3,648	4,609	5,296	2,722	1,994	3,466	6,533
Eldorado	605	683	736	857	1,160	1,278	629	441	736	1,382
Total Cadillac	3,175	3,482	3,505	4,505	5,769	6,574	3,351	2,405	4,202	7,915
Total GM	58,256	42,626	70,640	65,456	6,604	123,900	67,474	69,065	85,336	98,929
LTD (Ford)	7,912	6,090	9,022	6,061	14,992	7,244	9,799	5,466	12,423	7,028
Torino	6,636	3,660	7,026	3,425	11,191	4,034	7,093	2,737	9,759	3,852
Elite		1,884		1,899		2,592		1,889		2,488
Granada		4,309		4,042		6,048		3,807		5,562
Club Wagon	303	343	339	304	594	383	379	220	533	255
Maverick*	5,745	2,142	5,068	2,066	7,302	5,895	4,705	4,025	5,907	5,822
Mustang	7,180	3,430	6,962	4,500	10,545	15,550	6,142	6,610	8,853	9,769
Thunderbird	987	732	1,063	876	1,510	972	943	629	1,234	800
Pinto*	10,384	5,073	10,021	6,290	15,126	15,920	9,547	6,723	12,982	10,436
Total Ford	39,147	27,663	39,501	29,463	61,260	58,638	36,608	32,106	51,691	46,012
Marquis (Mercury)	1,547	1,129	1,941	1,376	3,552	1,781	1,770	1,291	2,122	1,561
Montego	1,802	953	1,935	1,050	2,999	1,340	1,635	799	1,970	1,223
Cougar	1,809	789	1,722	755	2,872	1,106	1,570	735	2,064	1,086
Monarch		1,179		1,486		1,991		1,573		1,932
Comet*	1,937	703	1,796	739	2,711	2,079	1,458	1,308	2,075	2,009
Total Mercury	7,095	4,753	7,394	5,406	12,134	8,297	6,433	5,706	8,231	7,811
Lincoln	720	785	998	801	1,245	1,082	605	796	822	966
Mark IV	975	891	735	942	1,688	1,060	911	550	1,042	795
Total L-M	8,790	6,429	9,127	7,149	15,067	10,439	7,949	7,052	10,095	9,572
Total Ford	47,937	34,092	48,628	36,612	76,327	69,077	44,557	39,158	61,786	55,584

* Indicates rebated models.

EXHIBIT 13
Continued

	Jan. 1–10		Jan. 11–20		Jan. 21–31		Feb. 1–10		Feb. 11–20	
	1974	1975	1974	1975	1974	1975	1974	1975	1974	1975
Gran Fury (Fury)	2,306	889	2,968	1,024	5,346	1,726*	2,866	2,067	3,786	2,819*
Fury (Satellite)	2,255	1,193	2,737	1,602	6,125	4,666*	2,640	1,000	3,803	3,295*
Barracuda	273		323		658		224		427	
Valiant	6,991	3,633	7,076	8,315	12,859	7,098	6,151	8,634*	10,305	6,999
Voyager		129		207		315		147		380
Total Plymouth	11,825	5,844	13,104	11,148	24,988	13,805	11,881	11,848	18,321	13,493
Chrysler	1,882	877	2,279	1,462	4,177	4,727*	2,323	979	2,874	2,396
Imperial	323	111	342	171	596	271	308	108	541	211
Cordoba		1,001		1,983		2,779		1,828		2,854
Total C-P	14,030	7,833	15,725	14,764	29,761	21,582	14,512	14,763	21,736	18,954
Monaco	1,246	539	1,498	847	3,353	2,438	1,479	545	2,096	2,093
Coronet	2,062	935	2,377	1,315	5,094	3,518	2,557	1,437	3,518	2,401*
Charger S.E.		439		820		1,154		427		745
Challenger	335		319		900		313		532	
Dart	5,106	2,351	4,948	5,273*	10,012	4,888	3,976	6,183*	6,512	5,473
Sportsman	739	371	861	589	1,784	963	684	376	1,154	1,092
Total Dodge	9,488	4,635	10,003	8,844	21,143	12,961	9,009	8,968	13,812	11,804
Total Chrysler	23,518	12,468	25,728	23,608	50,904	34,543	23,521	23,731	35,548	30,758
Total AMC	8,398	4,049	10,008	5,456	13,959	10,804	8,043	6,154	11,223	8,412
Total U.S. cars	138,109	93,235	155,004	131,132	257,794	238,324	145,595	138,108	193,893	193,683

*Indicates rebated models.
Source: Ward's Automotive Reports.

APPENDIXES

ECONOMIC ANALYSIS

Marketing managers find themselves engaging in both quantitative and qualitative types of analysis as they evaluate market opportunities and seek to develop appropriate marketing programs.

Some of the quantitative tools and techniques used in marketing are highly sophisticated and require a significant level of statistical and mathematical expertise. Others, involving relatively simple concepts and computations, represent fundamental skills which every marketing manager should possess. In almost all instances, it is necessary to determine the economic consequences of alternative courses of action and of adopting alternative sets of assumptions. This appendix discusses some of the basic terminology and calculations used in analyzing marketing problems, beginning with the concept of contribution *and how it is calculated.*

CONTRIBUTION

Contribution *refers to the funds available to the seller of an item after subtracting the variable costs associated with it. The commonly used term* unit contribution *refers to the contribution yielded by item sold. Assume, for example, that we sell a unit of a particular product to wholesalers at a price of $100, and that the variable manufacturing costs of that unit are $30. In addition, it costs us $3 per unit to ship the product to wholesalers, and we pay a 5 percent commission to our salespeople ($5 per unit). Under these circumstances, the variable costs associated with each unit of this product are $38 ($30 + $3 + $5). Since we receive $100 revenue for each unit we sell, our unit contribution is $62 ($100 − $38).*

This $62 unit contribution is available to cover the fixed manufacturing expenses, overheads, and marketing costs associated with the product and, hopefully, to provide a profit. Fixed costs are costs which remain fixed regardless of the volume of production. Thus, whether we produce 1,000 or 5,000 items, the cost of executive salaries remains fixed, as does rent, insurance, and other so-called overhead expenses. Fixed costs remain unchanged over some reasonable range of activity of the firm. Variable costs, on the other hand, are costs which are directly traceable to the volume of activity—the more we sell, the more raw *material we need, usually the more assembly workers we need, the more sales commission we pay. Variable costs are directly traceable to variations in volume of activity.*

BREAK EVEN

Break even means that our revenue is just enough to pay both for the variable and the fixed costs incurred. But only just that. We have no profit, we have no losses. We have only broken even.

As a bare minimum, most companies expect a product to break even, i.e., not to lose money. Depending on the situation, the appropriate time within which a product should break even may be short (a year, or a season) or long (perhaps as much as 5 years). For the sake of simplicity, we will assume that the appropriate time period for break even is 1 year.

One way to talk of break even is to say it occurs when the number of units we sell, multiplied by the unit contribution, is equal to the fixed costs. Thus we calculate break even as follows: BE = total fixed costs divided by unit contribution. If unit contribution is $62, for example, and fixed costs are $100,000, break even will occur when we produce and sell 1,613 units (that is, $100,000 ÷ $62). If we expect to produce and sell 1,613 units, we expect to break even. But if we produce 2,000 and sell 1,613, we have not broken even. We have incurred losses because our total variable costs are now $62 × 2,000, not $62 × 1,613.

PROFIT IMPACT

Few companies are content to operate at break even. Normally, they require that each product produces a positive impact on company profits. The impact which a particular product will have on company profits is easily calculated, as follows, using the same figures we have been using:

(Unit contribution × units prod. & sold) − fixed costs = profit impact
($62   ×   2,000   )
                    $124,000   − $100,000   = $24,000

Why do we call this $24,000 impact on profit (or profit impact) and not just plain profit? The answer is that there may be a few other costs yet to be charged against the product, such as corporate headquarters overhead, not just product-related overhead.

Suppose we have a certain profit target in mind—say we want to have a profit impact of $50,000. What will our production and sales have to be to achieve this target? The calculation is the same as the above, except that we add the $50,000 profit target to the fixed costs. With fixed costs now at $150,000 instead of $100,000, the resulting calculation gives us 2,419 units.

A similar technique may be used to calculate the effects of a change in our marketing program. Assume that with our present program we expect to make and sell 2,000 units of a product with a $62 unit contribution. With our fixed costs of $100,000, we saw that this yields a $24,000 profit impact. We now consider raising our advertising expenditure by $50,000, which would increase our fixed costs to $150,000. If we do so, how much volume would the new marketing program have to achieve to generate the same profit impact ($24,000) as our present program?

The calculation is as follows:

Present fixed cost + present profit impact + add'l fixed cost ÷ unit contrib. = required vol.
$100,000   + $24,000   + $50,000   ÷ $62   =   2,806

We would have to make and sell 2,806 units in order for the new program to yield the same profit impact as the old one which required sales of only 2,000 units. There are other ways to come up with the same answer, of course, but this way has at least the virtue of simple clarity for the amateur.

Suppose we improve our product by adding $3 per unit of variable cost. This cuts our unit contribution to $59. If all other costs, as well as prices, remain unchanged, how much would we have to sell to maintain our current profit impact of $24,000? The answer is ($100,000 + $24,000) ÷ $59 = 2,102 units.

In calculating the economic effects of a marketing program, one is generally forced to make a number of assumptions. The sales forecast is generally the most critical, but fixed costs, variable costs, and selling prices may also be uncertain. Under these circumstances, it is generally useful to calculate the profit impact of a marketing program under varying sets of assumptions.

Obviously, one can make break-even points or expected profit impact come out any way one wishes by making the appropriate assumptions about sales volumes and costs. For this reason, the marketing manager should become adept at appraising the realism of the assumptions on which calculations of these types are based.

MARKET SHARE ANALYSIS

One way of assessing the realism of a sales forecast is to calculate its implications for a firm's market share. Assume, for example, that the total market for the product mentioned in the previous examples is 10,000 units, that the market is not expanding, and that we presently sell 2,000 units. We therefore have a market share of 20 percent. The product manager recommends that we raise our advertising budget by $50,000, which means that we would have to make and sell 2,806 units to maintain our current profit impact. We shall have to make and sell 806 units above the present level, raising our market share from 20 to 28.06 percent. How likely is this? Can $50,000 of additional advertising accomplish that? Will our competitors give up 8 percent market share without fighting back?

When demand for a product is not static (as we have assumed in this example), calculation of probable effect on market share is more difficult. If we increase advertising by $50,000, for example, total demand for the product may increase. If this happens, some of our sales increase may come from increased market share, but some may also come from increased demand. Would the competition then be as likely to retaliate?

COMPUTATION OF MARGIN

When manufacturers produce an item for sale, or when retailers buy an item for resale, they decide on the price for which they hope to sell it. This price exceeds the manufacturing cost, or the cost paid by the merchant, by an amount termed the margin. (The terms markup and markon are also often used interchangeably with margin.) The margin is similar, though not necessarily the same, as unit contribution—a distinction we shall not attempt to clarify here.

Margin, cost, and selling price are related to each other in the following manner:

$$\begin{aligned} \text{Selling price} &= \text{margin} + \text{cost} \\ \$1 &= \$0.40 + \$0.60 \end{aligned}$$

Thus, we say that the retailer's selling price of an item consists of the cost to the retailer plus the margin. For many purposes it is useful to express the margin as a percentage. Theoretically, the 40-cent margin might be expressed either as a percentage of the cost or as a percentage of the selling price. If it were expressed as a percentage of the cost, the margin would be 66.67 percent; i.e., the 40-cent margin divided by the 60-cent cost equals 66.67 percent. When it is expressed as a percentage of the selling price, the margin is 40 percent— $\$0.40 \div \$1$. The commonly accepted practice is to express percentages (both as regards margins and costs) with net sales as the base. While this is the "commonly accepted" practice, some industries, firms, and individuals depart from that practice. We will follow the common practice.

If the cost is known and the percentage of margin on selling price is given, it is a simple matter to compute the selling price. Suppose, for example, that a retail merchant buys goods at a cost of $10 and wants a margin of $33\frac{1}{3}$ percent to cover expenses and have some chance of making a net profit. What should be the selling price? Since 100 percent of the selling price is made up of two parts (the cost and the margin), this means that $\$10 + 33\frac{1}{3}$ percent = 100 percent. It follows that the $10 cost must be $66\frac{2}{3}$ percent of the selling price. What is 100 percent—the selling price itself?

We have said that

Then:
$$\begin{aligned} 66\tfrac{2}{3}\% \times \text{selling price} &= \$10 \\ \text{Selling price} &= \$10 \div 66\tfrac{2}{3}\% \\ &= \$15 \end{aligned}$$

Similarly, if a wholesaler buys an article for 60 cents and wants a margin of 20 percent, the selling price is $60¢ \div 80\% = 75¢$.

Margin percentages are figured on the selling price at each level of business. If it costs a company 75 cents to manufacture an item and it wants a 25 percent margin, the selling price must be $1. If the wholesaler to whom the manufacturer sells the item for $1 wants a margin of 16⅔ percent, his selling price will be $1.20. And if the retailer who buys it from the wholesaler for $1.20 resells it to consumers at $2, his margin will be 40 percent.

Since some firms and industries use cost rather than selling price as the base for their percentage calculations, it is useful to know how to convert from one base to the other. On merchandise costing $6 and selling for $10, the margin is $4. This margin, which is 40 percent of the selling price, would be 66⅔ percent if computed on the basis of the cost. To make the conversion, from either the cost base or the selling-price base to the other, it helps to understand once more that selling price is composed of two parts, the margin and the cost, as follows:

$$\text{Cost} + \text{margin} = \text{selling price}$$
$$\$0.60 + \quad \$0.40 \quad = \quad \$1$$

$$\text{Margin as percent of selling price} = \frac{\$0.40}{\$1.00} = 40\%$$

If we want quickly to convert this margin, expressed as a percent of selling price, into a margin expressed as a percent of cost, we say:

1   If 40 percent is the margin on selling price

2   Then the remaining 60 percent must be the cost

3   $40\% \div 60\% = 66\frac{2}{3}\% = $ margin based on cost

The following formula invariably gets this conversion right:

$$\frac{\text{Percentage margin on price}}{100\% - \text{percentage margin on price}} = \text{percentage margin on cost}$$

$$\frac{40\%}{100\% - 40\%} = \frac{40\%}{60\%} \qquad = \qquad 66\frac{2}{3}\%$$

Suppose we have the opposite question: How to express a margin figured as a percent of cost into one figured as a percent of selling price? We say:

1   Cost is 100 percent, i.e., the denominator on which the margin was figured.

2   Since the margin on cost (in the above example) is 66⅔ percent

3   Then the selling price must be

$$\text{Cost} + \text{margin} = \text{selling price}$$
$$100\% + 66\frac{2}{3}\% = \quad 166\frac{2}{3}\%$$

4   Margin on percent of selling price $= 66\frac{2}{3}\% \div 166\frac{2}{3}\% = 40\%$

The following formula invariably gets this conversion right:

$$\frac{\text{Percentage margin on cost}}{100\% + \text{percentage margin cost}} = \text{percentage margin on selling price}$$

$$\frac{66\tfrac{2}{3}\%}{100\% + 66\tfrac{2}{3}\%} = \frac{66\tfrac{2}{3}\%}{166\tfrac{2}{3}\%} = 40\%$$

DISCOUNTS AND CHAIN DISCOUNTS

A common practice is for the manufacturer to suggest at what price his product should be sold by a retailer. If his "suggested retail price" is $100 while selling the item to the retailer for $60, he is, in effect, proposing a "suggested retail margin" of 40 percent, that is, ($100 − $60) ÷ $100 = 40 percent. In common usage it will be said that the manufacturer is offering a "trade discount" of 40 percent. Indeed, the manufacturer may actually quote his price to the retailer as "$100 less 40%." If the retailer chooses to sell the item for, say, $90 instead of $100, he will still have to pay "$100 less 40%," or $60. The retail margin will be $30 ÷ $90 = 33⅓ percent.

Occasionally, discounts from a suggested resale price will be computed in two or more increments. For example, a manufacturer might offer discounts of 40 percent + 5 percent on a product priced to be resold at $100. This means that in addition to the original discount (suggested margin) of 40 percent (i.e., $40), the manufacturer has allowed an additional 5 percent. This does not mean 40 percent plus 5 percent, or 45 percent. It means $100 − 40 percent less 5 percent of $100 − 40 percent. Thus the retailer pays ($100 − $40) − 5% + ($100 − $40) = $60 − $3 = $57. The 40 percent + 5 percent is called a chain discount. In chain discounts the specific percentage link in the chain that is referred to (say, 5 percent, as in the present example) is calculated on the price that is derived after the application of the prior link or links to the suggested retail price. This rather cumbersome practice of stating discounts (or margins) probably arose originally to advise customers of changes in a discount structure. Over the years, the method has become traditional in certain industries.

TERMS OF SALE

When a manufacturer sells to a wholesaler or distributor, who then in turn sells to a retailer, prices are also generally listed as discounts from a suggested retail price. A product suggested to sell for $100 at retail, with a suggested retail margin of 40 percent and a suggested wholesale margin of 20 percent, will be sold by the wholesaler to the retailer at a price of $60 (i.e., $100 less 40 percent), and will be purchased by the wholesaler from the manufacturer for $48 (i.e., $60 less 20 percent). Once again, the margin for a particular institution in the channel of distribution is applied to the price at which the institution sells its goods and services.

Terms of sales are a shorthand method of setting forth the conditions under which a company offers to sell its goods or services. They include, in addition to price, a statement of trade discounts, the date by which the amount is to be paid, and shipping responsibilities.

For example, terms of sale of "$50 per unit, 2/10 e.o.m., 60 days net, f.o.b. seller's plant" indicate that: (1) the price for which the product is being sold is $50, (2) a 2 percent trade discount off the price (i.e., $1) will be offered if the bill (or "invoice") is paid within a period ending 10 days after the end of the month in which the invoice is issued, (3) the total amount of the bill is due within 60 days of the invoice date, and (4) the title and responsibility for the subsequent transportation of the product passes from the seller to the buyer at the plant of the former.

Here, the letters e.o.m. stand for end of month. In their absence, to qualify for receipt of the 2 percent special discount would require paying the bill within 10 days after the date on the invoice. The letters f.o.b. stand for free on board, traditional means of expressing the physical location at which certain responsibilities for transportation and damage-claim litigation pass from seller to buyer. While these are just two of many different discount and shipping terms, they are perhaps the most commonly used in business today.

SUMMARY

When analyzing marketing problems, it is important to determine the economic consequences of alternative strategies, as well as of variations in the assumptions underlying production, marketing, and market data.

This appendix has reviewed several key concepts in economic analysis, including those of contribution, fixed and variable costs, break even, profit impact, and margins. It has also highlighted the basic arithmetical computations involved in undertaking economic analysis for marketing decisions.

EXERCISES

Horatio Alger has just become product manager for brand X. Brand X is a consumer product with a retail price of $1. Retail margins on the product are 33 percent, while wholesalers take a 12 percent margin.

Brand X and its direct competitors sell a total of 20 million units annually; brand X has 24 percent of this market.

Variable manufacturing costs for brand X are $0.09/unit. Fixed manufacturing costs are $900,000.

The advertising budget for brand X is $500,000. The brand X product manager's salary and expenses total $35,000. Salespeople are paid entirely by commission; this is 10 percent. Shipping costs, breakage, insurance, etc., are $0.02/unit.

1   *What is the unit contribution for brand X?*

2   *What is brand X's break-even point?*

3   *What market share does brand X need to break even?*

4   *What is brand X's profit impact?*

5   *Industry demand is expected to increase to 23 million units next year. Mr. Alger is considering raising his advertising budget to $1 million.*

a If the advertising budget is raised, how many units will brand X have to sell to break even?

b How many units will brand X have to sell for it to achieve the same profit impact that it did this year?

c What will brand X's market share have to be next year for its profit impact to be the same as this year?

d What will brand X's market share have to be for it to have a $1 million profit impact?

MARKET ANALYSIS

Market analysis is often a useful starting point for managers engaged in the planning and evaluation of marketing activities. By analyzing the structure and
dynamics of the market(s) in which the firm is competing (or wishes to compete), managers can gain insights into the performance of individual products
relative to the competition, evaluate future prospects, and develop marketing
strategies for their firms which are responsive to the challenges presented by
specific segments of the overall market.

Among the most significant questions facing managers in this respect are:

- How large is the market for the product in question? Is it growing or
shrinking? Why?
- What are the major forces influencing demand for this product?
- Can the market usefully be segmented, and, if so, along what dimensions?
- At what stage in the product life cycle is this market? Are we dealing with
a new product category or a mature and well-established one?
- Is demand consistent over time or does it fluctuate sharply in response
to temporal or cyclical factors?
- Who are the competitors serving this market and what are their market
shares? How and why have these shares been changing over time?
- What are the demographic characteristics of customers and potential
customers in this market?
- Are there any major customer needs or wants which are not currently
being satisfied?

THE NATURE OF PRIMARY DEMAND

The term primary demand is commonly used to refer to total industry demand
for a given product category.

Sometimes, it may be difficult to determine exactly how large the market
is. The problem is often one of definition: Is a portable tape recorder part of the
market for all tape recorders or is it part of the market for audio equipment of

all types? An unduly narrow definition of the market may result in the over-looking of potentially profitable marketing opportunities or in ignoring competi-tive threats from products which perform a similar or related function for the consumer. On the other hand, defining the market too broadly may fail to yield a useful basis for evaluating a specific product's performance and potential, or for planning future strategy.

Assessing the size of the market may range from a relatively simple task which can be expected to yield quite reliable information to a complex proce-dure, yielding only approximate "guesstimates." Many industry statistics are readily available through government statistical publications or are published through trade associations. In other instances, estimates can be purchased from professional research firms (such as Nielsen) which survey sales through a repre-sentative sample of retail outlets, or through specially commissioned market studies. Internally generated estimates may be developed from such sources as trade contacts or sales force reports.

Since market estimates may vary widely in accuracy, it is important to de-termine the source of the estimate and how the figures were derived in order to evaluate their credibility.

DETERMINANTS OF DEMAND

Having obtained some quantitative notion of the size of primary demand, it is desirable to examine the broad trend of demand patterns over time and fore-casts for the future. These trends should be reviewed with an eye to evaluating the forces which serve to determine demand levels for a particular product category.

Among these determinants may be the level of disposable personal in-comes, trends in life-styles, technological advances, economic expectations, etc. In many instances, the demand for one product is a derivative of the demand for a related one. Thus, the demand for jet aircraft determines the demand for jet engines; car radio sales are in large measure a function of new automobile production levels; and so forth.

Another often significant market influence is legislation. A change in fire regulations, for instance, may substantially increase primary demand for fire de-tection devices within the affected geographic area, while federal safety legisla-tion has spurred automobile safety belt sales (if not always their usage!).

MARKET SEGMENTATION

Market segmentation may be defined as the process of dividing the consumer market into meaningful buyer groups and then creating specific marketing pro-grams for one or more of the resulting segments with a view to achieving finan-cial and other corporate objectives. It represents a middle way between a *strategy of* market aggregation, *in which all consumers are treated similarly, and one of* total market disaggregation, *in which each consumer is treated uniquely.*

The concept of segmentation is based on the propositions that (1) consumers are different; (2) differences in consumers are related to differences in market behavior; and (3) segments of consumers can be isolated within the overall market. The benefits which may result from a segmentation approach include:

- *A more precise definition of the market in terms of the needs of specific groups, why they behave as they do, and possible ways of influencing behavior.*
- *Improved ability to identify competitive strengths and weaknesses, and opportunities for winning specific segments from the competition*
- *More efficient allocation of limited resources to develop programs which can best satisfy the needs of target segments*
- *Clarification of objectives and definition of performance standards*

The basic problem is to select segmentation variables which are likely to prove useful in a specific operational context. It can be argued that each of the following three criteria must be satisfied if meaningful market segments are to be developed. First, it must be possible to obtain information on the specific characteristics of interest. Second, management must be able to identify chosen segments within the overall market and efficiently focus marketing efforts on these segments. And third, the segments must be large enough (and/or sufficiently important to the organization) to merit the time and cost of separate attention.

The overall market for any given product can generally be segmented along several different dimensions. Thus, one can segment the market:

1 Geographically *(according to where consumers live or where they purchase and use the product)*
2 *By* demographic *characteristics of consumers (such as sex, age, income levels, stage in the family life cycle, education level, occupation)*
3 *By* consumption volume *or size of unit purchase*
4 *By the different* uses *to which the product is put*
5 *According to what are termed* psychographics *(variations in consumers' needs resulting from life style or personality characteristics)*
6 *By* product attributes *(such as size, price range, portability, technical features)*

It is often useful to segment a market along two or more dimensions at once; however, concurrent use of multiple methods of segmentation may lead to an unmanageable and meaningless number of market segments. The same consumer may fall into different segments in different marketing situations. For one product category, the most important variable may be the consumer's age; for others, it may be income level, the purpose for which he or she buys the product, or the type of retail outlet selected.

SELECTIVE DEMAND

The term selective demand *is used to designate the extent of a given market being obtained by a particular organization. Considered in relation to primary demand, it indicates the market share which a firm may possess or hopes to achieve. If a firm is only competing in a few market segments, it may be more useful to consider market share relative to these segments alone, than as a percentage of the overall market.*

In attempting to increase sales volume, firms are sometimes faced with a strategic choice between seeking to expand either primary or selective demand. If a firm already dominates an existing market (or segment), it may be appropriate to seek to stimulate consumer demand for that entire product category. As the total market grows, so should that firm's sales, even if its market share remains constant. A strategy of stimulating selective demand may be more appropriate when a firm has a relatively small share of a particular market. Selective demand stimulation involves promotion of brand awareness and preference, with a view to gaining market share from competing brands.

The choice of strategy (and sometimes a hybrid one may be appropriate) should be derived from careful analysis of market structure and trends, as well as evaluation of competitive strategies.

STAGE IN PRODUCT LIFE

One factor which may help to determine the potential for stimulating primary demand is the newness or maturity of the product category in question. Most products (other than fashion or fad items) go through a life cycle, beginning with an introductory phase and moving over time through growth, maturity, and decline phases to finish with withdrawal from the marketplace. Some, of course, die young.

This life cycle may be illustrated graphically as shown below.

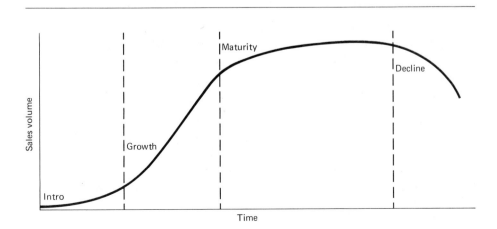

As sales expand, costs and prices typically fall and thus stimulate further growth in sales, accompanied perhaps by added product features and new uses. In time, however, the product may be displaced by new substitutes or the environment may change and eliminate consumers' need for this product category altogether.

TEMPORAL OR CYCLICAL VARIATIONS IN DEMAND

Market demand may not always be consistent over time. The demand for many products is highly seasonal, reflecting climatic variations, cultural or religious customs, or established societal practices such as beginning the school year in the autumn. For this reason, it is important to make seasonal adjustments for comparative purposes and for determining the overall trend of the market.

In other instances, there may be established cyclical variations in demand which, unless identified, can obscure any secular trend in sales.

These fluctuations may be very significant for planning future strategy. In addition to their implications for production and logistics scheduling, such fluctuations may influence the timing of promotional and selling activities. Some firms deliberately seek out two or more product lines with countercyclical demand patterns, so that one is in high demand at times when others are "out of season."

SUMMARY

This note has highlighted the importance for managers of understanding the structure and dynamics of markets in which they sell, or are considering selling. While qualitative evaluations often provide valuable insights, it is generally also necessary to express market characteristics in quantitative terms for purposes of planning and evaluation.

An understanding of the competitive structure of the market, the characteristics of the distribution channels serving it, and the needs and buying behavior of existing and potential consumers are also important adjuncts to market analysis. Each will be discussed in detail in subsequent appendixes on competitive analysis, trade analysis, and consumer analysis.

CONSUMER ANALYSIS

The market for any given product consists of all current or potential consumers for that product. In most marketing situations, consumers can choose between several alternative offerings in the same product category. Even in situations where there is no direct competition, people may be in a position to spend their money on a substitute product or not to purchase at all. It follows, then, that understanding consumers is central to developing an effective marketing program.

Asking questions about consumers as individuals enables the marketing manager to generate information concerning such issues as the needs of different consumer groups; how consumers make decisions and who is influential in those decisions; where, how, and when people buy; and how the products are used after purchase.

This understanding not only helps a marketing organization identify and select its principal target segments but also provides inputs to all the elements in the marketing mix. First, it helps organizations to develop goods and services whose characteristics meet the needs of target segments. Second, it helps to ensure that the resulting products are priced at levels which target consumers are able and willing to pay, and that suitable credit terms are available where needed. Third, it assists in selecting distribution outlets which are not only consistent with consumer life-styles and shopping patterns but also provide the desired amount of service and information for the product in question. And finally, it enables management to develop communications campaigns which are tailored to consumers' media habits and which convey the appropriate messages and appeals in a format that catches the target audience's attention.

CONSUMER VERSUS INDUSTRIAL BUYING BEHAVIOR

Although the term consumer is generally applied to individuals buying on their own or their family's behalf, organizations also consume goods and services. In many instances, a marketer may count both individuals and organizations as purchasers of the same product. For clarity, this appendix will use the terms consumer and industrial to differentiate between individual and organizational purchasers, although the latter term is sometimes a misnomer.

Some basic differences exist in the roles performed by consumer and industrial buyers. The former generally seek to fulfill personal needs, although in many instances they also serve as the family purchasing agent and have family needs in mind as well. Industrial buyers, by contrast, buy for the organization which they represent rather than for themselves. They tend to be better trained than consumers to evaluate the functional characteristics of most products which they buy, and to place more emphasis on such objective criteria as technical characteristics and performance. Unlike individual consumers, industrial buyers are often motivated by profit-related considerations and may therefore be required to justify their purchases on the basis of measurable performance.

This is not to say that all industrial purchases are made on an entirely rational basis. When buying a corporate jet, top executives may be swayed by differences in the appearance of competing aircraft. Purchasing agents may be influenced by considerations of friendship with a particular sales representative; and some industrial decision makers may have an emotional attachment (or dislike) for a specific supplier's brand name and image.

GROUP DECISION MAKING

Many purchase situations involve the participation of several people in the buying process. Participants in such group decision making are sometimes referred to collectively as the decision-making unit (DMU). It is important for marketers to understand the make-up of such DMUs and to be able to identify the role and needs of each of its participants.

Group involvement in the buying process tends to be the norm in individual purchasing situations. In many organizations, lists of approved suppliers are maintained for each regularly purchased product category, and a would-be seller's first task is to obtain the necessary approval. Such approval may require judgments by financial and production specialists on such issues as applicant's financial soundness, quality controls, and anticipated reliability of delivery.

The composition of the decision-making unit in an industrial buyer and the roles played by its members are likely to vary from firm to firm and from one type of purchase to another. In many instances, certain procedures are specified but the involvement of some parties is often limited to rubber-stamp approval for small or routine purchases. The level at which decisions are made also varies according to the nature of the purchase. A junior accountant may routinely initial an order for $25 worth of nails, but the company treasurer may be personally involved for weeks or even months on financial negotiations for a multimillion dollar purchase of sophisticated new plant machinery.

It is very important for marketers to be able to identify who will be involved in an industrial buying decision, what the nature of each individual's involvement will be, and what criteria each will employ. Top management's concerns in buying a new computer system will not necessarily be those of the managers whose departments will make the greatest use of the system. Likewise, these managers may employ somewhat different evaluation criteria from the data-processing personnel responsible for day-to-day operation of the machines.

Household decision making, by contrast, tends to be less formalized than in industrial situations and the roles played by family members less well defined. However, the extent and nature of group involvement in the various stages of the buying process may have important implications for marketing strategy in both industrial and consumer contexts. Consequently, marketers should seek to answer such questions as:

- Who initiates the buying process in terms of articulating the need for a particular product?
- Whose opinions influence the evaluation of alternative purchases?
- Who makes the final buying decision, and does any one individual have effective veto power?
- Who implements the actual purchase transaction?
- Who uses the product once it has been purchased?

It is possible to have situations in which the initiator, the influentials, the decision maker, the purchaser, and the user are all different people. For instance, a small child's teacher might suggest to its parents that playing with educational toys at home would be a good way to stimulate learning; the mother might then select a certain type of toy and identify some reputable brands after talking to friends with children of similar age; the father might undertake the actual purchase and choose a particular brand after looking around the store and consulting the salesperson; while the child would, of course, be the actual user.

In such a situation, the marketing program by the toy manufacturer might include careful product design to ensure its suitability for children in certain age groups; a public relations campaign directed at elementary school teachers; an advertising campaign directed at parents of young children, especially mothers; careful selection of retail outlets; a policy of regular calls by the field sales force to ensure that retail staff could offer knowledgeable advice to a broad range of different purchasers; and a point-of-purchase sales promotion campaign designed to achieve prominent and attractive displays in selected outlets.

At the opposite extreme are situations in which a consumer initiates the purchase, is not influenced by anybody else, then personally buys and uses the product. A repetitive purchase of a relatively inexpensive product, such as razor blades, typifies such a buying situation. However, in situations involving expensive outlays, new and unfamiliar products, or purchases with potentially important implications for the buyer, it is common for a consumer to receive solicited or unsolicited advice and even to be influenced by other people's behavior. The *degree of influence exerted by another party may reflect that person's perceived knowledge, skills, and competence relative to the product in question.*

People who rate high on such characteristics are sometimes termed opinion leaders, and their judgments are valued by other consumers. Opinion leadership is not necessarily transferable from one product category to another, so that within a given consumer's reference groups, the person who is always up to date on clothing fashion, the do-it-yourself expert, and the amateur photography specialist are likely to be three different people. Opinion leaders tend to have higher exposure than "followers" to relevant mass media (e.g., fashion magazines, do-it-yourself publications, and photography magazines) but not to mass media in general. If the marketer can identify and reach the opinion leaders for the product category that his or her firm is marketing, then it may be possible to leverage the communications campaign by word of mouth from opinion leaders to followers.

The usefulness of such demographic variables as age, sex, and income level in providing insights to understanding behavior may be greatly enhanced by combining them with the concept of the family life cycle. *The passage of birthdays may not be as crucial a determinant of needs and buying decisions as changes in an individual's family status, such as marriage, birth of a child, children going to school, last child leaving home, death of a spouse. Likewise, these different stages in the life cycle may have more important economic implications, in terms of disposable income level, than changes in gross income.*

DECISIONS TO ADOPT "NEW" PRODUCTS[1]

When faced with products which are new to them, consumers tend to move through several stages before deciding to make use of the product on a regular basis. These stages may be broadly defined as:

1 Awareness: *becoming aware of the product*

2 Knowledge: *becoming interested in the product and learning about its characteristics*

3 Evaluation: *evaluating it against other alternatives*

4 Trial: *trying it on a limited basis (e.g., renting the product, buying a sample, borrowing a neighbor's, taking it on a 10-day "no obligation" trial from the store)*

5 Purchase: *adopting it on a regular basis (buying a consumer durable, repurchasing a frequently purchased nondurable)*

6 Confirmation: *seeking reassurance that the right choice was made*

[1] *The term* new *is used in this context to describe products which are new to a particular consumer, as opposed to being new on the marketplace (in which case they are, of course, new to everybody).*

Consumers don't necessarily go through each of these stages in sequence for every product which is new to them. In some instances, particularly low-value products where there is minimum social or personal risk attached to ownership, awareness and purchase may take place simultaneously without intervening stages, as the consumer plucks the product from the shelf in an "impulse purchase."

However, it is helpful for marketers to recognize the existence of these various stages, since different elements in the marketing mix may be appropriate at different stages. The mass media are often employed to generate awareness of a new brand and then provide consumers with some basic information about it. Depending on the nature of the product and the buying situation, personal selling at the retail level may be helpful at the evaluation stage; alternatively, in supermarket selling, package design and copy may provide helpful inputs at this stage. Trial is often encouraged by "cents-off" coupons, offer of free or inexpensive samples, or simply eye-catching point-of-sale displays.

Purchase of a high-value consumer durable, such as a car, furniture, or central air conditioning, may depend heavily on the quality of personal selling activities at the retail level. Consumers may be prepared to spend a lot of time and effort on such a purchase, as they shop around for the right product and the best terms. A skilled salesperson should be able to assess when consumers are still in the information-gathering stage and when they are ready to consummate a purchase. Trial usage of the product, where feasible, can often be helpful in enabling consumers to make up their minds.

OBTAINING INFORMATION ABOUT CONSUMERS

If a firm is to develop an appropriate marketing strategy directed at specific consumer segments, it may need to collect data about consumer needs, characteristics, and behavior. Sometimes, such information may already be available for closely similar products, in terms of demographic and family life cycle characteristics, decision-making practices, and purchasing and use behavior. In other instances, special surveys may need to be commissioned. Where time and financial constraints make large-scale surveys impracticable, informal group discussions with people who are believed to be representative of potential consumers may yield useful insights, but it is dangerous to generalize too broadly from such research lest the subjects prove to be atypical.

In industrial marketing situations, industry publications may provide valuable information on the needs of different types of firms and even on typical purchasing practices within certain firms or industries. However, such information should rightly be augmented by the marketer's field sales force. Their job is not merely to sell but also to gather information about the needs and buying practices of specific customers or prospects, and to evaluate the particular concerns and roles of the various individuals who are found to participate in each organization's buying decisions.

When seeking information on what stage target consumers have reached in the purchase decision process for a particular brand, it is generally necessary to go out and obtain up-to-date data from the marketplace. Research may be needed to determine the level of consumer awareness for "our" brand versus the others. Consumer surveys may be needed to find out how knowledgeable consumers are about product features and how well they remember advertising copy; in many instances, consumers may also be asked whether they have tried the product and what their intentions are for the future. By looking at the "conversion ratio" from awareness to trial, and from trial to repurchase, marketing managers can better assess where their brand's strengths and weaknesses lie and what corrective strategy may be most appropriate. Professional survey firms are often employed to conduct such surveys on a continuing basis, so that management can look at trends in these measures over time for both its own and competing products.

SUMMARY

This appendix has emphasized the importance for marketing managers of understanding what consumers needs are, how consumers make decisions, and what their buying usage behavior is like. Needs may vary sharply from one segment to another, and it is obviously important to tailor product characteristics to the needs of the target segment(s) and promote them appropriately. Developing an understanding of consumer (and industrial) decision making places the marketer in a better position to influence such decisions. Recognizing the how, when, and where of buying behavior facilitates choice of distribution channels and strengthens the marketer's position at the point of sale. Finally, a continuing monitoring of actual and prospective purchasers ensures that the firm's strategy is up to date and takes account of the dynamic nature of the marketplace.

TRADE ANALYSIS

As has already been noted, manufacturers of both consumer and industrial products frequently find it necessary or advantageous to delegate a portion of their marketing functions to independent intermediaries (the "trade"). The trade may be defined here as those wholesalers, distributors, or retailers which take title to, and/or physical possession of, a manufacturer's products for the purpose of ultimate resale, either to another member of the trade (e.g., wholesaler to retailer) or to a final consumer (e.g., retailer to consumer, or distributor to industrial user). Generally, manufacturers who choose to market through such intermediaries, rather than directly to the final consumer, do so because their potential customers desire or require a greater amount of convenience, service, or assortment than the manufacturer itself could provide economically. Other reasons may reflect the nature of the expertise possessed by the distributors, or a desire to make distribution expenses a variable rather than a fixed cost.

IMPACT OF THE TRADE ON THE MARKETING PROGRAM

In delegating the physical distribution function, the manufacturer inevitably gives up direct control of certain elements in the marketing process which could have a major impact on the success of its marketing program. Nonexclusive wholesalers or retailers (i.e., intermediaries which carry competing products in a given product category) often give preferential support to the products of a particular manufacturer. An industrial products distributor, for example, might instruct its sales forces to make available the products of manufacturer A, but to concentrate on selling the products of manufacturer B whenever possible. To reinforce this instruction, the distributor might pay a higher rate of commission on the latter's products.

Similarly, a retailer of consumer products could provide preferential support to a particular brand in a product category by giving it extra space or preferential shelf location (in a self-service store), or by giving its salespeople incentives to sell one brand rather than another. In extreme cases, the appropriate nonexclusive intermediary for a particular product category (e.g., supermarkets for detergents) might simply refuse to stock a particular brand or item.

In product categories characterized by exclusive or semiexclusive distribution patterns, the trade also has considerable potential impact on the success of a manufacturer's marketing program. In such situations, the strength of the exclusive distributor or retailer franchised by the manufacturer in a given market area will often be the major determinant of its market share in that market. A manufacturer of fine men's suits, for example, will almost certainly do considerably better in a particular city if its suits are featured by the leading upscale department store or men's specialty store in that city than if it must settle for a retailer with a smaller or less affluent clientele.

FACTORS MOTIVATING TRADE BEHAVIOR

It is most important that manufacturers distributing their products through independent intermediaries understand the behavior patterns of such intermediaries and the factors which motivate their behavior. While such motivations are typically quite complex, they are generally closely related to the simple fact that the trade comprises independent profit-seeking business entities which are (understandably) far more interested in their own well-being than they are in the success or failure of the manufacturers which supply them.

While members of the trade vary greatly in size, sophistication, and objectives, they generally share a desire to maintain or increase profitability. In the distribution trades, profitability is largely a function of (1) traffic or customer base (i.e., how many customers buy from the intermediary in a given period), (2) sales volume per customer, (3) average gross margin, and (4) expenses of doing business. In making merchandising decisions (i.e., which products to carry, how to market them, how much support to give to individual brands or items), the wholesaler or retailer will generally assess the implications of a given decision for one or more variables in this profit equation.

Consider, for example, a retailer which is trying to decide which of several brands of color television sets to carry. After considerable deliberation, this retailer has narrowed its choice to two brands with markedly differing marketing programs. Brand A is intensively advertised by its manufacturer and has an excellent reputation for quality and value among consumers. It is widely distributed, however, with the result that retailer price competition has forced retail gross margins down to about $50 per unit. Brand B, conversely, is supported with only a limited amount of manufacturer's advertising and is thus not well known among consumers. However, the manufacturer's selling price for brand B is lower, and the few retailers which carry it have not chosen to promote price reductions to the consumer. As a result, the retailer could obtain a margin of $100 per unit on brand B, as compared with $50 per unit on brand A.

In deciding how to merchandise color television sets, the retailer in this situation would have three options. It could market brand A exclusively in the expectation that the "pull" generated by manufacturer advertising would (1) draw traffic to its store, (2) allow it to "close" a larger number of sales, or (3) reduce selling expenses because brand A would be relatively easy to sell. If it chose this option, the retailer would, in effect, be reasoning that increased volume or decreased selling expenses would outweigh brand A's relatively low gross margin.

As a second option, the retailer might decide to market brand B exclusively, on the premise that other factors (e.g., store location and reputation, other merchandise lines carried) would draw sufficient traffic to its store, and that its skilled sales personnel, in face-to-face contact with potential customers, would be able to counteract the information transmitted by brand A through advertising. While unit sales might be lower and selling expenses higher under this option than under the first option, the retailer might conclude that the higher potential gross margins on brand B would make it the more profitable alternative.

A third possibility would, of course, be to carry both lines despite the fact that doing so would increase inventory and space costs. If it followed this course, the retailer might find it advantageous to promote brand A heavily in its advertising in order to attract traffic to its store, but to instruct its sales personnel to try to sell brand B (at a higher margin) whenever possible. As a variant on this approach, the retailer might carry brand A exclusively, promote several models at very low prices and margins, and instruct its salespeople to use their influence to sell other models which carried higher margins.[1]

The choice a retailer would make, given these options, would, of course, depend largely on its overall merchandising strategy. The needs of a volume-oriented mass merchandiser would, for example, differ markedly from those of a traditional department store or a specialty appliance store. In designing a marketing program, it is thus necessary for a manufacturer planning to use intermediaries to identify the differing needs of various segments of the trade, and to incorporate elements intended to satisfy the needs of the trade segment(s) it plans to utilize.

In this sense, trade analysis is closely analogous to consumer analysis. For a given target segment of wholesalers or retailers, the manufacturer might usefully ask such questions as:

1   *What role does this product category play in this trade segment's merchandising mix (e.g., traffic generation or margin generation)?*

2   *How does this trade segment merchandise the product category in question (e.g., self-service versus personal selling)?*

3   *How well do the marketing programs of competitors satisfy the merchandising needs of this trade segment?*

---

[1] *In extreme forms, either of these approaches may be characterized as "bait-and-switch" merchandising, a practice which is considered unethical by consumer groups and, increasingly, as illegal by the Federal Trade Commission. While the distinction between "focused merchandising" and "bait-and-switch" tactics is difficult to define precisely, it is generally considered acceptable for a retailer to emphasize higher margin merchandise, provided that (1) an adequate quantity of the advertised merchandise is physically available for sale in good condition at the advertised price and (2) that retail sales personnel do not actually disparage the advertised item or brand.*

4   *What are the key motives of the individuals who actually develop and implement merchandising policies in this trade segment?*

5   *What differential advantage might be obtained through actions such as generous trade terms, extensive media advertising, sales training and merchandising assistance, improved delivery, frequent sales contact, and advertising assistance?*

It is frequently the case that the needs of one trade segment are in conflict with those of other trade segments. For instance, if a specialty store is looking for products which enhance its exclusive fashion image and provide high margins, its needs are unlikely to be satisfied by a brand marketed by mass merchandisers which favor well-known products that they can promote at low prices to stimulate traffic and volume. Under such circumstances, a manufacturer will generally be forced to choose one trade segment or the other and to design its marketing program with the needs of that trade segment in mind.

In practice, legal restrictions often make it impractical to design separate marketing programs for individual trade segments. In particular, the Robinson-Patman Act, and subsequent court interpretations of that act, require that manufacturers sell products of "like grade and quality" to all segments of a given level of distribution at the same price, except for quantity and similar discounts which can be justified by manufacturer cost savings, and that promotional allowances (e.g., cooperative advertising allowances) and merchandising assistance (e.g., display stocking) be made available to all members of the trade which carry the manufacturer's products on a proportional basis.

SUMMARY

The physical distribution function is often delegated to one or more independent intermediaries. While this may offer advantages for the manufacturer, it also results in some loss of control over certain elements in the marketing process.

In selecting distribution channels, a manufacturer should seek to understand the factors motivating trade behavior, so that the marketing program may be consistent with the needs of the independent intermediaries who will be distributing the product.

COMPETITIVE ANALYSIS

The success of a marketing program will often be highly dependent on actions taken by competitors during the life of that program. A product which is clearly superior to competitive offerings at the time of market entry may be just as clearly inferior 6 months to a year after entry if competitors have introduced new or improved products in the interim. Similarly, what appeared to be a "heavy" advertising budget, or a "competitive" price, may turn out to be inadequate if competitors choose to increase their advertising expenditures or lower their prices rather than give up market share.

For this reason, a thorough understanding of competitive behavior is a critical ingredient in the formulation of an effective marketing program. At one level, it is essential to obtain a clear picture of current competitive marketing patterns to ensure that the marketing program being formulated will appeal to a sufficient number of the potential customers in that program's target market segment(s). At a second level, it is necessary to know enough about one's competitors to be able to predict, with reasonable accuracy, what they are likely to do in the future.

OBTAINING INFORMATION ABOUT COMPETITORS

It is generally possible to obtain a clear picture of competitors' current marketing programs through a thorough examination of public and semipublic sources. Competitive products can be purchased on the open market and subjected to laboratory tests, consumer use studies, or both. Competitive advertising expenditures are regularly monitored and tabulated by a number of syndicated research services (e.g., Leading National Advertisers). Actual advertisements can be obtained from clipping services, or from firms which video-tape television commercials and record radio commercials. Articles in trade journals often contain information about competitors' sales forces, distribution channels, and marketing programs, or such information can be gathered through a survey of a competitor's customers. It is often possible to obtain a competitor's price list by simply writing and asking for it, or if necessary, such lists can generally be obtained from "friendly" customers. The marketer's own sales force is often well placed to obtain useful information about a competitor's strategy and marketing *practices through observation and questioning. However, it should be recognized that at some point intelligent information gathering shades into unethical industrial espionage.*

Data on market shares in a particular industry are frequently obtained from syndicated services such as Nielsen (mainly packaged goods) and Trendex (mainly consumer durables) or from industry trade journals. If necessary, a survey of customers in the target market can almost always be used to obtain a reliable estimate of competitive market shares, images, and marketing practices.

PREDICTING COMPETITIVE BEHAVIOR

The second level of competitive analysis—predicting what competitors will do in the future—is, of course, considerably more difficult. Generally, a good place to begin is to find out as much as possible about the competitor in question and its business in the product-market segment in which one is interested. What, for example, is the level of financial and managerial resources available to the competitor, and what commitment of resources to this product-market segment has it made in the past? Based on engineering and manufacturing cost estimates, and marketing data such as that described above, what does the competitor's income statement for its business in this product-market segment look like? How important are the revenue, profits, and cash flow generated by this business likely to be to this competitor? If it lowered its price, or increased its advertising in response to a competitive action, how much additional volume would it need to maintain its current cash flow? What has been this competitor's pattern of response to competitive actions in the past?

Asking and answering questions such as these should be useful in trying to put oneself into the shoes (and minds) of the managers whose actions one is trying to predict. While there are obvious dangers in this approach, a good question to ask is often, "How would I respond if I were in my competitor's situation?" Although there is clearly no certainty that the competitor would in fact respond as you would if you were in his or her place, it is generally a reasonable expectation that rational managers will respond in similar ways to a given situation. If one's competitors have in the past acted in what at least seemed to be an irrational manner, such a pattern must, of course, be taken into account. In many cases, what seems to be irrational competitive behavior may, however, simply reflect a lack of understanding of a competitor's situation.

In highly competitive markets it is often worthwhile to assign members of the marketing department to monitor and figuratively "get inside" the reasoning processes and behavior of individual competitors. When this has been done, individual managers may be asked to "role play" key competitors when it is necessary to predict competitive actions. In some cases, companies have found computerized data bases, game theory, and mathematical simulation techniques to be useful tools in making such predictions.

SUMMARY

Understanding competitive behavior is central to the formulation of an effective marketing program. First, it is important to have information on each of the elements in the competitors' own marketing programs. Second, the marketing manager should understand the nature of competing firms sufficiently well to be able to predict their future behavior in the marketplace.

SOURCES OF
MARKETING INFORMATION

The cases in this book contain both primary and secondary data available to executives of the organizations depicted. This is, perhaps, an appropriate point at which to caution the student that the typical case presents a relatively tight digest of potentially useful data, often computed and organized by the casewriter from a vast array of available information. In the "real world," managers must often go out and collect needed information for themselves, then digest and organize it into a suitable format for analysis and exposition.

As emphasized in the earlier text on Marketing Research (Part VI), it is unwise to initiate new field studies designed to generate primary data without first checking on the availability of existing secondary data. Much valuable marketing information on a given topic already exists, and the challenge for management lies in tracking this down and making any necessary reorganization and reanalysis of the available data.

Sources of secondary data can be divided into three categories:

1   Data generated internally within the firm

2   Data generated by other organizations with which the firm is associated in some way

3   Data generated by external, unrelated organizations

The identification, evaluation, and use of data from each of these categories will now be discussed in turn.

INTERNAL DATA

In the course of conducting their day-to-day business, firms and other organizations routinely collect an immense volume of data. However, whether these subsequently become useful inputs to future marketing decisions is very much a function of how the data are gathered, categorized, and stored.

Examples of such internal information are sales invoices, sales-force call reports, and dealer or distributor reports. Let us consider for a moment what can be gleaned from a study of sales invoices over a period of time. A sales invoice may include the following:

- *Date of sale*
- *Salesperson, outlet, and/or sales territory responsible for sale (often in numeric code)*
- *Name and address of customer (the customer's account number may include a code for type of business or industry)*
- *Type of item purchased*
- *Number of units purchased*
- *Price charged per unit*
- *Total dollar amount due*

If each invoice is entered into a computer file, it should not be difficult to develop programs for analysis of sales data which can yield such potentially useful marketing information as:

1 *Average and total sales over a given time period, in units and dollars, for:*
- *Specific product categories*
- *Individual customers*
- *Industry groupings*
- *Individual salespeople*
- *Specific sales outlets or territories*

2 *Proportion of total sales accounted for by:*
- *Different sizes of account (i.e., grouped by sales volume)*
- *Individual customers*
- *Industry groupings*
- *Individual salespeople, outlets, or territories*
- *Monthly (or other) selling periods*

In addition, there are almost unlimited opportunities for cross tabulations and other multivariate analysis of such data, using widely available statistical "library" packages or specially written computer programs. All too often, however, sales data are not stored in a way which makes them easily retrievable; as a result, management may be unable to generate even such basic data as profiles of the present product-customer mix or sales trends among specific customer segments.

Many organizations use their salespeople and distributors as two-way information channels between the firm and the marketplace. However, there have to be formalized procedures for collecting and storing market information thus generated if it is to be of more than just ephemeral value.

DATA FROM ASSOCIATED ORGANIZATIONS

Most organizations also have access to information which, while not internally generated, is restricted in its availability.

First, there are market intermediaries or service agencies with which the firm enjoys some form of ongoing relationship. Potential sources of useful market unformation, generally provided free of charge, may include the firm's wholesalers, manufacturers' representatives, dealers or retail outlets, as well as its advertising and public relations agencies.

Next are organizations which make available proprietary information to their members or subscribers. Trade associations in a particular industry often collect information for their members concerning market trends, industry sales, buyer intentions, etc. There are also commercial subscription research services—such as the Market Research Corporation of America (MRCA), A. C. Nielsen Co., Frost & Sullivan, or the Long Range Planning Service of the Stanford Research Institute (SRI)—which undertake studies and surveys on a continuing basis and sell the findings to any organization that wishes to purchase them.

MRCA and Nielsen specialize in continuous collection of data, notably information on products sold through food stores and drugstores. Nielsen obtains its retail data by auditing inventories and sales every 60 days in a scientifically designed sample of 2,000 stores nationwide in the United States. It also provides similar services in several foreign countries. The information received by Nielsen subscribers is limited to those product categories covered by the subscription agreement and includes total dollar and unit sales of the product class, sales of major brands (in total and by package), percentage of stores stocking an item, retailer inventory and stockturn, retail and wholesale selling prices, and dealer promotional activity. In addition to providing national data, Nielsen also provides breakdowns by geographic regions, city-size groupings, and different categories of stores.

MRCA provides information similar to Nielsen but collects its data through a national consumer panel of 7,500 households, who maintain a weekly diary in which they register purchases of specific food, drug, and household items. Consumer sales by brands are reported both by types of households (classified by various demographic variables) as well as by the types of stores from which purchases were made.

SRI and Frost & Sullivan undertake market studies of a wide range of industries and products, publishing a number of different reports each year. Various arrangements exist for purchasing such reports. A number of other commercial subscription services exist, often focusing on a specialized field of activity. Although commercial data of this nature are available to any subscriber, few libraries are able to afford the high cost of subscribing to such services.

EXTERNAL DATA

The array and volume of external secondary data applicable to marketing decisions are staggering. These data include publications by federal, state, and local governments; periodicals (newspapers, newsletters, magazines, and trade and academic journals); trade publications such as catalogs, pamphlets, brochures, and research studies; academic publications such as research reports, case studies, and dissertations; and, of course, published books.

One of the problems facing the manager is to decide where to start his or her search of external sources. Many large companies and organizations have excellent libraries of their own, keyed to topics of known interest to management. Even where the needed information is not available in-house, the reference librarians will probably know how to obtain it.

Managers whose employers lack such facilities must be prepared to do some work on their own.[1] Most universities and many public libraries have business sections with staff trained to help readers find needed information.

SOME EXAMPLES OF TYPES OF INFORMATION AVAILABLE

There are other ways than industrial espionage to obtain information on new products and processes. Sources such as patent disclosures, trade journals, competitors' catalogs, testing organizations, and the reports of such government agencies as the FDA, Bureau of Standards, and Department of Agriculture can yield valuable insights.

Useful information on distribution patterns can be obtained from the Census of Business, which lists retail and wholesale sales by type of outlet and geographic area, and from the Census of Manufacturers, which lists geographic and industry data on manufacturers, including costs of materials and production quantities.

A great deal of data is published on advertising costs and expenditures. The Publishers Information Bureau details advertising expenditures by medium for all advertisers of any substance. The Audit Bureau of Circulation, meantime, provides circulation data for magazines, while the Standard Rate and Data Service publishes reports detailing rates and specifications for buying advertising space or time in different media.

Information on the characteristics of different market areas may be obtained from such publications as the Rand McNally Commercial Atlas and Marketing Guide, the Sales Management Survey of Buying Power, and the Editor & Publisher Market Guide.

Trends and developments in different companies, industries, or product categories may be derived from articles in a huge range of trade, professional, and general interest publications, ranging from Fortune to Progressive Grocer and from Advertising Age to Modern Railroads.

---

[1] An excellent reference work is Business Information Sources by Lorna M. Daniells, University of California Press, 1976.

GOVERNMENT STATISTICS

The most voluminous source of basic marketing data is in the official statistics published by the federal government and its agencies, as well as by state and local governments. A good overview *of what is available can be obtained from the* Statistical Abstract of the United States. *Published every September by the Bureau of the Census, this contains some 1,300 tables from the most widely used governmental and private statistical series.*

In addition to the many periodic reports which are published by the Bureau of the Census (which include Censuses of Population, Housing, Agriculture, Manufacturers, Business, Transportation, and Mineral Industries), the Bureau also makes available both special tabulations and computer tapes of raw data.

The quality of state and local statistics varies widely. An example of a useful state statistical series is the data published in California on retail sales subject to sales tax, broken down by product category and county or city of sale.

USE OF INDEXES

Most people are familiar with the use of card catalogs to find books on a particular topic. Searches for periodical literature on a particular topic can be conducted in somewhat similar fashion through the medium of various specialist indexes. These are typically published annually in bound volumes, with regular updates throughout the year. These indexes include:

1   Business Periodicals Index (*similar in format to* Reader's Guide)

2   F & S Index of Corporations and Industries (*articles are listed (a) by industries and product categories using the standard industrial classification and (b) by name of corporation*)

3   F & S International (*articles from international publications are indexed (a) by SIC code, (b) by country, (c) by name of corporation*)

4   New York Times Index

5   Wall Street Journal Index (*articles from the* Wall Street Journal *are indexed both by topic headings and by corporations*)

Another useful index for marketers is Predicasts, *a volume of forecasts for numerous industries and product categories, with each abstract indicating both the size of the individual forecasts and a reference as to their source. Also of value is the* Public Affairs Information Service (PAIS), *which lists current books, pamphlets, articles, and government documents on topics that include economics, social conditions, and public affairs. Details of recent university dissertations, meantime, may be found in* Dissertation Abstracts International.

A major advance in information-retrieval technology is computer abstracting and indexing of periodical literature. Through use of key words, a computer search of literature on particular topics can be conducted very quickly, with abstracts of relevant articles being printed either on- or off-line.

SUMMARY

Managers should always explore the availability of secondary data before undertaking field research to collect primary data. Much valuable marketing information on a particular topic is often already available in the organization itself, in the form of internal accounting data (e.g., sales statistics), call reports from the sales force, communications from dealers and retailers, etc. Other information may be readily available in the library, through government statistical publications, periodical articles, trade association publications, published research reports, etc. Many firms have developed sophisticated marketing information systems to systematize collection and storage of all such information, as well as to facilitate its subsequent retrieval when needed by management.

However, a final word of warning is in order. The same caveats apply to use of secondary data as apply to primary data. Just because information appears in print does not always mean that it can be trusted. Data published to promote the interests of a particular group are often suspect. The careful user should therefore check into the research methodology employed to collect the data if he or she has any doubts about the competence or objectivity of the original researcher, with a view to identifying and evaluating possible sources of bias.

Marketing audit

I. Analyse customer
- # potential buyers
- # now buying - likes - dislikes

Profile development

II. where do customers live

III. where do buyers buy

IV. when do they buy

V. How they buy
- Brands
- Impulse
- Ect.

VI. who influences buying decision

Structure

I. How many competators?

II. How many brands
- share of mkt.

III. Product self
- Tangable, Service, Package, Brand

Complete

Price

I. Predicated by cost   Know B.E.

$$B.E. = \frac{TFC}{Net\ cont.}$$

$$NC = S.P/unt - V.C/unt$$

II. Dementions   shift function
- List price
- Storage

Promotion

Personal selling

Advertising

Sale Promotion
coupon
gifts

Publicity
free
Exclusive Sport